WHAT WENT WRONG WITH AFRICA

For Sietske and Vera

WHAT WENT WRONG WITH AFRICA?

A contemporary history

ROEL VAN DER VEEN

What went wrong with Africa?
A contemporary history

Roel van der Veen

KIT Publishers
Mauritskade 63
Postbus 95001
1090 HA Amsterdam
E-mail: publishers@kit.nl
Website: www.kit.nl

Original Title: *Afrika. Van de Koude Oorlog naar de 21e eeuw*

The English translation of this book was made possible by the Directorate-General for International Cooperation (DGIS) at the Ministry of Foreign Affairs of the Netherlands.

Cover Design: Ad van Helmond, Amsterdam
Cover Photo: *Samsam,* Amsterdam

Design: Nel Punt, Amsterdam
DTP: Henny Scholten, Amsterdam
Production: Meester & de Jonge, Lochem

Foreword

In 1995, after six years as an Asia specialist, I was transferred by my employer, the Dutch Ministry of Foreign Affairs, to the Sub-Saharan Africa Department in The Hague. I knew almost nothing about the region and went looking for a book that would give me a rapid introduction to Africa's recent history and problems. There is a great deal of fine writing about the continent, but I was never able to find a book that provided a digestible review of what had happened in Africa in recent years and why.

In the past few years I have written a lot about Africa for my work, in various positions in the Sub-Saharan Africa Department and the Strategic Policy Planning Unit at the Office of the Secretary-General. At one point it occurred to me that this work might serve as the basis for a book of my own – a book I still felt ought to exist. My work for the Ministry of Foreign Affairs undoubtedly had a strong influence on my approach, but in writing the book I always let myself be guided by my original concept: a general review of contemporary African history for all those with an interest in the continent.

During the final stages, many colleagues and friends made comments on parts of the manuscript and so enabled me to make considerable improvements to the text. However, I must confess that in some cases I deliberately ignored well-meaning advice to tone down some of my more outspoken statements. I hope that my provocative comments will enliven the debate on Africa and the role of the international community there. It goes without saying that I bear sole responsibility for whatever is written in these pages.

I would very much like to thank all those who read over the manuscript and commented on it, many of them colleagues at the Ministry of Foreign Affairs. I particularly want to mention the valuable comments made by Klaas van Walraven of the African Studies Centre in Leiden, and to thank Sandra Debets and her fellow documentalists and librarians at the Ministry for providing an intimidating flood of publications on Africa.

This book was written as a private project during a particularly hectic three-year period at home, in which our family was doubled in size by the arrival of two lovely daughters. My love and thanks to Margreet, who made it possible for me to complete this venture.

Finally, I would like to thank my former supervisor and good friend Jan Geert Siccama, who from the start provided moral and practical support and soon convinced me that my daydream would one day turn into this long-awaited book.

Roel van der Veen

TABLE OF CONTENTS

Country information

Country	Capital	Year of independence	Surface area (km²)	Population in 2003[1] (millions)	Per capita income in 2001[2] (USD)
Angola	Luanda	1975	1,246,700	13.9	701
Benin	Porto-Novo	1960	112,620	6.6	368
Botswana	Gaborone	1966	581,730	1.7	3,066
Burkina Faso	Ouagadougou	1960	274,000	12.2	215
Burundi	Bujumbura	1962	27,830	6.7	99
Cameroon	Yaoundé	1960	475,440	14.9	559
Central African Republic	Bangui	1960	622,980	3.8	257
Chad	N'Djamena	1960	1,284,000	8.3	202
Congo (Brazzaville)	Brazzaville	1960	342,000	3.2	886
Congo (Kinshasa)	Kinshasa	1960	2,344,860	54.6	99
Djibouti	Djibouti	1977	23,200	0.65	894
Equatorial Guinea	Malabo	1968	28,050	0.48	3,935
Eritrea	Asmara	1993	117,000	4.4	164
Ethiopia	Addis Ababa	1955	1,100,760	66.2	95
Gabon	Libreville	1960	267,670	1.3	3,437
Gambia	Banjul	1965	11,300	1.4	291
Ghana	Accra	1957	238,540	20.2	269
Guinea	Conakry	1958	245,860	8.4	394
Guinea-Bissau	Bissau	1974	36,120	1.3	162
Ivory Coast	Yamoussoukro	1960	322,460	17.3	634
Kenya	Nairobi	1963	580,370	31.5	371
Lesotho	Maseru	1966	30,350	2.3	386
Liberia	Monrovia	1847	97,750	2.9	*
Malawi	Lilongwe	1964	118,480	11.6	166
Mali	Bamako	1960	1,240,190	12	239
Mozambique	Maputo	1975	801,590	18	200
Namibia	Windhoek	1990	824,290	1.9	1,730
Niger	Niamey	1960	1,267,000	11.6	175
Nigeria	Abuja	1960	923,770	129.9	319
Rwanda	Kigali	1962	26,340	8.2	196
Senegal	Dakar	1960	196,720	10	476

Country	Capital	Year of independence	Surface area (km²)	Population in 2003[1] (millions)	Per capita income in 2001[2] (USD)
Sierra Leone	Freetown	1961	71,740	4.9	146
Somalia	Mogadishu	1960	637,660	10.6	*
South Africa	Pretoria	1910	1,221,040	45	2,620
Sudan	Khartoum	1956	2,505,810	32.5	395
Swaziland	Mbabane	1968	17,360	0.95	1,175
Tanzania	Dodoma	1961	945,090	35.5	271
Togo	Lomé	1960	56,790	4.8	270
Uganda	Kampala	1962	235,880	24.6	249
Zambia	Lusaka	1964	752,610	11.2	354
Zimbabwe	Harare	1980	390,760	13.1	706

* Not available

[1] Source: various Economist Intelligence Unit reports, 2003

[2] Source: UNDP Human Development Report, 2003 (figures for 2001)

Introduction

The last fifty years have seen unprecedented changes in people's standards of living all over the world. Despite explosive population growth, it proved possible to dramatically elevate the quality of life. Though poverty was the norm throughout human history, for many people a degree of prosperity came within reach. Some even began to take it for granted. In the late nineteenth and early twentieth century, mass production and consumption emerged, first in North America and then in Europe. After World War II, these innovations spread to the non-Western world. In the current period of globalisation, the percentage of the world's people living in extreme poverty, on less than one dollar a day, has continued to drop. From 30 percent in 1990, it fell to 23 percent by 2000, albeit of a much larger world population.[1] However we define poverty, it is clear that on average people's lives have improved, all over the world, on every continent.

Except Africa. Africa (more specifically, sub-Saharan or 'Black' Africa) is the only large, contiguous region left out of the worldwide rise in prosperity over the past fifty years. The percentage of Africans living in poverty has not dropped but risen. In nearly all African countries, the average income has fallen since decolonisation, which took place around 1960 in most cases. Even a confirmed optimist would hesitate to predict that life in Africa will get better in the years ahead. Alongside poverty, the troubling hallmarks of the continent today are misrule, violence, corruption and AIDS. The human development figures speak volumes.[2] So do the tales of travellers who returned to Africa in the early twenty-first century after visiting around the time of independence. The writer Paul Theroux, revisiting many parts of the continent after forty years, wrote: 'Africa is materially more decrepit than it was when I first knew it – hungrier, poorer, less educated, more pessimistic, more corrupt.'[3]

Many people think it surprising that prosperity has not come to Africa. In the heady years following independence, around 1960, the continent seemed to be making a fresh start, free at last of slavery and colonialism. On the face of it, Africa seemed no worse off than the other non-Western continents, Asia and Latin America. All three were made up of ex-colonies and were poor in comparison with the rich West. In France scholars invented a collective term for them: *Le Tiers Monde*, the Third World, as opposed to the West (the First World) and the Soviet-dominated Eastern Bloc (the Second World). His emphasis on vast political blocs and their interactions was typical of the times. Until the 1980s the vast differences within the Third World went largely unnoticed. All poor countries, it was felt, were in the same boat; they all had similar potential for development.

The first general theories about the future of the poor, newly independent countries were developed in the 1950s and 1960s in the United States, which had promoted the decolonisation of Europe's colonial empires. Officially, the postwar world order accorded 'sovereign equality' to all states, old and new, though in practical terms they were anything but equal; for one thing, most new countries were a good deal poorer. They seemed likely to succumb to the enticements of the socialist Eastern Bloc, which was locked in an ideological struggle with the United States and the rest of the Western world, a struggle that came to be known as the Cold War. In response, American scholars and politicians put forward the theory that the path to prosperity was the same for every country. If they would just let go of their 'traditional' ways of life, they could metamorphose into 'modern' societies. The most persuasive advocate of this 'modernisation theory' was Walt Whitman Rostow, whose book *The Stages of Economic Growth: A Non-Communist Manifesto* (1960) described the stages of the modernisation process that countries had to traverse in order to become 'developed'.[4] Poor countries became developing countries, countries on the road of development.

But modernisation theory soon fell out of favour in the development debate. Many felt it was too convenient for the West. In the 1960s and 1970s, there was real hope that many roads would lead to prosperity, or development. Why should Asian, African and Latin American countries follow the Western model? Wasn't the socialism of the Eastern Bloc an equally attractive paradigm? Or, it was thought, if countries wanted to stay out of the confrontation between the two blocs, they could pursue their own roads to a better future. Modernisation theory seemed to imply that there was just one, Western blueprint for escaping poverty; that was seen as an insult to the newly independent countries, with their very different cultures. Within the new international system emblematised by the United Nations, all countries were said to have equal status. The corollary, in many people's minds, was that they all had equal opportunities for development, and could choose whatever path suited them, just as they had chosen independence. Modernisation theory was abandoned not because it was shown to be scientifically incorrect; in fact, the jury was still out, since development had not yet reached the non-Western countries, with the exception of Japan. Rather, the theory fell from grace because at that time its conclusions and predictions were widely felt to be unacceptable.

Another factor behind the opposition to modernisation theory was the widespread opinion that Third World countries would probably never have a chance to develop, because the rich countries were maintaining an international system that worked against them. Until that changed, it was claimed, poor countries would never be able to move forward. The critics of modernisation theory, and of the international system, who advanced this argument were mainly Spanish-speaking and their conceptual framework was called dependency theory, after the Spanish word *dependencia*.[5] The most influential attempt to apply dependency theory to Africa was made by Walt Rodney, from the Caribbean country of Guyana, in *How Europe Underdeveloped Africa* (1972). However, the heyday of dependency theory, like that of modernisation theory, was short. In this case, it was clear that the theory failed to capture reality. Some poor countries, especially in East and Southeast Asia, proved perfectly capable of development. Apparently, the oppressive influence of the international system should not be overestimated.

Still, dependency theory was revived around the year 2000 by the antiglobalisation movement, which fiercely opposed the growing influence of capitalism on the international system after the collapse of the socialist Eastern Bloc. The movement claimed that capitalism's dark side was most evident in its dealings with poor countries. This new species of visceral aversion to capitalism formed the basis of an antiglobalist vision in Naomi Klein's *No Logo* (2000) and Noreena Hertz's *The Silent Takeover* (2001). It was predicted that as capitalism expanded its influence through globalisation, wages in poor countries would fall due to competition for international investment, in a race to the bottom. The result, the antiglobalists argued, would be growing poverty. Furthermore, open markets would let in a flood of foreign products with which domestic producers could not possibly compete. Finally, a narrow-minded focus on money would distract attention from environmental and social issues, causing living conditions to deteriorate further for many inhabitants of poor countries. According to the antiglobalist camp, fighting globalisation was the only way to give the poor of the world a chance at a better life.

The ideas of the antiglobalists are open to the same objections as dependency theory. They cannot explain why some parts of the world have succeeded in escaping the grip of capitalism and moving forward – or, more accurately, have moved forward thanks to capitalism – while other parts of the world, especially Africa, have not. Over time, Africa seems to have become utterly marginalised. Wages there are not lowered to attract international investment, nor do transnational companies make much effort to exploit what has become the world's least developed region. Africa's main problem is not that it is in a race to the bottom, but that it has not even managed to get into the game. Dependency and antiglobalist theories offer little insight into Africa's situation, aside from the thesis that an insufficiently competitive economy and open markets are a disastrous mix. Those theories will therefore not often be mentioned in the pages ahead. What I will discuss is the general significance of the international economy for Africa. Even though the continent has become ever more marginal to the world economy since independence, because of its internal weakness the international environment remains crucial. When examining the reasons for the continent's decline, international economic factors should be taken into account.

As some postcolonial regions pulled themselves out of poverty while others remained stuck or sunk even further, the Third World came apart. The contrast was so great that many researchers began to focus on regions or groups of countries, rather than the developing world as a whole. Africa (more precisely, sub-Saharan Africa) became a frequent object of scrutiny.

The issue then arose of why Africa was lagging behind the rest of the world. In the 1980s, a new school of thought put its finger on the sore spot: the poor performance of the African state. At the head of this school was the British scholar Basil Davidson, who made African history accessible to a wide public. In 1992, he published a book arguing that the European model of statehood which the colonial powers had brought to Africa – a model he called the nation-state – had become an obstacle to postcolonial development. The title of Davidson's work, *The Black Man's Burden*, summed it up neatly. His contention was that European state structures did not fit into African culture and society, and therefore stood in the way of development instead of promoting it. Africa's 'modern' states, he claimed, were making it impossible for the continent to move ahead.

Other scholars pointed to other features of the state in Africa, for instance its often inextricable links with society,[6] or its tendency to prey on its own people in increasingly criminal ways.[7] Still others emphasised how dependent on the international system the African state still was.[8] International institutions, particularly the World Bank, also criticised the functioning – or rather, the malfunctioning – of the African state.[9] Both scholars and policymakers focused on the state in their analyses.

In my view this approach, starting with the role of the state, is the best way to see the connections between the many aspects of recent African history. I will look at what the exact features of the state in Africa were, how they developed, and what they mean for the contemporary history – and the future – of the continent.

What approach will I take? First of all, I will place events in a broader historical context, a context that extends beyond Africa. If we limit our field of vision to events within Africa's geographical boundaries, then we lack any such context. Is Africa following its own path? If so, what path is that? Is Africa undergoing its own form of modernisation? If so, what is the essence of modernisation there? Such questions cannot be answered satisfactorily unless developments in Africa are compared with those elsewhere, in the light of a general theory.

That general framework will be provided by modernisation theory, which I believe is in need of rehabilitation. Since the 1960s, more and more countries in what used to be called the Third World have made great advances (especially in East and Southeast Asia), while others have lagged behind. We now have enough hard data to test scientifically whether modernisation theory is tenable. In the case of Africa, modernisation theory tells us that, if the continent remains stuck in the premodern stage, internal factors are probably to blame for its stagnation. Incidentally, those factors need not be economic. As Rostow put it, society should be seen as an organism, in which economic growth can result from noneconomic factors, such as political and social changes.[10]

At this point, we can shift to what in recent years has been identified as Africa's main problem: state failure. The state is by definition a society's central organisation. If it does not work properly, or at all, then it throws up obstacles to development and poses a threat to stability and social cohesion. If the failing state is not replaced by another, stronger one – an option that does not exist in Africa, at least not at this time – then chaos and anarchy are very likely to ensue. There have been plenty of instances of this chain of events in the since the end of the Cold War.

I will draw a link between the mechanism of state decline which we seek to identify and Africa's failure to achieve modernisation. It will be necessary to explicitly determine Africa's status within modernisation theory. That theory is often applied to the continent in an implicit, and perhaps flawed, way; constant references to African states as 'developing countries' show the powerful grip of modernisation theory on our thinking, but at the same time it must be pointed out that in most of Africa no development as understood in modernisation theory is in fact taking place. African countries are indeed poor countries, but they are not developing countries in any literal sense.

Meanwhile, the question arises of how 'modernisation' should be defined. The definitions supplied in the early literature – note 6 lists the foundational works – are variations on the theme of 'conditions conducive to economic growth'. In later years, however, 'modernisation' acquired quite wide-ranging connotations, creating a gap between later writing on modernisation and the term as originally used by Rostow and others. I will adhere to the original approach, in which the central issue was how a society can move from poverty to wealth. Tellingly, the final stage described in Rostow's *Stages of Economic Growth* was 'the age of high mass consumption'. In that spirit, I will adopt the following definitions. By a poor society, I mean a society with low production and low consumption and by a rich society, I mean a society of high production and high consumption. By modernisation, I mean the process of societal transformation required to move from poverty to wealth, from low to high production and consumption.[11]

Societies that have not embarked on this process of change, of economic growth, are by definition premodern. The term 'premodern' suggests a static society to many people, but that image is inaccurate. The pace of change is probably faster in modernising societies than in premodern societies, but premodern societies have a dynamism of their own. The difference between premodern societies and modernising ones is not their level of dynamism, but the result of that dynamism. In modernising societies the result is a structural (as opposed to incidental) increase in production and consumption, while in a premodern society the economy remains at the same level. Changes in premodern societies have no significant impact on the general standard of living.

Secondly, in addition to providing a broader historical context, I will emphasise the nexus of politics, economics, social relations and culture. There is nothing new about concentrating on political or socioeconomic relationships (perhaps drawing a distinction between social and economic relationships). They form the basis for historical work in the liberal and Marxist traditions, respectively. I will add the cultural dimension, the importance of which should not be underestimated in a study of the interaction between European state structures and African realities. Furthermore, modernisation theory ascribes the failure to achieve modernisation to country-internal obstacles, which include cultural issues. It has been said that 'culture is the mother, institutions are the children.'[12]

I define culture as 'the values, attitudes, beliefs, orientations, and underlying assumptions prevalent among people in a society'.[13] Obviously, these factors impact on the way a country's people live.[14] However, my chief interest is in the overlap between culture and the other domains mentioned above: political culture, economic culture and social culture. This approach has been underappreciated in previous work; in fact, it has been taboo. If one assumes that many (or all) roads could lead to prosperity, one tends to ignore countries' domestic circumstances. Any country-internal situation, and therefore any culture, is assumed to have the potential to generate prosperity. In theory, no culture is better, or more capable of modernisation, than any other. Now that Africa's development has fallen so far behind that of the rest of the world, there is good reason to question this assumption.

Of the domains to be examined in this study – politics, the economy, social relations and culture – culture is in no way subordinate to the others. I will not try to establish any order of importance or search for an 'ultimate cause'. This means I will disappoint liberals, who consider political factors to be crucial, socialists, for whom social and economic conditions take primacy, and conservatives, who tend to see culture as the ultimate source of success or failure. My interest is in the interaction between the four domains; changes in any one of them have an impact on the other three. This interaction can lead to large-scale transformations and start the engine of modernisation.

That brings me to the third element of my approach: the interaction between the internal and the international. Major recent issues will be discussed and analysed from both an internal African perspective and the international angle. The two will be considered jointly rather than separately, for it is the interplay between them that has been the mainspring of modern African history. The point of contact between these two very different worlds – African countries' internal affairs and the international context – is the position and role of Africa's ruling elites. When the colonial powers departed, these relatively small groups of individuals inherited the state structures and all that went with them. Among other things, this meant that they, as the new rulers of their countries, had to forge African power bases, while maintaining relations with the outside world. Many divergent and often conflicting interests, traditions, goals and ideals came together in the postwar African elites. They were like spiders in two crossed webs – the internal web of their own African societies, and the external web of the international system. The way in which African rulers survived (or otherwise) in these two webs, and what this meant for Africa, is the central theme of this book.

This approach makes it possible to examine all major facets of Africa's independent states as they relate to each other: internal and external factors, the political, cultural, economic and social domains, and the larger context of modernisation. This study will not be strictly limited to events during and after the Cold War but, where necessary, will also look back at the colonial period, since the predecessors of today's African states came into being then. Sometimes it will delve even further back in time, because the historical structure of Africa's societies and cultures bears on the performance of its contemporary states. While acknowledging the many differences between African societies, I will focus mainly on what they have in common.

Underlying this effort to explain the path Africa's states have taken since independence are several distinct groups of questions. The first concerns the fortunes and misfortunes of present-day African states. What are their problems, how did they arise and what impact do they have? What is the relationship between the elites and the general population? How does the state influence society and vice versa? Another group of questions relates to the international context. What are Africa's relations with the outside world, and how have those relations changed over the years? How do external factors affect the continent?

In addition, there are questions which, though not always directly related to African states and their elites, are of great relevance to them. How are the problems of the state linked to Africa's failure to develop economically and socially? How has the size, composition and density of the population changed, and what does this mean for African societies? What cultural, religious and ideological changes have affected Africa's states and their development? How do violence, lawlessness and instability fit into the picture? Other questions that arise concern remedies for the shortcomings of the state. What efforts have been made to get African states to function more effectively? What was the main focus of these efforts and what results have they had? Finally, how do developments in Africa differ from those in other parts of the world, and what will happen to Africa in the near future?

The structure of the book is as follows. The first two chapters deal roughly with the period 1960-1990, from the beginnings of independence to the end of the Cold War. Although African countries were formally independent in this period, there was still considerable international influence on the African state system. The first chapter focuses on political topics and the second chapter on economic ones; however, this should not be seen as a sharp dividing line, for major trends almost always affect the state and the population politically, economically, culturally, socially and in other ways. Moreover, as indicated, developments in Africa's international environment are always outlined and assessed in parallel with those within Africa.

Most of the book is devoted to the period since the end of the Cold War – the 1990s and the opening years of the twenty-first century. Chapters 3-10 discuss major themes from this period and the links between them. Chapter 3 looks at the democratisation of African politics and chapter 4 examines the idea that, as a result of all the changes Africa has been through, it may be on the eve of a renaissance. Chapters 5 and 6 focus on the collapse of state authority and the condition of the state system, covering such topics as civil and inter-state war, the disintegration of the social fabric and outright genocide. Chapter 7, on glob-alisation, turns to the international context once more, with particular emphasis on economic developments. Chapters 8 and 9 discuss major changes affecting the population, including international aid. Finally, chapter 10 looks at the stability (or otherwise) of Africa's states and its entire state system.

If the states – or indeed the state system – that we have observed in Africa over the past century were to become so unstable as to disintegrate altogether (as has already happened in Somalia), what would fill the gap? Is Robert Kaplan right to predict chaos and anarchy or could Africa embark on a new phase of state development? Will the continent develop novel state institutions of its own or will the European legacy survive? My thoughts on these questions are summed up in the concluding chapter, which examines why Africa's states, originally a force for modernisation, are now in many cases in the process of failing. The book concludes with a forecast of what Africa and its states will look like in twenty years' time.

I have mentioned that the term 'Africa' does not generally refer to the entire continent. When African countries gained independence (around 1960) there was still a feeling of Pan-African solidarity, but by the end of the Cold War this sense of unity had largely evaporated. North Africa showed a growing tendency to turn north to Europe, or east to the Arab and Muslim world, and was less concerned with the areas south of the Sahara. By the end of the twentieth century, the subcontinent known as sub-Saharan Africa had emerged as a natural unit. The countries of this 'Black' Africa share a number of material and cultural features, alongside their shared disappointment at the lack of progress since independence. It is sub-Saharan Africa that is the subject of this book, and accordingly the term 'Africans' will be used here to mean the inhabitants of Africa south of the Sahara.

Sub-Saharan Africa is made up of more than forty countries. Of course, there are considerable political, economic, cultural, social and other differences between them. It is precisely this enormous variation that is said to characterise Africa, and so generalisations about the entire subcontinent often meet with scepticism. Nevertheless, guides to Africa also describe striking resemblances between peoples that are in other respects far removed from each other. According to the authoritative work *Africa*, edited by Phyllis M. Martin and Patrick O'Meara: 'While a hallmark of African civilisations is their stunning cultural pluralism and tremendous diversity, there is also a basic traditional continuity that provides, simultaneously, a surprising degree of similarity between even widely separated societies.'[15]

Many of those similarities relate to state development, the topic of this study. I believe they provide a sufficient basis for generalisation. Unifying elements of this kind include Africa's physical environment, which has produced a low population density in almost all areas. This has in turn shaped Africa's political geography. In addition, African societies have quite similar (though, of course, not identical) demographic structures, degrees of technological development and levels of material welfare. Yet another common feature is their shared experience of colonialism and the post-colonial world. The methods of the colonial powers and of Africa's post-independence leaders have left their mark on the organisation and operation of African states.[16] This leads me to believe that it is just as reasonable – if not more so – to speak of a general African mode of state development as it is to speak of European or Asian modes.

Where appropriate, differences between regions (and in some cases between countries) will be indicated topic by topic. Generally, I will refer to the following regions: West Africa (made up of some twenty countries, almost all of them former French or British colonies), Central Africa (the two Congos and their neighbours), the Horn of Africa (the area around Ethiopia), East Africa (the smallest region, consisting of Kenya, Tanzania and Uganda) and Southern Africa (all the countries south of Central and East Africa). Maps of each region and of sub-Saharan Africa as a whole are included in the book. I occasionally refer to different groupings joined by a common history, such as the Anglophone or Francophone countries.

The islands off the coast of Africa will not be discussed here. With the exception of Madagascar, they are all very small and have had little or no impact on developments on the mainland. Most of them have mixed populations, for example of Asian, Arab, African and European descent. Almost nowhere is the African element politically or culturally dominant. I should mention that inclusion of the islands would have skewed in a positive sense the overall picture of Africa painted here. Some of the islands are tourist paradises, and so have fairly high standards of living.

Almost all the statistics in the book are from international organisations such as UN bodies, the World Bank and the IMF. With a few exceptions, the notes are limited to bibliographical references.

I
THE COLD WAR

African independence

Accra, 1957. In the first minutes of the sixth of March, in the great square bordering the ocean, Prime Minister Kwame Nkrumah addressed the multitude assembled in the cool night air to celebrate their newfound independence. 'Ghana, our beloved country, is forever free!', proclaimed Nkrumah, and the crowd cheered. The Union Jack was lowered and a new flag was hoisted, with horizontal red, yellow and green bands and a black star in the centre. The colony of the Gold Coast had passed into history. Aside from Liberia and Ethiopia, which had never been European colonies, Ghana was the first country in 'black' Africa to be free of the colonial yoke.

True, the British monarch was still the head of state and the governor-general would for a short time retain a ceremonial role, but the real leadership of the country was now in the hands of the African who had been prime minister ever since 1952. Just three years later, in 1960, Ghana was to break its last constitutional ties with Britain. The queen and governor-general would lose their authority and Ghana would become a republic, with Nkrumah as its president.

Both Ghana and President Nkrumah were in many ways emblematic of the new post-colonial Africa. Ghana had inherited the artificial structure which is a feature of so many African countries. Its name was taken from a Sahelian country that had prospered between the eighth and eleventh centuries as a staging post for caravans crossing the Sahara. That country lay more than a thousand kilometres northwest of its twentieth-century namesake on the Gulf of Guinea. The territory of modern Ghana had once been home to a flourishing empire, but in the 1950s there were political reasons for ignoring that fact. In the eighteenth and nineteenth centuries, before the British penetrated inland from the coast, the Asante empire had ruled most of present-day Ghana and the surrounding region. Its power was derived mainly from its position as a way station in the slave trade, between the African countries of the interior where the slaves were captured and the foreign settlements on the coast, where they were sold. In the newly independent state of Ghana, the Asante still formed the largest ethnic group, concentrated around their traditional capital of Kumasi in the west of the country. The other inhabitants of the ex-colonial territories that formed the new Ghana feared that the Asante would establish political ascendancy over the country. With British support, however, Asante dominance was averted: care was taken to ensure that the new rulers of independent Ghana were not Asante. Nkrumah, for example, came from a village on the coast of the country. The Asante responded to the new political situation by launching their own National Liberation Movement, which clashed with the Accra government in the 1950s and 1960s but was eventually defeated.

Nkrumah was not descended from a family of 'traditional' African chiefs. He owed his political career purely to the Western-style education that he had received, first from the British in Ghana and subsequently in the United States. The new Ghana he envisaged would have nothing to do with the local history of the Asante, Fante or other local ethnic groups; it was to be founded on the new Ghanaian citizenry, with their modern aspirations for Africa and for development. Nkrumah established himself as a champion of Pan-Africanism: the ideal of African unity and brotherhood. In his independence day address he said that Ghana's independence would be meaningless unless it was linked up with the total liberation of the continent. A year later, in 1958, he chaired the first Conference of Independent African States, held in Accra: an initiative that would eventually lead to the establishment of the Organisation of African Unity (OAU). Nkrumah's ultimate ambition was to achieve Pan-African unity. In 1959 he established a union with Guinea, which had just gained its independence from France, and in 1960 Mali joined too. However, this union was to remain a dead letter. In 1960 Nkrumah sent troops to Congo to support its prime minister, Patrice Lumumba. In this initial period of African independence, Ghana was the torchbearer of black Africa, the state to which many Africans throughout the continent (and beyond) looked with admiration and hope (and some others with a mixture of hope, envy and irritation).

Ghana's independence was a historic event, which must be seen against the backdrop of the global developments that followed World War II. The independence of India and Pakistan in 1947 had heralded a more general fragmentation of the British Empire. Africa was following in Asia's footsteps. For the British, Ghana was simply one more jewel lost from the imperial crown. But even in Africa, Ghana was not – judged by the standards and sentiments of the time – the first country to seek independence. All the countries of North Africa and even Sudan had already gained their independence in the 1950s. The wave of decolonisation sped south, hitting Ghana first in the sub-Saharan region. Ghana's independence was preceded by a number of measures designed to increase the country's autonomy. In 1951, for example, the colony was granted a constitution providing for an elected legislative assembly with the power to appoint ministers from among its members. In 1952, elections were held for the legislature, the first general elections in the country's history. Nkrumah, already a popular radical politician, stood for election from his prison cell. His party won a large majority and five days later Nkrumah was released from prison, reputedly having softened his demand for 'self-government now' to one of 'self-government soon'. He became prime minister in the new administration.

Many Africans felt that the independence of Ghana presaged the total liberation, reunification and rebirth of the African continent. The example set by Ghana under Nkrumah's inspiring leadership encouraged Africans throughout the continent to join the struggle against their colonial masters. Around 1960 there was a second wave of African independence (counting the wave in North Africa as the first) in which almost thirty black African colonies gained their freedom. After that, however, the movement faltered, mainly because of Portugal's point-blank refusal to work towards independence for its colonies and because of white hegemony in South Africa and the surrounding countries. These last bulwarks of colonialism did not begin to crumble until the mid-1970s.

Nevertheless, around 1960 most of Africa gained independence. Political power passed into the hands of new leaders: members of new elites, who had enjoyed Western higher education and frequently become politically active as a result. Since the start of World War II, politics in the colonies had become increasingly open and African parties had been established, with the aim of achieving first self-rule and eventually independence. Rather than providing a safe outlet for nationalist pressures, as the colonial powers had hoped, these politicians actually became the voices of nationalism. The representative assemblies in which they sat became forums for the expression of nationalist aspirations. However, the ambitions of the new African elites were in keeping with the Western ideal of modernisation, which had been introduced into Africa in the first half of the twentieth century. Apart from political freedom and independence, their priorities were economic development, social justice and autonomy or even autarky. The nationalists believed that these aims could never be achieved within the colonial system, another factor that made the liberation of Africa their top priority. They assumed that they would then achieve the rest of their goals more or less automatically.

Freedom for their continent was the prime objective of the Africans at the time of decolonisation. When looking at subsequent events, however, including those between the end of the Cold War and the early years of the twenty-first century, it is important to consider what became of their other goals. After all, it was these goals that most African leaders adopted (or claimed to adopt) as guidelines after they took power. At the time of independence, some nationalists (including Nkrumah) almost literally promised their followers heaven on earth. This can be attributed to the euphoria of the period, but later African governments – including those around the turn of the century – can rightly be judged on their success in achieving the other aims mentioned above (decolonisation, economic development, social justice and autonomy/autarky). Democracy was not one of Africa's main priorities at this stage. It was probably too closely associated with the Western values that had also produced colonialism. Moreover, it was unclear how to combine democracy with the socialist-style development advocated by many African leaders.

The transfer of power was primarily political in nature. The colonial power handed over to the new African government a territory with defined borders, the population living there, a physical infrastructure and the means of controlling it (an army and police), plus public institutions with a bureaucracy at their centre. That bureaucracy was itself composed of people with special knowledge and skills, and offices with telephones and other equipment.[17] In other words, the machinery of state was generally passed on in its entirety. It is important, however, not to overestimate the size of that machine. The European colonial powers had controlled Africa through indirect rule, with indigenous leaders as intermediaries. They themselves had built up few modern institutions. It was only in the twilight of colonialism, from the 1940s on, as the colonial powers began to concern themselves with the welfare of the indigenous population, that anything approaching a modern state apparatus really emerged.[18]

Even in the period of rapid growth following independence, the machinery of state in African countries remained modest by international standards. Public expenditure represented only a few per cent of gross national product (GNP), in contrast with the double digits usual for developed countries.[19] Much economic activity in Africa was directed at subsistence and was beyond the reach of the state. Even so, the many informal links between politicians and the private sector meant that the influence of the state on the economy was much greater than the low percentage of GNP may suggest.

It was the job of the new leaders to 'Africanise' the modern institutions they had inherited. Their success was frequently far from complete. In some cases, the former colonial power continued to exert a striking influence on the independent state. Such influence might extend to the army, or even the bureaucracy. Its scope was largely dependent on the interests and wishes of the former colonial power and the deals it had struck with the new African regime. For example, France's influence remained strong in most of its former colonies, but vanished almost entirely in Guinea after the country voted for greater autonomy in a referendum. Belgium tried to retain its influence in the newly independent Congo, but was largely unsuccessful because of the chaos surrounding decolonisation there.

What means did the governments of independent Africa have at their disposal to achieve their aims? The only income they had was from taxes (which were very low) and other levies. It had taken the colonial powers decades to set up these systems, which allowed the colonies to bear the costs of their own administration. European treasuries had frequently been drawn on to bridge financial gaps. The leaders of the new states no longer had this option (though often they did receive financial assistance from abroad). Nor were they given access to the profits of the modern enterprises established by the colonisers; these remained in the possession of the original owners and were not part of the property handed over. For the rest, the new governments were forced – as it were – to board a moving train: though the transfer of power brought many changes, a great deal of life simply rolled on as before. Major social changes like the expansion of the monetary economy and urbanisation had already begun before World War II and continued throughout the latter half of the twentieth century largely unaffected by decolonisation. It was up to the new leaders to establish their own power base in African society in the midst of this tangled web of continuity and change.

The Africanisation
of politics

The first leaders of independent Africa inherited states with colonial structures. Initially it was unclear how long these structures would survive. Although talk of a single great Pan-African union had virtually ceased, there were still plans to merge countries that had already achieved independence. Nkrumah's Ghana was at the forefront of this initiative. Nothing came of it, however, for various reasons.

Firstly, the larger countries resulting from these mergers would have been just as artificial as the newly independent countries – in a sense, even more so, since they would have had virtually no internal cohesion. The new African states all had colonial infrastructures which gave them a degree of internal unity and linked them to the former colonial power. With adjacent countries they often had no ties at all, apart perhaps from cross-border ethnic groups. Secondly, almost nobody dared to contemplate an entirely new order based, for example, on ethnicity. It was generally believed that this would open up a Pandora's box and lead to utter chaos. Thirdly, the ruling elites understood that it was not in their own interests to introduce a new political structure which would heighten the uncertainty of the already precarious situation in the early days of independence.

Eventually, therefore, the plans for new political entities faded into oblivion and it became clear that Africa would face the future with the national borders drawn by the European colonial powers. This principle was confirmed by the OAU, which was set up in 1963 in the Ethiopian capital Addis Ababa. Political borders within Africa were henceforth to be regarded as sacrosanct, however unnatural their origins, and indeed, they remained unchanged until the 1990s.

Although the borders inherited from the colonial powers were regarded as non-negotiable, the structures of state were to be 'Africanised'. That is to say, they were to be taken over by Africans. The speed and extent of this transition varied from one country to another. Under President Sékou Touré, Guinea made a clean break with France, whereas – at the other end of the spectrum – Ivory Coast continued for many years to employ French nationals in key government positions and thus experienced a far more gradual transition.

Another, possibly still more important aim of independent Africa was the Africanisation of the economy. The indigenous economy, almost entirely consisting of agriculture, animal husbandry (or associated activities) and trade, had always remained largely in African hands. Alongside it, however, the Europeans had established new economic ventures designed to meet demand and serve markets in the affluent North. Most of them were large-scale agricultural enterprises in the form of plantations for the supply of tropical products like palm oil, cocoa, coffee and peanuts, but some were businesses engaged in the extraction of minerals like copper, iron and gemstones. These colonial companies and their associated infrastructure had a major impact on local African communities because of the employment they created, but remained in a sense islands of modern business in a sea of economic underdevelopment. Most of the large profits they generally produced found their way to Europe. One of the aims of the new leaders was to nationalise ('Africanise') these enterprises, but in the first years of independence there was no real hope of this. Any such move was ruled out by the imbalance of power between the African governments and the Western economic interests involved.

This situation presented the new rulers with a huge problem. As a new elite, they lacked any real power base within African society and owed their position purely to their links with the former colonial powers. They had been selected to receive Western education not because they belonged to indigenous ruling families, but on the basis of individual merit. The decisive factor had not been their links within African society, but – on the contrary – their successful integration into the colonial, European-style culture. The new African elites had grown up within the colonial system and were its heirs. Once the colonial powers had withdrawn, they had to build support bases within their own African societies. In the countries which became independent around 1960, the struggle for independence had been too limited to forge an alliance between the general population and the new elite. The ideals of freedom and progress which the new leaders proclaimed when they came to power could certainly count on the enthusiastic support of the people and therefore produced a feeling of solidarity. But that feeling faded when the ideals proved too difficult to achieve.

Unlike the establishment in the West, the new African elites had no economic base within their own societies. A very few countries (Ivory Coast, Kenya and Botswana, for instance) had a black middle class, but in most African countries the elite carried on no economic activity of their own. They were entirely dependent on their control over the state apparatus bequeathed to them. For this reason, they had a supreme personal stake in safeguarding their position: their individual incomes (and, indeed, personal safety) depended on it.[20] The elite had no choice but literally to appropriate the state. Within just a few years of independence, the two had become indistinguishable. The tender shoots of democracy which the colonial powers had planted soon shrivelled and died. After all, politicians who lost elections forfeited their incomes. Given that the entire elite had to be absorbed into the machinery of state, the mechanism of cooptation worked flawlessly. With one or two high-principled exceptions, all its members were united in a one-party political system which itself became fully identified with the state.

In practice, the new elite regarded the independent state and its resources as their own property. Public revenue, part of it donated from abroad, was used not only to finance normal state expenditure in areas like defence, education and health, but also to fund private consumption, coopt rebellious compatriots and purchase and maintain a network of 'clients'. This took place first and foremost in the capital cities. Public funds were used to buy the support of the greatest possible number of local leaders, who in turn used them to maintain and if possible expand their own support bases. It is true that this system of clientelism (also known as patronage) produced national stability through informal networks of individuals, but it also damaged the political system. It encouraged corruption and was a major cause of the development of ever greater and less efficient bureaucracies. Although still relatively small by international standards, the mushrooming government bureaucracies in the cities absorbed more and more of the scarce resources available to the independent countries of Africa.

It should hardly be surprising that African politics became increasingly autocratic in the 1960s and 1970s. The necessary checks and balances entirely disappeared. Heads of state had absolute power and, as a result, tended to display capricious and often bizarre behaviour. The rise of autocracy in independent Africa can probably be best explained in Marxist terms.[21] Unlike elites in Western countries, the African elite (the Marxist 'ruling class') had no sources of income other than the state. It was therefore not in a position to dissociate itself from the state (to grant the state autonomy) in order to allow the political apparatus to arrive at a consensus with other sections of society (the 'oppressed classes') on a new distribution of resources. This kind of establishment-led consensus produces political stability and thereby protects the long-term interests of the ruling class as a whole (as well as producing a wider distribution of wealth).

However, the African elite could not afford to grant any autonomy to the postcolonial state. It had to identify with it in order to ensure its own economic survival. In Marxist terms, although a ruling class, it was immature. A situation in which members of the ruling class are forced to harness the limited resources of the state tends to produce an atmosphere of cut-throat individualism which threatens the long-term interests of the elite as a whole. European history presents comparable situations in which new and still immature ruling classes struggled to harness the power of the state. According to Marx, this was the context in which an 'adventurer', a 'Bonaparte' – often a member of the military – could seize and retain power because he was sufficiently independent from the other members of the ruling class to be able to stand impartially 'above' them, while at the same time (perhaps unconsciously) serving their long-term interests. This theory of 'Bonapartism' seems to offer a reasonable explanation of African autocracy: it was not a good thing, but it was the best political solution that the elite could find to the problem of ensuring their own survival as a ruling class under unfavourable economic conditions. It meant that, alongside patronage, the elites had another tool for managing the population: old-fashioned oppression.

This strategy kept most of the African leaders who inherited the colonies in power until the end of the Cold War, if they were not dislodged by a coup d'état in the interim. Given the circumstances in which they came to power, this was no mean achievement. Compared with states elsewhere in the world, the independent African states tended to be small. They had to get by with modest populations, extremely undeveloped economies and an inhospitable natural environment (despite rich natural resources in some areas). What is more, history had thrown their societies and cultures entirely out of balance. They were ruled by elites which, once their initial ideals began to fade, were linked to the rest of the population only through the strategic support that they purchased (and through oppression pure and simple). But this system of clientelism itself led to state inefficiency, which weakened the legitimacy of the rulers. It seems likely that the structure of the independent African states could not have remained intact for so long if based only on this weak national foundation. To find out what else was shoring it up, we shall have to look outside Africa, at the international environment.

International support

for the new states

World War II radically altered the international balance of power. After the war, the United States gained dominance but had to put up with a second new superpower: the Soviet Union. Britain, France and Germany lost some of their influence. Eventually the changes divided the globe: on the one side was the United States plus the countries of Western Europe and other allies (the 'West') and on the other the Soviet Union and its satellite states (the 'East'). The two camps were embroiled in an ongoing struggle over ideology, politics, economics and culture, but the conflict never flared up into a direct military confrontation; the war remained 'cold'. Nevertheless, the Cold War largely shaped the course of events on every continent for almost the entire second half of the twentieth century, right up to the fall of the Berlin Wall, which was regarded as its symbol.[22]

This was also true of Africa. In the years following World War II, almost the entire continent was in the hands of the European colonial powers (mainly Britain and France). The earliest result of the new world order, initially dominated principally by the United States, was considerable support for Africa's first steps towards decolonisation. Washington itself was keen to gain greater access to Africa and realised that this would be easier to achieve if it could deal directly with the Africans rather than with their colonial masters in Europe. Moreover, Washington feared that any postponement of decolonisation would play into the Soviet Union's hands. Anticolonial sentiments in Africa already tended to be linked to socialist or communist sympathies. This made it natural to look to the Soviet Union – which had also turned against the West. It was no accident that, soon after World War II, that prominent advocate of African independence and unity, Nkrumah, pronounced himself in favour of a Union of African Socialist Republics. In 1948 he was arrested and found to be in possession of a pamphlet entitled *The West African Soviet Republic*. Rapid decolonisation, it seemed, might be able to keep the new African rulers in the Western camp, especially given their close historical ties with Europe. But the longer the wait, the less certain this would become.

It was this Western (particularly American, British and French) analysis of the situation that powered the surprisingly rapid decolonisation of most of Africa around 1960. Its accuracy was demonstrated over the next few years, when Africa's Cold War began in earnest. Despite their official independence, the countries born of the British and French colonies frequently retained close links with the former colonial power, through either the British Commonwealth or the French *Communauté*. These new countries were almost all spared the armed conflicts that broke out in other parts of the 'Third World'. The same could not be said of the rest of Africa. The refusal of the authoritarian regime in Lisbon to grant independence to the Portuguese colonies in Africa produced, as had been predicted, an ideal seedbed for nationalist revolutionary violence, taking the form of local outbreaks of Cold War hostilities. It was a similar story in Southern Africa, where the small white community refused to hand over power to the black majority. The Belgian Congo became independent in 1960, but the process of decolonisation was so chaotic that armed conflict broke out, with substantial international intervention motivated by the country's valuable natural resources. In the 1970s, Cold War hostilities also erupted in the Horn of Africa, a region that had no great history of colonisation outside of its links with Italy.

However, apart from these violent conflicts (which are discussed in greater detail at the end of this chapter), the majority of the African colonies experienced a smooth and peaceful transition to independence. The result was a patchwork of independent states covering the continent. In view of the fact that the same process had taken place in Asia, it is fair to conclude that the international political structure was at this time moving rapidly towards a global system of independent statehood. This was seen as the most relevant form of political organisation. In principle, and increasingly in practice, the entire world was divided into states and together they formed a new world organisation: the United Nations (UN). In 1960, two resolutions of the General Assembly clarified which countries would become eligible for membership – a group that included all African colonies and ex-colonies. In cases of aggression, members were to have a right to protection by the international community, as laid down in the UN Charter.

The fact that the former African colonies were granted full membership of the international community signified a new view of what statehood was, or should be. Previously, states had needed to prove themselves in order to gain recognition by the outside world. The main criterion was effective control, or sovereignty, over a fixed territory and its population. States that failed to gain or maintain such control disappeared and had no place in the international system. In all probability, the new African states could not have met that criterion. However, the matter was never put to the test.

The new system of African states would have been unlikely to survive any substantial external pressure. It escaped such pressure thanks to its international environment: the support provided principally by France, Britain and the United States. It was this that made it possible for the new states to come into being and to make it through their early years.

They were not strong enough to present any threat to their neighbours. In contrast to 'traditional' systems of 'positive sovereignty' – in which states were responsible for maintaining their own authority – this new system in Africa has sometimes been referred to as a system of 'negative sovereignty', because of the decisive importance of international support, and the states involved in it have been called 'quasi-states'.[23] The most extreme cases of weak sovereignty were those in which a particular faction was able to gain control of a country simply by taking possession of the capital. The international connections that this supplied were decisive. For example, the capital was where letters from the UN were received. This kind of 'letterbox sovereignty' existed in Angola, for example, for many years.[24]

Despite numerous internal uprisings, this artificial system of African statehood guaranteed stability throughout the Cold War period, because of the advantages for all concerned. It gave the two superpowers the chance to compete for the favours of independent African regimes. The European powers were relieved of the burden of their colonial possessions, but the continuing close ties with their ex-colonies enabled them to retain many of the benefits. And the African territories were now independent, formally at any rate. For the governments of the new countries, the situation meant that they stood not only at the apex of national client networks, but that they themselves were the clients of foreign patrons. This made them the link between internal and external systems of clientelism. As the official representatives of their countries on the international stage, they were in an ideal position to attract aid (for example, in the form of money or arms) to reinforce their grasp on the domestic situation. This international legitimacy was generally the decisive factor in domestic power struggles.

At the start of the Cold War, when the East-West conflict had not yet assumed global proportions, most African governments faced a simple choice.[25] Close, stable ties with Western patrons would guarantee their domestic position. This was the most they could hope for. The Eastern Bloc countries did not present a realistic alternative. They were not interested in Africa and were in any case not in a position to provide the degree of support available from the West. In the mid-1970s, this started to change. While the United States declined in stature due to its problems in Vietnam, the Soviet Union stepped up its activities worldwide. By this time, there were plenty of opportunities for it to intervene in Africa's internal affairs: the struggle for independence in the Portuguese colonies was reaching a climax and the revolution in Ethiopia was destabilising the entire Horn of Africa. In this period of mounting tension between East and West, African governments sometimes had a serious choice to make between patrons. In the Horn of Africa, the situation produced a real *renversement des alliances*: Ethiopia and Somalia simply switched allegiance from one superpower to the other. But there was also scope for governments to sit on the fence, though it required a tricky political balancing act.

In a few places in Africa, the Soviet Union and its vassal states provided extensive military support. Overall, however, their influence over the continent remained very limited. The Eastern Bloc simply did not have the resources to compete successfully with the West so far from home. The West (particularly France) continued to invest in multifaceted relationships with Africa, including not just military and financial support, but also economic, monetary, political, cultural and development assistance. The African authorities were able to use this support to maintain the internal stability of their countries, frequently in a way that permitted them to line their own pockets.

The inability of the Eastern Bloc to offer a serious alternative to the West was a blow to many African governments. Given the history of colonialism, it is not surprising that there was much anti-Western and pro-socialist rhetoric in Africa during the Cold War, even if such rhetoric largely ignored the material existence of continuing close ties with the West and a virtual absence of new ties with the East. There was, however, widespread support for the socialist model of state-centred, planned development. The West was unconcerned. In the eyes of Western strategists, whose attention was absorbed by the global conflict between East and West, the application of this model of development in Africa presented no threat to political stability or security. And, indeed, there was some support in the West for the idea that it might sometimes be better for development not to follow the capitalist Western model. This is why it was possible for new African socialist 'people's republics' (including some in the relatively stable countries that had once been French colonies) to remain within the Western sphere of influence.

Anglophone Africa following decolonisation

For a large group of seventeen African countries, English remained the official – or, at any rate, an important – language following decolonisation. With a population of around 330 million, Anglophone Africa predominated at the millennium. At that date, Francophone Africa encompassed the same number of sub-Saharan countries but had a much smaller population (approximately 170 million). Between them, the two language groups constitute a large majority in the forty-odd African countries south of the Sahara. Their colonial past has endowed each of the two groups with certain shared characteristics (such as similar public institutions) and influenced their membership of international political organisations: the British Commonwealth of Nations and the *Communauté* (Community of Francophone Countries) respectively.

With the exception of isolated individuals like Cecil Rhodes, who aspired to create a single great British territory stretching from Cape Town to Cairo, British colonial expansion in Africa was generally undertaken with mild reluctance. Colonial acquisitions were usually motivated by private commercial interests, the desire to provide better protection for existing possessions or the threat of expansion by other European powers.[26] Even so, once the division of Africa between the European powers was virtually complete, the British found that they had not only inadvertently achieved Rhodes' dream – an uninterrupted British territory stretching from South Africa via southern Central Africa (now Zimbabwe, Zambia and Malawi), East Africa (now Tanzania, Kenya and Uganda) and the Sudan all the way to Egypt – but also possessed colonies scattered throughout the continent. These encompassed the greater part of Southern Africa, the whole of East Africa and large (if discontinuous) portions of West Africa. Although smaller areas had often been combined for administrative convenience, the colonial philosophy of the British government was not directed at uniting its territories. Each of the colonies was different, existed in isolation and had its own ties with Britain. These were not expected to be too close. For example, in British (unlike French) colonial theory, it was unthinkable for Africans from the colonies to occupy seats in parliament.

The individualised approach to the British colonies was reflected in the approach to independence. Following the loss of the Indian subcontinent in 1947, the retention of the remaining colonies was no longer a matter of life or death. The African colonies could be granted independence if the international situation or local circumstances made the move desirable. There was no question of a uniform approach. In 1956, Sudan was the first to go, in the wake of the international crisis concerning Egypt's nationalisation of the Suez Canal. The British were afraid that Egypt (in victorious mood following the withdrawal of the Western powers from the Canal zone) would turn its attentions to the British colony on its southern border: a large and thinly populated country straddling the dividing line between Arab North Africa and sub-Saharan black Africa. They saw that rapid independence for Sudan would prevent Egyptian President Gamal Abdel Nasser from using a war against colonialism as a pretext for territorial expansion and would turn an Egyptian occupation of Sudan into an act of aggression. In the event, the strategy proved successful. The largest country in Africa (in terms of territory) gained its independence, although it faced a turbulent future plagued by relentless civil strife between the Arab north and the African south.

It was in West Africa, however, that the struggle for independence south of the Sahara proceeded most rapidly. As we have seen, Ghana was the frontrunner in this region. Following independence in 1957, the country experienced several years of relative prosperity. However, the 1960s saw rapid political and economic decline in this model African state. The new constitution of 1960 had made the country a republic and given President Nkrumah sweeping powers. As time went on, his regime became increasingly dictatorial. Press freedom was limited and political opponents imprisoned. In 1964, amendments to the constitution created a one-party state and made Nkrumah president for life. He was to find it less easy to consolidate his power in practice: just two years later, while Nkrumah was on a visit to Beijing, a military coup put an end to his presidency. The first leader of an independent African state went into exile in Guinea, where his friend Sékou Touré provided a safe haven. Meanwhile, Ghana's economy had suffered since 1960 both from Nkrumah's attempts to introduce socialist economic policies and from the decline in the price of cocoa. There was a succession of coups and the standard of living steadily deteriorated. It was not until the 1980s that Ghana succeeded in halting its political and economic decline.

In 1960, Nigeria became the second of Britain's West African colonies to achieve independence. It was the only country in Africa to become a federation. Each of its original regions (Northern, Western and Eastern Nigeria) was dominated by a single ethnic group. (Later, the number of regions increased.) Together, the three regions made Nigeria by far the most populous country in Africa. Of the approximately 200 million Africans in 1960, no fewer than 40 million were Nigerians. The country's economic potential (based in part on the large oil fields discovered soon after independence) confirmed its status as a giant on the African scene. Nigeria too, however, failed to live up to its early promise. Democracy perished in 1966 and there was no improvement in the standard of living. The government had huge difficulty in maintaining the unity of a country with such ethnic diversity.

In Eastern Nigeria, the region with large oil fields, there was particular discontent with the management of the country. The Ibo who inhabited the region, which they themselves called Biafra, resented the growing practice of using local wealth to meet financial shortfalls in the rest of the country. In 1966, an Ibo resistance movement launched a war of secession. The federal army responded violently, prompting three years of bloody fighting in Biafra, where the situation was further exacerbated by a famine. Although the Biafrans proclaimed a people's republic, they were unable to internationalise the struggle and attract support from the Eastern Bloc. Despite some assistance from France, Biafra finally lost the war, following hostilities and associated misery that cost the lives of two million people. The unity of Nigeria was preserved, although skirmishes between the various ethnic groups continued to occur on a fairly regular basis. Because of the size of the country, the failure of Nigeria to realise its potential was a problem for the entire region.

The three countries in East Africa – Kenya, Tanzania and Uganda – had all been British colonies, but each of them experienced an entirely different process of development between independence and the 1980s. This was partly due to the influence of the Cold War, with its competing models of development. Perhaps surprisingly, these differences between the countries in the region (and even within the individual states) produced no great tension. The models of development in Kenya and Tanzania were diametrically opposed. Whereas Kenya opted for Western-style capitalism and offered generous facilities to transnational enterprises, Tanzania was determined to extirpate the capitalist spirit and establish an African form of socialism. Quite apart from the chaos in Uganda, these contrasting development ideologies, as well as personal differences between the leaders of the countries, made it extremely difficult to achieve cooperation in the East African Community (which was launched in 1967). Not surprisingly, therefore, attempts at regional cooperation ground to a halt in the 1970s and were not resumed until 1993, once relations between the three countries had improved. At that point, the three countries established the East African Cooperation, whose aims include the improvement of regional road and rail networks.

The Kenyan economy, in which white settlers had a considerable share, had long been one of the strongest in Africa. Following independence, it continued to expand at such a rate that per capita income increased despite the rapid rate of population growth (at one point the highest in the world at four per cent a year). President Jomo Kenyatta made the country a single-party state and ruled in an increasingly dictatorial fashion. At the time of his death, in 1978, Kenya's boom years had just been ended by the rising price of imported oil and the declining prices of the country's main export products. Kenyatta was succeeded by Daniel arap Moi, who had a much weaker power base in the country, if only because he was a member of an ethnic minority (the Kalenjin). Despite this, Moi proved able to survive tensions between different ethnic groups and an attempted coup in 1982 to remain head of state. But the period of prosperity was gone for good. The population continued to grow at a rapid rate while the economy stagnated and the quality of governance deteriorated. It was in a debilitated state that the country staggered into the 1990s.

The same was true of Tanzania, even though it had adopted a totally different course since independence. President Julius Nyerere, universally respected for his personal integrity, adhered to an ideal which he called *ujamaa*, a Swahili word meaning 'neighbourliness' or 'community spirit'. Rather than emphasising the importance of urban life and industrialisation, he concentrated on rural areas and agriculture. He believed that the sparse rural population of the country should be concentrated into larger villages, so that they could be given easier access to modern facilities like education, health care and clean drinking water. These villages could be connected to the road network and hence with the rest of the country. In two stages during the 1970s, more than eighty per cent of the rural population were relocated (on a non-voluntary basis, of course). The policy met with great resistance, but did eventually produce results. In the 1980s, according to UN researchers, educational and medical provision in rural areas of Tanzania was among the best in Africa. But these results were not achieved for the country as a whole. The socialist model of development produced no economic growth.

Tanzania's decision to adopt a form of socialism was connected with the union of the island of Zanzibar with the part of the mainland previously known as Tanganyika. Zanzibar was formally ruled by the Sultan of distant Oman. In January 1964 there was a revolution on the island, directed mainly against the local Afro-Arab elite. The new left-wing leadership sought international recognition of Zanzibar as an independent country and accordingly recognised the German Democratic Republic (becoming the first non-Eastern Bloc country to do so), as well as the other Eastern Bloc countries, North Korea, Cuba, and the socialist countries and freedom movements in Africa. The West was displeased by these events, which took place shortly after the Cuban missile crisis, and Zanzibar became known as the 'Cuba of Africa'. Yet there was no panic, nor any reason for it. Many of the people of Zanzibar, especially the black Africans, were far more moderate than their revolutionary leadership and had no desire for their small and impecunious island to become independent. They much preferred a union with Kenya and/or Tanganyika, which were at that time still discussing a possible East African Federation. Nothing ever came of that proposal, but Tanganyika proved willing to merge with Zanzibar. In April 1964 Tanganyika and Zanzibar united to become Tanzania.

The union between Tanganyika and Zanzibar certainly neutralised the radical elements on the island, as the Western countries had hoped, but at the same time it led to a certain alienation of Tanzania from the West, particularly because Zanzibar's socialist past could not be smoothed over without some trouble. Part of the problem was the issue of Germany. Zanzibar had the only embassy of the German Democratic Republic in Africa. Because Tanzania was reluctant simply to break off relations with East Germany (although was willing to replace the embassy with a consulate), West Germany reduced its support to the country. Nyerere was so offended that he refused all further assistance from the German Federal Republic. Relations with the United States and Britain also suffered. Tanzania became increasingly reliant on aid from socialist countries, as well as Scandinavia and the Netherlands. When Tanzania wanted to build a railroad to Zambia in order to enable that country to conduct its international trade without routing goods through Rhodesia and South Africa, the Western countries refused to finance the project. One Western ambassador wryly remarked to President Nyerere, 'I think you'll find that the railroad to Zambia passes through Zanzibar.'[27] The Tanzam railroad was eventually built by the People's Republic of China.

Relations between the United States and Tanzania improved during Jimmy Carter's presidency in the 1970s. By this time, relations with the main European countries had also been gradually restored. Despite his socialist sympathies, President Nyerere was admired in the West for his personal qualities. This could not, of course, protect Tanzania from the adverse economic effects of his policies and of the international crisis of the 1970s. Nyerere felt forced to borrow from the International Monetary Fund (IMF), but to the last refused to comply with the loan conditions, which he believed would mean dismantling his model. In 1986 he retired voluntarily from the presidency – a first in the postcolonial history of East Africa and rare anywhere on the continent. Right up to his death in 1999, he continued to play an important behind-the-scenes role in Tanzanian politics, although he could not prevent the country's further economic decline and changes in policy in the direction demanded by the IMF.

The stability of Kenya and Tanzania stood in sharp contrast to the instability of the third country in East Africa: Uganda. Once known as the pearl of Africa, Uganda was unable to live up to its initial promise once it had achieved independence. The socialist government of Milton Obote (more or less a kindred spirit of Tanzania's President Nyerere) did nothing to improve Uganda's economy. In 1971 Obote was deposed by a military coup headed by the commander-in-chief of the Ugandan army, General Idi Amin. The new president proved to be a cruel and arbitrary tyrant. His greatest victims were the economically important Asian population (who were, in fact, suffering all over East Africa as a result of the policy of economic Africanisation): they were forced to leave the country at short notice, abandoning all their possessions. Under Amin, there were massive abuses of human rights in Uganda. Nobody was safe. Even the Archbishop of Kampala was murdered, according to rumour by Amin himself. Within a few years of Amin coming to power, the country was in chaos.

In 1979, a risky invasion of Tanzania by the Ugandan army was Amin's downfall. Nyerere (who was giving Obote safe haven in his capital, Dar es Salaam) seized the opportunity to topple Amin. The Tanzanian army marched on Kampala, meeting little opposition. Amin fled the country and Obote was reinstated as president. However, his second period as head of state was no more successful than his first. His supporters engaged in widespread violence against members of Amin's regime and against certain ethnic groups. Armed uprisings continued until 1986, when a faction led by the minister of defence, Yoweri Museveni, seized power. Museveni had himself appointed president and succeeded in restoring stability to the country. In the late 1980s and early 1990s, Uganda gradually began to recover.

From 1960 onwards, events in Southern Africa were dominated by African resistance to the white domination of South Africa, Rhodesia, Namibia, Angola and Mozambique. This resistance was not only internal, but also external, from the newly independent 'frontline states' to the north. President Kenneth Kaunda's Zambia (the former British colony of Northern Rhodesia) was one of these frontline states, but neighbouring Malawi (the former British colony of Nyasaland) under President Hastings Banda caused much commotion in Africa by adopting a stubborn pro-South Africa stance motivated by economic considerations. The many tensions within Southern Africa made it an ideal terrain for the superpowers to extend their spheres of influence. This violent period in Southern Africa's history is discussed in detail later in this chapter.

Francophone Africa following decolonisation

Most Francophone African countries are in West Africa, a region roughly divided into two areas with contrasting ecologies and climates. In the north is the Sahel, an area of steppe with little precipitation, and between the Sahel and the coast is an area of savannah, merging into tropical rainforest in the coastal zone. With the single exception of Guinea, the Francophone countries (like their Anglophone counterparts) escaped the direct influence of the Cold War. And, again like the Anglophone countries, they displayed wide variations in development from the 1960s to the 1980s. Even so, Francophone Africa was more uniform than the Anglophone parts of the continent. The reason for this was the French policy of maintaining far closer ties with the former colonies than Britain thought desirable. Unlike Britain, France believed that the African colonies should remain, so far as possible, within its own sphere of political and cultural influence. France's *mission civilisatrice* was to disseminate its culture in Africa.

Around 1960, the French government successfully converted its colonies into a new community of nations (the *Communauté*), in which France continued to hold sway. The great political units of French West Africa and French Equatorial Africa were broken up. Talks on independence were held with the much smaller fragments of the French colonial empire which were to become separate nations and France then concluded with each of these new political units a separate bilateral treaty defining the limits to its sovereignty. The French government frequently continued to have a say in important matters like foreign policy, defence, the economy and the commodities and monetary policies of the former colonies. France also remained the leading aid donor. The 1948 *Communauté Française* (later to become the *Communauté Financière Africaine* or CFA) remained in existence, with its own currency (the CFA franc), the exchange value of which was guaranteed by France. The constitutions of the new countries were modelled on that of the French Fifth Republic and the education system remained French.

The French government had various reasons for this policy. It was one of the things that supported France's continuing claim to be a major world power and it helped to counter the influence of the Anglophone countries in Africa. In international organisations like the UN, France could rely on the support of its African allies. It could continue to pursue its mission of disseminating French culture around the world. And – of course – there were economic reasons, in particular the desire to retain its privileged access to the commodities and agricultural products of the countries concerned. French development assistance also had major economic benefits for the giver. It was closely tied to African imports of French products and the use of French technicians. But, alongside this French self-interest, there was also genuine anxiety about the future of the new African states. Around 1960, President Charles de Gaulle believed that they still did not have nearly enough structure to function properly as independent states. His government felt that the cost of maintaining a French presence in Africa, providing assistance in a wide range of areas and supporting the exchange value of the CFA franc was worth paying.

Once the French government under de Gaulle had concluded that African decolonisation was inevitable, it devoted itself to the task with great vigour. The process was carefully orchestrated by Paris, which organised a referendum in 1958 offering the African colonies the choice between independence on France's terms (that is, within limits but with continuing French assistance) or total independence with the loss of all their ties with France. The only one to opt for total independence was the small country of Guinea, led by the charismatic and self-reliant Ahmed Sékou Touré. The French government decided to make an example of the country. De Gaulle ordered all French government employees working there to leave immediately, taking with them every piece of government property they could. Before the end of the year, Guinea had become an independent sovereign state – but it had been stripped of virtually the entire machinery of government. The departing French had taken with them all of their supplies and equipment, right down to the official tele-phones and stationery. And all forms of French assistance and investment had been halted. The other countries were quick to learn the lesson of Guinea. France had little trouble in gaining their rapid consent to independence on French terms. In the majority, the process of independence was completed by the end of 1960. In August of that year, no fewer than eight French colonies became independent. The leaders of these new nations accepted the French deal with little resistance, since the limits on their full independence were offset by obvious advantages. French funding continued. Major African leaders who complied faith-fully with the agreements were kept in power by Paris, irrespective of the nature of their regime. The French secret service played an important role. Requests from various heads of state for French intervention in their countries were kept ready and waiting in Paris; only the date needed to be filled in.[28] From 1960 on, there was an average of one French military in-tervention a year in the former French colonies. France could rely on the tacit support of the other Western powers, including the United States. They saw the French presence in Africa as a major bulwark against possible infiltration by the Soviet Union. In 1983, when Libya once again intervened in the civil war in Chad, President Ronald Reagan of the United States reminded his French colleague President François Mitterrand of France's 'historic respon-sibility' to eliminate Libyan influence (probably backed by the Eastern Bloc) in this former French colony – a duty which was duly performed with the use of French military muscle.

Despite many coups and occasional ethnic clashes in countries of minor political sig-nificance, the Francophone countries were to remain peaceful compared to the rest of Africa. The monetary cooperation surrounding the CFA franc had a favourable influence on economic development. Right through to the mid-1980s, inflation in the CFA zone (actually two zones: Francophone West Africa and Central Africa) was considerably lower than elsewhere on the continent and the convertibility of the CFA franc was attractive to foreign investors. Since it made imports cheaper, it was also extremely attractive to the local elite. In addition, countries in the zone could count on substantial French development assistance. Partly for these reasons, the economies of the Francophone countries did rea-sonably well, despite being dealt a heavy blow by the crisis of the 1970s, when oil prices rose rapidly and the price of most African exports declined.

Political cooperation between France and Francophone Africa took firmer shape in 1973 when President Georges Pompidou organised a Franco-African summit. This was the first of a series of conferences, held alternately in France and in Africa, where the heads of state of France and Francophone Africa discussed topics of common interest. In time, heads of state of other African countries were also invited. The first were the leaders of the former Belgian colonies. Later, leaders of non-Francophone countries were also welcome to attend. Around 1990, these summits were to provide important encouragement for political reform in Africa, but during the Cold War years the emphasis was on political stability. To ensure it, the French government was not infrequently prepared to support African leaders who were indifferent to the development of their countries or who stopped at nothing to line their own pockets.

The development of Ivory Coast in the decades immediately following independence is perhaps the best advertisement for this approach. The relationship between Paris and the former independence fighter Félix Houphouët-Boigny, who became president in 1960, was always close. The president's loyalty to France was such that he never had to fear for his position, right up to his death in 1993. Numerous French nationals continued to be employed in the public institutions of Ivory Coast, especially in posts concerned with the economy. A few years after independence, there were actually more French nationals working in Ivory Coast than at any time during the colonial period. However, this did not prevent the entire apparatus of government becoming permeated with corruption and favouritism. Eventually, even the elderly president – nicknamed 'Le Vieux' – became infected with greed and megalomania. In 1983 he proclaimed his birthplace, the inland village of Yamoussoukro, the new capital of Ivory Coast and in the late 1980s he had a gigantic basilica built there: a replica of St Peter's in Rome, albeit – at the urgent request of the Vatican – on a slightly smaller scale.

Even during the colonial era, Houphouët's great African rival was Léopold Senghor, who became the first president of Senegal. Senghor, often dubbed the 'poet-president', felt himself to be both an African Frenchman and a French African. He refused to choose between the two cultures, preferring to draw sustenance from both. He was the first African to be admitted to the prestigious Académie Française, but was also fascinated by African culture. In an attempt to promote a sense of self-worth among Africans, he developed the term négritude to denote the entire world of African values and culture. As president, he had to content himself with the small country of Senegal. Once, in colonial times, Senegal and its capital Dakar had been the heart of all French West Africa. In 1960, however, it adopted a policy of isolation. At first Senghor ruled the country in a fairly autocratic manner and with relatively little success. In 1976, however, he decided to adopt a new course. Political prisoners were freed and Senegal became a multiparty democracy. In 1978 there were general elections, which he won by a large majority. In 1980 he stepped down voluntarily, appointing his prime minister, Abdou Diouf, to succeed him. In the forty years following independence, Senegal would have only two presidents.

The third most prominent former French colony (actually a trusteeship) was Cameroon. This republic was the result of a merger between a small British protectorate and a larger French one. Together they formed the Federal Republic of Cameroon, but barely a year later President Ahmadou Ahidjo proclaimed a United Republic. Tension between the Francophone and Anglophone parts of the country remained a constant feature in the history of Cameroon, with the English-speakers always feeling themselves to be at a disadvantage. Ahidjo ruled the country in autocratic fashion until he, quite unexpectedly, stepped down in 1982 and handed over power to his constitutional successor, Paul Biya. However, the elderly ex-president did not find it easy to relinquish his influence. The prolonged power struggle between him and his successor in the 1980s did little to improve the stability of the country. Ties with France remained close, although there were fewer French nationals in key positions in Cameroon than in countries like Ivory Coast or oil-rich Gabon.

These three leading countries – Ivory Coast, Senegal and Cameroon – were surrounded by many other new but smaller Francophone countries: Burkina Faso, Mali, Mauritania, Niger, Benin, Togo, Chad, the Central African Republic, Congo (Brazzaville) and Gabon. During the 1970s, some of the Sahelian countries were struck by famine as a result of drought. Economically, they had little to offer (apart from Gabon's oil). Partly because of a rapid rate of population growth, it was difficult for them to prevent a decline in the general standard of living. With the exception of Gabon, they were less politically stable than Ivory Coast, Senegal or Cameroon. There were occasional coups, but France refrained from intervening, preferring to keep watch from a distance. Cold War tensions had little impact on these countries.

After its rejection of a continuing relationship with France, Guinea was always the odd man out in Francophone Africa. In 1960 President Sékou Touré took his country out of the CFA zone and in 1965 he even broke off diplomatic relations with France. As a result, Guinea became completely isolated. No other Western country was prepared to risk offending France by offering assistance. For a time, Soviet or even Chinese support seemed to be an option but none was forthcoming in practice. Aid from the Soviet Union proved of little help, although the Russian snowploughs provided for the airport in tropical Conakry had a certain wry entertainment value. As early as 1961 the Soviet ambassador had to leave the country amid accusations of interference in Guinea's internal affairs. This put an end to any threat of a Cold War conflict involving Guinea. Nevertheless, Sékou Touré continued to rule the country in an oppressive manner and to pursue a Soviet-style approach to the economy. In 1979 he proclaimed a 'Revolutionary People's Republic'. Under his reign of terror, no fewer than a million people fled from Guinea. His sudden death in 1984 left a power vacuum which was immediately filled by the military. The new leaders abandoned the policy of isolationism and sought *rapprochement* with France and with Guinea's neighbouring countries.

From the Belgian Congo to Zaire

In the 1990s, Central Africa was the least stable region in the whole continent. The reasons for this were mainly historical. In the precolonial period, this vast region – originally largely covered with tropical rainforest – was home to a number of major kingdoms, including those of the Kongo, Luba and Lunda. In the second half of the nineteenth century, King Leopold of Belgium appropriated the region and turned it into his private fiefdom, called the Congo Free State after the mighty Congo river which, with its many tributaries, carries the water from the rainforest down to the Atlantic Ocean. Leopold's regime was brutal even by the standards of his day. After international and domestic pressure forced the king to relax his hold on the area in 1908, the Congo became a normal colony under Belgian rule and the worst atrocities were ended.

The area's promotion to the status of a Belgian colony produced some improvement in the lot of its people. Belgium established a more or less modern administration based in the capital, Leopoldville (today's Kinshasa), but displayed little interest in the rest of the country. The emphasis was on exploiting the country's wealth of raw materials and minerals (in particular, copper, cobalt, diamonds, gold, uranium and oil). Where profits could be made, as in Katanga, in the far southeast of the country, white settlements grew up, surrounded by concentrations of black workers. Attempts were made to supply the rest of the population with basic health care and education (mainly through missionary work), but this seldom extended further than primary schooling. No effort was made to establish, as in other African colonies, an elite of Western-style intellectuals who would eventually be able to take over the country. Brussels maintained that the colony was so undeveloped that it would have to remain under Belgian rule for generations to come. Its approach was completely based on the assumption that the Belgian presence would continue indefinitely. Even in the latter part of the 1950s, when the colonies in Asia had become independent and similar decolonisation seemed to be on the way in Africa, Brussels still foresaw no end to the Belgian presence in Central Africa for some decades to come.

The decolonisation of the Belgian Congo in 1960 was therefore a complete surprise to everyone, including those directly involved. With the rapid advance of the French and British colonies towards independence, and riots in Leopoldville, the Belgian government had woken up to the fact that decolonisation was inevitable. Their decision to withdraw as quickly as possible was based on two beliefs: firstly, that this would allow them to avoid the sacrifice of Belgian lives and resources in a conflict with Congolese nationalists (of whom there were as yet very few); secondly, that they might then retain more control over the Congolese economy and the undeveloped state. The Belgian government assumed that the main economic enterprises, the armed forces and the administration of the country (such as it was) would continue under Belgian management. The political and social structures handed over at independence on 30 June 1960 were little more than an empty shell.

In the vast jungles of Congo, with its many different peoples, there was really only the army to maintain or promote the unity of the country. Other public institutions were confined in Leopoldville and the other major towns. The structure that was handed over was largely Belgian. The king was replaced by a president with exclusively ceremonial duties, while political authority was invested in the prime minister. Between these two figures – the conservative President Joseph Kasavubu and the left-wing nationalist Prime Minister Patrice Lumumba – a power struggle quickly developed. The bicameral parliament had a nationalist majority. It may never be clear whether the Congolese government had any chance of retaining control over the country, given that there were virtually no administrative structures and the international environment was against it. What is certain, though, is that the clumsiness of the Congolese leaders exacerbated the situation, not only plunging the country into chaos but also entangling it in the web of Cold War intrigue.

Tensions started to emerge even as the independence ceremony was under way. In his speech, the Belgian king described Belgian rule in Congo as a heroic feat, while Prime Minister Lumumba emphasised the racial discrimination and brutal exploitation it had entailed. Less than a week later, a mutiny broke out in the army, with African troops rising up against the Belgian officers who still commanded them. Believing that independence would change nothing in practice, the army chief-of-staff (Lieutenant General Émile Janssens) had scoffed at the ambitions of the new Congolese government. The heart of the mutiny was in the mineral-rich area of Katanga, where the mutineers worked hand in hand with a local group resisting continuing rule from distant Leopoldville. The leader of the local uprising, Moise Tshombe, proclaimed the province independent. Belgian civilians were caught up in the ensuing fighting and some were killed. In July 1960, within a month of its official withdrawal from the country, Belgium intervened on its own initiative, uninvited by Lumumba and without international consultation. Lumumba had Janssens replaced with a Congolese army officer called Joseph-Désiré Mobutu.

The government in Leopoldville was itself unable to control the uprising in Katanga, but received help from the UN, provided on the initiative of the United States. This American move was motivated by Washington's fear that Lumumba would carry out his threats to call on the Soviet Union to help restore order in the country. Only 35 at the time and with no international experience, the young prime minister probably had no idea of the mistake he was making. Rather than playing off the West against the East, he was in fact signing his own death warrant. In 1960, the Soviet Union was in no state to intervene effectively in the heart of Africa – at the height of the struggle there were less than five hundred Russian and Czech advisors – while his threats made the Americans see red. For Washington, Lumumba was no longer an acceptable custodian of Congo's mineral resources. The conservative President Kasavubu was persuaded by the Americans to remove Lumumba as a political force. In the same year, during a journey in the interior, the prime minister was picked up by a group of combatants and taken to Kinshasa as a prisoner. He was subsequently handed over to his archenemies in Katanga, where he was promptly murdered.

For some time, the country was effectively divided into three. The capital, Leopoldville (now Kinshasa), was controlled by the conservatives (also known as neocolonialists, because of their ties with America). Elisabethville (now Lubumbashi), in the mining area of Katanga, was under the influence of the old colonial power, Belgium. Finally, Stanleyville (now Kisangani), in the northeast, was in the hands of the nationalist adherents of the murdered Lumumba. Thereafter, the United States played a major role in ensuring that the conservatives came to control the whole country. To this end it intervened both directly and via the UN, which was principally concerned to restore peace in the country. Without foreign interference, the nationalists would probably have won (at one time they held as much as two-thirds of the country), but the American support for the conservatives in the capital and for the official Congolese army was eventually to prove decisive. The new balance of power became clear in 1965, when the commander in chief of the army, General Mobutu, seized power in a coup d'état. He appointed himself president, dissolved the parliament, forbade all political activity and subsequently ruled by decree. With the help of the West, he was to keep control of the country for the next thirty-two years.

Mobutu enjoyed some initial popularity among the Congolese population. He had, after all, put an end to the civil war. But this support crumbled away during the long years of dictatorship. His rule was marked by the same paternalism practised by Belgium in the colonial period. His main priority was to control the country's territory for purposes of economic exploitation. Social development was seen as irrelevant and perhaps even counterproductive, since it would only encourage political unrest. Under Mobutu's regime, therefore, there was no real attempt to improve the general standard of living. Education and health care deteriorated rapidly after the churches, which had been critical of Mobutu, were banned from providing them. Organisations of any kind were taboo, with the sole exception of the revolutionary people's party – *Mouvement Populaire de la Révolution* (MPR) – set up in 1967.

In internal affairs, Mobutu relied partly on a system of 'divide and rule', but most of all on the army. Increasingly, it was drawn from his own ethnic group, the Ngbandi, native to the north of the country. Mobutu did attempt to attract wider domestic support through actions of a more or less symbolic nature, such as the development of an ideology of *authenticité* in the 1970s. This entailed an Africanisation of Congolese society and the Congolese state. For example, most of the remaining names from colonial times were changed and Congo became Zaire. In his own name, Mobutu replaced Joseph-Désiré with Sese Seko. Every measure he took was legitimised by reference to 'Zairisation'.

Without foreign military assistance, however, his regime could not have survived. In 1977 and 1978, there were two major uprisings in the mining area in the south. These were supported by Angola, where a Marxist regime had come to power after independence in 1975. These assaults on Mobutu's position could not have been suppressed without the Western military support provided both directly (primarily by Belgium and France) and indirectly through pro-Western African countries like Senegal, Morocco and Egypt. The communist sympathies nurtured by organisations opposing Mobutu's regime were sufficient reason for Washington to keep its vassal in power.

Under Mobutu, Zaire pursued an unambiguously pro-Western course, with just a few exceptions (such as the treatment of the major Western-owned private enterprises in the 1970s). Apart from the former French colony of Congo (Brazzaville), Central Africa remained free of communist influence. The West's hold on the country's mineral riches remained unshaken, though Mobutu demanded a good price for them. In stark contrast to the complete absence of economic development in the country as a whole, the personal fortune of the head of state grew to dizzying proportions. In the late 1970s, Mobutu was one of the richest men on earth. Around the same time, the worldwide economic recession drove up Congo's per capita national debt until it was among the highest in the world. During the 1980s, there was no real change in the situation. Fundamentally, the circumstances in Congo-Zaire were identical to those a century earlier: an authoritarian regime was using foreign support to maintain control of the interior from a remote capital (Leopoldville/Kinshasa). However, the Cold War was now drawing to a close. The Soviet Union no longer posed a threat to Central Africa and the West's interest in keeping Mobutu in power was waning. The end of the Cold War would herald a new era for the country.

Late decolonisation in

Southern Africa

Southern Africa is a vast region of plateaus, steppes, deserts and – further north, close to Central and East Africa – tropical rainforest. Today it accommodates ten different states, with borders that reflect the colonial history of the region. The southern tip of the continent, strategically located at the confluence of the Indian and Atlantic Oceans, is inhabited by the descendants of a large group of white European settlers (mainly Dutch and British). It was these descendants of European settlers who, in 1910, obtained independence for the Union of South Africa and so created the first modern independent state in the region. The majority of both the Atlantic and the Indian Ocean coastline in the region was then controlled by Portugal, the earliest European colonial power in Africa. These coastal areas and their hinterland formed the colonies of Angola and Mozambique. An intervening strip of Atlantic coastline (mostly desert) was once one of Germany's African colonies. Germany had to surrender it following its defeat in World War I, together with the other German possessions in Africa: Togo, Cameroon, Rwanda-Burundi and Tanganyika (the mainland portion of the territory that eventually became Tanzania). Following the departure of the Germans, South Africa was allowed to administer what was then known as South West Africa, initially on behalf of the League of Nations and later of the United Nations.

Scattered over the interior were other countries which had once been British colonies or protectorates. Three of them – Swaziland, Basutoland and Bechuanaland – had been taken under Britain's wing in the latter half of the nineteenth century in order to prevent northward migration by South African Afrikaners (descendants of Dutch settlers, who lived in a state of permanent friction with the British immigrants in the area). These thinly populated areas also became independent after World War II. By that time Lesotho (formerly Basutoland) was already entirely surrounded by South African territory and Swaziland and Botswana (formerly Bechuanaland) largely so. Immediately to the north of South Africa lay the white outpost of Rhodesia, for the time being still under British rule, and further north were Zambia and Malawi, both of which gained their independence from Britain in 1964.

Portugal had no intention of granting independence to its colonies, which it regarded as inalienable overseas provinces. Its colonies in Southern Africa were resource-rich Angola and poorer Mozambique. Portugal, like France, felt it had a mission to inculcate its own language and culture into the local population. In theory, an *assimilado*, a local who had assimilated Portuguese education and culture, presenting the right documentation could eventually acquire the same rights as white settlers. In practice, however, the Portuguese took a harder line than the French. There was little real assimilation; in Angola, only around thirty thousand Africans ever received Portuguese citizenship, and in Mozambique no more than a few hundred. Exploitation and oppression were routine. While France and Britain were reducing their presence in Africa during the years around independence in the 1950s and 1960s, the authoritarian government in Lisbon actually increased the Portuguese presence by encouraging emigration to Africa. The new Portuguese settlers found themselves surrounded by growing demands for independence. The struggle for independence in both colonies was to be shaped largely by the Cold War.

South Africa was the political, military and economic heavyweight of Southern Africa (and, indeed, the whole of sub-Saharan Africa). Because of the large numbers of white settlers, the history of the country had been entirely different from that of the rest of Africa. Because the settlers in South Africa had always intended to remain there permanently, there could be no question of a simple handover of power to the black population. The Union of South Africa had become independent in 1910 but power in the country remained entirely in the hands of whites. They had built up an economy which was as modern as any in the West in terms of its structure and productivity, but which was based on cheap black labour. Around 1990, South African production was almost equal to that of all the rest of Africa put together. Moreover, this powerful economy was located at a highly strategic point for international navigation and had access to a wealth of raw materials and minerals, including the uranium that was so important to the arms industry.

So it was that the black 'developing country' of South Africa harboured within its borders a prosperous and industrialised white nation. Interaction between the two worlds was confined almost entirely to the economic sphere. As the century wore on, successive white governments phased in a system of apartheid (racial segregation). In its most extreme form, this meant that, apart from supplying their labour for use in the white economy, blacks were forbidden to have any contact with whites or even to visit the same places. Racial segregation was codified in a wide range of legislation. The official justification was that separate development for each population group would produce the best results. The blacks, it was claimed, would automatically lose out if forced to compete with the whites. In actual fact, the system was far less neutral than the doctrine might suggest: for example, provision for health and education was far worse in the case of the black community than for whites, so there was no level playing field for development.

As more and more countries in Africa became independent, the fundamental inequality between blacks and whites in South Africa became a thorn in the flesh not only of the South African blacks, but of the whole of Africa and even of the entire Western world, because of the associations the system evoked with the racist doctrines of Nazi Germany. But as long as the Cold War continued, the white population of South Africa and the adjacent region could use the international environment to reinforce its own otherwise shaky strategic position. Internationally, the South African authorities presented the country as a bulwark against the advance of communism. The white people in the region saw themselves as an integral part of Western civilisation and, at the same time, as protecting the West's substantial economic interests in that part of the world. They saw the black population, both in South Africa and in the rest of the region (indeed, in the whole of Africa), as the enemy. In Cold War-speak, this meant that black Africa would opt for communism if it were to become independent. Accordingly, South Africa was opposed to independence for the rest of Africa, although it could not exercise any direct influence on the situation in distant countries. Closer to home, in Southern Africa, things were different. The black population of South West Africa could forget about independence for the time being, despite the dismay of the UN, which had formal authority over the region. Pretoria also forged successful alliances with Portugal to prevent independence for Angola and Mozambique.

South Africa owed this dominant role not only to its own considerable power but also to the support of the West (in particular the United States). As Cold War tensions increased, South Africa's offer to serve the West as a bastion against communism proved irresistible. During the 1950s, extensive arms shipments were made to South Africa and an agreement was concluded for the use of South African uranium in US nuclear weapons. Even so, the Americans were never entirely comfortable about their friendship with South Africa. They had ethical objections to apartheid and were repeatedly reminded of them both by the black community in the United States and by the newly independent black African states, which Washington was also supporting. The black states to the north of South Africa saw themselves as 'frontline states', with a responsibility to fight for the liberation of the whole of Africa south of their borders. Their aims included both the expulsion of the Portuguese from Angola and Mozambique and the end of white rule in South Africa, South West Africa and Rhodesia.

The former British colonies immediately set out to make life difficult for South Africa at meetings of the British Commonwealth. As early as 1961, shortly after the South African police had massacred black demonstrators in Sharpeville, South Africa realised that its position as a member of the Commonwealth was no longer tenable, and withdrew from the organisation. A few months later, the rift with Britain – which had joined in the criticism of apartheid – was widened by the proclamation of a republic. This meant that the British queen was no longer head of state in South Africa.

In Rhodesia, relations between Britain and the colony's white administration were becoming still more strained. Britain refused to grant independence to Rhodesia if white rule was to continue. In 1965, when it became clear that London would not back down from this position, the country's hardline white leader, Ian Smith, issued a unilateral declaration of independence. Relations with Britain were broken off. The white population of Rhodesia (a mere 250,000 out of a total population of five million) would henceforth stand alone against the black freedom fighters. In doing so, they received practical assistance from neighbouring Portuguese Mozambique and economic and military support from South Africa. Even so, the whites realised that they could not remain in conflict with the majority population indefinitely if they wished to maintain an acceptable standard of living and security for themselves. There was strong international pressure on Ian Smith and mounting African support for the black freedom fighters. In 1980, the white settlers gave up the struggle. For a few months Rhodesia returned to the formal authority of Britain, but only long enough to enable a handover of power to a black majority administration. In the same year, Rhodesia achieved internationally recognised independence under the new name of Zimbabwe (after the imposing ruins of an ancient empire).

In the Portuguese colonies of Angola and Mozambique, too, various liberation movements had also been increasing the military pressure on the white settlers. Following the 1974 coup d'état in Portugal, there was a complete U-turn on the issue of the colonies. The African wars in the colonies were unpopular and the new democratic government wanted to end them immediately. In great haste and within just a few months, the country divested itself of all its African colonies (as well as East Timor in Southeast Asia). In Angola and Mozambique, power was handed over to the liberation movement controlling the capital city: in Angola this was the MPLA in Luanda, while in Mozambique it was FRELIMO in Lourenço Marques (the name of which was immediately changed to Maputo). The leftist government of Portugal was indifferent to the fact that both these organisations were Marxist. Unfortunately, however, both countries (and Angola in particular) had a number of other liberation movements, each with its own sources of international support and ethnic and economic power bases. Consequently, the transfer of power did nothing to ensure national unity. This was to remain a problem so long as the Cold War continued to feed the flames of local rivalries.

Cold War hostilities were fiercest in Angola, where the main opposing parties were the government army (the former MPLA freedom fighters) supported by Soviet advisers and Cuban soldiers, and UNITA, backed by South Africa, Zaire, Zambia and – much more importantly – the United States. Although the two superpowers were represented only by soldiers from satellite states, the confrontation was so fierce than neither side was willing to back down. As a result, the main loser was the local population. The same was true in Mozambique, where the struggle between the government army (FRELIMO) and the RENAMO rebel movement (originating mainly from the Rhodesian security service) plunged the country into chaos and misery. This in itself fulfilled South Africa's main aim of ensuring that Angola and Mozambique could present no possible threat to the apartheid regime in Pretoria. No fewer than fifty thousand Cuban troops helped the regime in Luanda to keep control of a portion of the country. By the end of the 1980s, it was they who presented the last remaining potential threat to South Africa and Western interests in the region.

Washington managed to solve this problem by linking it to the independence of South West Africa/Namibia. As early as 1966, the UN had withdrawn South Africa's mandate to administer this territory, but the Pretoria government steadfastly refused to withdraw. The main Namibian liberation movement, the South West African People's Organisation (SWAPO), operated from bases within Angola. The fear in Pretoria and Washington was that an independent Namibia would open its doors to a Cuban military presence. In the late 1980s, the thaw in relations between East and West made it possible to come to a compromise. Under the watchful eyes of the two superpowers, Angola, South Africa and Cuba reached an agreement: South Africa would withdraw from Angola and Namibia, and would cease to support UNITA, if the Cubans withdrew from Angola within two years and Angola ceased to support the African National Congress, South Africa's main resistance movement. In November 1989, elections were held in Namibia and SWAPO won with a clear majority. The liberation movement formed a government and, a few months later, in March 1990, Namibia finally obtained independence.

The strategic importance of the Horn of Africa

The Horn of Africa – comprising the present-day countries of Ethiopia, Eritrea, Djibouti, Somalia and (according to some authorities) Sudan – is a transitional region between the Middle East and sub-Saharan Africa. At its heart is a savage mountain area, surrounded mainly by desert, lining both the Red Sea coast and, on the other side, the Nile. In racial and cultural terms, the peoples to the south of the mountains are part of sub-Saharan Africa, while those to the north have a different background. Although often darker in complexion, they are more closely related to the peoples of the Middle East, with whom they also have close cultural and religious ties. Relations between the Horn of Africa and the Middle East (and even Europe) are far more deeply rooted in history than those between the Horn and the rest of Africa, which are actually of recent date. To understand past and present events in the region, it is essential to appreciate the geographical position and ancient history of the Horn.

In the middle of the Horn of Africa is Ethiopia, the only country in Africa to have led an uninterrupted and almost entirely independent existence since ancient times. Ethiopia's roots go back to the kingdom of Aksum, which existed before the time of Christ in the northern mountain area and along the coast of the Red Sea. The kingdom expanded until for many centuries it encompassed the entire mountain region and much of the coast. The Ethiopian royal dynasty had lofty aspirations. It claimed to be descended from King Solomon and the Queen of Sheba (known to Ethiopians as the Queen of Aksum) and the rulers adopted the title *Negus Negast*, or King of Kings (in other words, emperor). For centuries, much of Ethiopian culture was Jewish in character, but the country was rapidly Christianised from the third century onward.[29] From the seventh century, dramatic changes occurred in the geopolitical position of the empire: it was encircled by Islam, which entered Africa along the Nile and came to dominate the entire Red Sea coast. Christian Ethiopia was driven back into the mountains and became almost completely isolated. Permanent tensions developed between it and the surrounding peoples with their new Islamic religion.

Except in a brief but almost fatal period of weakness in the sixteenth century, Ethiopia managed to maintain a position of political and military strength despite this cultural isolation. The empire was comparatively well-organised, whereas the surrounding peoples developed little if any form of government. The predominantly Islamised peoples of the desert and coast were grouped in clans or other small communities but seldom forged larger political units. This meant that their territories (particularly the Red Sea coast) were always an easy target for potential invaders. This became an important factor in modern times, when the Suez Canal was opened in 1869, establishing a new passage between Western Europe (then the centre of the world) and Asia (with the main European colonies) via the Red Sea. Instantly, the Horn of Africa became a key strategic area. All the great European powers wanted to possess a base close to the southern end of the Red Sea (which meant in or opposite the Horn of Africa). Britain was the first to achieve this ambition, when it captured the port of Aden, in Yemen. France followed suit in Obock (now part of Djibouti) and Italy in Abbas (now Assab). The territory occupied by Italy would expand after 1882 to become the colony of Eritrea.

The European conquests included not only small areas of Arab or Somali desert, but also the coast of Ethiopia. This northern part of the Ethiopian empire was sequestered by Italy and turned into the separate colony of Eritrea. It was only the astonishing Ethiopian defeat of the Italians in the battle of Adwa in 1896 that stopped Italy advancing inland and overthrowing the whole empire. Instead, the country retained its independence and was even able to take part in the large-scale European conquest of Africa in the closing years of the nineteenth century. Under Emperor Menelik II, Ethiopia conquered a large area in the south, doubling its territory. Many of the conquered peoples had previously had some form of contact with the empire (usually armed conflict), but did not share its Christian culture. As a result, twentieth-century Ethiopia was more ethnically and culturally diverse than ever. Consequently, it faced special difficulties during the Cold War period and thereafter. One problem area was the Ogaden desert, under Ethiopian rule but populated by Somali clans.

The state of Somalia is of very recent, postcolonial origin. The areas inhabited by Somalis – a large portion of the coast of the Horn of Africa and its low-lying hinterland – had been occupied in colonial times by Italy (Italian Somaliland), Britain (British Somaliland and British East Africa), France (around the city of Djibouti) and Ethiopia (the Ogaden). Italy was on the losing side during World War II and had to surrender its colonies to British administration. During the period of decolonisation, the territories previously known as Italian and British Somaliland were united to form the new state of Somalia, which became independent in 1960. The French refused to give up Djibouti, which they had turned into an important military base, and Ethiopia was equally unwilling to contemplate the inclusion of the Ogaden, given that it had come to regard it as an inseparable part of its national territory. However, the first Somali government refused to accept this state of affairs. Its key policy was the inclusion of all Somalis in a greater Somalia. To achieve this would require many adjustments to its borders. The French would have to give up Djibouti, Ethiopia the Ogaden and Kenya its northeastern province. Apart from Morocco, which aimed to annex the Western Sahara (then under Spanish administration), Somalia was the only country in Africa that did not comply with the OAU's taboo on changes in national borders.

Given the political situation in the Horn of Africa, Somalia's expansionary aspirations were unrealistic. Making foreign enemies might promote national unity between its warring clans, but Somalia was still an insignificant little country by any standard. Its population numbered around two million and eighty per cent of its inhabitants were tent-dwelling desert nomads. The country lacked even the rudiments of a modern economy. Its main income was from the export of bananas to Europe. However, none of these considerations prevented the Somali leaders from pursuing a policy of expansion. Judging Djibouti and Kenya to be impregnable due to their respectively French and British support, they turned their attention to Ethiopia. So it was that the traditional rivalry between Islam and Christianity in the Horn of Africa was restyled in the second half of the twentieth century to become part of the Cold War, with the Ogaden desert as the potential spoils of victory.

In 1956, with Egypt's nationalisation of the Suez Canal and the ensuing international crisis, the Red Sea and the Horn of Africa regained the strategic importance they had possessed almost a hundred years earlier. The United States could not leave the defence of the region to Western Europe, even though the French already had a strong military presence in little Djibouti. Washington's attention focused in particular on Ethiopia, where Emperor Haile Selassie showed himself an enthusiastic champion of close relations between Ethiopia and America. Substantial American military support would protect Ethiopia from Somali aggression and would at the same time guarantee the presence of a Western military base in this strategically vital region. But immediately after independence in 1960, Somalia also applied for American support. Economic aid was granted, but military assistance was withheld in order to avoid disturbing the balance of power between Somalia and Ethiopia. But this was precisely what the leaders in Mogadishu wanted to do. Accordingly, they seized the opportunity provided by the Cold War and in 1963 they played the Soviet card. The Somali government offered to promote Soviet interests in the region if the Russians would give Somalia the extra military muscle it needed to expand its territory. At first Moscow responded cautiously, but eventually Soviet military assistance started to flow into Somalia.

In this way, Ethiopia and Somalia used the international tension between the superpowers in the interests of their mutual rivalry and created an arms race in the region. The increasing military build-up continued despite the 1969 coup in Somalia, which established a military regime under Siad Barre. Somalia did change its tactics, however. It no longer displayed direct aggression towards its neighbours but attempted to undermine them by supporting local Somali 'liberation movements'. Its expansionary rhetoric waned and public support for the military regime became less general. The new government tended to rely on the support of only a few clans, while playing the others off against each other. Ties with the Soviets remained intact. Somalia became a 'socialist republic' and in 1974, when Nikolai Podgorny became the first Soviet president ever to visit Africa, Somalia was the chosen destination.

That same year, however, regional stability was threatened by a coup in Ethiopia. Emperor Haile Selassie was dethroned and a military junta seized power. In 1977 Colonel Mengistu Haile Mariam personally liquidated his rivals during a shoot-out in military headquarters in Addis Ababa, enabling himself to rule Ethiopia as a dictator. Mengistu belonged to a radical movement advocating a clean break with the Ethiopian past, including the country's ties with the United States. He embarked on a revolutionary socialist path towards complete modernisation of the country. The Americans were expelled and approaches were made to the Soviets. For Moscow this was almost too much of a good thing. Because South Yemen had also turned to the Soviet Union, all the countries around the southern end of the Red Sea were now Russian allies, but there were major tensions between them. In an attempt to resolve these and to create an atmosphere of mutual cooperation within a large socialist federation, a conference was held in Aden under the chairmanship of the Cuban president, Fidel Castro.

The approach was doomed to fail. The Somalis saw no advantage in such cooperation because it meant they would have to give up the dream of national expansion which had been the reason for approaching Moscow in the first place. In desperation, when it became clear that the Soviet Union preferred Ethiopia to Somalia, Siad Barre decided to take pre-emptive action. By this time, Somalia had one of the largest armies in Africa (as indeed did Ethiopia). While Mengistu's attacks on political opponents and rivals (the 'Red Terror') were causing chaos in Ethiopia, Somalia expelled its Eastern Bloc military advisers and embarked on a stealthy but swift invasion of southeastern Ethiopia. In an impressive logistical feat, Moscow responded by transferring its military base from Berbera in Somalia via Aden in South Yemen to Ethiopia in the space of just a few days. Cuban soldiers were flown in to strengthen Ethiopia's defences. By the end of 1977, Somalia was in possession of virtually the entire Ogaden, but the fruits of its conquest were mainly desert sand. The Somalis lacked the military might to strike at Ethiopia's heart and to end the war with a decisive victory.

Over the next few months, the roles were reversed. Ethiopia's Eastern Bloc support proved decisive: the Somali army was driven back over the border, losing almost all of its tanks and air power in the process. In a dramatic *renversement des alliances*, Somalia called on the Carter administration in Washington to supply military assistance. It drew a blank, spelling the final failure of the great Somali project after years of extraordinary effort. The country had failed to expand its territory, its huge army had been destroyed and no national development had been achieved. In the 1980s, Somalia would continue to receive economic assistance from the West (mainly from the United States and Italy), but – bereft of its dream of expansion – the state became mired ever deeper in clan rivalries.

Despite its victory in the Ogaden, Ethiopia was little better off. All the resources of the destitute country were absorbed by its military, since it also had to engage in military action in the north in order to put down a secessionist uprising in Eritrea. Eritrea had originally been taken from Ethiopia by Italy but was returned to Ethiopian rule as a mandated territory following World War II. In 1962, Emperor Haile Selassie formally annexed it, in effect restoring the situation prior to 1880. However, the Eritreans resisted reintegration into the Ethiopian empire. Historically, Eritrea had been far more open to the outside world than more inward-looking, 'traditional' Ethiopia. Its period as an Italian colony had heightened the contrast between the two countries. Annexation by Ethiopia was a signal that peaceful secession was no longer possible and instantly prompted violent hostilities.

The Eritrean struggle for independence continued from 1962 to 1991, making it the longest uninterrupted war in the history of twentieth-century Africa. The rebel province received virtually no support from the outside world. Despite its position on the Red Sea, it had less to offer the two superpowers than the far larger and potentially richer Ethiopia and they accordingly abstained from intervention in the dispute. Nevertheless, the war placed a heavy burden on the Ethiopian government, first under Emperor Haile Selassie and later under Mengistu. It cost one and a half million lives and ravaged large parts of Eritrea and northern Ethiopia. It was not until Soviet support for Mengistu started to dry up in the late 1980s that the rebel province finally got the upper hand. So it was that the formal independence of Eritrea in 1993 was ultimately made possible by the end of the Cold War.

The war in Sudan had no connection with the Cold War. Its historical roots lie far deeper. In the nineteenth century, when the British gained control of what is now Sudan, the north and centre were inhabited by Muslims of Arab extraction and the south by animistic black Africans. Under British rule, many southern Sudanese converted to Christianity, creating a sharper religious division between the two parts of the territory. After independence in the 1950s, the new, Islamic government in Khartoum embarked on a policy of dominance over the south, and met with armed resistance from the local population. Hostilities continued until 1972, when the south obtained a measure of autonomy. However, the 1980s saw a rise in Islamic fundamentalism in Sudan, prompting renewed north-south tensions. Fighting broke out again in 1983 and has dragged on ever since.

Africa and the shadow
of the Cold War

The Cold War had a major influence on Africa. Above all, it stabilised the patchwork of weak independent states. Most of the countries of Africa remained beyond the scope of tensions between the superpowers, even in the 1970s when these tensions boiled over in many other parts of the Third World. This positive effect was especially true of the ex-British and French colonies. These new countries enjoyed a relatively large measure of internal stability. This was partly due to the state structures built up during the colonial period, but the importance of their close continuing ties with their former colonial masters is undeniable. These meant that their leaders felt no need – and indeed had no chance – to turn to either of the superpowers. The only exception to the rule was Guinea, which deliberately broke off ties with France and was then, as it were, disowned by the West. In other former French colonies, like Benin and Congo (Brazzaville), the influence of the Cold War remained relatively slight. These countries borrowed their rhetoric and their economic policies from the Soviet Union but, since they received no material assistance from that quarter, they too remained within the Western sphere of influence and were not sucked into any serious East-West conflict.

The situation was quite different in almost all parts of Africa which had not been colonised by France or Britain. This historical difference created special local conditions which left these areas exposed to the global struggle between East and West. The most important special condition of all was the delay in granting independence to the Portuguese colonies. Over the years, the nationalist movements in Angola, Mozambique and Guinea-Bissau drew military and other support from the Eastern Bloc, inevitably evoking a response from the West. The mounting struggle in the Portuguese colonies, with the Cold War shaping events behind the scenes, only made it more difficult to reach the inescapable settlement in the form of independence. Both these (sometimes fierce) struggles for independence and the continual postponement of the transfer of power must be seen as consequences of the Cold War.

In the countries most directly influenced by the Cold War, another important consequence was the politicisation of the armed forces and the militarisation of politics.[30] In the new African states, whose internal political structures were still relatively undeveloped, it was only to be expected that the military would become more involved in national politics if international tensions affected national security. The armed forces began to take a firmer stance on issues like the national budget. Their foremost aim was to secure sufficient funds to procure military equipment. But their influence frequently went further than that and could even extend to the whole of national politics.

Even without the stimulus that the Cold War provided, internal conditions in most African states favoured an expanding role for the military, whether its leaders were already part of the elite or had to muscle their way into the elite. The position of the civilian leaders was often quite vulnerable. Military commanders had inherited troops and equipment which were intended for maintaining law and order, but which could equally well be used to stage a coup d'état. There was thus considerable temptation for them to seize power, dramatically enhancing their own authority and that of their clients. Apart from their monopoly on international contacts, the civilian leaders had almost no means of staving off the military. However, the veneer of legitimacy that they could provide sometimes enable them to reach some kind of settlement with the armed forces, a settlement that offered both groups the advantages of exploiting the state. The growing importance of the military in turn had major repercussions for the fledgling political cultures of the African countries. It gave an authoritarian twist to politics, at the expense of human rights and nascent democratic institutions. It also meant that development ended up low on the list of national priorities.

The Cold War damaged not only the political but also the socioeconomic development of the African countries that became most deeply involved. Military coups and other forms of political instability in themselves reduced the chances of healthy social development. Global tensions sometimes translated into increasing conflict between ethnic communities or clans in their struggle to control the state, or even just to hang on to a decent power position in their multi-ethnic society. And there was also, almost always, an inequitable distribution of government funding among sectors. Defence tended to receive the lion's share at the expense of the other, more development-oriented, sectors like education and health. The authorities often neglected their responsibility for development. Somalia was an extreme case of this widespread phenomenon. In those African countries drawn furthest into the Cold War, priorities shifted from development to security and military spending.

The Cold War also had major consequences for the security situation in Africa. Superpower rivalry increased the tension surrounding local conflicts, for example in the Horn of Africa and in the former Portuguese colonies in the south. Perhaps the rivalry between capitalism and communism in Africa (and elsewhere) served as a release valve for the aggression of the superpowers, unable as they were to engage each other directly in armed conflict in the presence of the nuclear deterrent. On the other hand, the United States and the Soviet Union were careful to ensure that their own or allied armed forces did not find themselves ranged directly against each other: the fear of escalation was as effective a deterrent in Africa as it was elsewhere. After the Cold War, however, African actors would no longer be restrained by the superpowers and could settle their differences freely. Deterrence was followed in those years by a kind of decompression. But the end of Cold War rivalry also left room for a positive new trend: international cooperation aimed at resolving local conflicts. Southern Africa was to benefit greatly from this development (see chapter 4, pp. 116-122).

African leaders were often aware of the dangers of excessive involvement in the global conflict between East and West. There was immediate and widespread interest in the deliberately neutral position advocated by the Non-Aligned Movement. This worldwide organisation was the brainchild of the leaders of the newly independent countries in Asia. In 1959, its first major, more or less formal, meeting was held in Bandung, Indonesia. It was attended not only by prominent figures like Sukarno (Indonesia), Jawaharlal Nehru (India) and Chou En Lai (China), but also by Gamal Abdel Nasser (Egypt) and Kwame Nkrumah (Ghana). In the years following this 'Afro-Asian' meeting in Bandung, ever more African countries joined the movement.

The desire of the African countries to occupy a distinct international position and to have their own political forum, separate from the great powers elsewhere in the world, was also expressed in the establishment of the OAU. This took place in 1963 in Addis Ababa, Ethiopia. The event demonstrated the survival of the old Pan-African ideal, but from the beginning there was also recognition that this was not likely to be achieved any time in the near future. To promote the stability of the member states, therefore, the organisation adopted the principle that national borders of independent countries were not to be disputed, however artificially those borders might have been drawn in colonial times. The African leaders were aware of the risk that any discussion of borders might open up a Pandora's box and ultimately destabilise the whole continent. The purpose of the OAU was to promote African unity through voluntary cooperation between the independent member states.

In the course of the 1970s, the European Community made its appearance as a new international player on the African stage, though at first it was primarily a co-financier of French policy. In 1975, the association agreements between the European Community and individual African countries were recast as the first Lomé Convention, an agreement between the countries of the European Community (later the European Union) and some seventy countries in Africa, the Caribbean and the Pacific (the 'ACP countries'). The Lomé Conventions, reviewed every five years, embraced both aid and trade, the latter in terms of access to the European market (see also chapter 7, p. 213).

Since it was not only the political environment but also the economic status of Africa around 1990 that determined the starting position of the continent for the post-Cold War period, chapter 2 provides a historical survey of the economy, with the emphasis on the reforms of the 1980s. The main effect of these were to liberalise Africa's economic systems. They were accompanied by liberalisation of its political systems, beginning as soon as the Cold War came to an end. This political transformation is the subject of chapter 3.

2
ECONOMIC DECLINE

Colonial influences on economic development

The African economy is marked by many coexisting forms and levels of economic activity. This is due partly to the rapid introduction, in historical terms, of new economic activities, and partly to the limited scope and success of these innovations. As a result, older systems and socioeconomic practices have inevitably survived, often continuing up to the present day. The oldest modes of subsistence – hunting, gathering and fishing – are still widely practised in parts of the continent. Livestock raising and agriculture have also been practised for centuries, initially for subsistence and then increasingly for sale on domestic and international markets. Over the course of the twentieth century, new trades and industries evolved. The final branch on the tree of economic activity emerged at the end of the twentieth century in the form of a large informal sector employing many people, notably in the service industry.

The driving force behind these economic activities was contact with the world beyond Africa, especially Europe. However, long before Africa and Europe had established significant ties, the African economy had already begun to diversify and trade links had been forged over immense distances, even extending to countries outside Africa. Of the distant regions with which Africa traded during the precolonial period, the most important were the Arabian Peninsula and Asia. Ships from these regions regularly put into the ports along the east coast of the continent, such as Massawa, Zeila, Lamu, Malindi, Mombasa, Zanzibar, Sofala and Kilwa. The main export product from East Africa was ivory, but large numbers of slaves were also traded. Because this trade was carried out by ship, it could be conducted on a larger scale than the trans-Saharan trade between West and North Africa, which relied on camel caravans transporting small quantities of goods, often of great value, such as gold, spices and salt. Slaves and ivory were traded in these regions as well. The trans-Saharan trade flourished during Europe's Middle Ages, with caravan routes leading to the towns of the Sahel on the southern edge of the desert. These towns, the most important of which was Timbuktu, were famed far beyond Africa.

Obviously, these economic activities influenced the social and political organisation of Africa. In regions where the economy was largely aimed at sustenance, small political units predominated, whereas in areas with more diversified economic and trade activity, larger polities tended to emerge. Political leaders used their power not just to amass wealth but also to redistribute some of it to their subjects, creating ties of dependence and loyalty. Investing in economic growth was virtually unheard of. Economic security and social stability took precedence over any perceived need to expand production and increase prosperity. This type of stable socioeconomic system was not unique to Africa but existed practically all over the world, with one or two exceptions: China underwent significant economic growth from around 800 to 1300, and Europe's economic growth began in the eleventh century. This European growth, which gained momentum in the nineteenth century during the first industrial revolution, would have major consequences in other parts of the world, where until then almost no growth had occurred.[31]

The long-distance trade across the Sahara led to the emergence of vast empires along the southern edge of the desert; these controlled the commercial activities on the African end. However, the arrival of European ships on the African coast, beginning with the Portuguese in the fifteenth century, had a major impact on the political and economic organisation of West Africa. Because these vessels could transport goods far more cheaply than the camel trains, the importance of the international trade routes through the African interior declined, to be replaced by ships carrying cargo around the continent by sea. This in turn diminished the political power and wealth of the rulers in the West African interior. The Portuguese also captured a large share of the trade between the east coast of Africa and Asia.

Throughout the rest of the continent, European influence was for many centuries either marginal or nonexistent. There were often no economic links between the inland regions and the coast, and for centuries Europeans were reluctant to venture into the African interior, chiefly due to fear of disease. They did, however, establish scattered trading settlements (known as factories) along the coast. From these – often fortified – sites they conducted trade with the interior through African middlemen. They dealt in products ranging from precious metals and spices to tropical crops. When the plantations established in Europe's 'New World' colonies (first for sugar and later for other crops) led to an explosive demand for manpower, Europeans also began trading in slaves. In the Americas an indigenous workforce was either unavailable in sufficient numbers or was regarded as unsuitable. The problem was solved by transporting Africans to the West as slaves. During this tragic period in African history, which reached its nadir around 1800, more than ten million Africans were taken abroad as slaves. The effects were wide-ranging and are to some extent still being felt in Africa today. The boom years of the slave trade plunged the continent into a trauma from which it has never fully recovered.

The economic and political effects of the trade were also immense. In the space of just a few years, a large proportion of Africa's workers were deported, often at the most productive stage of their lives. People in neighbouring regions often fled to avoid capture. In some places, normal social and economic activity was wholly abandoned, and agriculture must have suffered seriously from the interruption. Yet there were also Africans who benefited, politically and economically, from the slave trade. Slaves were captured in the African interior and transported to the coast entirely by Africans. These lucrative activities led to the emergence of new African states based on the slave trade, at a slight remove from the coast and just beyond the reach of European power. This African complicity in the slave trade, without which it could never have attained the same massive scale, still gives rise to argument concerning the extent of the 'collaboration' with the European slave traders. However, the driving force behind the slave trade lay outside Africa. It was demand for slaves in the Americas that made the trade so profitable for Africans and it was the availability of firearms that made it feasible.

In 1807 Great Britain, then the world's most powerful nation, declared the slave trade unlawful, and in the following decades the British fleet brought the bulk of the intercontinental traffic to an end. Beyond the reach of the British, however, transports of slaves continued on a smaller scale. This included international trade with the Arabian Peninsula. And in some parts of the African interior, the practice has survived into the present century, notably in those regions where Arabian and African cultures meet, such as Sudan and Mauritania. Europe's disengagement from the slave trade did not however sever the economic ties between Africa and Europe. In the latter half of the eighteenth and throughout the nineteenth century, an entirely new and revolutionary method of production evolved, starting in Great Britain. Inventions like the steam engine made it possible for factories to transform raw materials into finished products on an unprecedented scale. The industrial revolution, which swiftly spread to mainland Europe, dramatically altered economic relations between the European and African continents.

Just as the Europeans had needed slaves to compensate for the shortage of manpower in the Western hemisphere, they now needed raw materials for their new industries. There was also a demand for luxury products among wealthy Europeans. Operating from the trading settlements, the Europeans expanded the area they controlled along the African coast and established plantations for a wide range of tropical crops. Africa became a major exporter of palm oil, wax, rubber, cocoa, coffee, tea and sugar to Europe. The differences between this period and that of the slave trade may not be as great as they appear. It has been argued, in particular by African economists who are eager to show continuity in the Western exploitation of Africa, that the apparently striking differences between the two periods were simply due to the economic changes that took place in Europe and America, leading to a demand for different products. After the industrial revolution began the products that Europe needed for its industries and its affluent classes could be grown in Africa itself, and so it was no longer necessary to transport Africans out of their continent.[32]

Europe's enormous demand for raw materials to fuel the burgeoning industrial revolution and its growing power as a result of that revolution led it ever further into Africa. The process reached its climax at the end of the nineteenth century, when in the space of a few years the entire continent was divided up among the European powers. This marked the start of formal colonialism, with Africa now subject to European political and military control. However, it did not mean that Europe's influence over Africa was now total. The European presence was still restricted to the most profitable regions, although these regions were constantly expanding. Nevertheless, in large swaths of Africa Europe's influence was absent or marginal. These were regions where 'traditional' economic systems had remained intact: subsistence livestock-rearing and crop-growing formed the core of the economy. There were few if any markets; in economic terms, these regions were inward-looking.

Where the Europeans exercised day-to-day authority, there were major economic changes. Tropical crops were cultivated for trade on an extensive scale, either on large plantations or on smallholdings. Large-scale mining began, mainly in Southern and Central Africa. The biggest private investments were made in the mining industries of South Africa, Southern and Northern Rhodesia (now Zimbabwe and Zambia respectively) and the Belgian Congo. Although there are no reliable statistics covering this period, we can assume that Africa's economic output grew rapidly in the nineteenth and early twentieth centuries in terms of both the volume and range of products. This growth was later largely offset by the global economic crisis of the 1930s.

One important colonial innovation was the introduction of a cash economy. Money was needed to buy and sell goods; workers at European companies received cash and the colonial authorities began to collect taxes that had to be paid in the same form. Of course, this cash economy was concentrated around the European settlements, but it spread rapidly. More and more Africans began to work in the settlements, either voluntarily or under duress. Labour migration, which had probably always been quite widespread in Africa, became even more common. Often it was just the men who migrated, leaving their women and children behind in rural areas. Sizeable towns grew up around the centres of economic activity. Migration and urbanisation, which became familiar features of post-colonial Africa, had their origins in the colonial period or even before.

The colonial influence also prompted a shift in the division of labour between the sexes. In most regions of Africa, men and women had originally both worked the land. This was not the case in modern Europe, where farming was primarily a male preserve. European farms, mines and other commercial enterprises therefore employed African men but not women, who were left behind in their traditional economies, tending their own small plots. As a result, subsistence farming in Africa was increasingly taken over by women. If there was any surplus produce, it was they who brought it to market. The 'market mamas' so characteristic of West Africa in particular have their origins chiefly in the new division of labour imposed by the colonial economy.

The introduction of marketing boards in the colonial period also deserves mention. These were government agencies that bought up agricultural produce from African growers at a fixed price before selling it on elsewhere in the colony or abroad for a higher price. The purpose of this system was to guarantee the farmers a fixed minimum price despite fluctuations in the value of their products on the world market, by using the revenue generated in good years to shore up prices during bad ones. Of course, it also channelled profits from the agricultural sector to the state in the form of tax revenue. Following independence, the marketing boards would continue to be used to exploit the rural population, just as they had been under the colonial administration.

The growing output of the African economy in the colonial period was not matched by wider sharing of its benefits. The modern sectors of the economy, where this growth was taking place, were little more than outposts of the European economy, and the profits they generated therefore remained in European hands, with the exception of the wages paid to African workers. Although initiatives to promote development and improve the lot of the African population were put forward during the first half of the twentieth century, little or nothing came of them. It was not until after World War II that the European administrators in both the British and the French colonies drew up programmes for the development of the African economy. In the years just prior to independence, these took the form of three or five-year plans.

From the beginning of European rule in Africa, the European powers held the view that the colonial administrations should be self-sufficient.[33] The European authorities needed public funds chiefly to maintain order and security, to develop infrastructure and, as time went on, to fund education. Each colonial administration was supposed to generate these funds on its own. During the early decades of formal colonialism, they fell far short of this goal and additional funding had to be drawn from the treasuries at home. However, the colonial authorities in Africa were increasingly forced by their governments to look for ways of generating income locally. Gradually they became more successful. Taxes began to account for a growing share of their revenues. Direct taxation remained limited, but other levies, such as import and export duties, rose. Colonial administrations were increasingly able to obtain all the funds they needed from the local population. According to some analysts, this approach set the stage for the lifestyles adopted by the 'rent-seeking' post-independence African elites, who used the apparatus of government to extract 'rents', or uncompensated, unearned transfers of income.

The unique history of South Africa also had major economic repercussions. Farming, mining and industry were successively developed in this region, which was a colony in the original sense of the word (i.e. a place where colonists settled). This essentially Western economy exerted an enormous pull on the whole of Southern Africa. As a result, the aforementioned colonial trends of migration, urbanisation and the gender-based segregation of labour were felt here on a much larger scale than in the rest of Africa. South Africa evolved a social structure which was not only a more extreme version of the colonial characteristics of the rest of the continent but where, in addition, groups living alongside each other were separated by an immense economic and cultural divide. The gulf between these groups coincided with the racial fault line between black and white. The situation was a time bomb that began ticking more insistently when the rest of black Africa gained its independence.

The rise and fall of the

African economies

For many African countries, the years immediately following independence were economically successful. A new period of growth had begun straight after the global depression of the 1930s, which had hit Africa hard. The continent had been economically quite important during World War II, as it was sometimes the only supplier of products that the warring powers could no longer obtain from their usual sources. After the war, the top priority of the colonial powers had been to revitalise their own economies. This had both created considerable demand for African products and reduced the availability of European products in Africa. These circumstances had made it possible for Africa to begin industrialising. The African economy as a whole grew rapidly, and income – including that of the colonial administrations – went up. Some African colonies even made loans to Europe. By around 1960 the reconstruction of Europe was well under way, but the end of Africa's boom years was not yet in sight.

The first independent African governments placed almost all the emphasis in their economic policies on the most recent phase of the West's immensely successful development history (which was also the road chosen by the Eastern Bloc): namely, industrialisation. This was not just prompted by a desire to follow the example set by the West but was also a response to explosive population growth in Africa, which had accelerated rapidly following the introduction of Western medicines to combat infection during the first half of the twentieth century. Accelerating population growth – faster than anywhere else in the world due to the high African fertility rate – raised the question of what role this large future pool of potential workers could play in the economy. Agricultural development would not create many new jobs; in fact, the modernisation of farming methods generally reduces employment. The best solution was therefore felt to be the further expansion of the fledgling industrial sector. However, this could not be financed in the same way as it had been in the West, from the revenue generated through improvements in agriculture, since the agricultural sector in Africa was on the whole not nearly profitable enough for that. In any case, any profit that was generated (primarily from export crops) either disappeared abroad or was not used productively in Africa itself. There was, moreover, very little private capital in Africa. Instead, foreign loans and the authorities' own limited reserves were consistently used to fund industrial development.

From the very outset, the state played a key role in the industrialisation of Africa. It had assumed this role immediately after World War II, before the end of the colonial era. At that time, European savings were being channelled into reconstruction on the home front. It had in any case been recognised as early as the Depression that the state could and indeed should play a role in promoting economic development in Africa. The first independent governments felt this need even more urgently; African private investors had neither the means nor the experience to set up independent businesses. Public-sector involvement was also fuelled by an ideological argument, namely that the capitalist strategy pursued by the European powers had been a means of exploiting Africa. The strength of the Soviet Union at this time suggested that there was an alternative. It was thought that socialism (or communism, if you like), with a strong, central role for the state, could yield development without exploitation. Moreover, even the poorest citizens could feel that, through the state, they had a share in the means of production. State-owned industries therefore emerged in many African countries, alongside the European companies that maintained a presence on the continent. As a result, employment in the industrial sector continued to grow, until by around 1970 it accounted for nearly ten per cent of total employment across the continent. The growth of the economy in the 1960s and early 1970s was due to this new industrial sector.

The choice in favour of industrialisation was also a choice in favour of urban centres. Political stability depended on a reasonable standard of living for the rapidly growing urban population, or at least the prospect of one. For the African elite, who had inherited the key state positions, support from the residents of the towns and cities, even if merely passive, was vital. Above all, support was needed in the capital. In contrast to this direct link between political power and urban support, rural areas had far less political clout. They were simply too far away. In the countryside, personal ties with the elite led to even greater imbalances of power than in the cities, or else were totally absent. The inhabitants of rural areas led an isolated existence and were both economically and socially disadvantaged. Levels of political awareness and organisation were low. Since political challenges were unlikely to come from this quarter, investment in rural areas was not thought to be worthwhile. The state marketing boards simply removed agricultural produce from the countryside under a socialist redistribution system to sell in the cities or abroad. This provided revenue for the state and low-cost food for the urban population, but resulted in the farmers being paid less than they would have in a free market.

Rural Africa increasingly lost out under this policy until well into the 1980s, in terms of both food production and living standards. Since any profits were inevitably skimmed by the state, the sector had no capital to invest in modern means of production. This stood in stark contrast to developments elsewhere in the world, for example in Asia. Nor could assistance from outside the sector be expected. The state had no strategy for investment in agricultural production, physical infrastructure or the proper functioning of markets. Under these circumstances, the farming population was forced to concentrate on providing for itself. Rather the agricultural sector becoming an economic engine by modernising its means of production, more of it reverted to subsistence farming. The outside world, in the form of the state, had exerted such a negative influence on the living standards of the rural population that this appeared to be the best way of surviving. This inevitably had devastating consequences for the supply of food to the rest of the country, since it became increasingly difficult for the authorities to provide the urban population with food at affordable prices. As early as the 1970s food had to be imported from outside Africa – a disgraceful situation for a large continent with a small population, and a heavy burden on the public purse.

The vulnerability of Africa's food supply came to the fore in years of drought. The famines of the 1970s in the Sahel, along the southern edge of the Sahara, were particularly devastating. From Senegal on one side of the continent to Ethiopia on the other, tens of thousands of people and millions of animals starved to death. In the 1980s, it was famine in Ethiopia that once again attracted international attention. Ghana was struck by famine in 1982 and 1983. These disasters were linked to a variety of factors – drought, overpopulation, overgrazing, hostilities – but the main reason for the weakness of the African agricultural sector was neglect and even exploitation by government. Per capita food production fell over the 1980s in twenty-five of the thirty-six countries for which figures were available.[34] Although the total population living outside urban centres increased due to the overall rise in the population, the percentage of Africans living in rural areas and working the land declined from approximately eighty per cent in the 1960s to well below seventy per cent around 1990. Africa was less and less an agrarian continent.

Unfortunately, the decline in agriculture was not offset by growth in industry or the service sector. Africa did not become a more industrial continent.[35] In fact, industrialisation began to falter around 1970. The state-owned companies were operating less efficiently, partly due to the need to absorb large numbers of workers. Moreover, they were almost always incapable of keeping up with foreign competitors. Tariff barriers provided some protection; even so, losses mounted as the years went on. Company closures could not usually be contemplated due to the political implications. State-owned industries were a liability in financial terms, but they were a useful tool in domestic politics. Only with international support did Africa manage to sustain employment in industry at an average of just under ten per cent of the workforce. The 1970s and 1980s were a time of contraction rather than growth.

As we have seen, the years immediately following independence were economically successful, better even than those at the end of the colonial period. However, the 1970s saw the beginnings of an economic recession, followed in the 1980s by a full-blown economic crisis. The ideal of a self-sufficient, prosperous economy had come to nothing. The main economic sector, agriculture, had turned in on itself. The industrial sector could only be kept going in the face of substantial losses. There were no cohesive national economies with links between the various regions, or supply chains within and between sectors. In fact, Africa's economies had become ever more fragmented. Their international competitiveness and hence their profitability had fallen dramatically compared to every other continent. In around 1960, African countries were still holding their own against the East and Southeast Asian countries in terms of economic development, but by the 1980s a yawning gulf had opened between them.

The fact is that, despite the sometimes substantial differences between African countries, the continent as a whole fell far behind the rest of the world in economic terms. This suggests that Africa may have been beset by certain characteristics or problems that were less prevalent or even absent in developing countries on other continents. The traumatic effects of the slave trade and of colonialism may have been a factor in the often anti-Western and anti-capitalist approach that characterised postcolonial development. Perhaps for this reason, African governments tended to embrace a socialist model that eventually proved unable to produce development. The status of the new political elite (another legacy of the colonial era) further worsened this situation. The economic policies pursued by the African leaders were informed mainly by a desire to ensure their personal survival by powerfully reinforcing their own position within the state. As a result, these governments generally kept the value of their own currencies artificially high, which reduced the relative cost of imports (consumption) and made exports (production) comparatively costly. Other prongs of this approach included duties and subsidies. Food subsidies benefited the urban networks of the politicians (consumption) at the expense of the rural populations (production). And while this made it possible to build up a more or less loyal urban following, in the long term it was neither economically nor financially viable. Economic decline brought an end to the ideal of development. The rulers of these countries were primarily concerned with their own survival: 'Staying afloat was more important than going somewhere.'[36]

The unbalanced development of the African state and economy must be seen within the context of both African history and the international scene. The phases into which the continent's economic fortunes are divided almost exactly coincide with major developments in the global economy. Unlike in the period from 1940 to 1970, from the 1970s onwards economic changes in the rest of the world would have a largely negative impact on Africa's economies.

The oil crisis and the fall
of the Berlin Wall

The serious economic problems with which Africa has struggled in recent decades perhaps too readily create the impression of a weak continent that has always been easy prey to the world's political and economic superpowers. That picture is historically inaccurate. As mentioned, the final two decades of the colonial era and the years between independence and the 1970s were good ones for African industrialisation and exports. During this time, the African economy as a whole grew substantially. Alongside the pessimistic warnings about Africa's future economic prospects, there were also highly optimistic forecasts. Even after the first setback, in the form of the oil crisis of the mid-1970s and the simultaneous deterioration of the ratio between the prices of African exports and imports (the terms of trade), many continued to believe for some time that conditions would improve once more.

In 1973, Israel fought a bitter war with its Arab neighbours. The Organisation of the Petroleum Exporting Countries (OPEC), which was dominated by the Arab oil-producing nations, used its power over the world oil market as a political lever by sharply raising oil prices. The immediate consequences were that oil producers saw their incomes shoot up (in Africa this meant primarily Nigeria, Gabon and Angola), but that other countries, which were forced to import oil at progressively higher prices to keep their economies running, were spending more and more for the same volume of imports. Countries that needed large amounts of oil for their export industries were to some extent able to offset these higher import prices by passing them on in the prices of their exports. This generally made industrial outputs more expensive. As a result, African countries without their own oil (the vast majority) had to pay far more not only for their oil imports but also for the other – often industrial – products that they required. The terms of trade differential between industrial products and primary commodities (agricultural products and minerals) thus shifted in favour of the industrial products. During the mid-1980s, for example, Zaire and Zambia were being paid just over half of what they had been receiving ten years earlier for the same volume of copper exports (on which they were both heavily dependent).[37]

This body blow to the African economies was further aggravated by measures taken by the Western nations – which were by far the most important of Africa's export markets – to compensate for their own economic difficulties as a result of the rising price of oil. Practically all the developed countries began to make cutbacks which reduced their imports, including those from Africa. African exports began to decline during the 1970s. Yet import levels remained relatively high despite the higher costs. Inevitably, there was a price to pay, and practically all the African countries ran into financial difficulties. At precisely this time, however, banks in the developed world began to provide loans to these countries on quite favourable terms, making it possible to plug the financial gaps. This came about because the oil-exporting countries, most of which were in the Middle East, had placed their huge capital reserves with the Western banks, which then had to find somewhere to invest them. The restrictive economic policies pursued by the West, and the accompanying recession, meant that not all of these 'petrodollars' could be invested in the Western economies. The banks saw no alternative but to lend these surplus dollars to developing countries, including many in Africa. Before the oil crisis, the size of the collective public debt in Africa – just over five billion US dollars – had not been particularly noteworthy. However, from the second half of the 1970s onwards the size of loans to Africa began to rise very rapidly. By 1980 the collective debt burden in Africa had reached nearly USD 50 billion and by 1990 it had climbed to USD 150 billion.[38]

Borrowing is not unusual or inherently imprudent. All developing economies borrow, often in substantial amounts. This money is used to make investments that will boost production or raise productivity levels, which will in turn generate extra revenue, some of which can then be used to repay the loans. The improvements make it possible to take out new loans and bring about yet more improvements, and so on. Borrowing therefore often goes hand in hand with economic growth. In Africa, however, this was not the case. The money borrowed was used neither to boost production nor to increase productivity. More often it was used to redeem existing debts, pay public-sector wages, shore up loss-making state industries and pay for imports. These imports almost always consisted of consumer goods, rarely of capital goods. Politically and socially, these imports were crucial. The duties raised on them funded a large share of the national budget, and imports were used either directly or indirectly to fuel the clientelist networks that kept the continent's political and social systems up and running.

The decline in the terms of trade during the 1970s, caused by rising oil prices, was gradually intensified in subsequent years by another factor, an insidious process that had long gone unnoticed. The belief was that following years of economic downturn, the economy would recover once more, resulting in higher export prices for African goods and lower import prices. It was simply seen as a matter of waiting for better times, with the remaining reserves of the marketing boards (accumulated in earlier, more prosperous years) and new loans being used to tide things over in the interim. However, the much-hoped-for and much-needed improvement in the terms of trade did not materialise; in fact, the downward trend continued. In the 1980s the prices of primary products continued to fall against those of industrial products.

It gradually became clear that the falling terms of trade formed a structural problem. The underlying causes included the emergence of alternative products made of other materials, such as synthetics, and a widening of the product range. Then there were the effects of the evolving Western economy, which was turning out products (such as computers) that incorporated a large body of new and expensive knowledge, skills and information. These gained in economic importance compared with unsophisticated products such as agricultural commodities (tea, coffee, etc.) or raw materials, and this was reflected in the plummeting prices of the latter. There was no prospect of this process being reversed. In fact, it was far more likely that the rate of economic innovation in the West, and hence the relative decline of the African economy, would continue to accelerate. Africa's poor economic outlook generated pessimism about the continent's future. The changing world climate following the end of the Cold War quickened the pace of international economic developments. The term 'globalisation' was coined for this process, which during the 1990s was almost as important for areas on the margins of the global economy, including Africa, as it was for those at the centre (see chapter 7).

In the late 1980s the African economy sustained a second blow, caused by international developments following the end of the Cold War. The fall of the Berlin Wall in 1989 and the subsequent collapse of the Eastern Bloc reduced Africa's strategic significance. Some primary products, such as uranium from Niger and manganese from South Africa, suddenly lost their importance for the former adversaries in the North. The prices of these commodities soon slumped. Moreover, the former Eastern Bloc had now been opened up to the Western economy, releasing raw materials and other products onto the world market, again to the detriment of the prices for these products, which included some of Africa's major exports. Without a doubt, the end of the Cold War structurally weakened Africa's position in the global economy.

Economic decline and externally imposed reforms

Throughout the 1960s and 1970s and in later years, it was often claimed that economic progress in Africa, and in developing countries in general, could be achieved only by putting in place a new economic order. The poor countries were said to be caught in the economic grip of the rich ones. It was even argued that poverty in the Third World was due to the prosperity of the industrialised world (see also the introduction). However, from the 1980s onwards, belief in such a dependency relationship (*dependencia*) began to wane. Some developing countries had, after all, succeeded in fighting their way out of poverty. Prosperity in East and Southeast Asia rose sharply following improvements in agriculture, the development of a service sector and industrialisation.

Large parts of Latin America had also managed to pull themselves out of the poverty spiral. In fact, only Africa had been left behind. The result was less discussion about the development problems of the Third World and more about the problems of specific regions, especially Africa.

This change affected economic thinking about development. Around the 1970s, when analysts were examining the dependency relations between rich and poor, it seemed that there were two types of economies: first, those of the rich, industrialised world, and second, the developing economies. The central question was how poor countries could make economic progress. From this perspective, the situation of poor countries was fundamentally different from that of rich countries, mainly due to inferior initial conditions, their dependence on the prosperous West and their distinct social structures. These structures, it was argued, prevented the laws of economics that applied in the West from working in poor countries. Proponents of this 'structuralist' view attached relatively little importance to the free market and advocated a bigger role for the state in the economy.

However, when some Asian countries were successful at development despite the continued presence of 'underdeveloped' structures and the adverse nature of the global economy, the influence of structuralist thinking on the economy of developing countries weakened. Clearly, then, the structure of the worldwide economy did not have to change in order to give developing countries a chance to grow. South Korea, Taiwan, Singapore, Thailand and Malaysia had already proved this point. It was far more important for the governments of developing countries to pursue the right policies and turn international conditions to good effect. The fact that Africa's problems lay at its own door rather than beyond it was also shown by the experiences of the African oil-producing nations, notably Nigeria. Despite its extra revenue as a result of rising oil prices, it was no better off than African countries that had no oil (and therefore no oil revenue). The crux of the matter was whether or not the available funds were being used productively.

The return on investment in Africa had fallen dramatically in some sectors.[39] As a result, many transnational companies began focusing on just one or two sectors (such as the oil industry) where they knew there were still substantial profits to be made. This strategy ensured that the high risks involved would be commercially acceptable. This made it seem as though the return on investments in Africa was still considerable, while in truth this high average return was only achieved by disposing of activities in less remunerative sectors.[40] While for Asia, exports were the main engine of development, Africa's share of exports (excluding oil) on the world market fell from seven per cent in 1970 to four per cent in 1985.[41] Both the industrial and agricultural sectors either stagnated or declined. And with the population growing at a record rate of up to three per cent a year, Africa's economic and social problems mounted ever higher. This state of affairs was quite simply untenable; the African nations had to reform their economies and economic policies.

Because African production and marketing methods were now out of date and the continent's competitiveness was on the wane, debt (both internal and foreign) increased. International lenders began to realise that at least some of these countries were unlikely ever to repay what they had borrowed. In financial terms, Africa had become a bottomless pit. A radical overhaul of its economy was urgently needed to turn the tide. However, due to the political and social structure of the African countries, the chances of their governments being able or willing to carry through the necessary reforms under their own steam were remote. The initiative for change instead came from the international lenders themselves.

It was primarily the International Monetary Fund (IMF) and the World Bank that put pressure on African governments to carry out what were termed adjustment programmes, aimed at adapting these countries to the international economic environment. Since these reforms were generally focusing on the structures already in place (thereby to some extent vindicating the structuralists), the reform process was called structural adjustment. In reality, however, structural reform was only a second stage following a more fundamental adjustment, namely macroeconomic stabilisation. The African economies had to achieve financial equilibrium before they could be adjusted to fit into the global market.

The structural adjustment programmes therefore aimed to improve both internal balance (the budget) and external balance (the balance of payments). African governments were not allowed to spend more than they acquired in income and they had to take steps to tackle their high levels of inflation. Only when this had been achieved could the real work of structural adjustment begin, with financial assistance from the World Bank and other donors. The IMF and the World Bank set out how stabilisation and adjustment would take place without significant input from African governments, whose willingness to cooperate was in any case limited, given that the first priority of the reforms was to curb public spending. But these governments had no choice; they had become too financially dependent on the West to offer any genuine resistance. To keep the loans coming, they had to reform.

The first structural adjustment programmes were introduced around 1980. At first, their scale was modest but over time they became more and more comprehensive. They were introduced not just in Africa but also in developing countries on other continents. In the 1990s, even the industrialised nations were increasingly forced to adapt to the demands of the global market. To some extent, globalisation made it necessary for any country wanting to capture or retain a share in the global economy to carry out ongoing structural adjustment. In any case, at the time the programmes began, the African economies had gradually been driven to the margins and no longer played a significant global role. Structural adjustment was intended to change all that. Since the reform programmes lasted many years, by the second half of the 1980s and the early 1990s almost every African country was carrying one out, under the direction of the World Bank and the IMF. These were not standardised programmes, and they sometimes differed substantially from country to country. The measures that were included also changed over time as the designers learned from their mistakes. However, the programmes had a number of common characteristics.

First, they were designed to reduce the role of the state. The state's hold over the economy may have been understandable from a historical, political and social perspective, but its economic disadvantages had begun to predominate. 'Market forces' was the new rallying cry. The physical size of government was also a problem. Sprawling bureaucracies had to be scaled down, if only to bring their costs under control. The machinery of government placed too great a financial burden on the budget. Because African governments had borrowed heavily to reduce their budget deficits, rising global interest rates in the 1980s created an even bigger debt burden. These debts sometimes even outstripped a country's Gross National Product. The annual loan repayments of the larger countries very soon equalled a quarter to a third of their export revenue. Governments quickly began to print more money, which in turn pushed up inflation. By slashing public spending (mainly by scaling down the bureaucracy) and tightening monetary policy, the World Bank and IMF tried to stabilise the macroeconomic and financial situation in the African countries.

Second, they sought to expand the role of market forces. Mainly, this meant devaluing the local currencies, which in almost all cases had been kept artificially high to push down the relative cost of imports. This benefited the elite and urban consumers. The often drastic devaluations that were imposed therefore hit these groups hard but made life easier for producers, and for exporters in particular. Earlier policies had overemphasised consumption at the expense of production. Devaluation corrected this bias. In practice, however, the shift was less extreme than in theory, since there had almost always been a black market and this had injected some degree of competition into the system. The move to floating exchange rates was painful for government officials and others with fixed salaries paid in local currencies. The countries that had adopted the CFA franc as their currency did not at first take part in devaluation; France did not agree to the measure until 1994.

Third, the World Bank and the IMF insisted that governments sell off many of their almost invariably inefficient state-owned companies to the private sector. These were either companies that had been nationalised following independence or state-owned companies set up in the same period. Collectively, they were a huge drain on the state budget. The marketing boards also had to be closed down. These institutions, which had bought up agricultural produce from farmers at a fixed price before selling it on at a mark-up (which effectively created an export duty), were a major obstacle to a properly functioning rural economy. However, the closure of these boards came as a severe financial blow to the state. In many countries, the revenue collected by the marketing boards, especially the duties on exports, had formed a large share of the state budget. In Uganda, the sale of tea accounted for more than half the national income thanks to this method. Even in countries with a more diversified economy, such as Ivory Coast, the marketing boards had generated at least a quarter to a third of public revenue.[42] The abolition of these institutions was intended to provide an incentive for farmers, boosting production and ultimately creating a supply of cheaper food.

Finally, African states were generally expected to refrain from price-setting. Not only were fixed prices for agricultural produce abolished, but a wide range of subsidies and tariffs also disappeared in whole or part. These subsidies and tariffs had been designed to improve conditions for certain groups relative to others. Frequently they benefited consumers at the expense of producers. The abolition or reduction of food subsidies was, of course, a highly contentious measure. The same applied to the introduction of fees in some countries for services that had until then been free of charge, such as education or health care. People now had to start paying for the goods and services they received. The assumption was that this would persuade the public and organisations to adopt a more 'rational' (in the economic sense) approach to money, which would in time boost both productivity and returns on investment, and ultimately increase prosperity. The aim of dismantling protective tariff barriers which sheltered unproductive companies was to force these enterprises to become more competitive. In practice, however, this led to major difficulties because the companies were unable to adjust in time. The outcome: yet more company closures and lost jobs.

Effects of the structural
adjustment programmes

It is still almost impossible to obtain a reliable picture of the overall results and effects of the structural adjustment programmes in Africa. Evaluations of the adjustment process have simply perpetuated the debates of the Cold War period. Adherents of the market mechanism saw only the benefits of capitalism – a view seemingly vindicated by the collapse of the socialist model – and therefore initially refused to acknowledge any problems with the introduction of a free-market economy in Africa. This viewpoint was represented most notably by the international financial institutions themselves, who were the architects of the programmes. Although organisations cannot be expected to be the harshest critics of their own activities, the assessments made by the World Bank, which was closely monitoring the progress of the reforms, were nevertheless remarkably optimistic. Around 1990, its overall conclusion was that structural adjustment was working. It found that economic growth was highest in those countries where the reforms were being most effectively implemented. Countries that were not adapting were still in the economic doldrums. The remaining problems were the result, it concluded, of inadequate adjustment. Consequently, in the 1990s the World Bank's message to the stragglers was clear: their progress depended on liberalisation of their economies.

This irked practically everyone who was ideologically opposed to the market-based approach. That included large numbers of Africans, both in and out of government. But the fiercest criticism came from Westerners who had been involved in African development, sometimes for many years: field workers and members of action groups or universities. The main approach many of them advocated was development centred on the individual, a notion which paradoxically often translated into a high degree of state involvement, guidance and planning. The failure of this model in Africa, together with the collapse of the Eastern Bloc, had forced this group to rethink its views slightly, but they never went so far as to embrace the free market. The possibility that, like the socialist Eastern Bloc, Africa might also be lost to capitalism was too unpleasant for them to contemplate. Both their intellectual energies and their frustrations were therefore turned against the reforms that sought to liberalise Africa. Their barbs were directed at the IMF, the World Bank and structural adjustment. They were no longer able to halt the programmes – the international balance of power had shifted too radically – but they could at least highlight the failures of the approach. This produced a wealth of literature, sometimes general, sometimes highly detailed, with the message that structural adjustment was leading Africa down the road to ruin. Even when the need for liberalisation measures was accepted, they were said to be proceeding far too rapidly, in the wrong order, with unacceptable social costs and so on.

The mystery is how there came to be such widely differing views on the impact of the reforms. What made the situation in Africa open to so many interpretations? One explanation involves the statistical material concerning the results, or rather, the lack of such material. Structural adjustment was meant to generate clear economic improvements that would be reflected in figures on both the overall state of the economy (the 'macro level') and the situation of individuals and families (both producers and consumers, the 'micro level'), plus the structures in between, such as the agriculture and health care sectors (the 'meso level'). When no figures were available, it was anyone's guess whether or not the intended changes had occurred. Even when statistics were available, they were frequently so unreliable that they could be used to back up almost any interpretation. For example, the figures produced for whole countries sometimes only reflected the situation in the capital city.

A second reason that the results of the reforms received so many different interpretations was the difficulty of showing a link between the numerical data (on the few occasions where they were reliable) and the structural adjustment programmes themselves. Some economic and social trends had begun long before the launch of the reforms and continued to make themselves felt. Moreover, major global events sometimes took place while the reforms were being carried out, such as a large fluctuation in the price of a country's main export product on the world market. Nor was it clear in advance how long specific adjustment measures would take to have visible effects. Moreover, for political reasons, the reforms promised by African governments were by no means always implemented and were sometimes reversed at a later stage (see the final section of this chapter). Certain sectors, such as the financial sector, often remained completely untouched. As a result, evaluations of the effects of structural adjustment in Africa gave rise to a mass of often contradictory conclusions.

So was structural adjustment (in the period up to about 1990) successful or not? It is tempting to give an answer based on one's own ideological preferences, but that would add nothing to the debate. It is equally tempting to conclude that the truth lies somewhere in the middle, but this is also unsatisfactory. The fact is that the model of large-scale state intervention, with its panoply of rules and a minor role for market forces, failed in Africa. By the early 1980s the African economies had been thrown completely out of balance, financially and otherwise. Stabilisation was thus a prerequisite for the adjustment process, and it had to take place quickly. Without macroeconomic stability, countries would be incapable of development. Only socialist diehards and the most hard-headed advocates of 'people-centred' development were unwilling to recognise this. When they were carried through, the reforms that targeted macroeconomic stability were usually successful. External conditions, notably prices on the world market, sometimes greatly helped or hindered the process.

If we look at the cutbacks that governments made and at the additional revenue they generated in an attempt to balance their budgets, the picture varies from country to country. The way in which public expenditure was reduced had a large social impact, since it affected not just the salaries of government employees but also the costs of health care, education, food subsidies and so on (see the next-to-last section of this chapter). The picture on the income side is equally varied. The tax system improved in some countries, but in others the size and composition of public revenue barely changed, presumably because self-serving national elites gave a low priority to these reforms.

A key component of the structural adjustment programmes was 'getting the prices right'. Market forces were intended not just to set realistic values for local currencies but also to bring prices on the domestic market to more realistic levels. Initially this meant devaluing the national currencies, a process that took place only later in the CFA zones, where the CFA franc had a fixed value against the French franc (see next section).

While the deregulation of prices apparently improved domestic economies, it had disappointingly little impact on relations with other countries. In most cases, there was no real promotion of exports. The main problem was probably the low competitiveness of the private sector. Despite lower production costs, it remained difficult for African companies to capture a larger share of the international market. This was one reason that the anticipated boost for private enterprise did not materialise. Of course, it is reasonable to ask how quickly the private sector could be expected to respond. It is next to impossible to build up an efficient, competitive enterprise until a whole raft of conditions are in place: trained managers and personnel, for instance, and readily available capital. The environment also has to be conducive to private enterprise, with markets for products, labour and finance, plus legal and physical security. Often, many of these conditions were not satisfied.

A key aspect of many programmes was to make inefficient state-owned enterprises more cost-effective. In many cases, this meant privatisation. However, selling publicly owned companies to the private sector was a tricky proposition in countries where there were few, if any, entrepreneurs not connected to the government. As a result, the sale of state-owned enterprises was highly politicised. The companies often enjoyed a statutory monopoly that was later handed on to their market-based successors. Though not legally protected monopolies, these new private-sector enterprises benefited from the absence of competitors, as well as informal political protection that prevented such competitors from emerging.

As a result, economic monopolies passed into private hands. According to some commentators, this made the situation even worse, since there was no public stewardship of private monopolies as there had been under state ownership. According to others, privatisation did at least generate economic benefits, for example in the form of a less bureaucratic company structure, fewer inefficient rules and more competition, especially on the labour market. This generally cut production costs, which in turn benefited the consumer. Moreover, it was better to have private monopolies turning a profit than state monopolies that were a drain on the public purse.

Nevertheless, many companies, both public and private, were unable to manage without help and, in the face of mounting competition, were forced to cut back or even close down. Some countries underwent 'deindustrialisation', more or less completely dismantling their domestic industries. Workers found themselves jobless and had to fend for themselves. For lack of alternatives, many sought refuge in independent economic activities not subject to regulation or other forms of state interference. Activities in this informal sector ranged from selling newspapers in the street to giving language lessons. The informal sector began expanding rapidly during the economic recession of the 1970s and 1980s. Structural adjustment programmes aimed to remove a large number of regulations that were distorting the market or restricting economic growth so as to allow the formal sector to expand again and absorb workers from the informal sector. Unfortunately, this did not happen. Rather than expanding, the formal sector shrank still further, forcing yet more people to try their luck in the grey economy. As a result, the informal sector became the main source of employment almost throughout Africa. By about 1990 it included more than sixty per cent of the urban workforce.[43]

The barriers to starting a new business were formidable. Although the reforms did manage to improve the conditions under which new companies operated, fledgling businesses were often unable to weather the competition. The hopes of economic diversification were thus largely dashed. Moreover, countries continued to rely on just one or two export products. As before, oil was the economic mainstay in Nigeria, Angola and Gabon, tobacco in Malawi, coffee in Uganda and Burundi, and so forth. While the liberalisation of

Africa's economies sometimes improved matters locally, the small-scale entrepreneurs who benefited (many of whom were working in the informal sector) were either unable or unwilling to increase the scale of their activities, for example by producing for foreign markets. There was therefore almost no movement from the informal to the formal economy.

The reforms took root relatively well in the agricultural sector, and food production often rose substantially. However, other factors (such as rainfall) made it difficult to measure even the combined effect of the reforms on production and made it impossible to gauge their individual effects. However, the impact of structural adjustment on agriculture seemed generally favourable. The reforms were targeted mainly at removing or alleviating price distortions for producers (who had been paid far too little for their products due to tariffs) and consumers (who had not paid enough due to subsidies). Rural incomes went up, which improved the economy in many places, especially as the abolition of numerous regulations created opportunities for people to pursue economic activities outside farming. This expanded the range of small-scale economic activity in the countryside, blurring the strict division between rural areas (where the only activities were farming and livestock raising) and urban centres (where everything else was done). New growth clusters arose: small towns with 20,000 to 30,000 inhabitants, which were chiefly based on agriculture but expanded to include other economic pursuits. In general, the new emphasis on market forces worked well in the countryside, especially near urban areas that could be served without high transport costs. Unfortunately, life did not improve in remote areas, which had done relatively well out of government intervention. When this intervention was removed, the rise in transport costs often made it too expensive for farmers to reach their markets. Consequently, these areas sometimes reverted entirely to subsistence farming.

The CFA: a separate exchange rate,

a separate course

The reforms in the countries that formed part of the *Communauté Financière Africaine*, the region that had adopted the CFA franc as its common currency, differed from the rest of Africa on one fundamental point. Many years before, France had guaranteed these countries a fixed exchange rate of fifty CFA francs to one French franc. This fixed rate gave the economies of the participating countries a sound economic base, both internally and in terms of international trade, foreign investments and loans. Inflation levels were identical to those in France, and therefore low by African standards. Companies knew what they could buy abroad with the currency, including in the long-term, and they could always exchange their francs for hard currencies. In short, they knew where they stood in every regard. Unlike practically all the other African currencies, the CFA franc had a strength that was economically favourable.

The CFA member states (all former French colonies in Africa with the exception of Guinea) were however required to relinquish some of their sovereignty in exchange for membership. The link between their currencies and the French franc meant that the CFA's monetary policy was made in Paris. This strand of the colonial relationship had remained after independence; the ongoing link between the two monetary systems could in fact be regarded as a French neocolonial tactic since it prevented the CFA countries from promoting their own development through a unilateral monetary policy.

Many wondered whether the benefits of CFA membership outweighed the disadvantages. The governments of the participating countries evidently felt that they did. In 1962 Mali had withdrawn from the CFA and introduced its own franc in a bid to assert its independence, and the consequences had been disastrous. The Malian franc soon collapsed, with all the attendant problems. The government in Bamako did its best to be readmitted to the *Communauté* but did not succeed until the 1980s. Non-Francophone countries also showed interest in joining. In the 1980s, for example, Equatorial Guinea, a former Spanish colony whose neighbours were CFA members, gave up its own currency to become part of the CFA. France set limits on borrowing by CFA members and forced them to cap their budget deficits. One or two managed to get round this with creative accounting, by allowing public and semipublic enterprises (over whose finances Paris had no direct control) to run up huge debts. As a result, the debts of the Francophone countries sometimes appeared smaller than they really were.

One major disadvantage of the fixed exchange rate was the relative rise of the CFA franc as a result of the currency devaluations elsewhere in Africa and beyond. In the late 1980s, even the US dollar fell against the French franc. This undermined the competitiveness of the CFA countries, which found it increasingly difficult to export goods that other countries could supply more cheaply. During the 1980s, for example, vegetables from the Anglophone African countries supplanted those from the CFA on the European market. This led to extensive smuggling between the CFA countries and their non-CFA neighbours. Wages and prices in the CFA were generally high, but could not be sustained following the decline in its international economic competitiveness. Corrective measures needed to be taken.[44]

For the largest CFA member state, Senegal, whose capital of Dakar was home to the CFA central bank, the need to adapt came even sooner. In 1979 Senegal had become the first country in the world to receive a World Bank loan to carry out structural adjustment. Since independence in 1960, Senegal's economy had become lopsided. During the colonial era, it had been at the hub of French West Africa, and this had left it with the legacy of a large bureaucracy. Once the other colonies gained their independence and each went its own way, this bureaucracy needed to be scaled down substantially. The Senegalese government also pursued a socialist economic policy characterised by extensive nationalisation, regulation and other forms of state intervention. This was a major cause of its gradual economic slowdown and, finally, stagnation. Up to the mid-1960s, Senegal's economic growth rate was over three per cent a year, but it fell in the space of a decade to approximately one per cent before slipping below the one per cent mark around 1980.[45] Meanwhile, the population was growing at a rate of two to three per cent annually. Per capita output thus peaked in the early years of independence, after which it declined with progressive speed. Nevertheless, the government managed – with donor assistance – to maintain per capita income for many years. In the 1980s Senegal's average per capita income of approximately seven hundred US dollars a year (of which one hundred dollars came from external aid) was in fact the highest in the whole of West Africa. The country was therefore living beyond its means; systematically consuming more than it produced and making no significant investments.

An obvious first step would have been to drastically devalue the local currency, in order to reduce the price of Senegalese products abroad and hence boost exports. However, this was not an option, since the structure of the CFA system with its fixed exchange rate was not yet open to discussion. The initial emphasis was therefore on stabilising the macroeconomic situation and reducing the government's dominant role in the economy. These goals were only partially met. Although the government cut spending, for instance by dismissing civil servants, income remained low. Little attempt was made to impose duties on imports since this would have had an adverse effect on consumption by the country's elite. Nor was the tax system improved. A large share of public revenue continued to come from duties on petrol (the price of petrol in Senegal was two to three times higher than the world market price), which pushed up the costs of domestic economic activity. Inflation remained low thanks to Senegal's membership of the CFA but the national debt burden rose despite the steps taken. In the 1980s the country was forced to adopt increasingly stringent measures to avoid bankruptcy. More public employees were dismissed, public-sector pay was reduced, state-owned enterprises were privatised, subsidies were abolished and so on. A period of company closures and of growing unemployment now began, with the private sector unable to absorb the effects of the downturn in the state sector.

Senegal's dire financial and economic straits forced the authorities in Dakar to comply increasingly closely with the requirements imposed by the IMF and the World Bank in order to qualify for financial support. However, promises of reform were often not followed up or were kept only with great reluctance. Consequently, no real progress was made in the 1980s. Despite one or two improvements, the government remained inefficient, the scope for market forces limited, the private sector uncompetitive and the debt burden high. While standards of health care and education deteriorated as a result of the cutbacks, the economy continued to stagnate. By the early 1990s, the reform programmes in Senegal were still being carried out (though half-heartedly) but the light at the end of the tunnel was not yet in sight.

The economy of Ivory Coast – the biggest in Africa after South Africa's and Nigeria's – was even more important than that of Senegal. By the time Ivory Coast gained its independence, its economy was already fairly developed. During the 1960s, it had sustained an average annual growth rate of eleven per cent, and by the 1970s the economy was still growing by as much as six per cent a year. The Ivorian government pursued a stable pro-Western course in close consultation with France. There was heavy investment in the country's export production, especially from France. Ivory Coast became the world's main exporter of cocoa. Coffee, hardwoods, palm oil and rubber were also sold abroad in large volumes. The generally high prices for these products on the world market made Ivory Coast increasingly prosperous. By 1980 it had overtaken its neighbour, Ghana, which had been wealthier at the time of independence but since then had suffered from political instability and disastrous socialist policy.

Prosperity gave rise to overconfidence, which became more pronounced from the 1970s onward. The government in Abidjan launched a programme of measures to reduce the influence of foreign capital and external control of the economy. Its aim was to 'Ivorianise' the country's economy, especially its industrial sector. Because there was no home-grown private sector and no private financiers, the state took this task on itself. This gave rise to corruption and nepotism. The country's elite misused the programme to appoint their friends to the well-paid jobs previously held by foreigners, some of whom were permitted to stay on and continue managing their former companies in an 'advisory' capacity. The government also sought to diversify the economy. Though essentially a prudent move, this was handled badly. State-owned enterprises were set up in sectors that were unattractive to foreign capital. These state-owned companies, many of which were placed under poor local management, were unable to make a profit. Their losses were borne by the Treasury, whose coffers had already been depleted by the rise in oil prices. Still, the government did not rethink its policy. Instead, the losses were covered with borrowed money.

This led to a full-blown economic crisis in the 1980s, coinciding with another sharp rise in international oil prices, a global economic recession and a decline in the price of raw materials. Public revenue fell dramatically and the country's debts mounted. In 1981 the government began to adopt the IMF's recommendations, starting with the suspension of aid to state-owned enterprises. Wherever possible, these companies were either privatised or converted into cooperatives; failing that, they were closed down. Cutbacks were also made elsewhere. Between 1982 and 1985, for example, public spending was halved.[46] Expenditure on health care and education was reduced to bare bones. The IMF began making new loans to Ivory Coast in recognition of these cutbacks and after 1985 the economy picked up again slightly, though not for long, since in 1987 international prices for cocoa and coffee fell to below the farmers' cost price. This made it increasingly difficult to maintain state revenue through exports, even if only to pay off the country's debts. In 1990 there was another round of cutbacks: spending on education and health care was further curtailed, as was civil servants' pay. Government officials who were not dismissed saw their salaries slashed by forty per cent. Ivory Coast entered the 1990s with its economy in crisis.

The economic travails of Senegal and Ivory Coast reflected those of the other CFA countries, all of which were eventually forced to appeal to the international financial institutions for assistance. None of these countries were able to boost their economic growth by promoting exports. A related problem was contraband from non-CFA neighbours, whose products were often much cheaper thanks to their devalued currencies, leading to a rise in imports into the CFA. In theory, the CFA governments could have generated extra revenue by imposing duties on these imports, but that proved impossible. Higher import charges were unpopular in any form, since they pushed up consumer prices. Customs officers added to the problem, since they were more interested collecting bribes for themselves than duties for the authorities. As a result, much trade remained undeclared. Although there was little formal trade between African countries, in some places there was a substantial flow of unregistered cross-border buying and selling. For example, the high price of petrol in Benin created a lively illegal trade in the border region with Nigeria, earning the area the nickname of Kuwait. The Beninese bought cheap subsidised petrol from Nigeria, bribed the border guards and then sold it at a higher price in their own country. The problem in such situations was not only the price disparity between neighbouring countries, but also the fact many African customs officers regarded the duties they collected as a source of personal income.

In the early 1990s, the economic position of much of Francophone Western and Central Africa had become unfavourable due to the high fixed rate of the CFA franc. Within the increasingly liberalised global economy, the initial advantages of the CFA system had turned into disadvantages. Most CFA countries could no longer generate sufficient revenue to maintain the level of either investment or social spending. For France, the system became a greater financial burden by the year. The only question was how long France and the African member states would be able and willing to continue down this road.

Economic problems
in conflict regions

The pursuit of economic reform under peaceful conditions was by no means possible throughout the whole of Africa. In countries embroiled in enduring armed conflicts, such as Angola and Mozambique (which had not become independent from Portugal until 1975), the need for change was even greater than in other regions. Not only were these countries faced with the classic political and economic problems – inefficient government, low economic competitiveness, declining output, bureaucracy, corruption, mismanagement and the disorganisation of state-owned enterprises, the failed collectivisation of agriculture, a rising state budget and trade balance deficit, an overvalued currency and, as a result, parallel (i.e. black) markets – they were also forced into high defence spending and were struggling with a lack of internal security. All this eroded living standards. Shops ran out of merchandise and markets vanished because there was nothing left to sell. Imports were unaffordable. What little revenue governments did manage to generate was used to purchase arms. In the 1980s, after the withdrawal of Soviet aid, Mozambique's income dried up almost completely, while Angola's revenue remained at a reasonable level only due to its income from oil. With the exception of the oil sector in Angola, neither country made significant investments due to the lack of internal security.

Mozambique was therefore in greater need of a new economic policy than Angola. It joined the IMF and the World Bank in 1984, and began to discuss a structural adjustment programme. These talks progressed very slowly since the government in Maputo was inclined to view the liberalisation process merely as a new phase in the socialist development of Mozambique, whereas the international financial institutions saw it as a first stage in the complete dismantling of the country's planned economy. In 1987, a few months after the death of socialist president Somora Machel, the Mozambican government made a radical change of direction. It adopted a new programme of economic recovery designed to lead to a market economy. Public expenditure was drastically reduced, price controls were abandoned, the currency was floated, subsidies were abolished or restricted and loss-making state-owned enterprises were forced to borrow on the open market. The result of this policy was to attract new loans from the West and new development aid for investment. The shops were restocked and money could be earned once more. By the late 1980s, the Mozambican economy was growing by a few per cent a year. In 1990, however, this growth collapsed once more. The devaluation of the currency had reached enormous proportions: whereas in 1987, forty meticals had been equivalent to one dollar, by 1990 this had risen to a thousand meticals. This made foreign goods unaffordable.

The Angolan government spent approximately half of state revenue on defence, using it to develop the strongest, best-equipped army in black Africa. This left little over for investment. The economy worsened almost every year, partly due to the war. Mines ground to a standstill, farmers abandoned their fields and trade ceased. Only the extraction and export of oil continued, and the revenue was used to continue the war. Although in 1985 the socialist ruling party gave the formal go-ahead for liberalising the economy, little came of this for several years, since reform was undermined at all levels, both for ideological reasons and out of self-interest; even the lucrative senior posts in state-owned enterprises were under threat. In 1987 Angola applied to join the IMF in order to qualify for loans, but because of the ongoing war this request met with political objections from the United States, which backed the UNITA rebel movement. Washington was unwilling to relax its opposition to Angolan membership of the IMF until a peace settlement had been negotiated. For these political reasons, too, the war hampered economic recovery.

In Sudan, economic development was a low priority. Living conditions for many Sudanese were undermined by the tensions between the Arab (Muslim) north and the black African (Christian and animist) south. Rural areas suffered appallingly from the conflict and from neglect by the authorities. Although Sudan has relatively large tracts of high-quality agricultural land for its small population, it nevertheless endured repeated famines. The government constantly overspent, yet because it adopted a pro-Western stance and occasionally made one or two half-hearted attempts to liberalise the economy, it continued to receive loans to repay its debts. However, this changed during the 1980s when the government in Khartoum, inspired by the Islamic revolution in Iran, began to follow an increasingly pro-Islamic course. The civil war with the south flared up again and Sudanese terrorists carried out attacks in various countries. The United States suspended aid to Khartoum and added Sudan to its list of rogue states. Aid from the Middle East kept the country afloat for a while, but dried up when Khartoum sided with the Iraqi dictator Saddam Hussein during the Gulf War. Oil sales provided some respite, but since Sudan's pipelines and oil fields were a key target for southern rebels, even this source of income remained unreliable.

The independent countries bordering the strongholds of white rule in Southern Africa regarded themselves as 'frontline states'; although not formally at war with South Africa, Rhodesia or (until 1975) Angola and Mozambique, they nonetheless opposed them in ways that had economic repercussions. South Africa and its neighbours, with their highly developed economies and advanced infrastructures, would have made logical trading partners for the frontline states. Economically, this would have been far more attractive than looking for import and export opportunities along the coastline further to the north, where there were no decent port facilities and connections with the hinterland were poor. However, the frontline states refused on principle to make such choices on an economic basis (with the exception of Malawi, which remained on good terms with South Africa and Rhodesia for just this reason). It is difficult to assess what economic consequences this moral stance had for the frontline states, especially as it brought them the benefit of additional donor aid, not just from the West but also from socialist countries as a result of the Cold War. For example, the People's Republic of China financed and built a railway line from Zambia to the coast of Tanzania (the 'Tanzam Line') to promote international trade with Zambia, a landlocked country.

RECEIPT

No. 095370

DATE 11/30/04

RECEIVED FROM Sylvia

Thirty-one and 00/100 $31 00 DOLLARS

FOR RENT Books
FOR

○ CASH
○ CHECK
○ MONEY ORDER

FROM

BY

ACCOUNT	
PAYMENT	
BAL. DUE	

2701

The social costs
of the reforms

The economic stagnation or decline of almost all the African countries inevitably had social repercussions. By around 1990, many countries had lower per capita incomes than immediately after independence. Basic social services such as education and health care, the vast majority of which were state-run in Africa, were under constant threat of bankruptcy. Generally speaking, African governments were overspending. This could not continue, especially since these governments themselves were offering no prospect of improvement. It thus became necessary for the international donor community, which was after all financing Africa's deficits, to take the lead in introducing unavoidable economic cutbacks. The social impact of these measures would be felt by practically everyone in Africa. This sometimes created the impression that these international institutions and donors (especially the IMF and the World Bank) had actually caused the problem. But in fact, unsparing economic and social reforms were inevitable; the money had simply run out. The structural adjustment programmes provided loans to try to make the inevitable cutbacks more manageable and gradual than they would otherwise have been. They also guided the reforms so that the scarce resources available could be used as effectively as possible after the reform process. Finally, in many countries the programmes probably provided some protection for the most vulnerable population groups, who without external influence might well have paid more dearly for the excesses of their political and economic elites.[47]

The funds that were still available to Africa by the 1980s were certainly scarce. They amounted to far less, in fact, than was needed to maintain the standard of living. The structural adjustment programmes forced governments to make some painful choices. As frequently mentioned above, public spending had to be drastically curtailed. One of the ways this was done was by channelling most of the scarce funds into areas where they would generate the biggest economic returns. The social sectors were regarded as being largely consumptive without generating much wealth, at least not in the short term. Yet the fact is that hard investment was also reduced in order to limit the damage to basic social services as much as possible.

The cutbacks could not, after all, be based solely on economic factors. Social and moral imperatives also had to be considered. The public employees who lost their jobs may have been among the more affluent city-dwellers (and compared to the rural population could even have been called wealthy), but it should not be forgotten that they often provided for an entire clientele. The decision to reduce or stop paying their salaries could therefore adversely affect countless people, right down to the lowest social classes. And it sometimes raised a serious moral dilemma. Normally, investment in education was guaranteed to yield returns. But how (to cite the most extreme example) was a government to deal with children suffering from AIDS, whose parents had already succumbed to the disease? Should they be given additional supervision and counselling, which would cost money? These children were almost certain to die, so any money spent on them could not be justified in terms of economic growth. Yet surely they could not simply be left to their fate? In practice, non-economic factors often came into play.

How did structural adjustment affect African society? Naturally, the answer differs widely from country to country and from sector to sector, but in general it seems that social conditions did not dramatically worsen during the 1980s. Certainly a number of basic social indicators showed no perceptible deterioration. Life expectancy, for example, continued to rise. Whereas in 1973, Africans could on average be expected to live to about the age of 45, by 1985 this had risen to 49, and by 1991 average life expectancy had reached 51. Child mortality fell during the same period, from 137 per thousand births in 1973 to 118 in 1985 and to 107 in 1991. Literacy increased in percentage terms among both men and women, rising among men from 37% in 1973 to 56% in 1985, and reaching 62% in 1991. Among women, it rose from 11% in 1973 to 33% per cent in 1985, attaining 39% in 1991.[48]

However, these figures should not be allowed to give the impression that there were no serious problems. In the 1980s, many countries spent considerably less on education and health care than they had previously. One effect was a lower ratio of doctors and nurses to patients. While the population continued to grow rapidly, many qualified doctors and nurses were emigrating. And medical treatment and hospitalisation grew more expensive because patients were required to pay higher user fees for them. There were similar trends in the education sector, with a decline in the ratio of teachers to pupils. School fees went up and subsidies for school meals and textbooks were abolished.[49] Although these adverse developments had not yet appeared in the social indicators during the 1980s, by the 1990s they had.

Incomes were largely dependent on work. The decline of the formal sector was discussed above (pp. 66). Public employees saw their jobs disappear due to cutbacks and intense competition led many businesses to close their doors. Many who managed to keep their jobs saw their wages slashed. In addition to the direct effect this had on the workers concerned – whose jobs had kept them out of the worst poverty – there was also an indirect effect on those who depended on their wages. A single wage earner might well have been supporting large numbers of people, who were often among the poorest of the poor. On the other hand, employment in the informal sector rose sharply in many African countries. All the same, work in this sector did not provide the same security as 'real' employment. Moreover, it was not generally clear whether the growth of the informal sector entirely made up for the decline in employment in the formal sector. This differed from country to country. In countries where the informal sector grew more slowly, large groups of people saw their incomes plummet.

An additional question was what exactly incomes could buy. Each new structural adjustment loan from the international financial institutions enabled a country to start importing goods again. The shops and markets would be well stocked. The country's economic fortunes would appear to improve for a time until prices rose too sharply and the goods became unaffordable. Part of the reform process, after all, was to ensure that national currencies assumed their real value, which was much lower than the artificial exchange rate previously maintained by the government. This reduced purchasing power. Moreover, the public had to pay for products and services that had in the past been subsidised, such as food, education and health care. This increased the cost of living, especially in the towns and cities. The situation in rural areas was generally better: price rises were minimal since rural populations bought few imported products. Rural producers were also paid more for their output. As a result, purchasing power often increased outside the major cities.

So while the effects of the economic decline and the reforms were not detrimental to all population groups, the living standards of large sections of the population nevertheless worsened. This conclusion is supported by the average economic growth rates from the 1980s, which were lower than those of population growth. Per capita GNP in Africa fell between 1980 and 1992 by an average of 0.8 per cent per year.[50] Poverty either remained a serious problem or became one.

A new danger: the disintegration
of the state

As we have seen, the structural adjustment programmes were not an unqualified success. Yet looking back, it is clear that these programmes alone did not have the potential to restore economic growth. The fundamental issue was the African approach to the economy and the economic choices made by the leaders of the independent states. Furthermore, the physical and social infrastructure was inadequate to bring about the growth that was so sorely needed.

African economies were traditionally characterised by redistribution mechanisms designed to share wealth. In the exceptional cases where there was a substantial accumulation of riches, they were mainly put to economically passive use as a way of demonstrating affluence and drumming up political support, rather than being used for investment. The aim was economic and social security, not growth. A more or less equitable distribution of income was regarded as more important than an increase in output.[51] Colonialism introduced a different economic system to Africa, which gradually gained ground on the surface, and in some sectors more deeply. Following independence, cultural and social factors gave renewed importance to Africa's indigenous economic practices. The continent's new leaders had generally received a Western education, but they were quickly reabsorbed into the African system. Clientelist ties began to dominate the whole political and social spectrum. The modernisation that had taken place mainly in the 1950s and 1960s, but which since then had remained limited in scope, was swept along in this clientelist system. This tiny core of modernity was not enough to change the rest of society, and what was essentially a non-indigenous element was therefore simply subsumed into the traditional African social system. For instance, state-owned enterprises were clearly used for purposes of redistribution, not growth.

The economic growth of the 1950s and 1960s had shifted this redistribution system into high gear. However, when economic growth stalled and eventually reversed in the 1970s, it became increasingly difficult to maintain the same high level of redistribution. Foreign capital was used to plug the widening financial gap. These burgeoning loans created Africa's debt problem. The economic cutbacks that followed in the 1980s had far-reaching political and social effects as well as economic ones. The structural adjustment programmes pushed redistribution into the background and championed a return to the principles of the growth economy. Restructuring was designed in part to raise output but the reforms only succeeded in one or two sectors, notably agriculture.

Before growth could take place, many conditions had to be met – conditions that went much further than the requirements laid down by the structural adjustment programmes. One of these was the availability of a skilled workforce. Africa could not adequately satisfy this requirement with its existing educational system. The state of its physical infrastructure was also a serious drawback. Although many roads were being built in Africa, an equal number of existing roads were disappearing just as quickly through lack of maintenance, so that the network never truly expanded. At the end of the twentieth century, the railway network was still about the same size as it had been in the 1920s. Moreover, it was put to very little use. Various cultural conditions for growth were also absent, for example the work ethic, organisational and managerial capacity and trust. Legal certainty (the certainty that the law will be applied) was poor almost everywhere, as, in some places, was physical security.[52] If all this is taken into account, then it becomes more understandable why the adjustment programmes alone could not restore growth.[53]

Another problem was that some of the programmes were implemented late or only partially, or else in a manner entirely at variance with what had been agreed between the African authorities and the international financial institutions. Even when compared to other parts of the world that went through similar processes, Africa was notable for its slipshod approach to reform and lack of political commitment to it. The reason frequently given for this was that the social costs would otherwise have been unacceptable and would have led to political instability. It was therefore said to be better both for the population as a whole and for the elite if the international community did not to try to rush the reforms. Presumably the true explanation for the delays and circumventions lay rather more in the private interests of the political elite, many of whose members stood to lose some of their power (and hence their income) as a result of the reforms.

The problem was that the reforms still focused too narrowly on economic issues, without aiming at any real political change. The 1980s were, in political terms, the years of the old guard (the 'dinosaurs'), who included presidents Mobutu Sese Seko, Kenneth Kaunda and Daniel arap Moi. During this period, there was no monitoring of political decisions and no political transparency. As a result, the powerful benefited from privatisation (though it must be said that there were often no other entrepreneurs around). The government's misappropriation of public revenue grew increasingly shameless. It became gradually clear that the reforms would never make any headway until there was genuine political change. In countries with a reasonable standard of democratic governance (such as Ghana, Uganda and Mali), the results were encouraging. But in those with bad governance (such as Zaire), the reforms had no positive effects at all.

The variable results and the secondary effects of the reforms prompted a great deal of debate. The supporters and opponents of the adjustments, who were initially irreconcilable and diametrically opposed, eventually found their ideas converging to some extent. The IMF's critics – the 'structuralists' – gradually began to acknowledge the importance of exports, advocating the creation of a single African market. They also softened their traditional emphasis on industrialisation, acknowledging the importance of agriculture. For their part, the international financial institutions now accepted that the reforms had a social impact, often a large one. Around 1990, they declared themselves prepared to devote more attention to this social component, to development 'with a human face'. In the second half of the 1990s, this led to a new economic concept, that of pro-poor growth; in other words, economic growth that is generated primarily through the participation of the poor, who then reap the benefits of that growth. The IMF and the World Bank also relaxed some of the requirements they had imposed on African governments. Their blueprints dictating the nature and timing of reform, which had usually overlooked the diversity of the countries involved, became somewhat more flexible.

However, the main changes made to the reform programmes related to institutions, particularly state institutions. Their weakness in Africa, and in some cases their further erosion as a result of the reforms, gave rise to serious concern. The progressive disintegration of the state was increasingly seen as the main obstacle to the success of the reforms, and in fact as the number one African development problem. Rather than rebuilding institutional capacity, in many countries the reforms accelerated the disintegration of states, with all the tragic consequences one might expect (see chapter 5).

At the end of the Cold War, there were frequent complaints that the structural adjustment programmes were not working and that they should never have been carried out. However, this raises the question of what alternatives were available. Doing nothing was not an option. Governments had been on the brink of bankruptcy when they accepted (and in some cases initiated) the reforms. Without external assistance, their collapse would have been unavoidable. And even then, services such as education and health care would not have been able to survive since there was simply no more money for investments or imports. Africa had no choice but to make its way through the long dark tunnel of reform, though the light at the other end was still far from view.

The deterioration of certain areas, such as basic social services, could be repaired when economic growth returned. What was more serious, as mentioned, was the damage that had been done to the states themselves, whose already weak structures were further undermined by economic contraction and cutbacks. In some countries, it began to look as though the machinery of the state was sustaining irreparable structural damage that would seriously impair their long-term development prospects. But once again, we must ask ourselves what the alternatives were. It would have been absurd for the international community to continue underwriting ineffective, corrupt state systems that fed off clientelist networks. The quality of governance in these countries had to be radically improved and the relations between state and citizen had to be placed on an entirely new footing. However, the prospects for such a radical overhaul were far from promising. Where would Africa draw the strength it needed to reform the state? Yet surprisingly, the need for action overcame the obstacles. In 1989, Africa embarked on several years of remarkable democratisation.

3
DEMOCRATISATION

Upheaval in Benin

Africa's great wave of democratisation in the 1990s began in the small West African country of Benin.[54] Just a few months after the fall of the Berlin Wall, representatives of a wide range of political groups, including both supporters and opponents of the regime, convened a national conference in the seat of government, Cotonou, to discuss the country's woes. However, they did not leave it at that. Within a few days, the national conference declared itself sovereign, in other words, the highest authority in the country. General Mathieu Kérékou's regime, which had ruled the country with an iron hand for seventeen years, was forced to stand by as the political system underwent a radical transformation. The general offered no resistance, paving the way for a civilian candidate to triumph at the ballot box and assume power in early 1991. Benin thus became the first African country in which the civilian population managed to overthrow a military regime and remove a sitting president by means of elections.[55]

Located on the Gulf of Guinea, Benin is a little smaller than England and has almost seven million inhabitants, divided into three main groups. The Fon live in the southwest of the country. In precolonial times, this group formed the basis of the kingdom of Dahomey, as a result of which the country was named Dahomey when it gained independence in 1960. The Nagot or Yoruba, who are related to the Yoruba on the other side of the Nigerian border, live in the southeast of the country. The north of the country, which for a long time was almost entirely cut off from the coastal region, is home to various smaller groups, which, for the sake of convenience, are jointly referred to here as northerners. In 1975, Kérékou, who was a northerner, changed the name of the country from Dahomey, with which only the southwestern Fon identified, to Benin. This name also refers to a precolonial kingdom, but one that, strangely enough, was located largely on the territory of neighbouring Nigeria. However, the name was acceptable to the entire country.

During the colonial period, Dahomey was a remote backwater in the colony of French West Africa. As elsewhere in the French colonies, the French government permitted a small measure of political freedom and competition after World War II. Three people, each with his own ethnic-regional constituency (southwest, southeast and north), thus began to control Dahomeyan politics from the 1950s onwards and continued to do so after the official departure of the French in 1960. None of these three political blocs was able to achieve an electoral majority independently, and this resulted in the formation of coalitions whose composition varied frequently over the years. However, the three prominent politicians (also referred to as the 'triumvirate') were unable to establish a stable political system under their joint authority, and the military therefore repeatedly felt obliged to seize power in order to restore order and preserve national unity. Nevertheless, the armed forces lacked the will to govern the country for more than a few months or years at a time, or so it was believed for many years.

Another military coup, the sixth since Benin's independence, took place in 1972. Although nothing indicated at first that this one was different from its predecessors, the military leader of the coup, General Kérékou, announced in 1974 that the takeover should be regarded as a Marxist revolution. The people of Dahomey, which was shortly to become Benin, had unwittingly chosen the path of socialism. The reasons for this choice lay in the Cold War context, in which the logical outcome of the country's enduring anticolonial and anti-French sentiments was a choice in favour of the West's ideological adversary. As it happens, the international status of the country did not change as a result of this turn-around: the Eastern Bloc was unable to provide substantial aid and France continued to serve as the patron of its former colony, regardless of who was in power. The socialist features of the political system were negligible. A Marxist-Leninist party was established in 1977, but the military was unwilling to play second fiddle.

The revolution had more significant economic implications. Whatever economic activity existed in the People's Republic of Benin – which was not much, as the country has no resources or export products to speak of – was completely destroyed by socialist measures. The few existing private enterprises were nationalised, and a new range of state-owned enterprises, regulatory bodies and monopolies saw the light of day. These developments initially created employment, but the new enterprises proved to be entirely uncompetitive. All other products, including expensive ones from Western countries, proved cheaper than their Beninese equivalents. Exports had ceased almost entirely: export revenue dropped to just fifteen per cent of the value of imports. This situation eventually became too much even for France, which had continued to provide financial support to the regime. During the 1980s, the Beninese government became increasingly unable to pay the wages of the many public employees. Other economic activity had all but disappeared, and it was almost impossible to earn anything, even in the informal sector. When the government-appointed leader of the country's single, socialist trade union called for wages to be paid, he was replaced by somebody who did not issue such calls.

In 1988, the regime's financial bankruptcy spilled over into moral bankruptcy, when information leaked out that, in a desperate bid for revenue, it had planned to import and bury toxic waste from other countries for profit. As if that was not enough, the military, which was dominated by northerners, had selected the historical capital, Abomey, located in the middle of the densely populated southwestern territory of the Fon, as the prospective dumping ground. As a result of this plot, which – once revealed – was not carried out, and the collapse of the economy, the military regime's position had become untenable by the end of the 1980s. The government entered into negotiations with the World Bank and the IMF to secure financial assistance, which it could only obtain if it agreed to radically restructure the economy: the public sector had to be largely dismantled, the number of public employees had to be reduced and radical cutbacks were required across the board. While the parties were discussing these matters, mass strikes broke out in Cotonou. The protesters were united by their lack of income. This applied even to non-commanding members of the military, who had not received their wages in months.

The regime could see no way out of this dismal situation for the country or itself. By convening a broad-based conference, it hoped to encourage some form of national unity or even reconciliation that would make it easier to swallow the bitter medicine prescribed by the structural adjustment programme. Representatives of the protesters were given the opportunity to articulate their grievances at the conference. In addition to political opponents and returning exiles, the participants included representatives of the government, the military and many institutions that officially supported the government. The 488 delegates met for the first time on 19 February 1990, at a short distance from the hotel where a World Bank delegation was staying. It quickly became clear that there would be no declarations of support for the regime. The delegates rejected the government's agenda and refused to accept the president as chairman of the conference, electing the archbishop of Cotonou in his place.

For nine days, the national conference discussed the situation in the country as it saw fit. The population, which was able to follow the deliberations on radio and television, listened and watched with bated breath. The whole range of political, economic and social grievances was openly vented at this modern-day tribal council, while nobody defended the government. It was clear that the government would collapse in the absence of drastic military action, but Kérékou seemed unwilling to pursue this option under the watchful eye of the World Bank delegation. He understood that the military government would have to step down and decided to smooth the transition. He also apologised to the conference for the mistakes his government had made.

On 25 February 1990, the conference declared itself autonomous and sovereign. It established an interim government with twenty-seven members, including all the country's former presidents, and charged it with drafting a new constitution to replace the Marxist constitution of 1977 and with organising elections for a new parliament and a new president. As a result of these developments, General Kérékou became acting president of Benin, whose only responsibility was to see to it that the above-mentioned decisions were carried out. Actual power was placed in the hands of a new prime minister, a former World Bank official named Nicephore Soglo, who was considered neutral by the Beninese and enjoyed the backing of the World Bank and France.

The interim government drew up a liberal constitution that was adopted by referendum the same year. Parliamentary elections and presidential elections, the latter in two rounds, took place in February and March 1991 respectively. Having become a swift convert to democracy, Kérékou actually participated in the presidential elections, but was soundly defeated by Soglo, who was sworn in as president in April. Thus it happened that, within a period of two years, Benin's political order was transformed without bloodshed from a Marxist military dictatorship to a liberal democracy, in the civilian equivalent of a coup d'état. Civil society had assumed power and dealt a heavy blow to the predatory state. With the support of the population, the new government was ready to take on the immense task of reforming the economy, but, for the time being, the rest of Africa and the world were captivated by the success of Benin's peaceful transition to democracy.

Many paths to the one-party state

When considering the history of democracy and democratisation in Africa before the 1990s, it is important to determine first what these terms actually mean, all the more so because in recent years almost every regime in Africa, however dictatorial, has tended to describe itself as democratic. Let us understand democracy as meaning that the population controls the state and governs freely, if indirectly, by means of elected representatives. Democratisation is the process that is meant to lead to democracy. In the 1940s, Joseph Schumpeter formulated his by now classic definition of the democratic method: '...that institutional arrangement for arriving at political decisions in which individuals acquire the power to decide by means of a competitive struggle for the people's vote.'[56] This definition, which has been characterised as electoral democracy due to its emphasis on the electoral process, is nowadays regarded as minimalist.

In the 1970s, Robert Dahl expanded the concept of democracy by introducing the concept of polyarchy, which encompasses not only political competition and participation, but also a considerable number of individual freedoms (freedom of speech, the press, assembly and so forth), and makes democracy conditional on pluralism in society.[57] According to Dahl, political competition and participation only have meaning if human rights are also observed. Schumpeter's classic concept of 'electoral democracy' was thus expanded to 'liberal democracy', where 'liberal' refers in particular to the government-protected freedoms of both individuals and groups. Besides elections, 'liberal democracy' thus includes respect for civil rights. It is sometimes also emphasised, finally, that democracies may not contain substantial areas of activity that evade democratic control because they fall under the jurisdiction of the military, the bureaucracy or oligarchic groups. Though such reserved domains were larger in Latin America and Asia, they existed in Africa too; for example, military control of a country's main natural resources.

The political history of Africa differs greatly from that of Western countries, where democratic systems evolved over centuries of power struggles between various groups. Africa has been home to diverse state systems and areas with no state system at all.[58] Many precolonial African states had political systems that, by modern Western standards, contained no democratic features: systems centred around an authoritarian 'traditional' leader who, together with a select few, ruled over subjects who had no influence to speak of. The ruler's power was without limit and theoretically all-encompassing. All aspects of society fell under his authority and no separation existed between the public and private spheres. The ruler was closely connected to the spiritual world that is so important in Africa, and his authority was therefore of a sacred nature.[59] In some cases, he depended on a kind of 'witch doctor' to interpret the spiritual world.

But as noted above, there were many different state systems. Some were more or less democratic. In some cases, kings were appointed by (and from) aristocratic families that also kept them in check. In cases of serious failure, a leader could even be deposed. Institutional checks and balances often helped to maintain the balance of power.[60] In general, the king and his advisers occupied themselves solely with the most important affairs of state, such as military, financial and spiritual matters and the administration of justice at the highest level, while the remaining governmental duties were delegated to others. Most disputes, for instance, were settled by village chiefs, who also enjoyed a substantial amount of autonomy in other matters. Where important decisions were concerned, these chiefs organised councils in which all interested parties and even outsiders could voice their opinions, after which the elders of the village would withdraw until they had reached a decision. Decision-making was thus participatory, and consensus was pursued in an attempt to take account of all views. The population could also express discontent indirectly through stories, legends, proverbs and songs that poked fun at the authorities.[61]

Precolonial systems of government in Africa were often based on agreements concerning the rights and duties of the governing powers and the governed. Although these rights differed from modern human rights as formulated in the Universal Declaration of Human Rights, the systems nevertheless provided a certain degree of legal certainty. Precolonial Africa had many constitutions, although they were usually not written down.

African traditions and practices were rudely interrupted by colonisation. The continent's own political structures were forced to adapt to the new situation to survive, or simply disappeared. In their place, new colonial structures arose that made use of African systems of government but were themselves in no way African. This phenomenon was known as indirect rule. Existing African checks and balances were systematically undermined during the colonial period. African leaders, who had been incorporated into the system of indirect rule, no longer depended on the consent of their subjects for their power, which now rested solely on the backing of the colonial rulers. As a result of this disruption of the local sociopolitical balance, local rulers could more easily enforce their will on the population.[62]

The colonial system had its roots in Europe, which was going through turbulent years, politically and otherwise. In the early twentieth century, Europe made great advances in human rights and democratisation. Their impact was scarcely felt in Africa. Only a handful of Africans had been 'civilised' (to use the language of the period) by colonialism, by means of a European education, and thereby elevated from subject to citizen. The population of the colonies continued to be deprived of the human rights and democracy that were becoming the norm in Europe. Nevertheless, a small, Europeanised African elite became familiar with such ideas.

By the end of the nineteenth century, the idea began to take hold that the colonial powers were duty-bound to improve the lot of their colonial subjects. However, the colonial powers did almost nothing to put this idea into practice in Africa before World War II. Only after 1945, when it became clear that colonial relations were in need of rethinking, did things begin to change. In addition to social and economic reforms, France and Britain introduced political innovations with democratic characteristics. The French government, which had a policy of assimilating Africans into French culture, went further in this regard than the government of Britain, which believed in two separate worlds: a colonial European world and an indigenous African world. Hence, Africans in the French colonies could be assimilated into the French political system (and could even become members of the National Assembly) but the role of the Europeanised elite in the British colonies remained less significant. No noteworthy political innovations took place in the Portuguese colonies during this period. Although Portugal, like France, had a policy of assimilation, the country was so underdeveloped and undemocratic by European standards that it was unable to exert a modernising effect.

As noted in chapter 1, the French and British colonies in Africa gained independence around 1960. The first leaders of the newly independent states came from the new African elite created by France and the United Kingdom during the colonial period. These leaders inherited a tradition of centralised colonial power and everything this implied in terms of outlook, especially arrogance. In many respects, the European colonial order had reinforced the tradition of absolutism that held sway in many parts of Africa. This effect went much deeper than the democratic systems and constitutions, similar to those of France and other Western countries, which were not introduced until the end of the colonial period. Historically speaking, the first wave of African democratisation in the twilight of colonialism was a superficial phenomenon, but it did present a challenge for the newly independent political systems. Following independence, the political parties established in the colonial period began a new existence in their native African environment.

The fledgling democratic institutions and organisations did not survive for long. Not only were they regarded as foreign impositions, but they also failed to serve the interests of the new rulers. In contrast to the elites of Western countries, the African political elite had no economic resources of its own. Its members had generally reached the summit of national politics solely on the basis of their education and ties with former colonial rulers. They depended for their income on a central role in government. Elections paid off for some members of the elite, but left others – the members of the losing parties – high and dry. The victors gained access to the state institutions and their revenue, while others received nothing. Elections were thus a zero-sum game where the winners took all and the losers were left empty-handed. As the opposition was unable to survive economically without alternative sources of income, it was not difficult for the authorities to encourage opposition politicians to defect to the ruling party, and to neutralise the small hard core in other ways. This led to the emergence of the one-party system in Africa. As the single surviving party was sustained economically by the state, the two gradually merged, creating a one-party state.

In order to consolidate their power, the civil authorities had to cooperate with the military establishment. The nature of this cooperation differed from country to country and in some cases changed over time. However, the military always received or appropriated a portion of state revenue in exchange for its services. In some countries, civilians continued to call the shots with the support of the military, while, in others, the military ousted the civilian leadership and established a dictatorship. In fact, it was not always possible to make a meaningful distinction between political and military elites. The national leaders further strengthened their popular support base – initially built on their reputation as liberators who had freed their country from the yoke of colonialism – by exploiting traditional relations of patronage. In exchange for political support, clients received a share of the state pie. This frequently took the form of government jobs, which made a valuable gift in an underdeveloped economy where unemployment and uncertainty were the order of the day. The regimes thereby ensured themselves of a support base in the cities. In addition, they often received substantial aid from the major powers. Regardless of their performance, the African governments were thus quite firmly ensconced and could govern in an authoritarian manner. During this period, political freedom and popular influence on national government were non-existent in almost all African countries.

In fact, the period of one-party systems and military dictatorships, which began in the mid-1960s and effectively continued until the end of the Cold War, was not as homogeneous as the preceding account might suggest. There were some significant exceptions. For example, Botswana and Gambia boasted a certain amount of political pluralism and liberal democracy throughout this period, although the influence of the largest party on the state was quite substantial. Some one-party states permitted internal party elections in which multiple candidates participated. Multiparty systems occasionally emerged, sometimes to stay (as in Senegal from the 1970s onwards) but usually only to disappear again in short order. In spite of everything, the struggle for democracy remained alive in many places in this difficult time. During the process of renewed democratisation, which began in 1989, politicians sometimes fell back on these experiences when it came to forming political parties.

The call for social and political change

During the Cold War, democracy was the exception in Africa and a combination of authoritarian leadership, centralised decision-making and a lack of political freedom, pluralism and human rights was the rule. This situation was ideologically justified by reference to Africa's dismal socioeconomic condition. Freedom was not considered important for development and political pluralism was regarded as un-African; it would lead only to infighting and instability and would waste resources needed for development. The authoritarian regimes nonetheless failed to produce socioeconomic progress, regardless of their ideological slant. On the contrary, by the end of the 1980s, most African countries had reached rock bottom, financially, economically, socially, politically and morally. The people of Africa became increasingly restless and frustrated about the faded hope of a better future. As noted by the prominent Nigerian scholar Claude Ake: 'Poor leadership and structural constraints have turned the high expectations of independence into painful disappointment.'[63]

The changes that led to democratisation were set in motion by urban protests against deteriorating social conditions. Unemployment was high, and what was worse, people with jobs had often stopped receiving part or all of their wages. This not only affected ordinary civil servants, but also members of the armed forces and the many groups that were dependent on the state as a result of its pivotal role in the economy. Having almost completely run out of funds, African governments were no longer able to meet their responsibilities to their own citizens. In addition to the direct financial implications for public employees, there was a general decline in other job benefits. Social conditions for the population as a whole also suffered as a result of deteriorating health care and education, as well as price increases for basic necessities.

In many countries, the protests were led by students but others were usually quick to join in. After years of oppression and cooptation, however, there were no real leaders that could channel their energies in the service of a clear-cut programme. Initially, this made the protests look very similar to the demonstrations of discontent to which African regimes had become accustomed over the years. At first, therefore, the authorities saw no reason to respond differently than they had in the past: by making as many concessions to their critics as possible, for example, by delaying price increases, paying back wages and improving conditions for students, while bringing the remaining hard core firmly into line, if necessary by force. In the past, this strategy had almost always produced the desired effect, and it turned out to be relatively successful once again in countries that still had the resources to satisfy the demands of the population, such as Côte d'Ivoire and Gabon.

However, the key difference from previous years was the severity of the problems – not just economic, but moral and political – facing the African states, as a result of which they had lost all their legitimacy, even among the large urban groups that the elites had traditionally managed to hold onto by means of government jobs. Clientelist networks collapsed because governments could no longer afford to pay wages, and the material foundations underpinning the loyalty of the regime's supporters disappeared. In addition, the young were already too far removed from the old leaders to be able to see them as the freedom fighters of yore. Members of the new generation, especially students, were more likely to see the authorities as domestic oppressors of whom nothing good could be expected. Maintaining the status quo was therefore no longer as straightforward as in previous years.

This fundamental change at the domestic level – the imminent demise of the traditional postcolonial state due to bankruptcy and generational transition – went hand in hand with dramatic changes in the international context that had important implications for Africa. The end of the Cold War deprived the authoritarian African regimes of their strategic value. The major powers no longer considered it necessary to prop up African dictators and were therefore unwilling to continue subsidising their deficits. Instead of international aid, which the incumbent regimes had used to maintain their clientelist networks, the major powers now preferred to provide loans, and only on the condition that the regimes be radically overhauled. Cutbacks were unavoidable. This led to the further fragmentation of networks of patronage and removed the possibility of ending the crisis by appeasing a sufficient number of protesters. The time-honoured alternative of forcefully suppressing the protests was also out of the question, as such a move would have cost the leaders their last vestiges of Western support, making it even more difficult to solve the underlying problems. In many countries, the authorities could no longer see any way out of this sorry situation; they were checkmated.

It did not take the disaffected population long to realise that the authorities would no longer be able to end the crisis in a traditional manner. This insight lent a political dimension to what had so far been social protests. The shift happened more quickly in countries where some political freedom and pluralism had already existed than in countries that had little or no experience of non-authoritarian politics. A connection with structural adjustment programmes also emerged; protests were more political in character in countries where reforms (i.e. cutbacks) had aggravated the urban population's problems than in countries where economic reforms had not, or not yet, been implemented. Initial political demands concerned the abolition of onerous or oppressive government measures and practices and the expansion of popular influence over the running of the state; in other words, political liberalisation.

At this very time, in 1989 to be precise, these demands were backed up by an unexpected source: a report from the World Bank, an institution on which African governments were financially very much dependent. In this report, entitled *Sub-Saharan Africa: From Crisis to Sustainable Growth*, future aid was linked to the quality of governance in the countries concerned. The report did not discuss democratisation, but it did address freedom of speech, transparent decision-making and free political debate. The African leaders were unaccustomed to this and protested strongly that the World Bank and the former colonial powers had no business interfering in African affairs (although they were apparently welcome to foot the bill). Some leaders, including President Kenneth Kaunda of Zambia, went so far as to claim that multiparty democracy was unsuitable for Africans. In spite of their rhetoric, the African authorities realised that the West's new attitude indicated a fundamental shift in the relationship between African governments and the international donor community. The extent to which the times were changing was further emphasised in Central and Eastern Europe, where one regime after another was forced out over the course of a few months. The dramatic downfall of the Romanian dictator Nicolae Ceausescu, in particular, made a deep impression on many African potentates.

It started to dawn on the authorities that political liberalisation could not be halted, as there was simply no alternative. After a number of governments had reluctantly taken the first steps down this road, others followed. Social demands led to political demands, and political liberalisation (the destruction of authoritarian structures) was followed by democratisation (the construction of new democratic structures).[64] Countries drew on each other for models of democratic reform. Nowhere was this clearer than in Francophone Africa.

Democratisation in
Francophone Africa

The governments of almost all the countries that had been part of French West Africa and French Equatorial Africa were largely dependent on the economic, political and military support they had received from France since gaining independence. The domestic power of many African presidents was based on their relationship with the French government, and correctly interpreting the signals from Paris was therefore a matter of political life and death. This had not been a problem during the Cold War, when it was clear where everyone stood, but became significantly more complicated after 1989, when France started sending mixed political signals. While Benin's national conference was meeting in Cotonou, Jacques Chirac, the mayor of Paris who just a few years later became the French president, declared in Burkina Faso that multiparty systems were perhaps not suited to Africa. A few months later, in June 1990, the regular Franco-African summit took place in La Baule, France, under the chairmanship of President François Mitterrand, a social democrat. There, the French government for the first time made a connection between the depth of France's relations with its partner countries and their level of democracy. To the dismay of his audience, Mitterrand declared that African countries that flouted basic democratic principles and violated human rights could no longer count on France's support. In future, French support would be directly linked to the democratic calibre of the political systems of the recipient countries.

President Mitterrand's declaration made a deep impression on the African heads of state attending the summit, as well as on African groups seeking a change of government. The fact that France ultimately watered down its position somewhat did little to diminish the effect of his words. The democratisation process in Francophone Africa accelerated substantially in the months following the summit, despite the fact that the French government subsequently issued less stringent statements on political conditions for future aid. A year-and-a-half after the summit in La Baule, in November 1991, at the fourth conference of Francophone countries in Paris, President Mitterrand noted that African countries were free to determine the nature and pace of their democratisation processes, thereby indicating that France would wield the criterion of democracy in a flexible manner. At the Franco-African summit of 1992, which was held in the Gabonese capital of Libreville, France laid out its priorities in greater detail. According to some African leaders, it was sometimes difficult to further democracy, pursue socioeconomic development and maintain security simultaneously. In response, Prime Minister Pierre Bérégovoy of France noted that France's African allies should adhere to the following agenda: first security, then development and finally democratisation.

These qualifications somewhat reassured African leaders about France's position. Nevertheless, Mitterrand's statements in La Baule had given an enormous boost to the democracy movements in Francophone Africa. In 1990-1993, significant political changes took place in almost all Francophone countries in Africa, almost suggesting a domino effect. In fact, these reforms were not limited to Francophone Africa: the wave of democratisation of the early 1990s swept across the entire continent.

Even so, there was an important difference between developments in Francophone Africa and elsewhere on the continent. In almost all the Francophone countries in West and Central Africa (though not in the more remote Djibouti, Rwanda and Burundi), the above-mentioned changes were ushered in by so-called national conferences,[65] for which the groundbreaking conference of February 1990 in Benin served as an example. In countries where they did not take place, such as Côte d'Ivoire, Burkina Faso and Cameroon, antigovernment groups did call for such conferences, but the authorities managed to prevent them from taking place. Of all the Francophone African countries, only Senegal did not even experience a call for a national conference, which may be interpreted as a sign that the country's democracy (to which many critics have added the prefix 'quasi') had nevertheless managed to function in a more or less satisfactory manner in the eyes of opposition groups. In contrast, national conferences did not form part of the democratisation process in a single country outside Francophone Africa.[66]

No clear explanation exists for this phenomenon. Apart from the possibility that the countries concerned influenced each another, French political tradition might also have played a role. In an attempt to explain the different political developments that have taken place in Africa, for instance, a Zambian commentator described the resort to national conferences as the Jacobin model of civil revolution.[67] This comparison with the French Revolution, which took place two centuries earlier, is of course far from perfect, but it highlights a number of interesting similarities, such as the struggle of representatives from a patchwork of groups for a voice in a constituent assembly that sought to adopt a constitution and determine the future form of the state; the assembly's declaration of sovereignty, making it the highest authority in the state and adding legal force to its decisions; and the unchecked and therefore increasingly scathing criticism of the incumbent regime, as a result of which the confidence of the opposition movement grew and that of the regime declined in equal measure.

From a long-term perspective, the most important outcome of the debates that took place during the aforementioned national conferences may have been the new power of civil society. Alongside the similarities, there were substantial variations in the nature and development of these conferences, which were partly responsible for the success of the democratisation process in the Francophone countries.

The developments in Congo (Brazzaville) were most similar to the successful reforms in Benin. During the Cold War, a military regime under the leadership of General Denis Sassou-Nguesso had transformed the country into a people's republic, with a centralised government and a nationalised economy, which ended in bankruptcy in the late 1980s. During the summer of 1990, at the time of the summit in La Baule, the president of Congo renounced Marxism-Leninism and promised political reforms. Ultimately, however, he was unable to withstand public pressure to hold a similar conference to the one in Benin. The following February, as many as 1,200 representatives from various political parties and associations convened to establish a national conference. Unwilling to admit defeat, the government placed its hopes in its nominal supporters at the conference. This strategy proved to be a mistake. The vast majority of participants immediately began to criticise the regime. During the deliberations, which lasted until June, the government lost one battle after another; first the chairmanship of the conference went to the bishop of Owando, then the conference declared itself sovereign and superior to the government, appointing a transitional government to draft a new constitution and organise multiparty elections. A new, liberal constitution was adopted in March 1992. A few months later, in July 1992, Pascal Lissouba was elected president.

National conferences also played an important role in the Sahelian states of Mali and Niger. In March 1991, protests against the dictatorial regime of Moussa Traoré, who had ruled Mali for twenty-two years, led to bloody riots in the capital city of Bamako. Under the leadership of Colonel Amadou Toumani Touré (also known as ATT), the military staged a coup d'état, only to come face to face with the democracy movement. The organisers of the coup quickly decided to cooperate with the civil opposition. The two sides appointed a joint transitional government to organise a national conference, which lasted just two weeks, long enough to adopt a new constitution, an elections act and a charter for political parties. This was followed in April 1992 by a general election that launched the presidency of Alpha Oumar Konaré. ATT's short period of rule had given him a taste for power. After Konaré completed two terms of office, ATT won the 2002 election and succeeded him.

In neighbouring Niger, an even larger national conference lasting many months took place in 1991. After criticising the regime's performance at length, the more than one thousand participants managed to replace it by appointing a transitional government and organising elections. As a result of ethnic tension (including a Tuareg uprising in the north of the country) and opposition from the military, however, the new democratic government soon faced problems of its own.

One dictator survived a national conference through cunning, without resorting to force. President Omar Bongo had ruled oil-rich Gabon since 1967. Originating from a small ethnic group from the interior of the country, he was advanced by the French at the time of Gabon's independence as a neutral individual who could help reduce the tension resulting from ethnic rivalry between Gabon's political parties. Bongo banned all political parties, after which he founded a single party to lead the country. He managed to secure the loyalty of potential opponents by providing many members of the elite, from all ethnic backgrounds, with jobs in the expanding state institutions. France's extensive military support of Bongo's regime helped to keep political life stable in Gabon. However, his firm hold on power did not blind him to the signs of change. Even before the summit in La Baule, he decided to organise a national conference. When it was convened, the opposition appeared largely unaware of the opportunities that such a conference presented. The government therefore had little trouble keeping it under control. The conference was satisfied to play an advisory role, and a declaration of sovereignty was therefore not forthcoming. Although it resulted in a new constitution, the introduction of a multiparty system, elections and a freer press, the conference did not directly restrict the president's powers. In Gabon's liberalised political environment, Bongo managed to win both elections that took place during the 1990s, in 1993 and 1998.

Although the aforementioned national conferences were the first step towards greater democracy, the role of the military proved to be a decisive factor in the success of the opposition at replacing authoritarian regimes with democratic systems of governance in almost every country (with the exception of Gabon, as noted above). In Benin and Congo, the military offered little resistance to these changes. In Mali, they initially seized power themselves, but were willing to hand it over to a democratic government. In Niger, the military was significantly less cooperative in this regard, creating problems for the civil government. In the small country of Togo, which borders Benin, the military remained firmly behind General Gnassingbe Eyadéma, ensuring his political survival after Togo's national conference of July-August 1991. The regime ordered the 'adjournment' of the deliberations, and, in the ensuing months, the military dealt forcefully with the divided civil opposition and the transitional government appointed by the conference to organise the elections. Eyadéma's bloody regime, which began in 1967, thus continued into the twenty-first century.

Democratisation in
Anglophone Africa

Just as Benin had played an important role in Francophone Africa, so Zambia was pivotal to the democratisation process in Anglophone Africa during this period. Following its independence in 1964, Zambia was effectively ruled by one party and one person: Kenneth Kaunda. As a symbol of his country's independence and as a result of his fairly progressive policies, the president of Zambia enjoyed much prestige at home and abroad. However, the country's modest wealth and Kaunda's power were both entirely dependent on the sale of copper. When the price of copper on the world market dropped in the 1970s, Zambia's social provisions underwent the same deterioration that afflicted many other African countries during this period, with lost jobs or salary cuts for public employees, cutbacks in education and health care, and the lowering or elimination of many government subsidies. In spite of these measures, Zambia was as good as bankrupt by the late 1980s.

Rocketing food prices, due to lower subsidies, led to riots that were put down harshly by the regime. Calls for political reform were meanwhile becoming stronger. Kaunda agreed to elections with remarkable alacrity, apparently assuming that his position was secure despite the setbacks of recent years. This proved not to be the case. By the time of the elections, in 1991, the opposition had not yet managed to organise itself into distinct political parties, but proved single-minded in its desire for a new political system and a new leadership. It therefore united under the banner of the Movement for Multiparty Democracy, under the leadership of a trade unionist named Frederick Chiluba, who challenged Kaunda for the presidency. To the surprise of almost all concerned, Chiluba managed to defeat Kaunda at the polls. The latter accepted defeat and, after having served as president of Zambia for twenty-seven years, stepped aside in favour of Chiluba.

In certain respects, developments in neighbouring Malawi were similar to those in Zambia. There too, the person who had led the country since it gained independence in 1964, President Hastings Banda, was forced to surrender his position as a result of the democratisation process. In the 1960s, Banda had successfully resisted all challenges to his leadership and continued to rule the country in a rather totalitarian manner. In addition to declaring himself president for life in 1971, he was also chairman of the country's single party, which all Malawians were obliged to join. A youth movement (the Malawi Young Pioneers) and the police dealt harshly with all opposition to Banda, while the military was scarcely involved in the oppression. In 1992, after emerging calls for democratisation met with a bloody response from the regime, the military intervened on the side of the reformist groups. The youth movement was disarmed, and the officers informed the government that they too supported reform. Banda agreed to a referendum on the introduction of a multiparty system. In spite of the regime's attempts to influence the voting in its favour, however, a majority of voters appeared to favour democracy. In 1993-1994, the old system was gradually replaced by a new one. Banda's 'presidency for life' ended when, after taking second place in the presidential election, he handed over power to the victor, Bakili Muluzi, in 1994.

A little further to the north, Julius Nyerere, known as the father of Tanzanian independence, had bowed out on his own initiative. More so even than Kaunda, Nyerere symbolised a particular brand of African humanism. In 1965, he had declared Tanzania a one-party state, but twenty years later he decided, at least as far as he was concerned, that enough was enough and voluntarily stepped down – a unique step in the African context. Of course, Tanzania's single party, an amalgamation of the political forces on the mainland and the island of Zanzibar, appointed a successor, Ali Hassan Mwinyi, who came from Zanzibar. It was thus Mwinyi who came face to face with the population's demands for democratisation. With Nyerere, who had publicly declared in 1990 that the one-party state had been a mistake, still in the background, the party launched reforms. In 1992, it agreed to the establishment of multiple parties, although elections did not take place until 1995. The former single party, which still counted the ever-popular Nyerere within its ranks, managed to maintain its majority over the divided opposition. Its candidate, Benjamin Mkapa, a former student of Nyerere, became president. Due to the continued domination of one party and, effectively, one person (Nyerere, until his death in 1999), the political scene in Tanzania did not change radically, despite the introduction of a multiparty system.

The same applies even more strongly in the case of Kenya. Following independence, the country formally became a parliamentary democracy, but increasingly took on the character of a one-party state during the 1970s. In 1982, the transformation was officially complete. The regime took increasingly harsh action against the opposition during the 1980s, blotting its previously good record in the field of human rights. In 1991, the government reluctantly reintroduced a multiparty system, but this did not signal a change in the attitude of the authorities. Arrests, torture and even murder of political opponents remained the order of the day. The groups opposing the regime of President Daniel arap Moi at one point appeared to join forces under the banner of the Forum for Restoration of Democracy, but failed to maintain their unity. The forum broke up into separate groups, largely along ethnic lines. As a result, the governing party was able to emerge victorious from the December 1992 elections, and Moi held on to the presidency.

Events in Uganda – to complete this tour of East Africa – proceeded very differently from those in Tanzania and Kenya. In the 1960s, power was concentrated in the hands of Prime Minister Milton Obote, who later became president. Opposition parties were banned, and Obote's rule became increasingly authoritarian. In 1971, a military leader named Idi Amin came to power in a successful coup d'état. In the 1970s, General Amin proved to be a colourful, unpredictable and above all bloodthirsty dictator. A military incursion into Tanzania in 1979 brought an end to his rule. The Tanzanian army occupied Kampala, and Amin fled to Libya. After a period of anarchy, Obote returned to power in Uganda but was unable to rebuild the country or even restore order. In the meantime, more and more Ugandans were being driven from their homes by battles between various armed groups. In 1985, the leader of the main armed opposition group, Yoweri Museveni, seized power. Obote managed to escape to Zambia.

In 1986, Museveni became president of a country devastated by fifteen years of bloodshed. He did not regard democratisation at the national level as a solution to the instability that plagued Ugandan politics and suspended the scheduled elections, as well as all party-political activity (although he allowed the parties to exist as organisations). Only later, in 1989, did ordinary Ugandan citizens become eligible for election to a parliament that further comprised government-appointed members and representatives of various organisations. A committee created by Museveni recommended extending the suspension of party-political activities until 2000, and its advice was followed. A referendum was held in 2000 on the continuation of the existing political system. The government won and decided to maintain Museveni's 'no-party democracy' until 2004.

The president defended the system enthusiastically, arguing that Ugandan society – and, essentially, African society in general – was not diversified enough to sustain political parties on the basis of competing ideologies or interests. According to Museveni, most Africans were simply peasants who shared the same basic priorities. Any political parties they might form would be based on ethnic differences and would therefore only threaten social stability. The representatives of the old political parties did not accept this view, but remained unable to prise open Ugandan politics. However, central government did devolve some powers to the district level, which meant that the responsibility for a large number of tasks came to rest with local, elected bodies.

The striking difference in the international community's attitude towards the political situation in Kenya and neighbouring Uganda has been pointed out on many occasions. Kenya, formally a parliamentary democracy, was constantly subjected to heavy criticism, while Uganda, a no-party democracy, not only received the benefit of the doubt, but even enjoyed a certain amount of esteem at the international level. Obviously, a substantial part of this discrepancy can be traced back to the different histories of the two countries. In Kenya, after a hopeful start just after independence, the political situation deteriorated. The impact of democratisation measures in the early 1990s appeared to be minimal. At any rate, they had little or no effect on the country's political culture. Also, manipulation, violence and corruption have continued to characterise Kenyan politics, mainly due to the conduct of the authorities. Meanwhile, despite a lack of democratisation at the national level, Uganda's political development moved in the opposite direction. After the chaotic and violent years of Amin and Obote, the country found a new stability under Museveni, with disciplined armed forces and – in comparison with Kenya – a more efficient and less corrupt government. Museveni's idiosyncratic views on democracy did little to detract from its successes.

President Jerry Rawlings of Ghana was similarly admired by the international community, although he too could hardly be described as a paragon of democracy. In 1979, as an air force lieutenant, he carried out his first coup d'état against the military regime of the day. Rawlings used populist tactics to portray himself as a national hero who protected the man in the street from successive corrupt governments. For a long time, he did not take the slightest notice of national laws or even of the constitution. He also dealt harshly with his political opponents, not eschewing execution. Over time, however, he became less volatile, and, as an enduring central figure in Ghanaian politics, made increasing use of conventional political channels. In the early 1990s, this meant participating in the wave of democratisation. He created a national committee for democracy that organised meetings to discuss the future of the political system. This led to the establishment of a parliamentary democracy in 1992. Rawlings, who by then had been in power for ten years, took part in the elections as a presidential candidate. The opposition was divided. Some parties accused the government of electoral fraud and refused to participate in the elections any longer, although this may have had more to do with their own disappointing results. Under these circumstances, Rawlings easily won the elections and continued his career as a democratic president.

In Nigeria, an important country because of its large population and considerable regional influence, attempts to introduce democracy were stifled by the military. General Ibrahim Babangida, in power since 1985, attempted to bend the future political life of the country entirely to his will. In order to prevent several dozen ethnic and religious parties from causing political chaos, Babangida banned all of them. He then founded a party that was slightly to the right of the political centre and another that was slightly to the left of it. The Nigerian people had to make do with these two parties, whose names and even manifestos were determined by the military. Elections were scheduled for mid-1993. Despite the military's hold on this 'guided democracy', a presidential candidate not favoured by the military, an eccentric businessman named Moshood Abiola, appeared to be headed for victory in the election. Halfway through the counting of the votes, Babangida therefore, not surprisingly, declared the election invalid, but still stepped down soon afterwards. Abiola, who had become the leader of the opposition, declared victory and was subsequently imprisoned. All hope of democracy then evaporated under the new military leader and president, Sani Abacha, who banned political parties once more and oversaw years of harsh oppression of the population by the armed forces. During the first half of the 1990s, Nigeria thus formed the most salient example of failed democratisation in Africa.

The democratisation process in South Africa, the other predominantly Anglophone giant of Africa, took place in the framework of an even more important process, namely, the abolition of apartheid (see chapter 4, p. 116 et seq.). In neighbouring Zimbabwe, there was little to report in the way of democratisation. By abolishing apartheid in 1980, Zimbabwe had a fourteen-year lead on South Africa (where it continued until 1994), but it was roughly twenty years behind most African countries, where political power had moved into African hands around 1960. As a result, the inevitable crisis did not strike Zimbabwe's one-party system until the beginning of the twenty-first century, much later than in other African countries. The belated political and governmental deterioration of Zimbabwe and, potentially, South Africa is discussed in the penultimate section of chapter 10.

Failed democratisation in the Great Lakes region

The history of the Great Lakes region has been largely shaped by the ethnic makeup of its population.[68] With the exception of a small group known as the Twa, who account for roughly one per cent of the population, the inhabitants of the region belong to the Hutu and Tutsi ethnic groups. To this day, the historic differences between the two peoples, which the first Europeans to arrive in the region dubbed the enemy brothers at the sources of the Nile, have left a mark on the countries in the region. They also strongly influenced the efforts of Rwanda and Burundi's moves towards democratisation.

After the European powers partitioned Central Africa, the borders between British, German and Belgian colonial territory ran straight through the Great Lakes region. Long ago, the geological fault line known as the Great Rift Valley, which crosses the continent from north to south, led to the formation of hundreds of small bodies of water in this area, and a few large ones, such as Lake Victoria, Lake Tanganyika and Lake Kivu. Following partition, Britain controlled the northern shore of Lake Victoria, Germany controlled the southern shore up to Lake Kivu and Lake Tanganyika in the west, and Belgium controlled the area up to this boundary in the east.

The heart of the Great Lakes region, the kingdoms of Rwanda and Urundi (later Burundi), came under German control. In practice, Germany left almost everything as it was. The indigenous governments remained in place and were simply augmented by a handful of German supervisors. Germany's regime in the heart of Africa, with just six Germans in Rwanda and five in Urundi, was almost certainly the most extreme case of indirect rule. In World War I, this made it easy for the small Belgian contingent stationed in Congo to drive the Germans out of the region. Rwanda-Urundi became a Belgian mandate (governed by Belgium at the behest of the League of Nations) and, after World War II, a UN trust territory under Belgian control. In 1962, Rwanda and Burundi formally gained independence from the European powers.

Central Africa had been home to both Hutu and Tutsi since time immemorial. The Hutu, in particular, tended to emphasise their ethnic origins and thus the differences between the Tutsi and themselves. This was undoubtedly related to the numerical balance between the two groups: there were five times as many Hutu as Tutsi living in the region. As a logical consequence of this situation, the Tutsi generally tried to play down ethnic issues and the differences between the two groups, by arguing, for example, that the only distinction that mattered was the one between Rwandans and Burundians. Clearly, the meaning and application of ethnic labels largely depend on the situation in a particular time and place. In the countries neighbouring Rwanda and Burundi, relations between

Hutu and Tutsi were of a different nature. In Uganda, relations had been peaceful for such a long time that Hutu and Tutsi were sometimes treated as one ethnic group, but there were sharp differences between the two groups in the area alongside Lake Kivu in eastern Congo (Zaire).[69]

Traditionally, the Hutu grew crops and the Tutsi chiefly raised livestock. More importantly, the Tutsi were almost always in charge in the precolonial kingdoms. The Belgian colonial regime reinforced this uneven distribution of power and even provided a theory to justify it: in contrast to the short, stocky Hutu, who were descendants of the Bantu, the tall, athletic (read: 'aristocratic') Tutsi were descendants of the Hamites, a race originating from the Middle East and the northeast of Africa. The members of this group, according to this story, had not only been in close contact with European civilisation in the past, but could even be regarded as distant relations of the white man. This was the reason given for placing the internal government of the colonised territories in the hands of the minority Tutsi. However, during the limited democratisation that took place at the end of the colonial period, Hutu parties were able to seize power in Rwanda, while the Tutsi kingdom in Burundi survived until 1965.

The changing of the guard from the Tutsi to the Hutu in Rwanda did not take place without a struggle. During the first half of the 1960s, the Hutu removed the Tutsi from positions of power throughout almost the entire country. Many Tutsi lost their lives, and between 100,000 and 200,000 others fled to neighbouring countries, exacerbating tensions between Hutu and Tutsi in eastern Congo. In Burundi, the refugees strengthened the Tutsi leadership against the challenges of the Burundian Hutu. The kingdom sought to preserve a certain balance between Hutu and Tutsi, but the demographic predominance of the Hutu started to have an impact by the time of the 1965 elections. The Burundian Tutsi refused to accept this development and seized power through the Tutsi-controlled military, wiping out almost the entire Hutu leadership and abolishing the kingdom. In 1972, the two groups in Burundi were involved in a much larger and bloodier encounter. The Tutsi elite ultimately held on to power and took brutal revenge on the rebellious Hutu and their associates. Approximately 200,000 Burundians, most of them Hutu, were killed. For the Tutsi authorities, the Hutu threat was thereby averted until the end of the 1980s.

As a result of the change of power in Rwanda at the beginning of the 1960s, a considerable number of Tutsi refugees ended up in Rwanda's northern neighbour, Uganda, and were caught up in the country's political turbulence. During the 1980s, many of them, and their descendants, fought alongside Museveni, who belonged to a Tutsi-related group himself. After Museveni had secured his position in Uganda, the services of the battle-hardened Rwandan Tutsi warriors were no longer needed, and they were forced to find a new outlet for their energies. Their adjacent fatherland, where the Hutu had been in control continuously since independence, radiated a natural power of attraction. The refugees organised themselves into a military force, the Rwandan Patriotic Front (RPF), and prepared to invade Rwanda.

By the end of the 1980s, Rwanda and Burundi were both *de facto* one-party states, the first controlled by the Hutu and the second by the Tutsi. They experienced the same problems as other one-party states in Africa and were among the poorest countries on the continent, despite receiving large amounts of foreign aid. Rwanda had some good years, but much of its economic growth was cancelled out by rapid population growth. The shortage of productive land also became increasingly palpable, as Hutu agriculture and Tutsi nomadic livestock raising started to get in each other's way. The political systems of the two countries had hit a dead end: authoritarian leaders were totally uninterested in liberalisation, and oppression and corruption were the order of the day. The crisis became acute when, from 1987 onwards, prices of important export products such as coffee and tea began to drop rapidly.

Rwanda and Burundi were part of the French-led Francophone community. The autocratic leaders of the two countries could not ignore the warning issued by President Mitterrand in La Baule in June 1990 any more than their colleagues in the former French colonies. None of them could afford to forfeit foreign aid, especially from Belgium and France, in a time of political and economic crisis. In 1990, the Rwandan dictator, Juvénal Habyarimana, adopted a new constitution establishing a multiparty system, and various parties entered the political stage.

This new political openness began immediately after the Rwandan Tutsi refugees of the RPF had launched an invasion from Uganda. Their objectives were, first, the return of all Tutsi refugees to Rwanda and the restitution of their land and, second, the end of the Habyarimana regime, with its corruption and human rights violations. The attack by the well-trained and well-armed refugees caught the small Rwandan military by surprise. In all probability, the Rwandan government's plans to democratise the country's political system accelerated the plans of the invaders, as the existence of a dictatorship provided a good argument for overthrowing the government, an argument which could no longer be used if the system became democratic. In addition, as a result of the demographic balance, free elections would have unavoidably led to a Hutu-controlled government.

The attempt to democratise Rwanda was overshadowed by the fighting between the RPF and the government forces. Democracy was not the RPF's objective, and the Habyarimana regime took advantage of the fighting to delay political reforms. The war between the military and the RPF also led to a radical polarisation between Hutu and Tutsi. The government tried to create a united Hutu front by bringing leaders of new opposition parties into the government. From 1992 onwards, various coalition governments operated under the leadership of President Habyarimana, who continued to maintain a strong hold on power. The most important problem faced by the government was which attitude to adopt towards the invaders. For example, should it be trying to reach a power-sharing agreement with the Tutsi rebels?

The government opted for a dialogue that would lead to such an agreement. In 1993, the two sides reached a peace agreement in Arusha (Tanzania) as a result of intense international mediation and pressure. The RPF agreed to transform itself into a political party and join a transitional government with the members of the existing government and other political parties. In addition, both armies, which by now had considerably grown in size, were to be merged, although a majority of soldiers would be demobilised. Finally, returning Tutsi who had fled the country more than ten years earlier would not be able to reclaim their land. The French forces that had supported the Habyarimana regime in the war against the RPF left Rwanda, and a contingent of UN peacekeepers arrived to oversee the implementation of the Arusha agreement. However, the demobilisation of fighters and the distribution of political functions did not get off to a good start. Tensions in the country thus remained high, and violence flared up repeatedly.

As a result, the radical currents that regarded military confrontation as the answer, rather than dialogue and power-sharing, continued to grow.[70] In practice, the country was divided into three camps: Tutsi, moderate Hutu and extremist Hutu. These groups interacted in a complex manner. The Tutsi wanted to seize some or – if possible – all power in Rwanda. Their main opponents were the extremist Hutu, who wished to hold on to the power that the Hutu had held since Rwanda's independence. The third current consisted of moderate Hutu, who were tired of the failing Hutu regime and wanted to democratise the political system, allowing Tutsi involvement. The moderate Hutu were thus potentially useful for the Tutsi, but in the eyes of the extremist Hutu they were extremely dangerous, because they opened the door to a loss of Hutu power. The extremist Hutu regarded the moderate Hutu as traitors to the Hutu cause, which was unforgivable.

In Burundi, the Tutsi government and the Tutsi-controlled military had already brought an end to the oppression of the Hutu in 1988, after disturbances in the north of the country led to thousands of deaths. The government of President Pierre Buyoya, an army major who had seized power in a bloodless coup a year earlier, decided to form a government with an equal number of Hutu and Tutsi ministers, under the leadership of a Hutu prime minister. The government also made it easier for Hutu to find work in government institutions and education, but all command positions in the military remained in the hands of the Tutsi. In 1990 a newly drafted constitution established a multiparty system, on condition that parties were not organised along ethnic lines. The Hutu opposition thus failed to obtain a platform for its grievances. Although each of the new parties counted both Hutu and Tutsi among its leaders and members, it proved impossible to keep them from diverging along ethnic lines in the run-up to the 1993 elections, since the main issue in the country was the relationship between the Hutu and the Tutsi. As time went by, President Buyoya's governing party (Uprona) became more and more of a Tutsi bastion, while the main opposition party (Frodebu) increasingly positioned itself as a Hutu party. President Buyoya continued to control the state and all communication channels until the elections, presenting himself as 'the father of democracy' and a symbol of national unity. However, the population was already too ethnically polarised to allow Buyoya to triumph. The outcome of the elections was a surprising and resounding victory for the Hutu candidates.

The Tutsi elite was shocked by this outcome, but resigned itself to the facts. Buyoya stepped down and was succeeded by Melchior Ndadayé, a Hutu who had fled to Rwanda at the time of the 1972 massacre and had lived there ever since. As the new president, Ndadayé's task was to allow the Hutu to increase their power in Burundi, inevitably at the expense of the Tutsi. All this was based solely on the outcome of a mere election, while the Tutsi continued to dominate the military. Ndadayé was aware of the difficulty of his position and embarked on a moderate, conciliatory course. A national unity government was established under the leadership of a Tutsi, Africa's first female prime minister. In quick succession, Hutu were appointed to various key positions.

The Tutsi elite immediately came under a great deal of pressure. Tutsi students protested in the capital against what they regarded as a purely ethnic manoeuvre, and the military became increasingly restless. After an earlier attempt by rebellious troops to force their way into the president's residence, Tutsi soldiers assassinated the president, with the knowledge of their superiors. Various important Hutu ministers were also killed. Ordinary Hutu did not take these developments lying down. They attacked Tutsi families throughout the country, which in turn provoked a harsh response from the military. This outbreak of violence led to approximately 50,000 deaths. Under intense international pressure, the violence subsided and a certain equilibrium returned. In early 1994, Frodebu and Uprona, the largest parties in parliament, reached a temporary political compromise, which lead to the emergence of a new Hutu president, Cyprien Ntaryamira, and a Tutsi prime minister. Nevertheless, the situation in the country remained extremely tense, with Hutu and Tutsi almost entirely separated from each other.[71]

On the other side of Africa's Great Rift Valley, in the vast country of Zaire (now known as Congo), the Hutu and Tutsi in the east did not play a major role in national politics, which for many years had been controlled from the distant western capital of Kinshasa by President Mobutu Sese Seko. However, the end of the Cold War forced Mobutu to change his policies. Zairean opponents of the regime at home and abroad were calling for political and economic reform and when his main foreign allies – France, Belgium (the former colonial power) and the United States – added their voices, Mobutu introduced a number of changes. He stepped down as chairman of the country's single party (only to reassume the position at a later date) and allowed the formation of new political parties. He also withdrew from day-to-day politics to a certain extent, only to maintain his hold on power from a distance, far away from the country's almost insoluble problems, by controlling the armed forces, the central bank (and thereby the state's finances) and the country outside the capital (through the provincial governors). Under pressure from the opposition, Mobutu consented to hold a national conference, as elsewhere in Francophone Africa, which paved the way for the appointment of the leader of the opposition, Étienne Tshisekedi, as prime minister.

Tshisekedi's first objective was to depose Mobutu, whom he regarded as the main cause of the country's problems. Mobutu removed the prime minister instead, but Tshisekedi was reinstated by the broad-based opposition. Mobutu then formed his own government. This led to a standoff in which two competing governments both tried to gain control of the state's key institutions. Mobutu triumphed, not only because he had retained control of the military and other key institutions, but also by employing a policy of divide and rule (in the course of which he did not even hesitate to fan the flames of ethnic tension) and by successfully appeasing key foreign powers. These powers were becoming more and more concerned about the escalating violence in neighbouring Rwanda, which they feared would spread to Zaire. Under the circumstances, France gave more weight to its narrowly defined national interests in the Great Lakes region than to the principles it had articulated in La Baule. The truth was that France's position was not invulnerable in this formerly Belgian region. This became especially clear in Rwanda, in particular, where the RPF was fighting its way to the top under the leadership of a Ugandan-trained, English-speaking elite. As always, therefore, France continued to support the incumbent heads of state of Rwanda, Burundi and Zaire.

The failure of the democratisation process in these three countries had far-reaching consequences for the region's future. Levels of political tension remained high in all three countries, which continued to experience frequent outbreaks of violence. In Rwanda, the fighting between government forces and the RPF continued, resulting in the largest massacre in modern African history in 1994. Burundi did not experience a similar tragedy, but the violence there claimed many lives each year, while a political solution remained elusive. In Zaire, Mobutu, who continued to oppose democratisation, was forcibly driven out in 1996-1997, although his successor, Laurent Kabila, was no more of a democrat than he had been. For the remainder of the twentieth century, nobody was able to initiate a serious political dialogue in Zaire/Congo. Its complex relationships with its neighbours also went awry. By 1998, the entire region had descended into hostilities, which soon involved so many parties that the conflict in the Great Lakes became the largest war in African history (see chapter 6).

Obstacles to the development of democracy

Putting aside the major problems in countries such as Rwanda, Burundi and Zaire, Africa took great strides toward democracy in the early 1990s. However, this process of political transformation was impeded by a number of obstacles, mainly historical and social. These obstacles resulted from the complex interaction between indigenous African culture and imported Western culture, which had already lasted more than a century. As long as that may seem, however, it was a short historical period in which to make the leap from traditional African power structures (which in their own way were quite effective and sometimes had democratic features) to modern systems of governance. The development of democracy in Europe took many centuries. This seems to imply that obstacles to democratisation in Africa are structural; there is little or no possibility of eliminating them, certainly not in the short or medium term.

The nature of social relationships in Africa is the first obstacle to the development of democracy.[72] Political, economic and social relationships between individuals are often characterised by a patron-client pattern. Patrons occupy a certain social position, possess power and resources and are therefore able to grant favours, such as jobs, to others (clients). Such networks of patronage were responsible for the social structure of precolonial Africa, where unpredictable and insecure conditions made them a logical option. The same pattern had emerged under similar circumstances on other continents; for example, in Western Europe after the collapse of the Roman empire.[73] Networks of patronage persisted in colonial Africa and were even reinforced in certain areas, as the European powers operated by means of indirect rule. This meant that, in principle, the Europeans only interacted with patrons.

As we have seen, the state structures introduced by the colonial powers fell further and further into the grip of patronage networks in the postcolonial period. The patrons were almost always in control of the state and treated government resources as their personal property, using them to buy as much support as possible from local leaders, who did the same thing at a lower level. Although clientelism provides a certain degree of stability through informal, personal networks, it also has a highly corrosive effect on the political system: it encourages corruption, since the leadership (the patrons) are not held accountable for their decisions and it is impossible for the clients to apply checks and balances of any kind. Organised mistrust in the form of a parliament or a free press has no place in such a system, which tends to regard the opposition as the enemy.

The extended family is a major pillar of clientelism. Members of extended families are expected to care for their relations. This applies in particular to upwardly mobile family members who occupy senior government offices or other lucrative positions. Within this system, authoritarian conduct by patriarchs and their political cronies, as well as a flexible approach to the law (including corruption), are normal and widely accepted practices that are therefore difficult to eradicate. From time immemorial, clientelist networks have been organised along ethnic lines.

A second factor that can form an obstacle to the development of democracy is the ethnicisation of politics. Africa consists of a patchwork of ethnic groups, each with its own language and culture, and just a few African states (such as Botswana, Lesotho and Swaziland) possess a more or less homogeneous population from the point of view of language, culture or religion. Under dictatorial regimes, expressions of ethnic identity usually met with little or no tolerance, for reasons related to nation-building and the preservation of power, but they reappeared with the new political openness of the early 1990s. They received a boost from the emergence of new political organisations, especially political parties, which were often organised around a specific individual and supported by a particular ethnic group. Where the ideological differences between the parties were small, as a result of a country's still limited economic diversification, it was only natural that groups rallied around individuals, preferably from their own elites. Each elite had a bond with its ethnic support base and could be expected to use its political power to take care of its own. By the same token, leaders looked for followers within their own ethnic groups.

In many countries, Africa's ethnic realities thus led to the formation of ethnic political parties, which threatened to accentuate differences and fuel tension between population groups. It is this process that might be termed ethnicisation. The Great Lakes region offered an extreme example. Some countries therefore constitutionally prohibited the formation of political parties along ethnic lines, in part to encourage the formation of national parties, while other countries did not impose such restrictions. The still brief history of the new African political parties reveals a wide range of trends. In some cases, parties appeared to develop more distinct stands on political issues, thus taking on a more national character. In other cases, however, they lost their national character and split along ethnic lines. Kenya was a case in point; parties that still had aspired to a national, multiethnic support base at the time of the 1992 elections participated in the 1997 elections as ethnic parties.[74]

In fact, it seems that the basis – whether ethnic or otherwise – on which political parties are formed does not ultimately determine the success of a democratic system. The problem is usually not the manner in which groups wish to organise (or are organised from above) so much as the way in which they interact. The leaders of the different groups must arrive at practical agreements of which compromise and power-sharing are key elements. Almost all multicultural systems that have proved stable are based on power-sharing arrangements. At the beginning of the 1990s, however, African politics could boast few such arrangements. Key politicians focused on confrontation, instead of searching for consensus on important issues. Even on the eve of an election, the main players could sometimes not agree on how they would operate in the future, thereby encouraging the loser of the election to continue the struggle by other means. Modern African political culture, which is characterised by confrontation and a 'winner-takes-all' approach, is thus at odds with stable democratic governance.

A third obstacle to the development of a modern democracy is the manner in which power is traditionally exercised in Africa. The increase in the power of African authorities over their citizens and the omnipotence of the president ('presidentialism') correspond to a concept of power that is widespread in Africa, where power has always possessed a sacred and all-encompassing character. Rulers are able to assert their authority in all areas of life, from politics and the economy to social relations. No separation exists between the public and private spheres, and power knows no boundaries. The origins of this all-encompassing concept of power are located in a social framework that is based, as noted above, on networks of patronage. This framework is clearly very old. It has even been said that the omnipotence of the Egyptian pharaohs served as an example for rulers in other parts of Africa, in particular the rulers of the Sudanese states in and around the Sahara Desert. In these and other African political systems, the economy and other sectors of society could not be separated from power or politics. Power was centralised and always reached further than the purely political, pervading all areas of life in society.

Obviously, this concept of power is not unique to Africa. Furthermore, we have seen that the type of power restricted by checks and balances was in fact also present in precolonial Africa, but local political systems of this kind were almost entirely destroyed during the colonial period. The colonial authorities themselves also acted in an authoritarian manner, avoiding all forms of accountability to the African people. Following independence, the tradition of authoritarian leadership was often further nourished by the role of the military. Many African countries were ruled by the military for a prolonged period, and this had a considerable impact on the relationship between citizens and the state. The existence of a tradition of authoritarian power did not mean that the state had a totalitarian hold on society, however, as most African states were far too weak for this. In many places, especially in remote rural areas, the power of the state was more or less limited and offset by the local power of chieftains and patriarchs.

Africa's low level of socioeconomic development is a fourth obstacle to the development of a modern democracy. In Western countries, democratisation took place in the course of the nineteenth century, following a process of economic development, steady advances in civil rights and cumulative governmental reforms.[75] The African countries have an entirely different historical background. As a rule, they have only experienced advances in the field of human rights since the end of the Cold War, at the same time as democratisation. Their understandably weak tradition of human rights has occasionally given rise to incidents that had hitherto been rare in democracies, such as populations awarding power to autocratic leaders of their own free will or majorities stripping minorities of their rights. Such democracies, which are characterised by their inadequate respect for human rights, are sometimes referred to as illiberal democracies, in order to distinguish them from liberal democracies, which place a strong emphasis on the protection of individual human rights. In addition, some African countries have had democratic constitutions but failed to apply them adequately in practice. This failure can be ascribed to a lack of effective implementation mechanisms, but also to a certain amount of unwillingness on the part of the authorities. Alongside problems with the quality of the political system, which were definitely not limited to inadequate levels of democracy, there were other obstacles; for example, the institutional structures of many African countries were very poorly developed and had become weaker still as a result of cutbacks.

Experience has shown that Africa's low level of socioeconomic development does not make democratisation impossible, but it should nevertheless be regarded as a structural obstacle to the development of a stable and mature democracy. A robust private-sector economy makes citizens less dependent on income from or through the state, so that the individual economic stakes in the contest for state power are not as high. And in any case, people need a decent income in order to provide a solid material foundation on which to build a democracy. After all, it is the public that provides the government with the resources it needs to implement policy by paying taxes and it can use this avenue to compel the government to spend these resources in a certain manner and account for its expenditure.

The centuries-old battle cry of the American struggle for independence, 'no taxation without representation', indicates just how closely taxation is linked to democracy. A situation of limited economic development offers little scope for taxation and therefore provides an inadequate material basis for democracy. From the late 1970s, multilateral financial institutions and large bilateral donors were the main backers of African governments, which enabled them to function as the 'external parliaments' of African countries. This situation will not change until African governments become more dependent on revenue from their own populations. From the 1980s onwards, various countries improved their taxation systems somewhat, often in the framework of structural adjustment programmes.

A democracy also functions more effectively if citizens no longer need to devote most of their attention to acquiring basic necessities. Better socioeconomic conditions make the population less dependent on traditional patrons and thereby expand its range of choices, since clientelism encourages conformity and generally excludes real political debate. Moreover, in countries where the economy and society are still not very diversified, there are few ideological differences or conflicts of interest that can serve as a basis for political pluralism. Better socioeconomic conditions also include general education. On the whole, both the availability and quality of education were extremely inadequate in Africa around 1990. As a result of inadequate education, African countries were not making optimal use of their human resources. It is plausible that a link exists between standards of education and the quality of government, as well as between education and the potential for democratisation, particularly when education devotes attention to diversity, tolerance and human rights. Low levels of literacy and education, especially among women, hamper the active participation of the population in decision-making. More advanced education can promote understanding of, for example, development issues, economic phenomena and historical context. Insight into such processes leads to the kind of emancipation that is a prerequisite for democratisation.

The democratisation years:

an overview

During the 1989-1994 period, democratisation took place throughout Africa, although the nature of the political changes in each country and region depended in large part on local conditions. In almost all countries, popular social and political protests were at the root of the liberal reforms, but in a few reforms took place even in the absence of such protests. In each case this remarkable political turnaround usually started with the legalisation of political parties and the resultant demise of the one-party state. In addition, new constitutions officially ended the governing party's ties to the state and, in some cases, the military. Measures were also introduced to achieve a clearer separation of the three branches of government (the legislature, the executive and the judiciary). Another key change that appeared in many new constitutions was a limit on the number of presidential terms of office. In most cases, presidents were obliged to step down after a maximum of two five-year terms. To crown these achievements, the new political parties organised parliamentary and presidential elections.

Democratic transitions, in which autocratic governments were replaced by more democratic ones, took place in roughly a third of all African countries. In addition, at least ten other countries launched democratisation processes that met with delays of varying seriousness. In a similar number of countries, however, these processes ground to a complete halt (at least for the time being), while the remaining countries (of which there were very few) did not experience any democratisation at all.

By the end of 1994, only a minority of countries (sixteen to be exact) had held elections that deserved to be called free and fair. More than ten other countries also held elections during this period, but failed to comply with the international minimum standards. The remaining countries (also more than ten) did not hold elections at all. A large number of countries experienced political liberalisation (a relaxation of the authoritarian system that granted more political freedom to citizens), but as yet did not develop democratic structures.

Political pluralism increased almost everywhere in Africa. This manifested itself, first of all, in the rise of multiple political parties in almost all African countries. By 1994, the average African parliament contained six or seven parties, although one party – the governing party – often held a large majority of seats. This was a significant improvement on the situation in the 1970s and 1980s, but Africa continued to lag behind other continents with regard to pluralism in party politics.[76] The same could be said of civil-society organisations and the public media: significant improvements had occurred in relation to previous decades, but in comparison with other regions they remained weak.

The relationship between citizens and the state is determined in part by the power of civil society, which in Africa currently differs from country to country. African civil society is often described as weak. This may be fair as a general comparison with Western civil society, but does not by any means apply to all African countries. In some parts of Africa, all manner of traditional and modern non-governmental organisations (NGOs) are shooting up, many of them local in character. In recent years, poor political and socioeconomic conditions have also encouraged Africans to organise and pressure their governments to change course. The public has thus become part of the democratisation process, preventing it from remaining an exclusively elite issue and allowing it to take root in society. In some countries, incidentally, civil society may be dominated by a counter-elite whose primary interest is to seize power (see chapter 9, p. 292 *et seq.*). The influence of genuine civil-society interest groups, such as women's rights groups and farmers' associations, varies significantly from country to country.

In many respects, the democratisation of Africa from 1989 to 1994 was of great historical significance, however weak or incomplete the process may have been. In the first place, it was significant that it took place at all. Until that time, a certain level of socioeconomic development had generally been regarded as a prerequisite for democratisation. This supposed regularity even led Samuel Huntington to predict in 1990 that the so-called third wave of global democratisation would probably not reach Africa. According to Huntington, most impoverished societies would remain undemocratic as long as they remained poor.[77] On the basis of the African experience, in particular, it appears that the connection between political and socioeconomic development is more complex, to say the least. It is true that democracy performs better in more developed countries, but this does not mean that the spark of democratisation cannot ignite under poor socioeconomic conditions as well, especially if there is hope for a better future.

Democratisation was also important because it interrupted the ongoing centralisation of political power that had been taking place in Africa since its independence. Political decision-making and financial resources were increasingly concentrated in the capital, and in the hands of certain people. In almost all political systems this had culminated in 'presidentialism': all power was in the hands of the president. The successful changing of the guard by means of elections was therefore an important step on the way towards changing the system. In addition, the broadening of the political base of the regime as a result of democratisation also led to a wider distribution of power, even if that power usually remained within the elite. Various countries launched decentralisation programmes, and the centre began to lose influence to the periphery. Finally, the democratisation process was also historically significant, because it represented another victory of African civil society over the authorities (the first being decolonisation). This unexpected victory – often called the second liberation of Africa – provided the African population with an incentive to become more deeply involved in politics, which further strengthened democracy.

Nobel Prize winner Amartya Sen has written that 'a country does not have to be judged to be fit for democracy, rather it has to become fit through democracy.'[78] In Africa, too, democracy was regarded as a new means of building society and the state. The implications of democratisation were therefore not limited to the field of politics, but also related to the economy, social structures and relations between groups. The connection between democratisation and economic reform attracted much attention. Could democratic governments implement the structural adjustment programmes of the World Bank and the IMF, which required cutbacks and thus caused a deterioration in social conditions, for the urban population in particular? Numerous observers were of the opinion that only authoritarian regimes would be able to implement such unpopular measures, and they consequently suspected the international institutions of secretly opposing democratisation in order to rescue economic reforms.[79]

In the protests against such socioeconomic deterioration, there was an important difference between the cities and the countryside. The main impact of the cutbacks resulting from the adjustment programmes was felt in the cities, in the state's infrastructure and capacity. Because many African states still had next to no presence outside the cities, at least not as a source of services and funds, the countryside was almost untouched by the cutbacks. In fact, agriculture was one of the main sectors to benefit from the economic reforms. Another factor contributing to the urban character of the protests was that political problems generally occurred at the national, 'macro' level and less so at the intermediate or 'meso' level of districts and provinces. In many African countries, local government functioned better than its equivalent at the meso and macro level, presumably because the villages had preserved much of their old style of administration and because they were ethnically and culturally homogeneous. More so than the authorities in the national and provincial capitals, local authorities could boast a natural link to Africa's past and therefore enjoyed relatively high levels of legitimacy.

Unfavourable socioeconomic conditions stimulated important political developments all over Africa, but these developments were not so far-reaching that most countries were able to develop effective democracies within just a few years. The democratic governments that replaced the dictatorial regimes were almost always weak. In some cases, they started to display the same autocratic and corrupt behaviour as their predecessors. This should not come as a surprise, in light of the structural obstacles to democratic culture in Africa (see previous section). Examples of such obstacles include not only a tradition of authoritarian leadership, but also a social framework largely based on clientelism and ethnicity. Other aforementioned structural obstacles also had an impact, including the lack of a tradition of human rights and good governance, the continued weakness of civil society and low levels of socioeconomic development and education. In addition, insecurity and instability sometimes made it impossible to develop democratic political systems.

By 1994, the wave of democratisation had passed its crest. Instead of progress, the emphasis came to lie on consolidating what had been achieved in previous years. In some countries, democracy continued to strengthen, almost unnoticed, beneath the surface as it were. This led to renewed progress around 2000 (see chapter 10, pp. 325-331).

In other countries, however, democratisation turned into its exact opposite. This was connected to a negative side effect of the democratisation and pluralisation of African societies in the early 1990s, namely, widespread ethnic polarisation. This trend was visible all over the world around the same time, but was remarkably powerful in Africa, just as in the Balkans and the Caucasus. In particular, the impact of African ethnicisation increased as a result of the weakness of the African state, which was barely able to assert itself. In so far as it stimulated ethnicisation, democratisation therefore actually threatened the stability of the state, resulting in outbreaks of violence. Although there is clearly a connection between democratisation and ethnicisation in Africa, ethnicisation is also connected to other issues, such as economic decline, the decline of the nation-state and the rise of globalisation. In reality, ethnicisation has both positive and negative effects, but the negative ones were the most striking, particularly the escalating hostilities between ethnic groups. Besides democratisation, the spread of internal conflict thus became another leitmotif of African politics in the early 1990s. In 1994, new depths of horror were reached in the Rwandan genocide (see chapter 6).

Before we turn to those topics, the following chapter discusses a number of positive developments that accompanied democratisation, such as the end of several violent conflicts dating back to the Cold War (the highlight of which was the abolition of apartheid in South Africa), renewed economic growth and, above all, the emergence of a new African consciousness and optimism. In the mid-1990s, was Africa headed for a renaissance?

4
Renaissance

A period of promise

With the end of the Cold War, the world began changing fast. It was the spectacular political transformation of Central and Eastern Europe that attracted most attention, but in fact the reverberations of the fall of communism were felt almost everywhere, including Africa. After decades of decline, it seemed that change could only be for the better. The sense of new possibilities produced a surge of enthusiasm and energy throughout the continent. Its first impact was in the domain that had become the greatest barrier to development: politics. A wave of political reform swept over the majority of African countries, taking by surprise even those most directly involved, and raised the prospect of further – perhaps much more far-reaching – advances.

It was only to be expected that the end of the Cold War should have consequences for security in Africa. In some regions and countries, the rivalry between the superpowers had fanned the flames of pre-existing local conflicts. The wars in the Horn of Africa and Southern Africa were the prime examples. In the second half of the 1980s, however, the Soviet Union began to change its policies abroad as it found itself in ever-deeper difficulties at home. In 1988, President Mikhail Gorbachev suggested to the Americans they should join hands with the Soviet Union to resolve regional conflicts. This led to the departure of Cuban troops from Angola and to the independence of Namibia. Following the disintegration of the Soviet Union, Russia lost interest in Africa. Insofar as it still had a presence there, it was willing to work with Western countries to resolve problems, in return for support on issues closer to Moscow's heart. Accordingly, there was a general atmosphere of cooperation on the resolution of regional conflicts. As a result, the number of major conflicts in Africa declined in the first half of the 1990s from more than ten to around six or seven (the exact figures depending on the definition employed).[80] This naturally led to greater optimism about the continent's future.

These major advances in politics and security were matched by significant economic development in the first half of the 1990s. For years, the results of stabilisation and structural adjustment had been patchy and largely disappointing. Now, suddenly, there was an upturn in economic growth. In the mid-1990s, Africa achieved its highest economic growth figures since 1970. Admittedly, they varied widely from one country to another, but by 1995 the continent's average growth rate was high – as much as five per cent. After years in which productivity and income had stagnated, and even declined in real per capita terms due to rapid population growth, the expansion of the African economy began once again to outpace that of the continent's population. Was Africa finally becoming a growth market? Would it be able substantially to increase its share in the global economy and lay the basis for reducing poverty?

It was a period of great promise, despite major crises in places like Liberia and the Great Lakes region. Many countries in Africa saw simultaneous improvements in the political field, in security and on the economic front, producing new self-confidence and assertiveness. The new mood affected the whole continent, but was especially evident in Ghana. For a long time after independence, there had been little good news about the country. In the 1980s, however, it finally found its way out of the morass and onto the path it was to pursue over the whole of the next decade. Flight Lieutenant Jerry Rawlings, a populist leader, had restored civilian government after his first coup in 1979, but refused to do so following his second in 1981. He was to remain in power for the next twenty years. His military regime guaranteed stability and eventually introduced democratic reforms. The economic success of the country, with annual growth figures of almost ten per cent, initially deprived Ghana's political opposition of any hope of electoral success. This frustrated some groups and led the international community to doubt the democratic nature of Ghanaian politics. But as long as Ghana kept making economic progress year after year, the critics of the regime were fighting a rearguard action.

By and large, the same was true of Uganda. There too, there was reason to doubt whether the system was truly democratic and whether the regime was actually committed to democracy, but criticism was stifled by successes in the area of security (even more of a problem in Uganda than in Ghana) and in particular on the economic front. The reforms seemed to be successful and for some years the economy continued to expand at an unprecedented rate, sometimes as much as ten per cent a year.

A third example, this time in Francophone Africa, was Mali. In the 1990s its national economic growth figures began to exceed the average for the continent. This in itself was a huge achievement for a country which straddles the boundary between the Sahara and the Sahel and thus has to cope with an inhospitable climate. Democratisation in Mali went further than in Ghana or Uganda. Under President Alpha Oumar Konaré political opposition was allowed but had no real chance of success given his huge popularity. Critics thus charged that Mali remained to all intents and purposes a one-party state despite the ostensible liberalisation of the political system. This situation was typical of that in many African states making the transition to democracy, particularly in the Francophone parts of the continent. There was almost no multiparty system in which public support was evenly balanced enough to allow parties to alternate in government. One party always had the upper hand and was able to govern continuously without much reference to opposing views. Even so, major progress was certainly being achieved in Mali and elsewhere on aspects of democracy such as freedom of speech and transparent (i.e. clear and open) decision-making. Moreover, government was being decentralised in an attempt to bring politics closer to the people.

Mali also greatly improved its internal security. There had always been unrest among the indigenous nomadic Tuareg population in the north of the country. During the nineteenth century, the emergence of new boundaries in the Sahel had increasingly limited the freedom of movement of the desert nomads. This had led to clashes in the French colonial era. In 1916, for example, a mass Tuareg uprising against the colonial authorities was suppressed with much bloodshed.

Following the departure of the French, the Sahara and Sahel were carved up between a number of states. More than one and a half million desert nomads found themselves suddenly apportioned to Mali, Mauritania, Algeria, Niger or Chad. The new states maintained the policy of centralisation established in the colonial era and regarded the nomadic way of life as an anachronism. Accordingly, the governments of Mali and neighbouring states did their best to undermine the Tuareg way of life. To make matters worse, the desert tribes were hard hit by drought in the Sahel during the 1970s and 1980s. Increasingly, the only good land for grazing was in the south. But access to it was rapidly being blocked by the growth of the sedentary population, which was grabbing all the more or less arable land. As time went on, the shortage of water and arable land and the general antagonism of the authorities made life practically impossible for the Tuareg population of Mali (numbering some six hundred thousand). Some of them gave up their nomadic existence and migrated to the cities in the south; others resorted to desperate armed attacks on anyone straying into their territories.

In 1990, the violence was intensified by the return of many Tuareg from Libya, where they had acquired both arms and revolutionary ideas. Initially, the Malinese military regime responded with an iron fist. Hundreds perished in the fighting. However, the 1991 coup led by army officer Amadou Toumani Touré resulted in a change of policy. The government embarked on negotiations with the Tuareg which eventually, following the election of President Konaré in 1992, culminated in a national reconciliation pact. As part of a general policy of decentralisation, it was agreed that the north of Mali should be given a certain measure of autonomy, together with funding for development, the reintegration of Tuareg fighters into society and the return of refugees.

Nevertheless, there were new outbreaks of violence in 1993 and especially in 1994. The government was partly responsible, because it had failed to provide much of the promised funding. A more important factor, however, was a resurgence of traditional friction between the nomadic tribes. When negotiations recommenced in Tamanrasset, just over the border in southern Algeria, the Malinese government representatives had the additional task of achieving reconciliation among the Tuareg themselves. In the course of 1995, the violence finally subsided. Many of the over ten thousand combatants received jobs in the army, small businesses or agriculture. They were given financial support and an additional hundred US dollars for every weapon surrendered. The Tuareg uprising in Mali came to a symbolic end on 27 March 1996 when a huge pyre of three thousand weapons was publicly burned in Timbuktu in the presence of almost all those who had participated in the conflict and the negotiations.

Peace had been restored in northern Mali, but in many other places along the border between Arab North Africa and black sub-Saharan Africa tensions persisted and local skirmishes continued. The main reasons were the substantial political, religious, ideological, economic and cultural differences between the northern and southern parts of the Sahara desert, but the problem was exacerbated by the increasing marginalisation of the desert nomads. Desertification was making natural conditions in the less arable areas ever more difficult. Along the fringes of the desert, the sedentary population was increasing, as was the number of Tuareg. It was clear that many nomads would eventually be forced to settle and the twenty-first century might even see the end of the distinctive nomadic way of life that the Tuareg had pursued for thousands of years in and around the Sahara. Huge efforts, like those made in Mali, would be needed to prevent that process from erupting into violent conflict.

The struggle of the Tuareg in Mali, though vital to those directly involved, was of lesser significance for the continent as a whole. As chapter 1 shows, the Cold War had had a particular impact on three regions: Central Africa, the Horn of Africa and Southern Africa. In theory, therefore, that is where the end of the Cold War should have allowed the most progress to be made in terms of security, democratisation and economic development. This was borne out in parts of the Horn of Africa (Ethiopia and Eritrea) and in almost all of Southern Africa. These two regions are discussed below. In Central Africa, however, no progress was made in the 1990s. On the contrary, events like the collapse of Zaire (renamed the Democratic Republic of Congo) and the ethnic strife around the Great Lakes led to explosions of violence which made Central Africa the symbol of all that could go wrong in the continent (see chapters 5 and 6).

Peace in Ethiopia and Eritrea

The disappearance of Soviet support in the late 1980s made the position of the Ethiopian dictator Mengistu Haile Marian ever more precarious. By this time, his regime was so loathed for the misery it had caused – ranging from famine to political terror – that it was facing a large number of different resistance movements. Like the Mengistu regime, most of these had originally been Marxist. Over time, however, many of them had anticipated the defeat of communism by becoming true believers in liberal democracy and the market economy. They worked together within the Ethiopian People's Revolutionary Democratic Front (EPRDF). In the spring of 1991, the EPRDF and the Eritrean People's Liberation Front (EPLF) together inflicted a decisive military victory on Ethiopian government troops. Mengistu fled to Zimbabwe and the coalition of resistance fighters seized Addis Ababa. Matters were quickly settled with the EPLF, which was in control of the whole of Eritrea now that the Mengistu regime had collapsed. It was decided that the EPLF should be allowed to retain control over Eritrea until a nationwide referendum had been held in 1993 on the future of the province. The referendum proved to be a mere formality: over ninety per cent of those eligible to vote in Eritrea were in favour of independence and nobody disputed the result. On 24 May 1993, Eritrea became formally independent. This brought a provisional end to a war which had cost the lives of half a million Eritreans and over a million Ethiopians.

Eritrean independence gave Africa yet another new state with a small population (approximately three million) and virtually no natural resources. Hostilities had left the country in ruins. Almost everything had been destroyed. Half a million Eritreans had sought refuge abroad, mainly over the border in Sudan, and had to be repatriated. The resistance movement of the past had to be drastically trimmed down into a proper national army, although it was far from clear how veterans could be put to work in the primitive Eritrean economy. Despite all the problems, however, there was still some reason for optimism. First and foremost, of course, there was the euphoria that came with independence and peace. The lengthy struggle had created a feeling of self-assurance and solidarity that was unique in Africa. Now that they had won the war, the Eritreans were confident that they could deal with the problems of peace. Measures were taken to intensify this mood of national unity. Local government was reorganised into six zones, the borders of which were deliberately designed to produce the greatest possible ethnic mix. In addition, an eighteen-month period of compulsory military service was introduced for both sexes and had to be served in multiethnic units. It was hoped that the shared experience would help to produce a generation who saw themselves as Eritreans. For many women, however, the transition to peace brought problems as well as prospects: the exigencies of war had enabled them to occupy positions of sexual equality, but in the ensuing peace many found themselves forced back into more traditional subordinate roles.

The political leadership of the Eritrean People's Liberation Front became the government and as such enjoyed great legitimacy as a result of its victory in the war. There was no real internal opposition. Opponents of the EPLF had fled the country as far back as the early 1980s. Internally, the EPLF claimed to be democratic and to give all its members a say, but in practice it was primarily an authoritarian military organisation imposing a strong hierarchy and discipline. Not surprisingly, therefore, the new EPLF regime quickly imposed a ban on all forms of official opposition and created a one-party state. All public organisations were answerable to the governing party and there was no freedom of the press. Even so, in the years immediately following independence, Eritrea did not exhibit the inefficiency and corruption of the typical African one-party state. That was not at all the mood of the country. In fact, efficiency and integrity were the hallmarks of the new regime.

The new government tackled the development of the (even by African standards) destitute country with considerable vigour and striking assertiveness, even in its relations with Western aid agencies. Firm conditions and constraints were imposed on their activities. The basic philosophy was one of self-development. Foreign aid was to be no more than a stopgap. Acting on its own initiative, the government propelled the country into transition from the planned economy it had inherited to a new market-based system. The World Bank and the IMF applauded the move but remained on the sidelines. While maintaining a firm macroeconomic balance, the government liberalised trade, privatised state-owned enterprises and encouraged foreign investment in the country. However, in view of the almost entire absence of statistical material, little can be said with any certainty about the effect of these measures on the Eritrean economy immediately after independence. At the time, little was known even about government finances and people joked that Eritrea's Ministry of Finance consisted of an old shoebox full of loose papers. Yet after the drought crisis of 1993, the economy recovered rapidly, at times growing – it was thought – by up to ten per cent a year.

The main emphasis was on exports. The country's key trading partner was Ethiopia, with which Eritrea still shared a common currency (the birr). In 1992, the value of exports to Ethiopia had been fourteen million US dollars; by 1995 it had risen to fifty-six million. Over the same period, the value of total worldwide exports rose from one million to twenty-four million dollars.[81] Admittedly, imports also increased rapidly and the country still had a trade deficit, but it was clear that Eritrea – like the ancient Kingdom of Aksum – saw itself primarily as a trading nation. It was following the example of the rapidly emerging Asian tiger economies, likewise based on exports, and was particularly inspired by developments in Singapore (another small country which, like Eritrea, had few natural resources but was strategically located). Returning from a tour of growth economies in East and Southeast Asia, the Eritrean president declared that his country's future was to serve the Horn of Africa as Singapore served Asia: as its gateway and financial capital. It was a vision still far divorced from the immediate reality of life in Eritrea, but a major step forward compared to the wartime mentality of the recent past.

To Ethiopia, the loss of Eritrea was a heavy blow. Since the entire coastline lay within the breakaway province, the country lost its access to the Red Sea. Still, it had plenty of other assets. Its fifty-five million people made Ethiopia the second most populous country in sub-Saharan Africa (after Nigeria). Its ethnic diversity was vast. Many of its peoples had only recently come within its borders, having been conquered by the Ethiopian Empire in the late nineteenth century as part of the 'scramble for Africa'. Others were at the core of the ancient nation. Ethiopia was one of the few countries in Africa where there was a feeling of national unity based on a shared history. Unlike in Eritrea, however, where the war had forged national unity, in Ethiopia it had to some extent undermined the population's nationalist loyalties. Eritrea – long an integral part of Ethiopia – had seceded and other ethnic groups were likewise turning against the unitary Ethiopian state. The Amhara had led the country under both the imperial and the Mengistu regimes. The EPRDF was a coalition of several small, mainly ethnically-based armed resistance movements, of which the one from the northern province of Tigray (situated between Eritrea and the Amharan heartland) was by far the most powerful. It was the Tigray, comprising around ten per cent of the population of Ethiopia, who seized power in Addis Ababa when Mengistu fled.

The main aim of the transitional government was not, as in Eritrea, to promote national unity; on the contrary, it aimed to strengthen the position of the many different ethnic groups (to which it referred by the Leninist term 'nationalities') so that they would never again be ruled by the Amhara. To this end, local government was reorganised and areas like Shewa, Welo and Gojam, which had existed for centuries, made way for numbered regions with borders drawn as far as possible along ethnic lines. The idea was that each region should be dominated by a single large ethnic majority. The effect was to convert Ethiopia from a unitary state into a federation of ethnic regions. In the past, ethnicity had been of mainly cultural significance but now it became politicised. Amharic was no longer the official national language. Government and education were to be conducted in the local language of each region. For a long time, however, these policies existed only on paper, since there was insufficient local administrative capacity and funding for provisions such as textbooks in local languages to put them into practice. Outside Ethiopia, there were widespread doubts about the wisdom of these ethnic policies. The benefits of local autonomy and freedom had to be weighed against the disadvantage of the loss of national unity. Was it really prudent to reject a national Ethiopian identity in favour of a multitude of ethnicities? In some areas, the political changes produced new local rivalries and power struggles. Sometimes members of minority ethnic communities were driven out of a region or murdered, and their possessions were looted or destroyed. At times, such action even seemed to amount to campaigns of 'ethnic cleansing'.

In Ethiopia itself, however, the new policy of ethnically based decentralisation was hardly questioned. It had been designed by the Tigray resistance movement before the overthrow of Mengistu and put into practice immediately afterwards. Other ethnic groups had had no substantial say in it. The process was tightly controlled from Addis Ababa and attempts at consultation and democratisation soon broke down. For example, although the Oromo (in the centre and south of Ethiopia) numbered around twenty million and were therefore the largest ethnic group in the country, their resistance movement soon withdrew from national talks about new constitutional and other arrangements. They resumed the armed struggle, this time against the EPRDF regime in Addis Ababa (which managed to confine the uprising to a relatively small area of the country). As a counterweight to genuinely independent political movements like the Oromo and Somali Liberation Fronts (the latter based in the Ogaden desert), the EPRDF set up local ethnically based political parties. These were then absorbed into the government coalition, becoming in a sense the government's straw men in the regions. With help from the capital, they were able to win an easy victory in every election held in the 1990s. In practice, therefore, central government was able to maintain control of the entire country despite the ostensible policy of ethnic autonomy. Even so, it would be wrong to dismiss the elections (at local, regional and national level) as simply a charade. The parliamentary elections of 1995 were the first multiparty general elections in the history of Ethiopia. So there was some degree of democratisation, however limited.

The ethnic decentralisation policy culminated in the constitution of 1996, which was unique in Africa. On paper at least, Ethiopia became a democratic federation of ethnic states. For the first time in the history of modern Africa, there was even a right to secede, although any region wanting to do so faced a complex procedure taking several years, intended to nip any separatist ambitions in the bud. In the event, no region made any attempt to avail itself of the right, since even those regions most opposed to rule from Addis Ababa had local governments working hand in glove with the central EPRDF regime. And in fact most regions had no real reason to seek independence. In practice, therefore, Ethiopia's unique constitution had no effect on the unity of the country. It was speculated that the Tigray had only introduced the option in order to be able to exploit it themselves if there was ever any threat to their own grasp on central government. But so far there was no prospect of any such thing.

Like the Eritrean government, the EPRDF regime in Ethiopia placed great emphasis on the transition from central planning to a market economy, seeing this as a precondition for economic and social rehabilitation. Like Eritrea, Ethiopia was one of the poorest countries in Africa. Per capita income was only around a hundred US dollars a year. Up to three-quarters of the population were illiterate, average life expectancy was less than fifty years and twenty per cent of children died before the age of five. From 1993, however, the restoration of stability and the government's new policies began to bear fruit. The economic growth rate rose to as much as eight to twelve per cent a year. Private investment increased and inflation declined. Ethiopia, like Eritrea, appeared to have entered a new era.

After the many years of warfare, relations between the two countries were remarkably friendly. This cordiality was rooted in their history of shared military opposition to the Mengistu regime and the personal chemistry between the two leaders, President Isaias Afwerki of Eritrea and President Meles Zenawi of Ethiopia (who later became prime minister under the new constitution). Together they took action against neighbouring Somalia and Sudan, where events were taking a quite different course. Somalia was disintegrating and had ceased to present a threat to its neighbours, but the Islamic fundamentalist regime in Sudan was still trying to destabilise Ethiopia and Eritrea. Although around half of all Eritreans and Ethiopians were Islamic (the other half being Christian), their religious practices were completely different from those of the Sudanese Muslims, many of whom were fundamentalist. For some years, Ethiopia remained more or less neutral in relation to

Sudan, but became openly hostile when the Sudanese secret service made an assassination attempt on President Hosni Mubarak of Egypt during a visit to Addis Ababa. By contrast, Eritrea pursued a consistent policy of confrontation with the government of Sudan. Diplomatic relations were broken off and the government of Eritrea gave the Sudanese embassy in Asmara to the Sudanese National Democratic Alliance resistance movement (which was illegal in Sudan). Indeed, there were times when war between Sudan and Eritrea seemed inevitable. For the time being, however, hostilities in the Horn of Africa remained purely intrastate (within Sudan and Somalia) and it was not until 1998 that a new war would break out between nations.

Positive developments
in Southern Africa

In a sense, the Cold War had gone only too well for South Africa. The government in Pretoria had succeeded in destabilising the frontline states (especially Angola and Mozambique) and forcing them onto the defensive, without the Soviet Union and its satellites being able to intervene (with the exception of Cuba's support for the Angolan government). In the course of the 1980s, countries in the West had realised that there was no longer any strategic reason to support South Africa. Instead, they became increasingly sympathetic to the objections to the racist regime being voiced both in their own countries and by the independent black states. Accordingly, they introduced a wide range of sanctions, seriously damaging the South African economy (which was already in trouble because of the global recession). With the end of the Cold War finally in sight, the apartheid regime had to rethink the future of the country and the region.

In February 1990, after only a few months in office, President F.W. De Klerk announced in parliament that the African National Congress (ANC) and countless other opposition movements were to be legalised. This was followed by the release of political prisoners, most importantly ANC leader Nelson Mandela, who had been incarcerated for twenty-seven years, half of the time on Robben Island, several kilometres offshore from Cape Town. This surprise move by De Klerk was a milestone in the history of South Africa. It was a sign that at any rate a large part of the white minority realised that there was no future for white rule. It was also the first step towards a new political system.

However, the road to fundamental reform was to be far from straight or smooth. At times, white opponents attempted to reverse the process of change and it was only with great difficulty that the government was able to gain acceptance of its plans. In retrospect, however, the process of reform seems rapid and controlled. At the end of 1991, broad-based consultations commenced on a new, post-apartheid constitution and the following year the white community voted in a referendum in favour of the political reforms. Even so, reform did not spell the end of violence. Thousands died in conflicts associated with the political transition but the process itself was never really in jeopardy. Further encouragement for a nonviolent end to apartheid came in 1993 with the award of the Nobel Peace Prize to the two main actors in the drama, De Klerk and Mandela. In the same year, agreement was reached on the formation of a transitional government and this was followed in 1994 by South Africa's first all-race national elections.

The results were an accurate reflection of the racial/ethnic mix in South Africa. The ANC achieved a resounding victory with over sixty per cent of the vote and won a majority in seven of the nine provinces. However, most of the white community and a large proportion of the Coloureds voted for De Klerk's National Party, giving it twenty per cent of the overall vote. It was only in Western Cape province, around Cape Town, that it won a majority. Finally, the Inkatha Freedom Party, a Zulu political movement, won hands down in the black homeland KwaZulu-Natal, but attracted little support in the rest of the country (a total of ten per cent of the overall vote). As agreed in advance, a government of national unity was established under ANC leader Nelson Mandela. De Klerk and Thabo Mbeki, second in command of the ANC, both became deputy presidents.

South Africa officially became a 'rainbow' nation and its new constitution included an obligation to build a 'participatory' democracy. Although the exact meaning of the latter term remained rather unclear, it seemed at any rate to indicate that all sections of the community should have the right to participate in the political process.[82] This emphasis on public participation took root elsewhere in Africa and went much further than the definition of formal Western democracy, perhaps demonstrating an African need to win back something lost to the peoples of the continent during the colonial era.

In order to enable the nation to close the book on the apartheid era, both legally and morally, a Truth and Reconciliation Commission was set up under the chairmanship of Archbishop Desmond Tutu, who in 1984 had also received a Nobel Peace Prize. The commission was a unique institution enabling those who had committed violations of human rights to appear in public to discuss their actions, make a clean breast of their crimes and seek forgiveness. The commission had discretion to grant them legal amnesty. This mechanism enabled countless people, of every race and political creed, who were guilty of misconduct under the apartheid regime, to embark on the new era with a clean slate. The South African truth commission was emulated elsewhere, especially in Latin American countries (Chile, Argentina and Guatemala) grappling with a similar need to achieve closure following bloody episodes in their recent histories. In Africa, a similar commission was also appointed in Sierra Leone at the start of the new millennium.

As apartheid came to an end, the social position of black people in South Africa was ambiguous. On the one hand, they were usually better off than black people elsewhere in Africa, but on the other they were worse off than the whites in their own country. The average annual per capita income of the thirty-eight million black South Africans stood at around six hundred US dollars: similar to that in other relatively affluent African countries like Senegal, Ivory Coast and Zimbabwe. For this reason, South Africa has always attracted immigrants from adjacent countries and even much further away. In the mid-1990s, the country had some four million immigrants. The greatest social problem was not, therefore, the absolute poverty of the black population (although many were living in wretched conditions), but rather the economic gulf between black and white in the country. The six million whites enjoyed an annual per capita income of no less than fifteen thousand US dollars: comparable to that of many Western Europeans and twenty-five times that of black South Africans.

The end of apartheid in South Africa was an event of continental and even global significance. Many Africans saw it as marking the end of the colonial era; the black struggle for freedom in South Africa was the final stage in the liberation of the whole continent. Yet it was only the term 'apartheid' that was peculiar to South Africa (or even to Africa as a whole). Segregation was particularly glaring in South Africa, partly because of the huge economic gulf between the races, but more particularly because it was underpinned by a system of strict legislation. In fact, however, segregation between different ethnic groups also existed elsewhere in Africa, whether or not it was officially recognised. Along the whole northern fringe of sub-Saharan Africa, for example, there was social discrimination between Arabs and black Africans, a legacy of a far more ancient form of colonialism. The kind of discrimination varied from country to country and, in the case of Mauritania, even resulted in black Africans holding a status almost indistinguishable from slavery.[83] Even in some purely black African countries, there were social systems similar to apartheid (for example, between the Americo-Liberians and the rest of the population in Liberia or between the Hutu and the Tutsi in the Great Lakes region). These forms of apartheid between indigenous ethnic groups attracted far less international censure, probably because they were less obvious to the outside world and because there was no clear and direct connection with European colonialism.

In Namibia, apartheid was abolished when the South Africans withdrew in 1990. However, the new state still exhibited a racial, economic and social divide resembling that in South Africa, albeit involving far fewer people (the white community in Namibia numbered less than a hundred thousand out of a total population of one and a half million). Given the inexperience of the country's new black regime, there were doubts about its ability to deal sensitively with the potential for internal conflict in the country. These doubts were reinforced just before the transfer of power, when it became known that the South West African People's Organisation (SWAPO) – which had won a large majority in the UN-supervised elections – had just a few months earlier tortured and murdered hundreds of its own people on suspicion of treachery and other crimes during an internal clean-up operation in the camps inside Angola.

After this troubling revelation, the initial years of the SWAPO regime came as a relief. President Sam Nujoma proved to be a competent leader. There were no great political tensions and there was some growth in the country's economy. The main barrier to the rapid economic growth required to bring the black standard of living up to that of the whites was the overwhelming competition from Namibia's larger neighbour, South Africa, which monopolised international attention and investment following the end of apartheid. Otherwise, relations with Mandela's government were good. For example, when Mandela came to office in 1994, the major port of Walvis Bay, an exclave of South Africa, was returned to Namibia and all Namibia's debts to South Africa were cancelled at a stroke.

Mozambique was another country that benefited greatly from the end of the Cold War. In spite of its appalling record (fifteen years of civil war, with almost a million dead and society in ruins), the country was able to transform into an inspiring example for the rest of the continent. Cooperation between the superpowers and the withdrawal of South Africa's support for the RENAMO resistance movement forced a reconciliation between the two warring factions. The Mozambican government (in effect, the FRELIMO party of national unity) and RENAMO reached agreement on a new multiparty political system and a market economy. The military accord between the two sides was perhaps even more vital. In 1992, meeting in Rome, they agreed that the national and rebel armies should both be disbanded and that the two organisations should each supply fifteen thousand men to form a new national army. The remaining veterans were to be demobilised. They also agreed to general elections which took place in 1994, with RENAMO standing as a political party. The government obtained agreement that Mozambique would remain a unitary state and not, as RENAMO wished, become a federation.

The Rome peace accord attracted wide international support. The United Nations coordinated one of the largest ever aid operations, known as UNOMOZ, and a UN peacekeeping force provided logistical support for the implementation of the agreement. A crucial point was that every former combatant willing to return to civilian life received UN financial assistance, as well as food and medicines, for the first eighteen months after demobilisation. The fledgling political parties also received funding to enable them to prepare for the elections, although preferential treatment for the former militias disappointed and infuriated the smaller Mozambican parties, who found themselves virtually excluded from the elections.

FRELIMO won the elections, but its lead over RENAMO was surprisingly small. Indeed, the former rebel movement actually gained a majority in some provinces in the centre of the country. Nevertheless, FRELIMO resisted international pressure to form a government of national unity and instead appointed all members of the government and all the local governors from its own ranks. This risky move put the peace of Mozambique under strain but at the time the country was too exhausted by the recent hostilities to engage in a new round of civil warfare.

Reconstruction was rapid. The economy was hugely boosted by the presence of so many affluent foreigners, including thousands of UN staff. Until 1995, when the UN announced the end of the operation and withdrew, UNOMOZ cost the international community a million US dollars a day, and most of that amount was spent inside Mozambique.

By 1995, however, the successful recovery of Mozambique had had a snowball effect, attracting more than a hundred international aid agencies into the country. This did away with the last remnants of central government planning. The international aid effort was impossible to direct or control – each aid agency simply went its own way. Peace and the influx of foreign money (including that of the returning refugees) ushered in a period of prosperity. From 1993 onward, Mozambique showed growth rates in excess of five per cent a year. Although a large proportion of the investment was being financed from abroad through international loans and the result was a rapid increase in the country's national debt, economic growth was maintained for some years and parliamentary democracy survived. In 1999, general elections was held for a second time, with another FRELIMO victory.

The end of the bloody civil war in Angola opened up the prospect of a new, stable zone of peaceful reconstruction throughout Southern Africa. At first, the way seemed clear for a Mozambican-style peace process in Angola. Once again, the two superpowers cooperated, South Africa withdrew (as did the Cuban troops who were supporting the Angolan government forces) and an accord was struck between the government in Luanda and the main resistance movement, UNITA. The Estoril peace agreement, signed in Portugal, strongly resembled the Rome accord that had sealed the peace deal for Mozambique: it contained provisions on demobilisation, a new integrated army and a multiparty political system. In 1992, general elections were held, and won by the ruling party. For a few months peace returned, but then UNITA resumed the armed struggle. The Angolan peace process col-

lapsed. The civil war flared up as violently as before and was henceforth to continue uninterrupted until the assassination of UNITA leader Jonas Savimbi in 2002, making the war
in Angola one of the longest in the history of Africa.

One of the main reasons that it was difficult to establish peace in Angola was probably
the country's rich natural resources, which gave the opposing parties the means to purchase arms and support armies. This meant that there was no economic reason to abandon
hostilities. The income from the diamond trade was easily enough to enable UNITA to continue fighting, whereas electoral defeat had forced the movement to give up this lucrative
business. This was another reason, apart from personal motives, for Savimbi to continue
the struggle. Angola was, in a sense, too rich to make peace.

In Mozambique, the situation was completely different. The country was so lacking in
natural resources that it was impossible for a profitable wartime economy to emerge and
sustain the combatants. Thanks to wide international support, the hostile parties could be
drawn into a peace process. In the initial postwar years, Mozambique lived on international
aid, which at times made up as much as seventy per cent of its gross national product. In
Angola, by contrast, international aid barely exceeded ten per cent of GNP, not enough to
make it a decisive factor.

Botswana, in the heart of Southern Africa, is another country that should be mentioned in
a chapter about positive developments.[84] Once it had gained its independence in 1966, the
country began a steady process of reconstruction. Although roughly the size of France,
Botswana has a population of little more than one million. The capital, Gaborone, is more
like a village than a city. Indeed, much of Botswana lies in the Kalahari desert and it is in
many ways an insignificant country. Nevertheless, as soon as it gained its independence
from Britain, it became in virtually every respect a model for development elsewhere in
Africa. The country exhibited uninterrupted stability, democracy, respect for human rights
and economic growth. In the 1990s, average annual per capital income was around 3,000
US dollars, not only far outstripping that of every other country in black Africa (apart from
oil-producing Gabon), but more or less equalling the all-race average in South Africa and
exceeding that in Namibia.

Part of this economic success was due to diamond-mining, which really took off in the
1970s. International diamond prices rose almost every year, giving Botswana a relatively
large export income. Far more important, however, was the use the country made of the
money. Many other African countries with substantial mineral export earnings slid into
bankruptcy. Indeed, relatively easy money of this kind has frequently seemed to prevent
rather than promote national development.

Happily, Botswana was an exception to the rule. The government pursued cautious
economic policies giving top priority to macroeconomic stability. In almost every year
throughout the remainder of the twentieth century, the value of exports exceeded that of
imports and public income exceeded public spending. As a result, the country built up considerable financial reserves. The policy was that these should always be sufficient to fund
one year's imports, but in practice they were often even greater. Botswana was virtually free
of foreign debt. Its repayment behaviour was beyond reproach. Market mechanisms guaranteed efficient use of economic resources and the currency had a floating exchange rate
that rose gently but steadily, even against the South African rand. Although Botswana was
not without its problems, it was a striking success compared with other parts of Africa.

The great conundrum is why Botswana succeeded when virtually every other country in Africa failed. Undoubtedly, the reason lies in the sphere of government policy, so it may be better to rephrase the question and ask why the successive governments of Botswana succeeded in pursuing effective policies when almost all other African governments failed to do so. Part of the answer must lie in the stability and openness of Botswanan democracy, which allowed open debate on policies and a degree of public control over the actions of government. Public offices changed hands with few problems and even presidents came and went peacefully.

It is important, however, not to idealise Botswanan democracy. The country was led by a fairly authoritarian elite which never surrendered power. The government was invariably dominated by the same party. Despite a democratic system, the elite was able to do things more or less its own way, undisturbed by competing groups. It was not until around 1990 that other sections of society began to gain more influence in Botswana, as elsewhere in Africa. In the early 1990s this produced a broader and more genuine democracy.

The success of Botswana was due in part to special features of its national elite. They formed a united front with a common mission: the development of the country. This public good was not, as elsewhere on the continent, subordinated to personal ambitions. Perhaps this unity of purpose was encouraged by the maintenance of a democratic system, which made it possible for public offices to change hands without violence. In addition, the machinery of government was exceptionally professional and technocratic (in a positive sense) compared with that in most other African countries, and remained entirely unpoliticised.

A combination of factors may have been at work. First of all, the ethnic makeup of Botswana's population was quite homogenous. In addition, Botswana was one of the few countries in Africa with a black middle class (whose prosperity came from stockbreeding). Moreover, the intrinsic precariousness of Botswana's international position – as a small country wedged between larger neighbours constantly plagued by internal warfare – tended to restrain its aspirations and pretensions. Its close links with Britain were cherished and foreign expertise was bought in whenever it could be useful. A sound balance was struck between planning and market mechanisms. Indeed, government policies were based on a philosophy of constantly responding to the demands of the external situation, thereby avoiding unbalanced growth. It enabled Botswana to maximise its income from diamonds and its other limited resources and achieve small economic advances, year by year, that eventually put the country far ahead of the rest of Africa.

The improvements in the situation in Southern Africa boosted regional cooperation. Since 1980, the region had had a platform for cooperation in the form of the Southern African Development Coordination Conference (SADCC). This had originally been an organisation of frontline states, set up to reduce their economic dependence on the apartheid regime in South Africa. The end of apartheid in the region changed its purpose. In 1994, South Africa became a member and, because of its economic importance, the linchpin of the organisation. SADCC was renamed SADC, the Southern African Development Community, and adapted its aims accordingly. In addition to striving for development and economic progress, it now sought to promote intraregional trade and political cooperation (for example, to end the violence inside member state Angola). In 1996 it acquired a separate mechanism for cooperation in political, defence and security fields. SADC was heavily dominated by South Africa, which accounted for no less than eighty per cent of the member states' combined GNP. This meant that South Africa could act as an engine for development throughout the region, but also raised fears in the minds of the remaining members that they might be eclipsed by their powerful neighbour. Trade liberalisation might simply open up their markets to a flood of South African products. It was especially difficult for Zimbabwe, which had previously occupied a prominent position in the organisation, to play second fiddle to the new member.

Mbeki's African renaissance

African self-confidence was boosted by the political and economic progress achieved in many African countries in the first half of the 1990s and by newfound peace and security. Around the middle of the decade, therefore, greater optimism began to emerge alongside (though not entirely to replace) the previous mood of pessimism. Some governments began to herald a brighter future now within reach, both for their individual countries and for Africa as a whole, despite all the problems besetting the continent. In the early 1990s, the new mood found expression in the concept of the African renaissance. This became an important topic of debate for many years, both inside and outside Africa, with advocates and opponents pointing respectively to the successes and failures of contemporary African development.

The idea of a renaissance – literally a rebirth – originated in South Africa at the end of the apartheid era. It may have been conceived by Thabo Mbeki, the first black deputy president, and from 1999 president, of South Africa. At any rate, Mbeki and some other South African representatives were among the leading proponents of the idea. Although the term was used mainly in relation to South Africa, the ambitions surrounding it were much wider. It referred to a wide-ranging vision which encompassed the past, present and future of Africa, even if it was rather short on detail. What precisely was to be reborn? Who was to bring about this rebirth? Only the black population? What were the objectives and was there a reasonable prospect of achieving them?

In April 1998, Deputy President Mbeki delivered a lecture at the United Nations University in Tokyo entirely devoted to the African renaissance. He started by emphasising that Africans were no different from people elsewhere in the world: they had their own history with its many triumphs and tragedies. Their future could be as bright as they wanted to make it. After all, wasn't Africa the very cradle of humankind? Mbeki thought it necessary to approach the subject this way because the outside world had for centuries depicted Africans as terrifying savages; there were countless curious and sometimes even amusing examples of this tendency. Black as a colour had come to symbolise terror, evil and death. Such stereotypical thinking still influenced the modern view of Africa and encouraged prejudices about Africans, for example that they were more chaotic and violent than people in other parts of the world and might never be capable of organising their own continent and achieving development. In Africa, as elsewhere, people's thoughts about the future were largely dependent on their ideas of the past.

The West has only recently discovered the history of Africa. It was not until the second half of the twentieth century that its more glorious episodes became widely known to the Western public, in particular through the work of the British historian Basil Davidson. This lack of information may have indirectly influenced the views that Africans held of their own heritage. Gradually, historians began to piece together the grand tales of Africa's ancient civilisations: Ghana with its control of the gold trade, Benin (in present-day Nigeria) with its artistic prowess, the might of ancient Zimbabwe, the religious influence of Ethiopia and the centre of learning that was Timbuktu. Above all, ancient Egypt was identified as part of the African story. Europeans are used to viewing the civilisation of ancient Egypt as a precursor to that of Greece and therefore part of their own history, but the country of the Nile is, after all, geographically part of Africa. Moreover, Egyptian traditions on matters such as the status of kings travelled via Nubia (in present-day Sudan) to influence large parts of sub-Saharan Africa. Even if Egypt was not itself part of black Africa, it formed a major source of inspiration for the lands to the south. In his Tokyo lecture, Mbeki too looked back to Egypt and to other memorable episodes in the history of black Africa which he thought should not only make Africans proud of their past, but should demonstrate that there was no reason why Africa should not once again excel in the future. Africa's pride could be revived and reborn. In this way, the African renaissance could connect the past with the future.

But what was that future to be? The stress on the continent's history was not intended to encourage a return to a more or less mythical past. Events never repeat themselves exactly. In Tokyo, Mbeki spoke of a twenty-first century Africa of dignity, peace, stability and prosperity. African children should grow up to be citizens of the world, enjoying universal respect and equality. The continent had to put its house in order, both politically and economically. Governance in Africa had to improve dramatically. To Mbeki's mind, the days of military regimes and one-party states were numbered. Government had to become transparent and accountable. That was the only way to end the widespread corruption and abuse of power. The authorities would have to surrender their prominent role in the economy and promote the growth of the private sector. This would open the way to new jobs and new housing, safe drinking water, the eradication of hunger, high-quality education and health care and so forth. Recent successes in Africa proved that it was all possible, Mbeki claimed.

Critics of Mbeki pointed out the remarkable U-turn that had taken place in his thinking. Until just before the end of the apartheid regime, the ANC (in which Mbeki spent his whole political career) was not only closely linked to the South African Communist Party but also preached an ideology typical of many liberation movements in Africa; namely, one opposed to liberal democracy and the market-based economy. However, by the time the ANC came to power in South Africa, the world had changed dramatically. Socialism was a thing of the past. Adjustment to the new world order was by far the most sensible course for black African leaders to adopt. Mbeki's new philosophy of the African renaissance put a positive slant on (some would say spin-doctored) the act of submitting to the new reality.

Mbeki's concept of renaissance also invites questions of a more substantive sort. The African renaissance looks back to an entirely African past but forward to a future built mainly on ideals of progress inherited from the European Enlightenment. Can those ideals – such as democracy, social justice and welfare – be achieved on the basis of African traditions and values? And, if so, which traditions and values? What is to be preserved and what will have to change? Mbeki says almost nothing about this. His programme for the future is almost entirely Western in substance, and its African aspect seems to be mainly limited to the suggested motivation for adopting the proposed course. Africans were to take pride in their heritage in order to find the strength to make the necessary leap into the future. Through their readiness to learn from others, they could once again become their own liberators, this time not to win the continent's political freedom, but to achieve a better future for its entire population.

As chapter 1 shows, episodes like the slave trade and colonialism had left deep scars on the soul of Africa. These were not healed by the experience of the first decades of independence, but in fact exacerbated by a disappointing lack of progress. In this 'neocolonial' era, African governments and their subjects became dependent on foreign aid. Ideologies like Senghor's *négritude* or Nyerere's self-reliance were insufficient to maintain a sense of self-confidence once the euphoria of independence had worn off. Aid dependency breathed new life into the stereotypical colonial view of Africans as lethargic and undisciplined. To escape from it, people in Africa needed to adopt a new attitude: a sense of pride in their own history and heritage. It was this that Mbeki was trying to encourage with his idea of an African renaissance. Africa's attitude needed to change; a new self-confidence was needed to fuel an upsurge of initiative, creativity, individuality and enterprise.

But who exactly was to benefit from this renaissance? What did 'African' mean in this context? Was the renaissance to be confined to black Africa or would it encompass countries like Egypt (now mainly Arab)? More importantly still, where did the white population of Mbeki's own South Africa (who actually called themselves Afrikaners) fit into the picture? Mbeki wanted to exclude nobody. Like the struggle against apartheid, the African renaissance was to be inclusive and nonracial. But what were the implications of this for the relationship between, for example, the white South Africans and indigenous African traditions and values?

It seemed impossible to answer all of these questions within the ideology of the African renaissance. Nor was it actually necessary to do so. After all, the importance of the concept lay not in its comprehensiveness but in its power to inspire change. And in this respect, it was largely successful, despite the major setbacks of the late 1990s (such as the war in Central Africa). Large parts of Africa responded to Mbeki's exhortation.

In calling for an African renaissance, Mbeki was not merely describing current developments, but issuing a clarion call to take them further, or – in countries where no progress had yet been made – to make radical changes in policy. How did this relate to the principle of nonintervention in the affairs of other states, a doctrine Africa had clung to ever since independence? Perhaps it was the first sign of a more critical attitude towards other African governments. In the closing years of the twentieth century, there were some striking signs of such a shift. Mbeki suggested that Africa should be viewed as a single entity. Countries in the forefront of development had a duty to help those lagging behind. He personally called on military regimes, like that of the despotic General Sani Abacha in Nigeria, to make way for democratic governments. Democracy, he said, had to be introduced throughout Africa, although it was up to individual countries to decide the form of democracy best suited to their circumstances. He also advocated a greater role for the OAU, which in 1993 created a mechanism for conflict prevention, management and resolution in Africa. As far back as 1981 it had adopted a Charter on Human and People's Rights prescribing standards which African governments were expected to observe.

The doctrine of the African renaissance recognised the role of African governments. Good leaders produced good citizens. The quality of African leadership had for a long time left a great deal to be desired, not only by Western standards but also in the eyes of many Africans. To improve it, a new sort of leader was required: one who would be self-aware, honest, up-to-date and confident. By the mid-1990s, such leaders actually seemed to be emerging.

New leaders and a
wind of change?

The term 'new leaders' is used in both a broad and a narrow sense. In the first, it refers to all African rulers who, to put it simplistically, 'govern well' by international standards. Judged purely on key criteria such as reasonably successful reforms that promote a market economy and democracy and improvements in the quality of governance, leaders of this kind can be identified in all parts of Africa. In the narrower sense, however, the term 'new leaders' is used to refer to a particular group of four rulers who all shared a number of major characteristics. They were (in the order in which they took office) the president of Uganda, Yoweri Museveni (1986), the president and later prime minister of Ethiopia, Meles Zenawi (1991), the president of Eritrea, Isaias Afwerki (formally appointed at the time of independence in 1993) and the vice-president and minister of defence (and in practice 'strongman' and later president) of Rwanda, Paul Kagame (1994).[85]

A couple of the new leaders were relatively highly educated and they were all regarded as intelligent. They were also closely connected. Kagame had actually worked under Museveni as head of Ugandan military intelligence before he seized power in Rwanda, while Meles and Isaias had cooperated during the war in Ethiopia. The four shared an assertiveness that was regarded as 'progressive' by the international community and, with their self-confident and at times populist approach, displayed a panache new to African politics.

All four acquired great popularity in their own countries, although they also roused strong domestic opposition and even armed resistance. But, above all, they were popular in the West. The reason was simple: they were able to create order out of chaos and to offer hope of progress. Museveni liberated Uganda from its blood-soaked past under Amin and Obote, Meles and Isaias defeated the communist regime in Ethiopia and achieved Eritrea's relatively smooth transition to independence, and Kagame came to power in the wake of the Rwandan genocide.

The order imposed by these leaders was in itself a major advance and the sound economic policies they pursued also counted in their favour. Although their shared Marxist past might have been expected to predispose them in favour of a planned economy, they took free-market thinking in their stride and implemented reforms aimed at economic liberalisation. Even if the IMF was not always directly involved, the thrust of their reforms matched its basic policies. Success was not long in coming. The four countries were soon exhibiting remarkable rates of economic growth, assisted by extensive support from abroad as their 'new leaders' became the darlings of the international donor community.

Economically, this was justifiable; politically, much less so. None of the four leaders was a dyed-in-the-wool democrat. All had come to power following often prolonged guerrilla warfare against the established regimes. Elections had played no part in their accession and did not feature in the early years of their rule. First Museveni and then Kagame launched their own theories about the (at best limited) role of liberal democracy in the less developed parts of Africa (see chapter 3, pp. 94 and 96). It was not until around the millennium that there was any move to liberalise politics in Uganda and Rwanda. In Ethiopia, the ruling party set up its own straw men disguised as representatives of the country's ethnic groups and then entered into a political alliance with them. And Eritrea remained essentially a one-party state.

In all these countries, in other words, the political culture and system remained authoritarian. The political situation was, of course, more stable than under the chaotic regimes of the past, but these countries were by no means political pioneers compared to the rest of Africa. While democracy was being introduced in countries like Tanzania, Mali and Zambia, progress in Uganda, Ethiopia, Eritrea and Rwanda consisted primarily of restoring order and improving economic conditions. An effective state was a major priority. The new leaders placed great emphasis on strong government and public integrity. They gave the appearance of combating corruption in Africa, but in fact showed considerable favouritism towards their own families and 'clients' (especially in Uganda).

It was a striking paradox that the new leaders tailored some of their policies to international preferences (economic liberalism, effective and noncorrupt government and, in general, Western-style policies), while at the same time displaying great self-assurance in steering an autonomous course on other matters, such as the form of their own political systems or the solution to Africa's international problems. By successfully adapting to the international environment (going with the flow, as it were) they gained a degree of autonomy in other areas that was not available to governments which tried to swim against the tide from the start. One example of the assertiveness shown by the new leaders was their promotion of what were dubbed 'African values'. To the alarm of the West, these included the abhorrence of homosexuality expressed by Museveni (following in the footsteps of President Robert Mugabe of Zimbabwe and others in Africa).

The new leaders' approach to domestic and foreign policy-making was decided by their military and authoritarian background. Prolonged armed conflict tends to leave a legacy of factions unable to submit to the new order. The new leaders cracked down hard on such domestic opposition, much of it armed. This struggle sometimes entailed widespread violations of human rights, and arbitrary arrests of political opponents took place even in more peaceful times.

Nor did the new leaders shrink from an aggressive approach to international relations. Where diplomacy failed, they resorted to force. They broke with the OAU tradition of non-intervention in the internal affairs of other states, rousing the apprehension of many rulers of neighbouring countries. The importance of this approach was increased by the fact that the new leaders coordinated their foreign policies and not infrequently engaged in joint action. For example, they openly opposed the fundamentalist Islamic regime in Sudan (which supported the armed opposition in Eritrea, Ethiopia and Uganda) and they worked together to engineer the downfall of the Mobutu regime in Zaire. Their four countries formed a stable and powerful regional block extending from the Red Sea to the very heart of Africa. In 1996-1998 it seemed as if it was about to expand further. The regime in the Sudan came under heavy pressure and in Zaire Mobutu was forced to flee. It looked as if the country's new strongman, guerrilla leader Laurent Kabila, might set himself up as another 'new leader'. In the end, however, the conflicts of interest between Kabila and the leaders of the neighbouring countries proved to outweigh their shared interests. Instead of the group of new leaders expanding to include Kabila, 1998 saw the outbreak of a large-scale war which almost annihilated all hope of an African renaissance.

But even at the height of their popularity, the new leaders had already become the subject of Western criticism. This centred on their authoritarian approach to politics, which left little room for democracy and led to violations of human rights. Some critics even doubted whether they were new leaders, believing that they were simply clever enough to mislead the Western media and politicians. Whatever the truth of the matter, the new leaders became a focal point of the United States' policies on Africa as developed in the mid-1990s by the Clinton administration.

The United States' new
policies on Africa

At the end of the Cold War, the American government lost interest in Africa. There was no further geopolitical reason to care about events there, and the continent's widespread economic malaise made it of little financial interest. American development aid had had poor results, if only because the choice of countries had proved unfortunate: in the 1980s, American aid had been concentrated on Liberia, Sudan, Somalia and Zaire, all of which descended into chaos in the following decade. The Washington-orchestrated UN intervention in Somalia (Operation Restore Hope, see chapter 5, pp. 148-152) was a debacle. Not surprisingly, therefore, American involvement in Africa at the end of the George H.W. Bush administration (until January 1993) and the start of the Clinton administration was largely confined to humanitarian aid. The Afro-American lobby in Washington could do little to change this, although its influence did help to ensure that the American government remained alert to developments in Africa to which it might wish to respond in the future.

There was a general expectation that democratisation and the African renaissance would eventually bring about faster economic growth, and Washington was well aware of the positive developments outlined in this chapter. Gradually, forecasts of doom and gloom gave way to a new and optimistic vision of Africa. This time, the approach was not geopolitical but rather based on countries' internal politics and in particular the economic outlook of the continent. Africa could now be portrayed as having a future of democracy and prosperity in the twenty-first century. The continent was also seen as important because there was money to be made there, if not immediately then at least in the relatively short term. There was general support among both Democrats and Republicans for the political and economic liberalisation of Africa.

President Clinton used the 1997 world summit in Denver to showcase the United States' new policy on Africa. The Clinton initiative was the result of the new American interest in the continent, and its name – the Partnership for Economic Growth and Opportunity in Africa – gave a clear indication of the Americans' main interest: economic growth. Through partnership with the US, the new levels of economic growth already emerging in Africa were to be further heightened, creating opportunities both for Africans and for

Americans who wanted to do business with Africa. Washington planned to link its measures directly to the policies pursued by individual African countries: the better their policies (not judged on the basis of any stringent criteria, but in terms of sound financial management, scope for private enterprise and good governance), the more the countries would be allowed to benefit from preferential trade deals, investment guarantees and debt relief. This policy of 'building on success' did not view Africa as a single entity, but drew a clear distinction between those countries that were managing their affairs well (and therefore qualified as business partners) and those that were not.

The United States saw its own domestic market as the main means of promoting growth in African economies. The volume of trade between Africa and the US was already increasing, but it could be dramatically expanded if access to the American market were improved. To achieve this, President Clinton promised to introduce new legislation, for example to provide free access to the American market for an additional 1800 products from Africa. Those African countries that went furthest in opening up their own markets could expect even better access. In this way, reciprocity was built into the US scheme: it was to be a matter of tit for tat. The Americans also wanted to involve other industrialised countries in the arrangement. In cooperation with the World Trade Organisation (WTO) and other international agencies, they would help African countries create the conditions for trade liberalisation.

An important limitation on the American policy was that the products to be exempted from free trade included several which were economically important, for both the US and Africa. These included agricultural products, leather and textiles (although the US Congress made it easier to export textiles when reviewing the plans). In this respect, the short-term interests of the US triumphed over the principle of free trade. The question was how far these exemptions would inhibit the expansion of trade between Africa and the US. Some critics felt that lifting trade barriers for the 1800 additional products would have little impact so long as such key products continued to be excluded. On the other hand, it could also be argued that the partial removal of trade barriers would help to promote further diversification in the African economies, a matter which had been neglected in previous decades because of the preoccupation with certain traditional exports. As a result, African economies had tended to retain colonial structures of production and export. In the long run, some people felt, it might actually be a good thing if the African countries were encouraged to look for new products to export.

The United States was eager to improve the climate for both internal and external investment in Africa. To this end, it produced plans identifying a number of priorities. First and foremost, African countries were to abandon statutory distinctions between internal, African investors and those from abroad. Two new funds with a total value of 650 million US dollars would provide guarantees for American investment in Africa. Bilateral investment protection agreements would be signed with as many African countries as possible and the US also planned to advocate multilateral measures to ensure better protection for international investment. Partly in order to promote economic growth in Africa, the US also planned to participate in the recently announced HIPC debt initiative, in which donors would work together under the leadership of the World Bank to reduce the debts of the most heavily burdened developing countries on condition, of course, that they pursued sound economic policies (see chapter 9, p. 287 *et seq.*). The idea was that all African countries would qualify for certain trade liberalisation measures, investment promotion and support for regional cooperation but that countries willing to make reforms in order to accelerate economic growth could look forward to extra help. This might take the form of even greater market access, debt relief and technical assistance. In the long term, the administration envisaged free trade agreements with thriving African economies. However, the conditions to qualify for the extra trade liberalisation measures were so stringent that few African countries had any prospect of meeting them in the near future.

Alongside these economic plans, the Clinton initiative included measures to encourage democratisation, good governance, institutional strengthening, agriculture, health care and, above all, education. Although it held out the prospect of a large range of activities in these fields, it was clear from the modest amount of funding made available for them that no great impact was to be expected. The effect of the American plans was to be mainly indirect; the intention was to encourage African governments to devote more of their own resources to education and health care. Countries that did so could count on extra support from America.

The Clinton initiative was typically American in the sense that the administration confined its efforts to establishing a framework for profitable private enterprise. The US has traditionally had little faith in aid as a means of achieving development. Not surprisingly, therefore, the new policy paid little attention to traditional development cooperation, even though this would continue to be the main form of relations with the world's poorest countries for a long time to come. After all, they could not be expected to win export markets in the industrialised world overnight. The Clinton initiative ignored the fact that the share of the US gross national product devoted to development aid had fallen in the 1990s to 0.2 per cent and made no commitment to increase this amount.

Although the new American policy on Africa focused principally on countries which were already doing comparatively well, it did pay some attention to regions in armed conflict. Washington put forward its own plans for conflict prevention and peace enforcement. Following the failure of the operation in Somalia, these plans made no mention of the direct deployment of American troops, but emphasised international support for African peacekeeping forces. They were in fact simply a more detailed version of a plan that Washington had advocated a year earlier for the establishment of an African Crisis Response Force. The Americans wanted to cooperate with a number of European allies to train and equip African troops for deployment in theatres of conflict or humanitarian operations in Africa. The failure of the operation in Somalia had clearly had a major impact on American strategy towards conflicts in Africa: from now on, its involvement was to be strictly indirect.

For many years, the main job of the US administration's Africa desk had been to make sure that the president did not have to spend his valuable time on Africa's problems. Under Clinton, all this changed. Here was a president who actually wanted to be personally engaged with African affairs. The first major issue with which he became closely involved was the end of apartheid in South Africa. The revolutionary changes taking place in that country gave Washington an ideal opportunity to advance new policies. In 1994, immediately after his appointment as president of South Africa, Mandela visited the United States. Clinton took the opportunity to announce his plans to visit Africa in the course of his presidency. This was more startling than it may at first appear. It had been almost twenty years since a sitting US president had visited sub-Saharan Africa. The last one to do so had been

Jimmy Carter, who had made brief visits to Liberia and Nigeria in 1978. It was no coincidence that he too was a Democrat.

It was March 1998 before Clinton fulfilled his promise. But he did so in style. In a lightning diplomatic tour, he visited no fewer than six African countries in the space of eleven days, lavishing special attention on the new leaders. The trip was partly designed to improve the image of Africa in the minds of the American public. The wide media coverage was intended to focus on issues other than famine and warfare. The main emphasis was on the African renaissance, trade, investment and development, and the environment (although, unfortunately, the armed conflicts could not be entirely ignored).

Clinton's first destination was Ghana, an excellent example of a country that had succeeded in eliminating the most abject poverty through economic and political reform. He then moved on to South Africa, the most important stop from the strategic point of view. Since South Africa was a regional superpower with a military to match, the United States hoped that it would help to stabilise crisis areas not only in its own backyard in Southern Africa but also in the centre and west of the continent. But the South African government had its doubts. The feeling in Pretoria and Cape Town was that South Africa should beware of undue assertiveness, so soon after the ending of apartheid and the establishment of normal relations with the rest of Africa. Accordingly, military cooperation between South Africa and the United States remained a thorny issue.

From South Africa, the president travelled to Gaborone, the capital of Botswana. Clinton's visit was an acknowledgement of the achievements of this small country, but was also designed to focus attention on Africa's environmental problems. He to discussed measures to halt desertification and plans for nature conservation.

Going on to Kampala – where the Ugandans, with a keen sense of geopolitical realities, dubbed him the 'President of the World' – Clinton gave President Museveni the chance to demonstrate regional leadership by hosting a summit of leaders from the troubled Great Lakes region and the Horn of Africa. This was attended by Museveni's kindred spirits, the heads of state of Ethiopia and Eritrea, and the presidents of both Kenya and Tanzania.

This regional summit with Clinton may have given the impression that a new Pax Americana was emerging in East and Central Africa, but this was not entirely true. One of the main players on the regional stage was absent from the talks. Laurent Kabila, the new president of what had been Zaire and was now renamed the Democratic Republic of Congo, had always fiercely resisted attempts by the new leaders and by Washington to bring him into line. He had flatly declared that he wanted nothing to do with Clinton's visit. At the time, the aggressive attitude of the Congolese president could be shrugged off as an unpleasant footnote to the tour, but it was to prove the harbinger of fresh problems in the region. Kabila's attempts to retain his political independence later plunged Central Africa into a major war which tarnished the reputation of the new leaders (see chapter 6).

After Kampala, Clinton touched down in the neighbouring country of Rwanda before finally leaving the region. For security reasons he never actually left the airport at the Rwandan capital, Kigali, and his visit was intended simply to show respect for the victims of the 1994 genocide and express support for the Rwandan people and regime (under the new president, Kagame). Local reactions were mixed: while welcoming the demonstration of sympathy, the country would actually have preferred more concrete help with national reconstruction, which Clinton was unable to provide for budgetary reasons. However, he did apologise for not doing so.

The last of the countries on Clinton's tour of Africa was Senegal. There, the American president looked back on a shameful episode in the history of Afro-American relations: the slave trade. He visited Gorée Island which dominates Dakar harbour and was originally named 'Goede Rede' (Good Roadstead) by Dutch traders impressed by its quality as an anchorage. Once an entrepôt for slaves waiting to be loaded onto ships for the long voyage to the Western hemisphere, the island is now a world heritage site with many monuments to the horrors of slavery. The approximately thirty million citizens of the United States who are descended from African slaves – now known as Afro-Americans – are an important factor in contemporary American politics. Prior to the visit, there had been some debate about whether the president should apologise for America's participation in the slave trade but in the end Clinton chose not to.

Clinton's tour of Africa was spectacular from both the American and the African point of view, but its long-term effect was limited. Washington immediately turned its attention to other, more important issues. The new Africa policy never really got off the ground, firstly because no extra financial resources were made available, but also because few American politicians shared the president's optimism. Where he saw an African renaissance, they saw only poverty, corruption, death and destruction, and thought the US should keep well away from it. Work on the plans for trade and for the African peacekeeping force suffered endless delay and Clinton's presidency was almost over before much had been implemented.

In August 2000, in the last days of his presidency, Clinton paid another visit to Africa. This time, the trip attracted little attention, partly because it had little political significance. The political scene in the US was already dominated by the struggle to succeed Clinton and the president could launch no new American initiatives for Africa. He did, however, visit Nigeria to express encouragement for the democratic system that had been reinstated there in 1999 and to ask the country, as a member of OPEC and in the interests of the global economy, to help reduce the price of oil by increasing production. That done, he went on to Arusha in Tanzania to assist Nelson Mandela – now the former president of South Africa – in what was supposed to be the concluding stage of talks to end the civil war in Burundi. In the event, however, not even the presence of the American president could persuade the opposing parties to abandon their cutthroat enmity and sign a peace agreement. For the Africa policy of Clinton's successor, George W. Bush (the son of Clinton's predecessor), see chapter 10, pp. 344-346.

Under Clinton's successor, George W. Bush, US political interest in Africa declined. President Bush refused to consider any substantial increase in the low American aid budget. He felt it was mainly up to African governments to put their own house in order through democratisation, respect for human rights, observance of the rule of law and the pursuit of sober financial and economic policies. This would not only attract private investment from abroad, but also make foreign aid more effective.

Optimism versus pessimism

Clinton's 1998 initiative was significant as an attempt to end America's indifference to Africa. It made the continent a somewhat higher international priority, especially because the US expressed the intention of encouraging other industrialised countries to become active in Africa. This was not difficult to do, since Africa had been attracting almost universal attention in 1996 and 1997. The Asian growth economies were showing interest in it for the first time and even the United Nations Development Programme (UNDP) Human Development Reports, usually a source of pessimism, had become surprisingly optimistic in tone. In effect, therefore, the American initiative was more a symptom of international interest in the continent than a driving force.

The upturn in international interest had not, however, eliminated an extremely negative and pessimistic attitude towards Africa among some in the West. This attitude had actually been reinforced by the major setbacks of the 1970s and 1980s and some people now refused to believe in Africa's ability ever to catch up with the rest of the world and integrate into the global economic system. It was just too far behind and too different. In development terms (the main international yardstick), Africa was regarded as a lost continent. This image was so powerful that it could not be stamped out by a few years of good news. Even in the 1990s, pessimism continued to underlie attitudes towards Africa, despite the optimism about the continent's future that emerged alongside it.

Before proceeding to examine these ideas in more detail, it is important to identify the traditional holders of these opposing views. The pessimists were largely to be found in 'colonial' circles: people who had been against the transfer of power from the start and thought that independent Africa was bound to come to a sticky end. This current of belief continued to thrive among conservatives on the political right. By contrast, the optimists were to be found among the advocates of independence, and in particular among the progressives on the political left. They were often critical of relations between the West and the Third World (which they felt continued to be exploitative, even after decolonisation), but agreed with the first postindependence leaders of Africa that the continent could expect a bright future if it were only given a 'fair' chance. To preserve this positive image of Africa, reports of problems like growing corruption were swept under the carpet. People working in the development field in the 1970s and 1980s tended to be optimists. The collapse of communism (their underlying ideology or, at any rate, a source of inspiration for many of them) had made this group – if not less numerous – at least less clamorous.

But help was to come from an unexpected quarter. Emerging from the Cold War as the victors, the political right – libertarian democrats and capitalists – seized their opportunity to reshape the world. Democracy and the market-based economy were to reign supreme, even in Africa. No region, however backward or culturally divorced from the West, presented an intrinsic problem: it had simply opted for the wrong system. Political and economic liberalisation would soon put things right.

Although the debate between optimists and pessimists was conducted principally among Western intellectuals, it had very real consequences for Africa. After all, those most fervently for or against the new optimism included many Westerners who were professionally involved with the continent, whether as politicians, government officials or staff of NGOs.

They not only had a heavy influence on the international image of Africa, but also played a decisive role in establishing the international aid policies on which a considerable portion of the income of African countries depended.

While in the West, therefore, the debate on the negative or positive prospects for Africa might at times have seemed academic, for African leaders it was very far from it. For them, it was politically and economically crucial to project a positive image of development in their own countries and of their own style of government. Admittedly, African leaders had become better at this since independence, but the changes in the international situation following the end of the Cold War called for considerable adaptation. This was a problem for some of the long-established 'dinosaurs' surviving from the immediate postindependence era. Others, in particular the 'new leaders', knew how to strike the right tone and became the new darlings of the donor community. So the debate between optimists and the pessimists was in fact directly connected with aid to Africa.

The debate itself went as follows. To start with, around 1990 the deplorable state of Africa was clear to everybody and the pessimists had no serious challengers. The new optimists responded by looking for any faint glimmer of hope, which they then talked up and presented as the light at the end of the tunnel. The pessimists parried these attempts either by interpreting the same phenomena so differently that they could be completely discounted, or by identifying a host of equally significant adverse features or events to cancel out any hopeful signs.

If the optimists pointed to democratisation, the pessimists retorted that greater democracy had not always led to any significant change of power. And, they added, where power had indeed changed hands, it had produced little perceptible change in the style of government or in policies. In any case, any changes that did take place were unlikely to benefit the people of the countries concerned, or at least not in the foreseeable future. If the optimists called attention to a new and positive trend in the economy, the pessimists dismissed it out of hand. After all, they would argue, many major countries in Africa (including Nigeria, Congo and Sudan) had no share in it, and how could anybody think that the smaller countries could serve as an engine of growth for the bigger ones? It was far more likely that the smaller countries would be dragged down by the deadweight of their larger neighbours. Growth in foreign investment was minimal and, subtracting investments in oil and other minerals, it was virtually zero. If the optimists pointed to peace deals, there were always new outbreaks of war to prove the pessimists' contention that their significance was only local. And if the assertive style of government of the new leaders was thrown into the discussion, the pessimists referred knowingly to the unabashed way in which those same leaders committed violations of human rights.

These rhetorical exchanges could have gone on for ever. What changes could be regarded as presaging real improvement? Was democratisation to be seen as the start of something new and better, despite the unfavourable environment in which it was occurring? Were the signs of economic improvement harbingers of permanent recovery or merely passing spasms in a system that was chronically sick or perhaps even on its deathbed? What is quite certain is that, despite the enormous size of Africa and the diversity of its problems, there never were two diametrically opposed situations: one sunny and one pitch black. In some places, of course, the overall situation was a lot better than elsewhere, but the underlying problems were the same throughout the continent. Even where progress was being made, they lurked beneath the surface, and even in places where they dominated, it was surely at least theoretically possible to overcome them. Everywhere, the situation was a mixture of light and dark.

The debate on the future of Africa seldom addressed long-term, structural trends. Why was Africa virtually unable to achieve progress while developing countries elsewhere in the world were far more successful? Why had there been such a deterioration since independence, for example in Africa's position in the global economy? What were Africa's structural problems after independence? For answers to these questions, we shall focus – as promised – on the changes in the African states. These can provide a basis for the explanation of many events on the continent and eventually (in the closing section of the conclusions) for a discussion of the current prospects for Africa.

There is no doubt that the growing ineffectiveness of public institutions in Africa was responsible for many of the continent's problems. By the 1990s, this had reached such proportions in some countries that it led to escalating internal violence and ultimately to a major war in Central Africa. These events, which are the subject of the next two chapters, served throughout the 1990s as the main argument against any overly optimistic view of Africa's future. In 1998 they tipped the balance once again in favour of pessimism. By doing so, they undermined international support for the idea of an African renaissance. Nevertheless, that dream continued to live on in many parts of Africa, especially where it had started: in the minds of the postapartheid leaders of South Africa.

Nelson Mandela

The main proponent of the concept of an African renaissance may have been Thabo Mbeki, the first black deputy president of South Africa, but it was Nelson Mandela, the country's first black president, who personified the ideal. Mandela's own life story, of freedom after long years of imprisonment, reflected the whole history of the continent's transition from colonialism to independence. Accordingly, he became a figurehead of the renaissance movement. But Mandela was even more than that. Through the respect that his charm and absolute integrity earned him in his own country and abroad, he became the living symbol of Africa in the 1990s. Whenever cynics sneered that Africa never produced anything worthwhile except athletes and musicians, it was always possible to point to Mandela to prove the contrary. Mandela was Africa's homegrown saint.

Nelson Mandela was born in 1918 in Umtata, a town in Transkei, in the southeast of South Africa, near the Indian Ocean. At the height of his fame, attempts were made to match his origins to his later status. As befits a true leader, he was supposed to have royal blood in his veins. However, Mandela himself has always publicly rejected such attempts at myth-making. He was not the scion of a royal house, although his father's family did have the traditional status of advisers to a local African ruler and was therefore fairly prominent locally. His father died when Nelson was twelve and the child was placed in the care of the local king, who ensured that he received the best education available. The name Nelson was bestowed on him by a primary school teacher who felt that all children should have first names. At the age of twenty-three, Nelson Mandela went to Johannesburg, the largest city in South Africa, to study law.

There he experienced the apartheid system at first hand and quickly became politicised as a result. He played a major role in the revival of the ANC in the 1940s, when the black population were experiencing a period of relative prosperity that prompted an intensification of apartheid. At the time, Mandela was earning his living as a member of the first black law practice in South Africa, but he became increasingly involved in the resistance against apartheid. Arrests and trials followed, culminating in his 1964 sentence of life imprisonment for 'treason'. Mandela served his term in a variety of prisons, including fourteen years on Robben Island (a sort of 'Alcatraz' off the coast of Cape Town). His incarceration gave him long years in which to reflect and to think about his own future and that of his country. In the 1970s he was almost forgotten, but the ANC and in particular his wife Winnie – left at home with two daughters – did their utmost to keep his name alive as a national symbol of the struggle against apartheid. And they succeeded. When the white government decided to consult the black majority on the future of the country, Mandela was the obvious person to approach. In the 1980s, therefore, a string of secret talks took place between the members of the white regime and the prisoner on Robben Island. Eventually, Mandela was transferred to a prison on the mainland, and soon after that released.

In February 1990, after 27 years in prison, the great day had come. The release of Mandela was broadcast live around the world. It was as if the dignified, elderly figure – for Mandela was now seventy-four years old – had only to walk up to the television cameras to be universally accepted as leader. Black South Africa now had a lever with which to end apartheid. Mandela became the president of the ANC and chief negotiator in the talks on the ending of apartheid. The white South African community saw him as somebody who could be trusted, despite all he had suffered, and who would ensure that no bloody retribution was exacted for the events of the past. The transition was gradual and it was another four long years before it culminated in all-race general elections, held in 1994. This was the first time that Nelson Mandela had ever had the chance to vote. He won the elections with a huge majority and, at the age of seventy-eight, was sworn in as the country's president.

As agreed before the elections, Mandela formed a government of national unity whose task was to hold the country together now that it was a 'rainbow nation' (multicoloured rather than multiracial). With his aura of wisdom and integrity, Mandela was the ideal man for the job. As the country's first black president, he presented himself as the father of the nation and the embodiment of a unified South Africa. His success in nurturing a feeling of national unity was reinforced by several major international sporting victories. In 1995 South Africa triumphed on the rugby field (a white domain) when it won the World Cup and in 1996 on the football pitch (a black domain) when it carried off the African Cup of Nations. On both occasions, Mandela was a prominent and enthusiastic supporter, decked out in the appropriate team colours. His success in maintaining national unity throughout the almost bloodless transition from the apartheid era was the greatest feat of his political life. The difficulty of controlling such a process was demonstrated by the dramatic events in countries where discrimination similar to apartheid had been practised between black and black, especially in Liberia (see chapter 5) and Rwanda (see chapter 6).

However, Mandela's government of national unity was not destined to survive for long. The white Afrikaner National Party had claimed – and perhaps hoped – that it would be able to act as an intermediary between the black members of the government and mainly white institutions like the army, the local and international business community and governments in the West. In practice, this proved unworkable. Almost everybody wanted to deal directly with Mandela. Accordingly, there was little point in having a white presence in the government and in 1996 the National Party joined the opposition.

This was a major test for South African democracy and it passed with flying colours. The white withdrawal from the government caused no deterioration in relations between the different races in South Africa. Perhaps, however, it did make it even more difficult for Mandela's government to persuade the black population of the need for moderation in the way it ruled the country. Many people felt that the Truth and Reconciliation Commission was not the best way to deal with those who had committed violations of human rights during the apartheid era, particularly because the Commission uncovered an unexpectedly large amount of information about violations perpetrated by antiapartheid activists. However, Mandela's prestige was still sufficient to ensure that the Commission could continue its work.

No black government leader in history had ever had access to such a wealth of resources as the South African state now had at its fingertips. Even so, it was not possible immediately to solve the vast problems of inequality, poverty and unemployment that were the legacy of apartheid in South Africa. A careful balance had to be maintained between the need to redistribute resources and opportunities among the various sections of the population and the need to avoid killing the goose that laid the golden eggs. It was vital that the national and global business community should not lose confidence in the future of South Africa, since that would lead to an economic recession which would make it impossible to improve the standard of living of the black population. Mandela himself was closely involved in projects to improve conditions for black children, for example by providing school meals. Social inequality was just one of South Africa's many structural problems that could only begin to be addressed effectively through Mandela's personal intervention.

The abolition of apartheid instantly ended South Africa's political isolation. The world expected a great deal of the new regional power, but Mandela's government was hesitant about asserting itself, especially within Africa. Even so, the sudden elevation of Mandela to a prominent position in world affairs created friction between him and President Mugabe of Zimbabwe (who had been in office for fifteen years and had come to see himself as more than just the leader of a medium-sized African country).

Mandela was called on to intervene in all sorts of international issues. His successful management of the process of reconciliation between groups in his own country led to expectations that he could engineer peace elsewhere in Africa. But this proved not to be the case. South African efforts to broker peace in Central Africa were particularly unsuccessful. First of all, Mandela was turned down by Kabila when he tried to prevent further bloodshed during the overthrow of Mobutu. The rebel leader preferred to march directly on the capital, Kinshasa, rather than pause for talks with Mandela and his rival Mobutu that were likely to give him less than complete power over the country. Similarly, South Africa tried in vain to establish negotiations between the various hostile elements at the start of the major war in Central Africa.

That same year (1998), while Mandela was out of the country, the South African army joined with that of Botswana – officially under the flag of SADC – in invading the diminutive member state of Lesotho. The aim was to restore order in the small mountain enclave within South Africa, where elections had been followed by unrest and the risk of a coup by junior army officers. In large parts of Africa there was a storm of protest at what was seen as South Africa's arrogance in invading the tiny kingdom.

In fact, Mandela was never able to pursue any effective foreign policy. His inability was largely due to the struggle within government between the old right-wing white officials and new left-wing (black) ANC members. This raged not only within the Ministry of Foreign Affairs, but also in the army and the intelligence service. Nevertheless, the president's image remained untarnished by these foreign policy problems, both in South Africa and abroad.

In 1998 he passed responsibility for the day-to-day running of the country to Deputy President Mbeki, while himself retaining the official titles of president of South Africa and leader of the ANC. With Mandela as its icon, the ANC won an easy victory in the country's second all-race general elections. In view of his advanced age, however, Mandela had already said he was unwilling to serve the whole of a second term. In mid-1999 he stepped down as president of South Africa. Nevertheless, he remained involved in the process of national transition and acted outside the country as a facilitator of peace negotiations in Burundi, taking over the role from ex-President Nyerere of Tanzania following the latter's death.

The presidency of South Africa was taken over by Mbeki. Despite the wars that were plaguing the continent, he tried to revive interest in the idea of an African renaissance and at the end of the century presented a Millennium Partnership for the African Recovery (known for short as the Millennium Action Plan or MAP), drawn up by South Africa in cooperation with several other countries in Africa. This initiative was subsequently expanded by a number of African heads of state, including Mbeki, to form NEPAD, the New Partnership for Africa's Development (see chapter 9).

5
DISINTEGRATION

Failing states

Towards the end of the twentieth century, states all over the world were forced to adjust to new technological, economic, political, social and cultural developments. In order to survive, they needed to move forward. Many of these developments were facets of globalisation (see chapter 7) and first emerged in the 1980s, in other words, before the end of the Cold War. In fact, globalisation and its attendant changes played an important part in the ending of the Cold War, as Western states became more efficient and effective under the pressures of globalisation, while the Eastern Bloc collapsed under the challenge. Even so, the countries that survived the Cold War were forced to adjust their basic concepts of the nation-state. For example, control of a fixed territory, the foundation of the state par excellence, was challenged by the 'virtual reality' of new technologies, and state sovereignty proved no longer to be an absolute, but a divisible notion with relevance from the local to the supranational level.

Globalisation is first and foremost a technological and economic phenomenon whose greatest impact has been felt in the most developed regions of the world, in other words, in North America, Europe and parts of Asia. It largely bypassed Africa, due to the continent's lag in technological development and limited integration into world markets, although its indirect consequences were substantial, especially for the position of African states. The end of the Cold War, which, as noted, cannot be separated from globalisation, drastically altered the global balance of power. Africa lost its strategic significance, and, by extension, African governments saw their guarantees of stability fade from one day to the next.

From Ethiopia to Mozambique, the implications were enormous. African governments would have to fend for themselves in future, while the outside world looked on (at best). In order to survive, governing elites became more dependent upon their position in their own countries and their relationship with the rest of society. In developed countries, there is usually a complex interplay between state institutions, civil society and the private sector. These three elements not only contribute to social stability, but also complement each other. With the exception of South Africa, however, African countries were not familiar with this type of stable social system. In many cases, the governing elites had deliberately prevented the development of civil society and the private sector, placing all their bets on the state. When the structure of the state began to crumble, both the position of the elites and the cohesion of society were therefore in immediate danger. African society slowly started to disintegrate.

In hindsight, it is clear that the African states could never have stayed the course they embarked upon in the 1960s and 1970s. In fact, due to their low levels of socioeconomic development, their state structures had never amounted to very much to begin with. In addition, a state that has no counterweight, no system of checks and balances, will inevitably fall victim to corruption. In the African environment, in which relationships were more personal than professional and the distinction between the public and private spheres was almost non-existent, this phenomenon became very common. Throughout the continent, corruption took hold in state institutions, from the highest level to the lowest. Citizens had to bribe officials to receive basic government services. This was not just because civil servants were filling their own pockets; in addition from time to time, state power was systematically exploited to extort money from the population. In this manner, the state became a predator that fed on the resources of its citizens. This type of predatory state was far removed from the ideal of the state as an institution that promotes the development of its citizens and of society as a whole.[86]

The predatory state was not a new phenomenon in Africa. Its origins can be traced back to the colonialism of the 1930s, when certain groups first began to exploit state structures to generate private income. These groups essentially lived on 'rents' (payments extorted from productive economic sectors such as agriculture and trade). Following independence, this parasitic behaviour, which used the state as a instrument for living off society, continued to characterise the African elites and became increasingly significant.

As the economic situation deteriorated, the internal revenues of the state began to dry up, forcing the elite to look for new sources of income. Political and military rulers often organised dubious schemes for personal gain, such as backroom deals to export natural resources or illegal drug trafficking. These activities were sometimes more lucrative than official means of generating state revenue, despite the fact that the government was extorting as much money as it could from the population in addition to receiving foreign development aid. The state thus became a shadow state, constituting little more than a useful façade for the private machinations of its leaders.[87]

Under these circumstances, the population could no longer regard the government as an ally, and the state became an enemy that needed to be kept at a distance. Especially in remote rural areas, where extortion was at its worst, the population tried to keep the state at bay. At the same time, the state was also becoming less popular in the cities, due to a deterioration in the provision of services and staff cutbacks. In the 1980s, states all over Africa lost a substantial amount of legitimacy in the eyes of their populations. They were no longer in the least representative, not to mention democratic. The state's failure to promote development or even carry out its most basic tasks completed this dismal picture. The relationship between the citizens and the state was breaking down. This was exacerbated by the disintegration of traditional networks of patronage between the authorities and their clients in the cities, once the elite became short of funds and were less and less able to bestow government positions or smaller favours. On the contrary, lost jobs and an inability to meet expectations led to a dangerous rise in frustration and anger towards leading politicians.

In the 1980s, the bankruptcy of the African states presented the elites with a dilemma. Continuing on the same footing would destroy their societies, as next to nothing remained of the economic foundations of the state. However, the only alternative that presented itself, namely, the internationally supported structural adjustment programmes, did not offer a much better prospect. Through the IMF and the World Bank, international donors had instructed African states to restore financial stability, and this could not be achieved without cutbacks in public expenditure. In Africa, however, a higher proportion of public spending went to goods and services than in other parts of the world; basically, African governments spent a larger proportion on civil-service salaries than their counterparts in Europe or Asia, and less on investment. The required cutbacks were therefore bound to affect civil servants. As a result of lost public employment opportunities, the networks of patronage lost their importance and support for political leaders began to erode.

It is hardly surprising that African governments tried to delay these reforms – which were central to the adjustment programmes – for as long as possible. The people behind structural adjustment, most of whom were in Washington, were probably vaguely aware of the political repercussions of their demands, but were either unable or unwilling to take them into account. The struggling African governments would just have to sink or swim.

So what was the political and economic condition of the African state at the beginning of the 1990s? It is obviously difficult to speak of *the* African state, due to the great diversity among the more than forty countries of sub-Saharan Africa. Some states fared a great deal better than others, but none managed to evade the above-mentioned problems entirely. In different states, different factors dominated the overall picture. Some states appeared to have put the worst behind them and were back on track as a result of democratisation and institution-building, but in others disintegration was already so far advanced that it began to look doubtful whether the process could still be reversed.

The state's ability to carry out effective policies was frequently compromised. At the centre of power, in the capital's government buildings and primarily in the office of the president, policies were still being made, but the chances that they would actually be put into practice had become small. In fact, they varied according to the policy area in question. Policies regarding the security of the regime, which concerned the military and the police, and foreign policy, which concerned donor relations, had priority. African governments were also fairly active in the economic sphere, since the international financial institutions were monitoring this policy as part of the structural adjustment programmes. In some countries, however, government had all but ground to a halt in other policy areas. In many cases, civil servants still came to the office, at least for part of the formal working day, but their presence there was becoming increasingly symbolic. Their work was no longer aimed at achieving results, but instead took on a ritualistic nature. Despite its continued physical presence, the state had thus become non-existent from a practical point of view.

The term 'non-existent' sounds deceptively neutral. In reality, the failure of the African state constituted a very serious problem, whose magnitude was not yet fully appreciated in the early 1990s. In the absence of a functioning state, the simplest tasks in areas such as public safety, health care, education, infrastructure and water supply could not be performed – especially not in Africa, where there were few alternative providers of these services besides religious institutions. In many countries, the state aggravated existing social problems through corruption and predation. The social structure, based on clientelist networks, started to collapse, and some groups became estranged from the state, either because it was no longer able to reach them or because they were actively avoiding contact with it for reasons of self-preservation.

As the state's power base narrowed, the elite turned to ever smaller groups whose loyalty it could still afford to buy. As a rule, these were ethnically defined and were granted material privileges unavailable to other ethnic groups. Struggling governments abandoned the politics of consensus, despite the fact that it had served as the basis for societal support almost everywhere in Africa since the continent had gained independence. This politically motivated ethnic fragmentation gave rise to tensions that could not always be controlled. The failure of the state thus led to new internal security problems (discussed later in this chapter).

African states are often characterised as having a 'weak' hold on their societies. This is most meaningfully translated as 'ineffective', rather than, for instance, 'mild'. As little as the state was able to achieve, it was definitely not gentle, but remained as authoritarian as it had always been. The authorities fiercely defended what remained of their privileges. Depending on the stage of the state's decline, as well as other circumstances, they usually managed to prevent it from collapsing completely. Chapter 4 describes how the so-called 'new leaders' of Ethiopia, Eritrea, Uganda and Rwanda gave new life to their war-torn governmental structures through authoritarian measures. Other states failed completely, but did not collapse. Zaire is the best example of this.

Mobutu and the erosion of the Zairean state

Zaire (now known as Congo), which covers most of Central Africa, has always loomed large in African history. In addition to its location and sheer size, it undoubtedly derives its importance from its rich supply of natural resources. The greed of King Leopold of Belgium, who was eager to get his hands on Congo's wealth, was one of the main reasons for the international Berlin Conference of 1885, which established the rules for the partition of Africa by the European powers. The role of the country in the decolonisation process was equally noteworthy. The rapid decolonisation of Belgian Congo was a tumultuous affair, as were the first years of the country's independence. Under the leadership of President Mobutu Sese Seko, Zaire achieved a measure of stability (with the support of the United States, France and Belgium), which lasted for a surprisingly long time after the end of the Cold War. However, Mobutu's regime (1965-1997) did not provide a sound basis for the country's development. In fact, development was never a serious objective for Mobutu, and most areas of political and economic activity actually deteriorated. By the end of his regime, state institutions had been reduced to a husk and hardly any were still functioning.

Take the Ministry of the Interior. This would have ordinarily been an important institution in a country that is four times the size of France and has more than fifty million inhabitants. Instead, it was housed entirely within a single villa in Kinshasa. State institutions with larger premises, such as the Ministry of Foreign Affairs, had many empty rooms. Even the most basic activities were no longer carried out there. If Western ambassadors needed landing permits for emergency aid flights from their countries to Zaire, for example, they had to type them up on their own typewriters. However, since they were unable to place an official Zairean stamp on the permits, they had to comb the empty corridors and rooms of the ministry for a remaining official who could do it for them.

The country's tragic past – as a slave depot, exploited colony and Cold War pawn – points towards a series of historical injustices as the explanation for Zaire's collapse. It would appear that the country never stood a chance. This approach is too simple, however, as the history of Congo-Zaire-Congo (the country kept switching names) is not just a catalogue of misfortunes. Like almost all other African ex-colonies, Belgian Congo experienced a period of progress after World War II. The 1950s, in particular, were a decade of economic success. The hostilities immediately following independence temporarily brought an end to this, but progress subsequently continued where it had left off. Not until 1974 did the country enter its long downward spiral, with a drop in the price of copper on the world market and, subsequently, a disastrous campaign of 'Zaireanisation'.[88] The country fell into uninterrupted decline in the 1980s and 1990s.

Apart from the price of copper on the world market (an external variable that could not be influenced) Mobutu's policies provide the only explanation for the country's decline. Mobutu leaned heavily on Western countries and companies, and this enabled him to operate independently of his country's people. He thus required little domestic support to remain in power, and the bond that had developed between Mobutu and parts of the population when he put an end to domestic instability in the 1960s gradually disintegrated. The regime and the population both felt that they had to fend for themselves. In many respects, they actually succeeded in doing so (especially the regime), at least as long as the Cold War continued. After the end of the Cold War, however, the government's international ties started to weaken, and Mobutu became increasingly isolated. Being a consummate politician, he managed to hold on to power for a number of years more. Using a policy of divide and rule, he did not hesitate to set population groups against each other while simultaneously cultivating the image that only he – the captain of Zaire – could hold the divided country together. He has been jokingly described as a *pompier pyromane*, a pyromaniac fireman.[89]

If Nelson Mandela symbolises the promising aspects of recent African history, Mobutu serves as a symbol of its dark side. The manner in which he sacrificed his country's political and economic potential for the sake of self-enrichment is reminiscent of many other African presidents. However, Mobutu's position and conduct were more characteristic of Africa during the 1970s and 1980s than after the Cold War. During the 1990s, many long-serving African presidents – also referred to as 'dinosaurs' – came under fire from their own populations. One leader after another was forced to step down. The fact that Mobutu survived until 1996 was exceptional and, frankly, an anachronism. In that respect, he is not such an appropriate symbol of Africa's troubles after the Cold War, although his regime did bear a large share of the responsibility for a situation in Central Africa that largely determined the image of the whole continent at the end of the twentieth century.

Mobutu was extremely authoritarian, but did not control anything like the whole of the country, as state power was too weak for this purpose. At a distance from the capital and the provincial centres of power, local leaders were able to make their limited influence felt. But they were unable to influence national politics, which would remain in the hands of the president until he died or was driven out of the country.

It was to be the latter. The Rwandan genocide of 1994 brought the Tutsi-controlled RPF to power in Kigali and led to a massive influx of Rwandan refugees into eastern Zaire, where tensions between Hutu and Tutsi also began to escalate. In addition, the two groups continued their armed struggle on Zairean territory. Mobutu was powerless to stop the fighting; in fact, the Tutsi leaders in Rwanda managed to put pressure on the government in Kinshasa, supporting local Zairean exiles in their revolt against Mobutu. In 1996, the exiles began a march on Kinshasa under the command of the local rebel leader and smuggler Laurent Kabila. In a matter of weeks, they succeeded in breaking Mobutu's hold on power. Mobutu finally left Zaire in early 1997, only to die six months later in exile in Morocco. Kabila became the new strongman in Kinshasa.

However, few institutions remained for governing the country from Kinshasa, and the new president did not arrive in the capital with a substantial power base of his own. Kabila had been an opponent of the Mobutu regime for many years, but his power had never transcended the local level in eastern Zaire, and his name was unknown in the rest of the country. The fact that he had happened to find himself in a position to finally oust Mobutu made him a popular man in many Zairean circles, but did not mean that he could count on widespread support. Zaire was too fragmented for that, in every respect. The new president's circle of loyal supporters was even smaller than Mobutu's. In fact, Kabila's position in Kinshasa depended entirely on the support of foreign powers: primarily the RPF regime in Rwanda, under the leadership of then Vice President Paul Kagame, and the regime of President Yoweri Museveni of Uganda.

Kabila's close links with Museveni and Kagame, who were widely regarded as 'new leaders' (see chapter 4), seemed a hopeful sign that he too would try to rebuild the state, whether in an authoritarian manner or otherwise. The new president certainly did everything he could to emphasise the break with the Mobutu era. He replaced the name Zaire, which had been introduced by Mobutu, with the country's former name and the descriptive phrase 'democratic republic'.[90] This produced the peculiar result 'Democratic Republic of Congo' (DRC for short).[91] After all, the country could hardly be described as democratic, even if Kabila may at one time have entertained thoughts of democratisation. In addition, the term 'republic' only applied in the most formal sense. With regard to the original meaning of the term – *res publica* or 'public interest' – there were few countries in the world where the public interest received less attention than in Congo. This book will henceforth refer to the DRC simply as Congo, unless there is a risk of confusing it with the much smaller country of Congo (Brazzaville), which is located on the other side of the Congo River.

The new regime did not bring economic recovery to Congo, and Kabila continued his predecessor's poor policies. He allowed a lot of money to be printed, bringing inflation to dizzying heights, but also tried to maintain an artificially high exchange rate. That guaranteed the survival of the black market. In addition, the regime maintained restrictions on the use of foreign currency, plundered state-owned companies mercilessly and forced businesspeople, who had sometimes retained limited freedom of action under Mobutu, to place themselves increasingly 'at the disposal of the government'. In accordance with time-honoured African tradition, the political authorities tried to seize control of private economic power. Once they had succeeded in doing so, they tried to enrich themselves. In this respect, Kabila and his entourage were worthy successors to Mobutu, although there was less and less to steal in Kinshasa. The Congolese economy contracted further each year. At the millennium, perhaps as much as eighty per cent of state revenue went to the military and the security services. Less than two per cent of the state budget was spent on health care, and less than one per cent on education.

In early 2001, when Kablila was shot dead by one of his bodyguards, whatever political control remained in Congo was concentrated in the hands of his family and a small circle of loyal supporters. As a result, the number of potential successors was limited, and Kabila's son Joseph was immediately nominated. The succession was unconstitutional, as Joseph Kabila did not meet the constitutional requirements for holding the presidency (he was only thirty-one years old, rather than the required forty, and had not been born in Congo, but probably in Tanzania), but nobody made an issue of this. More remarkable even than the unconstitutionality of the succession was its monarchic character, which was a rarity for an independent African country. The monarchic succession in Kinshasa – 'Kabila is dead, long live Kabila' – demonstrated that the *res publica*, the public interest, had shrunk so much that it now covered just *one* family.[92]

The family and its supporters were entirely dependent on foreign powers. From 1997 until August 1998, those powers were Rwanda and Uganda, followed by Angola, Zimbabwe and Namibia. Territorial sovereignty was not much more than an illusion in many African states, but in Congo it was truly a fantasy.[93] Instead of state institutions, an administrative vacuum existed in the heart of Africa. Neighbouring heads of state were aware of this. Thus, President Museveni of Uganda once declared that Congo was just an area on the map, not a country. The situation was unstable; historically, political vacuums have always sucked in the surrounding countries. Museveni's assessment of the situation in Congo was undoubtedly at the root of the decision by Uganda and Rwanda to install a new government in Kinshasa in 1998, thereby plunging the whole of Central Africa into war (see chapter 6).

New threats

In the first years after independence, the deterioration of the state did not have a serious impact on daily life in Zaire. For some years – in fact, for two whole decades – living standards gradually declined throughout the continent. Services such as education and health care grew more and more scarce, but the social structure did not collapse.

During the 1990s, however, that began to change in countries whose security was under threat. As noted above, the state institutions responsible for maintaining peace and security were often the last affected by the disintegration of the state, but this did not mean that they remained intact. The armed forces and the rest of the security apparatus also began to operate less effectively. Professionalism declined, corruption could no longer be resisted and demoralisation took hold. Police and defence-related expenditure sometimes stagnated and sometimes declined as a result of cutbacks. In general, there was less 'bang for your buck'.

The decline of the security apparatus took place against a background of rising political, economic, social and ethnic tension. The power base of the elite was weakened by the bankruptcy of the state and the subsequent structural adjustment programmes, making it impossible to maintain all the networks of patronage. As a result, alternative centres of power had an opportunity to make a name for themselves. Such a change in the domestic balance of power is comparable to a change in the balance of power between states. Just as the relative decline of a hegemonic power can lead to war with newly ascendant powers, so too the weakened position of governing elites encouraged violent conflict within African states. The government's monopoly on violence is one of the main characteristics of the modern state. Its breakdown opens the way to internal conflict.

The risk of such conflict is greater in societies consisting of groups with different historical, linguistic, economic, religious and cultural characteristics. In such 'multicultural' societies, loyalty to subgroups can easily become more important than loyalty to the state. For struggling politicians, manipulating ethnic loyalties can be a simple and occasionally effective way of advancing their own interests. Inciting mutual feelings of hatred between population groups can lead to what, in the African context, has been described as 'tribalism': belligerent posturing by population groups in the supposed manner of 'old-fashioned tribes'.

The potential for violence in heterogeneous societies is reduced when significant distinctions do not coincide; for example, when local or religious minorities do not consist exclusively of rich or poor individuals, but display the same variety as the rest of the country when it comes to the distribution of wealth. Shared interests among individuals from different groups prevent too much tension from building. If there are no shared interests, which is often the case in Africa due to simple social structures, there is a greater risk of irreconcilable differences. In addition, if one group completely dominates another, there is a risk of revolutionary violence. For these reasons, violent conflicts often have their roots in political, economic and cultural inequality and discrimination, as well as marginalisation and exclusion. In consociational societies, in which distinct but equal groups live side by side, conflicts may arise if elites pit their followers against each other. In situations of this kind, power-sharing agreements among the elites can keep a lid on tensions.[94]

In some African countries, valuable natural resources were a major source of conflict. As long as the state was strong, it could prey on such resources, without regard to ordinary sources of state revenue like taxation. However, if ever the state's hold on natural resources weakened, other, non-state groups emerged that sought to wrest control of them by force. In cases where they succeeded, the state lost much of its revenue, and gained a rich and powerful rival.

The economic and political implications of this were considerable. Occasionally, governments that were powerless to combat such 'rebels' would single-handedly attempt to avert the danger with the help of private security organisations, which essentially consisted of mercenaries. These organisations were often remarkably professional and well equipped, and considerably more effective than what remained of the state's own armed forces. However, substantial risks came with delegating such a fundamental aspect of national sovereignty to private organisations. When the contract ended, so did the security. In addition, there was no link between the public and the security services, which further eroded the legitimacy of the state's actions. The rise of competing centres of power, each with its own economic base, clearly posed a danger to the continued integrity of the state.

In the 1990s, the rise of alternative centres of power within the territories of African states was a new phenomenon. During the Cold War, roving bandits had stood no chance against the armed forces of the internationally supported regimes in the capital. Now that this support had disappeared, warlords cropped up in various places, especially in locations where valuable resources, such as diamonds, could be exploited. Charles Taylor, in Liberia, was the first significant example.

However, it would be a inaccurate to view warlords as something entirely new to modern Africa. After all, how great were the differences between warlords like Taylor and 'legitimate' heads of state like Mobutu in Zaire and Samuel Doe in Liberia, when it came to their economic base and their relationship with the population? Heads of state also preyed on the resources in their territory, and had often derived their veneer of legitimacy solely from their role in the Cold War struggle. If Taylor was a roving bandit, could Mobutu not be described, with equal justification, as a stationary bandit?

One difference was that, in exchange for international support, the presidents of the Cold War period were obliged to abide by certain international rules. They were restricted to their own territories and had to refrain from interfering in neighbouring countries (though they did support rebel groups on occasion). The disappearance of the international order imposed by the Cold War turned the stationary bandit in the capital into little more than just another actor competing for power within the territory of the state. At the same time, the concept of territorial integrity was losing significance. If the international community cared so little about Africa's internal borders, why should the warlords care about them? If Liberian diamonds were a source of wealth and power, why not push through to the diamond fields of Sierra Leone to increase that wealth and power? Due to the influence of African renaissance ideology (see chapter 4), the borders between African states were already seen as more permeable. It was thought that this would promote the development of Africa as a whole. It was in some ways a nice idea, but in combination with the decline of the state it made national borders seem almost irrelevant. In this context, it is worth remembering that the borders in question had been drawn by the colonial powers, not by Africans, as a result of which they had always had a special status.

From a political, economic and military point of view, Africa's internal borders took on a new, far lower status in the 1990s. As national borders in the developed world lost their significance under the impact of globalisation, especially as a result of technological advances, the role of borders in Africa also changed. This change may have been of an entirely different nature, but it could be traced indirectly to the same process of globalisation.

In various African countries, complex military conflicts developed between all kinds of armed groups. In general, one of the objectives of the warring parties was to gain control of the capital and the remnants of state power. As long as state structures were responsible for international relations, which went together with status and, in particular, international aid, they were worth fighting for. For example, Taylor's ultimate goal was to be president of Liberia, as this would crown his career, legalise his lucrative diamond trade and allow him to tax the funds that were made available for humanitarian aid and post-conflict reconstruction. Although the certainty of international support disappeared after the end of the Cold War, state power often remained interesting to warlords because of its international aspects. As long as Africa continued to receive substantial amounts of foreign aid, which was distributed mainly through government channels that originated in the capital, the African state system would never vanish entirely.

Areas rich in mineral resources faced the toughest challenges. Africa's mineral resources have traditionally been regarded as a potential source of wealth, but in general they have brought the local population little more than economic exploitation and military conflict. In contrast, countries with less generous natural endowments, where agriculture is the main form of economic activity, have tended to enjoy relative tranquillity. It is true that most of rural Africa was heavily exploited, but at least it did not hold much interest for the warlords. Largely agricultural states therefore did not generally become embroiled in a fight for their survival.

In the 1990s, there was only one country in Africa where the local warring parties were no longer interested in seizing control of central government. State institutions became irrelevant once revenues from natural resources, regular economic activity (such as agriculture) and international aid had all dried up. The state in question – Somalia – simply disappeared.

The demise of Somalia

Somalia is more an example of failed state formation than of a failed state. For ten to fifteen years, the Somali leadership was building up an impressive war machine, but doing little else. After the armed forces were demolished, there was almost nothing left. This senseless course effectively made it impossible to stabilise the state. Most political, social and economic activity that was still taking place was financed from abroad. The relationship between the regime and the population was a mix of patronage and repression. The regime of Siad Barre, which had been in power since the coup d'état of 1969, continued to rely on assistance from the West even after its defeat in the Ogaden War.

In comparison to the other African countries, Somalia did not receive all that much aid, but what it did receive was absolutely indispensable due to the country's poor economic base. In the 1980s, development aid was the source of more than half of Somalia's GNP.[95] As the end of the Cold War approached, however, Western countries began losing interest in giving aid to Somalia. The extensive human rights abuses of the politically embattled Barre regime played into the hands of those who advocated discontinuing aid. This soon led to a vicious circle: the weakness of the government's power base led to violence against the population, and this led to a drop in international aid that further weakened the government's position.

In 1988-1989, the West froze almost all its structural aid to Somalia. This left the Barre regime unable to maintain control of the entire country. Rebel factions first seized large areas of rural Somalia, then moved on to the cities. In 1990, government forces even came under fire in the capital of Mogadishu. By January 1991, the regime was finished. The loyalist forces were comprehensively defeated, and the president fled the country.

Somalia was at the mercy of armed factions, which were organised along clan lines. There had always been sufficient fodder for internal strife in Somalia, and President Barre's policy of divide and rule had further strengthened animosity between clans. Weapons were widely available. Under the leadership of the warlords, the clans initially waged war against central government and, after the government collapsed, against each other. The main objective of these battles was the control of local economic activity, which was usually located in local population centres and their surrounding areas. This activity consisted of trade in legal and illegal goods, as well as agriculture, which was practiced alongside the rivers where the population centres were located. In 1991 and 1992, the fighting made normal economic activity almost impossible. The food supply was disrupted, and a widespread famine broke out. More than 100,000 Somalis died, and almost 1.5 million – a quarter of the population at the time – fled their homes to escape the famine and the violence.

The crisis led to calls for international humanitarian aid, but aid could not be distributed effectively in such a dangerous environment. For the warlords and their militias, foreign assistance was a potential source of revenue, but they realised that the funds would not start flowing if interclan fighting continued to spread. To turn the tide, various Somali clan leaders approached the United Nations for help in restoring central authority and rebuilding the country.

These requests were well-timed. The international community felt uncomfortable about the existence of a country without a government, a situation that had not arisen anywhere in the world since World War II. In its current condition, Somalia simply did not fit into the international state system, the basic paradigm of international politics (see chapter 1, pp. 27-30). Furthermore, Somalia's particularly barbaric brand of anarchy was an affront to the optimistic spirit of the 1990s, a decade of liberation and development.

Flushed with victory after winning the 1991 Gulf war against Iraq, the United States felt that the chaos and humanitarian emergency in Somalia could not be tolerated. President George H.W. Bush spoke of the 'new world order' that would succeed the Cold War and in which the United States would play a key role. Accordingly, US troops made up the core of a UN peacekeeping force that landed on the Somali coast in December 1992 and headed inland. The ambitious objectives of Operation Restore Hope were to restore security in the country, begin a process of national reconciliation, allow the numerous refugees and displaced persons to return to their homes and, obviously, provide humanitarian aid.

Against all expectations, the intervention, officially known as the United Nations Operation in Somalia (UNOSOM), ended in disaster. The various factions refused to cooperate with the peacekeepers, and the most powerful warlord in the capital of Mogadishu, General Mohamed Aidid, managed to evade arrest. Essentially a patron who had gone out of control, Aidid had appointed himself as Somalia's interim prime minister. He was in fact one of those who had requested the UN operation, but the international community still regarded him as one of the main instigators of the anarchy that gripped the country. The peacekeepers were disappointed by the attitude of the Somali clans that they were meant to disarm. Instead of being faced with an organised force that needed to be brought under control, the UN troops were continually confronted with new groups and individuals who trained their weapons on them. The losses on the international side were considerable, especially in comparison to the 1991 war against Iraq. During the hunt for Aidid, two helicopters were shot down, killing eighteen US soldiers. On the Somali side, there were probably about 500 fatalities, including civilians.

The United States was shocked by the hostility it encountered not only from the Somali fighters, but also from the civilian population. Accustomed to being welcomed as liberators, Americans became confused. Their confusion turned to disgust when they were confronted with the television images of a dead US soldier being dragged through the streets of Mogadishu to the cheers of Somali bystanders. The verdict of US public opinion was that such a barbaric country could not be saved, and the US government did not dispute this conclusion. The United States left Somalia in 1994. Apart from providing humanitarian aid, it had achieved nothing.

The UN diplomats also failed to attain their political objective of initiating a process of national reconciliation, though they did not immediately abandon their attempts to convince the clan leaders to agree to the establishment of a central government. Together with sixteen recognised factions, they discussed the reconstruction of the state at dozens of conferences, which ultimately led nowhere. The factions displayed little willingness to cooperate, and were often unable to do so anyway, as they lacked the necessary legitimacy and power. Their ability to destroy was much greater than their ability to create. In 1995, the

United Nations acknowledged the futility of its efforts and officially terminated UNOSOM, abandoning Somalia to the violent and arbitrary rule of clan leaders and warlords.

In hindsight, it is clear that some of the objectives of the UN operation were rather naïve. There was too little understanding at the time of what the disappearance of a state implied. It was believed that key Somali figures and groups would support the core of a new central government as soon as it had been established with international support. However, Somalia lacked not only a central government, but also subnational government institutions. The total absence of state structures meant that there was a critical lack of potential support for reconstruction. The UN operation also underestimated the forces of disintegration. The armed gangs that were responsible for the chaos that reigned in Somalia generally had no interest in the restoration of order, as their power, status and income derived from the use of force. As long as there was a chance of obtaining a share of the international aid, these gangs were reasonably interested in international involvement, but their interest in a political settlement for Somalia had faded completely by the end of the UN operation.

This did not mean that the violence in Somalia simply continued to escalate. The situation had reached its most tragic phase in the early 1990s, and many areas subsequently enjoyed a certain amount of tranquillity. This led to the emergence of local centres of power with more or less mutually recognised borders. At a certain point, most problems, ranging from disputes concerning the right to levy tolls to the theft of camels, had pretty much been fought out or otherwise resolved. To a certain extent, the fighting now retreated to the background, granting other members of society an opportunity to build up local government. In the north of the country, in particular, the population established the beginnings of new state structures. As early as 1990, a group in northwestern Somalia had declared the region independent under the name Somaliland. Interestingly enough, the borders of the new state, (which, incidentally, was recognised by nobody) coincided with those of the former colony of British Somaliland. As in the case of Eritrea, the force of the colonial borders thus asserted itself once again. In fact, border adjustments in post-colonial Africa always tended to focus on the colonial borders, however artificial they were.

A modest governmental structure developed in Somaliland, including means of maintaining public order. A start was made on the reconstruction of the region's physical infrastructure, and schools reopened. Trade started up again around the port of Berbera, bringing the town and its surrounding area a modest amount of wealth, which quickly exceeded the level of prosperity that had existed before the collapse of Somalia. This relative prosperity made it possible to fund the new government institutions.

Peace also returned to northeastern Somalia, sometimes referred to as Puntland. The fighting had not been so heavy there to begin with, as the region was inhabited by just one clan and had a tradition of political compromise. In addition, there were almost no armed groups, and this allowed civilians to maintain the upper hand. The port of Boosaaso stood at the centre of a minor of economic recovery, though nothing like that of the port of Berbera in Somaliland. Disputes concerning the control and spending of port dues hampered the funding of local government for a long time, but did not lead to eruptions of violence.

The remarkable recovery in the north stood in stark contrast to the rest of the country. The capital of Mogadishu and its surroundings, as well as the areas to the south of the capital, remained in the grip of lawlessness and violence. Political and military power was fragmented. General Aidid's once powerful faction had lost much of its power as a result of internal squabbling. In 1996, Aidid was killed in a shootout. He was succeeded by his son, who proved unable to command the same authority as his father. Mogadishu remained divided among groups that continued to clash, making it impossible to use the airport or the harbour. Trade suffered as a result, and it became increasingly difficult to make a living in the city. Thousands of Somalis who had come to the capital in the early 1990s in search of a better life began to leave again.

Armed youths terrorised civilians and made it impossible for the institutions in and around Mogadishu to function. International aid organisations were also unable to perform their functions properly. The few institutions that continued to operate often did so under difficult conditions. For example, they could not fire employees that appeared on hospital payrolls but did not actually do any work, because the individuals in question possessed firearms and could use them with impunity if they felt their interests were threatened. A separate development was the spread of fundamentalist Islam in central and southern Somalia, which led, among other things, to the deterioration of the status of women. Islamist groups also sowed unrest in the Ogaden desert and as far as the Ethiopian capital of Addis Ababa, where they carried out a number of bombings that provoked reprisals by the Ethiopian army.

However, the disappearance of the Somali state also led to a number of positive developments, especially in the north of the country, where there was relative order. Local private entrepreneurs rushed to fill the gap left by the state; for example, by taking responsibility for the supply of water and electricity. Such functions, which are performed in most countries by public utility companies, were usually performed very inefficiently in Africa. The new private service providers were expensive, but at least they were relatively efficient. Telecommunications was another area in which private entrepreneurs were able to achieve more, without state intervention, than supposedly functioning African states. In a certain sense, the private sector in Somalia was already in a position to benefit from the technological advances that accompanied globalisation. In the rest of Africa, however, the state still formed an obstacle to such progress.

In many cases, the market operated more efficiently in Somalia than elsewhere in Africa, with prices fluctuating in response to supply and demand. The Somali market even took over a number of functions that are normally performed exclusively by states, such as the issue of travel documents. In 2000, for example, the price of a Somali passport in the market of Mogadishu, where it was prepared on the spot in the space of five minutes, was roughly twenty dollars. In general, commercial transaction costs were still relatively high, because it was almost always necessary to pay for the 'protection' of the ruling clan and because the whole of Somalia was once again subject to the levying of tolls. The Somali shilling retained some of its value, even in the absence of a central bank, but the paper money began to look the worse for wear as the years went by, as for obvious reasons new banknotes were no longer being printed.

From 1997 onwards, in what was known as the Sodere peace process, Ethiopia tried to bring no less than twenty-six factions together in a National Salvation Council with a mandate to form a transitional government for Somalia. However, the faction led by the son of General Aidid refused to cooperate, and, more importantly, the northern region of Somaliland preferred to go it alone. Initiatives by Egypt and Djibouti to restore the unity of Somalia also failed to get results. In 2002, the Intergovernmental Authority on Development (IGAD), a regional organisation, started fresh peace talks in Kenya, which were again boycotted by Somaliland.

At the beginning of the twenty-first century, Somalia was therefore still a unique case in Africa and the world. To all intents and purposes, the Somali state had disappeared, but the country still appeared on every political map of Africa. According to the prevailing political order, there had to be a state on the territory in question, whether it existed or not. The international community no longer concerned itself with Somalia, but continued to wait for somebody who would claim to represent the country. International organisations, such as the United Nations, continued to reserve a seat for Somalia. This situation would endure as long as no further drastic changes occurred in the African state system.

Liberia's path to revolution

The small country of Liberia, which has a population of just over three million and is slightly smaller than England, was the scene of one of the most violent African conflicts of the 1990s. Its civil war was regarded both as a new phenomenon and as characteristic of Africa in the post-Cold War era, not so much because of its scale (with estimates of the number of deaths ranging from 60,000 to 200,000, it did not rank among the largest bloodbaths in postcolonial Africa), but due to the brutality and chaos, the abundance of warring factions, the use of child soldiers and the conduct of the warlords. Nevertheless, if the war in Liberia is considered from a wider perspective, it also appears to conform to established patterns. For example, the sequence of events was consistent with the general theory on the origin of revolutions; namely, that they are the result of the frustrated expectations of groups which, after enduring long periods of oppression, have recently been emancipated.[96] A parallel with the events surrounding the chaotic and hasty decolonisation of Belgian Congo also presents itself. To illustrate these points, let us turn first to the history of Liberia.

In 1822, philanthropists from the United States purchased Liberia, a hot and humid piece of land on the section of the West African coast where Africa and the Americas are closest together (opposite Brazil). It was to be a 'land of freedom' for emancipated slaves who were no longer needed on American plantations. A few thousand former slaves took advantage of this opportunity to return to Africa. The colonists and their descendants, referred to as Americo-Liberians, emerged as the new rulers of this as yet undeveloped section of the West African coast. They made their homes in the new settlement of Monrovia, which was named after James Monroe, then president of the United States. From the beginning, relations between the colonists and the indigenous population were tense. The former slaves regarded the native Liberians as savages that needed to be civilised and converted to Christianity.

The new rulers put the indigenous population to work under conditions best described as slavery. This ironic situation became most egregious when Liberia actually began to export slaves to the Spanish colony of Fernando Poo. This practice was discontinued after protests from Britain and the United States, but Liberia's domestic power structure remained similar to that in other African countries, which had been colonised by European powers. The country may not have been a colony in a formal sense, but it possessed all the relevant features. Power was concentrated in the hands of a small elite of foreign origin. Only the members of the elite enjoyed civil rights, while the rest of the population performed forced labour. The elite held colonialist attitudes that differentiated between civilised individuals and savages, and the administration of sixteen 'recognised tribes' was based on indirect rule by externally appointed tribal leaders.

Liberia thus did not differ notably from the rest of colonial Africa. It was an attractive country for foreign investors, especially from the United States and Germany, as they could do business directly with a small independent elite instead of with the European powers. Immediately after World War II, foreign investment in Liberia increased substantially, particularly in plantations and mining. The indigenous population was forced to perform the necessary labour. Liberia became a classic example of a rentier state.[97] The elite had a monopoly on state power and was able to collect revenue not only from the export of products obtained through forced labour, but also from foreign companies. It derived its wealth entirely from its position and had no economic base of its own. Some of the above-mentioned revenue was channelled to local leaders, who were responsible for maintaining order outside the capital.

Around 1960, when most of Africa was in the process of decolonisation, the Americo-Liberians in Monrovia (who made up just three per cent of the population) began to realise that the power structure in the country could not remain the same forever. At some point they would have to develop the interior and give the indigenous population a stake in the country's economic and political life. They constructed roads between Monrovia and the hinterland, built schools and allowed young men from the interior of the country to enter military service. Nevertheless, the government was in no great hurry. As long as the Cold War continued, it was safe inside the sphere of influence of its old patron, the United States. The Eastern Bloc had no foothold in Liberia.

It was ultimately the international economic recession of the 1970s and the related decline in revenues that put pressure on the elite. With the United States doing little for Liberia (although it did complain about human rights violations), the elite in Monrovia found itself in rocky financial straits. As a result, the internal system of patronage began to falter. In addition, after many years of growth, the economy began to stall. For ambitious young men from the 'sixteen tribes', who had now been educated and were looking for work, the only jobs available were in the military. Towards the end of the 1970s, the armed forces therefore contained a large number of restless young men who were demanding a larger slice of the national pie for themselves and their communities. Due to the poor economic prospects, frustration also mounted among the young urban unemployed.

The tensions reached a climax in 1979-1980. A number of demonstrators were shot dead in riots that erupted over an increase in the price of rice. The army was divided and indecisive. A number of junior officers, under the leadership of Master Sergeant Samuel Doe, carried out a bloody coup d'état, in which the president and some of his closest associates were killed. Other prominent members of the government were shot dead on the beach the following day. United under the banner of the People's Redemption Council, the rebels thus put an end to one-and-a-half centuries of uninterrupted Americo-Liberian rule. The violent nature of the takeover drew protests from neighbouring and Western countries, but this did not prevent Doe from eliminating his brothers in arms, whom he regarded as rivals, and then doing the same to other potential opponents. This completed the first stage of the Liberian revolution.

Liberia was going through a transition the rest of Africa had experienced about twenty years earlier. The international environment was probably to blame for this delay. The country was located in a neglected corner of the continent. In the rest of Africa, the situation in Liberia had either gone unnoticed or else been too delicate and politically inconvenient to attract much attention. While the large colonial empires were breaking apart, the international community had been blind to the apartheid in this independent country of former slaves. The strong, protective arm of the United States had discouraged other countries from interfering in Liberia, while the United States itself had focused on other issues during the Cold War. A small degree of emancipation finally got under way in Liberia, but quickly stalled due to the country's poor economic prospects. The domestic situation then became explosive. Liberia's rigid political system had no mechanisms for dealing with this kind of tension, and the international community was not there to provide political or military assistance. As a result, the old order – the *ancien régime* – perished in an orgy of violence.

It quickly became clear that matters would not end there. Doe's power base was narrow. He tried to take over the previous elite's system of patronage in order to gain the support of the interior of the country, but the continuing international recession made this extremely difficult. In addition, the violence and instability of the regime led to the near-total withdrawal of foreign investment and aid. There was substantial capital flight, and the ambitious project of an annual minimum wage of USD 2,400 per person was doomed from the start. The government tried to cover its financial deficits by plundering the country. The prospects of the indigenous population were no better in the 1980s than they had been previously, despite the removal of the Americo-Liberian regime. Doe failed to pursue practical policies and also proved unwilling to share power. In 1985, he organised a fraudulent election in order to become president. Several attempted coups d'état from within the army followed. Soldiers from the Nimba region, in the northeast of the country, came closest to succeeding. In retaliation, Doe allowed soldiers from his own ethnic group to wreak vengeance on the Nimba region. They burnt villages to the ground and murdered or drove out the population. Divisions along ethnic lines within the armed forces and the opposition movements, both in Liberia and among Liberian refugees, were a significant new development in the sphere of politics and security.

The battle for Monrovia

Towards the end of the 1980s, the largest group of Liberian rebels, exiles and refugees was located on the border with Ivory Coast. This group, of which Charles Taylor would eventually become the spokesman and leader, received arms from various countries, including Ivory Coast, Burkina Faso and Libya. Calling itself the National Patriotic Front of Liberia (NPFL), it became the strongest resistance movement opposing Doe's regime. Around Christmas 1989, probably with support from soldiers from Burkina Faso, the NPFL invaded the county of Nimba, where it was joined by local groups that were determined to force out the government in response to Doe's revenge. Thus began the march on Monrovia. As Taylor's forces advanced, they were joined by an increasing number of armed, but untrained, young men. Within a few weeks, the fighting, which killed thousands of people, had reached the capital. The end of Doe's regime was in sight.

At this point, the Economic Community of West African States (ECOWAS) took the surprising step of intervening. In its capacity as a peacemaker in Liberia, this regional organisation, which was established in 1975 and included almost all West African countries as members, operated under a formal UN Security Council mandate. It was encouraged and supported, financially and otherwise, by Western countries, which were thus spared the decision whether or not to intervene themselves.

However, the ECOWAS initiative cannot be fully understood without taking into account the special interests of the participating states, especially those of Nigeria, which had by far the strongest voice in the organisation. During the 1980s, a lively trade had developed between Anglophone and Francophone countries in West Africa, because the CFA franc had not been devalued, while the currencies of the Anglophone countries had been (see chapter 2). Nigerian products, often unlicensed imitations, thus became very cheap in Francophone countries. Often they were smuggled in, with the willing participation of Nigeria's political and military leaders. Nigerian leaders were also involved in other illegal activities, such as drug trafficking and money laundering.

Leading figures in almost all West African countries belonged to the networks that carried out such activities. Although they did so in a private capacity, and not, for instance, in their role as presidents or generals, these leaders did exploit the state power at their disposal. This 'criminalisation of the state', symptoms of which became visible throughout Africa from the 1980s onwards (see chapter 10, pp. 315-318), was linked to highly flexible international networks, in which one contact could easily be replaced with another.[98]

Nevertheless, these networks were also bound up with national interests, as determined by historical and other local factors. In West Africa, the main feature of this kind was the distinction between the Francophone countries, with their close ties to Paris, and the Anglophone group, which was much more independent of London and where Nigeria called the shots on account of its size. The differences between the two groups had theoretically been bridged by ECOWAS, but they were often still in evidence, especially in relations between Nigeria and Ivory Coast, which had supported Biafra's attempt to break away from Nigeria in the 1960s. The Nigerian network, under the leadership of President Ibrahim Babangida, included Doe's regime in Monrovia. Babangida was even the joint owner of Liberia's state oil company. In addition, there was a predominantly Francophone network of countries led by Ivory Coast, which also included Burkina Faso and, behind the scenes, even Libya.

The Liberian rebel leader, Charles Taylor, was allied with the Francophone network. When it became clear that he would succeed in capturing Monrovia, Nigeria sprang into action. The transition of Liberia from the Nigerian network to the Francophone network would be too harmful for the economic interests of the military leadership in the new Nigerian capital of Abuja. Furthermore, as a potential regional superpower, Nigeria had a strategic interest in intervening. Preparations for intervention were made under the cover of ECOWAS.[99] The international political climate worked to Nigeria's advantage. Western countries were concerned by the mounting violence in Libreria, but preferred not to intervene themselves. They therefore pushed for so-called African solutions, such as an African peacekeeping force. Francophone ECOWAS member states, which held an entirely different view of the war in Liberia than Nigeria, were urged to participate in the force by Western countries, which used development aid as leverage. A proper international military force thus reluctantly came into being, but did so under the overall leadership of Nigeria and with a heavy Nigerian predominance in all its components. The force was known as ECOMOG, which stood for ECOWAS Cease-Fire Monitoring Group, because its mission was to monitor compliance with the ceasefire.

When the ECOMOG soldiers arrived in Monrovia in mid-1990, the ECOWAS-imposed ceasefire was extremely fragile. Taylor's NPFL, which had almost conquered the capital, suddenly found itself face to face with a new enemy – officially an African peacekeeping operation, but in reality an invading Nigerian army. In the first few days of this new confrontation, a dramatic event occurred. Soldiers from a breakaway group of the NPFL tortured Doe to death in an area officially controlled by ECOMOG. The peacekeepers on the scene were unable or unwilling to intervene, and the shocking footage of the president's murder was broadcast all over the world. In Doe's place, ECOMOG established an interim government under the leadership of the widely respected Dr Amos Sawyer.

A relatively stable situation had emerged by the autumn of 1990. Dr Sawyer was the official president of Liberia, but his authority was limited to the capital of Monrovia, which was controlled by ECOMOG. The rest of the country was almost entirely in the hands of the NPFL, of which Taylor, after murdering his rivals, had become the undisputed leader. The NPFL was not strong enough to drive ECOMOG out of Monrovia, and the peacekeepers made no attempt to conquer the rest of the country, although partition was in nobody's interest. Violence erupted once again in 1992 after ECOMOG refused to negotiate a settlement with Taylor on the country's future. It is ironic that the intervention of the ECOMOG peacekeeping force, which prevented a decisive military victory by Taylor in 1990, prolonged the conflict until 1997. However, the leader of the NPFL also deserves a certain amount of the blame; Taylor knew that he was unable to defeat ECOMOG – or Nigeria – but still refused to work out a political compromise with the peacekeeping force.

After gaining control of the NPFL and the bulk of Liberia's territory in 1990, Taylor's next objective was the Liberian presidency. In 1992, he launched a frontal military assault on the capital, but ECOMOG managed to fight off the attack. None of the parties abandoned the notion of the Liberian state. Liberia may have been weak, like almost every other African state, and it may even have 'failed', but it was fundamental to everybody's plans. In Liberia, power traditionally went hand-in-hand with substantial revenues, which could be used to maintain a domestic network of patronage, as well as a comfortable private life. For the first couple of decades after World War II, those revenues were obtained mainly through contracts with foreign companies. From the 1970s onwards, this method was supplemented by all kinds of more or less illegal activities. And as for the future, Western governments had pledged extensive aid for reconstruction whenever the violence finally ended. Aid money would be a clear target for 'taxation', and that was a good enough reason to make the presidency in Monrovia the main objective of the struggle. Liberia was thus not destined to go the way of Somalia, which basically disintegrated around the same time.

Although Taylor controlled ninety per cent of Liberia's territory – which he referred to as Greater Liberia – he was unable to control the state's finances. In order to continue the battle for Monrovia, he therefore needed to generate additional revenue. This was not difficult. Liberia is extremely rich in natural resources, including diamonds, gold, tropical hardwood and iron ore. Furthermore, there was no need for a functioning, formal economy to produce and sell diamonds, as they could be smuggled out of the country and onto the world market in many different ways. The revenues were used to buy weapons and ammunition, as well as to recruit new fighters. The NPFL was not the only armed group that sought control of the diamond fields. Many breakaway groups and factions were fighting for a piece of this lucrative trade. At one point almost twenty different groups were involved. This led to the emergence of a genuine economy of violence, a mode of economic survival that formed both the engine and the objective of hostilities. As a result, the ethnic aspect of factionalism, which was still significant around 1990, gradually retreated to the background. The decisive factor in the formation and fragmentation of alliances (alongside the role of ECOMOG) was now the extent to which each faction could gain control of mineral resources.

For most young Liberian men and boys, the fighting in the interior of the country – and occasionally against ECOMOG in Monrovia – essentially formed the only activity through which they could support themselves. There was no legal alternative. The regular economy had collapsed, and the state's institutions had crumbled under the weight of the fighting, meaning that government jobs were no longer available. On the other hand, it was always possible to obtain a firearm, which could be used to earn a living.

This was not an entirely new development. Before the arrival of the Americo-Liberian state, which was a recent occurrence in certain areas, young men in Liberia's hinterland had found an outlet for their ambitions by attacking neighbouring villages or tribes. However, this was not a clear case of history repeating itself. The chaotic battles that characterised Liberia during the 1990s displayed certain similarities to the past, but simultaneously put an end to other traditions. For example, the rite of passage from boyhood to manhood (*poroh*) often could not be performed, because the jungle, where it had to take place, had become too dangerous.[100] Many male children thus joined the fighting without initiation or a mandate from their elders. In addition, warlords sometimes manipulated the *poroh*.[101] The new status that a firearm gave these young men all but destroyed their traditional respect for their elders, which was still one of the most important social ties in Africa. Thus, not only the Liberian state, but also Liberian society, swiftly disintegrated as a result of the fighting. This disintegration often penetrated to the most basic social unit, that of the family.

The conflict in Liberia seemed interminable, perpetuated as it was by the laws of the economy of violence. Hundreds of thousands of refugees crossed into neighbouring countries, and even the warring parties did not remain exclusively on Liberian territory. Taylor drew neighbouring Sierra Leone into the fighting, partly to capture the country's diamond fields (which were contiguous with Liberia's diamond fields and even richer), and partly to put pressure on the Sierra Leonean government to end its participation in ECOMOG. The spillover of the Liberian conflict into Sierra Leone would have fatal consequences for this small country (see next section).

Attempts were nevertheless made to contain or even end the fighting. Under pressure from Western countries, which had established an international contact group for Liberia, and from ECOMOG, the parties negotiated with each other from time to time and even established ceasefires. These never lasted, however, because the rewards of violence were too great for the fighters, and the lack of trust between the Nigerian leadership and Taylor, in particular, too deep.

This changed when General Sani Abacha came to power in Nigeria in 1993. The new military government wanted to put an end to Nigeria's substantial involvement in the fighting in Liberia and was therefore willing to strike a deal with Taylor. In Abuja, the parties this time concluded a peace agreement that would last. Under international supervision, Liberia held presidential elections, in which the rebel leaders were allowed to participate. Showing striking pragmatism, an overwhelming majority of Liberians voted for the man who, in practical terms, was already in control of the country: Charles Taylor. This shocked the West, which not only regarded Taylor as the main instigator of the violence that had consumed Liberia for years, but also believed that the presidency should not end up in the hands of the country's worst criminal. It was clear to all concerned, however, that the only way to end the fighting in Liberia was to install Taylor as president. The wandering warlord thus finally settled down, but without abandoning his raids in Sierra Leone. Taylor's ongoing armed incursions into a neighbouring country led the UN Security Council to impose sanctions on Liberia. Relations between the Taylor regime and the rest of the world remained tense.

Nor had peace been fully restored to Taylor's own country. Taylor quickly moved to eliminate all threats to his government. Rough handling awaited political opponents who did not escape the country in time. Oppression was the order of the day. It was only a matter of time before rebel groups (mostly consisting of fighters from earlier episodes of the Liberian wars) took up arms against the dictator. Liberia became the scene of renewed and sometimes heavy fighting, especially from 2002 onwards. The country's internal power struggle had international ramifications; it was one of the major factors destabilising the neighbouring country of Ivory Coast.

In 2003, the fighting again reached the centre of the capital, Monrovia. Taylor was forced to give up the presidency and accepted asylum in Nigeria. ECOWAS peacekeepers returned to Liberia and the country's political parties and rebel groups negotiated a settlement providing for a new, interim government. However, the international community had lost any confidence that Liberia could handle the situation on its own. The UN prepared to dispatch peacekeepers and play a large part in rebuilding the ravaged country.

Sierra Leone and the tragedy of Africa's youth

The war in Liberia is often mentioned in the same breath as the war in neighbouring Sierra Leone, and with good reason. In Sierra Leone, where fighting continued almost throughout the 1990s, violence also corroded the foundations of the state and society. Like Liberia, Sierra Leone experienced the combination of a corrupt government that pursued bad policies, an economic recession, widespread unemployment, frustrated youth, rich mineral resources (again diamonds, to which any party could as a rule help itself) and readily available light weapons. More important, however, was Sierra Leone's location, right next to Liberia, as well as the porous border between them, which let through rebels, weapons and diamonds. Sierra Leone, only about half the size of Liberia, could easily be destabilised by its larger neighbour. This was exactly what the Liberian war-lord Charles Taylor had in mind when he sent NPFL units across the border in 1991.

The attack on Sierra Leone's government combined Liberian and Sierra Leonean elements. The Liberians belonged to Taylor's NPFL, while the Sierra Leoneans had their own resistance movement, the Revolutionary United Front (RUF), which had been established by young people, most of them students, in the capital of Freetown. Disheartened by the lack of prospects and angered by the government's negative role, they had developed an ideology of their own at political gatherings during the 1970s. Interestingly enough, this ideology was not based on the socialism of the Eastern Bloc, but had its own unique, rather brutal features.

Muammar Gaddafi's Libya served as a source of inspiration. Revolutionaries from Sierra Leone always attended the yearly festivities surrounding his Green Book. Towards the end of the 1980s, thirty-five of them received military training in the Libyan city of Benghazi. Most of the members of this group later refrained from participating in the armed struggle in Sierra Leone, but the leadership of the RUF nevertheless consisted entirely of individuals who had been trained in Libya. Their assessment of the situation in Sierra Leone was simple: the country had immense wealth as a result of its ample supply of natural resources, but its riches were controlled by a small group (including many traders of Lebanese descent) that held all the political power. That had to change, but the time for talking was over. In the view of the RUF leadership, the solution to the country's political and economic problems was to be found in an explosion of destructive violence.[102]

The RUF was true to its principles. In 1991, in emulation of the rapid success of the NPFL's invasion of the Nimba region, it invaded a remote corner of Sierra Leone where the population was also heavily opposed to the government. However, the population was not as enthusiastic as it might have been about joining the uprising. Political opposition to the government could not be translated automatically into armed support for the RUF's destructive ideology. Large-scale recruitment was only possible among the unemployed and disadvantaged youth, which included boys and girls. These 'lumpen youth', who came from the capital of Freetown as well as the diamond fields in the interior, began to form the core of the RUF. Despite their lack of training and discipline, or perhaps because of it, they managed to force the government into a corner and destabilise the whole of society, just as their leaders had planned.

The military responded with a coup d'état in 1992. Young officers from the front in the interior of the country formed a new government, which took on the resistance movement with renewed zeal. However, the military had difficulty replenishing its ranks with new soldiers. In fact, it was only possible to recruit from the above-mentioned group of rootless young people, as a result of which the government forces quickly became known for perpetrating the same atrocities as the RUF. Ordinary, often somewhat older civilians therefore wanted nothing more to do with either side and organised armed units for their own defence, which quickly became a third party to the conflict. Foreign soldiers also participated in the fighting. Neighbouring Guinea sent troops to assist the government in Freetown, and ECOMOG dispatched a Nigerian battalion from Liberia to prevent the ECOMOG forces in Liberia from being attacked from Sierra Leone. The military situation was extremely complicated, especially along the border with Liberia, but in essence the entire country had descended into chaos.

This did not alter the fact that the RUF's success was limited at first. In 1992, the movement was driven almost entirely out of the country. It only managed to survive in a few camps along the border with Liberia, where it decided to change its military strategy. The leadership was forced to admit that the RUF was too weak to carry out a successful frontal military attack and opted for a guerrilla strategy of hit and run. Starting from the camps along the border, the movement established a network of small bases from which it could cover the entire country. Between 1994 and 1997, the RUF operated in this manner throughout Sierra Leone, without possessing real military power. The young fighters made a name for themselves by kidnapping, abducting and mutilating people on a massive scale. Thousands of civilians had their hands or feet chopped off. In this manner, the leadership of the RUF managed to strike terror into the hearts of the population. As a result, in spite of its military weakness, the movement was considered important enough to participate in the innumerable peace talks that were held to determine the country's fate.

Militarily, the RUF was defeated after the government purchased the assistance of a South African private security company known as Executive Outcomes. A few hundred of the company's highly skilled mercenaries trained the military in antiguerrilla tactics, provided logistical support with their own helicopters and supplied valuable information on the enemy's actions with their modern communications equipment. Even more significant, perhaps, was the increasing power of the population's own self-defence groups. In some areas, these groups cooperated with government forces, but in other areas they were able to maintain security on their own. A guerrilla army can only triumph when the population is sympathetic to its cause. The RUF never managed to win the hearts of the people.

In spite of the terror, the country remained more or less in one piece. It even managed to hold elections, which were won by a civilian, Ahmad Kabbah. President Kabbah's first priority was to implement the Abidjan Agreement, which had been concluded under pressure from the ECOWAS countries and the rest of the international community. The agreement included a ceasefire, the disarmament of the RUF's rebels and the transformation of the movement into a legitimate political party that would participate in governing the country; in essence, it was thus a power-sharing arrangement.

The peace agreement came to nothing. The RUF groups refused to disarm, and the government forces likewise failed to cooperate. The leaders of both parties may have been willing to end the fighting – though that was actually rather doubtful in the case of the RUF – but the thousands of young people who did the actual fighting were not. These young people, in both the RUF and the government forces, had nothing to gain from peace. Their lives depended on the conflict. Under normal circumstances, they would be unable to acquire what they obtained by plundering, and their status, which was based on their firearms and knives, would immediately disappear. Violence enabled them to command respect, or so they believed, and respect was something they would be deprived of in peacetime. Under pressure from these thousands of young people who wished to continue the fighting, a number of army units carried out a new coup d'état, a bloody one this time. President Kabbah managed to escape across the border.

This was too much for the numerous countries that were working on resolving the conflict in Sierra Leone. Nigeria was determined to triumph, and the ECOMOG troops intervened forcefully, liberating Freetown and enabling the return of President Kabbah. In 1999, a new peace agreement was concluded, this time in Lomé. The leader of the RUF,

Foday Sankoh, joined the government and settled in Freetown. To ensure that the agreement would be observed, the United Nations deployed UNAMSIL, a force of 17,000. It was the largest peacekeeping operation in the world at that time and the largest ever in Africa.

Once again, however, the agreement ran into significant practical problems. The fighters still refused to disarm, with all that entailed for the country's security. After a year, only a quarter of all weapons had been surrendered. The young fighters made life extremely difficult for the peacekeepers; for example, they denied the United Nations entry to the diamond fields in the interior of the country. In 2000, they even abducted a few hundred UN soldiers, who were later released, and heavy fighting erupted once again in the capital of Freetown. Until mid-2001, peace in Sierra Leone depended on the ability of the civilian population and the international community (United Nations, ECOMOG and aid organisations) to provide a counterweight to the desire of the young combatants on both sides to continue fighting. Britain, itself a former colonial power, dispatched several hundred marines to assist the government. As a result of substantial international support, in particular the effective British military contribution, the peace process eventually gained the upper hand.

The fate of Sierra Leone's young people is the most harrowing example of the tragedy of Africa's youth. Born into a world without prospects, they were caught up in a cycle of violence from which there was no escape. It was kill or be killed. Ordinary human values no longer applied to them. Abduction, torture and mutilation, such as the severing of hands, were part of their everyday experience. Drugs stilled their hunger and enabled them to live this kind of life day after day. Desertion was not an option, given the fear and hate they had already inspired. Young fighters who turned their backs on the RUF and fled the fighting would be executed for treason by their former comrades or, if they managed to evade them, shot in retribution by government soldiers or what in normal times would have been ordinary civilians. Return to a more or less normal way of life was impossible, as such a thing no longer existed in Sierra Leone. The conflict had to continue, with only a distant hope that one day, for whatever reason, it would come to an end.

Despite its rich supply of mineral resources, Sierra Leone has from time immemorial been one of the poorest countries in the world, by some measures the very poorest. The violence of the 1990s destroyed whatever material wealth there had been. More importantly, perhaps, it destroyed the country's social structure. The self-defence groups that formed all over the country demonstrated the resilience of society, but were also an expression of the fact that all other forms of social organisation had disappeared. By the end of the twentieth century, Sierra Leone had totally disintegrated. Although from that point onwards things could only improve, almost nobody even dared to imagine a brighter future. As a result of the fighting, life expectancy in Sierra Leone had dropped below thirty and, according to one estimate, was no higher than twenty-six, making it the lowest in the world.

In early 2002, after the British and the UN had brought a degree of stability to the country, peace was officially declared. A few months later, elections took place and were won easily by President Kabbah. Britain made a commitment to financially support the country's government for ten years, in the hope that this would restore international confidence in the country and attract foreign investment. In order to put its horrific past to rest, Sierra Leone set up a Truth and Reconciliation Commission. For the individuals bearing greatest responsibility for the atrocities, however, a Special Court was set up with both Sierra Leonean and international staff. The court produced some spectacular indictments, including one for RUF leader Foday Sankoh (who died in prison soon after) and one for the Liberian president, Charles Taylor (who had to flee Liberia and accept asylum in Nigeria). After order was restored, Sierra Leone could make rapid progress. However, being located in the middle of a highly unstable region, it was dependent on continued support from the international community, especially the British.

Proliferation of light weapons

Violence in Africa since the end of the Cold War, in particular the continuing violence within states, cannot be separated from the proliferation of weapons, especially light weapons. These are weapons that can be easily used or transported by individuals and small groups, such as rifles, handguns, hand grenades, mines and shoulder-mounted rocket launchers. Light weapons are easy to purchase, transport, use, maintain, repair and conceal. The best-known weapon of this kind is probably the AK-47 automatic rifle, also known as the Kalashnikov, tens of thousands of which can be found in Africa. In practice, however, ordinary tools and appliances must also be regarded as light weapons. In the region of the Great Lakes, in particular, many people have been killed with machetes, which are essentially agricultural tools (see chapter 6).

The word 'light' refers to the usual size of such weapons, rather than their potential in combat. An automatic rifle can fire hundreds of bullets a minute. Almost anyone could carry and use these compact weapons, even women and children, and that fact made them potentially full participants in hostilities. Male children, in particular, opted to fight, some even before reaching the age of ten.

In theory, anyone could purchase and use these weapons. Prices were low due to the abundant supply. In Uganda and Burundi, a Kalashnikov cost no more than a chicken.[103] In Kenya, which was not flooded with weapons to the same extent, the same rifle was more expensive, but hardly unaffordable: the same price as a goat. In Angola, finally, a rifle cost as much as a sack of grain, or about fifteen dollars. Once a group obtained weapons, it could use them to acquire more weapons. Control of natural resources also opened up plenty of opportunities to purchase weapons. In the mid-1990s, for example, the Angolan resistance movement UNITA is said to have spent almost half a billion dollars, which it raised from the sale of diamonds, on light weapons and ammunition on the black market.[104]

Light weapons played a crucial part in the disintegration of quite a few African societies. Liberia and Sierra Leone are the best examples of this, but the conflicts in Angola, Somalia and around the Great Lakes were also dominated by light weapons. This represented a significant change from the Cold War period, when warring parties in Africa, often governments or clearly recognisable resistance movements, received their weapons from the superpowers of the day and their allies. At that time, conflicts were the result of decisions at government level, and weapons were simply a means to carry out those decisions.

All that changed after the Cold War. The government was no longer the dominant actor, but just one of the players in a cast that also included armed factions, militias, gangs and clans. During the 1990s, the relatively orderly arms trade of the 1960s, 1970s and 1980s, run by centres of power in the global North, made way for a more diffuse arms trade, which could be traced to numerous countries around the world, in so far as it did not manage to conceal its origins entirely. The general availability of weapons was the final proof that the states concerned had lost their monopoly on violence. The termination of the violent conflicts that ensued thus required the cooperation of many parties, but most armed groups proved to have little interest in ceasefires and peace agreements. Light weapons provided power, status and a means to survive. In this sense, weapons were no longer just instruments of combat, but became a driving force behind Africa's conflicts.

It grew increasingly difficult to put an end to the scattered intrastate violence, which was often low intensity, but could flare up at any time. Agreements were only significant if they provided for the collection and destruction of weapons, but in practice this often proved the most difficult aspect to implement. Handing over weapons meant handing over power, with all the uncertainties that entailed for the lives of the owners. Young fighters preferred to hide their weapons, so that they could take them up again if the need presented itself. Furthermore, it was often less expensive for the military to give away weapons than to store or destroy them safely. Even after political problems had been resolved, it remained almost impossible to deal with the many weapons in circulation and, by extension, the threat they posed to social order. Furthermore, the weapons hardly ever stopped working and were easy to repair if they did. Their life expectancy was long, often longer than that of their users.

The violence that consumed Africa in the 1990s would never have flared up as it did, if not for the waning of state power and the above-mentioned changes in the nature of the arms trade. Almost all conflicts were fought mainly with light weapons. This applied in particular to conflicts in areas with mineral resources such as gold and diamonds for the plundering. In addition, many countries went through local conflicts of one kind or another, which were also fought with light weapons. Almost ninety per cent of fatalities resulted from these weapons. Most of the victims were civilians, including many women and children. This was in part because fighting could flare up in any location and the distinction between combatants and non-combatants was often difficult to make.

Light weapons also played a significant part in the large-scale conflict in Central Africa, which involved the regular forces of various states as well as several nongovernmental armed groups. In that conflict, however, it became clear that the greater the role of national authorities, the larger the weapons that appeared on the front. Around the Great Lakes, all available means were thrown into battle, from machetes to combat aircraft. A similar development took place in the conflicts in Sudan and Angola. In contrast, the new war between Ethiopia and Eritrea, which lasted from 1998 to 2000, was the only real war between states (see chapter 6, pp. 180-183), and it was therefore predominantly fought in a conventional manner; in other words, with standard military weaponry, ranging from automatic weapons to tanks and combat aircraft.

Where did this flood of weapons come from? Weapons such as machetes, which under normal circumstances have a different function, were obviously readily available, but began to be used for violent purposes once the fighting erupted. Other, 'real' weapons often came from elsewhere in Africa, either from the scene of a previous conflict (for example, the Mozambican civil war) or from the arms depots of foreign armed forces. As for the origin of the weapons, in other words, the countries where they were manufactured, Africa's role was very limited. Only South Africa has a significant, long-standing weapons industry of its own, which has remained in operation since the abolition of apartheid. South Africa currently supplies weapons to several African countries. In addition, Zimbabwe, Uganda and Kenya launched their own, if limited, weapons production programmes during in 1990s.

Central and Eastern European countries have been the main source of weapons for Africa. Their stockpiles had become superfluous, initially because of the disarmament treaties concluded in the final years of the Cold War and then as a result of the end of the East-West conflict. The new NATO member states were also obliged to standardise their arsenals, which made more weapons superfluous. Many of these weapons – not just light weapons, but also aircraft and tanks – ended up in Africa. Destroying them would have been expensive, while selling them – legally or otherwise – could actually raise some money. Hungary, Russia, Belarus, Ukraine and, in particular, Bulgaria carried on a lively trade. For many years, Bulgaria supplied weapons to almost all the warring parties in Africa, sometimes even to different sides in the same conflict.[105] In the above-mentioned countries, most of the companies involved were state-owned enterprises that had recently been privatised. The ringleaders often set up their own businesses to organise arms exports to third countries. This makes the arms trade very difficult to trace, all the more so because it is characterised by circuitous supply routes, false export licences, false invoices and false or missing end-user certificates. In fact, China is one of the few countries that openly supplies large quantities of weapons to African conflict areas.[106]

Due to the weakened position of African states, the arms trade with and within Africa is no longer predominantly a national issue. Individuals and non-state groups have now become the key players. Intermediaries, often ex-soldiers or former members of Eastern Bloc security services, also play a vital role. For them, wars are lucrative events that should be prolonged as long as possible. Not surprisingly, the private arms trade pays even less heed than governments to international measures aimed at preventing arms sales to certain groups, governments or countries. Countries subject to arms embargoes have thus been able to obtain weapons without much difficulty.

In spite of these serious problems, various international actors, including both countries and organisations, have remained actively involved in arms issues. Their multifaceted approach involves monitoring the production of weapons more effectively, limiting the arms trade and subjecting it to stricter controls, encouraging a transition from military production to non-military activities, laying down stricter codes of conduct, imposing arms embargoes in conflict areas, buying up surplus weapons and destroying them, limiting the availability of ammunition and so forth. In Africa, the regional organisations ECOWAS (in West Africa) and SADC (in Southern Africa) have made a particular effort to tackle arms issues in their regions.

Since 1998, the member states of the European Union have adhered to a code of conduct on arms exports, which provides that they may not authorise the sale of weapons that may cause or prolong violent conflicts or exacerbate existing tensions in the country of final destination. As early as 1991, the United Nations established a global arms register that was meant to list all transfers of conventional weapons. In practice, however, the register did not achieve very much in Africa, because many governments, of both arms-exporting states and the African states that purchased the weapons, failed to report their transactions. And obviously, the entire illegal arms trade went unreported. The arms register thus only provided a very partial picture of the African arms trade. Only a small number of countries, among them the member states of the European Union, report all their arms exports to the UN register.

Disintegration and violence
in perspective

In many African countries, society began more or less to break down after the end of the Cold War; in other words, there was a decline in social cohesion. In the governmental and administrative area, this decline was visible throughout most of the continent. The current chapter has referred to this process as the phenomenon of state failure. Instead of moving forward, most modern African states have gone into stagnation or even degenerated, causing significant problems for their societies. A few examples have been discussed in this chapter. In some countries, the breakdown was not limited to institutional structures, but permeated all areas of society, including the most fundamental level of all, that of the family and the everyday lives of ordinary people. However, disintegration that severe was always accompanied by violent conflict, as in the cases of Somalia, Liberia, Sierra Leone, Sudan and Angola. It is therefore important to re-examine the relationship between state failure and the outbreak of violent conflict. If all over Africa states fail, should we not expect to find fighting and chaos all over the continent as well?

Examination of the countries discussed in this chapter suggests that the above-mentioned relationship is, at the very least, not a direct one. Violence does not inevitably erupt in a failing state, but there is a greater chance that it will, because failing states are generally unable to maintain their monopoly on violence and to resolve political disputes or other domestic problems peacefully. However, violence did not erupt in many weak African states, and society continued to function there, despite poor governance. In cases where violence did erupt, there was usually another factor that ignited the conflict.

For example, the many failings of the Liberian state may have facilitated the country's civil war, but they were not the immediate cause of the conflict. In fact, on the eve of Samuel Doe's coup d'état in 1980, Liberia was not a particularly weak state. The outbreak of the war in Sierra Leone was similarly not the result of extreme weakness, but was largely due to the country's geographic location alongside Liberia.

The conflicts in Liberia and Sierra Leone highlight the extent to which rich natural resources can perpetuate conflict. As the state weakens, natural resources, instead of forming a source of wealth that can be used for development, become a liability than can ignite and prolong hostilities.[107] The impact of economic resources on Africa has differed from the European experience, in which states often plundered other states' resources. In order to do so successfully, they needed to build domestic unity, and attempts to capture foreign resources thus promoted state formation at home. In Africa, however, subnational groups generally plundered their own country's resources, which hindered state formation.

Other factors also left African society vulnerable to outbreaks of violence after the Cold War. The widespread availability of light weapons, in particular, was discussed in the previous section. In addition, the combination of rapid population growth and a poor socioeconomic outlook was an important factor. All over Africa, large groups of young people saw little or no prospect of improvement in their own countries. At the same time, however, the mass media showed them that living conditions were far better elsewhere in the world. This understandably generated considerable frustration, which sometimes led to violence.

The last significant factor in this context is the ethnic diversity of African societies, which provided politicians with an opportunity to manipulate and strengthen subnational loyalties. Politicians in trouble could always attempt to maintain or strengthen their authority by inciting ethnic conflict.

The total disintegration of the state and society in countries such as Liberia and Sierra Leone gave rise to dire predictions about Africa's future. Robert Kaplan's warning of 'the coming anarchy' is the best-known example.[108] Disintegration nevertheless appeared to have its limits. In particular, it did not automatically lead to violent conflict. In fact, its consequences were not exclusively negative. The loss of social cohesion also made it possible to adopt new forms of organisation, whether formal (for example, through democratisation) or informal (for example, by establishing networks using new technologies). This provided young people with a chance to extricate themselves from overly restrictive social networks.[109] Even the emergence of new social conflicts was not necessarily a bad thing, as such conflicts are an inevitable element of social change.

Disintegration thus has both positive and negative aspects. It is almost impossible to control politically, whether in Africa or in a broader international context, and attempts to influence the process therefore generally focus on preventing or reversing its negative side effects. State failure is currently addressed by promoting democratisation, institution-building and good governance, alongside efforts to prevent or resolve violent conflict. In practice, these policy approaches, which are still relatively new, have had great difficulty producing results. Experiences in the field of conflict prevention have been particularly disappointing. There are many reasons for this. For instance, many countries only invest significant political capital in ending a conflict after blood has already been spilled; in other words, when it is already too late to find a peaceful solution. By this time, economies of violence have already built up their own momentum, and the initial violence and casualties have created an atmosphere that is no longer conducive to peaceful resolution. The last section of chapter 6 discusses international conflict prevention in greater detail.

African countries have become more involved in African conflicts, in both positive and negative ways. They have become quicker to intervene in each other's affairs, even to the point of exporting violence. From the 1970s onwards, the ties between the elites in different countries became stronger, at least in West Africa. These ties, based on common economic interests, were often made official through marriages between presidential families. The British historian Stephen Ellis has even compared the networks connecting West African rulers to the marital ties connecting the royal houses of Europe during the eighteenth century.[110] These efforts to strengthen regional ties can be regarded as an expression of the waning power of the African rulers. Lacking support from their own people, the elites had continued to rely on international support. But when aid from the West dried up after the Cold War, African rulers were forced to seek allies closer to home, in their own regions. Some leaders, especially in Nigeria, exploited this situation to strengthen their own influence in the region.

The above-mentioned networks were not limited to official rulers, but also included rebel leaders and warlords. In Charles Taylor's days as a warlord in Liberia, for example, he already belonged to a network that included Ivory Coast and Burkina Faso. His capture of the Liberian presidency a few years later was symbolic of the ever fuzzier distinction between roving bandits and presidents, as the latter could increasingly be regarded as stationary bandits. In fact, even more traditional rulers such as President Mugabe of Zimbabwe had often been warlords of a kind, but in a different international environment. Mugabe acknowledged international borders, but only because this was obviously in his interests, since it brought in official international aid and allowed Zimbabwe to hold onto its seat at the United Nations. This situation changed in the 1990s. African governments began to intervene in the affairs of other states, and warlords had a chance to spread their wings. Weak yet rich, Congo was as attractive a target as it had been a century earlier, and its many neighbours plunged into the country on a massive scale. Some sought to profit from the situation in Congo, while others actually sought to prevent them from doing so. Whatever the political motive, however, Congo's riches were looted from all sides.

But intervention in other countries' affairs had another face: African regional organisations branched out into matters of peace and security. The ECOMOG operation in Liberia, initiated by ECOWAS, was the first of its kind. Although it should be judged generously as an initial attempt by African countries to take responsibility for peace on their own continent, the ECOMOG operation also highlighted the weaknesses of this approach. In particular, the peacekeeping force was a tool of the Nigerian military leadership, which used the troops to secure its own, predominantly economic, interests in the region. Moreover, ECOMOG provided a true reflection of its member countries, characterised as it was by mixed political, military and economic motives, corruption, excessive force, poor discipline, occasional cruelty and, more generally, disorganisation and ineffectiveness.[III]

International efforts to prevent conflict could not stop violence from erupting in Africa. In fact, the final years of the twentieth century saw the outbreak of the largest African war of the century, if not of all African history. Although the intensity of the violence was limited and no major battles took place, the fighting involved the whole of Central Africa, as well as parts of Southern Africa, East Africa and the Horn of Africa. The reason for this remarkable geographic spread was the situation in Central Africa, which managed to combine all the aforementioned determinants of conflict: a large failed state (Zaire/Congo), rich mineral resources, socioeconomic malaise, an abundant supply of light weapons, frustrated youth, a faltering process of democratisation, foreign intervention and mounting ethnic tension. The Congo war had a hellish prelude in the small country of Rwanda.

6
WAR

The genocide in Rwanda

6 April 1994, 8.30 p.m. A plane is making its approach to the airport at Kigali, the capital of Rwanda. In the darkness, a ground-fired missile streaks up and strikes the aircraft. It plunges down in flames. There are no survivors.

On board were the presidents of Rwanda itself and of neighbouring Burundi. Chapter 3 (pp. 96-101) describes how these two countries in the heart of Africa had for several years been in the grip of violent conflict between their two main ethnic groups: the Hutu (making up over eighty per cent of the region's population) and the Tutsi (making up over fifteen per cent). President Juvénal Habyarimana of Rwanda was a Hutu. He had been in conflict not only with the Tutsi who, in the shape of the RPF resistance movement, had invaded the country in 1990 from Uganda, but also with part of his own divided Hutu community. President Cyprien Ntaryamira of Burundi was also a Hutu. Just a few months prior to the missile attack, he had succeeded Melchior Ndadayé, the first elected Hutu president of Burundi, who had been assassinated by Tutsi army staff soon after his inauguration. Despite the numerical superiority of the Hutu in both countries, their political control of the area was far from automatic. Indeed, both countries had been ruled for a long time exclusively by Tutsi. Their democratisation, which began immediately after the end of the Cold War, was blocked in Rwanda by the RPF invasion and in Burundi by the opposition of the mainly Tutsi army. In both countries, the two groups were locked in a ruthless and unprincipled power struggle in which the ends were invariably taken to justify the means.

And the means included bringing down a presidential plane. Although the perpetrators were never identified, it was widely assumed that the plane had been shot down by Tutsi, perhaps belonging to the RPF. However, this was probably not the case. The hill outside Kigali from which the missile was fired was in the hands of members of Habyarimana's presidential guard and Belgian soldiers from the UN Assistance Mission for Rwanda (UNAMIR). This fact gave rise to widespread speculation, especially because witnesses claimed to have seen white men driving away at top speed immediately afterwards. In the light of events soon after the crash, however, it is more likely that the perpetrators were in fact Hutu, however odd this may seem. The president's Hutu community was divided into 'moderates' who wanted to share political power with other groups (both Hutu and Tutsi) and 'extremists', for whom the preservation of Hutu power was the only consideration. The extremists felt that President Habyarimana had made too many concessions in the Arusha peace agreement and could therefore no longer be relied upon to guarantee Hutu power in Rwanda. This meant that he was regarded as an enemy – for example, by members of his own presidential guard on the hill near the airport at Kigali. This is the most likely version of the events surrounding the attack on the president's plane.[112]

The downing of the plane was dramatic enough, but what followed was truly astonishing. Within an hour, blockades went up in the streets of the capital and houses were searched. People were gunned down on the spot, not just one or two, but large numbers. Whole families were massacred with rifles and knives. The perpetrators were soldiers from the army, backed up by irregular troops (mainly the Interahamwe militia). Their members, numbering around fifty thousand (as many as in the army), had been armed and given all other necessary support by the military.

The operation was conducted systematically. The execution squads had been furnished with lists of people to be killed. The first victims were high-ranking Hutu officials suspected of jeopardising Hutu power through their support for the Arusha peace agreement. Among them was the head of the transitional government, Agathe Uwilingiyimana. Her bodyguard consisted of ten Belgian soldiers who were members of the UN Assistance Mission. They were told to lay down their arms and accompany their captors to a military camp, where their throats were cut.

The death of the Belgian peacekeepers prompted Brussels to withdraw the Belgian contingent from Rwanda. Belgium's example was followed by other countries that had supplied troops for the UN Assistance Mission. The whole peacekeeping force in Rwanda (numbering 2,500 troops) was in effect dismantled. Its mandate had not permitted armed intervention in combat situations, nor was it equipped for such action. The hostilities in Rwanda escalated so rapidly that there was no time to organise more effective international intervention, even if there had been support for it among the leading members of the UN. Instead the foreign powers, headed by France, confined themselves to evacuating their own subjects and other Westerners from Rwanda. Left to itself, without the prying eyes of foreigners, the country became the scene of an appalling bloodbath, the nature and extent of which would only gradually dawn on the international community.

Once they had worked their way through the lists of people slated for execution, the army and militias began to systematically eliminate the whole Tutsi population. From the capital, the slaughter spread throughout the country. The chain of command was clear. Senior army officers gave the orders and made use of the machinery of civilian government. In many cases, the church (a highly respected institution in Rwanda) also played a questionable role. The killing was not random, as in Somalia or Liberia. On the contrary, it was highly organised, with the army and local government efficiently coordinating the execution squads. At first, one district was spared: Butare (in the south of the country), the only one in Rwanda headed by a Tutsi. After two weeks, however, the leadership in Kigali lost patience; the administration of Butare was replaced, militant Hutu were flown in and inflammatory rhetoric did the rest. Butare too was engulfed in the bloodbath.

The mass killings in Rwanda meet all the usual criteria for genocide. They were directed at a single racial category (the Tutsi) with the intention of wiping them off the face of the earth (in Rwanda at least). The massacres were literally intended as a 'final solution', like that envisaged by the Nazis for the Jews. Every Tutsi was to be killed – male or female, young or old, right down to babes in arms. Nobody was exempt. Women and girls were frequently raped before being killed. The instruments of slaughter were sometimes guns, often knives or simply whatever came to hand. Many of the bodies were mutilated. Mounds of corpses littered the streets. There was virtually no escape. The Tutsi minority was consistently outnumbered and had nowhere to go. Only a few isolated individuals managed to avoid the slaughter by hiding out for a long period, for example in an abandoned roof space or up a tree in the forest.

Insane as it may sound, the genocide was almost entirely successful. Estimates differ, but it appears that of the over nine hundred thousand Tutsi living in Rwanda in April 1994, only around a hundred and thirty thousand managed to escape death at the hands of their murderous fellow countrymen. The remaining eight hundred thousand or so were all killed.[113] This is an inconceivably large number. Imagine that the names of all the victims were to be listed here. Each page would contain approximately a hundred and fifty names (three to four on each line, given that Rwandan names tend to be long, and forty to fifty lines per page). So ten pages could contain the names of fifteen hundred murdered Tutsi, a hundred pages fifteen thousand names and a thousand pages a hundred and fifty thousand. But this would still only account for less than a fifth of all those who were killed. To list every single one of them would take more than five thousand pages (or more than ten books of this size) – and that would be only their names . . .

Admittedly the number of Jews murdered by the Nazis was far greater, but in that case the killings were spread over a period of years and involved what might be described as an industrial process. In 1994, Rwanda was a densely populated but preindustrial agricultural country. The genocide was carried out manually, but at a pace five times that of the annihilation of the Jews in Europe. Around eighty per cent of the killings took place in the six weeks following 6 April. What was Rwanda like during that period and in the months that followed? The country must have been littered with corpses. Some were dumped in anonymous mass graves, some were burnt to death collectively (for example, in churches or other places where the victims had sought refuge), and some were simply thrown into the rivers. The waters flowing out of Rwanda were full of human remains. In Lake Victoria they formed reefs of bodies.[114]

Towards the end of May, the genocide began to lose momentum, mainly because so few people were left to kill. The country had descended into chaos and normal social structures had completely broken down. The transitional government established on the basis of the Arusha peace agreement was gone, and the army and militias were preoccupied with the massacres. The invading Tutsi army, the Rwandan Patriotic Front (RPF), had stopped fighting following the Arusha agreement but now resumed its campaign. It was too late to save the bulk of the Tutsi population, but it could still reverse the balance of power in the country. It advanced steadily, occupying large areas, and in July seized the capital, Kigali.

Fearing retribution, the Hutu population fled before the advancing RPF forces. More than a million people sought refuge outside the country, where many of them were to suffer hunger, cholera and other hardships in the next chapter of the Rwandan tragedy. Meanwhile, in Rwanda, the RPF did its best to restore some sort of order. A new government was formed, based on the distribution of ministerial posts agreed to in Arusha, but with no extremist Hutu members. Their place was taken by members of the RPF. A Hutu was appointed as president, but the real power behind the government was the military leader, Paul Kagame. The post of vice-president was specially created for him, but in due course he acceded to the presidency.

Not surprisingly, the advance of the Tutsi army and its seizure of power were accompanied by a certain amount of bloodshed, with the emotions of the forces running high as a result of the genocide. Initially, the lack of reliable information from inside Rwanda and accounts by the Hutu who had fled to the neighbouring countries (and, naturally enough, were keen to play down their own part in the killings) led the international community to believe that a double genocide had occurred. Boutros Boutros-Ghali, the secretary-general of the United Nations, succinctly summed up the situation as one of Hutu massacring Tutsi and Tutsi massacring Hutu. This simplistic view was used to justify nonintervention. After all, what were ordinary people supposed to do if in some faraway country they decided to start cutting each others' throats?

Of course, not everyone shared this hands-off attitude. People around the world demanded that the international community take notice. Eventually, the French returned to Rwanda, mounting a humanitarian and military mission called Operation Turquoise, in the fear that otherwise Anglo-Saxon forces might enter the Francophone country.[115] By the time the French soldiers arrived in Hutu-controlled territory, the genocide had almost been completed and the RPF was rapidly advancing across the entire country. The leaders of the RPF were against the French presence, because they interpreted Operation Turquoise as a French move not to end the genocide but to defend what remained of the old regime and keep it in power. That proved to be impossible, but the French did rescue the Hutu elite, including the officials responsible for planning and executing the genocide, who were surrounded by RPF forces at the lakeside near Rwamagana. The Hutu leaders were evacuated, first to Zaire and then on to France and Belgium. Operation Turquoise was certainly highly controversial, both in Rwanda and elsewhere. After a few weeks, the French government called off the operation. It had not accomplished much, beyond making an extremely difficult situation even more complicated.

In any case, the idea that two genocides were taking place simultaneously was factually incorrect. True, the Tutsi army's advance and occupation of the country cost the lives of around a hundred thousand civilians, most of them Hutu, but – however shocking – it was in no way comparable to the genocide of the Tutsi. Although dreadful atrocities took place, no evidence has ever been found of any RPF plan to systematically exterminate the Hutu. Indeed, given the numerical ratio, any such plan would have been sheer absurdity. Even so, the RPF leadership cannot be entirely absolved of guilt for the genocide in Rwanda. By launching an invasion from Uganda, they deliberately placed the lives of the Tutsi population of Rwanda at risk. The RPF should have known that Hutu anger at the invasion was likely to be visited on innocent Tutsi civilians.

Finally, mention should be made of the slaughter of an estimated thirty thousand moderate Hutu by Hutu extremists. This brings the number of Rwandans killed in 1994 to a total far exceeding nine hundred thousand – an inconceivably large number, especially since the total population of Rwanda was only seven to eight million at the time the presidential plane was shot down.

Causes and consequences

The extermination of over ten per cent of the population of a country within the space of a few weeks is an incomprehensible event and clearly distinguishes the genocide in Rwanda from large-scale massacres elsewhere in Africa. In the early 1990s, Rwanda was certainly not a failing and disintegrating state. The violence that occurred was not the result of collapsing state authority that set off a violent struggle for power among splinter groups. On the contrary, it was the terrible efficiency of the state apparatus that made it possible to kill so many people in such a short time.

Rwanda had not descended into a state of chaos in which everybody was murdering everyone else, as people like the UN secretary-general (quoted in the previous section) wanted the world to believe. His description of the situation could not be viewed in isolation from its political implications. After all, if the Hutu and Tutsi population were indeed engaged in exterminating each other, as if in obedience to some law of nature, then there was no point in external intervention. After all, nature would always take its course.

In reality, however, there was just one well-organised group engaged in murdering a clearly defined section of the population. Even the chain of command was clear. The genocide was directed by Colonel Théoneste Bagosora. His deputy, the minister of defence, Major General Augustin Bizimana,[116] was in charge of the logistics of the operation and ensured that army units unwilling to participate in the genocide did not actively obstruct it. These two were supported by a wide range of people in Kigali, mainly army officers, who took care of the logistics. They had links with people in the each district, both in the gendarmerie (present throughout the country) and in civilian government. It was they who sent out the murder squads, mainly members of the army and young Interahamwe militiamen.

It is hard to believe that normal government institutions and public officials were prepared to countenance this operation and implement it with such care. But the preparations had been meticulous. As early as 1992, a 'zero network' of people within the army had begun planning the extermination of the civilian Tutsi population.[117] As time went on, the plans were more and more openly discussed. In the early months of 1994, the public was inflamed by radio broadcasts and, as it were, mentally prepared for the storm ahead.

The success of this approach was connected with the history of conflict between the Hutu and the Tutsi in Rwanda and the surrounding region. Large-scale violence between the two had been common in the past. As recently as 1993, for example, the assassination of the president of Burundi had led to around fifty thousand deaths. So the genocide in Rwanda was part of an established pattern, although the vast number of killings was exceptional even for the Great Lakes region.

The usual political and socioeconomic causes of conflict provide an inadequate explanation for the genocide, although there certainly was a political power struggle, as well as socioeconomic differences between the Hutu and the Tutsi. In an effort to identify factors which may have exacerbated the tensions between them, some researchers have pointed to the population density of the region around the Great Lakes.[118] With around two hundred people per square kilometre compared with a continental average of only twenty-five, Rwanda and Burundi were certainly by far the most densely populated parts of Africa. The hilly landscape of the two countries was relatively fertile, but even so the population was pushing the limit of what the land could support, given the primitive agricultural techniques still in use. Each year, an average farming family in Rwanda or Burundi had access to less land. Given the virtual absence of any means to modernise the economy, the ever-increasing population could be seen as a curse.

Another, primarily psychological, explanation is based on the observed fact that socioeconomic and other differences between the Hutu and Tutsi had actually been shrinking in the years before. The Hutu government in place since independence had gradually eroded the traditional socioeconomic superiority of the Tutsi. The two peoples were becoming ever more similar and the many mixed marriages taking place reflected this fact. Even so, it was primarily the tensions between the two that laid the foundation for the conflict. This is the same strange phenomenon that was witnessed in the former Yugoslavia, where an explosion of extreme violence occurred and 'ethnic' differences resurfaced after years of inter-marriage between people of Serb, Croat and other origin. The rapprochement that had taken place between the groups seems to logically contradict any attempt to explain the violence on the basis of the differences between them.

Dutch anthropologist Anton Blok has made an intriguing attempt to sort out this paradox by reference to Sigmund Freud's theory of the 'narcissism of minor differences'.[119] Freud noticed that individuals sometimes hugely exaggerate very minor differences between themselves and other people in order to confirm or strengthen their own identities. This is logical, since the individual identity is largely based on the idea of being different from other people. Accordingly, any blurring or elimination of such differences poses a threat to personal identity.

Blok applied this theory to ethnic groups. While political and sociological theorists had viewed the levelling of differences between the Hutu and the Tutsi as beneficial to the unity of the country, Freudian theory saw it as a threat. It made it increasingly difficult for individuals who had always regarded themselves as Hutu or Tutsi to maintain that self-image. When tensions in the country increased, people wanted to know who they were. The national Rwandan identity was clearly not yet firm enough to fill the vacuum. Under political pressure, the population reverted to the old contradistinctions, even though they had to exaggerate the tiny remaining differences out of all proportion in order to do so. In this way, the traditional Hutu and Tutsi enmity was revived and provided the basis for an explosion of violence.

What were the consequences of the genocide? By mid-1994, Rwanda was in ruins and its population was traumatised. In the years that followed, Rwandans were to remain the most introverted people in Africa. Many of them had been too deeply shocked by the atrocities ever to talk openly about them. Almost everybody had witnessed the murder and mutilation of friends, neighbours and colleagues. Families had been wiped out or torn apart. People used to living in the midst of relatives and in close-knit communities found themselves suddenly alone in the world. They had frequently been forced to abandon their homes and had no idea what they would find when they eventually returned. The country was full of wandering orphans and soon there was a new group of children, born of rape.

Suspicion was rife. Who had done what? Was anyone truly innocent? Many of the guilty sought refuge outside Rwanda, only to be cornered by RPF forces in Zaire/Congo. The new regime's troops captured many camps in the provinces of North and South Kivu, killing ex-combatants (if they had not managed to flee deeper into Congo) and forcing civilians to return to Rwanda. Undoubtedly, however, many of the perpetrators of the Rwandan genocide escaped retribution.

In the second half of 1994 and in 1995 over a hundred thousand Rwandans were arrested on suspicion of participation in the genocide. Given the extent of the slaughter, this was no very startling number, but it still swamped the Rwandan prisons and courts. It would take many years to try all the prisoners and meanwhile they were jammed together in small cells awaiting their turn. From 2001, therefore, an experimental attempt was made to speed up the process by taking groups of prisoners accused of playing relatively minor roles in the atrocities (for example, 'simply' having murdered a few fellow villagers) back to the places where they were said to have committed their crimes. There, the assembled community decided whether the accusations were true and, if so, what penalty should be imposed. The village assembly acted as both judge and jury. This approach ensured that thousands of young Rwandans received some form of trial or were returned to the community relatively quickly.

The United Nations also took over part of the task of trying alleged perpetrators of the genocide. In the Tanzanian city of Arusha, where the Rwandan peace agreement had been signed as recently as 1993, the UN set up an international tribunal to deal with the alleged ringleaders. The tribunal has been subjected to a barrage of criticism for its meticulous and therefore cumbersome approach. It has insisted, for example, that the evidence against the accused should be completely watertight, even though evidence in cases of genocide is generally extremely difficult to collect. Lawyers have managed to spin trials out to great lengths and – unlike the Rwandan courts – the UN tribunal cannot impose the death penalty. Critics have complained that this 'civilised' approach is in unreasonably sharp contrast to the barbaric deeds of which its beneficiaries stand accused.

Even so, the tribunal has been able to score some major victories. In 1999, for example, it became the first international tribunal ever to find a former head of government guilty of genocide. The leader in question was the former prime minister, Jean Kambanda, who received a life sentence. The tribunal hopes to be able to try a total of around a hundred major perpetrators, a task which it may not complete until 2008.

The lessons of Rwanda were too bitter for the international community to ignore.[120] Come what may, it was imperative to intervene to prevent any new genocide. The problem, however, was that military intervention in another country to prevent genocide was only legally possible with a mandate from the United Nations Security Council. And that kind of mandate was not easy to get. The North Atlantic Treaty Organisation (NATO) wanted to intervene when the Yugoslavian government was known to be taking increasingly aggressive action against the Albanian minority in the country (mainly resident in Kosovo), but was unable to obtain a mandate due to Russian opposition in the Security Council. It was to a large extent the shock of the Rwandan genocide of 1994 that made the Western countries decide in 1995 to take action in Kosovo independently of the UN. This produced the phenomenon of 'humanitarian intervention' (military intervention undertaken for humanitarian reasons without a mandate from the Security Council). The genocide in Rwanda also had an influence on the international community's attitude towards armed conflicts elsewhere in Africa. In early 2000, for example, a large-scale UN peacekeeping operation began in Sierra Leone (see p. 203).

An important lesson learned by the Rwandan Tutsi was that, at the end of the day, they could rely only on themselves. This was what motivated the firm action taken by the Tutsi, and in particular by the government of Rwanda, in the Great Lakes region from 1994 on. Following the genocide, the Rwandan government was fairly paranoid, displaying an exaggerated suspicion of the outside world that no doubt seemed justified to a group which had just survived genocide. An obvious comparison can be drawn with the Holocaust and the subsequent attitude of the Jewish state of Israel. Successive Israeli governments have invariably attached top priority to national security, if necessary subordinating other interests – including respect for the rule of international law – to that aim. Mindful of the historical background, the international community resigned itself to the situation.

Similarly, the security of the Tutsi was the overriding consideration for Rwanda's strongman, Paul Kagame. Where necessary, he was fully prepared to ignore international law. This made Rwanda, like Israel, a special case in the eyes of the world. Because of its dramatic history, Rwanda was given greater latitude than other countries. The greater part of the international community turned a blind eye its to transgressions. After all, it was difficult for countries that had virtually ignored the systematic extermination of a large part of the Rwandan population to censure the survivors when they took action to protect their own people. And so it was that the consequences of the Rwandan genocide helped pave the way to a war that would ravage the whole of Central Africa.

The Hutu extremists had gone a long way towards their aim of exterminating all the Tutsi in Rwanda. Out of the original population of over nine hundred thousand Tutsi, only around a hundred and thirty thousand had survived the slaughter. Nevertheless, the previous ratio between the two groups in the Rwandan population was swiftly restored. The new RPF-dominated government encouraged Tutsi emigrants to return from neighbouring countries, even if they had been living there for over twenty years. A total of approximately seven hundred and fifty thousand Tutsi streamed into Rwanda from Uganda, Burundi, Tanzania and Zaire. Their first move was to look for the homes and lands that they or their forefathers had once possessed. They found them in rack and ruin, occupied by other families, or abandoned (but perhaps eventually to be reclaimed by some returning displaced person or refugee). The country's turbulent recent past thus sowed the seeds of continuing strife. Assuming that the majority of those who had fled the genocide or its aftermath would eventually return to Rwanda, and given the new influx of Tutsi, there was no decline in the overall population of the country. Rwanda remained overpopulated, full of ethnic tensions and short on means of resolving them in a humane and conclusive way.

Central Africa's
Great War

Starting in April 1994, over a million refugees streamed out of Rwanda. Many of them had been implicated in the genocide. Most crossed the border into the Zairian province of North Kivu, an area larger than the whole of Rwanda but with a far smaller population. The huge influx of Rwandan refugees placed severe pressure on living conditions in the province, and the international community, ashamed of its failure to prevent the genocide in Rwanda, responded with a large-scale programme of humanitarian aid to ease their plight.

However, the conflict between the Hutu and the Tutsi was not yet over. Hutu militias tried to recover and regroup in Kivu in order to return to Rwanda and 'complete' the genocide. Naturally enough, the new Tutsi government in Kigali, led by Kagame, was determined to prevent this and counted on the support of President Mobutu of Zaire. He, however, saw no reason to assist; civil strife between ethnic groups in distant provinces presented no threat to the president in Kinshasa. But Mobutu had not reckoned on the determination of the new Tutsi leaders in Kigali, for whom the security of their own people was the be-all and end-all, even in their relations with the government of Zaire. If Mobutu would not cooperate, he would pay the price.

In October 1996, therefore, serious resistance to Mobutu emerged in eastern Zaire, instigated by the Rwandan army. One of the many Zairian resistance groups, which had previously been relatively weak, suddenly proved capable of successful military action. Its leader was the hitherto unknown Laurent Kabila and the group of local Zairian rebels included many people of Tutsi descent (known in Zaire as Banyamulenge).

The support of the Rwandan government must have made an enormous difference to Kabila.[121] At the start of his uprising, dramatic events occurred in the Rwandan refugee camps in eastern Zaire. Tutsi refugees were press-ganged into Kabila's rebel army or enlisted voluntarily, while Hutu opponents of the Kigali regime were killed on the spot or transported back to Rwanda (or in some cases Burundi), if they did not manage to escape by seeking refuge deeper inside Zaire. As Kabila's troops advanced westward towards Kinshasa, these Hutu refugees and fighters were driven ahead. The individual fate of these people – numbering hundreds of thousands – is generally unknown, but the mass graves discovered later speak volumes.

The collapse of the Mobutu regime in 1996-1997 seemed to herald a new era for Zaire. The outside world was persuaded that the nation, under Kabila's leadership, had rid themselves of the hated dictator. Many people in Africa and elsewhere felt that the fall of the 'dinosaur' heralded the end of the neocolonial era. Here was Africa engaged in its own liberation. But sentiments in the Democratic Republic of Congo (the new name that Kabila gave the country after taking power) were rather different. Many people felt far from liberated. It was difficult, especially for those in the capital, to get used to the Rwandans who surrounded the president. And, as time went on, the Rwandan support which had been necessary to bring Kabila to power, gradually undermined his authority in the nationalist city of Kinshasa.

If Kabila wanted to survive in Kinshasa, he would have to free himself from his role as a puppet of Kigali. He would need to build up powerful grassroots support for himself and get rid of his Rwandan advisors. Accordingly, Kabila began to adopt a more independent attitude. He refused to participate in a plan put forward by Uganda and Rwanda for economic cooperation, and eventually even integration, in the Great Lakes region. In order to construct an independent Congolese army from a ragtag bunch of ethnic militias, Kabila started to make use of the Mai Mai in the east of the country, who were traditionally the sworn enemies of all Rwandans, whether Hutu or Tutsi. He even began to use Hutu who had participated in the genocide for his own purposes. This increased the tension along the border with Rwanda and was probably the factor that eventually drove the Kigali government to take action. The chief-of-staff of the Congolese army, James Kabarehe, had previously served in the Rwandan armed forces. At the request of Rwanda, he now plotted to carry out a coup d'état in Kinshasa.[122]

Kabila realised the danger just in time. He dismissed Kabarehe and ordered his Rwandan advisors out of the capital and all Rwandan forces out of Congo. But Kagame was not about to give up quietly. On 1 August 1998, Rwandan forces in Kinshasa advanced on all the strategic points in the city. At the same time, a rebellion broke out in eastern Congo, along the border with Rwanda, looking suspiciously like a replay of Kabila's own uprising against Mobutu. This time, however, Rwanda's involvement was more overt: columns of

Rwandan army vehicles drove across the border into eastern Congo and Rwanda's ally Uganda declared its support for the 'insurgents'. In the small town of Goma on Lake Kivu, virtually on the Rwandan border, they set up an alternative Congolese government. Whatever might eventually transpire in distant Kinshasa, it was clear that the two countries were determined to bring order to the tumult of eastern Congo.

The Rwandan government tried to force events in the Congolese capital by launching a spectacular military airlift to faraway Kinshasa. However, the Rwandan military failed to seize the city, mainly because they found themselves unexpectedly facing a force of seven thousand foreign troops supporting the Congolese government. With lightning speed, Kabila had called on the help of Angola, which had also been instrumental in his rise to power. At this critical moment, with his control of the country at stake, he was prepared to accept the inevitable quid pro quo.

With Angola's help, Kabila was able to parry the direct Rwandan threat to his regime. The Rwandan military decided to withdraw overland to territory controlled by the UNITA rebels in northeastern Angola, whence they were eventually flown back to their own country. In the Congolese capital, however, tension persisted. The inflamed nationalist feelings of the Kinshasans turned them against all foreigners, in particular if they looked like Tutsi. The head of Kabila's private office went so far as to label all Tutsi in Congo microbes and vermin needing to be eradicated.[123] So it was that the most reckless of Rwanda's attempts to secure Congo for itself in the ethnic struggle in the Great Lakes region, or at least to neutralise the country, had the counterproductive effect of turning a considerable proportion of the Congolese people against Rwanda and fanning the flames of ethnic hostility.

That was not the end of the war in Congo. In fact, it was not really even the beginning, which came in August 1998, when Rwanda and Uganda launched a new offensive in the east of the country. Other countries joined with Angola in support of Kabila's regime. After that, the war in Congo and around the Great Lakes became exceedingly complex. It came to display every hallmark of contemporary warfare in Africa: a complicated internal situation; foreign intervention (not only by African states, but also by countries outside Africa and by international organisations); political, economic, social and cultural issues; participation by both 'new' and 'old' leaders; the involvement not only of regular national armies, but also of militias, gangs and young drifters with no future prospects; trading in arms, diamonds, oil and coffee concessions, typical of the economy of war; use of every kind of weapon from modern fighter aircraft to machetes; huge numbers of refugees and internally displaced persons, many of whom were involved in the hostilities; and a motley assortment of shifting internal and external coalitions.

Some order can be discerned amid this chaos if we distinguish between various levels of conflict.[124] The first, and by far the most important, distinction to make is that between the two regional power blocs: a 'Great Lakes' alliance of Rwanda, Uganda and, to a lesser extent, Burundi, versus Congo and the allies of President Kabila (Angola, Zimbabwe and Namibia). All these countries and their individual roles in the war are discussed below (pp. 185-189).

At stake in the conflict between the two blocs was their ability to retain or extend their geographical spheres of influence, in the interest of security or, in other words, physical control over ethnic groups and fighting forces. But there were also economic motives for the war. Congo is extremely rich in mineral resources and everyone wanted a share. Each country or faction occupying part of the territory of Congo immediately began to extract natural resources for its own gain. This meant that Congo was, in practice, carved up into a number of zones of occupation, even if their borders varied over time. None of the governments that were drawn into the fighting in Congo made any formal claim to its territory. It was not, therefore, a matter of openly declared territorial ambition at the expense of Congo, but rather of taking military and economic advantage of the weakness of the government in Kinshasa.

The second level of conflict was domestic. There was a long-running civil conflict going on between a shifting set of rebel groups and the government in Kinshasa. President Kabila's authority was challenged by a host of disparate and often mutually hostile groups and individuals. The role of this armed opposition within Congo cannot be viewed in isolation from the conflict that was being waged at international level. Foreign powers and Congolese resistance groups provided armed support for each other wherever they thought it useful to do so.

The situation in Congo and surrounding area was further complicated by a third level of conflict: civil wars in the adjacent countries which increasingly spilled over onto Congolese territory. The prime example was in Rwanda, where the postgenocide regime in Kigali was fighting armed Hutu groups in eastern Congo (many of whose members had served in the former Rwandan army). The Rwandan situation was one of the main causes of the war in Central Africa. But the governments of Uganda, Burundi and Angola also took armed action inside Congo against resistance movements formed of their own nationals.

Finally, the fourth level of conflict was fighting by armed groups like the Congolese militias, the Interahamwe (Hutu) and the Mai Mai (who had a different ethnic background), in the provinces of North and South Kivu in eastern Congo. These groups were initially thought to have no political goals of their own, but it eventually became clear that they were linked to President Kabila in Kinshasa. They often operated on the basis of informal instructions from the national Congolese army.

Large-scale warfare engulfing almost the entire continent was a new phenomenon in Africa. Over the centuries, the continent had experienced violent episodes of many kinds, but they had always been limited in scale, if only because of its low population density. The colonial era produced its own particular tensions and hostilities, but they were kept under control by the European powers. After independence, this situation persisted for the duration of the Cold War. The worldwide confrontation between East and West translated into many local conflicts within Africa, but the global superpowers were careful to prevent these from escalating to the point where they might themselves become directly involved.

With the end of the Cold War, the situation changed dramatically. International control was removed from the continent and African states were able to pursue independent policies, unconstrained by the superpowers. Unaccustomed as they were to such freedom, it took them some time to take advantage of it in their relations with their neighbours and more distant countries. Their delay in doing so was also due to the weakness of the ties between them, friendly or otherwise. Their isolation from each other was a result both of their historical background and of the virtual absence of physical infrastructure. Ideologically, it was reflected in the principle of nonintervention in the internal affairs of other African countries, which was a central provision of the OAU Charter.

However, new freedoms always attract people eager to exploit them. The rulers of countries like Uganda, Rwanda, Ethiopia and Eritrea, as members of the generation of 'new leaders' discussed in chapter 4 (pp. 125-127), saw no moral objection to interfering in the internal affairs of other countries, particularly neighbouring countries that had descended into chaos. One such country was Congo. The postgenocide government of Rwanda had given top priority to restoring order and security within its own borders, but was unable to achieve this without the cooperation of the authorities in its huge neighbour. First Mobutu and then, soon after his removal, his successor Kabila were uncooperative. The result was a new Rwandan intervention (supported by Uganda) in the Congolese political scene.

The new mentality on the part of Rwanda and Uganda's leaders encountered fierce resistance from the other countries in the region. Protest was voiced not only by the Francophone countries (especially nearby Congo (Brazzaville), Gabon, the Central African Republic and Chad) which – accustomed as they were to the order imposed by Paris – abhorred this kind of African international activism, but also by Angola, Zimbabwe, Namibia and Sudan. The war in Congo revealed a faultline between 'new-style' and 'old-style' international conduct on the part of African governments.

There were still other motives for participating in the war in Congo. Engaging in a foreign campaign was a proven means of distracting attention from domestic political problems. There was also the lure of Congo's mineral wealth. And considerations of prestige and power could also persuade countries to go to war, feeling that they would no longer count in the region if they lingered on the sidelines.

The motives of the various parties for taking part in the war and their roles in the hostilities are discussed in detail later in this chapter. First, however, it is worth considering the situation to the northeast of the Great Lakes. Around the same time that the new leaders Kagame and Museveni intervened in Congo, eventually precipitating a war in the whole of Central Africa, the new leaders of Ethiopia and Eritrea (Meles Zenawi and Isaias Afwerki) were also entangled in hostilities. Against each other.

Ethiopia and Eritrea
once again at war

The war between Ethiopia and Eritrea that broke out in the summer of 1998 was a complete surprise to the outside world and even to many experts on the Horn of Africa. In the preceding weeks there had been border skirmishes, but virtually nobody seriously expected hostilities of such magnitude. There was simply no real reason for them. In fact, cooperation between the two countries had been surprisingly good since Eritrea had broken away from Ethiopia in the early 1990s. The leaders of the two countries were on friendly terms. Moreover, Western governments were under the impression that both Meles Zenawi (in Ethiopia) and Isaias Afwerki (in Eritrea) sincerely wanted what was best for their two countries – something they did not necessarily believe of all African leaders – and this made the two of them popular among international donors.

Even after fighting was under way between the two armies, the world was still mystified about the exact nature of the rift. An answer was not forthcoming from the governments in question. They each refused to take responsibility for the war, claiming that it was the fault of the other for displaying aggression against a peace-loving neighbour. Observers could only guess at their underlying motives. And their guesses were heavily influenced by their personal feelings about the two countries.

Eritreans thought that Ethiopia had been unable to stomach the success of its former province and was out to put its small northern neighbour 'in its place'. They emphasised the economic and monetary situation; Eritrea had been gradually disentangling its affairs from those of Ethiopia, a process completed in 1997 when the Ethiopian currency, the birr, was replaced with a separate Eritrean currency, the nakfa. Ethiopians, on the other hand, laid all the blame on Eritrea, claiming that the successes of the past decade had given the authorities there an inflated sense of self-importance. Still, the exact purpose of the Eritrean attack remained unclear. The ostensible focus of the dispute was an arid and infertile patch of border territory offering nothing of any particular value either above or below ground. Nobody seriously believed that this minor border dispute was the real reason for the war.

The assertiveness (or, as some would have it, inflated ego) of the Eritrean regime may indeed have been the main reason. Having won its own independence by force of arms, a rare occurrence in Africa, Eritrea was determined to take control of its own development. No task seemed too great for the little country, with a population of just three million. Likewise, the government showed that it would stand for no nonsense in its relations with neighbouring states. In the internal conflict in Sudan, Eritrea openly supported the rebels against the government in Khartoum, correctly pointing to anti-Eritrean Islamic forces inside the Sudanese government. At times, little Eritrea actually seemed to be heading for an armed confrontation with its vast neighbour Sudan. It came even closer to war with Yemen, on the other side of the Red Sea, when the many islands in the straits between the two countries became a subject of dispute and the Eritrean navy began firing on the Yemenis. It took considerable international pressure to prevent further escalation of the conflict.

In fact, Ethiopia was the only adjacent country that Eritrea had not threatened with force since its independence. With its large population (twenty times the size of Eritrea's), Ethiopia was the natural leader in the Horn of Africa and perhaps it was precisely this fact that inflamed the Eritrean government. It is probable that Eritrea saw Ethiopia as a giant with feet of clay. After all, many people assumed that the Ethiopian government was dominated by people from the northern province of Tigray, bordering on Eritrea, and that the many other ethnic groups in Ethiopia would eventually attempt to cast off the Tigrayan yoke. Perhaps Eritrea thought that Ethiopia was already disintegrating and that the process could be accelerated by launching a vigorous and well-placed military attack on northern Ethiopia to break the power of Tigray. Ethiopia might then fragment, leaving little Eritrea, with its formidable armed forces, as the major power in the Horn of Africa.[125]

As it happened, however, the outcome of the Eritrean attack was very different. Ethiopia did not disintegrate but actually became more united. Although it was dominated by Tigrayans, the government in Addis Ababa showed a surprisingly bellicose spirit. Domestic political considerations played a major role. The prime minister, Meles Zenawi, used the war to strengthen his standing in the country. No leader ever wins popularity by relinquishing national territory. The independence of Eritrea following a successful war of secession was therefore a sore spot with the Ethiopian public and a potential Achilles' heel for the regime. The fact that Ethiopia had ceded the port of Assab to Eritrea was a particular problem. Although Assab had been part of the Italian colony of Eritrea, after Eritrea had once again become part of Ethiopia, the port had become part of a different Ethiopian province. For this reason, many people in Ethiopia felt that it had been unnecessary to cede the city to Eritrea. By doing so, Meles had deprived Ethiopia of direct access to the Red Sea. The critics complained that the government put Tigray's interests first, above those of the country as a whole. In order to end these and other doubts, the Ethiopian government responded harshly to the Eritrean attack on its border. It was determined to teach Eritrea a lesson it would never forget.

The result was one of the largest-scale wars in modern African history. The world looked on in amazement as hundreds of thousands of troops from two of the biggest and best-equipped armies in Africa fought each other tooth and nail. This was the exact opposite of the key security problem that had emerged in Africa since the end of the Cold War, that of weak states unable to control internal ethnic tensions. By contrast, the war between Ethiopia and Eritrea conformed to the standard Western model of armed confrontation between two countries, two governments and two armies. It involved powerful, centrally led organisations with such a grip on the minds of their soldiers that they were prepared without hesitation to leave their trenches and advance to almost certain death in very large numbers. In this sense, the war between Ethiopia and Eritrea was quite atypical of Africa and more reminiscent of the European battles of World War I.

On both sides of the border, nationalist feelings ran high.[126] The thousands of Ethiopians in Eritrea and the many Eritreans in Ethiopia paid the price. In 1998, Addis Ababa expelled no fewer than forty thousand of the latter, including people who had lived in Ethiopia for as long as thirty years. Others were interned in camps. Some were Ethiopian citizens; formal nationality was seen as less important than ethnic origin. With thousands of mixed marriages and countless other personal ties between Ethiopians and Eritreans, the result was many tragedies for individuals and their families.

Eventually both countries became weary of the war. There was a virtual stalemate on the battlefield, although Ethiopia eventually gained the upper hand. The human cost was high – probably around fifty thousand casualties on both sides – and the material damage was enormous. The area around the battlefields was ravaged and further back from the lines the bombardments had taken their toll on civilian life and property. To keep the war machine running, Ethiopia and Eritrea – both among the poorest countries in the world – each had to spend nearly half a million dollars a day. International aid to the two countries – previously darlings of the donor community – was halted, making it financially and economically ever more difficult to sustain such a large-scale war.

After a year of fighting, the governments of Ethiopia and Eritrea began to realise that they had to negotiate a ceasefire. There was little alternative, but they still needed to save face. International mediation by agencies like the OAU was the answer. The two countries met in Algiers (Algeria being the chairman of the OAU at the time) and, after months of wrangling over the details, finally signed a peace agreement in late December 2000.

Eritrea conceded to the establishment of a demilitarised zone within its territory on the border with Ethiopia so that peacekeepers from the United Nations Mission in Ethiopia and Eritrea (UNMEE) could monitor the ceasefire. UNMEE was led by the Netherlands and Canada. Eritrea was allowed to deploy police, but of course no soldiers, in the demilitarised zone. There was some tension when the Eritrean government sent frontline troops into the zone disguised as policemen (or militias). However, this did not really threaten the peace agreement. Meanwhile, the border between the two countries was to be precisely surveyed in order to engineer an agreement on the exact demarcation.

Continued fighting
in Sudan

In 1998, several countries bordering Sudan became involved in wars. This influenced the internal struggle between the north and south of the country. The conflict between Eritrea and Ethiopia gave the government in Khartoum some respite, since it meant that both neighbouring countries would concentrate their energies and resources on fighting each other rather than directing them against Sudan. It also reduced their support for the Sudanese resistance. Ugandan involvement in the war in Congo had a similar effect. The Sudanese government even allowed itself to be drawn into the latter conflict to some extent, by acquiring from Kabila the right to use airfields in northeastern Congo. This meant that the Sudan could provide direct support for Ugandan rebels operating on the border with Congo. In turn, this Sudanese strategy gave the government of Uganda an additional reason to send in troops to occupy part of Congo.

However, these international intrigues caused no more than a ripple in the civil war inside Sudan. The roots of the dispute lay far back in time. Through the Nile valley, Islamic influences filtered down from the Arab countries into what is now Sudan and hence into black Africa. A few hundred kilometres to the south of Khartoum, the advance of Middle Eastern culture was blocked in the early nineteenth century by the very different topography of southern Sudan (where the desert gives way to savannah and marshes) and also by the intervention of the British. From that time on, the territory that is now Sudan was divided into a northern area with a Muslim population of Arab extraction and a smaller southern area with a population of black Christians and animists.

From the moment of Sudan's independence, there were always great tensions, and frequently armed conflict, between the two areas. This conflict can be interpreted either as a political war of independence (waged by the south against the rest of the country) or as a cultural and religious war (waged by Arabs against black Africans). However, the most logical explanation is that it was a war waged by an expansionist Islam against the British presence and legacy in Sudan. When the British departed in 1955/1956, the Islamic advance resumed. The southern Sudanese had been opposed to British decolonisation, fearing that the northern Sudanese would step into the power vacuum. After a period of peace in the 1970s, the war flared up again in the 1980s when – mainly under the influence of the Islamic revolution in Iran – the government in Khartoum became increasingly fundamentalist and aggressive.

Throughout the 1990s and into the twenty-first century, the civil war raged on unabated, despite international attempts to end it. It was useless to point out the economic damage and human misery it was creating or the impossibility of a decisive military victory for either side. Khartoum was determined to achieve the political, military, religious, cultural and economic subjugation of the south. Indeed, it was difficult in practice to distinguish between these various dimensions. For example, Khartoum wanted to impose the same social constraints on women in the south as existed in the north. Government troops tried to prevent women in the south from engaging in trade, for example in foodstuffs.

However, such female trading activities were common throughout the whole of sub-Saharan Africa. A prohibition on it ran deeply counter to local cultural traditions and economic realities.

In 1989 the Sudanese army executed a coup d'état against the then civilian government. The inspirer of the coup and the strongman behind the newly installed military government was a religious leader and politician named Hassan al-Turabi. He was the ideologue of the National Islamic Front (NIF) and the brain behind the strategy for the islamisation of the country. Under his leadership, Sudan was to become the bastion of Islamic fundamentalism in sub-Saharan Africa.

In 1999, however, there was a rift between the army leaders and the fundamentalists. In a surprise move, the head of the army and military junta, Omar al-Bashir, managed to rid himself of Turabi. He then obtained confirmation of his presidency by calling elections in the part of the country controlled by the government. He won with a huge majority. Having consolidated his power in this way, he showed himself accommodating towards other parties, announcing his intention to include representatives of other parties in government and to end the war with the south by means of dialogue and negotiation. However, these plans were frustrated by Turabi. Although once the fiercest opponent of the rebels in the south, he now made overtures to them, suggesting that they should join forces with him against the 'oppressive' Bashir regime. He also called on the Sudanese people to rise up against the government. In 2001, Turabi was even detained for some time on suspicion of conspiring with the rebels in the south.

Politicians in northern Sudan were fairly easily able to form coalitions with turncoat rebel leaders in the south because the resistance in the south was heavily divided. Although the black African peoples in the region shared an unwillingness to be dominated by the Islamic, culturally Arab north, they had nothing else in common. Of the widely dispersed southern population of approximately five million, half were Dinka. The many much smaller minorities were afraid of a Dinka hegemony. This, combined with the very rudimentary physical infrastructure of the large southern region, with its many marshes and lakes, encouraged the different peoples and fighting forces to act in isolation from each other. Nevertheless, most remained affiliated in some way with the Sudan People's Liberation Army (SPLA), set up when the civil war resumed in the early 1980s.

During the Cold War, the SPLA received most of its support from the communist regime in Ethiopia, but after the fall of that government in 1991, it came more under the influence of the West (with support from the governments of Eritrea, Ethiopia and Uganda, which were likewise supported by the West). Unlike the old Soviet Union, the new Russian Federation had little interest in the war in Sudan. However, it still attempted to sell arms in exchange for hard currency – an offer the government in Khartoum was glad to accept on more than one occasion. China also assisted the Islamic regime, mainly in protecting the Sudanese oil industry.

In 1997, the government in Khartoum came under military pressure when the southern rebels, assisted by Eritrea, opened up a new front in the east of the country. This threatened the economically and militarily important link between Khartoum and the ports on the Red Sea coast. Relief came a year later when war broke out between Ethiopia and Eritrea, dramatically reducing the support they were able to give the Sudanese resistance movement. Eventually Eritrea even found itself under such pressure that it sought a rapprochement with Khartoum, but the war with Ethiopia petered out before any close link could be forged between Khartoum and Asmara.

Inevitably, the war in Sudan had serious consequences for the civilian population. None of the leaders in either the north or the south was much concerned with the development of the potentially wealthy country. The vast majority of the population, especially in the south, was poor and miserable. The lack of security was perhaps the worst problem. After the war was resumed in 1983, almost two million people perished and no fewer than four million were forced to flee the war zone. Most of them remained on Sudanese territory, often building shanties for themselves on the periphery of cities like Khartoum in the centre of the country or Nyala in the west. Others lived in camps in the south. Hundreds of thousands sought refuge in neighbouring countries, particularly Uganda.[127] For its food supplies, the south was dependent on international aid routed through Kenya. This cost the international community around a million dollars a day.

Africa's wars produced many child soldiers. By the turn of the century, there were around a hundred and twenty thousand of them. In the Sudan as elsewhere, children were heavily involved in the fighting, especially as members of southern resistance groups. There were local cultural reasons for this. Fighters were recruited through family connections. Following their initiation at around the age of twelve, boys were regarded as men and therefore suitable recruits. As the war dragged on, many child soldiers were orphans who had been born during the war and never had a normal family life. For them, the armed resistance group was a substitute family and its leader a proxy father. International pressure, in particular from the United Nations Children's Fund (UNICEF), brought about the discharge and demobilisation of some child soldiers, but they had difficulty adjusting to civilian life. There was even a fear that they would choose to return to the fray once they had been re-energised by a period of proper nourishment.

In both northern and southern Sudan there were widespread and extremely serious violations of human rights. The tradition of slavery and slave trading continued throughout the war. The northern army and related militias frequently raided the south in search of boys. To prevent them from joining the southern resistance groups, they abducted them and bore them off to the centre and north of the country, where they were forced to do all sorts of chores. As in previous centuries, Western aid organisations (in particular religious groups from the United States) attempted to purchase the freedom of these present-day slaves, openly collecting money for the purpose. This method attracted international criticism on the grounds that the payments created a financial incentive to capture slaves and that there was no guarantee that the newly emancipated slaves would not be immediately recaptured and put back on the market for 'liberation'.

Congo and the enemies
of Kabila

The drama in Sudan was not destined to retain the world's attention for long. By the millennium, it was the great war in Central Africa that was dominating the face of the continent. There were two reasons for this: the large number of belligerent parties and the duration of the hostilities. Instead of lasting just a few weeks, as the aggressors had expected, the war dragged on for years. Its complexity has already been discussed in this chapter. Very roughly speaking, the parties can be divided into two groups: on one side the enemies of the Congolese president, Laurent Kabila (see below), and on the other his allies (see next section), whatever their motives for taking part may have been.

On the subject of Kabila's opponents, it is arguable that the Congolese president was in fact his own worst enemy. Admittedly, he could not help the fundamental weakness of his position: without foreign assistance, he would never have obtained the presidency. But even with foreign support, Kabila never managed to do anything positive for Congo. In that respect, he was no better than Mobutu. Their regimes were similar in both style and policy, and Kabila's rule was – if possible – even worse for the country. Kabila lacked Mobutu's political instincts, and as a result actually plunged Congo into war.

Just as Mandela was in many respects the personification of all that was good in Africa (see last section of chapter 4), so Kabila became, in a sense, the embodiment of all that was wrong with the continent. He came to symbolise the disappointments of the 1990s, which were partly the result of unrealistically high expectations. Because Kabila had been brought to power by Museveni and Kagame, it was immediately assumed that he would be a 'new leader' of their calibre, someone who could get Congo back on track. In fact, however, Kabila proved to be a product of Africa's bad days in the 1970s and 1980s.

This was clear from the way he ran domestic politics, calling parliamentary and presidential elections only to postpone them, and finally suspending them entirely for the duration of the war. They were never to take place under his rule. He did, however, respond to national and international pressure to engage in political discussion with the opposition and other parties. And, just as Mobutu gave in to pressure and called a national assembly in 1991, so Kabila permitted religious leaders to organise a 'national consultation' in 2000. Representatives of government, industry, civil society and academia took part, together with traditional leaders. Even though Congolese rebel groups were not represented, the meeting rapidly transformed into an anti-Kabila forum demanding the resignation of the government, the liberation of political prisoners and the launch of a genuine national dialogue.[128]

Realising that the consultation was not working to his advantage, the president decided to establish a competing 'constituent assembly', the members of which were either appointed by him or at any rate on his side. But Kabila failed to control even this group; at its first meetings it attacked the government for the way it was running the country. But even more than criticising Kabila, the members of the constituent assembly were interested in lining their own pockets. If they were only there to applaud and rubberstamp Kabila's decisions, they wanted at least – as befitted true political clients – to be properly rewarded for their efforts. Kabila quickly lost patience with them. In October 2000, just two months after the official opening of this 'parliament', the president ordered the police to clear the offices of the representatives in the parliament building. The people of Congo would once again have to do without political spokesmen.

For those Congolese not averse to violence, there remained the option of armed opposition to the government in Kinshasa. Under Kabila, as in Mobutu's time, the country was full of armed gangs, militias and rebel movements, all operating in a disorganised way, with or without their own political agendas and support bases. What made them more dangerous during Kabila's presidency than in previous years was the certainty of substantial foreign support. Kabila himself had been the first Congolese rebel leader to benefit from such support, and now he risked falling victim to it. The weak armed forces available to the government in Kinshasa were capable of exercising some control over stray rebel groups, but not of resisting a serious attack by a foreign army.

The greatest problem for Kinshasa was the alternative government in Goma, which suddenly appeared on the scene in August 1998, simultaneously with the invasion of eastern Congo by joint forces from Rwanda and Uganda. This 'Goma regime' consisted of members of a resistance movement calling itself the Congolese Rally for Democracy (RCD). Apart from its self-proclaimed interest in democracy, nothing was known about this movement. Its leader, a history professor named Ernest Wamba dia Wamba, admitted that it had yet to draft a political manifesto. Furthermore, the Goma regime was still searching for a support base. The explanation for this curious state of affairs is that the RCD was actually a front for the Rwandan and Ugandan presence in Congo.

The later rupture between Kigali and Kampala was mirrored by a schism within the RCD. Wamba, whose leadership of the movement was already shaky, withdrew from Goma with his supporters and organised his own breakaway RCD further north, supported by Uganda. The Goma RCD continued to rely heavily on Rwandan support and pursued a purely military strategy, without bothering to develop any clear Congolese political identity. By contrast, Wamba's breakaway RCD adopted the strategy that Museveni had pursued in Uganda and built up a highly motivated militia via a programme of political education amongst its followers. Even so, Wamba's RCD remained too weak to be of much real use to Uganda and the Ugandan army gradually switched its support to another anti-Kabila group, the Movement for the Liberation of Congo (MLC), which was active throughout the north of the country. By the beginning of the new millennium, the MLC had become the most highly organised and motivated Congolese fighting force, with the potential to constitute a real threat to the government in Kinshasa.

However, the real military threat to Kabila came from abroad. The Rwandan and Ugandan invasion forces were among the most powerful armies in Africa. Rwanda had more than twenty thousand men in Congo and Uganda around ten thousand.[129] Rwanda's motive for intervening in Congo was clear enough: to conclude the unfinished conflict between the Tutsi and the Hutu. The motivation of the Ugandan government in Kampala was less obvious. It probably feared that its ambition to dominate the region would be in jeopardy if it did not intervene in Congo's affairs, but it also claimed a right to defend itself against rebel movements operating out of northeastern Congo. Kabila had fed this Ugandan fear by giving Sudan permission to use airfields in northeastern Congo to supply the anti-Kampala rebels.

Many people in the outside world accepted the security arguments cited by Rwanda and Uganda for invading Congo as reasonable and even legitimate. But the longer the occupation of eastern Congo went on, the more important the economic motives seemed to be. Kabila's enemies shared his awareness of the country's natural wealth. For a long time the plundering of Congo's resources by the neighbouring countries tended to be ignored but in 2001 the United Nations published a report focusing on this aspect of the affair.[130] Although the report was heavily criticised for overemphasising the roles of Uganda and Rwanda and for its occasional lack of hard evidence, it did put the presence of the two countries in eastern Congo in a new light.

According to the UN report, a special section had been set up inside the Rwandan army in Congo to plunder the economic resources of the occupied areas in a systematic way. Minerals were moved to Rwanda, bank vaults were emptied and production plants were dismantled and transferred piece by piece to Rwanda. The Rwandan army forced hundreds of prisoners to work in Congolese mines producing columbite-tantalite, coltan for short, a material used in the manufacture of mobile phones and therefore an extremely profitable trade commodity at the time. But other products, including gold, diamonds, timber and coffee, were also appropriated and sold. In this respect, Uganda was less systematic than Rwanda. The exploitation of Congo's wealth was mainly left to private individuals, although they needed political and military support to run their operations. For example, the leading Ugandan businessman in Congo was reportedly a younger brother of President Museveni. The governments of Rwanda and Uganda denied any involvement in these military and economic activities and claimed to be unfairly accused by the UN report.

But their activities in Congo were betrayed by their national export figures. Exports of gold from Uganda (which itself produced little of the metal) faithfully reflected the course of the war in Congo. They increased after Kabila came to power with the help of Uganda, dipped in 1998 following the breakdown in relations between Kabila and Uganda (and Rwanda), and immediately shot up again once Uganda had occupied part of eastern Congo.[131] From 1999 onward, Uganda and Rwanda engaged in more intensive economic exploitation of eastern Congo and were able to use the profits to meet much of the cost of their military operations. In this way, the occupation was not only economically selfsustaining but also became a source of income for the governments of both countries. As a result, there was no reason to bring the war to a rapid end. In the long run, it would be much more profitable for the governments in Kigali and Kampala to carve Congo up between them (although they would still have to demarcate their respective spheres of influence) than to allow eastern Congo to be absorbed into a new, unitary Congolese state.

However, the growing emphasis on economic interests meant that Rwanda and Uganda found themselves increasingly in competition with each other. It was not easy to demarcate the zones of occupation, if only because the personal economic interests of local military commanders sometimes overshadowed those of the governments in Kigali and Kampala. Perhaps President Kagame of Rwanda wished to demonstrate his independence from his patron Museveni, just as Kabila had demonstrated his independence from both of them. Whatever the reason, on no fewer than three occasions, widespread fighting broke out in Kisangani, the main city in northeastern Congo, between units of the Rwandan and Ugandan armies, with Rwanda maintaining the upper hand. Thousands perished, including many Congolese civilians, and hundreds of thousands of other civilians fled into the surrounding jungle. The fighting was only ended with difficulty and under heavy international pressure requiring the intervention of the UN Security Council itself. This surprising turn of events in eastern Congo dented the international image of both Rwanda and Uganda and gave Kabila the idea that time might be on his side.

The other member of the crumbling international front against Kabila was Burundi. Following the deaths of two Hutu presidents in 1993 and 1994, the country was riven by major internal tensions and there was no practical prospect of compromise or cooperation between the Hutu and Tutsi communities. In 1997 army leader and former president Pierre Buyoya led a coup which placed power firmly back in Tutsi hands. The international community responded by imposing sanctions. As long as Kabila was allied with Rwanda and Uganda, Buyoya's Tutsi regime in Burundi had nothing to fear from Congo. At that time, the Burundian (Hutu) resistance was operating mainly out of Tanzania. In 1998, however, the change in Kabila's policies put him on a conflict course with Burundi. For safety's sake, Buyoya had his soldiers occupy the Congolese side of Lake Tanganyika. At the same time, Burundian rebels were welcomed to Congo, because their aims were now consonant with Kabila's. Indeed, Kabila could make good use of these battle-hardened and highly motivated troops. Rewarding their commanders richly, he absorbed thousands of Burundian fighters into the Congolese army in the east of the country. They swiftly became its core.

From that point on, the international struggle surrounding Kabila was inseparable from the internal strife within Burundi. Acting via ex-President Mandela of South Africa and others, the international community brought heavy pressure to bear on Burundi to reach a political settlement. In Arusha, Tanzania, Buyoya's regime and no fewer than nineteen Burundian political parties signed an agreement ending the war. However, the armed resistance operating out of Congo refused to sign. Kabila could not afford to lose the support of the Burundian military, and offered their commanding officers persuasive financial inducements to fight on. The war in Congo had to continue and this had the effect of prolonging the civil war in Burundi which, in the last decade of the twentieth century, cost the lives of almost a quarter of a million people in that country.

Congo and Kabila's allies

In addition to around sixteen thousand Burundians, Kabila's army also included tens of thousands of Rwandans. The majority of them were exiled Hutu, many of whom had served in the Rwandan army under the pregenocide regime. They numbered no fewer than forty thousand and were highly motivated to fight, since they had a clear interest in winning the war. In addition, Angola, Zimbabwe and Namibia provided battalions led by their own officers. Other countries in the region, including Congo (Brazzaville), Gabon, the Central African Republic, Chad and Tanzania, supported Kabila less directly, either out of a belief in his right to defend himself against the illegal attack by Rwanda and Uganda or for pragmatic reasons, to preserve the balance of power in Central Africa. However, these countries provided no troops, either because they did not dare to or because they had too many domestic problems of their own. Finally, the war in Congo also involved irregular militias and mercenaries of many different nationalities. The whole miscellany was completed by military advisors from North Korea and also China. North Korea was probably hoping to be rewarded with Congolese uranium, which it could use for nuclear bombs, although it is highly uncertain whether Congo could in fact have provided it. Kabila probably paid the Asian countries in cobalt, a metal used in the aircraft industry.[132]

Kabila needed such copious and varied support simply to survive. Unaided, his own forces could never have fought the war. Admittedly, the Congolese army had around fifty thousand men, but it was poorly equipped and even the so-called elite troops were unreliable: more than half of the army was likely to desert if called upon to fight. To deal with this problem, frontline troops were paid regularly (unlike the others). To make matters worse, the Congolese army was divided between Swahili-speaking troops from the east of the country and Lingala-speakers from the west.[133] Since Kabila was from eastern Congo, those from that region now had the upper hand in the army. Since it was extremely important to them to keep control of soldiers from other parts of the country and to ensure that Kabila remained in power, they were the only members of the army who faced battle with any enthusiasm. The rest were almost always unwilling to engage in action. The same was true of the mood in the country at large. Although there had been a fierce nationalist response at the time of the Rwandan attack in 1998, especially in Kinshasa, this ebbed away later.

Amid his throng of allies, Kabila's own position was weak. An obvious way of strengthening it would have been to share power with prominent Congolese leaders with their own support networks. This might also have strengthened the regime's ethnic and regional power base. But Kabila's fear of losing his dictatorial grasp on power was clearly too great to allow him to adopt this course. He did precisely the opposite, and surrounded himself with people who – like himself – had lived for long periods outside Congo and therefore lacked any current power base within the country. The only real powers with which he was willing to ally himself – when driven by military necessity – were foreign governments. They sent whole battalions to Congo in order to prop up his regime. In essence, Kabila thereby placed large parts of the country in the hands of foreign powers. Rather than share sovereign authority, he preferred to share the territory of the country. Congo was carved up among armies and fighting forces which often operated as competing gangs. Kabila tried to remain the top dog, but there was no way he could retain control of the whole country under the circumstances.

A major section of the army over which the Congolese president had no control were the Angolans. Angola's intervention in Congo must be viewed in the light of its own civil war between the government and the UNITA resistance movement. In the early 1990s, there had been some hope that the internal struggle in Angola might be coming to an end. After reaching an agreement with the government, UNITA leader Jonas Savimbi stood for election, but was defeated. In a country operating on a winner-takes-all (and therefore loser-loses-all) principle, there proved to be no place for him in the postwar democratic system. This made it inevitable that he would decide to resume the civil war.

The Angolan civil war therefore entered a new phase, which resembled the previous one at first sight but differed from it in terms of the reduced international support for UNITA. By allowing the peace process to fail, the resistance movement had forfeited the sympathy of its former allies (in particular the United States and South Africa). Cut off from the sea (because the entire Angolan coastline was controlled by the government in Luanda), the resistance groups in the often remote areas of the interior found their ability to fight limited by their access to supplies of such essentials as weapons, munitions, petrol and spare parts for road vehicles.

All these things could be bought on the international market. The weapons came principally from the surplus arsenals of the former Eastern Bloc states. Bulgaria, Ukraine, Belarus and Russia were the biggest suppliers. Since UNITA's only trade and supply routes ran north through Congo, the power vacuum in that country gave the resistance movement a unique opportunity to rebuild its fighting capacity. By 1997-1998, on the eve of the war in Congo, UNITA had once again mustered an impressive army of up to sixty thousand well-armed rebels. The Angolan government awaited the new escalation of the civil war with apprehension. Knowing that it was facing a difficult challenge, it opted for the daring strategy of striking out at UNITA via Congo. If the movement's supply lines there could be cut, UNITA would eventually be forced to give up the struggle and government troops might be able to finish it off for good.

So Angola's military support for Kabila in the war in Congo was seen by the government in Luanda primarily as a means of opening up a second front in its own civil war. Kabila was a minor consideration. Given the considerable military threat on its own territory, however, Angola could not make many troops available. Four months after the start of the war in Congo, UNITA decided to launch a major offensive in Angola. Throughout 1999, there was large-scale fighting in the centre and north of Angola with modern military equipment. The government in Luanda was forced to move troops from Congo to the home front. But gradually the strategy of cutting off UNITA's supply lines through Congo started to take effect. Towards the end of 1999, the rebels faced a serious petrol shortage and malfunctioning equipment could not be repaired. For the next year, UNITA continued to lose ground and by the end of 2000 the entire territory of Angola was effectively back in the hands of government troops. As a regular army, UNITA had ceased to exist. This was a major success for the government in Luanda but did not automatically spell the end of the civil war. UNITA was not so easily finished off. The UNITA army fragmented into smaller forces, which hid out here and there in the interior and carried out small raids. The military front had disappeared, but the interior was still far from secure. The Angolan war entered another new phase, in which sporadic low-level violence threatened the security of the entire country.

Kabila benefited greatly from the strategy of the Angolan regime. The Angolan troops constituted a strong defensive line for his seat of government in Kinshasa and helped the Congolese army to maintain its military grip on strategic points elsewhere in the country. Modern Angolan planes and attack helicopters at bases just over the border inside Angola could be called in at any moment to provide support for ground troops. By the new millennium, although the Angolan government was still grappling with UNITA, its involvement in Congo's tangled affairs had nevertheless turned it into a regional superpower dominating the western area of Central Africa.

The result was that in Central Africa, as in the Horn of Africa, alliances were reshuffled. During the Cold War era, the governments of Zaire/Congo and Angola had belonged to opposing camps, with Kinshasa allied to Washington and Luanda to Moscow. The rules of the Cold War game had demanded that each of them try to undermine the other by supporting its rebels and in this sense, it had been a logical move for the Angolan government to support Laurent Kabila in his attempt to depose Mobutu. Once Kabila's coup succeeded, however, there was a Luanda-Kinshasa axis and Luanda's aim was to prevent groups in the Congolese interior seizing power from the government in Kinshasa.

Another powerful foreign ally of Kabila was Zimbabwe, which provided over ten thousand well-trained and highly disciplined soldiers, equipped with tanks, aircraft and a range of relatively up-to-date equipment — about a third of its army in total. Many people were surprised by President Mugabe's decision to intervene in the conflict on such a scale. But Mugabe had good reasons for doing so. Firstly, he envisaged a major future role in Africa for himself and his country and therefore could not afford to remain neutral. Moreover, by intervening to protect Kabila, he was defending the principle that one African country should not attack another. Mugabe's personal friendship with Kabila must also have been a factor. In the domestic sphere, a military action on foreign soil was a convenient way of distracting attention from the tensions that were starting to emerge as a result of political, economic and social decline (see chapter 10, pp. 335-339). Finally, the Zimbabwean elite were keen to join the scramble for a share in Congo's mineral wealth.

Kabila realised that this was a price he had to pay. He made an arrangement with Mugabe to fund the Zimbabwean war effort with the profits of various Congolese companies. At its heart was a provision that Zimbabwe's Ridgepointe Central Mining Group would take over the management of Gécamines, the Congolese mining company.

In the event, however, the financial benefits were smaller than Zimbabwe had hoped. Congo had virtually no hard currency and payments in its own currency were worthless to Zimbabwe. The only alternatives were barter and payments in kind, but these proved difficult to arrange. Congo's debts to Zimbabwe piled up swiftly, while Zimbabwe found itself in an economic crisis and was struggling with its own rapidly mounting debts. Within two years, Zimbabwe's role in the conflict had cost the country around two million dollars.[134] In itself, this was not a vast sum, but the country could not really afford its military involvement in Congo. Mugabe was aware of that, but was afraid of a domestic backlash if he withdrew. Moreover, his entourage was still hoping for a share in Congo's riches. So Zimbabwe remained actively involved in the war.

This catalogue of Kabila's allies would be incomplete without some mention of Namibia, the smallest country to engage more or less formally in the war on Kabila's side. According to the Namibian president, Sam Nujoma, a friend of Kabila's, Namibia had felt obliged to respond to Kabila's appeal for support from members of the Southern African Development Community (SADC). However, its military contribution was small – less than two thousand soldiers plus some ordnance – and played no significant role in the war. The economic benefit to Namibia consisted of the chance to supply fish to Congo in exchange for a share in Congo's diamond industry, made over to a brother-in-law of Nujoma.[135]

The Lusaka Accord:

untangling the web

The war in Central Africa can be regarded as Africa's First World War. It resembled its European counterpart of 1914-1918 in the swiftness and suddenness with which a whole region was plunged into violent conflict as multicountry coalitions engaged in hostilities. And in Africa, as in the Europe of 1914, people thought the war would soon be over. The aggressors thought that victory would be easy but the defence proved stronger than expected and a military stalemate developed. As time went on, the war has become almost a permanent feature of life in Central Africa.

The nature of the conflict was determined principally by the geography of Congo. The country was huge and thinly populated, with few transport links. Rivers (and, for the well-equipped armies, aviation) were important means of transport. Armies and fighting forces of all sorts roamed the vast country trying to find (or avoid) each other. In many areas, especially along the eastern border with Uganda, Rwanda and Burundi, a variety of armed groups operated with or against each other, sometimes creating complicated military situations.

For the more regular armies, however, the main targets were the Congolese mining areas, which offered rich pickings both to fund the war effort and to line the pockets of individual leaders. In such potentially wealthy areas, especially in the diamond-rich provinces of Kasai and Katanga (in the south and southeast of the country respectively) fronts developed on which a well-organised conventional war was fought. In the north there was a separate front, with fighting between the MLC resistance movement and troops defending the Congo River town of Mbandaka, gateway to Kinshasa.

There was no lack of weapons. The next-to-last section of chapter 5 describes the ease with which, from the 1990s on, all the warring parties in Africa could purchase arms on the international market. The main suppliers to the Congolese army were Zimbabwe (which was building up its own defence industry with help from China), Libya and Iran. Zimbabwe itself was using fighter aircraft supplied by Great Britain in the 1980s and equipment from the former Eastern Bloc. Rwanda obtained many weapons from South Africa, which had inherited a major arms industry from the apartheid regime. Uganda relied more on the former Eastern Bloc, but had also built three arms and munitions plants of its own. Almost all the national armies involved in the war supplied arms to irregular forces and militias.[136] The weapons were largely financed out of taxes on the export of minerals (such as diamonds) and other commodities from the occupied territories, but warring parties also obtained loans from foreign companies in exchange for mining concessions.[137]

Some countries and organisations strove to reduce the flow of arms into Central Africa. As early as 1993, the European Union imposed an arms embargo on Zaire as a means of putting pressure on Mobutu's dictatorial regime. In 1997, this embargo was automatically transferred to Congo. In 1994 a UN arms embargo was imposed on the non-state parties to the conflict in Rwanda. Efforts were also made to cut off funding to the combatants. Diamond certification was introduced in order to reduce the income of various parties in Congo and Angola (and, indeed, in Liberia and Sierra Leone) by restricting their access to the international market. However, the diamond trade was complex and convoluted, involving large numbers of shady middlemen. It would take years to bring it under control.

From the start of the war in 1998, the international community, with some Western and African countries leading the way, imposed heavy political and diplomatic pressure to abandon hostilities. All the countries involved suffered serious damage, with the exception of Angola, which was becoming more and more powerful while making relatively small sacrifices. On the initiative of Zambia, a neutral member of SADC, a major conference of all the warring parties was held in mid-1999 in the Zambian capital, Lusaka. In August, a year after the outbreak of war, this produced the Lusaka Accord, signed by six African heads of state and more than fifty rebel leaders, which was intended to lead the way to lasting peace in Congo.

The Lusaka Accord was in part a ceasefire agreement but went further. It was realistic, acknowledging the fundamental threats to regional security and sources of political instability. Since one crucial factor was the de facto absence of a Congolese state, the accord provided for a two-track approach: an end to hostilities, coupled with a domestic political dialogue within Congo, elections, a new national army and the restoration of government authority throughout the country. To promote internal dialogue, the OAU appointed Ketumile Masire, the former president of Botswana, to act as facilitator. However, Masire found it impossible to establish a dialogue between the government in Kinshasa and other parties in Congo. President Kabila was simply not a man for negotiated solutions, especially not at the expense of his own authority. Kabila felt justified in his refusal to engage in dialogue because no progress was achieved on the other track of the Lusaka Accord, the ending of hostilities.

The accord provided for a UN-mandated peace force to patrol the ceasefire, disarm belligerents and arrest war criminals. If such a force could truly be assembled, however, it would be some time before it could be put in place. The parties to the Lusaka Accord found themselves with no alternative to undertaking the initial supervision of the ceasefire on their own. The result was a peculiar situation in which the warring parties themselves had to monitor compliance with the agreement. They set up a joint military commission for the purpose, headed by a neutral chairman, again designated by the OAU.

Initially, the international community lent only moral support to the peace process. The problem was seen as too large and too complicated to do more. Africa would have to sort out its own affairs. In diplomatic jargon, this was known as finding 'African solutions to African problems'. Nevertheless, the United Nations did manage to make a start on assembling a peacekeeping force to monitor the implementation of the agreement in Congo. In 2000, the first part of the United Nations Organisation Mission in the Democratic Republic of Congo (MONUC) arrived in Central Africa. However, inadequate cooperation from the warring parties prevented it from playing a role of any importance.[138]

The main obstacle to ending the conflict was actually that none of the non-Congolese parties had anything to gain from the restoration of Congolese state authority over the entire territory. The many countries involved in the war – on whichever side – all preferred to see a weak government in Kinshasa. In the end, the only way for Rwanda and Uganda to guarantee the security of their borders was to do it themselves by occupying eastern Congo. Kabila's allies had other factors to consider, but the result was identical. Zimbabwe was increasingly war-weary and preoccupied by domestic difficulties, but this did not mean that President Mugabe could withdraw from Congo without loss of face. And without Zimbabwean troops on Congolese soil, his entourage could forget about the income from the Congolese mines. For the time being, therefore, Harare preferred to maintain its sphere of influence in southern Congo. Angola likewise had reasons to prefer the current situation, in which it was the most powerful country in west Central Africa. After all, a strong government in Kinshasa could not be expected to comply so readily with Angola's wishes.

The longer Congo's neighbours continued to occupy the country, dividing it into different spheres of influence, the more they came to rely on its practically inexhaustible mineral wealth. They exploited it with a dogged determination equalling that of the European powers in the colonial era.[139]

And the Congolese themselves? Did the majority of them favour the restoration of a unified state? The question was impossible to answer. There was undoubtedly a feeling of unity inside Congo, based on a century of shared history and recently reinforced by a surge of nationalism in response to the attacks from abroad. However, this had been insufficient to prevent rapid fragmentation of the country and its people over recent years. It was unclear which ethnic groups still hoped to see central state authority restored. It proved difficult to set in motion the internal Congolese dialogue for which the Lusaka Accord provided and which was intended to restore some semblance of normality to domestic politics. In August 2000, the Congolese government actually formally rejected the Lusaka Accord.

In the end, however, Kabila's opposition proved to be of little importance. His role in the drama was about to end. On 16 January 2001, Laurent Desiré Kabila was gunned down in his palace in Kinshasa by one of his own bodyguards. Bystanders immediately killed the assassin, so that nothing certain is known about the motive for the killing. Inevitably, some people suggested that he might have been acting on behalf of a foreign power, such as Rwanda, but no evidence of it was discovered. It is more likely that he had a personal grudge against the president, for example because he had been passed over for promotion or had not received his pay.

The murder of Kabila was sudden and unexpected, but not actually surprising. Kabila himself had always feared assassination. He was well aware of his weak power base and many enemies. He had always been afraid that, like his illustrious predecessor, Patrice Lumumba, he might fall victim to a Western plot or local treachery. Indeed, it was his para- noid suspicion of those around him that had made him expand the country's internal secu- rity system – probably the only part of the state apparatus that did expand under his regime.[140] The country was full of security officials spying on the population and on each other. Ethnic background was a major factor in staffing decisions. The more closely depart- ments worked with the palace, the more closely linked their staff had to be to Kabila's own ethnic group. The special presidential guard in charge of palace security was composed exclusively of people from Kabila's birthplace: Manono in the southeastern province of Katanga. In the end, however, all his efforts were in vain.

Following the death of the dictator, the regime's survival depended entirely on its foreign allies. At the funeral, the mood was embattled. The states that had fought against Kabila were asked not to send representatives. Of the Western nations, only Belgium had a politi- cal presence, in the person of its minister of foreign affairs. The Kinshasa public suspected the Belgians, like all the other white people present, of involvement in the murder. Belgian journalists were assaulted by a furious mob and Zimbabwean soldiers briefly detained a Belgian security official accompanying the minister. It was a clear illustration of how times had changed in Congo.

Behind the scenes, there was immediate consultation between a number of remaining members of Kabila's regime and the presidents of three friendly countries: Robert Mugabe of Zimbabwe, Sam Nujoma of Namibia and José Eduardo dos Santos of Angola. It was they who chose Kabila's successor: his young son Joseph. Although inexperienced and virtually unknown, Joseph Kabila immediately showed himself to be of a very different calibre from his father. He had an aura of integrity and was charming and open in his dealings with the outside world. Right from the start, he announced that peace was his main priority, fol- lowed by a better standard of living for the people of Congo (another new direction) and, finally, a greater role for the people in governing the country. In particular, he emphasised the need for greater democracy, although he stressed that it had to be introduced in an orderly fashion.

With the help of strong international pressure, Joseph Kabila succeeded in reviving the peace process. One after another, the neighbouring countries withdrew their armies, although Rwanda probably maintained a secret military presence in eastern Congo, an area that remained insecure. The UN gave its MONUC operation a stronger mandate, including the authority to enforce the peace. By 2003, the MONUC force was composed of some 10,000 soldiers from nationals around the world. The Congolese president embarked on good-faith talks with the rebel movements, which led to the installation of a transitional government in Kinshasa. All factions were represented in this government, which was led by Joseph Kabila but included four vice-presidents, thirty-five ministers and twenty-three deputy ministers from the various groups. The government, counting on generous international support, set itself the task of restoring Congo's state structures and organising elections in 2005.

The war had left the country in a humanitarian crisis. It was difficult enough to deliver public services to most of the provinces in peacetime; in wartime it was completely impossible. All over the country, basic services like health care, education and the provision of drinking water had virtually disappeared. The population was destitute. International humanitarian aid was only reaching some of the camps. By the turn of the century, more than one and a half million people were thought to have perished, two hundred thousand in combat and the rest as a result of malnutrition and disease. Still more had been uprooted. There were close to two million refugees and internally displaced persons. The widespread fighting, although generally of low intensity, was producing a genuine humanitarian disaster.

Refugees and internally displaced persons

With the war in Central Africa and the conflicts in Liberia and Sierra Leone, refugees once again became a major problem in Africa. Together, these hotspots produced an increasing number of refugees throughout the 1990s. This was in contrast to the trend elsewhere in the world: although the worldwide number of refugees had increased rapidly since the late 1970s, it stabilised in the mid-1990s at around fifteen or sixteen million.

In Africa, however, the number of refugees continued to grow even more rapidly than before. It had already increased in the 1980s, levelling off between three and four million.[141] By the mid-1990s it had risen to six million and by the end of the century it stood at eight million. At that time, Africa had more refugees than any other continent (in both absolute and relative terms). Disregarding those Africans who fled the continent entirely, and those who left their countries for economic or other non-political reasons (see chapter 8, pp. 257-260), Africa – with approximately ten per cent of the world population – was the source of roughly half the refugees on the planet. Add to this the many millions of people displaced within their own countries and the situation looks even more appalling.[142]

The traditional definition of a refugee, cited in the 1951 Geneva Convention relating to the Status of Refugees, is someone who has a 'well-founded fear of being persecuted for reasons of race, religion, nationality, membership of a particular social group or political opinion...'. However, this definition takes no account of the possibility that people may become refugees purely as a result of violent conflict and natural disasters – in Africa the two main reasons why people seek refuge outside their own home areas. The broader definition used by the United Nations High Commissioner for Refugees (UNHCR) is therefore more appropriate: namely, people who leave their country because they have a well-founded fear of being persecuted or because their safety is jeopardised by events seriously disturbing public order. The OAU (since 2002, the African Union; see chapter 7, p. 224) employs a similarly broad definition which can be understood to include even people who are uprooted by natural disasters. However, none of the definitions includes persons who are displaced but remain within their own country. In Africa, this is a large group and internally displaced persons often have the same problems as refugees, who have left their countries. In practice, however, UNHCR – the main organisation representing the interests of all these people – classes refugees and internally displaced persons together in the category of 'persons of concern'; in other words, people in need of help and protection.

Few of the many people uprooted in Congo could actually be helped or even counted. The total number of refugees and internally displaced persons in Africa has always been a matter of guesswork. By their very nature, refugee movements are dynamic and often involve a mixture of people: not only refugees in the strict sense but also internally displaced persons and economic migrants. Moreover, refugees and internally displaced persons often seek sanctuary in remote, inaccessible regions or among people sharing the same ethnic or linguistic background, making them difficult for outsiders to identify. Finally, governments may have political or other reasons for providing inaccurate estimates of their numbers.

Often, refugees are fleeing from natural disasters. In Africa, the consequences of such disasters have always been dire, mainly because of the fragility of social structures, especially in the poorest countries. Poverty makes communities vulnerable both to loss of human life and property damage. In absolute terms, of course, damage to property as a result of natural disasters has been far greater in rich communities than in poor ones. In terms of monetary value, seventy-five per cent of such damage has been suffered in rich countries.[143] However, Africans living under or just above the poverty line have always been extremely vulnerable to the effects of drought, flooding, earthquakes and storms. In addition to poverty, another reason for the increased vulnerability of communities and individuals has been the ever more serious degradation of the natural environment; for example, large-scale deforestation or the depletion of previously fertile soils.

In the period considered here, a more common cause of the growing number of refugees in Africa was the increase in the number, scope and duration of violent conflicts, especially civil conflicts. The civilian population was dragged into the fighting more and more often, producing a sharp rise in the number of casualties, including refugees and internally displaced persons. In civil wars like those in Somalia and Liberia, around ninety per cent of the dead and wounded were civilians. Local political leaders and warlords responsible for the fighting were indifferent to the fate of civilians and ignored the international laws of war and humanitarian law. Most conflicts were accompanied by widespread violations of human rights and caused untold human suffering. They produced large numbers of refugees and internally displaced persons. Around the turn of the century, one in five Africans was living in the midst of armed conflict. Although this was often what is classed as 'low-intensity violence', it was still sufficient reason for many to flee.

Women and girls were especially at risk. In various countries, especially around the Great Lakes and in West Africa, rape and other forms of sexual violence were widespread as a means of humiliating women and terrorising whole communities. Where such practices became common, they frequently provoked an exodus of refugees. Tragically enough, women and girls fleeing such situations often found themselves exposed to further sexual violence as refugees: from camps and elsewhere came reports of sexual abuse by policemen and other officials. Even within their own communities, they could be more at risk as traditional social structures and values crumbled under the pressures of refugee life. Sometimes the victims of sexual violence were actually rejected by their own communities. Since 1993, when it emerged that rape was widespread in Somali refugee camps inside Kenya, UNHCR has tried to take a systematic approach to sexual violence. It has issued guidelines for its own staff and other fieldworkers on ways of combating sexual violence and supporting victims.[144]

The elderly are another particularly vulnerable category of refugees. Malnutrition, inadequate medical care and poor accommodation expose them to particular risk of falling ill or dying. They also suffer more than other refugees as a result of the disintegration of social ties. During the 1990s, there was an increase in the number of elderly people becoming refugees without the support of younger members of their families or community. Like the sick, the disabled and single mothers with young children, they were often left behind in refugee camps when younger, fitter refugees were able to return home. Refugees in those categories continued to rely on support from international aid agencies for very long periods.

Although many organisations have been involved in assisting refugees in recent years, UNHCR has continued to play a central role. Its leading donors have been the United States, the European Union, Japan, the Netherlands and Great Britain. In Africa, UNHCR has had a presence in almost all areas where there were concentrations of refugees and internally displaced persons and it has taken responsibility for coordination with other aid organisations and the governments of the host countries. Nongovernmental aid agencies have carried out joint activities with UNHCR or have run their own independent projects. It has not been unknown for poorly qualified and inexperienced aid workers to act in an irresponsible and unprofessional manner, with adverse consequences for the refugees they were trying to help.[145]

More and more refugee aid operations had to take place in a politically sensitive environment. This sometimes politicised what was in principle purely humanitarian aid; local leaders and the indigenous population did not always regard aid workers as neutral.[146] The presence of fugitive murderers among the persons of concern in the camps – something that probably occurred on a large scale in Somalia, West Africa and the Great Lakes region – was also a problem. Aid workers had to decide whether to provide aid simply on humanitarian grounds or to distinguish between deserving and undeserving recipients. This was a particular problem in the case of Rwandan refugees in the camps in eastern Congo. Aid workers were unable to distinguish clearly between perpetrators and victims of the genocide, so that aid became politicised and even prolonged the hostilities.

The conflicts that led to the largest numbers of refugees in Africa were the disturbances in Congo following independence (1960-1967), the failed Biafran war of secession in Nigeria (1967-1970), the eventually successful Eritrean war of secession from Ethiopia (1962-1991) and the prolonged civil wars in Sudan, Chad, Angola and Mozambique. In the 1990s, virtually every country in Africa was affected by the refugee problem, either as a source of refugees or as a recipient, and often as both. The main movements of refugees occurred in the Great Lakes region, the Horn of Africa and West Africa around Liberia and Sierra Leone.

The sudden arrival of refugees, sometimes in hundreds of thousands, always posed major problems for the host area. Vital commodities like water, soil and firewood could all quickly be exhausted and social disruption and cultural clashes sometimes ensued if the newcomers were very different from the local population.

The capacity of any host population to absorb refugees is inevitably limited. In the cases considered here, the limit was reached sooner if refugees were offered aid while the local population remained without necessities such as food and medical care. For this reason, aid agencies increasingly resorted to providing material assistance not only to refugees, but also to the indigenous host population. By establishing special projects in areas with large concentrations of refugees, they attempted to make the situation more acceptable to the population and government of the country. Governments of host countries could, in fact, sometimes derive political advantage from accepting refugees. For example, the position of President Mobutu of Zaire was briefly strengthened as a result of the contribution that the international community asked him to make from 1993 on to the solution of the problem of refugees from Rwanda and Burundi.

But taking in and caring for refugees – however successful it sometimes was – could not be a permanent solution to the problem. In the 1990s, as refugee numbers skyrocketed, the attitude of the international community began to change. Increasingly, states tried to close their borders to new refugees and to repatriate those who had already arrived. As a result, attention shifted from the problems of refugees in host countries to the problems they faced on return to their countries of origin.

By the turn of the century, it was generally accepted that voluntary return to the country of origin and reintegration into the home community was the best solution for a very large proportion of the refugees in Africa. This strategy had a number of advantages: refugees were no longer permanently uprooted, the indefinite presence of large numbers of refugees in host countries, which sometimes had entirely different cultures, was avoided and the limited financial resources provided by donors could be used to promote development in the countries of origin. On the other hand, the new strategy obliged donors to become involved in repatriating and reintegrating refugees.

In general, refugees and internally displaced persons were only prepared to return home if they thought that their safety would be guaranteed both during the journey and after their return. Nevertheless, refugees throughout Africa began to return spontaneously to their own countries, even if those countries were still the scene of armed conflict. The situation for refugees in the country where they had been granted temporary asylum was often so precarious that they preferred to return *en masse*, even if life at home was likely to be arduous. In 1991-1992, for example, half a million Ethiopians left Somalia to return to their own country, because the situation in Somalia had become too dangerous.

One country that solved a large-scale refugee problem was Mozambique. In 1992, when a peace agreement ended the civil war, there were no fewer than 1.7 million Mozambican refugees in the surrounding countries. The plan for their return and reintegration into Mozambican society was developed and carried out under the leadership of UNHCR, in cooperation with countless agencies, and funded by a variety of international donors. The initial emphasis was, inevitably, on repatriating the refugees, but from 1994 the stress shifted to reintegration. This included food aid until the first harvest, distribution of seed and agricultural tools, and the restoration of basic facilities like water systems, roads, bridges, schools and health centres. The underlying idea was that the refugee problem could only be permanently solved if the returnees were offered some prospect of improving their standard of living.

This strategy for reintegration was carried out mainly through Quick Impact Projects (QIPs). The QIP approach involved responding quickly and directly to the needs of a community or area, usually by making a one-off contribution of financial or physical resources. It was then up to the local population to ensure that the QIP had lasting results. For this reason, it was important for all the beneficiaries to participate actively. A total of almost fifteen hundred QIPs were implemented in Mozambique, dispersed over ten provinces. The preferred location was an area with many returnees and poor basic facilities. Because activities focused on particular areas rather than specific groups, they benefited both those who had fled and those who had stayed. These reintegration activities were important as a first step from emergency assistance towards longer-term development aid.[147]

The international community's approach to refugees had traditionally been reactive: once movements of refugees had occurred, emergency aid was organised and longer-term assistance followed in due course. Towards the close of the twentieth century, however, the persistence and steady growth of the refugee problem in Africa brought a dawning realisation that a new approach was required. In addition to setting up camps and providing assistance, there was a need to reduce or if possible prevent refugee movements at the source. Crisis prevention and conflict management policies were as a rule more humane, as well as far less expensive, than simply responding to the consequences of war. They were better not only for potential refugees, but also for African societies in their entirety. For Africa to retain its stability and have any chance of development, it was important wherever possible to prevent disputes, political or otherwise, from escalating into armed conflicts.

Conflict prevention
on the agenda

As mentioned above, the number of violent conflicts in Africa and the number of states and other parties involved in them increased rapidly in the closing years of the twentieth century. They included not only wars between countries but also civil strife, and were frequently a combination of the two. The promise of the immediate post-Cold War era, with the prospect of cooperation rather than rivalry between the main international powers, had fizzled out and the disadvantages of the new world order began to make themselves felt, in particular in the form of declining international solidarity with Africa. Added to the tendency towards disintegration (see chapter 5), this increased the risk that violence would flare up. In view of the devastating impact of armed strife on countries and communities, conflict prevention came into the spotlight, in international politics and diplomacy as well as in Africa itself. After all, an ounce of prevention was worth a pound of cure. The longer the delay in intervening, the higher the cost in terms of human life and damage to property. Moreover, the more the violence escalated, the more difficult it became to resolve a conflict. Nevertheless, it was easier to pay lip service to conflict prevention than to put it into practice.

It is hard to prove that conflict prevention has been successful in any specific case. After all, it is impossible to say with any certainty whether tensions which in fact have not escalated would have done so without preventive measures. Even so, there was soon a general belief that conflict prevention was not proving as effective as had been expected.

Early warning of impending conflicts was not the problem. Indeed, there tended to be far too many warnings. Not only were national and international nongovernmental organisations monitoring potential and actual problem areas all over the world, but parties directly involved always sounded the alarm, often because they stood to gain personally from international intervention in a conflict that had not yet got out of hand.

The problem tended to occur at the stage of moving from early warning to early action. When should action be taken in response to an early warning, and who was to take it? There were usually deep-rooted causes of violence and in Africa these generally had to do with the declining effectiveness of state institutions. This was not easy to remedy in the short term. It was not enough simply to call on the hostile parties to keep calm and negotiate a solution, or to send an envoy to preach that message in the potential trouble spot. Moreover, the powers that really counted in international security tended to give higher priority to places where violence had already escalated than to situations which still seemed to be under control. Accordingly, initiatives to end conflict remained more common than measures to prevent it. That was why, for example, the international community took no action in response to the many signs of an impeding genocide in Rwanda. The warnings were disbelieved, ignored or disregarded.

The poor results of international conflict prevention have led to a flood of reports on the subject.[148] From small NGOs in faraway places to the secretary-general of the United Nations, everyone has had something to say on the subject. A striking feature of their contributions to the debate has been a preoccupation with the causes of conflict. To some extent, this has to do with the difficulty of devising effective measures, but it is also connected with the absence of a convincing conflict theory. There seems to have been a general assumption that problems and solutions should be of the same kind. For instance, a complex problem was thought to require a complex solution, and it was believed to be impossible to understand the solution without understanding the problem. Discovering that kind of connection between the cause and the solution would indeed be extremely useful for policymakers, but in practice it has proved an elusive goal.

As almost all studies in the field have indicated, conflicts tend to arise from a combination of causes.[149] Violence most frequently results where no political mechanisms are available for nonviolent conflict regulation. Hence, conflict prevention goes hand in hand with the establishment of legitimate states and the solution is almost always political. Sometimes the build-up of tension immediately preceding an outburst of violence can spur the necessary reform, but often it is too late by that stage. One major case in which that political reform is often put off is when it could be damaging to the powers that be. From their point of view, it may be logical to defend through violence what they would stand to lose in the event of a peaceful solution.

If the state is disintegrating, the situation may be more complicated. Conflict prevention is almost impossible if state institutions are not functioning effectively. By increasing the capacity of the state and promoting democratisation (and, importantly, forms of power-sharing), donors can help African countries to manage their own internal conflicts in a peaceful manner. Where conflicts have arisen primarily as a result of the disintegration of the state structures, the emphasis should be placed on institutional strengthening and better governance. Measures of this kind are regarded as a form of structural conflict prevention.[150]

It is almost impossible to put an end to violence if the state is disintegrating. Many conflicts in Africa have involved countless parties and there was often no arrangement that suited everybody. Even if the leaders were content with the outcome of negotiation, the question was whether their supporters would accept it; they often had their own reasons to prolong the armed struggle, for example because they had better chances of earning a living that way than in the peacetime economy.

The role of the international community in preventing and resolving armed conflicts in Africa has been complicated by rivalries among the main powers involved. There has almost always been a split separating France from Britain and the United States. Paris interpreted the growing power of Museveni and Kagame in Central Africa as an Anglophone conspiracy against the traditional hegemony of France in that part of the continent. Anglo-French rivalry has also been a factor in West Africa. London was determined to retain its position as the main player in Sierra Leone and was therefore disturbed by the French government's support for President Charles Taylor of Liberia, who had made a pact with the rebels in Sierra Leone and had good relations with the French-speaking countries of Ivory Coast and Burkina Faso. Although France's rivalries with Britain and the United States were never overt – after all, they were allies and were officially pursuing the same aims in Africa – these countries' covert pursuit of their own national interests in Africa nevertheless constituted a major obstacle to conflict prevention or resolution.

The rivalry between the British and the French in West Africa abated somewhat when France took on the task of stabilising the Ivory Coast in 2002. Now that the French had assumed a role similar to that of the British in Sierra Leone, the two countries were brought closer together by adversity. Since it looked as though neither Sierra Leone nor Ivory Coast would be ready to stand on its own two feet for quite a while, both Britain and France felt stuck; it would be extremely difficult for either one to extricate itself in the near future. They were both victims of circumstance, who could at least use each other's moral support.

In the 1990s, there was increasing demand for UN intervention to prevent or end conflicts, but it was usually requested at the close of a conflict rather than the beginning, to prevent violence in the first place. It was no great problem for the UN to meet the demand. After the Cold War, it became easier for the members of the Security Council to cooperate and to agree on the dispatch of UN peacekeeping forces. In the 1990s, therefore, UN operations were launched in a variety of African countries, including Angola (UNAVEM), Liberia (UNOMIL), Rwanda (UNAMIR), Sierra Leone (UNAMSIL), Ethiopia/Eritrea (UNMEE), Congo (MONUC), Ivory Coast (MINUCI) and again Liberia. Despite all this activity, there was widespread criticism of the UN, focusing on of its ineffectiveness. After hundreds of UN peacekeepers were taken hostage in Sierra Leone in 2000, a critical internal report was released. The Brahimi Report on UN peace operations argued that UN peacekeeping forces should be allowed to take firmer action in future.[151]

A related problem was the fairly universal unwillingness of UN member states to take part in peacekeeping operations and the consequent delays in launching them. If the UN wanted to respond effectively to warnings and to prevent escalation, time was of the essence. The earlier the intervention, the greater the chance of success. Violence quickly leads to polarisation and hatred, making a political solution ever more difficult to achieve. Even so, the members of the UN showed little willingness to provide military personnel or even equipment for use in preventive action in Africa, let alone to respond quickly. For this reason, various countries, including the Netherlands and Canada, suggested the creation of a UN rapid reaction force on permanent standby. However, the idea met with little support among the permanent members of the Security Council. Most Western countries were still willing to provide financial and logistical support for peacekeeping operations, but – following the failure of the operation in Somalia – they generally refused to send their troops to Africa.

Around the turn of the century, the biggest peacekeeping operation in the history of the United Nations was conducted in Sierra Leone. The situation there was problematic because, while the international community was determined that there should never again be such a bloodbath, none of the potential suppliers of troops had any particular national interest to pursue. Sierra Leone's former colonial master, Britain, proved to be the only Western country prepared to deploy its own troops in the country. The British marines were indispensable in getting the peace process started in Sierra Leone, where they were assisted by non-Western UN member states, which still tended to be willing to undertake peacekeeping duties in Africa if paid well. The other Western states confined themselves to supplying financial or other support for a peacekeeping force made up of troops from developing countries. It seemed as though the tone had been set for the future of international peacekeeping in Africa. In 2002, the French took on a similar role, as the core of an international peacekeeping operation in Ivory Coast, as did the United States in Liberia in 2003 (though with a far smaller presence on the ground).

More and more, it was up to African countries to keep the peace on their own continent. They were aware of the challenge. As early as 1991, a major pan-African conference was held on the subject in Lagos, Nigeria. The OAU and the various regional organisations set up departments of conflict prevention. The successor to the OAU, the African Union, made plans for a peace and security council of its own. ECOWAS went furthest in promoting peace and security in its own region, by playing an large, active role in conflict resolution in Liberia and Sierra Leone. Western countries saw this as a good example of an African solution to an African problem.

The West did, however, help African countries and organisations to build up their own peacekeeping capacity. France, the United States and Britain were especially active in this area and began working together to provide such support. The French programme for the Reinforcement of African Peacekeeping Capacities (RECAMP) was the biggest of its kind, providing equipment, training, technical support, transport and funding to help set up potential African peacekeeping forces. In 1996-1998, five West African countries took part in a first major peacekeeping exercise. In the 1998-2000 exercise in Gabon, there were eight, and in 2002 there was a still larger exercise in Tanzania in East Africa, involving more than ten African countries and twenty international donors. On that occasion there were not only troop manoeuvres, but also theoretical training in political and military matters for the officers.

7
GLOBALISATION

The world economy:

a runaway train

Since the early 1990s the term 'globalisation' has come into vogue. Globalisation has been briefly mentioned a number of times in previous chapters, for example in connection with the end of the Cold War (chapter 1) and in the discussion of structural adjustment programmes (chapter 2). As we turn to the main economic trends in Africa since 1990, it is only logical to take globalisation as our starting point. Globalisation is a mainly economic process that has had far-reaching effects worldwide. Since the 1990s, 'globalisation' has become an umbrella term embracing a whole series of economic, political, technological, social and cultural phenomena. It therefore makes sense to refer to the years since the Cold War as the age of globalisation. This is equally applicable to Africa. However marginal that continent's position may have been by world standards, globalisation nevertheless had a major impact there.

If we think of globalisation as a process of increasing international interconnectedness, it is clear that it has been going on for a long time. It is tempting to go back many centuries and say that it all began with Columbus, who brought an entirely New World into contact with the Old World. Yet even the discovery of America in 1492 was merely a milestone in a process that had been going on for hundreds of years – the discovery just speeded things up. In the seventeenth and eighteenth centuries, Europe's scattered trading links with other continents became more structured, bringing us another step closer to 'globalisation'. Yet there was still no single worldwide trading system, but only separate Asian and Atlantic ones. During that period Africa was absorbed into the Atlantic trading system along with Europe and America, albeit mainly as a source of slaves. In the nineteenth century, modern colonialism expanded what had hitherto been chiefly economic ties between Africa and Europe into all kinds of other links, again mostly not of Africa's choosing. Despite later decolonisation, Africa's role in the global system has remained a dependent one.

If international economic ties have been growing stronger for centuries, why do we speak of the age of globalisation as beginning in the late twentieth century? What is so new about this period that it justifies the new name? Globalisation is seen as a new stage of the industrial revolution, the first stage of which was industrialisation, with its origins in eighteenth-century Britain. Like earlier stages, globalisation is driven by technological advances. The main engine of globalisation is innovation in information and communications technology (ICT). This technology has increased the importance of knowledge in the economy and society (whence the term 'knowledge society') and linked the world in a new and much more efficient way, with especially far-reaching economic and financial effects. This in turn has triggered other kinds of changes, spreading the effects of the process further and further through society. Another important spur to globalisation was the collapse of the Eastern Bloc, which speeded up the process of interconnection by greatly increasing, at one fell swoop, the number of countries in which it could take place. The impact of globalisation was eventually felt in almost every part of the world.

In the 1990s the world economy grew by more than three per cent a year, and trade by over six per cent.[152] This expansion mainly involved the production of services, but large quantities of new goods were also produced. The main economic players since World War II – the United States, Western Europe and Japan – maintained much the same shares of world trade relative to each other, but there was a major increase in the total volume when the field of play expanded to include Asia, Latin America and Central and Eastern Europe. The greatest acceleration, however, was in international movements of money and capital. The number of foreign exchange transactions worldwide tripled between 1986 and 1992. There was also a new trend in foreign direct investment (FDI), which averaged 77 billion US dollars a year in the mid-1980s; just ten years later, in 1995, this figure had risen to 315 billion.[153]

Not only was all this symptomatic of the steady structural changes taking place in the global economy, but it triggered further changes. The balance of power between the players on the world stage was shifting. The nation state no longer reigned supreme. As a result of deregulation and privatisation, the modern state was forced to give up some of its tasks to the private sector. It also had to transfer tasks and responsibilities to supranational institutions such as the European Union, and at the same time it relinquished powers to lower levels, either through a controlled process of decentralisation or a chaotic process of disintegration. Creating a favourable business climate became a key task of government. Large private companies, which had thoroughly modernised their organisation and working procedures, became the new leaders on the world stage. By the end of the twentieth century the one hundred biggest 'economies' were divided almost fifty-fifty between countries and private companies. The companies were often mainly active in their own regions; truly global businesses were a rarity. They had a major influence on government policy. In the developed world the same could be said of nongovernmental organisations, which likewise increased their influence on the decision-making process.

Critics compared these constant innovations to a runaway train careering wildly out of control. There was increasing pressure from society to regain a grip on the process, culminating in a true anti-globalisation movement. Many politicians, too, were unhappy about what increasingly appeared to be 'cowboy capitalism', and called for a more orderly international economic system. Yet the process could not be reversed. Globalisation had given a major boost to the economies of Western and many other countries. It was justified in ideological terms with reference to the former battle between East and West, which had unmistakably been won by the West. At the same time, this international trend was very much in line with both classic liberalism and the internationalism of social democracy. Culturally there was a link with cosmopolitanism, only this time in a form that was readily accessible to the general population.

At first most people in the West were convinced that globalisation was bound to be good for every region in the world, including the poorest, such as Africa. Open economies, freer markets and deregulation were having an immensely positive impact on their own welfare, so why should they not be extended to other parts of the world? In particular, the success of the East and Southeast Asian countries (although the state had in fact played a major part in their development) and the failure of former communist and poor developing countries appeared to support the thesis that there was one royal road – perhaps only one possible road – to development. However, it was soon apparent that the free play of economic forces could upset the balance within countries, between countries and between entire regions. Moreover, Africa had a number of serious deficiencies, such as weak governments, political instability and low competitiveness. With these unfavourable initial conditions, the question was to what extent the continent could meet the challenges of globalisation.

In the grip of the international market

As indicated in the previous section, globalisation is an umbrella term that covers a number of diverse but related trends, particularly in the economy and finance. However, the impact of globalisation on nation-states and national economies depends on where they stand in the globalisation process. It varies according to whether the country or continent mainly plays a propelling, independent role (as does North America) or a more dependent one. Africa is economically the world's weakest continent, and was unable to offer much resistance to outside influence. Above all, this vulnerability had major consequences for its economy, but because of the many-faceted nature of globalisation, it also had a considerable political, technological, social and cultural impact. The changes in all these areas will be discussed in the remainder of this book. The end of this chapter will focus on the technological and cultural impact. The social implications will be examined in chapters 8 and 9, and the political ones will mainly be discussed in chapter 10.

The political aspects of globalisation were by no means confined to the role of the state in Africa or to attempts to influence economic and monetary policy through structural adjustment. Outside influence was also brought to bear on the relationship between states and their citizens in Africa. Among other things, efforts were made to promote good governance, institution-building, respect for human rights and democratisation. Both inside and outside the political field, foreign pressure interacted with autonomous developments in African countries. The relevant political issues, including what happened after the wave of democratisation between 1989 and 1994, are the subject of chapter 10. In short, this chapter will mainly address the economic effects of globalisation, with most other areas of impact reserved for later chapters.

As early as the 1980s, Africa had encountered the economic aspects of globalisation in the form of structural adjustment programmes imposed by the international financial institutions in cooperation with the donor community. There were whole series of programmes, in some cases extending right into the twenty-first century; as emphasised in chapter 2, brief or half-hearted reform would not have been sufficient. Structural adjustment measures began to be adopted in the 1990s, owing largely to the adverse social impact of the first generation of programmes on the local population. Rising unemployment in the formal sector and cutbacks in basic social services took a heavy toll in some countries, and there was little new growth to compensate. Moreover, that growth was quite unevenly distributed, and often benefited only a small group of people. Often they were members of the political elite, whose power enabled them to take advantage of the reforms. Privatisation of state-owned enterprises, almost always a key component of structural adjustment programmes, was usually a failure. Instead of ensuring that economic power was more widely distributed and that a group of independent entrepreneurs could emerge to build up the private sector, privatisation in many cases merely helped politicians increase their personal wealth.

Despite the best intentions, the structural adjustment programmes tended to strengthen rather than weaken politicians' grip on the economy in many countries. They also seemed to result in more corruption. Politicians sometimes misused their power in the most brazen manner for personal financial gain. For example, well-conceived commercial plans to restore and relaunch the colonial railway line from the Ethiopian capital Addis Ababa to Djibouti on the Red Sea, which would have greatly increased Ethiopia's export capacity, were never implemented because they were not in the personal interests of ministers who controlled road transport to the coast. In 2000, the directors of a large international brewery in Congo (Kinshasa) were jailed on trumped-up charges. The real reason was that the company had refused to help a local brewery – which was owned by a member of the cabinet – increase its market share. Corruption, lawlessness and abuse of power thus had a disastrous effect on opportunities for foreign investment almost everywhere in Africa.

Another crucial obstacle was the limited role of market forces in some sectors of the economy. Markets for certain products were dominated by a small number of businesses or even individuals. Women, ethnic minorities and the poor sometimes had little or no access to markets for various practical reasons, such as lack of organisation, infrastructure or collateral. In general, the structural adjustment programmes led to freer markets almost everywhere. However, in some remote areas where subsidies had enabled trade to develop in spite of high transport costs, the reverse was true. In such areas the abolition of subsidies meant that people could no longer get to the market, and they were thrown back into an economy of self-sufficiency. At the same time, the erosion of state support left certain regions and groups economically and socially isolated.

The adverse impact of the structural adjustment programmes should not be overstated, but it cannot be denied that their results were generally disappointing. They did not take sufficient account of the political and social situation in Africa. Many felt that both the benefits and the disadvantages of the reforms were unequally distributed over society. Critics of the programmes had complained about this for years, and eventually some of their criticism got through to policymakers in Washington and elsewhere. In the 1990s this resulted in a second generation of reform packages.

However, the core of the reforms was essentially the same. For example, the prime importance of achieving and maintaining macroeconomic stability was not open to debate, and faster economic growth remained the ultimate aim. The African economies were so small that no headway whatsoever could be made unless production increased. Africa contained about ten per cent of the world's population but produced only about one per cent of its goods and services.[154] Around 1990, an average African country with a population of around ten million produced no more goods and services than the average Dutch municipality.

In the 1990s most African countries succeeded in keeping their budgets and balances of trade in reasonable equilibrium. This was a considerable achievement, given that the international terms of trade for African products were deteriorating year by year. This trend continued into the twenty-first century, particularly as the knowledge incorporated into goods and services became more important, and hence more valuable. Human knowledge and skills were growing more and more significant as sources of new prosperity, and this was precisely the area in which Africa was weakest. Its main products were crops and raw materials, whose relative value was declining. In the closing years of the twentieth century, the value of one unit of African exports was falling by more than three per cent a year, while the equivalent figure for imports was rising by over two per cent. The result was that the terms of trade were deteriorating by more than five per cent a year.[155]

Behind these figures lay a crucial problem for African development. According to standard economic thinking, which was, naturally, espoused by the World Bank, Africa (like every other continent and country) would do best to concentrate on the products that it could bring to market most cheaply compared with other countries. These were primary products, raw materials and agricultural products – in other words, the things Africa had possessed in abundance since time immemorial. In theory, the best way for Africa to catch up with other continents was to exploit its 'comparative advantage' in this fashion. However, the structural deterioration of the terms of trade made this extremely difficult. According to African critics of this development strategy, Africa would never even begin to catch up with other regions in this way, let alone close the gap altogether. Yet there was no alternative. What could Africa do that would be any better? Compete in areas in which it had no comparative advantage? That would by definition be even harder. So the continent was caught in an economic bind. Its share of world trade was just two per cent, and the share of non-primary products in this figure was virtually nil.[156]

Whichever path was chosen, it was clear that Africa would have to become more competitive – and this was not going to happen if reforms merely led to social dislocation and an overall deterioration in people's living standards (particularly the quality of education). The second generation of structural adjustment programmes was intended to tackle these adverse effects. Growth objectives were broadened. The goal was no longer growth as such, but growth that would benefit a much larger group of people. The standard of basic social services such as education and health care had to be maintained. Policymakers also began to take account of the implications for women, a large portion of whom had been reduced to poverty. There was greater emphasis on institution-building and the environment. Around 2000 the integration of economic and social approaches led to the emergence of the term 'pro-poor growth', which was internationally adopted as the guiding principle for reform. The idea was that growth should take place in such a way that it would substantially help to reduce poverty, mainly by creating new jobs. However, translating this into practical policy measures proved no easy matter.

Furthermore, given its dependent position within the international system, Africa's interest lay in an international order that would protect it against arbitrariness and instability and at the same time give it some latitude to develop in its own way. This would have to involve something more than a development policy that was solely dictated by market forces, especially given the rigours of the financial market. What African countries needed was an institutional framework that would provide some protection for their own production while leaving sufficient room on the world market for newcomers or re-entrants. However, developing countries played only a modest, defensive part in the debate on the reform of the international system in the 1990s, for example the discussion about the establishment and design of the WTO. They were often very conservative, and clung tightly to out-dated structures. This was because they were convinced that poor countries would not ben-efit from further integration of the world economy or from global harmonisation.

The devaluation of
the CFA franc

As we have seen, the fact that the CFA franc was pegged to the French franc meant that structural adjustment programmes in Francophone West and Central Africa could only be partly implemented (see chapter 2, pp. 69-73). The currency's high fixed rate of exchange had gradually made the dozen or so African countries that made up the CFA zone more and more uncompetitive. They were pricing themselves out of the international market. Paris, which absorbed the losses, was also faced with increasing costs. For years any change to the once so successful system seemed unthinkable, but in the end it became inevitable. The turning point came in 1993, when wealthy West Africans began exchanging the local currency for hard French francs in anticipation of devaluation. Under the prevailing rules they were allowed to do so without restriction. The CFA franc already began to lose value as a result, but Paris maintained the fixed exchange rate for some time – until January 1994, when the French finance minister and the Managing Director of the IMF met in Dakar for joint consultations with various Francophone African heads of state and finance ministers, and the axe finally fell.

When the shops in Abidjan and Dakar, Libreville and Bangui, Yaoundé and Lomé reopened on 13 January 1994, the prices of most products shot up as shopkeepers suddenly found themselves having to pay twice as much for goods from outside the CFA zone. Paris had decided the fate of the local currency. Although the French government had not actu-ally abolished pegging, it had unilaterally decided to devalue the CFA franc. The value of the 'African franc' was still guaranteed, thus preserving the basis for monetary union between France and its former colonies, but the difference was dramatic. On 12 January one French franc could be bought for fifty CFA francs; a day later the rate had doubled.

Economically speaking, the devaluation of the CFA franc brought Francophone Africa down to earth with a bump. For years the region had been living beyond its means, but now it had to face reality. There were immediate balance-of-trade problems. Suddenly twice as much local currency was needed to pay back international loans. France gave several coun-tries additional support on a transitional basis by way of compensation. The impact on the people of Francophone Africa varied. In general, countries that were more closely tied into the international economic system – coastal states such as Cameroon, Ivory Coast and Senegal – were hit harder than more isolated ones such as Burkina Faso, Mali and Niger. The former group was immediately confronted with the new exchange rate in its dealings with the outside world. Furthermore, city-dwellers were hit harder by the change than those in rural areas, since their patterns of consumption were more international. There was little immediate impact on farmers in remote villages in the Sahel or along the Congo in Central Africa. In short, economies dominated by consumption took more of a buffeting than ones based on production – which was the whole idea.

The devaluation forced Senegal to slash its high import levels. Foreign products were now simply unaffordable – and this included not just luxuries for the local elite, but even staple foods such as rice, which was imported from Asia. Senegal had to become self-supporting once more, and did not find it easy. The sector that responded best was agriculture. Many farmers switched from commercial crops to millet for personal consumption and to feed people in the cities, who nevertheless had to pay a good deal more for their staple foods. The devaluation had a serious impact on industry. Like Ivory Coast, Senegal had built up a sizeable local industrial sector (especially in food processing) which was protected by an import substitution policy. When the tariff barriers were broken down, these businesses were badly hit. Senegalese industry did not manage to recover in the 1990s. Private enterprise was unable to fill the gap left by the shrunken public sector. It was therefore left to the informal sector to give the many people in search of work some kind of income, however paltry. There was major growth in one or two service sectors. For example, the tourist industry expanded considerably, with a sharp rise in the number of tourists coming to Senegal after the devaluation. Another economic effect was that smuggling from Gambia, which had been substantial, now ceased.

Ivory Coast, which already had its share of economic problems, responded stoically to the devaluation and the resulting fall in purchasing power. The country was entirely preoccupied with the death of President Félix Houphouët-Boigny. There was a rumour that publication of the decision to devalue the CFA franc had been delayed until the president, who suffered from prostate cancer, was dead – not only in order to spare the feelings of *Le Vieux*, who had been a pillar of Franco-African relations, but also to stave off the possibility of fierce public protest. Once the devaluation had taken place, however, the fifty per cent reduction in the value of the CFA franc had a favourable impact on the country's economy. Exports began to pick up again after a while, the economy started re-expanding and the government had a bit more money to spend. In the second half of the 1990s, for the first time in years, Ivory Coast was again able to invest in education and health care.

As already mentioned, it was the more isolated economies that generally benefited most from the devaluation. Obviously, countries such as Mali also faced higher prices for imports as a result of the new exchange rate, but the Sahel countries simply did not import as much as coastal states like Senegal and Ivory Coast. Since independence, the Malian economy had been badly damaged by its leaders' policies and excessive government interference in the economy, leading to disequilibrium, inefficiency, corruption and a steady decline in living standards. In the 1970s those problems were compounded by the serious drought in the Sahel, which reduced the economy to its most basic function, that of providing food for the population. In 1982 the government of Mali was forced to apply to the World Bank and the IMF for support. The resulting reforms included massive cutbacks in government spending, but the currency, the CFA franc, could not be touched. As a result, Mali also had to deal with an influx of cheap products smuggled in from countries that were not part of the CFA zone, such as Guinea, Ghana and Nigeria. Even products from newly industrialising countries in distant Asia reached the capital, Bamako, and local private industry, which was still in its infancy, could hardly compete. The result was that businesses in the Bamako area closed down and unemployment rose.

The tide turned when the CFA franc was devalued at the beginning of 1994. Purchasing power in urban areas declined as imported goods became more expensive, but on the bright side, both imports and smuggling greatly decreased. Local products were able to compete once more, and it was rural areas that benefited most. Mali could once again export cattle to the coast of West Africa, where it had previously lost ground owing to the high exchange rate of the CFA franc and competition from Argentinian and European meat (which could be marketed cheaply in Africa because it was subsidised). Cotton production and exports also increased rapidly, and Mali became the leading cotton exporter in sub-Saharan Africa. In addition, cotton industry by-products were used domestically in products such as clothing and cattle feed. The production and export of gold, activities for which the country had once been noted, were successfully relaunched in 1997. Government finances improved because spending was kept under control, and more effective tax collection caused revenue to increase every year.

The small business sector generally expanded, encouraged by rising purchasing power in rural areas and the country's greater competitiveness internationally. The informal sector began to flourish. For example, a great deal of building work was carried out all over the country, mainly by people building dwellings for themselves. Food production visibly improved, thanks in part to a series of years with abundant rainfall, as well as new techniques for irrigated rice-growing along the Niger. By the end of the twentieth century Mali was producing more food than it needed, despite a persistently high rate of population growth. Nevertheless, food prices remained high, owing in part to strong demand from Senegal and Ivory Coast. With economic growth averaging about seven per cent in the closing years of the twentieth century, Mali underwent a remarkable economic recovery. One major obstacle to further growth was the electricity supply, which was still in government hands. The country's inefficient state-owned enterprises were unable to keep up with demand for electricity, which was growing by fifteen per cent a year.

The devaluation of the CFA franc had a similar impact in each of the six Central African countries that used the currency: Cameroon, Gabon, Congo (Brazzaville), the Central African Republic, Chad and Spanish-speaking Equatorial Guinea. Here, too, the value of the CFA franc was cut by fifty per cent in January 1994. Living standards in these countries were on average somewhat lower than in West Africa, except in Gabon, which is a medium-sized oil exporter and a member of OPEC. These Central African countries were also less integrated into the world economy than West Africa.

After the devaluation, the economies of most of these countries revived somewhat, although not enough to raise the living standards of the rapidly growing population. However, the macroeconomic situation stabilised and the inflation triggered by the devaluation was brought back under control. Exports of agricultural and other raw materials increased. Again farmers benefited most from the devaluation, even though the price of such products as imported fertiliser increased. And again the urban population – less numerous here than in West Africa – by and large lost out. City-dwellers bought more expensive imported products more often and had to pay higher prices for food, while the number of salaried jobs was falling. Central Africa remained generally unattractive to foreign investors, except for the oil sector. Wage and price levels were relatively high, productivity was low, export opportunities were scarce and domestic markets were small, although after the devaluation they were no longer flooded with goods smuggled in from neighbouring countries that did not use the CFA franc.

The CFA franc thus remained pegged to the French franc. It was not until the end of the twentieth century that this special monetary relationship again came under threat, this time from Europe. During this period a majority of the member states of the European Union, including France, began making preparations for the introduction of a common currency, the euro. The euro would eventually replace the national currencies of the participating member states – including the French franc. This meant that the CFA franc would henceforth be pegged to the euro, but naturally only if the participating European countries consented. The link with the CFA franc, and with France's former African territories in general, mattered far less to most European Union member states than it did to the former colonial power, France. The African countries that belonged to the CFA zone strongly urged Europe to maintain the monetary union, claiming that its benefits still far outweighed its disadvantages. The European countries involved took the view that the introduction of the euro should not harm the CFA countries, and agreed to maintain the monetary union provided that the costs were covered by the French treasury in Paris rather than the new European Central Bank in Frankfurt. France accepted this condition, and so the CFA franc is now pegged to the euro.

Relative decline in trade
and investment

Globalisation was boosted not only by technological innovation, but also by the fact that national economies were opened up. International trade and movements of capital were liberalised, and countries saw their volumes of trade and investment grow as a result. However, this was not necessarily the case in African countries. Their figures did not always decline in absolute terms, but in relative terms, as a percentage of the world total, they certainly did. The rate of growth in the rest of the world was so staggering that stagnation in Africa was tantamount to decline.

Trade figures provide a measure of how dynamic an economy is, and trade can also be seen as a gateway to investment. Foreign businesses often prefer to get to know African partners by trading with them before taking the more risky step of investment. This section focuses on trade between African and non-African countries. Although not completely negligible, intra-African trade was very limited. Only about ten per cent of Africa's international trade was with other African countries, for several reasons. There was little economic diversification, so that countries in the same region usually produced more or less the same products and hence had no reason to trade with one another. Ties between neighbouring countries were often weaker than those with more distant partners such as the former colonial power in Europe, making long-distance trade easier. However, when there were considerable differences in the values of neighbouring currencies, as there were between CFA and non-CFA countries in the years before the devaluation, intra-African trade could sometimes be profitable. Often such trade took the form of smuggling, which declined at the end of the century, once nearly all African currencies were realistically valued.

In the 1960s world trade with Africa accounted for about three per cent of overall trade. This percentage then declined slowly, falling to two per cent by the 1990s. At first sight this may not seem so terrible, until it is noted that South Africa accounts for almost half of the total, leaving just 1.2 per cent for the other forty-plus countries in sub-Saharan Africa. That is very little for a region that is home to ten per cent of the world's population. If nothing else, this figure illustrates just how marginal a role Africa now plays in the world economy. In the past few decades there has been no appreciable diversification in the products exported by African countries. In other words, most of that 1.2 per cent still consisted of raw materials and agricultural products. What was worse, Africa was falling behind, relatively speaking, even in these traditional export sectors. Its share of the often rapidly expanding world market for raw materials and agricultural products was also to shrinking. In the 1990s there were virtually no industrial or handicraft products among Africa's exports. Products of this type made in African countries could not compete on the world market in terms of either price or quality.

One of the reasons often cited for the decline in African trade has been the difficulty African goods are said to have in gaining access to the large markets of the industrialised world. Europe and the United States have erected tariff barriers for both processed and unprocessed agricultural products and textiles. Fish and processed fish products cannot easily be exported to Europe. There are often quality standards which African products can only meet with great difficulty. On the other hand, under the Lomé Conventions (subsequently the Cotonou Agreement) and the General System of Preferences, very many products have almost unlimited access to the markets of the European Union and the United States respectively. In 2001 the European Union granted the very poorest countries unlimited access to its markets for nearly all products. Another obstacle to production and export by African countries are the subsidies that governments in Europe and North America pay their farmers.

Often, the policies pursued by African governments also stood in the way of African trade. Numerous rules and restrictions made it complicated and expensive to export goods, which were less competitive as a result. Transport was often run by state-owned enterprises. Sometimes they had been privatised in structural adjustment programmes, but continued to operate as monopolies. Trade with Africa generated the highest transport costs in the world. Instead of being streamlined, the rules governing imports often differed from product to product, and procedures were bureaucratic and impenetrable. In some cases local exports were heavily taxed, as were imports that were needed for local production. African governments remained reluctant to adopt measures that would encourage trade – far more reluctant than the governments of Latin American countries, which faced the same fundamental problems. Africans were less confident than Latin Americans that liberalisation would boost trade and hence the economy.

Nevertheless, the African economies responded to liberalisation in the same way as economies elsewhere. Deregulation and improved procedures did cause trade to pick up. The countries that went furthest in this process, especially Uganda and Ghana, achieved the best results, both at the outset (in the 1980s) and afterwards (right into the twenty-first century). The volume of African trade was remarkably small compared with other continents, but was average in relation to the size of African economies. Where governments succeeded in improving their trade policies, the volume of trade grew.[157] In the 1990s, African exports increased by more than four per cent a year (compared with only one per cent in the 1980s), but the deterioration in the terms of trade meant that the increase in dollar income was only 2.2 per cent a year.[158]

The nature of African exports did not essentially change. In the vast majority of countries, primary products were still the main exports. In four countries – Nigeria, Angola, Gabon and Congo (Brazzaville) – oil remained the mainstay of the economy. Then there was a group of ten mostly small countries that mainly depended on services (such as tourism), foreign aid and remittances from migrants. These included Benin, Burkina Faso, Djibouti, Eritrea, Gambia, Lesotho and Mozambique. Only a few, mainly larger, countries had export income from a variety of sources: South Africa (predictably), Kenya, Senegal and Cameroon.[159]

The pattern for investment was similar to that for trade: investment in Africa around the turn of the century was negligible in comparison with the world as a whole, but in relation to the small economies in which it took place it was of considerable and indeed increasing importance. At the same time, better use of existing productive capacity made economic growth possible almost everywhere in Africa, although this usually required an injection of capital. Economic growth and investment are closely connected. Africa did not have much capital of its own, and poverty naturally meant that very little could be saved. In some countries, moreover, the assets present were not always used. African savings (money that could be used for investment) were the lowest in the world. In 1980, domestic savings in Africa equalled 16 per cent of the continent's total GNP; twenty years later, in 2000, this figure had fallen to 14 per cent. By comparison, domestic savings in East Asia rose from 35 to 37 per cent of GNP over the same period. During that period, African consumption rose to more than 80 per cent of GNP.

There were considerable differences in savings between African countries, and the role of government also varied. Public revenue increased in some countries as a result of structural adjustment, but in other countries it fell. A case in point was Zambia. The Zambian government was notorious for its unsuccessful development policies, under both President Kenneth Kaunda and his successor President Frederick Chiluba. When sovereignty was transferred in 1964, Zambia was relatively well developed, with sufficient earnings from copper mining to be classified as a middle-income country. Yet, despite its natural resources and the absence of domestic problems, Zambia gradually went downhill. As foreign aid increased, the ruling elite lost all sense of responsibility. In the 1980s the international financial institutions had to intervene to stop the country going bankrupt. Wearisome negotiations between the Zambian government and the IMF and World Bank dragged on throughout the 1990s. Scarcely any of the policy changes that Zambia agreed to were actually carried out. Even so, donors continued to provide funding.

One of Zambia's main problems was a shortage of public revenue. The copper mines were generating less income than in earlier years. The government earned very little from excise duty or services such as issuing driving licences. Of the little that did get paid, a great deal disappeared into the pockets of individuals and the remainder was quite inadequate. Far from rising, tax revenue actually began to fall from 1996 onwards. The small group of wealthy Zambians who could have formed the government's power base were by then paying almost nothing at all. The poor no longer had material links with the state and the rich were rapidly shedding theirs. This left the Zambian government increasingly dependent on foreign support. In the 1990s, public revenue declined from 20 to 17 per cent of GNP. Domestic Zambian investment fell from 30-40 per cent of total investment in the years following independence to 10-15 per cent in the 1990s.[160] Domestic development efforts had been almost entirely replaced by financial injections from abroad.

In Zambia and elsewhere in Africa, wealthy people (politicians and entrepreneurs – the two categories often overlapped) had sufficient international contacts to get their assets safely out of the country. They would not usually have dreamed of investing their money at home. Governments were expected to use their own revenue for investment; since independence, this had been the policy in many African countries, for ideological reasons and for lack of any alternative. However, cutbacks in public spending as part of structural adjustment, and failure to make sufficient use of taxation (for political reasons), had dried up this source of investment. What remained were the remittances that migrants in Europe, the Middle East or North America sent home to their families in Africa. The sums involved were often considerable. Migrants in some European countries sent home amounts comparable to the official development aid given by those countries. In Africa the money was used to build houses, start small businesses or purchase basic necessities.

For large-scale projects designed to introduce modern, competitive production methods, African countries were dependent on capital from other continents. Funds could be obtained in the form of development aid, but aid was not always aimed at increasing or improving productive capacity. Moreover, in the age of globalisation, in which everything else seemed by definition to be growing rapidly, the total amount of development aid to Africa actually declined. In 1990 development aid still accounted for a major share of overall investment in Africa, but by 2000 it had become relatively insignificant. Just as in the colonial period around 1900, overseas private capital began to overshadow public funds. This was one of the most important changes that could be attributed to globalisation.

From the 1990s onwards it was no longer clear just how much was being invested in Africa. African governments often felt that in a liberalising world there was no longer any need for them to keep data on capital flows. Moreover, the institutions previously responsible for recording such things as foreign investment, in connection with structural adjustment programmes, had been abolished. As a result, much private investment was never officially registered. International institutions such as the UN Conference on Trade and Development (UNCTAD), the IMF and the World Bank published figures that were often highly divergent and, as detailed country-by-country research made clear, consistently too low.[161] Only an approximate assessment can therefore be made of the amount of foreign private investment in Africa.

The surprising discovery was that this capital flow, which increased rapidly during the 1990s, reached almost all African countries, not just the richest. Admittedly, South Africa was by far the largest recipient, but the interesting thing was that, in relation to the size of their economies, it was the poorest African countries that received the most investment. Investment in South Africa equalled about 5 per cent of the country's GNP, but in countries like Tanzania and Uganda the figure was up around 10-15 per cent – as high as in the fastest-growing Asian and Latin American economies.

The main component of this flow of capital to Africa was direct investment, which increased rapidly during the 1990s. The total around 1990 was just over one billion US dollars a year, but by mid-decade this had increased to some five billion dollars a year.[162] South Africa's share of this rose from just over 10 per cent in 1991 to 37 per cent in 1997. Its share of the new investment funds for Africa (discussed below) was as high as 90 per cent.[163] The international financial and economic world evidently saw South Africa as a unique case – the only economy on the entire continent that could be termed an 'emerging market' (see pp. 230-233). The bulk of international private investment went into emerging markets. However, after a number of crises in countries such as Russia (August 1998) and Brazil (January 1999), investors lost a great deal of their confidence in these markets. Some investment was rerouted to poorer countries in regions such as Africa, which thereby suddenly had access to additional capital.

What is especially noteworthy is that sources of private capital became more diverse. Prominent among the new investors were South African companies, which often had their headquarters in Western countries (a legacy of the apartheid era). South Africa became a leading economic power in other parts of the continent. East and Southeast Asian countries also began to invest in Africa. Japan's role was relatively minor – the main players were South Korea, Taiwan, Singapore, Malaysia and China (including Hong Kong). Most of this Asian investment was in construction and communications. However, the Asian crisis of the late 1990s reduced Asian investment in Africa. Other important new investors were ethnically Asian entrepreneurs who had once lived and worked in East or Southern Africa, many of whom had been forced to leave in the 1970s. They channelled large amounts of money back to Africa in order to set up or expand businesses there. These groups gained ground at the expense of traditional European and North American investors. It was American investment that was scaled back the most, despite the Clinton government's Africa policy, which was specifically aimed at encouraging American businesses to invest in Africa.

However, the fastest-growing flow of capital came from investment funds. These did not amount to much in the years before 1990, but from 1992-1993 onwards that changed fast. The South African funds grew in value to more than eight billion US dollars, and the Pan-African funds to about 700 million dollars. In addition, African businesses made up a share (probably between five and ten per cent) of certain global funds and emerging market funds.[164] This was a major source of capital for countries such as Zimbabwe and Zambia. In the closing years of the twentieth century more and more Pan-African funds popped up – about twenty by 2000. Stock exchanges were opened outside South Africa. In Francophone Africa, branch offices emerged; for example, the Abidjan stock exchange in Ivory Coast opened a branch in the Malian capital of Bamako. These exchanges were, of course, tiny by international standards, but nevertheless they formed part of a somewhat more modern approach to business finance.

During this period, relatively little capital reached Africa in the form of commercial bank loans. Hardly any long-term loans were granted, although some countries did receive non-guaranteed short-term loans. Estimates of the total amount varied greatly, but were never high. More funds were generated by bond issues – about one billion US dollars a year. Since most African states were not sufficiently creditworthy to issue bonds, only a few could take advantage of this source of funding. South Africa was once again at the forefront, followed by Nigeria and Namibia.

Slow economic growth

The crucial question is whether economic reform, trade and investment led to the growth that was needed to resurrect Africa's economies after two decades of stagnation and even decline, and whether globalisation was ultimately good for the economy. At first the answer appeared to be yes. That may surprise many people who associate Africa with scenes of fighting, famine and misery or have heard criticism heaped on the structural adjustment programmes. However, the figures for the mid-1990s, imprecise though they often are, definitely support a positive conclusion. If we look at the African economy as a whole, it is true that growth was very slow immediately after the end of the Cold War, but it later picked up. Economically speaking the best year was 1996, with a growth rate of 5.8 per cent. Growth then slowed down again, initially to 3-4 per cent a year. A few countries such as Mozambique, Uganda and Ghana stayed well above this level, and almost none fell far below it. The least developed countries usually achieved growth rates that were above the continental average.[165] By the end of the century it was the oil-exporting countries that were growing fastest, thanks to high oil prices.

Given the slow rate of growth at the beginning and the decline at the end of the decade, the rate of growth in the 1990s as a whole was only 2.8 per cent (still somewhat better than the figure of 2.5 per cent for the 1980s).[166] This equalled the average rate of population growth. Progress in per capita terms was thus nil. Furthermore, growth was very unevenly distributed, and large groups did not benefit from it at all. As a result, the average per capita income in these groups continued to fall in the 1990s, a phenomenon discussed in more detail in the next chapter. Even so, the declining trend that had prevailed during the Cold War was to some extent reversed. On balance, the situation stabilised. Under extremely difficult internal and external conditions, through very painful reforms, economic decline had been brought to a halt almost everywhere by the mid-1990s.

This was no mean achievement. Although in certain countries the expected profits in some sectors were considerable, so were the obstacles and risks. The overall political and social situation in Africa was far from attractive to potential investors. Markets were small and purchasing power limited. Employees had little or no experience in manufacturing. Labour productivity was low, and so was the level of education; many employees were illiterate. Entrepreneurial skills were scarce. African producers were not usually aware of the standards that prevailed on the world market, for example with regard to product quality. Hardly any countries had a well-developed financial sector, and apart from South Africa they were all technologically backward. Despite years of massive international assistance in developing such things as road systems, Africa's physical infrastructure was in decay. Perhaps more important, however, were the political circumstances. Corruption was practically ubiquitous, abuse of power was common, lawlessness and insecurity prevailed, and political unrest could lead to instability – hardly an attractive environment for long-term investment.

Accordingly, investors began turning away from Africa again in the second half of the 1990s. Extensive fighting broke out in the Great Lakes region, and Ethiopia and Eritrea came into conflict once more (see chapter 6). This cast a shadow on the picture that outsiders – including potential investors – had of Africa. At the same time, African countries were making little progress with economic and administrative reform. Of the world's continents, Africa continued to have the worst governance and the worst policies. The relatively rapid growth achieved in the mid-1990s could not be maintained. After peaking in 1996, the growth rate declined year by year, and by the opening years of the twenty-first century it had fallen to an average of just two per cent. Furthermore, prospects were gloomy, since Africa was feeling the impact of the worldwide slump that followed the attacks of 11 September 2001 in the United States.

The continent therefore failed to increase its share in the globally expanding economy in a lasting way. Its exports were still largely limited to agricultural products and raw materials. Apart from South Africa, no African country succeeded in making industrial or handicraft products that the rest of the world wanted to buy. In the decades immediately after independence, African countries, with their relatively closed economies, had been unable to build up significant industries of their own and capture a larger share of the world market. Yet in the more open economic climate of globalisation, from the 1990s onwards, they seemed unable to do any better. It should be noted that Africa had not yet done nearly enough to adapt to the new situation, and that most governments were very reluctant and in some cases openly unwilling to tread the path of liberalisation. In any case, however, the economic outlook was far from rosy. With rates of economic growth often lower than the rate of population growth, there was no way to raise living standards.

Yet, despite these persistent economic problems, there had been major changes in the structure of the African economy over the preceding decades. In the period from about 1960 (when many countries became independent) to the end of the century, the first conspicuous trend is the dramatic decline in the share of agriculture (including stockbreeding) in the economy. In 1960 agriculture still accounted for 40 per cent of Africa's GNP, but by 2000 this figure had fallen to just 21 per cent. Strikingly, however, the leading position was not taken over by industry, which grew very little over the same period; its share only rose from 26 to 30 per cent. The processing industry's share increased from 9 to 15 per cent.

Really substantial growth occurred outside these traditional economic sectors, namely in services, whose share of the economy grew from 34 per cent in 1960 to 50 per cent in 2000.[167] Admittedly, growth in the service sector was a worldwide phenomenon in the age of globalisation, but the situation in Africa was unusual in that most of the work done in this sector was 'informal', i.e. there was no contact with or use of formal structures or agreements. There were fewer and fewer institutionalised jobs in the public sector as a result of the structural adjustment programmes, and there was insufficient growth in the formal private sector to make up for this loss. By 2000 only a small part of the working-age population had work in the formal sector. This left people with no option but to start working for themselves.

The term 'informal sector' summons up a picture of newspaper vendors and tiny shops, but the sector should not be underestimated. It had the flexibility to respond readily to new developments and gaps in the market, and it generated a good deal of employment and income, much of it for women. Incomes were sometimes much higher than the African average of USD 1,500 a year.[168] The informal sector could be seen as a breeding ground for entrepreneurs. Yet microbusinesses and small businesses very seldom developed into bigger ones. This was due to a lack of know-how, training, credit and perhaps the necessary entrepreneurial skills. Often small 'businesses' were not run in a businesslike fashion at all.

Many African businesses run by locals were also hampered by social and cultural factors; above all, the patronage system. If African entrepreneurs turned a profit – the ultimate goal of any business – then friends, relations, acquaintances and quite possibly many others turned up to claimed their share. The few fortunate businesspeople who managed to amass a little wealth were under enormous pressure to spread it around. This pressure cannot usually be ignored. In some cases, those who refused to share suffered unpleasant consequences. The means used to force people to part with some of their profits sometimes even included witchcraft.[169]

Foreign businesspeople in Africa felt little or no such pressure. Often, they came from cultures where the nuclear family had clear boundaries; those who fell within them had a right to share in the wealth and all others did not. Almost nowhere in Africa was there a clearly defined notion of the nuclear family, and so in effect the claims of solidarity knew no bounds. Some African businesspeople even migrated to escape the pressure from their own relations and the other people around him. Others decided to give up on the business world, since it only led to trouble with family and friends. In short, clientelism held private enterprise and personal development in a stranglehold, perpetuating the status quo in both societal and individual terms. The Swiss anthropologist David Signer concluded that in Africa failure can be forgiven, but not success.[170] This attitude formed a major barrier to economic growth and development.

Other cultural factors may have played a part. Many Africans preferred to be thought of as wheeler-dealers rather than managers. Legality was the exception, not the rule. The motto seemed to be 'anything goes'. For example, a street vendor who cheated his customers by giving short measure was seldom the object of public censure. Instead, such trickery at other people's expense was considered clever or sharp, even admirable. President Konaré of Mali, on the other hand, called this a *culture de tricherie*, a culture of double-dealing.[171] He added that this widespread habit made it difficult to do serious business, since people did not trust each other enough to work together financially.

The rise of the informal sector was good for the economy and for society. However, this unintended effect of the structural adjustment programmes of the 1980s was bad for the state, since it could not make any money out of it. The informal sector was in some ways a law unto itself, and it paid no tax. As a result, African governments lost control of much of the economy in the space of a few years. The impact was mixed: the economy had to manage without the benefits normally provided by government, such as adequate infrastructure, but on the other hand it was spared the state's predatory attentions. In the informal sector, individuals were beyond the reach of government and could no longer be bled dry.

In order to complete our economic and financial survey, we must look at Africa's debts. The continent's massive debts partly date back to the pre-globalisation period, but are also partly the result of loans connected with structural adjustment programmes. Furthermore, the amounts African countries had to pay their creditors (interest plus capital) were so large, even after the end of the Cold War, that Africa's economic position cannot be correctly assessed simply by looking at inflows of capital to the continent. Outflows of capital are important too.

In fact, there is nothing odd about high repayments on loans and the resulting large outflows of capital. That is what happens when a country borrows money instead of receiving donations. Accordingly, the indebtedness of African countries must be seen in the light of a more general problem they faced in the age of globalisation; namely, their inability to generate sufficient returns on investment. Borrowed money must yield a profit, if only so that the loan can be repaid. When loans were used for purposes of redistribution and consumption, as happened so often in Africa, it frequently became impossible to repay them. Africa's economic – or rather, uneconomic – system was one reason for its debt problem and hence its marginal position in the globalising world. This issue is discussed in chapter 9 (pp. 281-284).

Regional cooperation
and African unity

At the beginning of this chapter, we saw that globalisation undermined the authority of the state. Particularly in the most developed parts of the world (such as Western Europe), states saw their sovereignty leak away in two directions, as tasks and powers were transferred either to supranational organisations or to subnational levels of government. The main motive for growing international cooperation was economic, while state tasks were often transferred to lower levels for cultural reasons. The same processes took place in Africa, except that the results were very much coloured by the weakness of the state. There is a link between a state's strength and its willingness to give up tasks and powers. Paradoxically, voluntary and orderly transfers of authority only take place when the state is in a position of strength and legitimacy. Weak states tend to cling desperately to their limited power.

Given the shaky power base of Africa's elites, it had not seemed likely that they would voluntarily strengthen either regional (supranational) organisations or local government at home. The fact that both of these things did occur across large parts of the continent in the 1990s cannot therefore be explained solely with reference to the African environment. There were certainly good substantive reasons for greater regional cooperation and for decentralisation, but African rulers could not be expected to pursue such policies of their own volition. Only strong international pressure could induce them to do so. Such pressure was only effective when donors backed it up with promises of funding. The policies that Western countries wanted to see (whether regional cooperation or decentralisation) were of interest to Africa's elites because they created new opportunities for patronage and clientelism. In practice, the supranational and subnational institutional development and 'capacity-building' advocated by the international community often simply led to the creation of new jobs for local elites. This section will look at regional and continental cooperation between African states. Decentralisation will be discussed in chapter 10 (pp. 322-325).

There was regional cooperation in Africa even in the colonial period, but it received an additional boost when independence came. Visions of African unity could not be realised, but the new leaders quickly agreed on the need for greater regional cooperation, especially in the economic sphere. The small newly independent countries would, it was thought, have a better chance of developing jointly, shielded by a system of common tariffs, than separately. In the 1960s and 1970s this led to the creation of a vast array of African regional organisations – so many, in fact, that in the second half of the twentieth century there was officially more regional cooperation in Africa than on any other continent. However, there is little point in listing these organisations, for most of them proved extremely ineffective, never moving beyond the conference hall or the drawing board. The participating countries were often eager to reduce or even abolish reciprocal tariffs and other barriers to trade, in other words to create free-trade areas of one kind or another. The idea was that they would complement each other economically. Yet they were unable to make real progress, for two reasons.

First of all, almost all the African economies were so tiny that they formed only a small market even when merged. Consequently, economic cooperation made no tangible difference to potential foreign investors. Only in the case of SADC was regional cooperation an interesting prospect for foreign firms, due to the large South African market. The European Union therefore worked to negotiate a free-trade agreement with South Africa or SADC (see p. 231). However, this was an exception to the general rule. In reality, the small national markets were not even properly integrated into a regional market. The participating countries were usually full of good intentions, but that was all. Far too little was done to harmonise national legislation in preparation for a free trade area, let alone a common market. National political leaders were unable, or unwilling, to put in the effort.

The second structural problem was that the participating countries' economies were almost totally undiversified. They all had the same kind of one-sided structure, based on the production and export of primary products. This meant they had little incentive to trade with each other. Trade between members of African regional organisations seldom exceeded 5-10 per cent of their total exports.[172]

The failure of regional economic cooperation in Africa contrasted starkly with developments elsewhere. In many regions, internal trade and investment often grew so fast that it was more accurate to speak of regionalisation than globalisation. This was true of trade blocs such as the European Union, NAFTA in North America and ASEAN in Southeast Asia. In the 1990s internal trade within the European Union – the most powerful trade bloc in the world – accounted for no less than seventy per cent of member states' total trade.

In the 1990s intraregional trade in Africa declined rather than increased, as more and more national currencies were allowed to find their true value. This made prices more realistic and more convergent, so that reciprocal trade was even less profitable. On the other hand, African regional integration was encouraged by the structural adjustment programmes, which involved trade liberalisation. That made it easier for neighbouring countries to work together. There was also some domestic pressure from groups of entrepreneurs who wanted to start exporting and therefore had an interest in regional cooperation. If regionalisation is seen as a step on the way towards further global integration, we must conclude that Africa was unable to take this step because it was economically underdeveloped.

Africa's regional organisations extended their range of activity in the 1990s, however. They began to tackle political issues as well as economic ones, particularly in the field of peace and security. It earlier chapters it was noted that African countries became more involved in each other's internal affairs after the end of the Cold War. This was a logical response to Africa's problems with regard to war and peace, but it created new problems. With support from the United States and Europe, the African organisations began to take on conflict prevention and crisis management. This was in the interest of both Africa and the West; it meant that there was less need for Western countries to become directly involved in African conflicts, and that African countries obtained the funds they needed to create or expand their capacity, which was of vital importance in helping national politicians maintain their power bases. Both sides could also claim that primary responsibility for preventing or ending violent conflict lay with countries in the region. In assuming this broader range of political tasks, the African regional organisations appeared by the turn of the century to be shrugging off some of their former apathy.

There were many regional organisations in West Africa, with the Francophone ones linked to Paris. The most important one was the Economic Community of West African States (ECOWAS), established in 1975. It included all the West African countries, irrespective of their colonial past. The ultimate goal of setting up a common market remained a long way off. There was also little progress towards other goals, such as the establishment of West African citizenship, with a single passport. What did bring ECOWAS into the international limelight was its decision to take a hand in ending the violence first in Liberia and later in Sierra Leone – the first time a purely African multilateral force had ever carried out a peace operation.

The greatest boost to regional cooperation in Southern Africa was the abolition of apartheid in South Africa. When South Africa joined SADC, the face of the organisation changed completely. The medium-sized states that had shaped SADC during the struggle against apartheid now saw themselves overshadowed by their former foe. The members found it difficult to reach agreement, due to fears that South Africa wanted to use SADC to gain economic control over the others. There was similar distrust about initial attempts at political and security cooperation.

Other parts of Africa had even less meaningful regional cooperation, although in the 1990s the East African Community (EAC) received something of a shot in the arm. The organisations in Central Africa existed only on paper. In 1986 a body was set up in the Horn of Africa to combat the effects of drought and desertification. In 1996 it was expanded and given a new lease of life as the Intergovernmental Authority on Development (IGAD). However, IGAD's efforts to promote development were thwarted by the extensive fighting in the region, and it began to focus on crisis management instead. In particular, it attempted to mediate in the conflicts in Sudan and Somalia.

For the record, there were many international – but not exclusively African – organisations (such as the UN's many specialised agencies) working in Africa. The fact that Africa was lagging behind in its development was a source of great concern at UN headquarters in New York and Geneva. One special initiative after another was launched in support of African development. However, the international organisations working in Africa had the same characteristics as the African regional organisations:, in the words of a top official, they were 'strong on principles, weak on tactics and nonexistent when it came to action'. As a result, the United Nations generally played only a marginal role in Africa. The fact that from 1996 onwards the UN Secretary-General was an African – the Ghanaian diplomat Kofi Annan – was of purely symbolic value.

The gulf between high-flown ideals and practical implementation was greatest of all in the Organisation of African Unity (OAU). African unity existed only in ideological and psychological terms, in the sense of an invented common past. In other respects, for example culturally or economically, Africa was largely fragmented. General characteristics that could be labelled African have been discussed in various chapters, such as the weak position of national elites and the all-pervading nature of political power. These traits led to less continental cooperation rather than more. Accordingly, OAU meetings were mainly publicity stunts. In the 1990s, however, the organisation was able to take advantage of the increased international interest in crisis management. In 1999-2000 it helped to end the war between Ethiopia and Eritrea by acting as an intermediary.

Around the turn of the century there was an unexpected call for African unity, but from a suspect quarter: the North African state of Libya. After years of isolation, not only from the international community but even within the Arab world, President Gaddafi of Libya had a plan to put himself back in the public eye. At special meetings of heads of state and government of OAU member states in Gaddafi's birthplace, Syrte, in September 1999 and March 2001, African leaders decided to replace the OAU with an African Union. Gaddafi had radical plans for the new organisation, but the delegates decided to restrict themselves for the time being to implementing the 1991 Abuja Treaty, which provided for an African central bank, African monetary union, an African court of justice and an African parliament.

These more modest goals were still totally unrealistic. African leaders naturally wanted to reap the benefits of such a union, but they were equally well aware that even a watered-down version of the treaty could not be implemented. However, it cost them nothing to sign Gaddafi's declarations, and some countries even did well out of it. For example, on the eve of the March 2001 summit the Libyan leader paid up the overdue OAU contributions of ten African countries so that their heads of government could once more take full part in top-level African talks. The leaders also knew that a joint African initiative would undoubtedly draw in new international funding. Gaddafi played to this in his speeches by emphasising what he saw as Africa's shared heritage. This led to the curious spectacle of an Arab leader proclaiming to a largely black audience, 'They sold us as slaves...'. However, he went even further in his identification with black Africa when he told his black audience that the world had first been dominated by the yellow race and then by the white race, and that the time had now come for the black race to rule the world. The proclamation of African Union – 'the greatest union in the world' – was the first step in this direction. Gaddafi's bizarre flirtation with sub-Saharan Africa was not backed by other Arab countries. The presidents of Libya's neighbours were conspicuous by their absence. In fact, the only country eager to proceed with the African Union was Libya. A Ministry for African Union was set up in Tripoli in anticipation.

The plan to set up an African Union was followed up at the summit of African leaders in the Zambian capital Lusaka in mid-2001. A formal decision was taken to dissolve the OAU (which had been established in 1963) in a year's time. The African Union was to replace the OAU and further promote cooperation and integration across the continent. It was to be modelled on the European Union, with a common market, common institutions and a common currency. The heads of government attending the Lusaka summit, with the African Secretary-General of the UN as guest of honour, were well aware that the road to real African union would be a long one and that the ultimate goal – a stable, prosperous continent – would be hard to attain. In order to set Africa on that road, President Mbeki of South Africa launched his Millennium Action Plan (MAP), later incorporated into the New Partnership for Africa's Development (NEPAD – see chapter 9, p. 296). In July 2002 the big step was finally taken. At a summit in Durban, South Africa, the African Union officially replaced the OAU.

To return briefly to President Gaddafi, he backed his policy of wooing black Africa with a generous invitation to Africans to come and work in his Libyan paradise. Thousands came legally, and many others illegally, to Tripoli and other Libyan cities. They did not even need visas or passports, just their national identity cards. In 2000 there were about half a million black Africans in Libya (which had a population of about six million).

However, integration did not take place. The Africans kept to themselves, and there was little fraternisation in the streets. There were countless incidents between Arabs and black Africans, at first on a small scale as a result of theft and other misdemeanours. In mid-2000 the unrest erupted into mass rioting in which dozens of black Africans were killed and hundreds injured. Most of the victims were from Ghana, Nigeria, Niger, Chad and Sudan. The Libyan police were instructed to protect the immigrants, but it was a hopeless task. The embassy of Niger was looted. To reduce the tension, the Libyan authorities eventually moved thousands of black Africans out of the capital to tent camps in the desert on the edge of the city. The government did all it could to calm things down and make sure that African ambassadors would not issue public appeals to their compatriots to return home. That would have meant a humiliating failure for Gaddafi's African policy and the end of his new role as Africa's Great Leader.

Incidentally, he did not see this role as being confined to Africa. According to Gaddafi, Libya could build bridges between Africa and Europe. Before intercontinental relations could improve, said the colonel, a number of obstacles would need to be removed, including what he saw as continuing French and Spanish colonialism in Africa. For example, Djibouti, the Canary Islands and various other European possessions would have to be given back to Africa. Gaddafi's overtures to black Africa and his attempts to muddy African-European relations were meant to reinforce what Libya saw as welcome signs of unrest in Africa, especially the spread of Islam. As noted in the last section of chapter 7, this spread could be seen as a protest against the poor living conditions and prospects of much of Africa's population – a protest aimed at the West.

Africa's close historical links with Europe were quite definitely a source of rancour and formed an easy target, especially as some predicted that Africa would become a mere appendage of Europe as a result of the regionalisation and globalisation process. According to this reasoning, there were three powerful economic blocs that would make the poorer countries in their regions utterly dependent on them. North America (NAFTA) would have Latin America as its back yard, Japan and China would hold sway over the rest of East and Southeast Asia, and the European Union would dominate not only Eastern Europe, but also Africa. This is therefore a good point to look at the relationship between Europe and Africa.

Continuing economic dependence
on Europe

As a result of its geographical proximity and historical ties, Europe was the continent that was most closely involved in Africa. Some European countries still had close links with former colonies. Relations with the leading European colonial powers, Britain and France, were discussed in chapter 1.

France has always found it particularly important to maintain influence in Africa, although it made major changes to its African policy in the 1990s, mainly in response to the conflicts in Central Africa. France not only pulled out troops and equipment, but also moderated its ambitions. Paris acknowledged that it could no longer guarantee the authority and safety of the presidents of Francophone countries. As a result, relations between France and Francophone Africa became less important to both parties. In addition, France began establishing closer relations with a number of non-Francophone African countries. In the late 1990s, for example, Paris focused particular attention on South Africa and Nigeria.

The smaller former colonial powers, Belgium and Portugal, were unable to branch out in this way. They did what they could to maintain the ties with their former colonies. Like France, Belgium saw its influence wane as a result of the turbulent events in Central Africa, which it could only observe from the sidelines. Portugal's role had already become negligible following the chaotic decolonisation process, although Lisbon attempted to keep the Portuguese-speaking countries together by setting up a Lusophone Community. Within the European Union, Portugal specifically presented itself as a country that had special ties with Africa.

Germany, Italy and Spain had only a small role in Africa. Of the remaining European countries, none of which had a colonial past in Africa, the Netherlands and the Scandinavian countries built up links with various African countries through development cooperation. As far as other European countries were concerned, Africa remained an unknown continent with which they had little or no direct contact.

With the first step towards European integration and the establishment of a supranational organisation in Europe under the Treaty of Rome in 1957, one question that immediately arose was whether the organisation should establish relations with other countries and regions, such as Africa, in its own right, in addition to member states' bilateral links. The French government insisted that its special relationship with Francophone African countries be acknowledged and given a place in the new European structures. This led to association agreements between the European Community and Francophone countries, agreements that were later merged into the Yaoundé Convention.

This special status for France's former colonies only came to an end when Britain joined the European Community in 1973. Germany and the Netherlands, which had never been happy with the emphasis on the Francophone countries, joined forces with Britain to promote a more inclusive relationship between Europe and what were then starting to be known as developing countries.[73] The idea was that an agreement should be signed between the European Community and all its member states' former colonies in Africa. The handful of African countries that had never been European colonies were subsequently added to this list, as well as the small island states in the Caribbean and the Pacific. In 1975 the first convention between the European Community and this group of dozens of countries, jointly known as the ACP (Africa, Caribbean and Pacific) countries, was signed in Lomé, the capital of the West African state of Togo.

What made this meeting so unusual was not only the number of participating countries, but also the emphasis on signing a convention. Years of negotiations preceded each renewal of the convention, which took place every five years. Under international law, any country that was a party to the convention, however poor, could enforce compliance with all of its provisions. Naturally the convention included a substantial aid component. This aid, which in fact was about equal to the amount provided by the individual member states combined (around 20 billion euros a year), was mainly in the form of programme aid: various forms of financial aid not linked to specific projects. It was mainly intended for improvements to infrastructure, rural development and food supply.

However, the agreement was not just about aid. The special thing about the Lomé Conventions was that they acknowledged the importance of trade between Europe and the African countries. The Lomé countries were granted trade advantages by the European Community (later the European Union). No import duties were levied on the vast majority of African exports. This preferential treatment was not reciprocal: the African countries were allowed to impose tariffs on similar products from Europe. In the 1970s and 1980s this was seen as a major advantage for African countries, but the accompanying protectionism eventually proved more of an economic drawback.

In any case, there was no free access to the European market for a number of agricultural products that were produced in both Europe and the ACP countries, although import duties on them were reduced. Textile products and leather were also excluded. Of course, these exceptions constituted barriers to African exports to Europe. The products concerned had great export potential for the ACP countries– otherwise Europe would not have seen any need to make exceptions. Spectacular estimates circulated of the potential income Africa was losing as a result of the remaining trade barriers. However, this should be put in proper perspective. Even the many products on which no import duties at all were levied were exported in limited quantities, and exports of some products even declined over the years. Often, African products were of poor quality, failed to meet all kinds of health, packaging and other standards and were relatively expensive – in short, they could not compete internationally. Even with free access to the European market, African products were still often no match for, say, Asian ones.

In 2001 the European Union decided to open up its markets to all products from countries where per capita income was less than one US dollar a day. There were forty-eight such countries, the majority of them in Africa. At the urging of France, Spain and other southern European member states which wanted to protect their own agricultural sectors, exceptions were made for three products. A quota was maintained for banana imports until 2006 and import tariffs were to remain in force for sugar and rice until 2009. As a result of this measure, exports from the poorest countries to Europe were expected to rise by fifteen per cent.

The chief remaining problem for African economies was the large subsidies that the European Union paid its farmers. Although not alone in this, Europe was certainly the most extreme, paying twice as much subsidy per farmer as the United States or Japan. On an annual basis the subsidies that rich countries paid their farmers at the end of the twentieth century were equivalent in value to Africa's total production.[174] This enabled industrialised countries to sell their agricultural products, especially meat and dairy products, well below the market price, even in developing countries.

This unfair competition, which was even more distorted due to Europe's habit of dumping surplus products below cost price on the African market, was a serious obstacle to the development of a healthy agricultural sector in African countries, and hence the development of African economies as a whole. The EU's Common Agricultural Policy, which was responsible for this, became notorious for its inconsistency with European development policy. This was euphemistically referred to as 'incoherence', which meant that policies interfered with each other. European development policy attempted to strengthen African agriculture, seen as part of the economy in general, but European agricultural policy weakened it.

Incoherence took many forms. In 1997, for example, the European Union signed an agreement with the government of Senegal under which it paid for the right to fish in Senegalese waters. This had benefits for both parties: it gave the Senegalese government greater financial latitude, and fishermen from the southern member states of the EU had access to well-stocked waters once more. The people who lost out in all this were the fishermen on the Senegalese coast. For centuries they had set out to sea in their small boats, and their catch had formed the basis for the coastal economy. The sale of fishing rights to foreign fishermen drastically reduced stocks in their traditional fishing grounds. None of the money that the government had earned from the agreement was passed on to them. Yet Senegal's fishermen had long been receiving support from individual member states of the Union, which provided aid so that small-scale fisheries could be modernised. The European Union and its member states were thus pursuing different policies, with conflicting effects.

However, the incoherence between different areas of policy within the European Union was even more striking. There were various reasons for it. In part, it was clearly a reflection of the conflicting interests of groups and institutions within the EU, probably aggravated by the Union's convoluted, obscure decision-making procedures. Moreover, development cooperation did not have an important place in European politics as a whole. Ignorance of the impact of European agricultural policy on developing countries may also have played a part.[175] By the beginning of the twenty-first century, however, European development ministers had policy coherence at the top of their agendas, and a debate on agriculture began in the rich countries.

The Lomé Conventions also set up compensation funds to protect developing countries against loss of income from exports. The Stabex Fund could be used to cover falls in prices of agricultural products, and the Sysmin Fund for falls in the prices of mining products. The idea was to guarantee poor countries more or less fixed incomes from their exports and so counter the effects of fluctuations in world market prices. Cocoa-producing countries, in particular, benefited from this in the short term. In the long term, however, the funds had a serious drawback. Interference with the price mechanism meant that prices could no longer perform their economic function. When world market prices fell, developing countries no longer had an incentive to switch to other export products. This problem was aggravated by the fact that prices of raw materials turned out not to be fluctuating but to be falling constantly for structural reasons. The funds were soon exhausted, but African economies continued to focus on the wrong products. The unintended effect of subsidies, from Europe and other donors, was to help preserve reliance on one or two main exports in many African countries at a time when there was an urgent need for diversification.

In the 1990s the subject matter of the Lomé Conventions was broadened to reflect the new recognition that the main reasons for Africa's failure to develop were political in nature. In 1991, for the first time, European development ministers began to focus on human rights and democratisation. The same issues were reemphasised in the Maastricht Treaty on European Union in 1992 and again when the Fourth Lomé Convention was revised in 1995. As a result of ongoing and imminent violent conflicts in Africa, conflict prevention also climbed higher and higher up the political agenda. In fact, this was an extremely delicate matter for the European Union, since various member states – particularly France, Britain and Belgium – were themselves involved in Africa's conflicts. The same was, of course, true of the United States. Their often traditional links with certain parties meant that EU member states sometimes backed different sides in the same conflict. The historical role that they had played in Africa often made it difficult for the EU to adopt a clear, joint position.

In 2000, Lomé was no longer the place where the new agreement was signed. This time the honour fell to Cotonou in neighbouring Benin. The bulk of the funds committed took the form of programme aid. Stabex and Sysmin each absorbed less than ten per cent of the budget. Large sums were also allocated as 'venture capital' for economic development, support for structural adjustment and emergency aid. Like the Lomé Conventions, the Cotonou Agreement drew largely on the European Development Fund. This fund did not fall under the ordinary European budget, but was periodically replenished (normally every five years) by separate contributions from member states.

Although the formal ties between Europe and Africa gradually became looser in the age of globalisation, Europe was still of crucial importance to Africa. The EU member states quite simply formed the largest trade bloc in the world and Africa's main trading partner. About half of African countries' total imports and exports were with Europe. More than half of their aid came from Europe. Together the EU and its member states were the largest group of donors to developing countries, and the EU was the largest contributor to institutions such as the World Bank and the UNDP. There were consultative structures such as Lomé/Cotonou and those between France and the Francophone countries, but there had never been broad top-level consultations between Africa and Europe. In 2000 it was felt that the time had come.

In April of that year, after lengthy, laborious preparations, the heads of state and government of the African countries (including those in North Africa) and the member states of the EU met in the Egyptian capital Cairo for a two-day exchange of ideas on political and economic issues and development cooperation. Topics ranged from the integration of Africa into the global economy to the prevention of violence against women. No specific decisions were reached. Africa's self-appointed new leader, Colonel Gaddafi of Libya, made a long-winded speech in which he dwelt on European imperialism in Africa. Apart from disrupting the programme, the speech had little effect. The European delegates listened impassively, and the Africans were mainly distrustful of Libya. At the end the assembled leaders reached agreement on a noncommittal declaration. The significance of this first-ever African-European summit lay not so much in its achievements as in the sheer fact that it took place. Leaders who had not been on speaking terms were once more able to discuss such things as the conflict in Sudan. Some felt the most important decision reached at the summit was that another intercontinental meeting would be held in 2003, this time in Europe (Lisbon). This second summit, however, was postponed because the European participants were unwilling to meet President Robert Mugabe of Zimbabwe there.

In contrast to the links between Africa and the United States (see chapter 4, pp. 127-132) and between Africa and Europe, there were scarcely any historical ties between Africa and Asia. While many Asians had worked in Africa since colonial times, apart from that, relations were mainly economic. At the end of the twentieth century this situation changed somewhat as the Asian 'tigers' began to make large investments in Africa.

Investment in Africa from Japan, Asia's largest economy, remained rather limited. However, Japan did begin providing development aid. In fact, in the 1990s Japan was the world's biggest donor country. Japan's assistance was mainly directed to poor countries in Asia; only about ten per cent of it was spent in Africa. What is more, Japanese aid was quite strongly linked to Japan's national interests. For example, much of it was used to support Japanese businesses in Africa. Nevertheless, Japan made much of its aid to Africa. Every few years it hosted a huge conference in Tokyo, where many African heads of state turned out to discuss their countries' relationship with Japan.

There was also some movement in Africa's relations with China, itself still a developing country. During the Cold War, for strategic reasons, China had maintained a presence in a number of African countries, but in the years that followed, it withdrew. In 2000, however, Beijing reappointed itself leader of the developing countries. Completely out of the blue, China invited African leaders to a summit meeting in Beijing. Officially, the Chinese leadership's purpose was to strengthen Sino-African friendship and promote economic and commercial cooperation at the beginning of the new millennium. However, the representatives of 44 African countries, including four presidents, were also told by the Chinese head of state that they should do more to resist Western domination. Furthermore, China wanted to provide experts, write off African countries' debts and set up a fund to encourage Chinese businesses to invest in Africa. In comparison with the economic and financial ties between Africa and the West, however, China's actions, and the funds it made available, were purely symbolic.

Relations with the Middle East can be summed up briefly. There were many people from the Middle East (especially Lebanon and Syria) working in Africa, for example as small independent entrepreneurs. There were also fairly close trading links between some African countries and the Middle East. In addition, various Arab members of OPEC gave African countries and groups financial support.[176]

South Africa: an emerging market

As mentioned, one key feature of globalisation was a worldwide increase in private investment. However, private investment in Africa was on a much smaller scale than elsewhere in the world. Official aid (development aid, roughly speaking) remained the main source of external funding for almost all African countries. Only in a few of them – Angola, Botswana, Ivory Coast and Ghana – were both private and public investment significant. The only large African country to depend mainly on private investment was South Africa.[177] As Africa's economic powerhouse, the country was the only one in Africa (apart from Nigeria, very briefly) to be granted the prestigious title of emerging market in the newly globalising world. An emerging market is one that is large enough and has sufficient growth potential to be attractive to international businesses. It was thought that in the age of globalisation such economies would attract so much private capital that they would become permanently integrated into the global economy. The criteria, apart from population size and per capita income (i.e. a country's purchasing power), were infrastructure, skills and expected political stability.

South Africa scored relatively well on all these criteria, far better than any other African country. Nigeria and Ethiopia had larger populations, but purchasing power in both countries was minimal (except for that of the Nigerian elite, who had grown rich on oil). Throughout Africa, infrastructure and skills were insufficient to attract international businesses. In some cases the political prospects were so uncertain that foreign businesses preferred to postpone investment. Of course, the situation varied from country to country. Countries with ample oil stocks were always attractive to major oil companies. Some other

African countries (such as Ghana, Ivory Coast, Kenya and Zimbabwe) were economically more versatile and may even have had reasonable prospects, but their economies were too small and their political futures too uncertain to attract much international interest.

That left South Africa. With production amounting to a full forty per cent of the continent's total GNP, South Africa was in a league of its own. Internationally the country was on a par with such emerging economic powers as Brazil, Russia and some Asian states. Its economic strength was the result of a long history that had begun with colonisation by the Dutch and the British. This led to a complex relationship with the local black population, culminating in the apartheid system, which had various implications for the country's economic development. On the one hand, apartheid limited South Africa's chances of integration into the world economy, because many Western countries refused to trade with it in protest; on the other hand, this very rejection forced South Africa to be economically completely independent, which gave the economy a powerful boost. In the first half of the 1990s apartheid was abolished and the reins of power passed largely into black hands. This made South Africa the only country in Africa where political and economic power did not coincide, for economic power was still in white hands. It was unclear whether this situation would last and whether the country would remain stable (see chapter 10, pp. 335-339). In any case, the international community was enthusiastic about the peaceful end to apartheid and there was great willingness to invest in the new South Africa. Its prospects were thus encouraging.

South Africa's post-apartheid governments, first under Mandela and De Klerk, then under Mandela only and finally under Mbeki, made the most of the international enthusiasm. They pursued neoliberal policies designed to attract foreign investment. This was considered necessary in order to develop the country further and spread the benefits of development more widely, since domestic savings, at just fifteen percent of Gross Domestic Product (GDP), were far too low for domestic investors to provide the bulk of the investment needed. With a savings ratio of fifteen per cent, South Africa put itself at the mercy of the international capital market. This hitherto protectionist country opened up to the outside world, regionally (it joined SADC, thereby increasing that organisation's economic importance) as well as globally. Negotiations began on a free-trade agreement with the European Union. However, some EU countries were so concerned about South Africa's competitive edge as a rival exporter of products that were significant for their economies, that they tried to introduce all kinds of exemptions. Years of wrangling over details drained the agreement of much of its substance. When it was eventually signed, many felt that a valuable opportunity had been wasted.

Despite these problems, South Africa became more and more integrated into the global economy. This left it increasingly vulnerable to the caprices of the international capital market that so typified the first few years of globalisation. The crises of 1998-1999 in Asia, Russia and Brazil were seen as a potential threat to all emerging markets. In fact, South Africa did not remain totally unscathed, even though the adverse impact was cushioned by the government's austere financial and monetary policies. However, the economic growth rate of three per cent a year that had prevailed immediately after the end of apartheid could not be kept up, and in 1997, 1998 and 1999 the South African economy grew by just one per cent a year. It was not until 2000 that growth picked up again, to over three per cent a year.[78] The economy as a whole was doing well at the start of the millennium, with inflation down to five per cent and the budget deficit down to three per cent. The Johannesburg stock exchange (the biggest in Africa) broke record after record, and internationally South Africa gained a reputation as one of the most promising emerging markets.

Apart from economic growth, the main goals of South African economic policy were higher employment and fairer distribution of wealth. This policy was known as GEAR (Growth, Employment and Redistribution). Higher employment was crucial in order to increase the incomes of the black majority and thus distribute wealth more equitably. In practice, however, the policy had little effect. While population growth was increasing the potential workforce by 350,000 a year, the number of formal jobs fell by half a million in the years after apartheid was abolished. Employment rose to a staggering thirty-five per cent. Despite the strength of the economy, the social crisis persisted. Wealth remained largely concentrated in the hands of the few; in 2000 about one South African in five had less than one US dollar a day to live on.

These developments made it clear that economic growth did not automatically lead to higher employment or fairer distribution of wealth. Accordingly, there was increased pressure on the ANC to abandon its free-market policies, especially from the South African Communist Party and the socialist trade union congress COSATU. Although they both supported the ANC-led government, they were very much opposed to a free-market approach. President Mbeki acknowledged that too few jobs had been created. In particular, investment by large transnational companies had not created as many new jobs as expected. However, he insisted that the government could not and should not create jobs itself. On the other hand, he added, it could do more to encourage enterprise among the black population. President Mbeki then announced a new revolution in South Africa – not a political one this time (like the abolition of apartheid), but an economic one. From 2000 onwards the more controversial components of GEAR, such as privatisation, labour market flexibilisation and measures to assist small and medium-sized businesses, were rushed into practice under the name 'Mbekonomics'.

In turning South Africa into a new economic power, great use was made of the technological advances that are such an important part of the globalisation process. In the field of information and communications technology (ICT), the country was on a par with Europe and far ahead of other African countries. Of the 2,250,000 people in Africa with mobile phones at the end of the 1990s, two million were South Africans.[179] The government supported wider use of mobile phones all over the country, in part by setting up mini-telecentres and telephone shops in various rural areas. Three quarters of the nearly one million African Internet users were South African, and so were almost all the African websites.[180]

The government placed great emphasis on technological progress. In 1996 South Africa even hosted the Global Information Society and Development Conference. At that meeting the government raised the problem of universal access to ICT within countries (including access for disadvantaged population groups and remote areas). South Africa's technological development also had an impact on neighbouring countries. Southern Africa as a whole was the most advanced region in Africa when it came to ICT.

Africa joins the techno-
logical revolution

From the mid-1990s onwards there was an explosion of ICT innovations and applications around the world. The ICT sector was no longer just a new economic sector in which goods and services were produced. Instead, it had a major impact on the entire economy through its influence on other sectors. Information became an integral part of almost all economic activity, and it was knowledge that fuelled this 'new economy'. The application of new knowledge and information made it possible to generate even more knowledge and information, in a mutually reinforcing loop. The human brain was no longer just the power that controlled all production systems, but a productive force in its own right. As a result, education and training rapidly grew more important. The gap between developed countries – North America, followed by Japan and several other East Asian countries and then Europe – and developing countries widened. Developing countries played a limited part in the technological revolution, with a few exceptions such as India, which was among the leaders.

Africa's poor educational systems and technical capabilities left it at the bottom of the ladder. It was by far the least computerised part of the world, and lacked the basic infrastructure that was needed in order to use computers. ICT skills were non-existent or very limited. Where use was made of ICT, it was 'passive', i.e. it was entirely focused on routine data processing rather than creative use of information, for example computer-assisted decision-making.

In 1996 there was one personal computer for every three hundred Africans, compared with one television set for every thirty and one radio for every five.[181] In the 1990s, then, the radio was still the most important mass medium. However, the Internet spread rapidly in the years that followed (see later in this section), so that these 1996 figures were soon out of date. As for fixed telephony – which was of great importance, since telephone lines are the basis for the Internet – the situation in 1996 was not much better, with just one telephone for every fifty Africans. In some sparsely populated countries this figure was even lower. However, the almost complete lack of telephone lines created opportunities to rapidly introduce new technology, such as digital circuits and optic fibres. Newcomers were able to take full advantage of the latest developments. Rwanda used part of the aid it received following the genocide to set up a modern telephone system. Rural Botswana also made a successful leap to high-tech communications.

Mobile phones had the potential to revolutionise communications in Africa. At the end of the Cold War there were only six African countries where mobile phones could be used, but by the turn of the century they could probably be used in every single one. Most mobile services were introduced and maintained by private companies. However, coverage often remained limited to capital cities and main routes. Perhaps the main advantage of mobile telephony was that it circumvented the problems associated with ordinary fixed telephones. In almost every country, conventional telephony was in the hands of state-owned enterprises which provided poor service. It often took years before applications for telephone were handled. At the end of the 1990s more than one million Africans were on waiting lists for fixed telephones. Even if people had a telephone, it could break down for all kinds of reasons. The systems were least reliable in the rainy season owing to water on the lines.

Mobile phones, on the other hand, provided rudimentary telephone services in areas where the prospects of having fixed lines were poor. If linked to the Internet, they also made it possible (at least to some extent) to supply rapidly growing markets – an essential contribution to overall economic growth. The business community put great pressure on governments to further privatise Africa's telecommunication sector, a step which was necessary in order to improve facilities and cut costs. In the 1990s, privatisation became the trend in African telecommunications. Yet, despite all this progress, Central, East and West Africa still had the lowest density of telecommunication services in the world.[182]

From the mid-1990s onwards the Internet grew exceptionally fast in Africa. In 1995 only four African countries were connected, but by the turn of the century all but one or two were. Over the same period the number of providers increased from just over 300 to more than 10,000.[183] After South Africa, the most flourishing Internet markets were in Ivory Coast, Senegal, Ghana, Kenya, Tanzania, Uganda and Zimbabwe. Yet the gap between South Africa and the rest was still quite large. In South Africa one person in sixty-five is an Internet user; the equivalent figure for the rest of Africa is one in five thousand. The world average is one in forty, and in the industrialised world the figure is as high as one in six.[184] A few large transnational providers such as AfricaOnline and CompuServe link various African countries to the United States, Britain and France. Internet access is unevenly distributed in all African countries. Services are mainly concentrated in capital cities and fan out from there. The number of cafés, kiosks and professional buildings (schools, hospitals, police stations, etc.) that are online is rapidly increasing. However, it costs a lot to use the Internet in Africa – more than in the United States and Europe. The countries where it costs most are those with only one provider, which to make matters worse is often owned by the national telecommunication company. This is yet another reason that privatisation and liberalisation are essential; they allow more providers access to the market. Members of government have usually had personal commercial motives to postpone these reforms, as well as budgetary and political reasons. Heads of state and ministers have had interests in national telecommunication companies. They could not do without the tax revenue. Moreover, they wanted to control access to news. Yet in Africa as elsewhere, the trend towards freer markets could not be reversed. However reluctantly, country after country decided to liberalise its ICT market.

Moreover, the benefits in terms of national and individual development could not be ignored. The business sector badly needed modern communication technology. That technology brought African producers into direct contact with potential customers all over the world and greatly reduced the influence of powerful, costly middlemen. In principle, ICT products and services could be produced and sold anywhere in the world, but Africa's role in this field remained negligible.

New technology did, however, find a place in education, with South Africa way out ahead once more. The University of South Africa offered complete online courses. There was even an African Virtual University for high-level scientific studies and online reference facilities, to which more than ten African countries were connected.[185] As elsewhere in the world, the potential for ICT in Africa is almost endless, with benefits for government, business, civil society and individuals.

Although when it comes to exploiting the potential of ICT the state can make a difference in all kinds of ways – from providing basic infrastructure and drawing up rules to allocating frequencies – the interesting thing about ICT in Africa was just how much was done through nongovernmental channels. We have already seen some examples in the former Somalia (see chapter 5, pp. 148-152). Governments could quite easily make a positive contribution by privatising utilities and other companies and by deregulating markets. Major leaps forward could sometimes be achieved with the help of new technology. It seemed it might be possible for Africa to start closing the large gap that had separated it from the rest of the world.

At the same time, many African governments were drawing up long-term plans to develop the ICT infrastructure in the public sector and in the country as a whole. They received plenty of international support for this, for in the eyes of the international development community ICT had become a gauge of the extent to which Africa could keep up in this age of technological breakthrough. Would Africa have to drop out of the race to develop in the highly modern global society and resign itself permanently to a place on the sidelines, or would international support in the area of ICT enable it to remain involved?

Leaving aside the symbolic significance of ICT, it is a field of vital economic importance for Africa's terms of trade and therefore for the continent's economic future. The prices of ICT products and services may not continue to rise, but they will remain relatively high, since technology-intensive goods and services generate high added value. Countries which are unable to use, let alone produce, advanced technological equipment and know-how will find themselves at a serious disadvantage. This technological challenge is one of the greatest Africa has to face in the age of globalisation.

Yet it is not the only challenge. There are political ones, too. Civil-society groups are rapidly becoming more organised, and in the hands of the opposition the new technology is a potential threat to governments. In theory, a single mobile phone is all an activist needs to organise a demonstration quickly in some unexpected place. So far, however, the political impact of new technology in Africa has been minor.

Cultural and religious

responses

The social changes wrought by globalisation were far-reaching and naturally had an impact on culture. 'Cultural confusion' was the term African delegates used to sum up this cultural impact at a meeting on the influence of globalisation in Africa, held in Tanzania in September 1998.[186] All at once, the ideologies Africans had used to interpret the world around them were no longer tenable. Socialism had been buried, nationalism was dying a natural death and even development no longer seemed to be a realistic ideology for Africa. What was to replace them? Liberalism and capitalism could hardly be publicly embraced. In Africa they were tolerated at best, not actively supported. The prevailing mood was therefore one of confusion and uncertainty.

This confusion and uncertainty arose against a background of continuing cultural homogenisation at a global level. This homogenisation – which in practice meant Westernisation or even Americanisation – was stronger and had begun earlier outside Africa, spreading outwards from the United States. It was homogenisation of culture in the broadest sense of the term, including such diverse areas as communication, consciousness and consumption. Consumer culture exerted a particular pull on the imagination. In the 1970s, Cola-Cola was the emblem of this process. In the 1990s, when the trend had progressed a good deal further, it was the McDonald's hamburger chain that came to symbolise it.

In Africa, however, 'McDonaldisation' did not yet amount to much. Africa's ties with the West were still too tenuous. The all-pervading sociocultural changes seen above all in the West, but also to some extent in Asia and Latin America (such as internationalisation, the beginnings of a functional network society and, as we have seen, technologisation), had hardly made an impression in Africa. Society had become rather individualised by traditional African standards, but by global standards Africa was still a continent with strong community ties. As the cultures of the world converged and a 'global village' took shape, Africa remained on the fringes.

Africa was not yet part of this global village (or rather, global city), yet contact with other continents was increasing, especially on an individual level. Growing international migration from Africa (see chapter 8, pp. 257-260), which is part and parcel of globalisation, forged new international links. Those links were reinforced by religious developments. Together with the collapse of secular ideologies, Africans' sense of social and often also personal insecurity led to a spectacular growth in religion. Of the major international religions, it was Islam and Christianity that benefited most. Both offered their members a place in a network extending to all parts of the world. Muslims and Christians were part of a greater whole and could use this frame of reference not only to reinterpret their world, but also to derive practical benefits from contacts with coreligionists. Through Islam one was part of a world that extended far beyond the Sahara into former Yugoslavia and Indonesia, and Africans' conversion to Christianity (often by Pentecostalists) brought them into contact with Europe and America.

Although Islam and Christianity originated outside Africa, the form they took in Africa owed so much to local influences that their spread should be seen as an authentically African development rather than a religious invasion. One reason for their popularity was that in times of uncertainty people sought succour in religions with simple ethical principles. Islam was especially attractive from this point of view. In Africa religion and politics are difficult to keep apart, and so the spread of religion was reflected in politics.[187] This was primarily true of Islam, in which there is no separation of mosque and state in any case, but African Christianity also had political significance. One African country, Zambia, even officially called itself a Christian nation.

The simultaneous rise in the popularity of Christianity and Islam in Africa around the turn of the millennium supports the hypothesis that religions may to a large extent shape the twenty-first century. At the same time, it illustrates a general ambivalence towards modernisation. On the one hand (particularly in the case of Christianity) new technologies often opened the way for new ideas, while on the other (particularly in the case of Islam) contact with the modern world not infrequently led to rejection and resistance. The recent acceleration of the modernisation process in the form of globalisation brought these contrasts even more sharply into focus, especially in places where the impact of globalisation was not altogether positive, as in Africa.[188]

This ambivalent attitude towards modernisation goes back many centuries. It can be found not only in the response of non-Western cultures to Western expansion, but also within the West. The modernising current has almost always been dominant, and throughout history dominant cultures have always inspired ambivalence. On the one hand the dominant culture is adopted, at least in part, not only because it is good at improving living standards, but also because, for example, it is fashionable. This may adversely affect the image of one's own, subordinate, culture, or indeed one's entire self-image. On the other hand, however, there is resistance to the dominant culture because it is supposedly no good, alien, second-rate or vulgar. This is usually accompanied by romanticisation of one's own culture. All these features can be found not only in the global South, but also in the European response to the dominant American culture. On the one hand Europe adopts a great deal from America, but on the other there is an undercurrent of anti-Americanism.

The impact of globalisation around the millennium has been different from that of modernisation in earlier centuries, if only because of technological progress. Before economic globalisation could make a serious impact on Africa, the continent was connected to the Internet and television had penetrated nearly everywhere. This had an effect of its own. The differences in wealth that exist between countries and within countries literally became visible to the majority of the world's population. This too encouraged ambivalence between wanting to adopt a culture and rejecting it. Most of all, however, Africa's self-image was adversely affected by comparison with other cultures. Whereas once owning enough cattle had been equated with wealth, on closer examination, those few paltry cows did not seem like much compared with what people elsewhere in the world owned and considered important. Although nothing had changed 'on the ground', the spread of technology had altered the self-image of both individuals and cultures. The result was often lower self-esteem, and people began to think of themselves as poor.

After independence, African ambivalence towards modernisation and the West had found a natural ally in socialism. Its collapse was greeted with disbelief and dismay. Socialism left behind an ideological vacuum. The simultaneous, sudden rise of no-holds-barred capitalism confirmed people's worst fears. The absence of local African forms of protest against the West helps to explain the recent popularity of Islam in Africa, since this religion has always been a rallying point for people and groups who, for whatever reason, wanted to challenge Europe and above all America.

In Africa, as elsewhere, the attraction of Islam may well be mainly due to its element of politico-cultural protest. This threatened to further disrupt relations between America – which was more the object of criticism than Europe and at the same time more aware of these issues – and the Islamic world. It has already been speculated that the traditionally regional battle between Christianity and Islam could therefore emerge in a new, global form – as a struggle between modernisation and those opposed to it.[189] The outlines of such a struggle, which could become violent, became apparent on a small scale in Africa. Of course, this struggle also had its roots in international power politics (see chapter 10, pp. 344-349).

At the same time, there was a current of opinion that wanted to combine Western secular influences with local African strengths, in order to improve living standards throughout the continent. This was the essence of the African renaissance (see chapter 4). Local cultural differences were also magnified and enhanced. This can be seen as the African version of the particularism that all over the world formed the psychological counterweight to cultural homogenisation. As a result of homogenisation, people increasingly dressed the same way, ate the same products, watched the same television programmes and so on (not only within countries but throughout continents or even worldwide). But there were many who instead felt the need to emphasise their own specificity, the aspects that distinguished individuals or groups from one another. In many countries this led to a revival of local culture and subnational identity.

The increasing importance of ethnicity ('ethnicisation') in Africa in the 1990s has already been referred to a number of times, often in the context of violent conflict. Since there was very little cultural homogenisation in Africa, this can hardly be seen as the main cause of the countermovement. Unlike in many Western countries, reflection on one's own identity was probably not the mainspring. In Africa, ethnicisation had much more to do with political factors. Incidentally, it is important to emphasise that the need for a group identity is a normal human characteristic. The choice of group or groups from which to derive that identity usually depends on a combination of family ties (in the broadest sense), racial characteristics, language, religion, a shared past and a common enemy.

Ethnic affinities change over time, and the relationship with the form of political organisation (the state) is important here. In the modern Western nation-state, the ethnic group came to coincide with the national population. In Africa, where the state was imposed from outside without regard for the feelings of group identity that existed among the population, such a bond between the state and the people living within its borders scarcely emerged.[190] In some cases, notably Lesotho and Swaziland, the state coincided with an ethnic group, but the vast majority of African countries were home to numerous ethnic groups.

In the 1960s, independence brought about a wave of popular enthusiasm that marked the beginning of a new sense of national identity. Many African rulers reinforced this sense of nationalism (which was useful for assimilating subnational groups) by making concessions to local identity in their policies, for example when allocating jobs in the civil service or in connection with development projects. The decay of the state in the period that followed made it impossible to continue with such policies. The structural adjustment programmes of the 1980s reduced states' income so drastically that the ruling elites could no longer keep all or even most of the ethnic groups in their countries satisfied. From the rulers' point of view, state resources (which were now extremely limited) had to be used as strategically as possible. That meant focusing on the ethnic group that would guarantee them the most, or the most reliable, political support – in other words, their own ethnic group. It is not hard to guess how other ethnic groups responded to such changes of policy. Groups came into conflict and began to turn their backs on the state or at the very least demand their own tangible share of its benefits. National loyalties gave way to subnational ones.

The motive behind ethnicisation was often the sense of being at a disadvantage compared with other ethnic groups. The emphasis was thus on conflict with other groups rather than social cohesion. Under certain circumstances a group's frustration about its relatively unfavourable position would erupt into violence. Then ethnicisation turned into tribalisation, with ethnic groups fighting each other within states just as tribes had done in the past. In this way the decay of the state contributed to a link between globalisation and particularism or ethnicisation – a special link that only existed in Africa.

Despite Africa's marginal position within the international economic system, globalisation thus had a crucial impact on the continent. All this took place against the backdrop of major changes in African society. For decades the population had been growing by several per cent a year. This was one factor that led to a dramatic change in the structure of the population. In the space of a few years a sizeable proportion of the population migrated from rural areas to the cities, which grew explosively. In turn, these changes had an impact on political, economic, social and cultural conditions. Demographic trends are therefore an essential aspect of any history of Africa. They will be discussed in the next chapter.

8
A NEW POPULATION

The population triples

The nature of any society is largely determined by the groups that make it up. Therefore, no survey of Africa would be complete without a survey of its demographics. I will restrict myself to discussing some general trends in population size, the age composition of the population and its social consequences, population movements and human impact on the natural environment.[191] We will see that the African population has changed so much and in so many ways that as we move into the new millennium, we can now almost speak of a 'new population', with characteristics that are new to Africa. At the end of the chapter, I will discuss the spread of AIDS in Africa.

In 1960, when many African countries gained their independence, the global population was three billion. Those were the years of the worldwide population explosion, when the average growth rate reached 2 per cent a year (2.4 per cent in developing countries). Forty years later, on the threshold of the twenty-first century, the global population had more than doubled to over six billion. During this time, the average population growth rate had fallen to 1.4 per cent a year (1.7 per cent in developing countries). However, Africa's growth rate was higher and reached its peak later. Population growth in sub-Saharan Africa between 1960 and 2000 was far higher than the doubling that occurred in the rest of the world, and in fact the continent's population more than tripled. There were 200 million sub-Saharan Africans in 1960; twenty years later, in 1980, there were 380 million, and another twenty years on, in 2000, this figure had reached 650 million. The fastest growth occurred in the 1980s, when the population across the continent grew by more than 3 per cent a year. This was an extremely rapid rise compared with the 1 per cent recorded in the 1940s and even the 2.5 per cent reached in the 1960s.[192] It was not until the 1990s that annual population growth first began to tail off, though Africa's growth rate remained the highest of any continent.

It has only been a few decades since Africa became populated to any substantial degree. Since the dawn of humanity, the continent had remained relatively empty for millions of years and had been dominated by wildlife, like other parts of the world. However, Africa remained in this state longer than other continents. There were probably only around fifteen million people living in Africa by the beginning of the first millennium AD. Europe, which is a third of the size of the African continent, already had thirty million inhabitants by this time. As the African population gradually increased to thirty million during the first millennium AD, the ethnic balance changed. The Bantu peoples began to spread from their heartland in Central Africa to other parts of the continent, displacing the Pygmies and Bushmen. By 1500 the African population had reached some forty million. During the centuries of the international slave trade, demographic trends differed widely from region to region. In some coastal parts of modern-day Guinea, Congo and Angola, the population periodically declined, yet across the continent as a whole it continued to rise slowly. By 1800 there were sixty million people in Africa and by 1900 the total had climbed to around ninety million. Only after that did the growth rate rise substantially, although even then it did not climb above one per cent a year in the first half of the twentieth century.[193]

Africa's extremely low population density in the precolonial era influenced the structure of African society. For example, local elites often found it very difficult to win the loyalty of the populace, simply because there weren't enough people around. Precolonial states of this kind are sometimes referred to as 'contest states' because they engaged in a form of interstate competition.[194] They did not compete for land, as was often the case in Europe, but for manpower. People were frequently able to evade the authority of a particular state simply by moving to a different region. The authorities in these states generally had not yet developed an effective monopoly of violence. As a result, there were often rival subcentres within states. Another consequence of the low population density was that there was little pressure to boost productivity, since there was always enough to feed what was then still a small population. Most people grew their own crops or kept their own livestock. This form of political and economic organisation gradually drew to an end in the nineteenth and early twentieth centuries, when European settlers began to introduce new systems of government.

The growth rate of a population is determined partly by immigration and emigration. In the colonial period, there was a considerable influx of non-African peoples into Africa, especially in certain areas, notably Southern Africa (the Dutch, British and Portuguese), East Africa (the British) and West and Central Africa (mainly the French). However, more people left the continent than entered it. The largest group of emigrants were not the colonists who left around or after independence, but black Africans. In the nineteenth century, most of the Africans who had left the continent were transported to other countries as slaves, but starting in the late twentieth century, many emigrated in search of a better life (see the third-to-last section of this chapter for an account of this recent wave of migration). However, the influx and outflow of people over the centuries had little influence on the total population.

Of far greater importance were the birth and death rates. Birth rates probably remained low until well into the colonial era, mainly due to the length of time that mothers continued to breast-feed their babies (sometimes more than two years), which substantially reduces fertility. However, social developments in later decades, such as the introduction of milk powder, increased fertility rates. Other important factors included poor education for girls, insufficient contraception and, more generally, poverty. Children were regarded as workers who could supplement family incomes, and sometimes as a kind of pension plan for their parents. In recent years, in countries where girls have better access to education, where contraceptives are more widely available and where there is less poverty, women have tended to have fewer children. From 1990, the average number of children per woman throughout Africa finally began to ease downwards, from 6.1 in 1990 to 5.7 in 1995. This decline was sharpest in countries that were marginally more prosperous (and where fertility had been lower to begin with) and slowest in the poorest countries (where fertility was higher).[195]

The decline in death rates in the twentieth century did even more to accelerate population growth. Africa, or at least its more tropical regions, has always been seen as posing high risks to human health. Its inhabitants waged a constant battle against a wide range of tropical diseases, as a result of which life expectancy was low. Portuguese travellers who visited Angola in the sixteenth century estimated average life expectancy there to be just twenty to twenty-five years. Infant mortality was particularly high. Western medicine, which was not introduced into Africa on a large scale until the twentieth century, therefore had an enormous impact. Treatment of infectious diseases, which began in the 1920s, was particularly effective in reducing infant mortality. Although in the first half of the twentieth century thirty to forty per cent of all children were still dying before the age of five, the mortality rate declined sharply among older children. Life expectancy consequently rose steeply, from just thirty-nine in 1950 to fifty-two in 1990.[196] However, this trend was undermined by the growing number of deaths from AIDS in the 1990s, which caused life expectancy to fall once more. By the new millennium, the AIDS epidemic was placing a severe burden on the overall social development of large parts of Africa. The emergence of AIDS and its consequences will therefore be dealt with separately in the final two sections of this chapter.

The combination of longer lives and higher birth rates in the second half of the twentieth century yielded a mind-boggling growth rate, which may well have been the highest in the world. Kenya was probably the record-holder, with a growth rate of more than four per cent for some years. In the colonial period, Kenya's population had been quite small: just over 2 million in 1920 and approximately 3.5 million in 1940. By the time the country gained its independence in 1963, its population had swelled to 8 million before doubling in just sixteen years to 16 million in 1979. After this, the growth rate tailed off slightly, and it took more than twenty years for the population to more or less double again, to 30 million in 2000.[197] The same principle applied in other African countries. Tanzania's population, 8 million in 1950, rose to 35 million by 2000. Ethiopia's population of 12 million in 1950 rose to 60 million by 2000.

This exceptional growth rate had major repercussions for the makeup of the population. For example, the proportion of young people in Africa became higher than in other parts of the developing world and far higher than in the industrialised world. This gave the population pyramid a very broad base. In Mali, for example, the youngest age group (children below the age of five) accounted for almost ten per cent of the entire population, compared to no more than three per cent in the industrialised world.[198] Children under fifteen accounted for nearly half the population of almost every African country. In Mali, fifty per cent of the population was under fifteen and sixty per cent was under eighteen. Moreover, these age groups were not evenly distributed throughout the country. Since it was mainly the young who migrated from rural to urban areas, the average age was lowest in the cities. By the year 2000, three out of four inhabitants of the Senegalese capital, Dakar, were below the age of thirty.[199] Population growth, coupled with a declining average age, altered the character of society, opening up an unprecedented generation gap between young and old and making life difficult for the older generation (see below).

The sharp rise in the population naturally led to an equally sharp increase in population density. With a surface area of 30 million km², Africa is the world's second largest continent after Asia (which is 45 million km²), and larger than either North or South America. Africa is also far bigger than Europe, which covers just 10 million km². Though it depends on where we draw the border of the Sahara, approximately 5 million km² lie in North Africa, with the remaining 25 million km² in sub-Saharan Africa. In 1960, when the African sub-Saharan population totalled roughly two hundred million, average population density was therefore eight people per km². By the year 2000, after the population had more than trebled, this had risen to more than twenty-six people per km². Even so, population density was still extremely low compared with other continents. France, which is quite sparsely populated by Western standards, still has four times as many people per km² as Africa. The Netherlands, which is very densely populated, accommodates as many as sixteen million people on just 40,000 km², giving it a population density of four hundred inhabitants per km². This means that on any given area of land, there are an average of sixteen people in the Netherlands for every one person in Africa.

At first sight, then, an increase in the African population would not seem likely to create any problems. Despite Africa's extensive tracts of inarable land and the paucity of alternative economic activities, it was thought that the African population would be able to provide for itself without any difficulty, even if it were to double in size once more. If we assume that the Africans have the right to appropriate as much land from nature as the Europeans or Asians have done on their continents, then there is enough room in Africa. The fact that we tend to think of Africa as a continent blessed with vast tracts of untamed wilderness and an abundance of wildlife is entirely due to its small population. Other continents once had a similar wealth of flora and fauna, but human encroachment began much earlier in these parts of the world. Nevertheless, at the millennium, the speed with which Africa was losing its natural environment was alarming. Moreover, since Africa's population had only recently started to grow significantly, making it almost the only place in the world where large animals still roamed in the wild, the question arose as to whether the preservation of that wildlife should be a responsibility of the global community rather than of Africa alone. We will return to the relationship between man and nature after the next section.

Mass migration

to the cities

Although, relatively speaking, Africa's population density was not yet a cause for concern, its rapidly expanding population was distributed unevenly across the continent, with the vast majority concentrated in the cities. In recent years the population of African cities has grown faster than the population of the continent as a whole, outstripping every other part of the world. The African population has more than trebled since 1960, but the combined population of Africa's capital cities has increased tenfold. Around 1960, the average capital city in Africa had roughly fifty thousand inhabitants. By the year 2000, nearly half of those capital cities had a population of over a million. They were the main locus of Africa's explosive urbanisation. However, smaller cities and towns also grew. In 1960, when much of West Africa was gaining its independence, the region had only seventeen cities with more than a hundred thousand inhabitants. By 1990, there were ninety. The expectation is that there will be as many as three hundred by 2020.[200]

In 1960, there was only one city with over a million inhabitants in sub-Saharan Africa: Johannesburg, in South Africa, whose historical and economic background made it difficult to regard it as an entirely black African city. It was joined in the years that followed by Addis Ababa, Lagos and Kinshasa. However, it was not until the 1990s that many African capitals had a population of more than a million (including Accra, Abidjan, Dakar, Nairobi, Dar es Salaam and Lusaka). By the year 2000, there were some twenty to thirty such cities in black Africa. The top-heavy political and economic structures of these countries meant that urbanisation was almost exclusively confined to their capital cities and that, unlike more developed economies, they had no network of provincial centres or smaller towns to link the capital with rural areas. In Africa, these two worlds remained separated by a vast gulf.

Only two countries in Africa had a truly multifaceted urban structure with a network of provincial centres and several cities with a population of over a million: South Africa, with its diversified and distributed economy, and Nigeria, with its exceptional federal structure. The capital cities of the Nigerian states each formed the hub of an independent political and economic network, which gave them an urban character of their own.

In the 1990s, three African countries tried to ease the population pressure on their capital cities by promoting a hitherto insignificant settlement to the status of the new capital city. All three initiatives involved moving the population inland from the coast, either for ideological reasons (because a focus on the coast symbolised ties with the country's former colonial rulers) or in keeping with a new vision of the country's future, based on developing the interior. These efforts were quite transparently modelled on the establishment of Brasilia in the Brazilian interior in the 1960s. However, in the early twenty-first century, two of Africa's new capital cities – Dodoma in Tanzania and Yamoussoukro in Ivory Coast – were still sleepy backwaters that were wholly incapable of competing with their elder siblings Dar es Salaam and Abidjan. Only Abuja, which had replaced Lagos as Nigeria's capital, was growing rapidly. It was the only one of the three to which the government had actually moved.

Africa had traditionally had a mainly rural population, and until the mid-twentieth century it was the least urbanised continent in the world. Its cities had begun developing very slowly in colonial times. Take Bamako, the capital of Mali, in the African interior. By the year 2000, it was a vast agglomeration of huts stretching along both sides of the river Niger, in a spot where a hundred years earlier there had been nothing worth mentioning. In the nineteenth century the French colonial authorities had chosen its site as a future administrative centre for the interior, which was still little explored by Europeans. This was done in typical arm's-length fashion from Dakar, many miles away. As a result, the choice of location was not well thought out and led to an unexpected surprise; Bamako could not be reached by sailing up the Niger. Despite this shortcoming, it held on to its newly acquired status as the local administrative centre. The railway line from Dakar to Bamako had to be extended to Koulikoro, a village located at the point where the Niger became navigable. A river port was built there. The first train arrived in Bamako in 1904 from distant Senegal. It was then a fishing village with a population of just a thousand, but it soon began to expand around the grey stone railway station.

In 1960, by which time it had a population of around a hundred thousand, it became the capital of newly independent Mali. Since then, it has grown steadily and its character has changed. As a former French outpost, Bamako had for decades had the air of a miniature Paris on the edge of the desert, with a predominantly colonial architectural style and atmosphere. However, the city's rapid growth pushed this distinctively French influence into the background, and Bamako increasingly took on the appearance of a bustling and colourful African town. The old centre became dilapidated and some of its buildings were demolished to make way for new government offices and high-rises. The quiet, sleepy town became increasingly chaotic, a tangle of minibuses, motorbikes and people trying to sell each other everything under the sun. Bamako gradually became the heart of Mali in every sense. More than half the paid work in the country was to be found there. The city was also the source of half the country's tax revenue and expenditure. However, these funds were not nearly sufficient to manage the growth of the city effectively, and as a result, the most basic amenities were generally absent. The further one travelled from the city centre, the more haphazard the neighbourhoods became. There were slum dwellings made of breeze blocks and loam with corrugated iron roofs. Most of these ad hoc shanty towns had once been home to a specific ethnic group, but they had become increasingly heterogeneous as the urban population had grown more mobile. In just forty years of independence, the population of Bamako had grown tenfold, reaching more than a million. Trains were still running twice a week between Bamako and Dakar, from the river Niger to the Atlantic Ocean.

Bamako's urban development is typical of the many capital cities that were founded as administrative centres by the colonial authorities, such as Lagos, Nairobi, Dakar and Abidjan. The work that these cities provided and the money to be made there drew people away from the countryside. This influx accelerated dramatically following independence. In the 1970s and 1980s, urban growth in Africa averaged five to six per cent a year, which was approximately double the rate of population growth. The new national capitals exerted a magnetic force, and in just a few years' time became veritable metropolises.

Why did cities, and capital cities in particular, grow so rapidly? The main reason was mass migration from the surrounding countryside. This was not exclusively an African phenomenon. On most other continents, however, one of the prime reasons why people moved to the city was the modernisation of agriculture, which not only increased production but also reduced the need for manpower. Africa was an exception to this rule, since farming methods had not been modernised. The lamentable neglect of rural areas in Africa meant that production did not rise. In fact, it fell from the 1970s onwards.[201] The rural population, on the other hand, grew rapidly. And because farming methods remained largely unchanged, it became necessary to use more and more land for cultivating crops. A growing number of farmers had to make a living by growing crops on land that had never been cultivated before. And under the pressure of a growing population, it became more and more difficult to make a decent living by working fertile soil. Without mechanisation or the benefits of a 'green revolution', African farmers therefore continued to toil away on the economic margins, often in conditions of extreme poverty. It is little wonder that the young in particular, who saw no future for themselves in the countryside, were drawn to neighbouring towns or to the capital in search of work, where, from a distance at least, money looked easy to come by. There appeared to be plenty of jobs available in the urban centres, and there was the added possibility of making useful contacts. Following independence, African governments encouraged this exodus to the cities through a policy that favoured urban dwellers over their rural counterparts, and through the culture of clientelism, which was often confined to the capital cities.

The natural expansion of the urban population was a second important factor in the rapid growth of the African cities. As urban centres expanded, this became a more important growth factor than rural migration. The first generation of rural immigrants brought with them the family pattern they had grown up with; namely, the tendency to have large numbers of children. However, the average family size decreased in subsequent urban generations, in line with the global trend.

The third main reason for the speed of urban population growth in quite a few African countries was the civil wars that were raging there, causing displaced persons, and refugees from neighbouring countries, to pour into the cities in search of a safe haven. Starting in the 1980s, the capitals of the former Portuguese colonies, Luanda in Angola and Maputo in Mozambique, expanded as a result of this form of migration, as did Khartoum, the capital of Sudan. Kinshasa expanded disproportionately due to the war in and around Congo, especially in the 1990s, becoming one of the continent's biggest urban agglomerations. The population of Monrovia, the capital of Liberia, and that of Freetown, the capital of neighbouring Sierra Leone, have also grown explosively as a result of conflict, although their populations have remained low compared with those of other African capital cities.

Despite the sharp rise in the populations of the new African capitals, it was only in their centres that they even vaguely resembled the prototypical global metropolis. There, high-rise development sent the message that these were cities to be reckoned with. The city centres housed the government buildings, hotels, schools, universities and office complexes. Their streets had at some stage been paved, even if they were no longer adequately maintained, and if the country had a wealthy elite, such as the oil barons in Nigeria, then strikingly large numbers of Mercedes, Porsches and other expensive cars might be seen manoeuvring around the potholes. Some of these city centres were bordered by old colonial districts or prestigious new developments, but moving out from the centre, these very quickly gave way to ramshackle neighbourhoods and eventually to slums. The slums covered a large majority of the surface area in all the major African cities, since the facilities in the city centres were wholly insufficient to cope with the huge influx of new arrivals. There were practically no paved roads, sewage systems, safe drinking water or electricity. Slum-dwellers were simply left to fend for themselves as best they could.

The rural immigrants lost hold of their original cultural identity. They were sometimes left feeling uprooted. The social world of the African city-dwellers began to drift further and further apart from that of the rural population. Social ties loosened, including those with blood relations. Over time, fewer people were supported by the income of a single individual, reflecting the growing individualisation in the cities. On the other hand, this progressive individualisation and the anonymity of the city sometimes strengthened the need for a group identity, a fact which perpetuated or even strengthened ethnic ties in some urban districts.

The process of urbanisation radically changed the economic, social and cultural environment in which Africans lived. What is more, this change took place fast. Whereas in 1950, only ten per cent of Africans were living in more or less urban areas, by the year 2000 this had risen to as much as forty per cent. Forecasts suggested that early in the twenty-first century, more than half of all Africans would be living in cities. Southern and Central Africa were the most highly urbanised African regions, followed at some remove by West and East Africa, with East Africa experiencing the fastest growth.

However, the speed of urbanisation on the continent as a whole began to slow down in the 1990s.[202] Presumably, this was mainly due to structural adjustment programmes, which often generated higher incomes in rural areas than in the cities, and consequently reduced the incentive to migrate to urban areas.[203]

Another likely factor is that mass migration led to a deterioration in living conditions in the cities. The sheer numbers of people flocking into the large African metropolises drove them to the brink of collapse. By the year 2000, some of Africa's cities were home to more than five million people. The largest was Lagos, with a population of thirteen million. Given their woeful shortage of manpower and funds, it was simply impossible for the authorities of these cities to impose any order on the chaos through elementary social provisions such as schools, markets, access roads or public taps. Moreover, the residents of the outlying slums had little incentive to improve their housing on their own initiative, since most residents of these informal overspill communities did not own the land they used. As a result, they could in theory be evicted from their homes at any time. Life in these outlying suburbs was therefore full of frustration and misery.

The situation was worsened by the high incidence of crime. From the 1990s onward, African cities very rapidly became unsafe, especially for people with something to lose. In particular, there were large numbers of armed attacks and burglaries, both by individual criminals and by gangs. Trade in drugs also increased. Violence and insecurity made entire neighbourhoods ungovernable and impossible to police. There was a combination of causes: unemployment and poor prospects, social inequality and indifference, the growing inadequacy of the official crime prevention and crime-fighting agencies, corruption throughout society, the decline of social norms and the uprooted anonymity of urban life. For many years, the level of crime in Johannesburg, one of Africa's most unsafe cities, was attributed to the former apartheid system, but in fact the city's problems were typical of the continent as a whole, albeit exacerbated by the specifically South African environment. Insecurity in African cities was a major disincentive to foreign investment and therefore to employment, creating a vicious circle. The cities also became less attractive, even terrifying, places to live.

This state of affairs put pressure on the relationship between the cities and the national authorities. City-dwellers had traditionally formed the power base for African politicians, but that support gradually began to crumble, partly due to the problems described above. The percentage of urbanites who belonged to a network of political patronage declined steadily in the 1990s and the number of people with no political, social or economic loyalties increased. This latter group, who generally looked to the informal sector for their economic survival, wanted little to do with politics. They had lost confidence in the government and were therefore a potential threat to the authorities, who not unnaturally feared that the dissatisfaction in the cities might flare into a violent explosion that would turn against them. However, in the twentieth century at least, things did not reach this stage.

The large African cities were wholly unable to emulate the positive social and economic role played by cities in more developed regions. They displayed some of the features of modern city life, such as streetlights at night, traffic jams, cinemas showing the latest films, discotheques and other forms of entertainment, but it was little more than a façade. They were unable to turn themselves into true economic engines by expanding their knowledge and skills base, through labour specialisation or by generating technological and business innovation. In fact, the only positive development was that urbanisation helped to stem overall population growth.

The environment
ravaged

Humanity may have taken its first steps in Africa, but this does not mean that the continent was generally very suitable for human habitation. Not surprisingly, in a continent as large as Africa, the range of ecosystems was huge, from deserts and steppes to savannahs, swamps, rainforests and mountain ranges. Some parts of Africa were temperate and hospitable but more often nature was a scourge, bringing tropical heat, barren or poor soil and an abundance of life-threatening diseases.[204] The natural climate, which was often hostile to man, resulted in a high mortality rate and largely accounted for the low population density. This inhospitable climate was a major reason European travellers and colonialists left Africa unexplored for so long and made only limited forays into the interior. The chances of surviving such expeditions were low. It was not until the twentieth century, with the development of effective medicines against infectious disease, that Africa became a slightly less dangerous place and the number of inhabitants quickly began to multiply.

Starting in the late twentieth century, various groups began to displace one another in some regions. In the Sahel, for example, farmers needing more land began to push nomadic herdsmen from their traditional pastures. Man also became a serious threat to wildlife. On other continents, the struggle between the human and animal populations had already been 'won' much earlier by man, but in Africa this struggle was just beginning. It was the last continent in which herds of large animals still roamed the wild. However, the areas where this was still possible shrunk year by year.

The environment was under even greater threat in areas of armed conflict. The war in the Great Lakes region, for example, had devastating effects on wildlife and the landscape. In eastern Zaire, most of the forest around the Hutu refugee camps was destroyed. The mountain gorillas that had inhabited it also disappeared, presumably because they had been hunted down for food. Armed conflicts generally had a more severe impact on rural areas than on cities. In some regions, the countryside was completely depopulated, both directly as a result of hostilities and indirectly because the fighting made it impossible to harvest crops, depriving locals of their livelihood. Those who stayed were reduced to subsistence farming, or, if that was no longer possible, to hunting. Some groups, such as those in the western region of southern Sudan, who had been unable to grow crops successfully for many years, were reduced to a way of life reminiscent of the Stone Age. They became hunter-gatherers once more, a practice that brought some species of gazelle close to extinction.

One of the biggest threats facing Africa's environment was the irreparable loss of biodiversity; in other words, the decline in the number of plant and animal species. This was largely due to the appropriation of natural habitats for human activity; tropical rainforests and low-lying wetlands were at the greatest risk. Semiarid regions were affected by soil erosion, the loss of vegetation and evermore serious shortages of water. The sum total was desertification, the expansion of the desert at the cost of other, wetter climates. In some steppe and savannah areas, stock breeding brought about the almost complete decimation of the indigenous fauna. Illegal hunting also took a heavy toll on wildlife, and posed a threat to endangered species. The relationship between man and nature had become unbalanced, especially in vulnerable areas. The encroachment of agriculture in the Sahel, for instance, posed a serious threat to the surviving elephant population. These elephants, each of which consumed around 150 kilograms of vegetation a day, in turn constituted a threat to the farmers, sometimes destroying their entire crop. Efforts to restore the natural equilibrium between man, crops, water and animals seemed doomed to fail.[205]

Human activity not only destroyed some ecosystems but also polluted many others. This was a particularly serious problem in the rapidly expanding cities, where air, soil and water pollution were often so severe that they threatened public health. Temporary settlements such as refugee camps were also frequent sources of environmental degradation and destruction.

Africa's per capita energy consumption is only a fraction of that in the industrialised world. The continent therefore cannot share in the blame for the overall rise in global temperatures, which is largely due to high fossil fuel consumption in developed countries. Africa would sooner or later suffer the effects of this phenomenon, but the natural disasters that took place there in the beginning of the twenty-first century could not yet be attributed with certainty to this phenomenon. In the year 2000, for instance, the heavy flooding in Mozambique and its neighbouring countries was caused by a combination of natural phenomena, to which a slight rise in the sea level may have contributed. This rise, which was due to the melting of the polar ice cap, makes the coast of Africa increasingly susceptible to flooding.

Global warming had another kind of impact on Africa; it endangered the few areas of permafrost on this tropical continent. The layer of snow covering Africa's highest peak, Mount Kilimanjaro, on the border between Tanzania and Kenya, gradually began to melt. This prompted fears that the famous scene of wild animals grazing at the foot of the snow-covered mountain – for many people the symbol of Africa – would disappear forever in a few years' time.

At the turn of the century, only one in twenty Africans had access to electricity. Fossil fuels were mostly used for transport. The vast majority of Africans met their energy needs by using biomass, in the form of wood and charcoal. Biomass generated over ninety per cent of the energy consumed in Africa and was practically the only available source of fuel in rural areas (along with batteries and kerosene in some cases). However, deforestation and soil erosion made it increasingly difficult for these energy sources to provide for the growing population. Africa had a vast range of potential alternatives, but they remained unexploited.[206]

One question that was frequently arose was to what extent the destruction of the natural environment was linked to economic development, or the lack of it. This debate was heavily influenced by ideology and moral standpoints. Was it the poor who were despoiling the environment, or the wealthy? Should environmental degradation be blamed on poverty in general or was it aggravated by economic reforms? The only link that could be made between poverty and environmental degradation was through the population explosion. Poor Africans, who accounted for the vast majority of that population, had seen little change in their lifestyle. Instead, the growing effects of poverty on the natural environment were due mainly to the growing numbers of poor people. Take the consumption of wood for cooking and heating, for example. In a rural environment with a low population density, the natural supply of wood could easily keep pace with demand. However, the population explosion made this increasingly difficult, and wood became scarce in and around Africa's major cities. Gatherers of firewood had to travel ever greater distances to find enough to meet their daily needs. And as a result, the countryside around the cities became increasingly bare.

Many attempts to link economic progress and environmental degradation focused on the activities of the World Bank, which together with the IMF led the process of economic reform in Africa. The potential environmental impact of the World Bank's work was subject to increasing scrutiny. Up to the 1980s, it frequently extended aid in the form of large-scale projects, and little attention was given to possible repercussions for the environment. However, during the 1980s, the World Bank changed its tack. It abandoned the project-based approach, which was found to have too little positive impact, and shifted to influencing the policies of countries receiving aid. At the same time, it gave more and more thought to the environmental impact of aid. Immediately after the publication of the Brundtland Commission's report in 1987, which was highly critical of the World Bank's environmental policy, it set up a separate environment department. During the 1990s, this department became an important arm of the organisation, exercising considerable influence on structural adjustment programmes.[207] This did not end the debate on the environmental impact of these programmes, which was the topic of countless studies. Nobody, however, managed to draw any clear conclusions.[208]

International scrutiny of the environmental impact of the activities of the World Bank and other international organisations in Africa distracted donors from the attitude of African governments and ordinary Africans. Rich or poor, they generally failed to appreciate the importance of protecting the natural environment. This was not unusual in itself. At the equivalent stage of development, none of the other continents had shown any particular concern for environmental protection. With so many serious problems of poverty and underdevelopment, environmental protection was either given low priority or was not even recognised as an issue. As an explanation of why African countries did so little to protect the environment, this is far more plausible than the oft-heard argument that they could not afford it. International donors did, after all, provide substantial financial support for environmental activities in developing countries.

The lack of concern for environmental protection shown by African governments, civil society and the general public posed a major stumbling block to international development cooperation. Most Western countries used targets to calculate the amount of money they should set aside for specific sectors, including the environment. For political reasons they set aside a certain sum each year for environmental cooperation with Africa.[209] But donors also insisted that development cooperation must be 'demand-driven'; in other words, that the wishes of the recipient countries should guide aid efforts. So before donors could spend any money on environmental cooperation, African governments and civil society first had to ask for such aid, which they rarely did.

Very occasionally, if there was some economic gain to be made from improving environmental management, for example by improving game reserves and opening them up to tourists, African governments might add environmental cooperation to their to-do lists. Some major economic successes were achieved through ecotourism, so there was no shortage of new initiatives in this area.

Limited appreciation of the need to protect wildlife and the environment, along with armed conflict, poverty, unsustainable economic development, the rapid spread of humanity across the continent and the growing consumption of non-biodegradable materials such as plastics severely damaged Africa's environment in the late twentieth century. Some of this damage was irreparable; for instance, some species became extinct. However, environmental problems were not so devastating that they precipitated armed conflict, as the American political analyst Robert Kaplan had predicted they would.[210] Africans saw environmental degradation primarily as a practical and aesthetic problem. Yet for humanity as a whole, the disappearance of Africa's vast tracts of unspoiled landscape – the last great wilderness on earth – represented the loss of a major part of our global heritage.

A poor outlook
for the elderly

The first part of this chapter gave a detailed account of the rapid population growth in Africa over recent decades. It noted that not only had the population increased, but that on average Africans were also living longer. Improvements in medical and sanitary provisions and in diet, housing and hygiene standards gradually raised average life expectancy to fifty by the early 1990s. In some countries, it rose even further, although only in South Africa did it climb above sixty (to sixty-four).[211] While average life expectancy rose more sharply on other continents, the trend in Africa was clearly positive and the proportion of elderly people in the population steadily increased. This, together with a number of important social changes, altered the place of the elderly in society. The first signs of the contemporary problem of an ageing population became apparent in Africa in the 1990s.

The elderly traditionally played an important role in most African communities, acting as intermediaries between their own communities and the all-important spiritual world. As repositories of their communities' religious heritage, they maintained links with the ancestors. They also carried with them a more practical cultural legacy which, in the absence of formal education, they passed on to others. They understood the structure of their village and the relationships within their communities (which could be important when marriages were being planned), they resolved disputes, they could forecast the weather and they knew ways to survive in difficult circumstances. As the Malian poet Hampate Ba put it, 'Each time an elder dies, a whole library goes up in flames.'[212] The elderly were treated with respect. They remained part of society by continuing to help cultivate the land, tend vegetable patches, cook meals, mind the livestock or care for their grandchildren. The extended family systems encouraged reciprocal care between the generations. The elderly did not simply receive help from the younger generation but also played an active role wherever they could.

The elderly in Africa were cared for either by their families or by a slightly larger group, depending on local customs. Compared with the same age group in other parts of the world, they were by no means badly treated. They generally lived with their immediate relatives, retained their social status and shared in whatever the rest of the group had. If the surrounding countryside was unproductive, as was quite often the case in Africa, the group would sometimes go hungry. There was then little in the way of special care available for the elderly. Health care in Africa focused mainly on preventing and treating infectious diseases, and on maternity and child care. Medical care for the elderly was either unavailable or unaffordable. Some people preferred to keep the little money they had for a dignified funeral rather than spend it on medical treatment.

In recent decades, however, Africa has undergone a series of important social changes that have made life more difficult for the elderly. Extended families have gradually been replaced by nuclear family units, beginning in the rapidly expanding cities. Many young people have left rural areas for the cities or even emigrated to other countries. These developments have weakened the social position of the elderly, and in many places, the traditional networks that would automatically have cared for them no longer exist.

There were no alternatives to this informal, personalised care in rural areas, but even in the cities, little was done to develop a 'modern' system of care for the elderly. Almost nowhere in black Africa were there formal old age provisions. For instance, there were no group homes for the elderly, although some cities (e.g. in Ghana) did provide a very limited day care service for older people. A few isolated experiments were also carried out to assess the feasibility of local social security systems based on small-scale credit programmes, for example in Mozambique.[213]

A growing number of elderly people had to rely on their own incomes to pay for accommodation, food and health care. However, due to the high unemployment across the whole continent, it was often impossible for them to find paid work on their own. Those who had been in formal employment were generally paid a pension, although inflation reduced its value as time went on. Some elderly people still had a few possessions of their own.

Of immense importance to the individual status of elderly people was the respect they commanded. As well as courtesy, this included a degree of affection, admiration and veneration. However, not all elderly people could expect to receive such treatment simply because they had reached a certain age. Individual characteristics and personality also played a decisive role. The elderly were judged by what they had achieved in life, and above all by whether they had managed to send their children to school or give them some form of education which would enable them to get a job. Building your own house was also important in many cultures. If you had not managed to do so, then you could be ostracised by your children and your local community. Such individuals had a very hard life, often filled with hunger and misery. Elderly men who were shown little respect because they had achieved too little in life were particularly prone to end up destitute. Society was generally less hard on women who found themselves in a similar situation.[214]

The vast majority of elderly people were in fact women, often with no family to care for them. As in other parts of the world, women in Africa tend to live longer than men. They frequently marry older men but are less likely than men to remarry following divorce or the death of their partner. Elderly women may have been more fortunate than their male counterparts in being able to rely on the generosity of their local communities, but they also suffered more discrimination under a range of laws and social customs. In some African countries, women could lose their homes, land or part of their income when their husbands died. They were less able to support themselves economically, for example because they had been given less education, had no access to credit and were paid less than men for doing the same jobs. Sometimes they could only obtain work on the margins of the informal sector, where there were no social provisions whatsoever. Single older women also risked being accused of witchcraft, especially if the community in which they lived was going through a bad patch. In the 1990s, thousands of elderly women were forced to flee their communities each year for this reason, and over a thousand were murdered on suspicion of witchcraft.[215]

Demographic trends were less favourable for the elderly in Africa than in other parts of the world. Although the industrialised West had a proportionally larger elderly population than anywhere else, this growth had been gradual and had been cushioned by a strong economy. By contrast, the 'greying' of the population in the developing countries often took place against a background of unremitting poverty.

Although the size of the elderly population grew much faster in Asia and Latin America than it did in the prosperous West, this growth was matched by a simultaneous rapid increase in the number of young people. In Asia and Latin America, the population growth rate had begun to decline once more, but a large workforce had emerged, composed of young people who were having fewer children and would presumably be able to financially support the expanding numbers of elderly people.

Most of the developing countries in Asia and Latin America could take advantage of this demographic bonus, but not those in Africa. Although in Africa the percentage of elderly people was lower than in the rest of the former Third World (in the year 2000, between three and four per cent of the African population was over the age of sixty), in absolute terms the number of older people was growing rapidly (to around twenty-five million by 2000), whereas the workforce that would need to support them was growing less quickly and in some countries was even in decline. This was due to the rapid spread of the deadly HIV/AIDS virus throughout Africa in the 1990s (see the final two sections of this chapter). The death rate in the 15-to-45 age group rose alarmingly throughout the continent. Not only did this leave the elderly with fewer caregivers, but it meant that they themselves often had to take on the extra work of caring for the many AIDS victims and orphans. In this indirect fashion, the elderly were severely affected by the AIDS epidemic.

Frustration among
the youth

The proportion of young people as a percentage of the overall population rose spectacularly. Around 1990, more than half of all Africans were below the age of eighteen. These young people grew up with a worldview that was often radically different from their parents'. For example, they had had no personal experience of colonialism, and knew only what they had been told about it. The sole political reality for them was the independent African state. If young people wanted to engage in political opposition against a particular group – and there were plenty of reasons for doing so in Africa at the end of the twentieth century – then it was not foreign imperialists or exploiters who formed the natural targets of their antipathy, but their own governments.

This wave of young people surged into a world of dramatic change. Africa may have lagged behind other parts of the world in terms of economic development, technological innovation and the network society, but these changes did gradually begin to affect the continent. Partly under the influence of the international mass media, African society underwent a degree of individualisation that affected both young and old. This, combined with growing Westernisation, sometimes altered the relationship between the generations.

However, different communities reacted to this trend in strikingly different ways. Some of them opposed 'modernisation' and the influx of Western influences in general (see the end of chapter 7).

Despite its poor quality, the spread of formal education across the continent also widened the gap between the views and perceptions of young people and those of their elders. Even with the sharp increase in the number of young Africans the percentage of African children attending school continued to rise for many years. It peaked around 1980, by which time four out of five children were attending primary school. Following the collapse of government funding, this figure began to decline to around seventy-five per cent during the early 1990s, after which it recovered slightly. While the figures represented a clear improvement, they were still far lower than in other parts of the world. This applied to primary, secondary and tertiary education alike. Although the number of children attending secondary school and going on to university in Africa continued to rise at a modest rate in the late twentieth century, it remained extremely low compared to other continents. In 1980, two out of every ten children attended secondary school; by 2000 this had risen to three out of ten (although in the poorest countries, such as the Sahel, it was only one in ten). In the year 2000, one in forty young people attended university, compared with less than one in a hundred in 1980.[216]

Even leaving aside the generally very poor quality of all types of education in Africa, the numbers of young people attending secondary school or higher education were far too low in most African countries to boost levels of knowledge and broaden the intellectual elites. There were simply not enough suitable, sufficiently qualified people to fully analyse the problems with which these countries were struggling, to draw up plans to resolve them and to carry out those plans. African governments and private enterprises faced a severe shortage of manpower. There were also too few people with an adequate grasp of politics or sufficient political awareness to provide a sound basis for broadening or diversifying African politics.

As problematic as this was for African states and for the future of the continent, young people were primarily concerned about their own economic prospects, which were gloomy to say the least. Until around 1980, school-leavers could often automatically count on a job in government, but after that time it became much more difficult, and by the 1990s it had become almost impossible. Prospects for young people were worst in rural areas, a fact which prompted them to migrate to the cities in droves. Although urban centres had lost some of their attraction due to the decline in the availability of public-sector jobs, they still exercised a pull. Despite the fact that urban amenities were increasingly unable to cope in the face of mismanagement and a mass influx of newcomers, they were still better than those in the impoverished countryside. The chances of finding work were still best in the city. Almost all public and private investment took place in the urban centres. Moreover, cities enjoyed a level of prestige that was systematically encouraged by the state. In the decades following independence, securing a job with the government (and the fringe benefits that went with it) was promoted as the highest attainment to which a young person could aspire. The anonymity and freedom offered by city life was also attractive to young people who wanted to escape what they experienced as claustrophobic traditional village structures and social customs.

Not all urbanites benefited from greater anonymity and individuality, however. Lost amid the faceless masses of the big city, some longed for a return to their former identity and customs. This led communities in some urban districts to revive what they regarded as their traditions. Young city-dwellers began re-emphasising their traditional identities. It would therefore be inaccurate to describe young African urbanites as 'modern' in contrast to 'traditional' villagers. They were in fact more likely to be a mixture of the old and new.

This mixture is exemplified by the young people of Kinshasa who crossed the border into Angola in search of diamonds and dollars following the collapse of the Mobutu regime in the mid-1990s. Their hunt for wealth could only marginally be described as a modern economic activity. While these youngsters were in the field, they concentrated on amassing wealth; they did not spend any of it. However, once they returned to the capital, this economic constipation turned into diarrhoea; in just a few days, they spent the money they had acquired on gold chains, transistor radios, sunglasses and sex. This mirrored the ancient pattern of the hunt, which was surrounded by countless rituals. By taking part in this 'modern' version of hunting, the young city-dweller could become a person of consequence. It was a rite of passage aimed at self-aggrandisement. The more wealth you amassed, the more you spent, the more women you had and the more debts you incurred, the more important you became. It had nothing to do with modern economic principles and everything to do with ancient methods of redistributing wealth and building personal networks. These were no longer the traditional rural networks whose rules where made by elders, but new urban networks of young people.[217]

Unemployment was a huge problem, not just in rural areas but also in the cities. The government was effectively no longer recruiting and the formal private sector was creating very few new jobs. Those entering the labour market were forced to make a living for themselves in the informal sector, which they did with varying degrees of success. Girls, who were on average not as educated as boys, had fewer opportunities on the job market. As a result, they tended to migrate to the cities less often. Those who did sometimes found work in the informal sector but it usually provided only a meagre income. Prostitution was more lucrative and this partly accounted for the sharp rise in the proportion of teenage mothers in African cities.

Young adults in urban families often carried on living with their parents longer as a matter of economic necessity, since without work they could not afford homes of their own. There were other reasons that young people were unable to find a social niche, as their parents had a generation earlier. Without an income, young people could not start a family. And without a family, they could not gain access to the adult world. Young adults with no children had no status in their communities.

The inability to become a full member of society had important consequences for the way in which many young people viewed their culture and themselves. Traditional norms and values, such as those governing the relationship between the generations, relations between men and women, the ownership of property or the use of force, were undermined. Disappointed and frustrated, some young people turned to drugs or joined gangs. Some tried to escape their marginal status by pursuing a career in crime or as an armed fighter, or, in less extreme cases, through religion or emigration. These young people were easy prey for criminals, warlords and pimps. It was almost impossible for young men to avoid being caught up in the fighting in regions worst hit by armed conflicts. Above, the section on the war in Sierra Leone (see chapter 5, pp. 158-162) discusses the tragedy of its young people, who lived – and frequently died – in a culture of violence.

To the prosperous West
in search of a better life

Migration is a common and widespread pheno-menon in Africa. Africans had been moving from place to place for millennia before they began their mass migration to the cities in the twentieth century. They sometimes travelled large distances, even crossing national borders. During the colonial era, those borders were usually quite arbitrarily drawn, often cutting right across a group's ancestral territory. Obvi-ously, quite a lot of movement across the border took place in such areas. This included a good deal of seasonal migration, either in search of work or to take herds to pasture. A more recent development is mass migration prompted by famine or war (see chapter 6, pp. 196-200). This section looks at migration as part of the search for a better life.

Those who migrate in search of better prospects are often termed 'economic refugees'. However, this description is not entirely accurate, since these people tend not to be living in the direst poverty (as the term might lead you to expect), but doing relatively well in eco-nomic terms. It is precisely these individuals who were able to take the preliminary steps required for international travel, such as going to the city, gathering information about other countries, making contact with people who can help to organise their journey and paying for the trip. Almost all economic migrants were young men in the prime of life, to whom the decision to leave their local area was not an act of despair but a carefully thought out strategy to improve their own lives and those of the dependants they left behind. These mi-grants did not usually include impoverished farmers who lived below the poverty line, since they generally knew nothing of other countries and were in no position to travel to them.

In the colonial period and for some years following independence, most migrants travelled to the former colonial power. Gradually, however, migration to neighbouring states, which had been taking place for many years, increased. This local migration was relatively straight-forward since Africa's borders were easy to cross in many places. It was therefore not too difficult to evade the border guards or to get across more or less legally. Modern vehicles and improved communication also made traffic between African countries slightly easier and cheaper. As a result, international migration came within reach of a growing number of Africans. This affected the entire continent, though not surprisingly the most popular destinations were the countries with the strongest economies.

South Africa was first among them. During apartheid, millions of black Africans trav-elled to South Africa from neighbouring countries to find work. The formidable South African mining industry was heavily reliant on workers from Lesotho and other neigh-bouring states. Following the end of apartheid in 1994, large-scale migration from the rest of the continent to South Africa began in earnest, and included not only job-seekers from Southern Africa but also refugees from Congo and Rwanda, traders from Senegal and Mali, and many others. According to some estimates, South Africa had received between two and four million immigrants by the year 2000.

However, this enormous wave of immigrants led to a number of painful situations and debates. Pan-African solidarity and equality were much vaunted by the new South African government, but in the face of high unemployment and crime, the voters were unimpressed by such ideals. Both ordinary South Africans and the country's Minister of Home Affairs, Dr Mangosuthu Buthelezi, who was responsible for migration, felt that unemployment, crime and AIDS would disappear from South Africa if immigrants were to leave the country.[218]

West Africa is another region with high levels of international migration. Traditionally, many men from the Sahel would travel to the coastal states in search of temporary or permanent jobs. The wealthy state of Ivory Coast was a particularly popular destination. In the colonial era, economic migrants usually made for the coastal plantations with their export crops. Later, cities like Abidjan and its surroundings began to draw more people. Migration from the Sahel to the coast was so common that it became part of the regional culture. In fact, some young Malian men were not allowed to marry until they had made the journey to Ivory Coast.[219] By the turn of the century, roughly a quarter of the Ivorian population consisted of immigrants. They included several million Malians and Burkinabe, plus hundreds of thousands from other neighbouring countries, most of them refugees from Liberia.

Here, too, the consequences of mass migration were not restricted to the economy but were also reflected in political tensions. The large influx of Muslims from the Sahel region threatened the traditional political dominance of the Roman Catholics in Ivory Coast. In 1999, the country's Muslim opposition leader, Alassane Ouattara, who was said to have been born in Burkina Faso, appeared to stand a good chance of winning the presidency of Ivory Coast. However, this was unacceptable to native-born Ivorians and shook the country's political establishment to its foundations. The army staged a coup, but when their military leader General Robert Guei himself failed to win the presidency, the army put forward Laurent Gbagbo, who, though an opponent of theirs, was at least a member of the Christian political elite. This shows how mass immigration fuelled the growing political instability of the once peaceful and prosperous state of Ivory Coast.

The political events in Ivory Coast also reflected one of the paradoxes of globalisation, namely that it brought about a huge increase in mobility yet also prompted a growing preoccupation with roots and local identity. This frequently led to the exclusion of others, usually newcomers. The same trend was visible in other regions. International migration by Africans was not, of course, restricted to their own continent. Globalisation made it easier for them to move further afield. Through the international media, many young Africans had become familiar with the lives and spending patterns of their contemporaries in the West. This gave them high aspirations and fuelled their frustration about the obstacles to social and economic reform at home. As a result, they often regarded their stay in the capital as the first stage of a journey that would lead them on to Europe or North America. The slave trade of past centuries was thus gradually followed by a voluntary global mass migration of Africans.

For the host countries in the West, this was the third wave of immigrants they had received from the world's poor regions since the end of the Second World War. The first wave had begun in the middle of the twentieth century, set off by the process of decolonisation. Most of those Africans had gone to France and the United Kingdom. The second wave had overlapped with the first one and was fuelled by rapid economic growth in Western Europe during the 1960s. At the time, business and industry in Europe had badly needed a source of preferably cheap and, if necessary, unskilled labour. This led to a wave of immigrants to the North, mainly from the Mediterranean countries. Unlike the North Africans, most of whom came from Morocco, black Africans played almost no part in this mass migration. The third wave of immigrants, many of whom labelled themselves asylum-seekers, began to arrive in the mid-1980s, and since then their numbers have continued to increase. In 1980, just under twenty thousand people applied for asylum in Europe but by the 1990s this number had risen to more than half a million a year.[220] This was the clearest difference between the third wave of migration and the two previous ones, namely that the latest influx appeared to be tied up with new global trends and therefore to have a permanent character. It had its origins in the huge economic gulf between the rich and poor countries, combined with improvements in communication and transport.

Africans were in fact a minority in this 'globalised migration'.[221] Unlike the populations of Latin America and above all Asia, Africans were rarely in a position to make the intercontinental journey to Europe or North America. They had neither the organisational capacity to migrate in large groups nor the financial means for migration. Migration to the West often cost more than four thousand dollars per person. However, there was no lack of motivation to leave their countries; Africans from all levels of society openly admitted that they would prefer to build lives outside their own continent. Intercontinental migrants from Africa included a relatively high percentage of people fleeing political instability, mainly from the Horn of Africa: Somalis, Ethiopians, Eritreans and Sudanese. Among the politically stable countries, Ghana was the main source of emigrants. This was primarily due to its flourishing Pentecostal Council, a church-based organisation with branches throughout the industrialised world, which helped its members to emigrate.

Intercontinental migrants initially focused on Europe, but over time more and more of them headed for North America. As their numbers grew, the rich countries tried to stem the flow, in the realisation that unlike the two previous migration waves, this one would not end until steps were taken. Moreover, the admission of large groups of immigrants which were big enough to form their own subcultures stood in the way of full integration into the societies of the host countries. Despite the successful integration of countless individual immigrants, social and cultural islands with 'Third World characteristics' began to form in Europe and North America. An ethnic underclass emerged in the West, characterised by extensive poverty, unemployment, a high dropout rate and crime. Occasionally, immigrants exported political tensions from their own regions to the host nations, some of which resulted in terrorist attacks. However, apart from those committed by militant Sudanese or Somalis, these incidents rarely involved African immigrants.

Not only did migration to the prosperous West have major personal consequences for the immigrants, it also affected the communities and countries they left behind. No matter how poor the immigrants might have seemed to Western eyes, they often managed to save some money to send home. This extra income amounted to billions of dollars each year, and provided a welcome supplement to the generally negligible savings of those on the home front. Moreover, African governments tended to encourage rather than to discourage migration, given that jobs on the continent were scarce, the better educated citizens were often critical of the prevailing regime and remittances from abroad injected some capital into the country. Occasionally, local groups sent one member to the West to generate capital. This practice was particularly common among Somalis. Migration of this kind was not just an individual choice but a social endeavour. And in theory, when they returned home, immigrants could use the knowledge and experience they had gained to help their own societies develop, although in practice it rarely worked out that way. Most immigrants did not in fact return. The opposite was more common, namely a loss of expertise and skilled personnel known as brain drain. Doctors and other highly qualified professionals from African countries could, after all, usually earn far more and enjoy a more comfortable life in prosperous countries than they could at home. And of course it was precisely those people who tended to have the contacts and the means to emigrate.

The loss of workers in the most productive phase of their lives, regardless of whether they were skilled or unskilled, was the biggest problem facing the countries of origin. Migrants were by definition people with initiative, which they could have used to promote the development of their own countries. The argument that their departure reduced unemployment does not hold water, since these productive individuals could have created economic growth in their home countries, thereby generating more employment. Migration left a relative surplus of children, elderly people and women in some regions, giving rise to a host of economic problems. During the 1990s, this trend was dramatically heightened by the AIDS epidemic, which mainly affected these same productive individuals, between fifteen and forty-five years of age. Migration and AIDS were a huge drain on Africa, leading to the further destabilisation of society.

The rapid spread of the AIDS epidemic

Infectious diseases have had a more devastating impact in Africa than on any other continent. Modern medicines, especially antibiotics, reduced the incidence of many of these diseases in the second half of the twentieth century. This resulted in a sharp rise in average life expectancy in Africa. However, as the century drew to a close, this progress came to an end when the financial and organisational problems of African states began to undermine their health care systems. As a result, medical facilities were either wound down or became unaffordable for much of the population following the introduction of mandatory user fees. This gave diseases the chance to spread once more.

Africa's health situation around 2000 was poor compared to that of other continents. Diseases that could in theory strike anywhere in the world, such as tuberculosis and malaria, became increasingly concentrated in Africa. Approximately 0.9 million of the 1.1 million people who died of malaria each year were African. River blindness (onchocerciasis) and sleeping sickness (trypanosomiasis) occurred almost nowhere else. Infectious diseases and malnutrition took a particularly heavy toll among children. In Africa, a child died every three seconds.[222] Sierra Leone, where health care had completely collapsed as the country unravelled, had the highest infant mortality rate, followed by Angola and Niger.

Africa was also occasionally prone to attack from mysterious, previously unknown infectious diseases. In 1976, an illness broke out in a number of villages on the Ebola River in Congo (Brazzaville), then the People's Republic of Congo. The symptoms began with a headache which quickly gave way to a high fever and internal haemorrhaging, progressing very rapidly to bleeding from the ears, nose, anus and even the eyes. The skin became flaccid and slimy and the internal organs also began to dissolve. Within ten days, the virus that caused the illness had the body completely in its grip, by which time death was inevitable. There was no known cure and the condition was highly contagious. Even the bodies of its victims could contaminate bystanders, and burials were therefore conducted with a minimum of ceremony, often with the help of bulldozers. The Ebola virus was subsequently detected in the United States, the Philippines, and one or two other countries, but only in animals, which showed symptoms of the illness but did not die. Scientists concluded that the virus was not passed from animals to humans, except now and again in Africa, with fatal consequences.

According to one theory, certain animals in the African jungle were carriers of the virus but were not affected by it. Under exceptional circumstances, notably during a rainy season following a period of drought, an epidemic might break out among the many animals drawn by a sudden surplus of food in the jungle. These animals then spread the virus, which was subsequently passed on to humans. The theory maintained that each outbreak of the Ebola virus among the human population in Africa had followed a similar train of events. What is more, the far-reaching penetration of the jungle by humans, as a result of the population explosion, played a key role. In 1994 and 1995, there were several outbreaks of Ebola in Ivory Coast, Gabon and Congo (Kinshasa). The last of these outbreaks, near the town of Kikwit, claimed nearly three hundred lives. In the year 2000, there was an outbreak of the Ebola virus in Uganda which killed around thirty people. Presumably the virus had been carried back to Uganda by soldiers returning from Congo. In all, the Ebola virus claimed approximately a thousand lives.

An almost equally mysterious disease emanating from the African jungle had far greater repercussions than Ebola. In 1982, it was given the name of Acquired Immune Deficiency Syndrome, or AIDS. Once again, the cause was a virus (HIV) which had been passed from animals to humans, probably during the colonial era by people in West or Central Africa eating chimpanzees with AIDS. As a result of increasing mobility, the virus then spread from Africa across the globe, causing great distress and panic. In the developed countries, the epidemic was largely brought under control within a few years, but in many developing countries, particularly in Southeast Asia and the Caribbean, the spread of AIDS reached catastrophic proportions. However, Africa was the worst hit. There, AIDS spread so rapidly that by the turn of the century it had led to the total disruption of society in some countries.

In the early 1980s, AIDS was identified in the United States as an entirely new and unique illness whose main symptom was the failure of the immune system. It initially appeared to affect only homosexual men, but shortly afterwards it was also detected in heterosexual men and women, and in children. It was unclear for some time precisely how the disease was passed to humans; this caused considerable panic and, in retrospect, led to some unnecessarily stringent prevention measures. In response, Western governments began to launch extensive information campaigns. In 1987, for example, the British government sent every household a leaflet headed 'Don't die of ignorance'.

According to the World Health Organisation (WHO), by 1990 the official total of AIDS sufferers in the world had reached over three hundred thousand. The actual figure was probably closer to a million. The number of people who were HIV-positive was by then around ten million.[223] This included some three million women who had given birth to seven hundred thousand HIV-infected babies. The virus could be passed from mother to child during either pregnancy or labour. It could also be transferred via the mother's milk. It was not until the 1990s that drugs were developed which had some success in slowing the spread of the disease. However, a preventative treatment or cure was not found, and the number of AIDS victims continued to rise.

In 1996 the United Nations established UNAIDS, an agency that assumed special responsibility for the fight against AIDS. UNAIDS took over all the AIDS-related tasks from a variety of other organisations, such as WHO, UNICEF, UNFPA, UNDP, UNESCO and the World Bank, whose efforts to combat the disease had been fragmented and only marginally effective. WHO in particular had been heavily criticised for giving too little attention to primary care and treatment and focusing too much attention on medical issues and vaccinations, an approach that had yielded few results. After its first few years of operation, UNAIDS was able to report that despite the ongoing spread of the epidemic, there were now at least some countries where the number of new recorded infections had finally begun to decline as a result of extensive information campaigns advocating safe sex. For the first time, there was now slightly more optimism about the chances of controlling the spread of AIDS, either by changing people's behaviour or with the help of medicines. Even so, the scale of the problem had reached overwhelming proportions: around forty million people had been infected with HIV by the year 2000, with sixteen thousand new cases each day.

By the mid-1980s it had become clear that many Africans were suffering from AIDS, especially in Central Africa. In Uganda, a local ailment known as slim disease was found to be AIDS. Plasma research was used to identify the first person who could be diagnosed with some certainty as having had AIDS: an inhabitant of the Belgian Congo who had died in 1959. WHO came up with a more clinical definition of the disease to make it easier for the African countries to calculate and report on the number of AIDS sufferers; the original US method of diagnosing AIDS had been based on laboratory data that could not be obtained in most African countries. Some African countries asked WHO for help in combating the epidemic. In 1986, Zambia became the first African country to launch its own national AIDS awareness campaign, in which dance, drama and songs were used to teach schoolchildren about the disease. The speed with which Zambia responded to the crisis remained exceptional in Africa and was probably due in part to the personal commitment of the country's president, Dr Kenneth Kaunda, who in 1987 announced that his own son had died of AIDS.

In the 1980s, the HIV virus began to spread across the continent more quickly. At the start of the decade, no more than one per cent of the population had been infected in any African country (with the exception of Uganda, where two per cent of the population was HIV-positive), but by the end of the decade this percentage had risen to several per cent in a number of countries. Uganda headed this doleful list with an infection rate of possibly as much as ten per cent of the population. In the absence of effective countermeasures, the epidemic spread further in the 1990s. Uganda shared the dubious honour of an infection rate over ten per cent with a growing number of countries. Southern Africa was hit hardest. Zimbabwe was the unenviable record holder, with a quarter of the population infected, closely followed by Botswana and Namibia. In large parts of West Africa, especially in Senegal and the Sahel states, the epidemic remained largely under control with an average infection rate of around one per cent.[224] By the year 2000, AIDS had become the world's fourth main cause of death, but in Africa it was number one, followed by tuberculosis in second place and malaria in third. Twenty-nine of the thirty-four countries most severely affected by AIDS at the turn of the century were in Africa.[225]

By the start of the twenty-first century, more than twenty-three million Africans were HIV-positive; this was seventy per cent of the worldwide total (though Africa is home to only ten per cent of the global population). The percentage of HIV-positive children in Africa was higher still. As many as nine out of every ten HIV-infected babies born in 1999 (including those infected through breastfeeding in the same year) were African.[226] This came to a total of almost half a million newborns. Moreover, children of any age could be indirectly affected by the disease if their parents or guardians died of AIDS. In Africa, AIDS orphans became a large and distinct group. There were over a million in Uganda alone.[227] By the turn of the century, the total number of AIDS orphans in Africa had reached ten million. In some cities, fifteen per cent of children were AIDS orphans.[228]

Most of those who succumbed to the HIV virus were the most sexually active members of society, mainly young, working city-dwellers. Young girls were especially at risk. In some countries, these girls were more likely to die of AIDS than to complete secondary school. Not only did Africa have the highest infection rate in the world, it also had the lowest availability of treatment and care. The economic and social buffers on which families could fall back in times of crisis were already quite weak and were further compromised by the epidemic.

AIDS spread much faster in the global South than it did in the North. So severely was the African population affected that the AIDS epidemic was well on its way to claiming more victims worldwide than any other in history. By 2001, the disease had claimed a total of twenty-two million lives worldwide, fifteen million in Africa alone. The Spanish influenza epidemic of 1918 had killed some twenty million, while the Black Death of 1347-1353, which had affected great swathes of Europe, North Africa and the Middle East, had left between twenty and twenty-five million people dead.[229] However, the new Black Death, in Africa and around the world, had just begun. In terms of absolute numbers of victims, AIDS would go down as the deadliest epidemic of all time.

AIDS and Africa: the
progress of a virus

Why was AIDS so devastating in Africa? In many other parts of the world, it was largely brought under control, whereas in Africa (and in one or two other places) it spread like an oil slick. By the late 1990s, some 5,500 people were dying of AIDS each day in Africa, which was more than the total number (4,000) that had succumbed to AIDS in the Netherlands over more than twenty years. This is particularly remarkable given that the victories in the fight against AIDS during that time had little to do with the usual strengths of the developed world, such as capital, information and social organisation. After all, it did not take much money to combat AIDS effectively, the information required was widely available and the disease affected rich and poor alike. To understand why AIDS had such a devastating impact in Africa, we must turn to other, more specifically African factors. There are two likely reasons why Africa has failed to tackle the

AIDS epidemic adequately. The first is cultural and the second (once again) relates to state structures and the elites that run them.

The general characteristics of the AIDS epidemic in Africa reveal the influence of cultural factors. Clearly, the continent does not have a single homogeneous culture; the differences between regions and between countries are often substantial. Nevertheless, the following overall picture emerges. Unlike in other parts of the world, where AIDS affected mainly drug users and homosexual men, in Africa the epidemic was not concentrated within distinct groups but ravaged large parts of the population. The virus was generally transmitted through the most common form of sexual intercourse, namely that between men and women. This was only possible because a substantial proportion of sexually active individuals were having unprotected sex with at least two partners, one from whom the virus was contracted and another to whom it was passed on.

The reasons for this situation were complex. Promiscuity was just one of them and maybe not even the most important. Also of great significance were environments with extremely loose social structures which people could easily enter and leave. This encouraged shifting patterns of interaction. Such environments included migrant communities or conflict situations in areas where social rules had broken down in whole or part. In such situations, people rarely used condoms, even if they were available. AIDS was also widespread in regular armies. Wars – and peacekeeping operations – encouraged the spread of the epidemic. Naturally, women suffered most from men's recklessness; only in Africa were more women HIV-positive than men, a phenomenon that can only be explained by reference to the large power imbalance between the sexes.[230] Many men played the macho, dismissing sexual restraint and contraception. As a result, girls were forced to be sexually active at a very young age, sometimes as young as ten. The very large group of HIV-positive children consisted mainly of girls. Traditional customs could also encourage the spread of the virus. For example, the Masai in East Africa had a centuries-old practice in which the widow of a deceased man was expected to marry his brother. This was designed to give the woman and her children some degree of economic security. But since many of the husbands who had died had been AIDS victims, it encouraged the transmission of the virus.[231]

Whereas the developed world and one or two developing countries had managed to bring about a major change of sexual conduct, convincing people to practise safe sex, Africa failed to make a similar shift. This was primarily due to an inability or unwillingness to adapt to the new situation. Old habits simply proved impossible to break; deep-rooted cultural patterns could not be altered in just a few years. To make matters worse, the public was given conflicting advice. Scientists and, following their lead, representatives of NGOs and other organisations advocated the use of condoms. However, the churches preached celibacy, at least outside marriage. Traditional medicine men, who wielded considerable influence in large parts of Africa, hawked natural remedies, which were generally ineffective. So it was not immediately clear to the public how to avoid getting AIDS or how to treat it. This generally meant they did nothing at all, especially as it was difficult for them to form any clear idea of the disease. HIV/AIDS usually went undetected for years and was transmitted through one of the most basic forms of human contact. Many Africans had great difficulty understanding such a threat and adapting their behaviour accordingly.

African governments could reasonably have been expected to issue clear and comprehensive information about the disease to the public. In practice, however, they did next to nothing. Many remote districts and villages could simply not be reached due to poor physical infrastructure or the ineffectiveness of local authorities. Yet this was only a small part of the problem. For the most part, AIDS was not spreading in these distant regions, which were often too remote to be reached by the disease, but rather in the main population centres and along the country's busiest roads. African governments could therefore in principle have informed risk groups adequately, but they seldom did. When the epidemic first broke out in the 1980s, they first tended to deny the problem, then to lay the blame elsewhere. Rarely did they give the impression of understanding just what was happening, and even if they did, they presumably felt that such a message would be too unpopular to communicate bluntly. The indifference of the national elites to the welfare of ordinary men and women doubtless also played a role. Some leaders even took the cynical view that, while AIDS was a humanitarian tragedy, it nevertheless solved the problem of high unemployment. Yet while governments could ignore the suffering of ordinary people in villages and cities for quite a while, it could not do so indefinitely. AIDS eventually reached the centres of African power and wealth.

One of the few African governments to issue clear and uncompromising statements about AIDS was that of South Africa. However, the pronouncements made by the South African president, Thabo Mbeki, ideologue of the African renaissance (see chapter 4) and a politician who commanded a high level of respect in the West, were rather curious. Following the lead of one or two international AIDS 'dissidents', Mbeki called into question the cause and diagnosis of the disease. He suggested that AIDS was not caused by the HIV virus and that it would not spread as extensively through Africa as the 'experts' had wanted the world to believe. Of far greater concern, he argued, were diseases like tuberculosis and malaria. These illnesses had indeed made a comeback in the preceding years, though the mainstream scientific view was that this was the result of AIDS, which weakened the human immune system and made the body more susceptible to opportunistic infections, notably tuberculosis. Mbeki also claimed that AIDS was caused or encouraged chiefly by poor or unhygienic living conditions, in short, by poverty. Ongoing development and poverty alleviation, he said, would therefore automatically eradicate the disease; as developments in the prosperous North had shown, without poverty there would be no AIDS.

Mbeki's pronouncements were praised by African groups and commentators, who saw his unorthodox statements as a weapon against what they regarded as the Western 'AIDS mafia'. However, AIDS experts refused to let Mbeki's comments go unchallenged, and continually urged him to rethink his stance. After all, the fact that a statesman like Mbeki, who had inherited some of the stature of his predecessor Nelson Mandela, was making such statements about AIDS, was a severe blow to efforts to tackle the disease effectively in Africa. In South Africa, the epidemic had already reached catastrophic proportions, but the rest of Africa was also influenced by the South African president's views. Mbeki's stance was bound to result in further postponement of effective measures to deal with the disease, pushing up the death toll by several thousand and eventually, perhaps, even by several million.

The struggle between the opposing views reached a climax at the international AIDS conference in Durban in 2000, which was hosted by President Mbeki. It would then become clear whether the president was going to uphold his original standpoint and perhaps even win over some of his fellow African leaders, which would have been disastrous for the fight against AIDS in Africa, or whether he would return to the scientific mainstream, thereby paving the way for a discussion of how to curb the epidemic. Mbeki's spokesman, who had so fiercely and enthusiastically propounded the unorthodox theory, was replaced immediately prior to the conference. AIDS experts saw this as a sign that Mbeki might now have changed his stance. Soon after, however, it was revealed that the former spokesman had died suddenly, and it was not long before it transpired that he had succumbed to AIDS. 'Obviously died of poverty,' some international experts dryly observed.

After this, Mbeki cautiously returned to the generally accepted theories on AIDS. To save face, he continued to insist that scientists must remain open to alternative explanations, a position with which nobody could disagree. In the meantime, politicians could no longer evade their responsibilities. Mbeki duly urged young people to wait as long as possible before having sex, and, if they did have intercourse, to use condoms.

However, Mbeki still had a few tricks up his sleeve. Although he had finally been persuaded that AIDS was indeed caused by a virus, he now declared that drugs were the new remedy against the disease. He went on to argue that poor countries like South Africa would not be able to obtain them because international pharmaceutical companies were keeping their prices artificially high. According to Mbeki, South Africa therefore intended to turn its back on official patent regulations and buy cheaper medicines from India, Thailand and Brazil, whose governments were commissioning the production of generic anti-AIDS drugs. The pharmaceutical companies responded with formal charges against the South African government, but withdrew them later in the face of international pressure and even brought down the prices of their products.

This appeared to be a breakthrough, since it opened the way for South Africa to purchase cheap AIDS drugs or else manufacture them itself. In fact, the country's travails had just begun. According to Mbeki, on closer inspection the medicines had been found to be poisonous (by which he meant that they had side effects) and could not be used. Moreover, he claimed that South Africa could not, after all, afford even to buy the cheaper drugs.

These confusing sidesteps repeatedly delayed any real moves to tackle AIDS. And although anti-AIDS drugs had become more effective, experts insisted that they did not provide a solution to Africa's AIDS problem. Not only were they unable to cure or prevent the disease, but the high cost of the drugs, the difficulty of reaching patients in remote areas and failure to take the medicines according to the prescription also stood in the way of even a short-term reduction in the number of sufferers. Getting the African public to take anti-AIDS drugs correctly would be even more difficult than persuading them to use condoms.

Because the South African government failed to launch an effective AIDS awareness campaign, the life expectancy of South Africans fell from sixty-five in 1990 to fifty-five in 2000. One-tenth of the population was infected, with young girls particularly at risk. When the government failed to take adequate measures, local communities organised their own initiatives. In particular, mothers began to take steps to protect their daughters from the almost inevitable fate of HIV infection. An important part of these preventative measures was to spread the idea that sexual intercourse before adulthood had to stop. In the province of Kwazulu-Natal, this led to the reinstatement of traditions surrounding virginity. Dressed in traditional costume, girls below the age of eighteen were required to submit themselves to inspections to see if they were abiding by the rules of chastity. In fact, these rituals were less about upholding traditions than about mothers wanting to protect their children. It may have been a step backwards for women's liberation but mothers saw it as the only way of keeping their daughters alive.

Not all African governments failed to act, however; some managed to deliver a clear message about AIDS. These public awareness campaigns always focused on the need to practice safe sex. This was still the only effective way of curbing the epidemic, both in rich countries and in Africa. The government of Uganda, which was the worst affected country in Africa during the early years of the epidemic, launched a campaign under the presidency of Yoweri Museveni which was designed to reform the sexual conduct of Ugandan men. The campaign slogan, 'zero grazing', was the Ugandan version of 'no hanky-panky'. The authorities also distributed free condoms, a vital element in any effective AIDS policy. However, to ensure that the policy worked, considerable energy and care had to be spent on reaching the target group (much of the population) in a way that would lead to a genuine change of conduct. This was something that no government could accomplish alone. Civil society, religious organisations and, perhaps most important of all, peer groups, were essential forums for getting the message across.

Senegal was the leading African success story when it came to efforts to combat, or in fact prevent, AIDS. The Senegalese government began taking effective measures as early as 1985, when the epidemic was still in its infancy. Information about AIDS was distributed to all the country's schools. Social groupings and religious leaders were pivotal in convincing the population of the seriousness of the situation and explaining how to avoid infection. The government abolished import duties on condoms, which were soon widely and inexpensively available. As a result, their use rose sharply. Senegal thus became one of the few African countries to successfully check the spread of the disease and by the start of the twenty-first century, the level of HIV infection had been limited to approximately one per cent of the population. Problems did arise, however, following the return of Senegalese troops who had served with the peacekeeping force ECOMOG in other parts of West Africa, many of whom brought AIDS home with them.

The vast majority of African governments failed to keep or bring AIDS under control; some of them did not even make serious efforts to do so. The personal and social repercussions of this failure were enormous. The life expectancy of new born infants in Africa fell by seven years in the 1990s.[232] The death rate rose alarmingly, especially among those on whom the economy relied most: people aged between fifteen and forty-five. Not surprisingly, Africa's health care systems were unable to cope with the sheer number of patients. In many countries, AIDS patients occupied the majority of hospital beds. Moreover, other diseases re-emerged as AIDS weakened the immune system. Illness and death also thinned the ranks of medical personnel. The same applied to the education system; in some regions, AIDS killed an entire generation of teachers. Ill health or other AIDS-related problems forced students to abandon their studies, for example because they had to return home to help out following the deaths of their parents. Both supply and demand in the education sector therefore declined. Private enterprises saw growing numbers of their employees die or leave work due to AIDS. The disease eventually became a more common reason for leaving work than retirement. While it was often not too difficult to replace unskilled workers, the practical difficulties were much greater when AIDS struck down individuals who held a company's knowledge and expertise. In some countries, private enterprises therefore began to launch their own AIDS awareness campaigns.

The devastating impact of AIDS on African societies will continue to be felt until well into the twenty-first century. Yet at the same time, the effect of the disease on the continent's development should not be overestimated. There is a strong tendency to view AIDS chiefly as a 'development issue'. Certainly, the disease is making economic development extremely difficult in African countries, especially by wiping out so many of the most productive members of society. However, it is important to recall that Africa had strayed from the path of development well before the outbreak of AIDS, and for very different reasons (political, social, cultural and economic in nature). Even without the AIDS epidemic, little development would have taken place. The very fact that the disease could spread unchecked for so long was due to the same factors that had stood in the way of development. Once again, state weakness, and more specifically, a lack of commitment by governments and elites to the welfare of the general population, was a large part of the problem. In the case of AIDS, matters were made worse by the persistence of certain cultural patterns of behaviour.

To help prevent the further spread of the disease, it would be more straightforward and presumably also more effective to return to seeing AIDS simply as an illness, as a medical problem which can be brought under control by a change in sexual conduct.

Finally, let us return to the overall demographic picture of Africa. If we look to the long term, there are alarming signs that Africa is still trapped in the classic demographic pattern of a preindustrial society. This pattern is characterised by high birth and death rates, which keep the population more or less constant in the long run. In good years, the population increases due to a decline in the mortality rate, but this growth is cancelled out in bad years, when famines or epidemics cause the death rate to rise sharply. Growing industrialisation prompts a fundamental demographic shift. It begins with a decline in the death rate, leading to a sharp increase in the population. This is followed by a decline in the birth rate, after which the population stabilises once more at a higher level. Within this process, industrialisation is always combined with rapid population growth and urbanisation.[233]

We saw that in the twentieth century Africa experienced both rapid population growth and urbanisation, but also that the industrialisation process stalled following a hesitant start in the 1950s and 1960s. By the end of the century, a process of deindustrialisation was under way in some African countries, resulting in the loss of what little industry had developed. And although the birth rate did fall towards the end of the century, this decline does not appear to have been big enough to reflect the necessary 'demographic transition'.[234] It is in any case unlikely that a transition to a fundamentally different demographic pattern could be accomplished without the industrialisation of society. Without industrialisation, why should we expect a lasting decline in the birth and death rates in Africa?

The AIDS epidemic lent these questions new urgency. It increased the death rate exponentially, causing Africa to revert to the classic preindustrial pattern of a high birth and death rate. Due to the lack of industrialisation, this pattern was also a better fit with the nature of African society. By the early twenty-first century, the key question was whether the AIDS epidemic would continue to spread so fast that it would largely cancel out the population explosion of the second half of the twentieth century. If even greater numbers of Africans died of AIDS, would that throw back the continent, albeit at a higher level, to a preindustrial demographic equilibrium?

9
Poverty and aid

Absolute and relative poverty

Those who have known only the prosperity of the West in the last few decades sometimes find it difficult to understand that, until quite recently, poverty was the natural state of most of the world's population. It can be hard to appreciate that the real question is not why so many people have remained poor, but why some have managed to escape poverty while others have not. Presumably something unusual happened in the West and, later on, in other areas to make this change possible. The poverty of the vast majority of Africans, which began with the first humans hundreds of thousands of years ago and has lasted into the twenty-first century, has been too consistent and unchanging to justify searching for a historical cause.[235]

Nor can we point to static social structures as a possible cause of Africa's poverty, since this ignores the internal dynamism that in fact characterises African society. What is more, the world altered dramatically in the latter half of the twentieth century, and Africa with it. Yet while much changed, none of these changes led to a substantial reduction in the extensive poverty that besets the continent. There is no simple explanation as to why this is so. This book therefore examines in greater depth why, despite the rising prosperity elsewhere in the world and the widespread changes that took place on the continent itself, Africa failed to break free of poverty after gaining independence.

Our study of poverty in Africa will be most meaningful if we compare it with parts of the world where poverty was eradicated or substantially reduced in the second half of the twentieth century. This happened in large parts of Asia and Latin America, as well as in the West.[236] Interestingly, both of these continents, together with Africa, were until recently seen as 'Third World' countries ('Third' after the 'First' and 'Second' Worlds, the West and the former Eastern Bloc respectively). The term 'Third World' has since fallen into disuse, not just because the 'Second World' disappeared after the fall of the Iron Curtain and the break-up of the Soviet Union, but above all because the gulf between Africa, Asia and Latin America in the crucial area of development had widened so much since the 1980s that it became unreasonable to group these three continents. So by analogy with the question of why some countries have managed to escape poverty while others have not, the key question about the differences between 'Third World' continents is: why did parts of Asia and Latin America become less poor and in some cases even fairly prosperous, while a similar rise in prosperity did not take place in black Africa? Why did Africa fail to attain prosperity despite the efforts of so many people, Africans and others?

Around the millennium, it was Asia, not Africa, that had the largest poor population. This was simply because Africa's total population was so much smaller than Asia's. India alone had a billion inhabitants by the year 2000, roughly four hundred million of whom were living below the poverty line. In the same year, sub-Saharan Africa had a population of six hundred and fifty million, three hundred million of whom were living in poverty. In many ways, Africa rather than Asia was the most poverty-stricken continent. Much of the Asian continent managed to struggle free of poverty in the late twentieth century and many millions of Asians succeeded in materially improving their lives. By the year 2000, the number of people enjoying at least a modicum of prosperity in Asia was many times greater than in Africa. Asia had a variety of social classes, whereas Africa was homogenous with practically universal poverty outside the capital cities. This may always have been the case, but with the advent of globalisation and vastly improved intercontinental communications, poverty started to become increasingly unacceptable to Africans. New emphasis was placed on relative poverty; Africa was becoming ever poorer around the end of the twentieth century, simply because the other continents were growing ever richer.

More than any other continent, Africa became associated with poverty, prompting some to draw attention to the remarkable contrast between the living conditions of its people and its natural bounty; above all, its natural resources. What are we to make of Africa's profusion of oil, gold and diamonds? There is no question that some parts of the continent contain immense riches waiting to be mined. Yet some qualification is required when considering the continent as a whole. After all, it is only logical that so large a continent should have considerable stocks of fossil fuels, minerals, metals and precious stones. The same is true of other continents. Moreover, when it comes to other crucial factors such as soil fertility, Africa does not score very highly. Europe and North America, and even large tracts of Asia, are far better suited to agriculture than Africa. This fact was important on the road towards prosperity. The vast majority of Africans did not live in an environment that was well suited to sustainable development.[237]

The way raw materials are used is another factor. With the exception of South Africa, no African economies managed to convert natural resources into a form of wealth that benefited more than a small elite. Consequently, countries with large natural endowments, such as Nigeria and Zambia, were economically no better off than those without such resources. In fact, natural resources often fuelled domestic tensions, on balance worsening rather than alleviating poverty and misery in the countries where they were found (such as Liberia, Sierra Leone, Congo and Angola). The political and social structures of independent Africa were such that natural resources tended to perpetuate poverty rather than bring prosperity.

The link between poverty and armed conflict in Africa is unclear. Poverty alone cannot have led directly to the outbreak of such conflicts, because it had been part of everyday life in Africa since time immemorial, whereas violent conflicts had not. In addition, one of the characteristics of poverty is that it restricts the ability to act, including the capacity to engage in armed opposition. On the other hand, for those who wanted to fan a conflict, Africa's large reservoir of impoverished people provided a useful source of combatants; poverty lowers the threshold for participating in armed conflict, since the poor have less to lose than those with a degree of material prosperity. In particular, the many young men who were frustrated by their poor economic prospects were relatively easy to draw into civil wars. The social and economic effects of these struggles were always devastating. A handful of individuals (primarily the leaders) were able to derive real material benefit from the conflict, while a larger group of fighters at least drew more income from the plunder that accompanied the fighting than they could have obtained in peacetime. This economy of violence was another major factor for prolonging the conflict. However, for the majority of those caught up in the hostilities – mostly civilians in conflict areas – impoverishment was the result. In short, armed conflicts were a direct cause, though not a direct effect, of poverty.[238]

So what exactly is poverty, in objective terms? The simplest way of looking at it is from the financial perspective. The criterion of one dollar a day per person has been used as a standard definition of poverty for many years, mainly by economists. Anyone living below this threshold is defined as poor. Obviously, this income poverty is a very crude measure which becomes less useful when local circumstances are studied in more detail. For example, what an individual can buy with one dollar can vary quite widely within a country, or even within a small area. An income of one a dollar a day might make you much poorer or richer in one place than in another. Even so, this approach was often taken because of its simplicity; since it was a quick way of gaining an impression of the poverty situation. According to this criterion, there were, as mentioned, more than three hundred million people living in poverty in Africa at the beginning of the twenty-first century, out of a total population of six hundred and fifty million. Nearly half of all Africans were poor.

In addition to the simple dollar-a-day yardstick, there was another that tied in more closely with what poverty really meant in practice. There are, after all, many dimensions to poverty: economic, social, political and psychological. This second yardstick saw poverty not just as a low income, but also as inadequate control over productive facilities, lack of political influence and poor access to services such as health care (including contraception), education, water and sanitation. Other components frequently added were lack of information and insufficient awareness that public services were available. This was a form of social marginalisation or exclusion that was closely linked to poverty and that threatened people's self-reliance and independence. This human poverty approach was undoubtedly closer to reality than the criterion of one dollar a day, but it was too complicated to serve as the basis for a poverty line. It was not clear what percentage of the population was poor by these standards.

Another approach to the poverty phenomenon was put forward by the Indian Nobel laureate Amartya Sen, who was discussed in chapter 3 in connection with the importance of democracy. In his book *Development as Freedom* (published in 1999), Sen argued that poverty is effectively equivalent to a lack of freedom. People who are poor are not free. If development takes place, people become more prosperous and have more choices. They thus become more free. Poverty is a lack of opportunity, a lack of choice. This does not underplay the importance of a lack of income, since that is one of the main reasons that poor people cannot lead the sort of lives that they regard as better or more valuable. Obtaining income or education is, however, viewed as means rather than an end in itself. Sen's theory thus draws a connection between poverty and human rights issues (see pp. 278-281). This yardstick also very clearly defines Africa as a poor continent, although it is impossible to say just how poor.

What did Africa's poor feel was the worst thing about poverty? In the late 1990s, the World Bank sponsored a project entitled Voices of the Poor, in which sixty thousand poor people around the world were interviewed about their living conditions. The overall impression was that their lives had grown harder in recent years due to the erosion of their traditional social support systems. As a result, poor families often had only themselves to rely on, which made them more vulnerable. The survey found that poor people regarded the social and psychological aspects of poverty as the most important. Many interviewees said they wanted to belong to a group and did not like having to be wholly self-reliant. They felt cut off from society and totally excluded from facilities that were meant for the entire population. They also felt that they were treated badly (often 'like dogs') by service providers, retailers, tradesmen and government officials. Their relationship with state institutions was particularly bad. Almost all the respondents said that they had no confidence whatsoever in the government, that they were never given any help by the state and that officials were corrupt. Oddly enough, nongovernmental organisations (NGOs) emerged from the survey as only slightly better than the government itself. The poor expressed the most confidence in religious institutions and indigenous local organisations.[239]

Only rarely did respondents mention shortage of income as their main problem. A far greater concern was the difficulty of obtaining loans and getting by when times were especially hard; those with little income are less able to borrow. Over half the poor people in Africa were trying to make a living in the informal sector. Their biggest practical problem was food security; many spent their entire time simply trying to scrape together their next meal. Availability of food was far less of a problem for the poor on other continents. This showed not just how appalling the African food security situation had become, but also how severe poverty was in Africa; for over a hundred million Africans, life was little more than a basic struggle to survive the next twenty-four hours. The situation for most of the poor in Africa had not improved since 1990. While food security probably improved in rural areas, it worsened for many city-dwellers. Per capita income in Africa fell by approximately one per cent in the 1990s.[240]

The poor continent

A closer look at the extent of poverty in Africa in the 1990s reveals a wide disparity between percentages and absolute figures. In percentage terms, little changed, with a probable decline in the number of poor people from 48 per cent in 1990 to 46 per cent in 1998.[241] However, due to rapid population growth, these percentages applied to populations of very different sizes. Consequently, a relative decline in the percentage could still mean a sharp rise in the absolute number of poor people, from 240 million in 1990 to just under 300 million in 2000. This phenomenon of a relative improvement but a worsening in absolute terms was also seen in South Asia and Latin America in the same period. The numbers of poor people in Eastern Europe and Central Asia rose, in both absolute and relative terms. East and Southeast Asia, on the other hand, recorded the fastest progress in poverty reduction. Despite the growth in the population, the percentage of poor people there fell from just under 30 per cent in 1990 to around 15 per cent in 2000. Much of this drop was due to favourable developments in China.

If we look solely at the rise or fall in the number of poor people since the end of the Cold War, then East and Southeast Asia show the best results, with the number of poor people dropping by approximately 140 million. The number of poor people in the Middle East and North Africa remained largely constant, while in Europe and Latin America it rose slightly. The number of poor people in South Asia and in sub-Saharan Africa rose sharply. By the new millennium, global poverty was becoming increasingly concentrated in these two regions. There were now roughly fifty million more poor people in South Asia and an additional sixty million in sub-Saharan Africa. Considering Africa's small population, it is clear that after 1990, poverty in Africa affected a relatively large group.[242]

Some blamed Africa's relative decline on globalisation. As the world's poorest and most dependent continent, Africa was seen as particularly susceptible to the predatory forces of international capitalism. Yet there was little sign of a 'race to the bottom' between developing countries, with wages forced further and further down as a way of attracting international investment. Africa was insufficiently integrated into the global economy to be led by international market forces or the competitive drive. Wage levels in Africa were not low enough to attract potential investors; moreover, political instability, physical insecurity and lack of facilities did far more to keep investors away. On the global level, there was growing inequality between countries, with significant social repercussions. The share in global income of the poorest twenty per cent of the world's countries fell in the last decades of the twentieth century, but not to the benefit of the highest income group. Instead it has benefited the middle-income countries, mainly in Asia.[243]

Social inequalities in African countries remained as wide as ever. Around 2000, the gulf between rich and poor was probably wider in Africa than on any other continent, although some estimates suggest that it was wider in Latin American countries, with their feudal traditions.[244] The source of this yawning gap was, as always, the structure of society, particularly the legacy of colonialism and decolonisation. The African inheritors of the former colonial states had become a new ruling class. The typical social structure that emerged within a few years after independence had two distinct parts: a small group of haves and a very large group of have-nots. The smaller group – the national elite – held all the country's means of production, while the rest had nothing. A Marxist interpretation would have identified two distinct classes. The gulf between the two was widened by the fact that one – the elite – also held all the political and economic power.

Marxist commentators had always maintained that such a concentration of total power would also occur in the West at the height of liberal capitalism, but this proved not to be the case. In Africa, this concentration of power was much more clearly present. Setting aside influences from abroad, some of which were quite considerable, practically all the power in the country was held by a small elite. This group had a monopoly on contacts with the West, for example in connection with economic globalisation and international development cooperation. The masses formed an almost destitute underclass that could survive only through clientelist ties with the elite and through charity. Confusingly, during the Cold War, many wealthy African rulers called themselves Marxists and used Marxist rhetoric to conceal the true situation in their countries.

The national elites had accumulated so much wealth, especially in countries with vast natural resources, that they could have brought about greater stability by redistributing it more effectively. Why did this almost never happen in Africa? There were several reasons. The main factor was the role of the military. In most states the civilian authorities either had to share power with the army and its commanders or came to depend on them more and more. Alongside redistribution of wealth, the army provided other means of maintaining stability. Elites used military authority in many ways, including downright oppression, to keep people in line. This political role of the military allowed leaders to divert more money into their own pockets and keep a relatively firm grip on their own position. Of course, the military commanders who served them had to be rewarded, at the expense of patronage networks involving other social groups. This development was made possible by the lack of checks and balances in African societies, and it further damaged the few checks and balances that remained.

There were other reasons that redistribution rarely became a force for stability. Long-serving presidents – who were common in Africa – gradually lost interest in wide-reaching patronage networks and instead tended to focus on their own personal projects. Félix Houphouët-Boigny used part of the fortune he amassed in his forty years as president of Ivory Coast to build a huge cathedral in his hometown, Yamoussoukro. He may have felt that this grandiose gesture would be so awe-inspiring that it would win him more support than ordinary redistribution of wealth. Another factor may have been the fading of the national ideals which had been so strong at the time of independence. This tendency under-mined countries' sense of national solidarity. Finally, social developments such as individ-ualisation, urbanisation and globalisation also had a negative impact on redistribution.

However, there were exceptions to these general trends. South Africa, for example, had one of the widest social gulfs in the world, even though the elite was quite large. Following the abolition of apartheid, the white elite's share in the country's wealth shrunk, mainly because the black population grew much faster.[245] There were also countries with an entirely black population where the trend was favourable. For instance, overall income disparities in Uganda and Ghana narrowed in the 1990s following reforms.[246] Although there were areas and groups in both countries that became poorer, poverty was nevertheless reduced in relative and absolute terms. And there were other countries in Africa, such as Ethiopia and Mauritania, where reforms were likewise successful in reducing poverty after the Cold War.

In most countries, rapid population growth was a major obstacle to combating poverty. Even if a country was pursuing reasonable policies, and even if circumstances were fa-vourable, as in Mali in the 1990s, it remained extremely difficult to reduce poverty. Fol-lowing the introduction of democracy in 1991, Mali was able to invest more in education and health care, despite government cutbacks, but it was impossible to keep pace with the population explosion.

The small size of African economies also posed a fundamental problem. Most African governments set aside a percentage of their GNP for education and health care comparable to that in other countries, and sometimes even slightly higher.[247] This had been the case ever since independence. So in some cases, lack of progress was due less to an unwilling-ness on the part of African governments to set aside resources for these sectors than to the fact that little could be achieved with such percentages, for a relatively small population of just a few million spread over a large area, due to the low levels of GNP involved. The sum available for the education and health care of each citizen was minuscule. Moreover, due to mediocre policies and governance, funds were not used optimally, which made the situa-tion in these sectors even worse.

Whereas almost everywhere else in the world, rapid strides were being made in educa-tion, African countries continued to lag behind (see chapter 8, p. 255). In the 1980s, the aver-age percentage of children attending primary school began to decline from roughly eighty to seventy per cent. More children in the cities attended primary school than in rural areas, more boys attended than girls and only a tiny proportion of the poorest children went to school. Less than a quarter of all African children attended secondary school; those who did were almost all better-off city-dwellers. Less than three per cent of young people went on to attend an African university. Since, like primary and secondary schools, universities were often very poor, members of the elite who could afford to do so sent their children to universities in the West. Africa had almost no capacity to prepare its own people for senior jobs in government, industry or the social sector.

Another consequence of poverty was the decline in health care (see also chapter 8, p. 263 *et seq.*). Child mortality in Africa rose to a level that contrasted starkly with that in other parts of the world. One out of ten newborn infants died.[248] Illness and death also began to loom larger in the lives of most adult Africans. The healthy lifespan of the average African adult decreased. On average, Africans spent fewer years in good health than the people of any other continent. In 2000, the World Health Organisation (WHO) surveyed life expectancy and the severity and duration of illnesses in all the countries of the world. This enabled it to evaluate the impact of armed conflicts and AIDS on populations. The survey revealed how many years on average a country's people were likely to live in good health. The ten countries at the bottom of the list were all African. The people of Ethiopia, Mali, Zimbabwe, Rwanda and Zambia averaged approximately thirty years. Right at the bottom was Sierra Leone, with just twenty-five years of good health. The list was headed by the world's richest countries, whose people could expect an average of more than seventy years in good health.

The health of the African population was undermined by food shortages, which were especially hard on children. If they were underfed for even a brief period, their weight lagged behind their height. If this went on for longer still, then they remained short for their age. The incidence of these symptoms of malnourishment rose most sharply in the poorest African countries, although there were also areas where the situation improved, usually in the cities.[249] Children remained especially vulnerable. Millions of orphans were forced to eke out a living on the streets of large cities. There they were exposed to all sorts of dangers; for instance, they could be drawn into violent conflicts. Children living in war-torn regions were most at risk, particularly those in Angola, Sierra Leone and Liberia.

Strong yet vulnerable

women

The 'feminisation' of poverty – that was the jargon used by development workers involved with Africa to highlight the increasing tendency, starting in the 1990s, for poverty to affect women most. Although there are few if any reliable statistics on the subject, experts believe that the proportion of women among Africa's poor increased after the end of the Cold War. The figures available certainly show that women and girls are in the majority in poor groups. They are particularly vulnerable. Obviously not all African women are poor, yet there are factors in African culture, society, economy, social relations and politics that frequently put women at a disadvantage to men, so that the most vulnerable women easily fall into or remain mired in poverty.

During the 1990s, in most African countries, twenty to thirty per cent of families (sometimes more) had a single woman as their main breadwinner.[250] The typical scenario was that the male head of household abandoned his family, leaving his wife or female partner with children (often quite a few) for whom she was obliged to provide. This meant working hard. In all African countries, women put in a longer working day than men. The average working day for a woman in the 1990s might well have been half as long again as that of a man.[251] Women were responsible for fetching water and firewood, and many also tilled the land. Food production in Africa (with the exception of the Sahel) was regarded as women's work. Furthermore, women's generally low status had visible repercussions in the agriculture sector. Women had less access to artificial fertiliser, for example, and so in the Sahel, where men and women both worked the land, land cultivated by men yielded some twenty to forty per cent more than that cultivated by women. Due to a whole range of cultural factors and legal restrictions, women had less access to means of production, including land, and to credit. Only one per cent of agricultural credit went to women.

One crucial difference between men and women was their unequal access to education. On average, women received less, and the higher the level of education involved, the greater the disparity between the sexes. Nevertheless, there was substantial variation among African countries. Lesotho, where fewer boys went to school than girls, was an extreme example. This was because boys often had to tend livestock in the mountains and many parents felt that their sons would ultimately be better off with a job in the mines in South Africa, for which they did not require an education. But in all other African countries, girls were under-represented in schools. This naturally had an impact on literacy. Around the turn of the century, only thirty-six per cent of women and girls could read and write, compared with just under sixty per cent of men and boys. Incidentally, this low level of participation by girls in education was not due to lack of money; even among the wealthier population groups, fewer girls attended school than boys. Instead, the reasons were social and cultural. However, the percentage of girls receiving an education did rise faster among the wealthy than among the poor.[252]

The unequal status of women was deeply embedded in culture and society and occasionally sanctioned by law. It was a constant source of difficulty in women's everyday lives. The sexual role of women was a particularly sensitive and crucial issue. In many countries (not just those that were preponderantly Muslim), it began with the circumcision of young girls. Men controlled sexual relationships, and their will was law. Moderation was not valued. It is telling that President Mobutu of Zaire called himself 'the cock who leaves no hen untouched'. It was difficult, if not impossible, for a woman to refuse a man sexual favours, especially if he was older or exercised some form of religious authority. In 2001, a major sex scandal shook the Roman Catholic Church following the revelation of widespread sexual abuse of nuns, mainly in Africa. These women had become targets because they were regarded as unlikely to be infected with HIV. Some of those who had become pregnant had been forced to have abortions, while others had been forced to take birth control pills.

Many African women of all kinds were unable to avoid being forced to have sex and thereby being infected with HIV. Africa was the only continent where more women than men became HIV-positive. In Ethiopia, Malawi, Tanzania, Zambia and Zimbabwe, among fifteen to nineteen-year-olds, between five and six girls became infected for every boy.[253] HIV was especially common among pregnant women. Over twenty per cent of pregnant women throughout Southern Africa were HIV-positive. Across almost the whole of Africa, women were at risk of being infected because they did not have the power to decide where, when or how to have sex. Many could not even discuss sexual or reproductive health matters with their partners or children.

The rise of Islam, accompanied in some regions by the introduction of *sharia* law, further weakened the social and legal status of women. Yet at the same time, many African countries saw the growth of a movement to obtain a more equal status for women. By the turn of the century, for example, fifteen African countries had outlawed female circumcision. Some countries took measures against rape, forced marriages and dowry murders and adapted other laws.

The degree to which women were able to improve their social status, through legislative reform or by other means, essentially depended on how well they were represented in politics and government. It was there that decisions were taken affecting countless facets of women's lives. However, the low levels of literacy and education among women, which were on average below those of men, hampered their active participation in politics. Higher levels of education could have instilled a better understanding of development processes, economic trends and historical contexts. Insight into such processes would encourage women's liberation. In the often highly patriarchal societies in which they lived, women found it difficult to exercise their political rights as voters, candidates or elected officials.

In many African countries, participation in politics became one of the priorities of the national women's movement. This led to a broad range of initiatives: civics classes for women, partnerships between women's organisations and NGOs in support of elections, training for female political leaders, support for female candidates and campaigns for constitutional amendments. Thanks to such initiatives, African governments became more open to women's participation in politics and government. The constitutions of Uganda, Namibia and Tanzania set minimum numbers of women MPs, and SADC, the regional organisation for Southern Africa, determined that by 2005, at least thirty per cent of all political and administrative decision-makers had to be women. Even so, women were severely under-represented in the political institutions of almost all African countries. They accounted for just six per cent of the MPs in national parliaments and only two per cent of the members of government. The governments of half the African countries consisted exclusively of men.[254] And from independence onwards, only one African country had a female head of state: Liberia, where Ruth Perry was interim president from 1996-1997.

Yet no matter how low the status of women and girls was, the same social order and rules that sanctioned discrimination also protected them. An even greater threat to them was the erosion or collapse of social structures which took place in varying degrees in many countries. Regions in conflict were marked by lawlessness and impunity. The only law that prevailed there was the law of the gun. Young men, and sometimes even children, made daily use of intimidation and brute force, making life intolerable for many women and girls. Armed fighters who found themselves on the losing side in conflicts sometimes vented their frustration by raping and torturing women on their return home.

Aid to and through women became a priority, both in international humanitarian aid and in regular development cooperation. There was almost universal agreement that development funds would yield greater returns if they were given to women. Men often spent their money on radios, bicycles and watches, whereas women invested in their families' future, by saving and sending their children to school. Studies revealed that a variety of phenomena were correlated with discrimination against women: greater poverty, lower economic growth, poorer policy and governance, higher infant mortality and shorter life expectancy. The more involved women were in government and business, the lower the incidence of corruption.[255] Development progressed fastest if girls were sent to school. More educated girls tended to have children later in life, when they were better able to provide for them.

The human rights situation:
political poverty

According to Amartya Sen, poverty goes together with unfreedom, and greater freedom with greater development (see p. 271). There is a clear connection here with human rights, and not just with economic and social rights, which relate to minimum standards of material security, but also with classic civil and political rights, such as freedom of expression, freedom of assembly, religious freedom, freedom from torture and the right to elect representatives. To uphold these rights, governments generally do not have to do a thing; in fact, they have to refrain from certain actions. To protect freedom of expression, for example, governments must leave their critics alone rather than arrest them. In a sense, this makes these rights easy to uphold, even in poor countries.

Although independent African states generally showed little respect for the civil and political rights of their citizens, that does not imply that most Africans were not 'free'. Only at the height of the Cold War, around the time that a few countries were declaring themselves 'democratic people's republics', did governments try to control all aspects of their citizens' lives with no regard for their liberty. This ideology could have led to totalitarian systems in some African countries, as it had in other parts of the world. However, this did not happen due to the absence of a cultural basis. African cultures simply did not have the neurotic compulsiveness required for totalitarianism. In any case, African state structures were far too weak and ineffective to maintain a totalitarian system. Even if governments had wanted to exercise total control, they would have lacked the necessary organisation, resources and mentality to make such a system work.

So while most Africans lived in poverty, they did not lack liberty. Even in major cities, the government was often far too remote to make life even more difficult for its citizens by violating their civil or political rights. As state institutions broke down, governments gradually lost their hold on their populations. Yet this did not mean governments and states were weak in the sense that they handled their citizens with kid gloves. On the contrary, when states were capable of cracking down, they did so. Here and there, the decline of the state even exacerbated this tendency towards oppression. Human rights remained under threat.

An opinion poll conducted in six African countries around the turn of the century found that many Africans were confused about political freedoms. A large number regarded freedom as a birthright, as 'the right to everything' or as control over their own lives. When asked about more specific political freedoms, they generally cited freedom of expression, including the freedom to voice an opinion, freedom of the press and freedom of dress.[256]

The gradual advance of political liberalisation brought with it greater political freedom for the population. In many African countries, including some that had undergone democratisation, journalists who criticised the government were persecuted; even so, freedom of the press marginally improved across the continent. There was also growth in privately operated media. Government censorship and control of information decreased, though television and radio were subject to more legal restrictions than the print media. Freedom of the press was greatest in Mali, Benin, Botswana and South Africa and most restricted in Sudan, Equatorial Guinea and Congo (Kinshasa).[257]

Despite the spread of liberalisation, there were still arbitrary arrests throughout the continent and people were still sentenced without trial, or without a fair trial. Individuals who challenged the views of their governments ran a risk –even if those governments were democratic – of being detained without any formal charge being brought against them. What is more, African jails, some of which were little more than detention camps, were quite simply appalling. Detainees were forced to live in cramped and crowded conditions, and the level of hygiene was very low, encouraging the spread of disease. Prisoners were frequently mistreated or tortured.

The death penalty can be imposed in almost all African countries. Most Africans regarded capital punishment as a normal and necessary punishment for certain crimes, not just for atrocities such as the genocide in Rwanda, but also for less serious misdeeds. However, in response to strong international opposition, many African countries no longer carried out executions. In others, such as Kenya and Cameroon, death sentences continued to be both imposed and carried out. At the millennium, around a hundred people were awaiting execution in Kenya. Extrajudicial executions were also carried out in many African countries.

The previous section discussed the wide gulf between the political, economic and social status of men and women in many African countries. Another striking human rights issue was the level of discrimination based on sexual orientation. Some African politicians declared homosexuality inimical to African culture and African values. Some went further still; President Mugabe of Zimbabwe claimed that homosexuals were 'worse than pigs'. In some countries, homosexuality was banned by law but not actively prosecuted. In Namibia, where the constitution prohibited homosexuality, President Nujoma called on the police in 2001 to arrest all homosexual men and women, but nothing came of this in practice.

Africa has its own human rights charter and associated institutions and procedures, based on those of other continents.[258] The charter was drawn up around 1980 at the initiative of the Organisation of African Unity (OAU), which in 2002 was transformed into the African Union. By the beginning of the twenty-first century, all the member states of the African Union had become parties to the charter. The African Commission on Human and Peoples' Rights is responsible for monitoring compliance with it. Violations of the rights enshrined in the charter can be reported to the Commission by states, individuals or NGOs.

In the 1990s, many African countries also set up national commissions to scrutinise their own human rights records. The first was established in Togo in 1989. By the year 2000, more than half of all African countries either had set up or were in the process of setting up such commissions. However, only three of them earned a good reputation by actually bringing violations to light: those in South Africa, Ghana and Uganda. The rest had no real authority and were too unwilling to stick their necks out for victims of human rights abuses. They appeared to have been established mainly to ward off criticism from the international community. As a result, they did not make ordinary Africans feel any safer.[259]

One striking aspect of the OAU/African Union's approach to human rights was its recognition of collective rights. The official name of the African human rights charter was the African Charter on Human and Peoples' Rights. Collective rights were included partly because African cultures have traditionally been centred on the community and on the communal, defining the individual chiefly through his place in the social order or group. A second reason is the emphasis placed on economic, social and cultural rights in developing countries. Unlike classic civil and political rights, which apply to the individual, economic, social and cultural rights are more group-oriented. On the other hand, studies have shown that by the beginning of the twenty-first century, Africans were saying they considered individual rights to be more important than collective rights.[260] In this respect, they were no different from people on other continents.

In the area of collective rights, although the African Charter includes the established economic, social and cultural rights enshrined in the UN system, it particularly emphasises the need to eliminate colonialism, neocolonialism, apartheid, Zionism and 'aggressive foreign military bases'. So although there is a link with human rights in their more traditional form, the Charter primarily reflects the international political agendas of African governments at the time of the Cold War. They were not especially concerned with protecting and upholding the rights of their own people more effectively. Instead, the message they wanted to convey was that Africa's human rights problems were caused by hostile foreign powers. They simply ignored their own share of responsibility.

In fact, they tended to see themselves as victims, in the same category as the citizens whose rights they violated. Human rights became a weapon that they could use to their own benefit in international politics. The more guilt the African governments could make the rich countries feel, the bigger the financial rewards for the ruling elites. They used their gains both for self-enrichment and to buy internal stability through patronage. Laying the blame on foreign powers also forestalled domestic criticism of African rulers. If the outside world and Africa's history were to blame for its problems, why criticise African governments? This attitude, which influenced many decisions by those governments, persisted even after the end of the Cold War, and briefly but spectacularly resurfaced at the United Nations World Conference against Racism, held in Durban, South Africa, in 2001.

The African states, which like those of other continents took a joint position at the conference, had no real interest in combating racism in Africa. This was surprising given the extreme violence that had flared up across the continent, especially in the 1990s, in which race (or 'ethnicity') had played a significant role, such as the struggle between the Hutu and Tutsi in the Great Lakes region. Since African governments had tended to fan the flames rather than try to reconcile the warring factions, the conference should have called on them to resolve their conflicts and impose specific sanctions on those found to be guilty of inciting racial hatred. It could also have launched many other initiatives to defuse racial tensions among the population, for example through education.

In fact, it did none of these things. African governments simply did not want the world to scrutinise their own human rights performance. Instead, they preferred to focus entirely on the past, targeting the slave trade and colonialism, and demanding compensation for the victims of slavery. They called for the creation of an International Compensation Scheme and a Development Reparation Fund to be financed by Western governments and voluntary contributions from private individuals in sectors that had benefited directly or indirectly from intercontinental racist activities. It was unclear precisely who should be regarded as the victims, but the African governments were of course more than willing to act as their representatives.

The African Group in the UN represented the whole of continental Africa, including the Arab north. Oddly enough, it was an Arab member, Egypt, that was the driving force behind the African position. This was surprising, since the Arab world had historically played a very large role in the African slave trade. This involvement went on for much longer than that of the West, and in fact continues to this day in some parts of Africa (especially Sudan and other states on the edge of the Sahara). Moreover, Egypt's colonialist activities in Africa – which included slavery – began in ancient times and lasted until well into the nineteenth century, extending as far as the country's military power could reach. However, the North African countries did not feel any sense of culpability. In fact, together with the black Africans, they tended instead to see themselves as the victims of Western expansionism and its attendant evils.

The antiracism conference in Durban ended in failure. This was chiefly because it tried to equate Zionism with racism, but the issue of slavery was also divisive. Western nations, while willing to accept their share of the blame for slavery, were reluctant to pay compensation. In any case, the modern-day victims of racism who needed protection, in Africa and elsewhere, were people suffering at the hands of their own governments. Since these governments had managed to shrug off their responsibilities, ordinary Africans could expect few active steps to protect their rights. The situation remained bleak.

Mounting debts

Let us now return to the material side of poverty. Poverty can include debt. Individuals have personal debt and countries have national debts. While it is impossible to determine the total household debt burden of the African population, we can nevertheless reach some conclusions about national debt. In the 1990s, African countries owed two to three hundred billion dollars to foreign creditors. Given that the population expanded from five to six hundred million in the same decade, this represented a debt burden of approximately five hundred dollars per person, which was more than the average annual income in most parts of the continent. Yet while this shows the size of Africa's debt problem, it also suggests a debt burden for individuals that they did not actually experience. The vast majority of Africans never came into contact with either public loans or public debt, since their connections with their own governments, which negotiated the loans, were too weak. The money was seldom used to pay for activities that benefited the general populace, and much of the debt incurred was cancelled, or restructured and then not often repaid in full. For most Africans, the loans and debts of their governments thus existed only on paper.

Obviously, these debts were not evenly spread across the continent. Almost all of Africa's poorest countries, such as Burkina Faso, Burundi, Cameroon, the two Congos, Ethiopia, Ghana and Guinea, had large debt burdens. However, so did wealthy oil producers like Nigeria and Gabon. Only a handful of the poorest countries had more moderate debts; these included Benin, Chad, Gambia, Kenya, Senegal, Togo and Zimbabwe. Among the poorest countries, only Eritrea and Lesotho had practically no debts at all. The same applied to a few of the wealthier countries: South Africa, Botswana, Swaziland and Djibouti.[261] South Africa's debts were almost all internal.

Approximately three-quarters of Africa's foreign debt came from loans made by either foreign governments or international institutions.[262] These debts were often the legacies of concessional loans; that is, loans with favourable, non-commercial conditions. This usually meant a low annual rate of interest (one per cent or less) and a longer grace period and repayment term (often ten years for the grace period and twenty-five to forty years for the repayment term). In 1980, Africa's debt to multilateral organisations totalled ten billion dollars; it rose to twenty-three billion dollars by 1985, to forty-four billion by 1990 and to fifty-eight billion by 1994.[263] Forty billion was provided by the World Bank and the IMF, mostly as part of structural adjustment programmes. The rest was lent by the European Union (under the Lomé Conventions), the African Development Bank (which lent a surprisingly large amount to countries that were wholly uncreditworthy) and other multilateral banks and organisations.

In truth, almost all African countries were even more financially dependent on the World Bank and the IMF than these figures suggest. Throughout the 1990s, other multilateral organisations and bilateral donors began to adopt the criteria applied by these international financial institutions. As a result, it became increasingly difficult for African countries to play one donor off against another, for instance by turning to a second rich country if they were refused aid by the first. After the Cold War, this time-tested strategy became almost totally ineffective for developing countries. International lenders began presenting a unified front, coordinated by the World Bank and the IMF. In an effort to gain or to remain in favour with these two leading institutions, debtor states began to focus on paying off structural adjustment loans, almost to the exclusion of any other kind. The ability to keep to strict payment schedules was highly valued by the financial institutions, and it largely determined whether any new loans were issued. A staggering ninety per cent of multilateral loans were repaid on time.

However, this jeopardised the repayment of other, notably bilateral, loans, most of which were part of development aid from the industrialised nations. In the 1990s, a mere twenty per cent of these loans were repaid. Although bilateral loans were generally far smaller than multilateral loans, the share of bilateral loans in the debt burden grew much faster than the multilateral share.

Total foreign commercial debt (debt to foreign lenders in the private sector) probably remained largely unchanged at around sixty-seven billion dollars. In 1980, this form of debt made up approximately three-quarters of Africa's total debt, but by 1994 this share had fallen to just a third. If we exclude South Africa, which had a high level of commercial borrowing, then the share of commercial loans in Africa's total debt fell to less than a quarter by the mid-1990s.[264]

By that time, Africa's debt equalled around seventy per cent of its total annual output, with some fluctuation. This was substantially higher in other regions, where the debt burden rarely rose above forty per cent of GNP.[265] Given that public debt is generally repaid using export revenue, we can see how difficult the situation was for Africa, where the public debt burden was two to three times as great as revenue from the export of goods and services.[266]

The growth of debt in Africa was very much stimulated by the policies of the international financial institutions, especially the World Bank, which tried to promote economic growth on the continent by providing loans. In the mindset of officials at those institutions, the more loans they could convince African authorities to take out, the better they were doing. Even though most of the loans were concessional (i.e., their terms were favourable), they did have to be repaid, with interest. African countries were usually unable to do so, due to their premodern domestic environments, in which the main objective was not to invest the money in an economically sound way, but to use it for social and political purposes. Consumption took priority over production, and the money thus used could not be repaid. When new loans continued to be provided, the resulting situation most resembled a contemporary variation on debt bondage; countries were kept under pressure through debts they would never be able to repay.

These debts hung like millstones around the necks of the African economies, regardless of whether they were performing well or badly. As a result, there was increasing support for cancelling most of the continent's debt. A large-scale debt relief operation was proposed, raising the issue of whether to distinguish between governments whose economic policies met generally accepted standards and those that were guilty of economic mismanagement. In the latter case, wouldn't debt relief be seen as a reward for poor policy? And would it really have a positive economic impact?

The World Bank and the IMF, which prepared the debt relief programme in cooperation with leading donors in the mid-1990s, decided to proceed selectively. In 1996 they came up with a special debt initiative for poor countries with high debt burdens, known as the Heavily Indebted Poor Countries (HIPC) initiative. To qualify for debt relief, would-be beneficiaries had to have a sound economic track record going back several years. How well they had implemented their structural adjustment programmes was also crucial. Not only did the programme make debt relief a reward for good policy, it also made it more likely to have a positive effect on the economy. The aim was to reduce a country's debt burden enough to create a manageable financial situation.

Around the world, there were around forty highly indebted poor countries that could in principle benefit from the HIPC initiative. Once the World Bank and the IMF had approved the policies being pursued by their governments, the first African countries to have their debts reduced were Burkina Faso, Mali, Mozambique and Uganda. The debt relief package for the four countries totalled three billion dollars, or six billion dollars if we include accrued interest.[267] The World Bank and the IMF also considered requests for debt relief from many other African countries.

The costs of the HIPC initiative were shared by the multilateral and bilateral creditor groups in proportion to their outstanding claims. The bilateral creditors (the rich nations with outstanding loans to the HIPCs) decided how they would share these costs in the Paris Club, which sets bilateral debt repayment schedules. The World Bank and the IMF were able to bear the costs of cancelling their own HIPC debts, but other multilateral institutions had to ask their rich member states for extra financial support to help them meet the costs of their HIPC debt relief operations. Some countries had their official debt (that is, both bilateral and multilateral debt) cancelled by the Paris Club and their commercial debt cancelled by its counterpart, the London Club. The scope of the HIPC programme was constantly expanding, partly at the urging of Jubilee 2000, an ad hoc alliance of supporters of developing countries, who called on the rich nations to cancel the debts of the world's poor countries as a magnanimous gesture at the start of the new millennium.

The aims and approach of development cooperation

Even after African colonies gained their independence, some strands of their relationship with the former colonial powers continued in a new form; namely, humanitarian aid and measures to improve the lives of the general population. Although the (newly appointed) governments of the fledgling nations bore primary responsibility for their development, the former colonial powers and other rich countries remained closely involved, either out of a sense of enlightened self-interest (since rich business partners were always preferable to poor ones) or for humanitarian reasons. The 1960s saw the birth of an extensive international 'development industry' of industrialised nations and international organisations, whose budgets grew in absolute terms year after year until well into the 1990s. The nature of these development activities changed continually to reflect the latest theories and the *Zeitgeist*. By the turn of the century, the field was known as 'international cooperation' or 'development cooperation'.

The policy areas in which rich and poor countries worked together, and the approaches they took, were quite varied and changed constantly from the 1960s onward. It was not until the 1990s that the wealthy nations and international development organisations finally reached a broad consensus on what they wanted to achieve. Surprisingly, perhaps, this shared goal was not 'development', which was regarded as too complex and controversial in meaning to serve as a primary aim. On the other hand, it became easier over time to agree that poverty reduction should be the central focus of development cooperation. Almost everyone was willing to view poverty as the main problem of underdevelopment, and so poverty reduction became the key goal of international development efforts.

This consensus had become possible because, in the 1990s, a start had been made on integrating the economic and social approaches to development. Although the World Bank's World Development Report 1990 had brought poverty alleviation into the limelight, international institutions like the World Bank and the IMF had for many years tackled development issues largely from an economic point of view. They had approached development primarily, though perhaps not exclusively, in terms of economic growth, which they regarded as the engine and hence as the essence of development. Other international organisations (notably the UN agencies) and bilateral donors had viewed development far more from a social perspective. They emphasised the ways that people's living conditions needed to change before development could be said to have taken place.

In the 1990s, the advocates of both approaches began to find themselves on common ground. They decided that the two philosophies were in fact not opposed, but complementary. The international financial institutions accepted that, while economic growth was still necessary, this alone was not enough to bring about development. For their part, the donors came to recognise the importance of economic growth, yet continued to insist that it must be pro-poor; in other words, that growth must be used to benefit the poor and reduce poverty. This view was reflected in *Voices of the Poor*, a three-volume series commissioned by the World Bank and published around the turn of the century. The World Bank's

World Development Report 2000/2001, with the revealing title *Attacking Poverty*, was also wholly devoted to poverty reduction.

The World Bank also tried to make Poverty Reduction Strategy Papers (PRSPs) the basis for international development aid. These national poverty reduction strategies had to be drawn up by the governments of the developing countries themselves, in consultation with the broadest possible range of local organisations, to encourage strong grassroots support in the country concerned. The first African governments submitted their PRSPs around the turn of the century. Uganda's came to be regarded as a model.

This approach, based on national strategies, ascribed a key role to the individual developing countries. More generally, since the end of the Cold War, the international community had held a series of international conferences on key development cooperation issues, at the initiative of the United Nations. These conferences not only developed strategies but also set targets against which progress could be measured later. Topics included education (in Jomtien, Thailand in 1990), the rights of the child (in New York in 1990), environment and development (in Rio de Janeiro in 1992), food and nutrition (in Rome in 1992), human rights (in Vienna in 1993), population and development (in Cairo in 1994), social development (in Copenhagen in 1995), women and development (in Beijing in 1995), human settlements (in Istanbul in 1996) and food security (in Rome in 1996). The level of development aid from rich countries was discussed in Monterrey, Mexico in 2002. The participating countries used these conferences to work towards international consensus on specific development goals under the umbrella of poverty reduction.

The United Nations Millennium Declaration of 2000 set out eight goals or 'pledges' which the international community agreed to pursue. The leading donors, all of whom were members of the Development Assistance Committee of the Organisation for Economic Cooperation and Development (OECD/DAC), used these goals as a springboard for a public relations offensive aimed at raising awareness of the aims of international development aid. The eight pledges covered the whole developing world, not just Africa, and the eighth had to do with international aid for developing countries. The pledges took the situation in 1990 as their baseline, and their target date was 2015. The sole exception was the target for girls' participation in education, which declared that as early as 2005, as many girls should be receiving an education as boys.

Not surprisingly, at the top of the DAC list was poverty reduction, with the donors agreeing that between 1990 and 2015, they would try to halve the percentage of people living in extreme poverty (less than one dollar a day). The second goal was to make sure that by 2015, all children would be attending school (compared to eighty per cent in 1990). Third on the list was the girls' education target for 2005, mentioned above.

The fourth goal was to reduce infant mortality and deaths among children below the age of five by two-thirds between 1990 and 2015. The fifth was to reduce the number of women dying in childbirth by three-quarters in the same period. The sixth pledge concerned reproductive health care, that is, health care relating to sex and reproduction. The aim was to make this care available to all who wanted it by 2015. Further, donors pledged to protect and better manage the natural and physical environment, establishing a link between development and environmental concerns. The seventh goal stated that if development were to be sustainable, the environment must not be allowed to deteriorate any further. All countries were therefore called on to launch their own strategies for sustainable development by 2005, to ensure a reversal of the trend of degradation or loss of natural resources, both nationally and globally, by 2015.

The eighth pledge was different in character. It called for a world-wide partnership for development. Its main objectives included developing a fair, rule-based, predictable and non-discriminatory trading system, giving products from poor countries better access to rich-country markets, and increasing aid to poor countries that made progress with poverty reduction.

The fact that the donor community had agreed on a set of targets, and even given some indication of how these targets were to be met, generated great enthusiasm in the international development world. This enthusiasm perhaps owed more to the fact that all those involved in the development process had for the first time reached agreement about what they wanted to achieve (everyone was finally 'on the same page') rather than to the belief that this approach would be far more effective than previous methods. Now and again it was sardonically remarked that development cooperation was the only area in which people still appeared to believe that societies could be remade, or at least steered in the right direction.

Yet there was another factor at work. A new approach known as results-based management was making the governments of Western nations increasingly anxious to set targets and make detailed plans. The work of policymakers was no longer defined in terms of input – that is, in terms of the manpower and funds used to carry it out – but in terms of outcomes, or the results to be obtained. For example, in the fight against crime, the important thing was no longer how much money was being spent or how many policemen were on patrol (both of which were forms of input), but the results of these measures; in other words whether crime levels were actually declining (a form of outcome). It was hoped that this method would spur government agencies, which lacked the natural competition of the private sector, to greater effectiveness.

Admittedly, this approach had a certain logic. To begin with, it set clear targets, which could in theory increase motivation. However, there were practical difficulties. Responsibility for each goal was distributed among a large number of organisations and individuals, so while it could provide extra motivation, this method could also encourage participants to pass the buck. Obviously, whether or not a target was met also greatly depended on external factors, most of which could not be controlled. Initial experiences with results-based management were therefore not particularly encouraging. Yet was this really the first time such an approach had been tried? Hadn't the socialist planned economies functioned – or rather malfunctioned – along these lines? 'If targets work, then the Soviet Union would have worked,' was how the British economist John Kay dryly summed up the results-based approach.[268] However, such warnings went largely unheeded.

The new international consensus was not restricted to the eight goals, but gradually began to extend to the way development cooperation was put into practice. This trend was fuelled by dissatisfaction about the effectiveness of aid. The new approach gave a leading role to the recipient country. Experience had shown that development aid would have little impact if the state receiving it functioned badly, or not at all. Emphasising individual projects in areas such as education, health care, infrastructure or agriculture had been the staple approach to development cooperation. But projects could not achieve lasting results if the context was unfavourable; for example, if the authorities were not doing their jobs properly. The role of the state was therefore reassessed, with new emphasis on the quality of governance and policy. If the state fell short in those areas, there was no point in giving aid (see chapter 10, pp. 318-322).

These new insights, which were authoritatively expressed in the World Bank's report *Assessing Aid* (1998), gathered pace throughout the donor community and led some donors to shift their emphasis from project aid to programme aid. Programme aid can take many different forms. Essentially, it is financial support linked not to projects but to the overall development policy and programmes of a recipient country. It is therefore channelled through the national authorities of the recipient countries, creating a direct link to state structures. Donors' new insights also led them to give more support to state institutions. Capacity building and institutional development became key development cooperation activities. A large proportion of the international aid to Africa was no longer directed at the national or local level, but now consisted either of programmes targeting an intermediate level or a particular sector (the 'meso' level), or of a package of activities aimed at different levels.

A second important change was the new emphasis placed on the input of participants in the developing countries, whether they came from government or, for instance, from civil-society organisations. 'Ownership', as it was known in development jargon, had to be in the hands of the developing countries themselves. The word was not used purely in its literal sense, but instead suggested responsibility, participation or even motivation. It was felt that this largely psychological notion deserved a bigger role in development cooperation; people in poor countries who were directly involved in development needed to see both policies and specific activities as 'their own' (see pp. 297-304).

If governments of developing countries wanted international aid, they therefore had to show evidence of good policy and good governance, and to accept ownership and the responsibilities it brought. However, this is not to suggest that the new-style development relationship only imposed responsibilities on the developing countries. The donors also made specific commitments, particularly in the eighth pledge, and they promised to coordinate their activities better. The Special Programme for Africa (SPA) played an important role in these developments. The SPA, which was established in 1987, was an informal forum chaired by the World Bank in which donors could coordinate their efforts in support of economic reform in Africa. This generally involved coordinating funds and activities in order to boost the effectiveness of aid. But in the eyes of many, the most important promise they made was to give more financial aid.

Money and effectiveness

Money plays an important role in development cooperation, both practically and symbolically. Investments often cost money – sometimes a great deal. And while not all reforms increase costs (some in fact save money), aid is frequently used to oil the gears when trying to wring concessions from African governments. If Western states do not open up their wallets, then there is generally no place for them at the negotiating table. Rich countries themselves often point to the financial contributions they make as a measure of their solidarity with the world's poor. The usual yardstick is the percentage of GNP they set aside for development cooperation. In the 1970s, the rich countries agreed to gradually increase their aid to the Third World to 0.7 per cent of their GNP.

In reality, only one or two of the more prosperous countries reached this target. Scandinavian countries and the Netherlands made the biggest relative contributions, giving between 0.7 and 0.9 per cent of their GNP by the year 2000. The larger countries gave less. France came closest to the target, giving just under 0.5 per cent of its GNP. After 1990, most countries slightly reduced the percentage of GNP they allocated to aid, a trend that led to the term 'donor fatigue'. Germany and Britain froze their contributions at around 0.3 per cent, while the United States gave just 0.1 per cent. Surprisingly, perhaps, it was the only large non-Western donor, Japan, that gave the most in absolute terms for many years: almost ten billion dollars, more than 0.2 per cent of its substantial GNP.[269] In 2002, the United States moved to the top of the list.

The total amount that wealthy countries spent on development cooperation worldwide came to over fifty billion dollars a year. This was sizeable, especially in view of the limited opportunities to spend it effectively. Yet compared to some of the losses that poor countries suffer due to the policies of rich countries, fifty billion dollars is not all that much. If rich countries were to lift all their trade restrictions on imports from developing countries, developing countries could potentially generate several times that amount in additional revenue. Moreover, if rich countries were to stop subsidising some of their own products and dumping them in poor countries, the developing world could make tens of billions of dollars more.

The donor fatigue of the 1990s, coupled with growing competition for development aid by countries in Eastern Europe and Central Asia, gradually ate away at the funds that had been reserved for Africa since the end of the Cold War. This reversed the trend of previous decades. Prior to the 1990s, Africans had received more per capita aid each year, partly because right from the start of development cooperation in the 1960s the total amount increased annually. By 1970 aid to Africa had reached an annual amount of two US dollars per person. By 1980 it had gone up to twenty dollars and by 1990 it had reached thirty dollars. This was a huge increase, especially considering the explosive growth of the African population. In 1991, at thirty-two dollars per person, the absolute level of foreign aid peaked. Because the African population continued to expand rapidly, per capita aid began to fall sharply from that year onward, from thirty-two dollars in 1991 to just twenty dollars in 1998.[270] On average, foreign aid accounted for ten to twelve per cent of the GNP of African countries, although the exact percentage differed substantially from country to country.[271] Of course, foreign aid often made up a much higher percentage of the recipients' government budgets. For most African countries (thirty-five of them) development aid was the main form of external financing.[272]

However, it was not so much the amount of international development aid that mattered when it came to attaining development goals; far more important was how it was spent. There were some indications that too much aid could be 'addictive'. Studies suggested that aid was used less productively if it rose above a certain percentage of a country's GNP.[273] Since the 1960s, a total of developing countries worldwide had received approximately a trillion dollars in international aid, about half of which (more than 500 billion dollars) had gone to Africa.[274] The results had generally been unimpressive.

So did international aid make a demonstrable contribution to development or poverty reduction, or did it in fact make little difference? Might international aid even have slowed down or held back development? There are no clear answers to these questions. The saga of development in the former Third World is quite complex, and because almost all poor countries received aid, it is not easy to gauge precisely what its overall effect was. Some countries, for example, made progress while receiving aid. Others made progress without aid. Still others received aid but did not make any progress, and a fourth group neither made progress nor received aid.

However, not all of these scenarios were played out in Africa between the 1960s and 1990s. Few African countries made any progress at all in this period. Only Botswana took major strides. And although one or two other countries, such as Senegal and Ivory Coast, performed relatively well, all this meant was that they were stagnating rather than shrinking. They only stood out because practically every other African country was in decline.

Given that all the African countries were receiving foreign aid in one form or another – most of them in substantial amounts – it might seem logical to draw a negative link between aid and development. Yet this would also be too simplistic, since there need not be any causal relationship between the two. Moreover, even if there is such a connection, then it is not immediately obvious which is the cause and which is the effect. Africa's decline may explain why it attracted so much aid; in other words, perhaps it was its underdevelopment that led donors to give aid, rather than aid causing underdevelopment. It is, of course, also possible that, without aid, Africa's decline might have been more severe. A causal link cannot be established easily, and not at all unless other factors are taken into account.

It became even more difficult to identify a causal link between aid and development from the 1990s onward. Until then, aid had been used mainly to stimulate development by fuelling change. The basic idea was: aid first, development second. After 1990, however, this approach underwent a fundamental change. International development cooperation began to focus on countries with a record of sound policy and governance, where development was on the horizon or already under way. This was intended to foster to a close connection between development and aid, in which each would bring more of the other. In one or two African countries this approach worked, notably in Uganda and Ghana. In the 1990s, the percentage of Ugandans below the poverty line fell from fifty-six per cent in 1992-1993 to forty-four per cent in 1997-1998, and to thirty-five per cent in 1999-2000, despite the country's rapid population growth.[275] Ghana recorded a similar trend, and there were one or two other countries, such as Mali and Benin, where, with a little good will, we could also identify positive developments.

A World Bank study of ten African countries identified a link between progress and the structural adjustment programmes in the 1990s.[276] In countries where the structural reforms had been successful – again, primarily Uganda and Ghana – foreign aid had played a major, positive role. Conversely, substantial international aid to countries with poor policies had simply led to the entrenchment and continuation of those policies. Attaching conditions to aid had had no effect on poor performers. In general, aid had been largely ineffective as a means of steering developing countries in the right direction. In Africa, policies were influenced mainly by domestic political considerations.[277] These conclusions matched the predictions of the World Bank's development theory, which maintained that reasonable, or even 'good', policy and governance had to be in place before development aid could achieve results.

Even so, the study also concluded that, when actually deciding what countries should receive aid, donors made little distinction between those that had carried through successful reforms – and where there were consequently good conditions for development – and those that were lagging behind. There was a major drawback to focusing aid on successful reformers with good policy and governance: few countries in Africa actually met these criteria. So amidst mounting political and public pressure to give more aid to Africa, the opportunities to spend that aid in an effective way remained limited. Inevitably, this meant that aid was also given to countries with dubious track records on both governance and policy, and even to some that utterly failed to meet the criteria.

The resulting relationship between the quantity of aid and the worthiness of its recipients, especially in Africa, could almost be called perverse. This was partly due to the self-imposed requirement of some donors to spend a fixed amount each year on development cooperation, a requirement adhered to ever more stringently as Africa slipped further into decline. African rulers could always be certain that aid would come, if not from one donor, then from another. And if the donors failed to deliver at the start or even in the middle of the year, then they would be sure to come through in November or December, when they were forced to relax their criteria in order to use up their budgets in time. The aid budget for Africa was simply too large for the kind of systematic, selective policy that was needed to ensure effectiveness according to the new theory. The new consensus was that aid should no longer be given automatically; it now had to be earned. The expected results were development successes that would be emulated in neighbouring states, paving the way to prosperity across the continent. However, this approach was constantly being undermined, by both the sheer size of the aid budget for Africa and the need to spend it quickly.

The debt relief plan for Highly Indebted Poor Countries (HIPCs) (see p. 283) illustrates these difficulties. The original idea behind the initiative was that, before HIPCs could have their debts cancelled, they would have to prove that they had pursued sound policies for a number of years. At the core of this approach was a desire to influence national policies. Yet the original criteria were diluted by pressure from the international public and from donors eager to use up their budgets. The result was more and more spending on debt relief. Eventually, even countries with highly dubious records were able to obtain short-term relief. One of these was Cameroon, which in 2001 was granted debt relief under the HIPC programme despite being high on the list of the world's most corrupt countries and having an abysmal record on policy and governance. Such decisions undermined the positive effect that the HIPC initiative might have had on development. Policy successes were subverted rather than propagated, since even governments that had made no effort to improve their policies were rewarded with aid.

The 20/20 initiative encountered similar problems. In 1995, the World Summit for Social Development launched this initiative. Developing countries were to set aside twenty per cent of their budget for basic social services (such as basic education and primary health care) and donor countries would set aside twenty per cent of their aid budgets for the same purpose. In practice, however, this link (which was never formalised) was soon abandoned. This was because some donors were so concerned about meeting their twenty per cent spending commitment that they paid little attention to what the developing countries were doing.

They thereby risked achieving the exact opposite of what they had intended. Instead of encouraging developing countries to take responsibility for their own social programmes (by setting aside twenty per cent of their own public funding), the 20/20 initiative gives them the opportunity to have them subsidised by foreign donors. If this is allowed to continue, then it could result in the creation of a wide range of social services for which there is no local basis. And while that would be unlikely to greatly worry the local population, it would thrust Africa back into the nineteenth century, when amenities were provided by foreign missionaries. Although things have not yet reached this stage, African governments know perfectly well that when push comes to shove they can ignore the conditions imposed on them by foreign donors, whether for the HIPC programme or for the 20/20 initiative. The extra funding allocated to these initiatives may, therefore, even impede the long-term development of the recipient countries.

Was Africa any closer to the international donor community's eight development goals by the start of the new millennium? Six of the goals had set 2015 as their target date, so there was still a long way to go. Moreover, the donors had taken 1990 as their baseline; back then, the new approach of rewarding good governance and good policy had barely begun. It was too early to draw any firm conclusions, positive or negative, from the interim results.

By the turn of the century, the following progress had been made (not just in Africa, but globally).[278] The world was more or less on schedule for four of the eight goals: reducing poverty, raising the percentage of children attending school, improving the availability of reproductive health care and increasing the number of countries with national sustainable development strategies. Some progress had also been made in reducing mortality rates for newborn infants and children below the age of five. However, there had been no real reduction in maternal death rates. Nor had any appreciable progress been made in increasing the proportion of girls in education, which was particularly striking because 2005 was the target year for sending as many girls as boys to school. When it came to assessing Africa's progress, the only possible conclusion was that it was still no nearer to the most important development goals.[279]

A final issue relating to the effectiveness of development aid is its concentration on countries with no access to the capital market. Some developing countries, notably in Asia, had built up sufficient commercial creditworthiness to borrow money from private lenders. Donor countries decided to shift their focus accordingly, to countries that were not as far along the road of development. The only African country with genuine access to the capital market was South Africa, which for political reasons (to encourage a clean break with the apartheid system) was nevertheless receiving substantial amounts of international aid. The rest of Africa had little or no access to private capital. Why was this? Clearly, one reason why more private capital was not finding its way to the continent was the poor quality of governance and policy in so many African countries.

As a result, development aid was funnelled towards countries where the prevailing criteria suggested it could not be used effectively. For example, many African countries receiving foreign aid were high on Transparency International's corruption index. Due to inefficiency and corruption, each dollar spent on development cooperation generated less than a dollar's worth of results. Fortunately, this rule did not apply across the board. A few poor countries achieved reasonable standards of governance and policy; they included Ghana, Uganda, and, despite their war with one another, Ethiopia and Eritrea. These examples showed that better governance and, above all, better policy need not always be costly, and can even generate revenue. The shortage of private investment, even in these well-performing countries, was largely due to other factors, such as their negative image overseas. Foreign investors often steered clear of a country for the simple reason that it was located in Africa.

So what picture should African governments be painting of their domestic situations in order to obtain as much development aid as possible? Should it be one of misery and powerlessness (in accordance with the traditional theory of international development) or of an effective government that is beginning to take control of internal developments (in line with the theory that rose to prominence in the 1990s)? In practice, donors' decisions about which countries would receive aid had little to do with effective poverty reduction, but were based chiefly on other considerations. Donors like the United States, France and Japan were motivated mainly by geopolitical factors and the aim of supporting their own companies. For many other countries, humanitarian concerns took primacy, especially when it came to aid for Africa. For that reason, putting on the traditional guise of helplessness was usually the most effective way for African authorities to obtain aid.

To be sure, there were some genuine failed states, but many African governments put on an exaggerated show of incapacity, especially in the social and economic spheres. This sometimes raised suspicions that development was simply not at the top of their agenda. For example, during the war with Eritrea in 1998-2000, Ethiopia managed to supply the right kind of diesel for its tanks and food for its soldiers as soon as they were needed, in villages that had never seen a schoolbook or medicines for tuberculosis, supposedly because the authorities lacked the capacity to provide them.[280] This suggests that efforts to promote more effective development cooperation often floundered due to the priorities of African political systems and their leaders.

Aid and politics

We have seen that aid is not allocated solely on the basis of humanitarian or development considerations. Foreign policy is a major factor in donors' decisions. Choices about which countries to support are influenced by historical ties and geopolitical factors. The relationship between France and Francophone Africa is the best example. Yet even these links weakened during the 1990s, as the French government grew more critical of some of its former colonies and became more open to cooperation with non-Francophone African countries such as South Africa and Nigeria. However, France's rivalry with the United Kingdom and the United States, which it regarded as an Anglophone bloc, continued to shape its decisions, especially in the Great Lakes region.

Donors' economic motives could also influence their development policies. Some gave 'tied aid', which had to be spent in the donor country. For instance, an African country might be given funds to buy supplies or build roads, but the goods or services would have to be purchased from businesses in the donor country. This strengthened economic ties and allowed the private sector in the donor country to benefit from the development aid provided by its own government. Some donors barely distinguished between aid and export credits for domestic companies. Tied aid made development activities more expensive and less effective by obstructing market forces. Some countries thus held that all aid should be 'untied' and that the recipient countries should be allowed to decide how and where to spend it. The Netherlands and the Scandinavian countries were the leading advocates of untied aid, while France and Japan preferred to give large proportions of tied aid.

Yet the effectiveness of aid was not determined solely by the political motives of the giver; it was also heavily influenced by political dynamics within Africa. Almost all Western institutions and individuals with Africa's interest at heart have always assumed that the continent's development was also the main priority of African leaders. In donors' eyes, development was the only conceivable goal. This assumption was fuelled by the many declarations and statements to this effect that African authorities made to their Western associates. Obviously, there were some critical scholars, mostly Marxists and dependency theorists (see the introduction), who pointed out that African development policy was not getting anywhere, but their arguments were either ignored or countered with the claim that the obstacles to progress were personal or incidental in nature, not structural.

It was not until the 1990s that structural problems were widely recognised as undermining most development initiatives and efforts to reduce poverty in Africa. This conclusion was not fully accepted, however, until sharp critiques had come from unexpected quarters, such as the universally respected Nigerian historian Claude Ake. Ake caused shock waves by arguing that poverty reduction and internal development were by no means the main priorities of African governments. These goals, whose supreme importance seemed so obvious to the West, looked much less compelling to African elites. Given their fragile political and economic power bases, they had what they saw as higher priorities than development. It was not that Africa's leaders were against progress; most of them simply had more pressing concerns.

Development cooperation must therefore be seen in the context not just of external financing, but also of domestic politics. Accounting for ten to twenty per cent of the continent's GNP, and a much larger share of government budgets, international aid was not entirely indispensable,[281] but it was very important, in part because it shored up the political status quo and created internal stability. Both states and individual leaders benefited from aid in many ways. It was difficult to separate the two, largely because leaders often used the state for their own ends. Some of the aid was skimmed off, either for government purposes other than those originally intended or else simply for personal use. In the 1990s, growing scrutiny of the way funds were managed and accounted for made large-scale misappropriation increasingly difficult. Extreme forms of abuse, such as the Ethiopian government's decision in the 1980s to tax foreign emergency aid to its starving people, became increasingly rare.[282] On the other hand, the growing tendency to channel aid through the central state budget was a godsend for the ruling elites. Provided they showed evidence of good policy and good governance, African governments could obtain financing for their activities in some sectors. This assistance, which was almost always accompanied by institution-building, strengthened the rulers' ties to the supporters who ensured their survival. In this way, channelling aid through state budgets made it easier for African elites to maintain or even fortify their patronage networks.

Development cooperation also had secondary benefits for African leaders, mainly in the form of international contacts. Not only did foreign representatives come to Africa, but their African counterparts were also invited to attend meetings and conferences in donor countries. In addition to giving African delegates the opportunity to shop in London or Paris, these visits were a chance to acquire international experience and forge new contacts. This gave them major advantages over their rivals in the small African political arena. There were generally very few people in African countries with political, administrative or academic skills. In fact, there were too few educated people to create a flourishing civil society or academic world alongside the apparatus of government. It was therefore only logical for highly skilled individuals, whether they worked inside or outside government, to try to tap into foreign financing. They could then use the contacts they made to arrange for their children to study abroad, or even to leave Africa themselves if they had to, which they often did. Even if university graduates managed to find government jobs, their employment conditions and fringe benefits were often far worse than those on other continents. By the turn of the century, around a third of African university graduates (a very small group to begin with) were living and working outside Africa. Some Africans established exceptionally good relations with the representatives of donor countries, international organisations and research institutes, reaping countless invitations to seminars and conferences. This small group of Africans, who became fully-fledged participants in international dialogue, led extremely busy, globetrotting lives.

Because Western donors dealt largely with this small group, a situation similar to that in the colonial period began to emerge. Then, white colonialists had struck deals with the representatives of black elites, and both had inhabited a world far removed from the everyday lives of ordinary Africans. However, it should also be remembered that, in both colonial and post-colonial Africa, the elites also formed part of another, African, world. This double web, in which the elites served as a link between domestic African networks and international circles of donors, operated in many respects like the colonial system of indirect rule, in which black elites had formed a link between the foreign rulers and the African population.

The policy of channelling aid through the state provided these leaders with an ongoing incentive to think nationally rather than in terms of subnational ethnic groups. This tied in well with the historical background of African elites, who had inherited state structures – and little else – from the departing colonial authorities. The state was their only source of income, and only when it was no longer sufficient to meet their needs did they explore other options. These might include natural resources, such as diamonds, gold or oil, or the illegal drug trade. Leaders who had managed to find an alternative source of funds no longer felt the need to think in national terms.

Life was more difficult for those who were not (or were no longer) part of the established order, but aspired to become part of it. For decades, the only way to secure advancement was generally to join the ruling party, but sometimes this was not possible for ideological or personal reasons, such as a poor relationship with the current leader. However, the years after the Cold War, with their emphasis on democratisation, pluralism and civil society, provided an alternative. Many Western nongovernmental organisations distrusted African governments and preferred to keep their distance from them. Instead, they sought partnerships with African nongovernmental organisations like themselves. These partnerships always involved funding for the activities of the African NGOs. This attracted the interest of African activists and socially committed individuals, as well as would-be politicians.

African NGOs are often very different from their Western counterparts. The latter generally have a clearly defined social goal and substantial public support. As a result, they have independent sources of funding. This is rarely the case in Africa. With one or two exceptions, none of the African NGOs which popped up in thousands during the 1990s had a well-defined political or social goal. Their programmes were generally as unclear as those of the emerging African political parties. The one element binding an organisation was usually an individual who for personal reasons wanted to develop a stronger network of clients. If this individual pulled out, the NGO ceased to exist.

These NGOs seldom had any real foundation in society, let alone substantial funds of their own. Most were in fact established principally to tap foreign sources of revenue. They often did not decide what type of image or programme to present until meeting with Western organisations. Then they adapted to the wishes of their Western sponsors. The more funds they managed to raise, the larger their support base became and the more political power they accrued. And while even the most successful African NGOs could never genuinely compete with their governments, they could nevertheless chip away at government authority and erode the country's political stability. And that was doubtless precisely what some of their leaders intended to do. Many Western sponsors failed to uncover the hidden political and personal agendas of some of these African NGOs, and their idealism and naiveté made then easy prey.

African governments were also careful to take account of the sensitivities of Western donors when making policies on domestic NGOs. Sometimes they even used civil society to drum up international support. The government of Tanzania, for example, held extensive talks with Tanzanian NGOs while drafting the country's PRSP. This drew fulsome praise from the donor community, which was eager to see evidence of broad-based support for African governments' approaches to poverty reduction. However, the obvious question was why the government had chosen these particular NGOs to consult with and who exactly they represented. Many NGO representatives in fact turned out to be former public officials or others who had links with government. Interestingly, the country's parliament, which should have provided the real representatives of the people, was effectively left out of the consultations.

African governments were far less dependent on foreign benefactors for their survival than African NGOs. Unsurprisingly, however, they tried to get their hands on as much foreign financing as possible, for their country, for themselves and for their supporters. As a result, they became adept at tailoring their policies and rhetoric, at least on paper, to what was expected of them. This can be illustrated by an anecdote about talks on development cooperation in the early 1990s between the Netherlands and an African country that shall remain nameless. The African spokesman began by delivering a speech on his country's development policy that he had clearly written for a similar meeting the day before with the United States delegation (a fact that was visible to the head of the Dutch delegation, who was sitting close to him). In some places, the typewritten text had been adapted in pen for the Dutch delegation: the policy priority 'strengthening the private sector' (a favourite of the Americans) had been crossed out and replaced with 'rural development' and 'improving the position of women', which were two focal points of Dutch development policy.

Clearly, African governments were happy to tell donors whatever they wanted to hear. From their perspective, this behaviour was entirely rational. After all, what they most needed was money and other forms of support that would help to ensure their political survival. They simply adapted their stories (or their 'discourse', to use the postmodernist term) to the expectations of their audience.[283] Moreover, the picture they painted was more or less the same for every donor. It only changed significantly when the audience was a domestic one, since African rulers depended for their survival not only on foreign networks such as the 'international community' and their personal contacts, but also on domestic ones. Foreign observers were vaguely aware that when African leaders addressed their own supporters, they frequently discussed very different issues from those they emphasised around donors. Furthermore, what they said at home was often difficult to reconcile with the policies they described at international meetings. The easiest thing was to ignore such discrepancies whenever possible, taking the position that outsiders should not stick their noses into African political rhetoric intended for domestic audiences.

Although better coordination among international donors may have made it easier for African governments to satisfy all their Western sponsors, growing democratisation and openness at home made it more difficult for them to satisfy their own people and keep all their stories straight. The British historian Stephen Ellis has compared African rulers to jugglers who have to keep several balls in the air at once: in one hand, their various discourses for foreign donors and in the other, their stories for domestic audiences. African politicians had no choice but to keep all these balls aloft. Those who failed to do so could not expect to stay in office for long.

The dawn of the twenty-first century inspired African leaders to launch new plans for the development of their continent. South Africa put forward a Millennium Action Plan (MAP), the Economic Commission for Africa in Addis Ababa put forward a Compact for African Recovery, and Senegal presented the Omega plan. In these plans, African authorities accepted certain obligations and asked the international community to pitch in. During the Organisation of African Unity (OAU) summit in Lusaka in July 2001, at which it decided to rename itself the African Union, the heads of state acknowledged that it might be asking too much of donors to support all three plans. They therefore agreed to merge the proposals into a single New African Initiative (NAI).

This joint African initiative, which was soon christened the New Partnership for Africa's Development (NEPAD), covered a wide range of topics, from strengthening peace and security to promoting the private sector. It also proposed a reassessment of the cooperative ties between Africa and its partners in the North. It assumed an aid relationship based on reciprocal commitment; in other words, one in which both the African governments and the donors set down their obligations in contractual form. This was a wholly new approach to what was perhaps the thorniest problem affecting development cooperation, namely the unequal status of donors and recipient countries. It touches on both the politics and the psychology of the relationship between rich and poor.

The psychology of aid

The relationship between developing countries and international donors has always been characterised by fundamental inequality.[284] As the term 'development aid' suggests, the rich industrialised nations were almost unilaterally able to dictate the nature and form that the relationship should take. Rich countries' ideas about development have changed profoundly over recent decades and this has led to a recognition that development is a complex process influenced by many factors within the recipient countries, such as the political landscape, respect for human rights, economic and social policy, the environment and the status of women. Donors tried to make provisions for all these factors, and this generally resulted in a form of cooperation that was tied to certain conditions, a characteristic referred to as the conditionality of aid.

Although the individual conditions placed on cooperation were sound, the approach as a whole was rather unsuccessful. The World Bank was the first to admit this; its researchers attributed the systematic decline in its returns on investment in the late 1980s largely to an increase in conditionality.[285] In the 1990s, it became clear that aid could only be effective within a favourable policy environment, defined chiefly in macroeconomic terms, using the criteria of a balanced budget, low inflation, a realistic exchange rate and well-functioning markets.[286] Aid did not appear to encourage the creation of such a policy environment. For instance, a World Bank survey found that the policy environment in countries receiving less aid sometimes improved, whereas it often worsened in countries to which the flow of aid had increased.[287]

This is not just unfortunate; in view of the consequences for the people of the countries concerned, it is tragic. Yet it was not entirely unexpected. It is, after all, a well-known psychological phenomenon that people make more effort to achieve what really matters to them than to achieve what others think should matter to them. An analysis of the relationships between seven donors and seven African countries concluded that inadequate 'ownership' by African countries was the main reason for the ineffectiveness of aid (see also pp. 284-287).[288] These findings were confirmed by many other publications.[289] The problem of ownership was most acutely visible in development cooperation between the West and Africa. It was less of an issue in relations with Asia or Latin America, since economic development in these countries had often reached the stage where Western conditions were less readily accepted.[290] However, Africa's poor development record meant fewer opportunities for Africans themselves to exercise influence or make policy, not just because they lacked the power to do so but also because their countries' failure to develop had undermined their self-confidence.

Discussions on how to resolve this problem raised a fundamental question: to what extent was it possible for donors to hand over ownership to developing countries? Ownership was surely something individuals had or took, rather than something they were given. The term 'ownership' concealed a contradiction in terms. States which had the capacity to chart their own course were already exercising ownership without it ever being handed to them. Only states that were seen as incapable of finding their own path were given ownership, despite donors' suspicions that they did not have the capacity to exercise it. The term may have masked the fundamental imbalance of power but it did nothing to correct it. This problem was constantly hovering in the background whenever donors pursued a policy based on ownership. How could they give the concept any kind of substance?

The contradiction between conditionality and ownership was not new. The tensions to which this gave rise could be seen as simply the latest manifestation of an age-old clash between encroaching Western culture and the local cultures of Africa and other continents. During the colonial era, this confrontation between cultures had taken various forms, and it continued to adopt new guises in the postcolonial period. By the twentieth century, the relationship between Western and non-Western cultures was becoming increasingly centred on the concept of development. The West justifiably claimed to know a great deal about development (its power and wealth were, after all, founded on it) and it had a natural desire to attach this knowledge to the aid it granted. On the receiving end, many developing countries obviously welcomed development, yet were unwilling to embrace it at the cost of their own cultures and identities. They also had an understandable reluctance to accept all the rich countries' proposals wholesale. Instead, they wanted to retain some control over their own development. During the 1980s, this was the source of the tension between ownership and conditionality, all the more so because the progressive increase in 'macro aid' (funds channelled directly into the national treasury of poor countries) made donors feel more entitled to set conditions.

In the 1990s, after the World Bank concluded that the effectiveness of aid could be improved only by increasing ownership among the people directly involved in the recipient countries, this principle was soon embraced by practically the entire international donor community. The authorities in African countries immediately seized on this consensus to extricate themselves from some of the onerous conditions attached to aid. In all kinds of contexts, they tried to justify their choices to donors by asserting their right to ownership. This took place both at the highest levels of national policy, where governments tried to circumnavigate the IMF's conditions for financial aid,[291] and in individual projects, where a recipient government might use the principle of ownership to justify diverting supplies intended for the project for other ends, to the great irritation of donors.[292]

Economic adversity forced many African governments to seek financial support from abroad. However, this did not necessarily mean that they always complied faithfully with the conditions set by donors. Negotiations between African governments and international donors were highly ritualistic in nature. Governments promised to meet donors' requirements, yet everyone knew that 'unforeseen circumstances' would largely prevent this from actually happening. For their part, the donors would warn recipient governments that they would suspend aid if this or that condition were not met, but this, too, was generally known to be an empty threat, given that such a move was generally considered 'too extreme'. On paper, then, it was possible to come up with a compromise that, while accepted by both sides, was in practice carried out half-heartedly, or not at all.

This affected not just the economic sphere but also spilled over into the political arena, partly due to the wave of democratisation that followed the Cold War. As a result, Western countries tried to impose their own version of democracy on African countries. They believed that democracy could not work without political parties, a view that many Africans did not think was correct, at any rate not at that stage in Africa's development. Nor was it clear what might form the basis for African political parties. Most of the continent's elites were unwilling to see the rise of parties divided along ethnic or religious lines. One solution, at least for a while, might have been a system based on locally elected representatives. This would have tied in with traditional systems that were in place in certain regions. However, donors not only felt that such systems entailed major disadvantages, but even went so far as to obstruct their further development. They preferred simply to go on insisting that

African countries set up political parties. Tanzania, for example, eventually dutifully responded by establishing a multiparty system in which the parties were little more than empty shells created purely to satisfy the donors.[293] Uganda, whose political system was not based on parties, also caved in under donor pressure and promised to introduce a multiparty system in 2004.

At the other end of the spectrum were the African governments that insisted on going their own way. Though perhaps headed for better results, they created many problems for themselves when negotiating with donors. The best example was Eritrea. This former Ethiopian province had unilaterally broken away from Addis Ababa and now wanted to take its development into its own hands. Donors were welcome to provide assistance, but only on the Eritrean government's terms. Otherwise they were asked to stay away. This applied particularly to foreign NGOs. According to the country's president, these organisations represented an outmoded approach to development, since they had a low degree of transparency, extremely inflexible procedures and high costs. Furthermore, they did not fit into government policy. Eritrea was also reluctant to accept grants, taking the position that there were too many conditions attached to them. The Eritrean president claimed that these conditions reduced efficiency by thirty to forty per cent and that he therefore preferred loans.

Eritrea's stance presented a donor like the Netherlands with unusual problems. Proposed funding sometimes had to be withdrawn at the last moment at Eritrea's request, which complicated financial planning. Or a training institute might suddenly, inexplicably, have to be moved from the site originally chosen for it on wholly justifiable grounds by the Dutch architect. In another instance, a training institute designed by an Eritrean architect was hopelessly outdated by Dutch criteria. Should the Netherlands have simply paid up, even when projects failed to meet its standards? Or should 'he who pays the piper call the tune'? Should a donor pay for a plan that it believes is far from optimal? There were more questions than answers.

Let us now return to the origins of ownership. The international donor community believed that in order to boost the effectiveness of aid, recipient countries should have more ownership of development cooperation. But precisely whom in the recipient countries did they have in mind? Opinions differed, but donors tended to focus on two groups, the authorities and local beneficiaries. Was it then primarily the donors who defined the concept of ownership? Generally speaking, it was. This may seem contradictory, but it was just the way development cooperation worked. Even so, individuals in developing countries did become more deeply involved in discussions about ownership. In Africa, these were generally the more sophisticated individuals (in other words, the elites) in the capital cities, especially those involved in national government. These groups used the ownership debate to bring African wishes to the fore.

At first it seemed clear that countries had taken ownership of national policies; governments made their own choices and assumed responsibility for them, preferably with a popular mandate. Ownership was right where it was supposed to be, namely in the hands of political leaders. This situation was cheered by the DAC members in their report *Shaping the 21st Century* (1996). Yet at the same time, the freedom of African governments to steer their own course had been reduced in recent years by the forward march of economic globalisation. More and more, the world was becoming a marketplace and countries had to tailor their policies to this economic reality if they wanted to make real progress. This perhaps applied even more strongly to Africa than to any other continent. Africa was still barely integrated into the international economy, yet it relied heavily on that economy for its development. The need to achieve integration made adaptation all the more urgent. As a result, Africa's freedom of choice was limited, above all in the economic sphere, but also politically and in other areas (chapter 7 addresses the effects of globalisation on Africa).

It was unclear precisely what remained of African ownership under these circumstances. The World Bank maintained that even complex reform programmes, such as structural adjustment, had a more sustainable result when there was more ownership by stakeholders in the developing countries themselves.[294] However, this remark was clearly prompted less by enthusiasm for the freedom to set policy priorities than by the desire to persuade developing countries to accept externally prescribed policies as their own. The DAC report *Shaping the 21st Century* may have advocated far-reaching ownership for developing-country partners, but it nevertheless expected their governments to subscribe to an impressive list of objectives in all sorts of policy areas when drawing up their development strategies. At the top of the list was adherence to 'appropriate macroeconomic policies'.[295]

So for national authorities responsible for development strategies, ownership was something of a paradox. It seemed to work only if African countries fell into line with international requirements and carried through the reforms prescribed by donors. This created opportunities for economic growth, which could in turn fuel development in sectors like education or transport. This approach was taken by a new generation of African leaders, of whom Uganda's President Museveni is probably the best example. They remade themselves to meet the demands of the new international economy. Some countries even managed to internalise the externally imposed requirements almost completely. This was the case in Ethiopia and even more so in Eritrea, both of which carried out structural reforms with the primary aim of adapting their economies to the global market, without any major involvement by the international financial institutions. The governments of these countries insisted that the programmes they were implementing were their own, thereby establishing ownership in the form of structural adjustment without conditionality.[296]

The new self-awareness of these governments also left its mark on their societies. Their take-charge attitude often left NGOs with little breathing room, posing a threat to ownership below the national level. This created a development dilemma. The creation of effective state structures, including local institutions, was crucial for Africa's development.[297] And the economic recovery taking place in some countries opened the door to stronger states. Of course this did not necessarily have to make it more difficult for NGOs to play a role in development activities, since an expanding government might even encourage these groups to organise more effectively for the benefit of development projects, especially at local level. However, in many African countries, the expansion of government influence undermined the authority of civil society, above all in its dealings with governments but often with respect to donors as well. Obviously, this made it more difficult for these organisations to take ownership of anything.

This lent new urgency to the question of precisely who was expected to exercise ownership in Africa. Several times now we have discussed the predatory nature of the African state, whose leaders exploited state power to prey on much of the population. It was primarily up to Africans to correct this situation, with assistance from the international community. The purpose of international development cooperation was to help build African states that were capable of bringing about their own development. Nevertheless, in individual cases the interests of different groups of Africans could clash. In such situations, donors relied chiefly on their assessment of the legitimacy of the authorities involved. They looked not just at the formal legitimacy gained through a popular mandate, but also at whatever practical legitimacy the authorities had built up through their development activities. Donors had to decide what stance to adopt on a country-by-country and even a case-by-case basis. Consequently, they always had to consider the potential political and social impact of their cooperation activities, and how they might affect the balance of power in recipient countries.

Boosting African ownership – whether that of African governments or of the groups directly involved in cooperation – should not be seen as a new development goal in its own right, but as a practical strategy to enhance the effects of international cooperation with Africa. It was meant to benefit not only the recipients but also the donor countries, by making their tax revenue go further. Yet because promoting ownership could conflict with other key development aims, such as establishing a sound and stable policy environment or building an effective state, frequent tensions arose. As a result, ownership could not always be given top priority. More often, it was a matter of searching for compromise, of assessing the pros and cons and deciding how much weight to give ownership. This meant that all the parties involved in an activity had to identify opportunities for ownership and make the most of them.

For their part, donors had to change their policies and organisational structures. They had the capacity to take unilateral measures that would strengthen the commitment, involvement, responsibility and hopefully even the motivation of their partners in developing countries. What held them back were their own bloated, byzantine bureaucracies, which had been designed to keep a firm grip on ownership rather than relinquishing it. Some donors placed ownership in the larger context of development cooperation with Africa, notably by trying to address the tensions between ownership and conditionality. Other initiatives were specifically geared to boosting ownership by Africans.

One goal was to give aid with fewer strings attached. Donors took a first step towards this goal: better coordination, with each donor imposing the same conditions. A second goal was more effective dialogue between donors and developing countries. Donors needed to listen more carefully to Africa's representatives. They faced the considerable challenge of changing their own attitude, though organisational reforms could also help. For example, their dialogue with recipients could be given more of an ongoing character and more of it could take place in Africa. The many brief missions sent out from the capitals of donor countries had to be replaced with permanent local representatives wherever possible. The consultative groups, usually chaired by the World Bank, in which the donor community would meet the recipient government to discuss its policies and potential roles for donors, were no longer to convene in Western cities such as Paris or Washington, but in the recipient country. The role of chair had to be given to the recipient government, so that it could coordinate the donors itself. However, the dialogue was to continue to take the form of negotiations. Donors could not dictate terms to the recipient country, nor could they simply give the recipients whatever they wanted.

It was decided that cooperation between donors and African countries had to be based on national development strategies developed by the aid recipients. Yet in the 1990s, medium and long-term strategies were almost unheard-of. Around the turn of the century, PRSPs were introduced as a tool for development planning, emphasising the principle of ownership. PRSPs were to serve as the development plans of the national governments of developing countries and had to be drafted in close consultation with civil society and other local groups. In some countries, such as Uganda, this worked reasonably well from the outset, but in others, such as Senegal, development planning remained the preserve of the government, to the exclusion of civil society.

African governments could not afford policies that ignored the exigencies of structural macroeconomic stability and the global market. If in spite of this they insisted on pursuing an alternative strategy, then donors had no choice but to withhold aid, regardless of how much ownership that strategy enjoyed. Ownership may have been a necessary requirement for development, but it was by no means sufficient. Donors could not support poor policy decisions, no matter how firmly recipients stood behind them.

Many donors moved towards programme aid (general, non-project-based financial support) and away from project aid. Programme aid could take many forms. There were also hybrids of programme and project aid. Generally speaking, programme aid was more strongly geared to achieving a long-term impact than project aid, mainly because it was anchored in the development policies of the recipient countries. However, making it work was quite a challenge. In preparing programme aid, donors therefore had to spend a considerable time negotiating with national authorities in order to identify their priorities, discuss their policies in various sectors, put forward proposals for key areas of cooperation and so on. Once again it was crucial for conditionality to be applied mainly after the fact rather than in advance; aid could only be granted if a good policy environment was already in place. Good intentions were not enough. Only if the policy environment were deemed adequate would donors consider pooling their aid in a fund for a specific sector or policy goal, under the overall management of the recipient country itself. In addition to long-term effectiveness, programme aid had other advantages over project aid; it was easier to coordinate and because there was more input from local institutions, it sometimes gave a large boost to local institutional development.

Aid had to be flexible. That meant cutting down on conditions and procedures. The sheer number of donor countries, each of which had different rules and expectations, imposed a heavy burden on the Africans involved in international cooperation. It was not just psychologically debilitating; it also undermined practical efforts to generate more ownership among Africans. If the donors were genuinely to take a back seat, then besides simplifying their procedures for giving aid, they also had to work harder on coordination both with other donors and with recipients. The inadequacy of donor coordination was an old and thorny problem, but it had to be tackled if recipient countries were to exercise more ownership.

Donors had to show greater flexibility, but not at the expense of transparency. Donors and recipients had to conclude clear agreements governing all aspects of cooperation (though not necessarily right at the outset). Who would be responsible for what? The procedures governing cooperation, including the financial aspects, had to be unambiguous. On this particular point, donor governments could not afford to be flexible, since back in their own countries they were accountable for the way aid money was spent. Financial accountability on the part of the recipients was a crucial aspect of good governance, which in turn was a key factor in development. Obviously, poor oversight of authorities in many African countries posed a problem. Partly for this reason, capacity-building became a central element of policies to boost African ownership. As a result, more ownership in the long term sometimes required more donor intervention in the short term. This illustrated the fluid nature of ownership. Once the institutional structures of recipient countries became more reliable, donors could gradually transfer more responsibility to them. However, donors had to be careful not to send their own development workers to areas where qualified Africans were on hand to do the same jobs. African ownership benefited enormously in instances where Western development specialists abandoned this self-serving practice. Donors were expected to call in their own experts only if it had been firmly established that no local expertise was available.

At the beginning of the twenty-first century, the World Bank and even the IMF were singing the praises of ownership as a way of achieving better development results. More generally, they acknowledged that their own economic strategies had failed to attain the desired goal of economic progress. Yet these specifications had probably been not so much misguided as incomplete. After all, a new economic policy could achieve little without sufficient attention to political and cultural factors, such as the way institutions worked (or failed to work). Moreover, these political and cultural factors could not be influenced by the international financial institutions; money was of little relevance. The World Bank and the IMF could not override the internal workings of African society, despite all their knowledge of what constituted good policy.

The international financial institutions in any case had a poor image in Africa, which was not surprising given that they were so often the bearers of bad news. People in Africa's Francophone countries even referred to the World Bank (*Banque Mondiale*) as the Deadly Bank (*Banque Mortelle*) and to the IMF as the Intransigent Monetary Fund (*Front Monétaire Intransigeant*).[298] In an effort to improve their image, delegations from both institutions paid combined – and increasingly 'Africanised' – visits to African capitals. In 2001, World Bank president James Wolfensohn and IMF director Horst Köhler sat down with around twenty African heads of state during a tour of the continent. Their general message was that the international financial institutions would now be listening more closely to Africa's needs and concerns. The African leaders' job was to tell them how, and how quickly, they wanted to tackle the continent's problems, which could cover anything from the AIDS epidemic and armed conflict to corruption and economic malaise.

Critics dismissed this new approach as a publicity stunt. The World Bank and IMF stressed that it should not be seen as a sign of uncertainty but as the logical extension of encouraging African ownership. After all, development could only succeed if Africans themselves took the lead. However, this theoretical argument entirely failed to take account of the political conditions in African countries. The national elites, who were the main contacts for the international financial institutions, were not in a position to make development their priority. That would have required a fundamental shift in Africa's political culture (at the very least). While this was not entirely unthinkable, especially if there were inspiring success stories, past decades had shown just how firmly entrenched Africa's political culture was in African society. If the necessary reforms were to take place, they would doubtless fundamentally alter the relationship between the public and its leaders and therefore inevitably erode the power base of the ruling elites. This was one of the many fundamental dilemmas facing African states; if they wanted to make social and economic progress, they had to make decisions that would ultimately undermine the authority of the decision-makers. It is no wonder that African rulers preferred talk to action.

But even if African governments were to make the development of their countries a serious priority, a donor policy based on conscientiously applying the principle of owner-ship would inevitably give rise to new problems. After all, how were African rulers to decide which steps would lead to sustainable economic and social development? The donors all too readily assumed that the African elites knew how to solve the problems besetting their countries, but in many cases this was highly questionable. The elites lived at a considerable remove from the impoverished majority. Yet consulting the poor rather than the elites was no solution either. Poor people obviously had insight into their own difficulties and could doubtless suggest practical ways to deal with them, but they did not necessarily know what fundamental changes were called for. Outsiders were too quick to assume that poverty turned people into development experts. But how could the poor of Africa have gained an understanding of development mechanisms? They had never experienced any actual devel-opment, nor, in most cases, had they had any dealings with organisations or individuals from non-African countries who knew what development was like. Ownership exposed this problem but did nothing to solve it.

The Netherlands: a committed partner for Africa

Let us close this chapter by looking at relations with Africa from the perspective of one specific rich country, namely the Netherlands. Although the Netherlands is a medium-sized country, it has always been one of the world's biggest donors and felt a special bond with Africa. From the mid-1990s, the Netherlands aimed to spend half of its foreign aid on Africa; Africa came to occupy a far more important place in Dutch foreign policy, including development cooperation, than might be expected given the limited scope of Dutch interests on the continent. Commercial relations with Africa were extremely modest; during the 1990s they accounted for only one per cent of Dutch exports (mainly chemicals, capital goods and agricultural products). The volume of imports from Africa (mostly raw materials and mining products) was slightly larger, but still came to less than 1.5 per cent of total Dutch imports. Dutch companies have invested little in Africa, with the exception of South Africa and Nigeria.[299] The only significant historical, cultural and linguistic ties between the Netherlands and the continent were with South Africa; there were weaker links with Namibia, Zimbabwe and a few other countries. Ghana and Senegal boasted the remains of seventeenth and eighteenth-century Dutch forts, a legacy of the slave trade. Another point of contact between the Netherlands and Africa was the steadily expanding population of African immigrants in the Netherlands. During dis-cussions on national policy in The Hague, there were ever stronger demands to restrict the number of asylum-seekers and immigrants entering the country, from Africa and else-where.

There were two motives for the increasing emphasis on Africa. The first was the general belief that the Netherlands would gain more by a flourishing Africa than by an impoverished one. Yet while this argument was obviously valid, it could not really explain the extent of the Netherlands' interest. More important perhaps was the humanitarian concern felt for poor countries by many Dutch politicians and large sections of Dutch society. After the end of the Cold War, this concern increasingly focused on Africa – by far the world's most impoverished and needy continent. This sense of solidarity also ensured that the Netherlands' relations with Africa continued to centre on development cooperation. To this end, the country maintained a network of embassies in Africa that was far more extensive than those of many similar Western countries.[300]

From 1990 to 1998, Dutch policy on Africa was dominated by the Minister for Development Cooperation, Jan Pronk, during his two successive terms in office. Pronk brought to the post an intense personal commitment to the continent which earned him the nickname of Minister for Africa.[301] Under his enthusiastic administration, Dutch development cooperation expanded to cover almost every country in Africa and practically every imaginable issue. In the belief that development touches all aspects of a country (its politics, economy, security and so on), the Netherlands became involved in many different activities and took part in many consultative forums. Before long, it had devised large numbers of 'spearheads' and development activities. The impact of all these initiatives was largely seen as indirect; not only was the Netherlands doing something practical in the field, but by continuing to take part in discussions and negotiations, it could also influence the more general course of events in its partner countries. Dutch development aid was therefore used to buy a place, as it were, at every negotiating table.

One of Pronk's initiatives was to set up the Global Coalition for Africa (GCA) in conjunction with the World Bank and a group of prominent Africans. The GCA, which was established in 1990, was an informal gathering for discussion in which donors, African leaders (always including a fair number of presidents) and representatives of African and international organisations could exchange ideas on sensitive issues. Each meeting had a main topic, such as AIDS, democratisation, corruption, poor economic performance or international cooperation. The GCA was a unique forum where participants were free to voice their opinions without having to make formal decisions. Although development cooperation was the rationale for the meeting, participants could bring up any subject they chose.

However, now that the Netherlands was coming to see development cooperation as less of a stand-alone policy and as part of something bigger – a national 'Africa policy', perhaps – the question was what exactly it hoped to achieve through such a policy. This question was not seriously considered until the 1994-1998 government period, during a foreign policy review under the first coalition led by Wim Kok.[302] One of the aims of the review was to ensure that, in the interests of a more effective foreign policy, the Netherlands spoke with one voice. Over the years, the rapid profusion of international contacts had led almost all the Dutch ministries to start conducting their own separate foreign policies. These activities had to be centrally coordinated, a role that was logically assumed by the Minister of Foreign Affairs. His main partner for relations with Africa was the Minister for Development Cooperation. Both were based in the foreign ministry, and the same officials who served the foreign minister were also responsible for development activities (at least the bilateral ones). The first new statement of Africa policy following the review was *Africa South of the Sahara* (1998) which made sustainable development the prime objective.

The second Kok government (1998-2002) included new foreign and development ministers, each of whom brought their own personal emphasis to their portfolios. These new departures were described in the *Memorandum on Africa* (1999). The main goal of the government's Africa policy was fleshed out in two sections of this report: one reflecting the commitment of the new Minister for Development Cooperation, Eveline Herfkens, to promoting good policy and good governance, and the other setting out a clear role for the Minister of Foreign Affairs, Jozias van Aartsen, in fostering peace and stability on the continent.

Although the emphasis was still on development cooperation, Herfkens cut many of the ministry's numerous activities. She was influenced by the new approach at the World Bank, believing that aid would only be effective in a context of reasonably good governance and policy.[103] To be effective, development aid had to be administered selectively. The Netherlands therefore drastically reduced the number of countries with which it had a long-term bilateral relationship. The criteria for selection were the level of poverty and the quality of governance and policy. This change of tack was also reflected in a switch of emphasis from 'combating poverty' to 'poverty reduction' as the main objective of development cooperation. Combating poverty was a donor-led activity, driven by the emotional engagement of donors who were not necessarily so concerned about effectiveness. Poverty reduction, in contrast, reflected the new emphasis on the role of the recipient countries. It was now their job to get the most out of aid; the donors merely assisted. This approach was dispassionate and focused on getting results; specifically, reducing poverty.

The Netherlands continued to allocate large amounts of public funding to development cooperation. Only Norway and Denmark spent a higher percentage of their GNP. Around the turn of the century, the Netherlands was the sixth largest donor in absolute terms, roughly on par with the United Kingdom and giving twice as much as Canada or Sweden. The Netherlands was proud that at a time when most wealthy countries were cutting back on aid for developing countries, it was one of the few to maintain its development budget at 0.8 per cent of GNP. This meant a sharp increase in expenditure; due to the rapid growth of the Dutch economy in the 1990s, the annual amount set aside for international aid rose incrementally from five billion guilders (less than three billion US dollars) in 1990 to more than eight billion guilders (over 4.5 billion US dollars) in 2001. The Dutch development budget alone was more or less equivalent to the entire GNP of a typical African country like Uganda or Senegal, and about ten times that of a small country like Eritrea.

All this Dutch aid had to be spent wisely, which presented the ministers and their officials with a daunting challenge. The entire development budget had to be used up each year. It was no longer politically acceptable to allow funds to accumulate from year to year, as they had in the 1980s. The development cooperation budget was growing by some half a million US dollars a day. The need to find valid uses for all this money produced some unintended side effects. Because the government had decided not to hire any new officials, an unchanging number of people had to manage a growing volume of development funding. At the same time, accounting procedures and other administrative requirements were also demanding an increasing share of their attention. One way of spending development aid responsibly was by allocating a smaller portion of the budget to minor, relatively low-cost projects, since a project costing fifty thousand US dollars often generated the same volume of paperwork as one costing two million. In other words, the transition from project to programme aid was prompted not just by major policy considerations but also by a need to reduce the administrative burden on staff. It was not until after the year 2000 that the foreign ministry finally acknowledged it would need more staff in order to manage its aid money effectively.

In an effort to fully use up its development cooperation budget, the Dutch government set aside large amounts of money each year for macro aid and debt relief. The Netherlands was a key donor in both these areas. Even though it had long since ceased to issue any loans to developing countries, restricting itself to grants, it was still frequently involved in debt relief operations. This was because developing countries had debts to multilateral organisations (which were generally funded in part the Netherlands) and to private Dutch companies. Companies doing business in certain high-risk countries could reinsure their risks with the Dutch state. This programme was put to greatest use in Nigeria. By the beginning of the twenty-first century, the Nigerian government owed approximately two billion US dollars to Dutch companies, which transferred these debts to the Dutch state. If the Paris Club ever decided to collectively cancel these debts, the Netherlands would sustain quite a loss.

Due to its large aid budget, the Netherlands used to have more uncommitted funding than other donors, which could be freely spent in a wide range of sectors. Although by the turn of the century, Dutch aid was no longer dispersed among quite as many areas, the Netherlands was still active in promoting good governance and good policy, strengthening the position of women, building institutions, preventing conflict, fostering peace, combating the spread of small arms, fighting corruption, encouraging democratisation, promoting respect for human rights, supporting nature conservation and environmental protection, fostering a positive climate for the private sector, strengthening civil society, improving basic education, protecting vulnerable groups (such as refugees, children and the elderly), fighting AIDS, encouraging decentralisation, promoting corporate social responsibility and the list goes on.

The Netherlands did not feel that it should set the agenda for cooperation unilaterally. Instead, it shifted more and more responsibility to developing countries. Development had to be demand-driven, with more ownership by recipients. This policy was put into practice in the mid-1990s. The first step was to move development-related tasks and responsibilities from the ministry in The Hague to the Dutch embassies in the developing world. Dialogue with recipients could then be conducted far more easily and directly, and in greater detail. The Netherlands also simplified its procedures for development cooperation.

The keystone of the policy on ownership was the introduction of the sector-wide approach by Minister Herfkens. This became the centrepiece of bilateral development cooperation, and was implemented in a limited group of countries selected on the basis of poverty and the quality of their governance and policy. According to the new school of thought on development, if a country was poor enough, and if its record on governance and policy was acceptable, then a donor like the Netherlands could help to reduce poverty there effectively through direct financial support for local activities. The Netherlands accordingly shifted its support from stand-alone projects to sectors chosen in consultation with the recipient country (often health care, basic education or rural development), based on that country's plans.[304]

Around the turn of the century, the Netherlands established long-term aid relationships of this kind with around twenty developing countries. In order to include African countries on its list, the Dutch government had to slightly relax its criteria, since they did not score very well on either policy or governance compared with developing countries in Asia, Latin America and Southeastern Europe. However, the Dutch government did not want to draw up a list of partner countries on which African countries barely featured. After all, if development cooperation had a future, then surely it had to lie in Africa. Where could the value of development cooperation be demonstrated if not on the 'poor continent'? In the end, over half the countries on the list were African. This made it possible for the Netherlands to meet its self-imposed goal of spending half of its bilateral aid on Africa.

Since this sectoral aid almost always included funding for institutional development, Dutch development cooperation became more focused on supporting and consolidating African state structures. The Minister for Development Cooperation was well aware of the importance of effective state institutions for the development of Africa, so much so that her policy sometimes led to tensions with members of the Dutch parliament and nongovernmental development organisations, who criticised what they saw as her *étatisme* (overemphasis on the state). These organisations and MPs believed that where African state structures were functioning poorly, NGOs should serve as the leading channel for development funds. In fact, ten per cent of the development cooperation budget was set aside to be used quite freely by selected Dutch NGOs, even under Herfkens, allowing them to retain a key role in Dutch development efforts. This construct was unique to the Netherlands.

The Netherlands also provided aid to Africa and other parts of the world through multilateral channels in the form of contributions to international organisations. In view of the advantages of multilateral aid – automatic donor coordination, simpler dialogue procedures with the recipient countries and more in-house expertise – the Dutch government decided to channel more funding, up to approximately a third of its budget, through international organisations. These organisations were always carefully screened for effectiveness. The Netherlands was especially critical of the European Union's aid activities.

In addition to calling for better donor coordination, the Dutch government increasingly emphasised the need for coherence, meaning consistency in all aspects of its relationship with poor countries: not just development cooperation, but also trade, agriculture and other sectors that were crucial for development and poverty reduction. The Netherlands also sought to ensure that key EU policies were brought more into line with development goals. Special emphasis was placed on reviewing the Common Agricultural Policy, harmonising product standards, concluding fisheries accords with African countries and reforming trade policy. At the turn of the century, the Netherlands was instrumental in opening up the EU market for almost all products from the least developed countries.

Within the Foreign Ministry, the development minister worked closely with the foreign minister in many areas. Soon after taking office in 1998, Van Aartsen had made Africa a top priority. His own role in relations with the continent was mainly to promote security and stability. Between 1999 and 2000, the Netherlands had a seat on the United Nations Security Council, the most powerful international forum for issues of politics and security. The Dutch government saw an opportunity to launch a high-profile initiative that would help Van Aartsen to fulfil his mandate in Africa. Two major issues that the Netherlands brought to the attention of the Security Council were the spread of small arms and the dire general situation in Africa. The Netherlands also headed the 2000-2001 UNMEE peace-keeping operation, which monitored the ceasefire between Ethiopia and Eritrea. Finally, the Netherlands and its EU partners helped to strengthen Africa's regional capacity to prevent and manage conflict, and supported peace processes in a number of conflict situations.

In 2002, the Netherlands was rocked by political turbulence. After a dramatic election, the social democrats entered the opposition and a coalition of Christian democrats, libertarians and a small third party formed a new government. Both the foreign minister, Jaap de Hoop Scheffer, and the development minister, Agnes van Ardenne, were drawn from the Christian democratic party (De Hoop Scheffer soon moved on to become Secretary-General of NATO). From the start, they made Africa a top priority of their joint policies. However, the economic recession hitting the Netherlands had a more striking impact. The link between the country's GNP and its development aid budget led to financial trouble. In the preceding years, a better and better job had been done of using up this budget completely and on time, thanks to more careful planning. For the first time ever, it was necessary to make painful cuts in development spending, because new development initiatives continued to be taken while the funds available did not rise as expected.

These financial circumstances, along with the Netherlands' interest in making aid more effective, led to a reduction (once again) of the number of countries with which the country carried on an ongoing bilateral development relationship. Aid efforts also focused on specific areas: basic education (including adult education in basic skills such as reading and writing), the fight against AIDS, reproductive health care and the environment. New emphasis was placed on encouraging private enterprise in developing countries. Still, the basic theme remained the same; as far as possible, all activities were to promote the quality of governance and policies.

However, the Netherlands became less strict about the quality of governance when selecting partner countries, letting go of the theory that in a significant group of countries governance and policies were already good enough to make direct support an effective means of poverty reduction. In practice, this effect had not been observed. In only a few parts of Africa was poverty on the decline, and it was clear enough why; even in the Netherlands' official partner countries, governance and policies were not good enough to bring about development. The criteria for partnership were therefore revised. Rather than countries where good governance and policies were already present, the Netherlands started looking for countries where the conditions were in place to improve governance and policies through aid.

This subtle shift reflected a changing view of the situation in Africa. It was no longer credible that the continent was making real progress, that poverty was being forced into retreat in a process that could be promoted through traditional modes of development cooperation. Instead, there was a growing recognition that, in more and more cases, the basic conditions for development were no longer present; this was especially true of state stability. Instead of directly contributing to development, donors had to shift their emphasis to ensuring the presence of those basic conditions, in the hope that development might follow at a later stage. The instability of African states also led the Netherlands, and other European states, to think more carefully about their own interests, in connection with issues like migration and the threat of terrorism. The 2003 Dutch policy memorandum on Africa, entitled *Strong People, Weak States*, put top priority on promoting peace, security and stability.

The new emphasis had financial repercussions. Hardly any forms of military expenditure met the international criteria for official development assistance (ODA), and that posed a major problem for a country that prided itself on its high level of ODA spending. The guidelines on aid to Africa began to look outdated, not only to the Netherlands but to the donor community in general. Within the OECD, the international organisation for donor countries, a debate arose about whether it should be possible to finance peace missions and the like using ODA. The Netherlands set up a 'stability fund' for this purpose. Though its contribution was modest in scale, by taking part in peace missions the Netherlands remained engaged even with Africa's worst crises.

10
STABILITY

A patchwork of
weak states

As the new millennium approached, a new question arose: how stable was Africa, really? Somalia had ceased to exist some years earlier and other states appeared to be heading in the same direction, either because state structures were losing whatever significance they had once had or because violence was tearing them apart. After the Cold War the number of conflict situations had at first declined, but it shot up again from 1997 onwards.[305] As mentioned in chapters 5 and 6, a massive conflict involving numerous countries flared up in Central Africa, a war broke out in the Horn of Africa between Ethiopia and Eritrea, and various other conflagrations (in Liberia, Sierra Leone, Angola and Sudan) proved difficult or impossible to extinguish. A particularly ominous sign was the spread of violence not just within states but between them. Since independence, African states had usually coexisted peacefully, but that period seemed to have come to an end. The sense of solidarity among African leaders was wavering in the face of increasing assertiveness and even aggression.

Below the surface, too, African society was changing in almost every respect. The ties between leaders and their people became looser. Governments saw their authority weaken. Corruption was rife, and in extreme cases entire states turned into hotbeds of crime. Ethnicisation was widespread, and in one or two places the fabric of society totally disintegrated. Children were becoming the majority; by the year 2000, one in two Africans was under eighteen. Life expectancy, which had been rising for more than fifty years, levelled off and then began to fall. Africa was the only continent where this happened, mainly owing to the devastating impact of the AIDS epidemic. More and more Africans migrated from rural to urban areas and, if they could, went abroad, preferably leaving Africa. All these dramatic changes were evidence of a society in flux, not to say turmoil.

It is hardly surprising, then, that some observers felt the changes in Africa were drastic enough to threaten the stability of its state system. This was a fundamentally new development, for Africa had been remarkably stable for the past century. Although the continent had been colonised and then decolonised, the process had not led to major violent conflicts as it had in other parts of the world. Despite major violent conflicts in the Horn of Africa and in Southern Africa, this relative stability persisted throughout the Cold War. After that, however, Africa was largely left to fend for itself and within a few years the stability of its states was being called into question. Though it had previously occurred to almost no one, it now became clear that African states were inherently very weak and might actually be incapable of surviving without outside assistance. What implications would this have? Would the stability that the continent had known for a century end in a great 'African world war' at the beginning of the twenty-first century? Only a few years earlier such a thing would have been inconceivable. Robert Kaplan, a well-known commentator, predicted increasing chaos and misery.[306]

All this is sufficient reason to look more closely at the stability of the continent. African states are undeniably weak – but does this mean that Africa's entire system of states is just as weak, or even on the verge of collapse? Weak components do not form a powerful whole, so Africa's regional and continental organisations are, perforce, weak and do little to promote stability on their own. African countries are only marginally interdependent. It may therefore make more sense to talk of a patchwork of separate, weak states than of a system of African states. This patchwork will persist as long as its components – the states – continue to do so.

Around the turn of the millennium, African states nevertheless appeared surprisingly resilient. Even the violent conflicts in the second half of the 1990s did not generally lead to state failure. People began to feel that the worst-case scenario – the end of several states and possibly the collapse of the whole system into utter chaos – would probably not materialise. No other countries had gone the way of Somalia. Around 2000 the worst of the dust began to settle. Ethiopia and Eritrea ended their bloody struggle, there was a period of relative calm in Liberia and Sierra Leone, and negotiations got under way in the Great Lakes region.

It was the colonial borders, which were thought to be so weak, that preserved order in Africa after the Cold War ended. Although colonialism was partly responsible for the weakness of Africa's present-day state institutions, since it had introduced forms of organisation that were alien and artificial in the African setting, it had also given the continent solid organisational boundaries by absorbing it into the international system. These boundaries were backed up by the global political and economic order and determined the thrust of political and military activity in Africa after independence. This gave the patchwork a certain strength which ensured that the whole, in fact, was stronger than the sum of its parts.

The facts speak for themselves. The only state to actually disappear, Somalia, was not colonial in origin but was a product of the decolonisation process in 1960, when Italian and British Somaliland were merged to form a single country. Various other attempts at cooperation or mergers between states were either a failure (an example being Senegambia) or led to nagging problems, such as the Zanzibar question in Tanzania or the Anglo-French conflict in Cameroon. The only new states to survive were those with colonial origins, such as Eritrea and, apparently, Somaliland (the former British Somaliland). Their success contrasted with failed attempts to secede by areas that had never been separate colonies, such as Biafra in Nigeria, Katanga in Congo (Kinshasa), Casamance in Senegal and the Caprivi Strip in Namibia. In general, British and French colonies had become the strongest independent states.

There was thus no fundamental change in the state system, which continued to be made up of more or less the same countries. The international community began making more vigorous efforts to help restore order in African countries that were in conflict or to reconstruct them afterwards. Although many had been indifferent to the fate of Somalia, war-torn Sierra Leone and Liberia received full international attention some years later. Large-scale rescue operations were launched to help these countries back onto their feet. A major driving force behind this renewed commitment to Africa was the United Nations. The global organisation did all it could to keep Africa on the world political agenda. One publication after another appeared, special conferences were held and so forth. The message was always that the rest of the world must not ignore Africa's distress. Africa was part of the world community, which had a moral duty to give the suffering continent a helping hand.

Significantly, the leader of the international community during this period was an African – and not just any African. In a post many described as impossible, the unassuming Ghanaian diplomat Kofi Annan became one of the brightest stars in the international firmament. He was universally praised. There were those who called Annan the rock star of diplomacy. Many considered him the best Secretary-General the United Nations had ever had and he had no difficulty securing a second five-year term in 2002. His prestige was considerable. He succeeded in reforming the UN's sluggish bureaucracy and producing critical reports on UN failures (during the genocide in Rwanda, for instance), and he mediated in countless international crises. In 2001, together with the UN, he was awarded the Nobel Peace Prize. Annan was seen as completely honest, with powerful moral authority. He was a natural leader who never seemed overbearing. His main themes were poverty reduction, the fight against AIDS, democratisation, respect for human rights, conflict prevention, and of course keeping Africa high on the international agenda.

Keeping Africa in the spotlight was important because in many respects it had drifted to the margins of the international community. Its share in the world economy was shrinking steadily. Politically and strategically, Africa had become utterly insignificant. Yet this did not necessarily mean that ties between Africa and the rest of the world had grown much looser. Chapter 9 pointed out how important Africa is to international organisations and the 'development industry'. Its institutional and financial ties – including debts – were considerable. The continent was also tied into the international system through the activities of transnational companies and its growing role in the international underground economy, especially the drug trade. However, the main thing that kept Africa anchored to the outside world was the personal contacts of the national elites. The international networks in which they operated were a stabilising factor. The only reason that Africans could be part of these networks at all was that they represented African states. Had it not been for this special role, they would have had no international contacts and hence much less status. This could have had all kinds of serious implications for the individuals in question. Their international ties constantly forced them to think and act in national terms, and this enhanced domestic stability.

Yet African rulers' international ties did not determine how they behaved back in their own countries. Since independence, their domestic politics had developed in its own way, with considerable emphasis on patronage and oppression. At the same time, there were institutions whose outlook was entirely national – above all the armed forces, at least until they became ethnicised in many countries. The national language can also be seen as a unifying factor. Although usually European – French, English or Portuguese – it was still the only language that the leaders of a country's ethnic groups had in common. On the other hand, one can point to a number of factors that undermined national unity, such as the high degree of ethnic diversity, often accompanied by internal conflict which aggravated existing tensions. Their countries' failure to develop also made national identity less important to many Africans. This increased the incentive to try out alternative forms of organisation.

A crucial issue for state stability was whether most of the population identified with the country as a whole or with a subnational unit such as an ethnic group. Not only did ethnic loyalties and a sense of ethnic identity persist in Africa, they actually grew stronger in many places in the course of the 1990s. In a sense, states and ethnic groups were competing for the people's favours. This should not be seen as a struggle between natural ties to ethnic groups and artificial ties to the postcolonial states. What may at first appear to be natural ties nearly always turn out, on closer inspection, to have been artificially constructed by rulers earlier on. Whether these fabricated identities actually work mainly depends on the circumstances in which they are introduced. The question is whether potential supporters benefit from rallying behind the new leader, or whether other options are preferable. All states are born out of power politics and are in that sense artificial, whether in Europe, in Africa or anywhere else.[307] Peoples, as they develop, tend to adapt to states rather than the other way round.[308]

Changing circumstances also cause group identities to evolve over time. Like states, ethnic groups come and go. The formation of ethnic groups (or 'tribes') in colonial times was essentially the same process as the creation of a sense of national unity after independence.[309] Yet from the 1960s onwards, the newly emerging feelings of nationhood displayed a different character from shifting ethnic identities. Ethnic groupings, whether or not 'frozen' during the colonial period, were almost always based on internal African developments. To take one important example, although the Hutu and Tutsi identities were largely determined by the Belgian authorities in the first half of the twentieth century, the Belgians had simply embroidered on pre-existing local affiliations. The same was true in other parts of Africa. However, things were different when it came to forming modern states. This development had entirely European roots (as far as Africans were concerned it came out of the blue) and was totally at odds with local tradition. That does not necessarily tell us anything about its ultimate impact but in the competition with ethnic sentiments it was definitely a disadvantage. The struggle between the two types of identity – ethnic and national – was later influenced by such factors as democratisation (which sometimes encouraged ethnicisation) and changes in international aid flows, more and more of which were channelled through states.

Interaction between different African states was an increasingly important factor in the continent's stability. This was a new phenomenon which was made possible above all by the decline in international involvement in Africa and the changing nature of that involvement. Major international powers were making increasing use of African countries and regional organisations to promote stability in the region. It was South Africa and Nigeria, the largest military powers on the continent, that benefited most. The buildup of African peacekeeping capacity enhanced their regional and even continental status. These 'pillars of stability' will be discussed in more detail later in this chapter.

The stability of states is ultimately determined by domestic rather than international factors. The most important of these was the way in which the apparatus of the state functioned in Africa. Much has already been said about this in connection with state failure. However, there is another major reason the machinery of state often failed to function properly, namely corruption, which spread continuously in the 1990s and was a major source of social problems.

Rampant corruption and
increasing crime

After the Cold War, African states were increasingly hampered by rampant corruption. Every discussion of corruption in Africa begins with the statement that it is not a specifically African phenomenon. Corruption is universal, and may always have been with us. Africans do not carry some special gene that makes them more susceptible to corruption than anyone else. Having said this, there is still every reason to look more closely at the phenomenon of corruption in Africa, for there can be no doubt that it has spread rapidly there in recent decades.

Back in the 1980s corruption was already recognised as a problem that had to be tackled. In the 1990s there was hope that democratisation would do away with corruption, by bringing greater openness and more effective monitoring of government. However, this did not happen – quite the contrary, in fact. In the 1990s corruption continued to spread in almost every part of the continent. This was reflected in the corruption index that Transparency International began producing in 1993. Over the years, more and more African countries were included, and they almost always ended up low on the list, among the most corrupt. By the turn of the century they were starting to rival Asian countries. In 1999 Cameroon was branded the most corrupt country in the world, and in 2000 that dubious honour fell to Nigeria. In 2001, 2002 and 2003, Nigeria finished second after Bangladesh. These lists made it clear that corruption was prevalent, and not just in Cameroon and Nigeria, but as a far more widespread African phenomenon. What was the explanation?

'Opportunity makes the thief,' as the saying goes, and this undoubtedly applies to corruption. But what is it in general – leaving Africa aside for a moment – that provides opportunities for corruption? What circumstances are most conducive to it? These have been neatly summed up in the following formula: power plus freedom of action minus accountability.[310] Whenever people find themselves in circumstances in which they can act as they see fit, without being accountable to anything or anyone afterwards, there is every opportunity for corruption. Such circumstances probably exist on a small scale all over the world, and hence so does corruption. On a large scale, things are different. In most countries, individuals do not have the requisite authority or freedom of action, and even if they do they can be held accountable afterwards. Only authoritarian systems in which the executive completely dominates the legislature and the judiciary are a breeding ground for large-scale corruption. These circumstances were well-attested in many Asian countries and became increasingly prevalent in Africa. Power was gradually centralised and state officials were not accountable to anyone.

African states have other features that encourage corruption. These have to do with the prevailing notion of power. Power in postcolonial Africa is not prepared to accept restrictions, but attempts to be all-pervading. Even in African countries where separation of powers has been introduced, there is pressure to reverse it and concentrate everything in the hands of the executive. The economy, like the rest of society, is usually in thrall to the country's political leaders. No distinction is made between the public and private spheres. The personal nature of social ties in Africa is also a key factor. People with special relationships are expected to help each other even if this is inappropriate in Western terms. This reveals the cultural relativity of corruption; much of what is judged corrupt in Western countries is not seen by Africans as a crime or even a problem.

This should not be taken to mean that African cultures are inherently corrupt, even by Western standards. The cultural traits that encourage corruption are essentially a protective mechanism.[311] In societies that lack impersonal safeguards against unemployment, disease, violence or poverty, it is inevitable that people will ally themselves with powerful citizens in order to obtain help, in the form of money or other favours. However, all lasting ties are reciprocal – there must also be something in it for the benefactor. Apart from popularity and social status, this may be, for example, political support.

Corruption is a method of accumulating wealth, for rich and poor alike. In combination with patronage networks, it is also a means of redistributing both public and private resources. In some cases this was more or less deliberate government policy. The state helped redistribute resources by spending state funds on public and semipublic enterprises, which usually operated at a loss. Employees who ought to have been fired were not, and enterprises survived even though there was no longer any financial or economic basis for their existence. The government kept them going for political and social rather than economic reasons. In addition, there was voluntary redistribution by rich and powerful Africans to maintain the loyalty of their clientele. Public resources were used for this purpose wherever possible.

This redistribution mechanism came into action when people had power over others, for example because they held government posts which enabled them to extort money from those who needed services ('ordinary' corruption). Corruption depended on power rather than wealth. Even poor people could indulge in it whenever they found potential victims who were unable to defend themselves. For example, foreigners arriving at the border of an African country were sometimes robbed by the local population before being allowed to pass through.[312] Other vulnerable groups included white farmers in Southern Africa and, above all, foreign-born entrepreneurs who had settled in Africa, such as Lebanese and Syrian shopkeepers in West Africa and Asian businessmen in East Africa. They could not count on the authorities to protect them and were often forced to part with their money in all kinds of illegal ways.

Not only did corruption have serious personal consequences for the victims, but it also made it difficult for states to improve their policies, for example by liberalising their markets. Africa lagged well behind other parts of the world in this respect, and even more so in practice than in theory. For example, businesses in Tanzania complained about being pestered with demands for types of tax that no longer officially existed. Government tax collectors clung to their confusing tangle of rules for as long as they could in the hope of collecting more revenue, part of which went straight into their own pockets. These 'public servants' fought against any attempt to simplify the system.

It was above all the adverse impact of corruption on the development of African countries that made international donors press for anticorruption campaigns in Africa. In the 1990s, anticorruption measures were taken in numerous African countries. Perhaps the most vigorous campaign was launched by the IMF. The main target was Kenya, whose government agencies were so utterly venal that in 1997 the IMF decided to suspend all aid to the country. Ties were re-established in 2000. The IMF said it would grant new loans only if anticorruption reforms were carried out. Curiously enough, the person the IMF had to negotiate with was the well-known white Kenyan Richard Leakey. He had spent years investigating the origins of man in East Africa, but had since gone into politics. The Kenyan government had unexpectedly made an offer to put him in charge of the civil service, which he accepted. His first task, boosting the country's economy, could only be accomplished by improving relations with the international financial institutions.

It was agreed that Kenya would only embark on new development projects with the consent of the IMF, which also compelled the government to introduce a new financial system, with a key role for the finance ministry. Only this ministry was henceforth authorised to spend money at the district level – even the powerful Office of the President could no longer do so. This drastically reduced the number of officials who could embezzle, making monitoring easier. All Kenyans in government service were required by law to declare their assets. Only the president was exempted from this requirement – his ministers were not. However, the large number of ministerial posts (and hence plum jobs under the president) remained unchanged, although the number of ministries was halved. The IMF paid weekly visits to the Central Bank to check the books. Its tough stance helped Leakey and his team of fraud-busters to clean up some of Kenya's state-owned enterprises. A number of corrupt senior officials were dismissed. However, there were limits to what the cleanup could achieve; the president and his entourage were left untouched. They had sufficient power and political skill to delay and frustrate the anticorruption campaign.

Many Africans greatly welcomed efforts to fight corruption in their continent. They also felt that things had gone too far. There were limits to what was acceptable. Some things were universally acknowledged to be excesses or even crimes. Over the last quarter of a century, as a result of political changes, the generally accepted social system began to break down in many African countries. Normal social behaviour degenerated into corruption. The patronage system, though its original function was to preserve social stability, gradually became a basis for criminal activity.

Crime was on the increase all over Africa, especially in urban areas. This often reflected a rise in small-scale offences committed by individuals or small groups, from pilfering to armed robbery. Within a frighteningly short time African cities became much less safe, and some societies, such as South Africa's, became thoroughly crime-ridden.

Large-scale organised crime also grew rapidly after 1990, partly owing to the changing international situation. Globalisation, with its porous frontiers, deregulation and better communications, made it ever easier for international networks to operate more or less unnoticed. Illicit trade expanded swiftly and covered a variety of commodities, from weapons and protected animal species to people (who were usually smuggled to Western Europe) and drugs. Illegal traffic in drugs became a lucrative activity for groups in West Africa, with their hub in Nigeria.[313] These networks consisted not only of Africans, but also of Latin Americans, Arabs and Asians living in Africa. Although local use of substances such as amphetamines, heroin and cocaine was rapidly increasing in West Africa and elsewhere on the continent, most of the trade involved drugs in transit to other parts of the world. Heroin from the Golden Triangle in Asia was shipped on to the United States and cocaine from Colombia and neighbouring countries found its way to Western Europe via West Africa.

Organised criminals sometimes operated independently from states but in other cases had links with them. In the 1990s many government officials became more willing to engage in lucrative illegal activities because of the financial distress brought on by structural adjustment programmes, economic problems and dwindling foreign aid. It was increasingly difficult for them to continue funding their networks of domestic clients. Crime, with or without the use of state power, was a way to replenish shrinking financial reserves. It was usually a sideline, but in some countries illegal transactions started to become a mainstay of the regime. Once again, in some circles this was not necessarily seen as unacceptable. Political and moral codes of conduct based on family, ethnicity and other ties left a good deal more latitude than in many non-African cultures. In some circumstances deceit could be a valued social skill and if it resulted in a glamorous lifestyle, people were even more inclined to condone it.[314]

Some regimes were a tissue of corruption and crime. The most extreme example was probably the Taylor government in Liberia (1997-2003), which can only be described as a bandit regime. Liberia was involved in various kinds of illicit trade. Its leaders placed themselves and their relatives in positions from which they could control the revenue. Ministers sat on the boards of humanitarian organisations and Taylor's own wife was put in charge of Liberia's emergency relief agency. Some donors decided to stop giving emergency aid to the destitute country because the money was certain to end up in the wrong hands and would never reach the people it was meant for.

Reassessing the role
of the state

Back in the 1980s, the international financial institutions were the first to be confronted with the serious problems besetting African countries. One state after another went bankrupt. How were these institutions to respond to the constant requests for financial support? In the structural adjustment programmes that were subsequently introduced, new loans were granted only if the government in question agreed to change its policies. This nearly always involved reducing the budget deficit, liberalising trade, privatising state enterprises and letting the currency float. The aim was to put state finances in order and improve the economic situation. However, this goal was not fully realised. The measures often conflicted with rulers' interests, and they did what they could to subvert reform. Even if measures were adopted in theory, there were complications in practice. Simply emphasising better policies was not enough.

The crucial problem was the dysfunction of African states. The only chance for improvement would come through a change in African policies and governance. The unexpected wave of political liberalisation after the Cold War got things moving, and for a number of years economic and political liberalisation went hand in hand. International support for this trend was known as the Washington consensus. However, the relative successes of the mid-1990s did not last. The outbreak of major new violent conflicts made instability another serious problem for African states. Their weakness was a threat to domestic security, and after the Al Qaeda attacks on the United States in 2001, failed states were also considered a threat to international security.

The role of the state had to be thoroughly reassessed. The international development community was slow to recognise that African state structures were an obstacle to development. For a long time, donors did what they could to avoid criticising African politicians and political systems, feeling that because Africa was now independent, its politics were its own business. Western countries had generally assumed that African political systems were up to their task. By the 1990s this view was no longer tenable. The all too conspicuous malfunctioning of African states was making aid ineffective.

This development ran roughly in parallel with new international thinking about the role of the state. All over the world, in accordance with the neoliberal orthodoxy that emerged just after the Cold War, the state was being rolled back. The smaller, the better, where government was concerned. This conveniently overlooked the tasks that the state did have and that could not be assumed by private institutions. The most important one, of course, was maintaining law and order, but the state also turned out to be indispensable to the economy. Business could only run smoothly in a climate of political and economic stability, physical safety and good infrastructure – things that only the state could provide. The state and the private sector were thus not only rivals, but allies as well. For markets to function properly, states were needed to draw up and enforce the rules. Without sufficient government intervention, the most that could be achieved was a wild-west economy based on chaotic, unbridled capitalism, rather than a flourishing private sector. On closer inspection, the state and the market turned out to be highly interdependent.

States might have been expensive to maintain compared with private companies, but they were nevertheless essential. Without effective states, society would pay an increasingly high price in terms of the economy, living standards, public safety, international security and so on. The state was a house that not only had to remain standing but also needed maintenance. This was something the market would not provide. All this led to a rediscovery of the importance of institutions and a new appreciation of the state.[315] Moreover, in the numerous cases in which the development of the private sector had gone together with a general rise in prosperity, the state had nearly always played a major part.[316] This was true of both the rich industrialised countries of Europe, with their mixed economies and their 'social market capitalism', and the countries of East and Southeast Asia, which had developed under the guidance of strong governments.[317] However, whereas in many Asian countries the state had been a powerful force for development, in Africa it had almost invariably been an obstacle to it.[318]

The new emphasis on the importance of the state in developing countries was a faint echo of what Gunnar Myrdal had said back in the 1960s. The Swedish economist had asserted that a key feature of states in developing countries was that they were 'weak' – or, as we now say, prone to 'failure'. Poor countries could not develop unless these weak states were strengthened. These views were several decades ahead of their time. In the international development policies of the 1970s and 1980s, the state played only a subordinate role. It was not until the 1990s that attention was focused once more on the operation of the state, both with a view to preventing violent conflict and in connection with development. Some even argued that instead of poverty reduction, the main goal of development cooperation should be to improve administrative structures – or, as we now put it, to promote good governance.[319]

Yet this too would have been too one-sided. What mattered was not just effective administration, but also what exactly it was meant to achieve; in other words, not just good governance, but good policies as well. Both were needed. Myrdal underestimated the importance of the right policies. He noted that the communist states of the Eastern Bloc were strong and concluded that they would therefore contribute to development, overlooking the possibility that poor policies might lead to total failure. This blind spot of Myrdal's was typical of the time, when it was fairly widely assumed that there were various roads to prosperity. However, the many failures of the 1970s and 1980s showed that this was not true in practice.

A final comment about Myrdal's intriguing work concerns his assertion that the chief characteristic of a weak state was its lack of control over the public. People could easily evade the law. It was everyone for himself, and the overall impact in terms of development was minimal. Strong states, he claimed, had to 'capture' or discipline their citizens; in short, influence their behaviour. Myrdal thereby linked the state and politics with culture, something almost no-one has attempted since. 'Culture' had become almost sacred and untouchable. On the assumption that many roads led to Rome (i.e. to prosperity), hardly anyone noticed that certain cultural characteristics of developing countries were obstacles to progress. Even after 2000, culture still appeared sacrosanct. States were supposed to maintain law and order, provide services, 'facilitate' and do any number of things, but at no time did anyone say that they were supposed to influence their people's behaviour, i.e. their culture. The only exception to this was perhaps the fight against corruption. Even in the fight against AIDS, attempts to influence people's behaviour were effectively taboo.

The only international donor that consistently paid attention to African states was France. Other countries tended to take a cynical view of this, since the French approach, which involved maintaining cordial relations with the most notorious African leaders, mainly served French national interests. Yet there was also a historical element. The state as an organisation has traditionally played a larger role in France than in other Western countries. Napoleon formulated the reasons for French étatisme as follows: 'Men are powerless to secure the future; institutions alone fix the destiny of nations.'[320] Accordingly, at the end of the Cold War, when the special relationship between France and the Francophone African countries was no longer so self-evident, France was the first Western country to press strongly for more democracy in African politics (see chapter 3, pp. 89-92).

The new general emphasis on Africa's states showed that Africa's state system and individual state structures, which had become increasingly ineffective since independence, would not be abandoned without a struggle. The interests of Africa's national elites, in particular, were far too great. Without states, all they would have left would be their foreign bank accounts. Other African groups, such as NGOs pressing for social change, also had an interest in the continued existence of Africa's states, albeit with improvements. There was support from this quarter for international policies aimed at good governance and for restoring stability in countries racked by violent conflict. The robust UN operation in Sierra Leone was the best example of this. International intervention put an end to the chaos that had engulfed the country, and gave the Sierra Leonean state a new lease on life. However, the full commitment of the former colonial power, Britain, was required. Sierra Leone became an unofficial British protectorate. This shows just how dependent some parts of Africa had become on international support for the stability of their state structures.

In countries that were still stable, the emphasis shifted to the political aspects of the state: democratisation, human rights and good governance. Efforts were made to increase states' administrative capacity by encouraging better governance. There were several criteria for 'good governance'. First of all, government had to be physically present, which was by no means the case everywhere. Secondly, it had to be effective, goal-oriented, transparent and well-monitored, and not corrupt. If the conditions were met, donors felt they should channel aid through state structures. They provided funds for direct use by the recipient states. Many states had not reached this stage in every respect, but this direct form of aid was often feasible in specific sectors, such as education or health care. In such cases, donors spoke of a sector-wide approach.

Most developing countries had pledged, in general international declarations such as the Millennium Declaration of 2000, to promote democratisation, human rights and good governance (see chapter 9, pp. 284-287). Further details were laid down in more specific agreements. The most important of these was the Cotonou Agreement of 2000 (the successor to the five Lomé Conventions), in which the EU's partner countries in Africa, the Caribbean and the Pacific undertook to promote democracy, human rights and good governance and to fight corruption. If in the EU's opinion a country was doing little or nothing in these areas, it had to hold talks with the EU. These talks became known as article 96 consultations (on democratisation, human rights and good governance) and article 97 consultations (on corruption). If partner countries failed to respond adequately to EU criticism, sanctions could be imposed. From 2001 onwards, a number of African countries had Cotonou consultations with the European Union. The first of these were Taylor's Liberia (under both articles 96 and 97) and Mugabe's Zimbabwe (under article 96).

Owing to the new emphasis in international aid on improving governance both indirectly (through pressure brought to bear in article 96 consultations, for example) and directly (through institution-building), the goal of poverty reduction faded somewhat into the background. In most African countries, governance and policy were simply not good enough to make poverty reduction an immediate option. Too many preliminary steps had yet be taken on the road to full statehood. Ironically, just as international agreement had been reached on poverty reduction goals (the seven pledges focusing on developing countries), they were becoming rather irrelevant to development cooperation in Africa. Given the way in which African political systems worked and the quality of state structures, the seven pledges could not be fulfilled in the foreseeable future. Instead of small, neatly-defined projects, development cooperation began to focus on more abstract efforts to improve structures.

Development cooperation also proved rather ineffective in promoting private enterprise, which most poor people saw as the best way to escape from poverty.[321] Donors searched hard for ways to strengthen the business sector in developing countries in ways that would particularly benefit the poor.[322] Examples included improved market access, freer markets, development of the financial sector, knowledge development and capacity-building, special support for women and improvements to physical infrastructure. Above all, the private sector also had an interest in better state structures. The private economy could not manage without support from the public sector. It was the state's job to provide an 'enabling environment' for businesses of all sizes. Here again, the focus was on somewhat abstract structural improvements.

However, structures only function properly if they are linked to people in the right way. African states had few positive ties with their people. Patronage systems did allow elites to interact with their supporters, but the latter had practically no influence on the state. It was hoped that democratisation would change all this by turning citizens into co-owners of the state (see pp. 325-331). Another problem was the distance – physical as well as figurative – between the strongly centralised African states and their citizens. The further people were from the centre of power, the looser their ties with the government. The answer was sought in decentralisation.

Attempts at decentralisation

A limited degree of decentralisation took place in one or two parts of Africa even before the end of the Cold War, with powers, tasks and funds being transferred from central government to local authorities. This became a key component of the democratisation process in the early 1990s. Democratisation and decentralisation went hand in hand and were mutually reinforcing. Both were needed in order to get ordinary Africans more involved in public affairs and make them citizens rather than subjects. This, it was hoped, would strengthen both state structures and people's sense of national identity. Decentralisation could also help reduce tension between groups in different parts of the country by granting them more local autonomy. This was an important aspect of the decentralisation that followed the genocide in Rwanda, as well as in Mali after fighting with the Tuaregs came to an end.

There were also more general administrative arguments in favour of decentralisation. It would reduce the burden on central government. Cutting red tape would speed up decision-making. Administration, coordination and monitoring would be easier. A decentralised government would be better at providing public services than a centralised one, for instance. These services would improve in both quality and quantity and would also be cheaper. Leaders who were close to the public would be more aware of their needs and wishes. This could serve as a basis for local policy, which the local population would not only support but would also have an incentive to help implement.

People would thus be well informed of what was happening, which would make it easier for them to monitor their leaders. Groups that had always been on the fringes, remote from government decisions and services, would have the opportunity to make their lives better. People who had never been able to take action to improve their lot could now do so in cooperation with the local authorities. Local government could cooperate or even merge with local activist groups. In general, decentralisation was expected to improve the social and economic conditions in which people lived and to strengthen local democracy.

However, not everyone in central government was eager to see this happen. The far-reaching centralisation of African states had a logic of its own, and, as this book has emphasised at various points, the national elites did well out of it. Improved local government and living conditions were not sufficient reason for the rulers in the capitals to relinquish any of their power or influence. They only would do so under pressure. Similar pressure was needed to get democratisation going – pressure from both African society and international donors to improve the often miserable conditions in African countries.

Accordingly, those with vested interests attempted to limit the decentralisation process. Almost nowhere did a general transfer of powers, tasks and funds take place.

Often the process got no further than what is known as deconcentration, with the local authorities remaining under strict central government control. Decentralisation may involve various ways of dividing authority between the central government and local authorities or civil-society organisations. These include deconcentration and delegation, in which the central government still retains statutory authority over the specific responsibilities that have been transferred. Another form is devolution, in which statutory authority and responsibility are transferred to lower tiers of government. Finally, there is privatisation, which can be seen as an extreme form of decentralisation. When privatisation took place in Africa, informal links with government usually remained, because the companies were taken over by holders of state offices, such as ministers.

The decentralisation process in Uganda was one of the first and most successful of its kind anywhere on the continent, and is therefore often taken as a model for the rest of Africa. President Museveni, whose National Resistance Movement came to power in 1986, wanted a clean break with the past. This included decentralisation of the highly centralised Ugandan state. The idea was to make local communities self-governing. Local 'resistance councils' were set up, primarily to protect law and order and public safety from village up to district level. They were also expected to mobilise the population to take part in development projects, and succeeded fairly well in doing this. The populace gained confidence in the councils, partly because they had access to funds from central government. The councils oversaw numerous local initiatives and soon came to be seen as agencies of the people. They also formed the lowest tier of the court system, and monitored the performance of office-holders.

Despite their rather bureaucratic structure, the resistance councils had considerable freedom in matters of policy. There was very little control from the top. As a result, they were somewhat distrusted by central state institutions such as the central judiciary and the police. By the mid-1990s their status had gradually been codified, which confirmed the success of political and administrative devolution; the local authorities had their own legal powers and responsibilities, separate from those of central government. From 1992 onwards the entire decentralisation programme was overseen by a Ministry of Local Government in the capital, Kampala. The decentralised system was finally incorporated into the Ugandan constitution in 1995. Local government became responsible for such things as primary education, health care, water and roads. This decentralisation process was successful because it was part of a broader process of administrative reform in Uganda. However, the disadvantage of giving the resistance councils formal bureaucratic status was that it turned them from instruments of the people into fully-fledged state institutions which, by their very nature, were at a slight remove from the public.

In any case, decentralisation in Uganda was only relatively successful. There were plenty of difficulties along the way. Similar, but even more extreme, problems arose elsewhere in Africa. In general, very few funds were transferred to lower tiers of government. There were also too few people at local level capable of drawing up and implementing policies. Such people were hard enough to find in the capital, let alone at the district or village level. It has sometimes been claimed that decentralisation in Africa was due not so much to a wish to organise things better, as to the poor performance of central government – 'decentralisation by failure'. Central problems became local ones. An example was corruption. Simply shifting the problem did not solve it. Corruption at lower levels, where people were at the mercy of local political bosses and away from the gaze of the national press, was often much harder to fight than in the capital. Decentralisation also distributed financial authority among more people, which increased the probability of corruption. Government funds were particularly prone to leak away at lower levels. One important measure in the fight against corruption was therefore to limit the number of officials allowed to handle funds. This clashed with the campaign of decentralisation.

There was considerable variation in local government in Africa, sometimes even within countries. In some regions modern local institutions such as town councils were set up, in others traditional chiefs had considerable authority, in still others there was a mixture of these forms. The traditional chiefs tried to use decentralisation and democratisation to enhance their political status. They presented themselves as the true leaders and representatives of the people. Unofficially they often had a great deal of influence and authority, but officially – with a very few exceptions – there was no place for them in the independent African states. If they managed to acquire important local positions as a result of decentralisation, it in a sense meant a return to the indirect rule of the colonial period, except that now the chiefs were answerable to their own national elite rather than a European colonial administration. However, this did not happen on a large scale, for traditional authorities were rivals of the modern African states. Relying too much on them would have posed an unacceptable risk for Africa's new leaders, who preferred to try and build up local government on more modern lines. In the rapidly growing cities, which mostly had no traditional power structures, the development of local institutions lagged far behind what was needed. In a metropolis such as Lagos, in Nigeria, neighbourhood services were usually provided by informal networks that had no connection with the state. In both urban and rural areas, local government sometimes had fierce competition from NGOs. Thanks to their links with international donors, NGOs often had access to funding that left local government in the shade. Prior to decentralisation, they had stepped in to fill the gaps left by failing states. In Kenya, for instance, about half of the country's health care was provided by NGOs. They had got used to going their own way, free from state authority, which they often saw as an obstacle or an adversary. Decentralisation brought them back under the government umbrella, which they did not always like.

In general, decentralisation only slightly improved people's lives. There were no resounding successes as there had been in some parts of Asia; in the Indian state of Kerala, for instance, more kilometres of roads were constructed, more latrines built and more schools opened after decentralisation than in all the years before it.[323] The problems of local government in Africa were too great for this to be possible. Decentralisation had no real impact on the nature of development projects. The emphasis was still on building physical infrastructure, such as schoolhouses and roads, which were then left to deteriorate for want of funding, motivation or organisation.

Although local government was sometimes just as hierarchical, secretive and corrupt as central government, decentralisation did encourage progress in some areas. The continent gradually became more democratic. Until about 1980, scarcely any part of Africa held local elections, but by the mid-1990s they were being held in fourteen African countries.[324] Decentralisation proved a major catalyst for democratisation, since its purpose was not only to give citizens a say in the development of their country and their local area, but also to provide them with the necessary institutions, such as local elections and councils.

Democratisation around the turn of the millennium

Almost everywhere in Africa, the relationship between citizens and the state is one of distrust. As citizens see it, the state has no legitimacy. There are no strong material ties between the state and its citizens; the state provides almost no services and citizens make little or no financial contribution to the state. An important way to create healthy ties between the state and its citizens is democratisation. Since the end of the Cold War, attempts have been made to breathe new life into African states in this way.[325] Between 1989 and 1994, as described in chapter 3, Africa's political systems rapidly became more democratic. Democratisation then stagnated for a few years. In Central Africa the obstacles were too great for political reform to have any chance of succeeding. Autocratic regimes in major countries across the length and breadth of the continent continued to resist change, for instance in Nigeria (where the military had been continuously in power since 1982), Cameroon (run by President Paul Biya since 1982), Zimbabwe (run by President Robert Mugabe since 1980) and Kenya (run by President Daniel arap Moi since 1979).

In 1998, however, the tide again turned in favour of democratisation, with the unexpected death of the Nigerian dictator General Sani Abacha. Suddenly change was in the air in Africa's largest dictatorship (see next section). Other countries also made progress. By the turn of the century it was clear that Africa was still perfectly capable of further democratisation. Some familiar old hands left the scene peacefully, the most prominent being President Abdou Diouf of Senegal, President Jerry Rawlings of Ghana and President Daniel arap Moi of Kenya. Only ten years earlier, peaceful transitions of this kind would have been unthinkable in Africa. They showed that, despite the apparent standstill in the mid-1990s, in many places democracy had been making steady progress beneath the surface.

Senegal was known as a relatively democratic country, but that did not mean that the transfer of power went off easily. Since independence in 1960 the country had had only two presidents: Léopold Senghor (1960-1981) and Abdou Diouf (since 1981). They were leaders of the same party, known since the 1970s as the Socialist Party. Two other political parties were allowed by the Constitution; the rest had no official status. One of the official opposition leaders was Abdoulaye Wade, who gradually gained in popularity through long years in opposition. In the 1988 elections, Diouf's Socialist Party won over seventy per cent of the vote, but by 1993 this figure had fallen to fifty-eight per cent (with Wade capturing one third of the vote). This was a sign that the party's power was waning. It allowed members of the opposition to join the cabinet, ostensibly to give the opposition a greater say, although some said the real purpose was to absorb it into the system. This led to a curious situation in which opposition ministers could, and did, openly criticise government policy.

In the 2000 presidential election, Diouf again stood for office. This time his share of the vote fell to forty-one per cent, which was not enough to be elected in the first round. In the second round Diouf lost to Wade. The handover of power was surprisingly smooth. The country's mood was euphoric when Wade, who was by then seventy-four and had spent his whole life fighting for democracy in Senegal, acceded to the presidency without difficulty. In the 2001 parliamentary elections, his coalition won a majority in parliament. For the first time ever, the Socialist Party went into opposition. A new constitution was immediately adopted in order to institutionalise the changes that had taken place in the country. It stipulated that a president could not remain in office for more than two terms.

In Ghana, the media played an important and perhaps even decisive role in the democratisation process. Free, independent media are often seen as essential to democracy. Freedom of speech is the criterion; the freer the media, the more respect there will be for human rights and the more democratic the country will be. Free media give the public more information and a clearer picture of how government operates. This makes it possible to hold authorities accountable for their acts. In Ghana, the new constitution of 1992 gave the media a chance to be independent after years of authoritarian control. It emphasised their responsibility for monitoring the government. In 1994, private businesses and individuals gained access to radio and television. In the runup to the 1996 election, the candidates were allotted almost equal amounts of broadcasting time. However, it was the strongman, Rawlings, who won again.

At the next election, in 2000, Rawlings had completed the two four-year terms of office he was allowed under the 1992 constitution, and so he could not take part. He abided by the constitution and stepped down, though he did back the ruling party's candidate to succeed him. The election was a contest between two fairly unknown and inexperienced candidates, and the ruling party's man enjoyed the support of the government apparatus. However, journalists were no longer blind to dirty tricks, and mercilessly exposed cases of vote-buying, forged identity cards and secret voter registration. The preparations for the election were discussed in public, building public confidence in the fairness of the proceedings. On the two election days, when armed groups came to the polling stations, ostensibly to maintain order but in reality to intimidate voters, the media called on the security forces to defend the constitution and appealed to voters not to let themselves be intimidated. The result was a relatively fair election which was unexpectedly won by the opposition candidate. The ruling party acknowledged its defeat and went into opposition, and President Kufuor succeeded Rawlings as Ghana's leader.

The third major country to undergo further democratisation was Kenya, which has only had two presidents in forty years of independence. Jomo Kenyatta, known as the father of the nation, ruled until his death in 1978, when he was succeeded by his deputy Daniel arap Moi. Moi has since completed five terms of office and would undoubtedly have become president for life were it not for the democratisation of the early 1990s, which made his political life much more complicated. Like many other African countries, Kenya adopted a constitution providing that a president could not remain in office for more than two terms. This meant that Moi would have to stand down in 2002. All the members of the political elite, from which his successor could be expected to come, were dependent on the president. A shrewd political strategist, Moi took his time designating an heir apparent so that he could keep a firm grip on the large ruling party. The opposition was easily divided.

Kenya's political system was stuck fast. Its rulers took a hard line, especially in the 1992 and 1997 elections, which the government was determined to win. Violence broke out on both occasions, and in total about three thousand people were killed. Between elections, on the other hand, force was not usually necessary. The country's steady decline over the previous twenty years had left its people dejected and apathetic. Most Kenyans had given up any hopes for the better, including the hope that Moi would go. Rather than revolt, they tried to leave the country or waited for the problem to go away naturally when Moi died. Meanwhile, most people's standard of living was deteriorating. The population continued to swell rapidly, but the economy did not grow.

That was the situation when Kenyans went to the polls in late 2002. Under great pressure, Moi had decided not to stand for election again, but it seemed as though he had taken the necessary measures to ensure that he could continue pulling the strings from behind the scenes even after the transfer of authority. He had chosen a successor from within the ruling KANU party: Uhuru Kenyatta, the son of Kenya's founding father Mzee Jomo Kenyatta. In elections that were generally taken as a sign of Kenya's political coming of age, Kenyatta and KANU lost unexpectedly to the united opposition parties under the leadership of Emilio Kibaki. The traditional dominance of KANU, which had ruled the country continuously since independence, came to a sudden end. For Kenya, a new era was beginning.

During the first wave of democratisation, following the end of the Cold War, many African countries had adopted new constitutions setting a two-term limit for the presidency. In countries where people were protesting against entrenched dictators, this took some of the pressure off, since it opened up the prospect that they would be succeeded by someone else after a clearly defined period (usually two five-year terms). This gave the sitting presidents ten years to think about how to deal with the problem. By no means all heads of state were prepared to accept the term limit, as Rawlings had done in Ghana. In most countries, the president's second term of office was scheduled to expire in the opening years of the new century. Leaders who wanted to keep on running things in the same old way, such as President Conté of Guinea, President Eyadéma of Togo and President Nujoma of Namibia, held referendums in an attempt to get the restriction removed from the constitution. They asked the people to support them on the grounds that the country would get into serious difficulties if they were not re-elected. What was actually taking place was a crucial battle between the old political system and a newer, more democratic one. If the restrictions on the length of time a president could remain in office were lifted, this would be a serious blow to the democratisation process.

In 1991, bowing to both domestic and international pressure, President Conté of poverty-stricken Guinea, who had been brought to power by a military coup in 1984, was persuaded to adopt a new constitution. It restricted the length of the presidency, prescribed that the president must not be older than seventy (Conté was almost that age) and allowed more than one political party. In 1993 and 1998 there were elections, both of which were won by the president, but only with the help of massive fraud and a good deal of bloodshed. Even so, Conté's presidency was due to end in 2003. As early as 2001 the president – who attempted to avoid the age limit by claiming to have been born 'around 1934' – began making clear public statements that the country could not manage without him, and organised 'spontaneous' demonstrations by supporters begging him to stay. A chaotic referendum held later that year was boycotted by the opposition. It was accompanied by serious intimidation of the electorate (including arrests, torture and disappearances) and protests from the European Union and other quarters. The results were unsurprising. The system – which was gravely harmful to everyone in Guinea but a small group in the immediate vicinity of the president – carried on as before.

Togo had the same problems as Guinea; in this small West African country too, the political situation was a serious obstacle to development. In 1967, just three years after independence, General Gnassingbé Eyadéma seized power in a military coup. For decades he ruled Togo harshly, indeed cruelly. Until 1991, when the wave of democratisation reached Togo, it was officially a one-party state. In that year other political parties were allowed for the first time. The new constitution of 1992 limited the number of terms that the president could remain in office. In reality, however, Togolese politics were not liberalised in the 1990s. The regime remained authoritarian and oppressive. The country was dominated by the army, which in turn was dominated by the president. Even so, elections were held in 1994 and 1998. The people badly wanted a change, but the country's rulers just as badly wanted to stay put. As a result, both elections were accompanied by extensive violence and fraud. Especially in 1998, the government and the army made it quite clear that voting was not meant to change anything. Numerous people were summarily executed during the election period, and the European Union suspended aid to Togo in protest.

In 1999 the president reached an agreement with the opposition in which he promised to abide by the constitution and not to stand for re-election. However, in the run-up to the 2003 elections he changed his mind. On the very last day of 2002, when most people's attention was focused elsewhere, the government and parliament amended the constitution to allow the president to remain in office. All major opposition candidates were barred from running against him, guaranteeing him an easy victory over a little-known opponent. It seemed that Eyadéma's political style was the same in the twenty-first century as it had been since the 1960s. Togo fell into gradual decline and observers started to wonder whether it could remain stable.

Political developments in Namibia – where President Nujoma was in the same awkward position – will be described in more detail later in this chapter. For now we will round off this brief survey of African countries with Togo's neighbour, Benin. What happened to the fledgling democracy that had led the way in Africa's democratisation process? The answer was rather unexpected. Democracy survived, but General Kérékou, who had ruled the country with an iron hand from 1972 until his fall in 1991, made a startling comeback in the 1996 election. The presidency of the technocrat Nicéphore Soglo, who had worked outside Benin (at the World Bank) for years, had not been a success. Having been abroad for so long, he lacked the domestic support on which African leaders' power is based: the pyramid with the president/patron at its apex and numerous tiers of clients underneath. Nor could Soglo build up such a network quickly, for he had little money to spend. What was worse, he immediately took painful structural adjustment measures to bring the country's economy back under control. This made him highly unpopular. The devaluation of the CFA franc in 1994 did not help either. The 1996 election was once again a contest between Soglo and Kérékou but this time the winner was Kérékou (who still had a good deal of backing from his former clients). Soglo went into opposition.

In his second period in office, Kérékou was no longer the Marxist dictator he had been in the 1970s and 1980s. During the riots at the end of the Cold War he had renounced Marxism and at the close of the national conference he had even publicly converted to Christianity as a repentant sinner. Kérékou's new image was that of the pious Christian, which made him acceptable to the people of Benin once more. With the help of his extensive domestic network, incomparably more powerful than Soglo's (which scarcely existed), he made a successful political comeback at the head of a coalition of numerous small parties. International donors continued to support Benin and Kérékou pursued a policy of economic reform. He also tried not to curtail democracy and freedom in the country. In stark contrast to neighbouring Togo, Benin enjoyed freedom of speech and freedom of the press. The army had withdrawn from politics and there were no political prisoners. Its macroeconomic policy was sound and its government budget almost balanced. The economy slowly began to grow. In 2001 Kérékou and Soglo contested the presidential election for the third time. Kérékou won again, this time in the knowledge that this would be his last term of office as president. He promised to abide by the constitution.

How firmly had democratic ideas and ideals taken root among the people of Africa ten years after the Cold War? Very firmly, according to a study by the American political scientists Michael Bratton and Robert Mattes, who also concluded that, for Africans, the meaning of democracy had undergone a clear change in the 1990s.[326] During the Cold War, Africans were made to associate democracy with the dictatorship of a single party and the promise of economic development. The 1990s saw a shift towards a much more liberal notion of democracy. To the majority of those interviewed (nearly seventy per cent), democracy was mainly a matter of politics, especially political procedures such as protection of human rights, participation in decision-making and voting in elections. Yet it was not just a question of procedures. A considerable number of Africans also felt that democracy would have to produce results; above all, economic results. Apparently they were confident that it would, for a full three quarters of the people interviewed said they preferred democracy to any other political system – a higher percentage than on some other continents.

In countries where democratisation had taken place, people were strongly opposed to the idea of a return to undemocratic politics, even if the new democratic system was far from perfect and there were major economic and other problems. Dictatorial regimes, whether civilian or military, were categorically rejected. Even the more traditional African authorities – chiefs or councils of elders – were not popular, at least in countries where people were familiar with them, such as Ghana or Botswana. Advocates of traditional forms of government were mainly to be found in countries where those forms had never existed.

This widespread support for democracy in Africa raises questions about the link with education, since levels of education tend to be low across the continent. In Western countries, support for democracy increases with people's level of education. In Africa, the opposite would seem to be the case. Educated Africans often had their doubts about granting political influence to the illiterate, ignorant masses, whom they feared would behave rashly and irresponsibly. The highly educated were also the most critical of how African democracies worked in practice. This meant that the strongest support for democracy came from the broad mass of citizens with little or no formal education. Bratton and Mattes concluded that 'although popular support for democracy is almost a mile wide, it may be only an inch deep.'[327]

With the spread of democracy across the continent, the number of peaceful changes of government increased. Until the early 1990s, almost no former African presidents were still living peacefully in their own countries. Of the 180 changes of government that occurred in the four decades between 1960 and 1999, more than 100 were violent, the result of a coup, invasion or war. Sixty to seventy per cent of the heads of state involved came to a bad end.[328] The turn of the century was the first time that Africa had a group of former presidents who could feel safe in their own countries and elsewhere in Africa and the world. This meant that, like other continents, Africa could at last avail itself of the experience and wisdom of what were often 'elder statesmen', for example in connection with regional or continental cooperation or conflict prevention.

Quite apart from the expectation that democracy would have a favourable effect on the quality of policy and governance, the democratic system had a positive psychological impact. Heads of state or government who live in fear of their lives mainly focus on the short term and on what decisions mean for them personally. This naturally conflicts with the long-term interests of society. By reducing the personal danger to rulers, democracy allows them to serve broader interests. The American scholar Arthur Goldsmith demonstrated a link between the degree of threat posed to rulers by their political environment and the extent to which, for example, they took steps to liberalise the economy. The more peaceful the power struggle, the more open countries were in economic and other respects. Heads of state in democratic systems were also less inclined to embezzle state funds.[329]

Elections were a recurring source of uncertainty. In the first few decades after independence, they were not intended to give the opposition (if there was one) any illusion that it might assume power. Until 1980, elections had never led to a change of government anywhere in Africa. The situation then gradually began to change, gathering momentum after the end of the Cold War. Almost eighty elections were held in the 1990s and a quarter of them were won by the opposition.[330] This was a signal that the elites in African countries were no longer an unbreakable bloc.

But was it a sign that the structure of African societies was changing? Hardly.[331] Individuals remained linked through vertical patron-client relationships. Although the size and density of clientelist networks did decrease as a result of economic problems, they were not replaced by horizontal links between people with common interests, as had happened in rich countries in the past (first in the guilds, and later in the socialist movement). Instead, the result in Africa was individualisation and social disintegration. Basically, however, the social structures of African countries remained unchanged during the years of democratisation. Patronage was still the main social nexus.

This seriously restricted the new parliaments' room for manoeuvre. They were not mouthpieces for emerging social forces. The importance of parliaments in the early days of Western democracies had lain not so much in the fact that they monitored the government as in their right of initiative; that is, the right to propose legislation. There were far more ideas, and a far broader range of ideas, circulating in the early Western parliaments than in their governments, which were above all bastions of the elite. Parliaments opened up politics, bringing democracy to life and opening the way to better legislation. Only later, in more mature democracies, once the differences between parliament and the government were no longer so great, did it become parliament's main task to monitor the government.

The inexperienced African parliaments were unable to make effective use of their right of initiative. Governments usually left members of parliament out of the loop when important issues were discussed. Undoubtedly in response to pressure from international donors, African governments were often more interested in talking to nongovernmental organisations than to the official representatives of the people. In Tanzania, for example, parliament never succeeded in acquiring any influence. Important political decisions were cooked up at meetings of the largest party (the former single party) – no other parties were involved. This was effectively a continuation of the one-party system, with parliament as a kind of low-ranking advisory committee. The old political tradition of keeping differences of opinion out of public view was maintained. Only occasionally did a representative of a small opposition party risk voicing criticism of any kind.

Democratisation did not bring economic progress to Africa. The general relationship between democracy and prosperity is fairly complicated. It is true that all countries where prosperity is widespread have democratic systems. But the reverse is not true; there are plenty of countries with democratic systems that are still underdeveloped and poor. Democracy thus by no means guarantees economic success. Moreover, there are countries with undemocratic systems that have made considerable economic progress and reduced poverty substantially, such as Indonesia under Suharto (except in his final years) and China after Deng Xiaoping's reforms. But here again, the reverse – that authoritarian regimes always bring greater prosperity – is not automatically true either. In numerous historical instances, political, social and economic conditions were all equally dreadful. The creation of prosperity can coexist with democracy, dictatorship or any other political system.

Winds of democratisation

in Nigeria

In many African countries, the desire of much of the population for political change, along with international pressure for reform, met with resistance from the established order. At the end of the Cold War, this confrontation culminated in political transformation almost throughout the continent. This second liberation of Africa, this time from its own despotic rulers, occurred at different times for different countries, depending on numerous, sometimes unpredictable factors. For example, Nigeria's army appeared to have Africa's most populous country in a firm and dispiriting grip, but things suddenly changed when the dictator General Abacha died in 1998.

The first attempt to establish a democratic system in Nigeria, immediately after the Cold War, had been suppressed by the military. In 1993 there was a chaotic election which was suspended by the country's generals halfway through. To the extent that one could talk of a result, it was clear that Chief Moshool Abiola, a wealthy businessman, had won. However, the defence minister General Sani Abacha seized power, and Abiola (who claimed to be the lawful president) was flung into jail, along with many others. The army subsequently held the country in an iron grip ('ruled' or 'governed' would be too flattering). As democratic, civilian rule rapidly gained ground in the rest of Africa, Nigeria's military rulers became increasingly anachronistic. Oddly enough, they were quite willing to support democratisation through peacekeeping operations in Liberia and Sierra Leone, two small countries in the region that had fallen prey to violence and anarchy. Nigeria was exporting a commodity – democracy – that it did not have at home.

This was not the only curious contrast. Nigeria's policy of subsidising domestic oil consumption (to keep the price of petrol artificially low) led to another bizarre situation. So much oil was being smuggled abroad to be sold at a profit that Nigeria, an oil exporter and a member of OPEC, could not satisfy domestic demand for petrol and often had to import oil from its neighbours. The military rulers had other strange policies. They largely ignored their duty as a government to provide the public with services such as education and health care, but they did get involved in commercial ventures such as shopping centres and cinemas. Bowing to strong international pressure, the main foreign oil companies with operations in Nigeria gradually began providing social services for the people of the Niger delta (where the oil wells were situated). Private corporations such as Shell thus ended up providing for the public, while the government engaged in private enterprise.

These anomalies were symptomatic of the consistently unbalanced development of the Nigerian state. Since intervening to preserve the unity of the country in the Biafran war (1966-1969), the army had felt utterly superior to civilian politicians. Military leaders continued to dominate national politics, using harsh, repressive measures to keep the numerous conflicts in this ethnic and religious powder keg from escalating into wholesale violence. Their methods included widespread violations of human rights, which reached their nadir when protests by inhabitants of the southern Niger delta were crushed. The area supplied the bulk of Nigeria's oil, but received very few public services of any kind in return. Instead, the environment was seriously contaminated, by the oil wells, by sabotage and above all by theft; holes were drilled over the entire length of the pipelines and the leaking oil was drawn off illegally into receptacles ranging from buckets to full-scale lorries. The pollution was horrendous and a smouldering cigarette butt could spark off a disaster that left dozens dead. The internationally renowned author Ken Saro-Wiwa spoke up on behalf of the small Ogoni group in the delta region, but his protests displeased the country's rulers, and in 1995 he was hanged along with eight others.

The international community was shocked, and the Abacha regime gradually became a pariah. Quite apart from its human rights violations, it was criticised on almost every other count. The military were doing nothing to improve the lives of ordinary people. The economy was on the brink of collapse. Debts piled up despite plentiful oil earnings. Corruption spread like wildfire, and Nigeria became one of the most corrupt countries in the world. The higher up people were in the hierarchy, the more public revenue they embezzled. President Abacha himself is believed to have stolen about ten billion US dollars. Senior Nigerians became involved in illegal international trade, particularly in drugs. In 1998, just as everyone was wondering how the country would ever get out of the mess it was in, Abacha unexpectedly died.

He was succeeded by his second-in-command, General Abdulsalami Abubakar. The new ruler immediately came under strong pressure to seize this opportunity for a fresh start. Realising that he would be well advised not to follow in Abacha's footsteps, he announced a new election and a return to civilian government. Abubakar would later mainly be remembered as the man who ensured a successful transition to democracy, but in other respects his hands were far from clean. Some say the new military leader had a hand in the unexpected death in prison of Chief Abiola, the winner of the 1993 election. If released, Abiola would immediately have laid claim to the presidency. Getting rid of him allowed the army to keep control of the transition to a new regime. It also bought Abacha's successors the time they needed to embezzle state funds. Confirming Goldsmith's aforementioned theory drawing a link between the degree of threat to rulers (Abubakar knew someone else would take his place in a few months' time) and the degree of corruption, the military used the year between Abacha's death and the advent of a civilian regime to feather their own nests as lavishly as they could. General Abubakar is said to have ended his one-year term of office a full four billion US dollars richer.

Yet the tide of democracy could not be turned. The 1999 election was a contest between the leaders of three new political parties. The winner was Olusegun Obasanjo, a former general with an impressive record. In 1960 he had been an officer with the UN peacekeeping force in Congo. Some years later he had played a decisive role in the federal army's victory over Biafran separatists. In the 1970s he had briefly been the head of a military government. Under Abacha he had been jailed for criticising the state of the country. His death sentence had been commuted to fifteen years' imprisonment. When Abacha died, Obasanjo was released and immediately went into politics as a civilian. While in jail he had felt a religious (Christian) calling to pull his country and the rest of Africa out of the quagmire. He set about this task as soon as he was elected. Even before appointing his team of ministers, he announced measures to tackle human rights violations and corruption and to improve the situation in the Niger delta. Obasanjo clearly wanted to make a clean sweep.

The country received plenty of international aid and oil prices were high, so there was no shortage of government revenue. Gradually, however, it became clear how difficult it was to change Nigeria's deep-rooted habits and structures. With a growth rate of four to five per cent a year, the economy appeared to be recovering, but this was entirely due to the rise in oil prices. When they fell in 2001, the government immediately found itself in trouble once more. There was no growth in other economic sectors. One of the greatest problems was the country's bureaucracy. On paper it looked capable of getting something done but in practice precious little was achieved. One main reason was corruption. A census of government officials revealed no fewer than 40,000 people on the payroll who had no business being there. They were no longer working for the government but were still receiving their wages. In fact, some of them had never even existed.[332] At the same time, government institutions were simply not equipped to make policy changes. Civil servants were only trained to carry out projects, not to draw up and implement policies or create a healthy climate for business.

Moreover, Nigeria's political and social system did not put the country's abundance of natural resources to good use. Oil earnings were used not to improve living standards but to support a relatively large and immensely rich elite which had been fragmented by the federal system and Nigeria's ethnic diversity. This wealth allowed the emergence of numerous parallel networks of clients which competed with each other and so undermined domestic stability.

In his fight against corruption, President Obasanjo attempted to establish a new culture in the country. All new ministers were required to follow a course organised by Transparency International, an international NGO set up to tackle corruption around the globe. Despite his efforts, however, it took a long time for significant measures to be adopted. In fact, the growth in oil earnings probably caused corruption to spread. Ironically, although the president had been a faithful supporter of Transparency International for years, the organisation had no choice but to keep Nigeria on the list of most corrupt countries during his term of office. Corruption had a huge impact, ranging from a poor international image for the country to poverty in many areas.

Obasanjo also attempted to improve human rights practices. A new committee was set up to investigate human rights violations under his military predecessors. Not surprisingly, the former dictators did little to cooperate, but the president did succeed in somewhat reducing the role of the army in politics and society and expanding civil rights. However, there was a dark side. With its numerous ethnic groups and its religious divisions, Nigeria was probably the most difficult country in Africa to hold together in a single state. A sense of nationhood failed to materialise, and as the years passed religious affinities, in particular, grew stronger. Many new mosques and churches were built and religious radicalism was on the rise. If religious or ethnic groups did not clash of their own accord, there were always politicians ready to exploit day-to-day tensions for their own purposes. Hostilities between groups could break out at any moment, anywhere in the country. Under military rule they had been firmly suppressed and the media had not been allowed to mention the subject. In the new climate of openness, the press was now able to describe in detail not only the (usually harsh) measures by the army to restore order, but also the clashes between groups. This often triggered reactions elsewhere in the country, sometimes leading to further hostilities. Under Obasanjo, Nigeria found itself trapped in a downward spiral of violence that threatened its stability.

Religion – above all, the dividing line between Muslims and Christians – began to figure even larger in the violent incidents. Half of Nigeria's people are Muslim, and the rest are mainly Christian. The Muslims mainly live in the dry northern part of the country, while most Christians (and animists) live in the humid south. For centuries there was almost no contact between these extremely different zones, but British colonialism brought them together in a single country. Since independence, distributing power among the representatives of these two groups had proved a very tricky balancing act. The last military rulers had been Muslims from the north, but Obasanjo was a Christian from the south. As a result, the democratic revolution gave some northerners the feeling that they were being left behind by the south. Religion was seized on as a means of opposing the central government through the northern states, in which the northern Muslims still formed a clear majority. Nigeria was constitutionally a secular federal state, but around the turn of the century Islamic *sharia* law was introduced in one northern state after another. In a sense it was being reintroduced, for in colonial days the British had tolerated Islamic law in the northern states as an extreme form of indirect rule.

Introduction of *sharia* not only led to friction between some national leaders and the states concerned, but also heightened tensions between Muslims and Christians, especially in the northern and central parts of the country. In areas where *sharia* had been introduced, thieves could have their hands chopped off and people found guilty of sexual misdemeanours could be stoned to death. In some places women had to be veiled whenever out of doors, and ideally were expected to remain indoors. Christians living in these areas were horrified, especially as it was not clear where the upsurge of Islamic fundamentalism would end. Some northern leaders were calling openly for Nigeria to become an Islamic state. There were scattered outbreaks of violence. Precisely in this period came the Al Qaeda attacks on the United States of 11 September 2001, which aggravated the existing antagonism between Muslims and Christians in Nigeria. Several thousand people were killed in religious conflicts in the course of 2001. Many Nigerians who were in an ethnic or religious minority in their area were expelled, or fled. Hundreds of thousands of people were displaced. Democratisation had not done Nigeria's stability as a nation any good.

Yet – and this is the final Nigerian paradox – none of this stopped Nigeria's rulers under Obasanjo, who was re-elected in 2003, from continuing with peacekeeping activities in West Africa and taking similar initiatives in the rest of the continent. As instability mounted at home, Nigeria was helping to promote continental stability. The new capital, Abuja, became a familiar venue for peace negotiations. Nigeria again sent troops to Liberia (in 2003), Nigerian observers took part in the UN peacekeeping mission in Congo (MONUC), and Nigeria even wanted to help resolve the crisis in Zimbabwe.

Delayed decline in
Southern Africa

The crisis in Zimbabwe around the opening of the twenty-first century ushered in the final stage of a steady deterioration. This slide had begun in the 1980s but only really got going in the following decade. The cause was President Mugabe's government. The head of state became increasingly dictatorial. The government's policies, economic and otherwise, were unsatisfactory by general standards and the country was governed in an increasingly chaotic fashion. There was less and less room for criticism in the press or from the opposition, and it was sometimes harshly suppressed. More and more jobs went to thugs in the service of political leaders. Mugabe and his clientele ever more egregiously abused their power, shamelessly lining their pockets.

The result was that by the 1990s what had once been a fairly prosperous country by African standards was on the verge of collapse. The economy, wrecked by bad policies and looted by the country's political elite, was shrinking by several per cent a year. The consequences for the man in the street were only too apparent; by the year 2000 he was earning thirty per cent less than when apartheid had ended in 1980. Inflation was high, the currency was worthless and there was widespread unemployment. Nor was the country much better off in political and moral terms. Although several political parties were officially authorised, in practice Mugabe's ruling party ran Zimbabwe very much like a one-party state.

The separation of powers (the executive, legislature and judiciary) also gradually degenerated. Parliament no longer had any say in how the country was run, and the judiciary, which had had previously some independent influence, came increasingly under attack. Decisions by the Supreme Court or other courts that were not to the government's liking were simply ignored and the judges who had ventured to make them were replaced by people with a clearer understanding of what the government wanted. Freedom of the press was curtailed. With the exception of the vast tracts of land owned by white farmers, the political elite was now in control of everything in the country that still brought in any money. A model African nation until the 1980s, Zimbabwe had by the 1990s degenerated into a textbook predatory state.

Plenty of other African states displayed similar behaviour, yet many others had changed for the better since the Cold War. In the 1990s, political freedom increased in many African countries, the powers of the executive were reduced, economic policies improved, political leaders loosened their hold on the economy somewhat and corruption was tackled. The results were seldom very satisfactory, but at least the trend was clear. What Zimbabwe went through from the 1990s onwards instead seemed more like a repeat of developments that had taken place in other African countries a decade or two earlier.

The reason for this anachronism may lie in the fact that the end of apartheid in Rhodesia – and the emergence of an independent black Zimbabwe – came some twenty years later than the decolonisation of most African countries, in 1980 rather than around 1960.

Only then did Zimbabwe embark on the same processes of Africanisation that had already taken place elsewhere on the continent. There appeared to be a fixed pattern which African countries were unable to escape, however late they became independent. African political and cultural characteristics, which had of course been profoundly influenced by colonialism and apartheid over the years, still had much the same impact and results everywhere. Whereas most African countries became politically, economically and morally bankrupt in the 1980s, Zimbabwe did so twenty years later.

Rulers who find themselves under pressure often look for external foes to distract attention from domestic problems. In the 1980s, Africa's rulers could only take out their anger and frustration on the World Bank and the IMF. These institutions were seen as neo-colonial powers and came to symbolise the big bad outside world. Many rulers did not suffer the political consequences of their countries' decline until after the Cold War, when democratisation could no longer be held in check. Zimbabwe's President Mugabe, who had been under similar pressure since the end of the 1990s, had other ways of distracting the public. Interaction between African states had increased to the point where it was thinkable for one African country to mount a military campaign in another. Zimbabwe's extensive involvement in the fighting in Central Africa, which had the potential to generate additional revenue for the country's political and military leaders, was also designed to whip up nationalistic feelings and support for the government back home.

However, a more effective target was the domestic legacy of colonialism: the white Zimbabweans. About five per cent of the population was white. Most were farmers, who still owned the best land. At the time of Zimbabwe's independence, 250,000 out of 300,000 white farmers had left the country. The 50,000 who remained did so at the explicit request of the Zimbabwean government, which told them 'Zimbabwe needs you.' They were the linchpin of the country's economy. When sovereignty was transferred in 1980, it was agreed that the good agricultural land would be redistributed in order to narrow the huge socioeconomic gulf between whites and blacks. However, this was on condition that the white farmers would receive financial compensation for the loss of their land. As the years passed, less and less money was available for this purpose. The economy was going downhill fast and the country's leaders preferred to put whatever money was left in their own pockets. For years the white farmers were protected by the continuing independence of the judiciary and the watchful eye of foreign powers, especially Britain.

All this changed when Mugabe began to feel his authority was under threat. He decided to make the struggle against the white farmers his new front, and began calling them enemies of the state. If they refused to voluntarily surrender their land without compensation, they would have to be driven off it by force. To do this, the government employed gangs of thugs who for nationalistic reasons were dubbed 'war veterans' – a reference to the independence struggle against Rhodesia's white rulers in the 1960s and 1970s. Most of these 'war veterans', however, had not even been born at the time. The results of their intervention were dramatic: thousands of farmers were dispossessed, dozens of whites were killed together with many hundreds of blacks working on the farms (who realised that the seizures would destroy their only chance of a decent income) and the independent judiciary collapsed (after initially daring to declare the land grab illegal). There was fierce criticism abroad and growing chaos at home. The benefit to the black population was nil. Many more jobs were lost, and all the land seized went to the president's cronies. The army chief received more than ten farms.

It was clear that Mugabe had his back to the wall and was desperate. But how was Zimbabwe to rid itself of this tyrant? The country still had elections. A large section of the black population, fairly well educated but now reduced to poverty, turned a deaf ear to Mugabe's bloated nationalism and anticolonialism. Despite intimidation and other forms of violence against the opposition, a movement arose with the aim of taking over the leadership of the country. The army, whose leaders were inextricably tied to Mugabe, expressed its unwavering support for the president, and made clear that a change of leadership as a result of the 2002 election would not be tolerated.

It was in this political climate that Zimbabweans went to the polls in March 2002. The many ways in which the government made it difficult or impossible for people to vote, the acts of intimidation and the irregularities, both minor and major, made it one of the most fraudulent elections in the history of Africa. Opposition leader Morgan Tsvangirai, who had a strong lead in all the opinion polls, was briefly arrested on charges of high treason just before and again just after the election. His party's head offices were looted and burnt to the ground by government thugs. Assuming the votes were actually counted, it was done in the absence of independent observers. To no-one's surprise, Mugabe was officially proclaimed the winner. While the president talked of a victory over imperialism, a dumbfounded world looked on at the ruling elite's unabashed refusal to relinquish its power. Zimbabwe was suspended from the British Commonwealth and became an international pariah.

Events in Zimbabwe naturally made people wonder whether the same thing could happen in its larger neighbour, South Africa. South Africa's history and population were very similar to those of Zimbabwe. However, everything in South Africa happened on a much larger scale than in Zimbabwe, and so events there had a much wider impact. The South African economy, for instance, was twenty times the size of Zimbabwe's. This was due to the far stronger colonial (i.e. white) presence in South Africa, as a result of which apartheid was not abolished there until much later (in 1994, fourteen years after Zimbabwe). Would South Africa go into decline just like Zimbabwe (and the rest of Africa before it), but with a similar time lag?

Hardly anyone dared speculate about this, for fear of being politically incorrect.[333] Any suggestion that South Africa might not be able to achieve widespread prosperity under black rule could all too easily be interpreted as racist. Scant attention was paid to the adverse impact on the state, and hence on society, of an ANC government policy that was generally held to be unavoidable and indeed just – namely, discrimination in favour of blacks (for example, when taking on new government staff) to counterbalance discrimination in favour of whites under apartheid. In the apartheid era, whites had on average received a far better education than blacks. The logical result of appointing more blacks to government posts was therefore a decline in quality and capacity. This was sometimes manifested in surprising ways. From about 2000 onwards, for example, the South African government no longer had the capacity to spend all the funds allocated for reducing the poverty of the black population (a key policy goal).

There were other problematic developments, although they could hardly be blamed entirely on the ANC government. They were chiefly due to South Africa's complex history. First among them was the growth in crime, which was increasingly prevalent in the cities. The country had the highest peacetime murder rate in the world. More than half of its people were afraid of falling victim to crime in their own communities. Some neighbourhoods were controlled by armed gangs.[334] People with material assets to protect took refuge behind high walls, complete with barbed wire and guards. A veritable bunker mentality took hold among South Africa's citizenry. There was also a rapid expansion in more organised forms of crime, from drug trafficking to money laundering.

During the isolation of the apartheid regime, the South African police had never had to deal with transnational crime. When South Africa opened up in the post-apartheid era, criminal organisations more or less had a free hand. The causes of the equally rapid growth in smaller-scale crime – from theft to murder – are harder to understand. Again, the police had not traditionally been concerned with fighting these types of crime, since their work under apartheid was above all political. Apartheid-era perpetrators may have seen apartheid as a justification for crimes committed against whites, and this attitude did not essentially change after apartheid was abolished. However, this does not explain the often equally vicious crimes committed by blacks against blacks. The cause may lie in factors found elsewhere in Africa, such as weakening social ties and respect for norms, combined with reduced government capacity to fight crime.

South African society was plagued not only with crime, but also with racism. There was a universal tendency to view the country's social problems in racist terms. The abolition of apartheid had not put an end to this. Many whites tended to explain the black government's problems by saying 'they just aren't up to it'. Conversely, criticism from whites, even if they had supported the abolition of apartheid (and did their utmost not to appear racist), was dismissed by black leaders because of the colour of the critics' skin. Black South Africans also discriminated against 'real blacks' (black immigrants from neighbouring countries), whose skin colour was supposedly different.[335] Racism was especially persistent in rural areas, but was also found in cities. Real life in South Africa contrasted starkly with the official ideology of the rainbow nation in which people of all colours lived together in harmony.

These serious problems came to the surface even before the ANC government launched its Africanisation policy. During Nelson Mandela's term as president from 1994 to 1999, however, there was no sign of the phenomena that are now familiar to us from the recent history of the rest of black Africa. The situation began to change under President Mbeki, very gradually. Political leaders began to behave as though the ANC were the only party in a one-party system. There was less tolerance of press criticism, and the opposition was largely ignored. The powers-that-be became increasingly arrogant, often dismissing criticism on the grounds that it came from 'suspect' (i.e. white) quarters. The general policy of discrimination in favour of blacks often went too far, leading to embezzlement and corruption. Policies were sometimes good (like the policy on social housing) but often unpredictable, and sometimes just plain bad (a prime example being the policy on AIDS). The bureaucracy was swollen with officials who were not always qualified for their tasks. More and more often, there were remarks to the effect that criticism by the free press, or the decisions of an independent judiciary, should not always be accepted.

The ANC leadership (whose political power in the country is absolute) will find it difficult to avoid the temptation to make money out of the system and to hand out government funds to their supporters. As we have seen elsewhere in Africa, misconduct of that kind diminishes a government's authority in society, trading it in for strong support from a small entourage. This ties the rulers and their supporters into an inextricable patron-client relationship, for patrons cannot manage without their clients and vice versa.

In many African countries, this system only came under pressure when countries went bankrupt and rulers could no longer cater to their clients' needs. In South Africa, however, such a scenario is inconceivable. The country's economy is far too large (as large as those of the rest of the continent put together) and is moreover largely in white hands. The ANC leadership will be unable to gain control of substantial parts of the economy without major crises, as in Zimbabwe under Mugabe. Yet the South African government will be tempted to go at least some way down this path. President Mbeki has said that if economic empowerment were to remain beyond the reach of those who gained power when apartheid ended, the ANC would continue to function as a liberation movement. This raises the spectre of Zimbabwe once more.

However, things need not reach that stage. Present-day South Africa has a number of advantages over Zimbabwe and the rest of Africa. The world is now more aware of the ways in which the political situation could veer out of control. International interests in South Africa – political as well as economic – are substantial enough that other countries will be inclined to respond faster. There is an international consensus that South Africa's transition to the post-apartheid era must not be allowed to fail.

Another question is whether neighbouring Namibia, which has been independent since 1990, will follow the same political and economic path. The official policy of the government in Windhoek is to promote national reconciliation and build up a democratic, market-oriented society. There is little social tension in the country. However, there have been some less encouraging signs. The Namibian government, which is dominated by the former liberation movement SWAPO, is displaying growing intolerance towards a variety of groups it has accused of undesirable conduct, including critical journalists, Afrikaans-speakers and homosexuals. The behaviour of the president and his SWAPO party is increasingly imperious. The worst sign, however, is SWAPO's amendment to the constitution in 1998, which allowed the president to remain in office for an additional, third term. President Nujoma may even stay on for a fourth consecutive term.

It appears as if South Africa, with Namibia in its wake, is just setting out on the path travelled by the vast majority of African countries since independence. It is hard to predict just how far down that path the two countries will go. However, there is a distinct likelihood of substantial political, economic and social decline. This will in turn have implications for other countries in Southern Africa, which are largely dependent on the South African giant for trade, investment and stability. If South Africa's economy is weakened, this will impair the overall development of the region, including such relatively distant countries as Zambia and Malawi.

The road to statehood: disappointment and determination

In this section, we will briefly turn to recent trends in the decline and emergence of state structures. Obviously, we cannot look at every single country. However, that will not be necessary, for the crucial factors are the same throughout

Africa: the creation of 'modern' states in the colonial era and their Africanisation since independence. Still, there are significant variations on this theme, and sometimes major differences even between neighbouring countries. This is possible because neighbouring countries often have very little to do with one another. There is little infrastructure linking them, and regional organisations are too weak to encourage uniformity. Both ends of the state formation spectrum are to be found within a single region, the Horn of Africa, where Africa's strongest states, Ethiopia and Eritrea, are right next door to its weakest one, the 'non-state' of Somalia.

In the northern part of the former Somalia, particularly in Somaliland but also in what is known as Puntland, there have recently been developments that suggest the emergence of new state structures. However, they have not received international recognition, which (as always when it comes to Africa) is entirely focused on the possible revival of a state of Somalia, controlling all of its former territory. Around the year 2000, on the basis of agreements between clans, a number of prominent Somalis set up a transitional government in a few buildings in Mogadishu. The idea was that it would develop into a true Somali government. The transitional government received diplomatic and financial support from various countries outside Africa. This included help setting up an army and a police force that could stand up to the militias of the warlords, each of whom held sway over his own piece of the country.

At the other end of the spectrum were Eritrea and Ethiopia. Both countries' state structures had emerged fairly unscathed from the war between them in 1998-2000. The indecisive outcome had prevented collapse. However, the leaders of both countries came under fire from political opponents, who wondered aloud whether the war had achieved far too little in the light of the huge sacrifices people had made. The feeling in Eritrea was that this small nation's considerable energy should now at last be directed towards more pacific goals. This 'African Sparta' should transform itself – as Germany and Japan had done in the past under international pressure – into a country whose industrious people would improve their living standards by the sweat of their brow. In the mid-1990s President Isaias Afwerki had dreamt of turning Eritrea into the Horn of Africa's financial centre and international port (rather like Singapore in Southeast Asia), but as a result of the war with Ethiopia this dream faded into the background.

After the war, Ethiopia's prime minister Meles Zenawi ran into considerable opposition from students, as well as from his former allies in the Tigray People's Liberation Front (TPLF), who accused him of insufficient perseverance in the final stages of the struggle with Eritrea. This group, which had strong revanchist feelings towards Eritrea, felt that the Ethiopian army should have completed its march on the Eritrean capital Asmara. These former socialists also felt that, by pursuing a policy of liberalisation, Meles was letting the United States and the IMF call the tune. The prime minister responded to this erosion of his Tigray power base by strengthening ties with non-Tigray groups in the ruling EPRDF coalition, so that he could build up an image as a national Ethiopian statesman. These changes had the potential to diversify, and hence to strengthen, national politics.

The Horn of Africa also included the special case of Sudan, which might have been better off partitioned in the first place. The country displayed a variety of instability that was exceptional in Africa; the problem was not that state structures were being eroded from within, as elsewhere on the continent, but that there were two fairly distinct groups which in the long run would probably be better off living separately than within a single state. But in 2003, there were finally signs that the civil war between the north and the south might be coming to an end. Under strong international pressure, the Khartoum government looked willing to abandon its policy of Islamic expansion.

Even after decades of fighting, by no means all southerners were convinced that secession would be the best alternative. Although the southern peoples had a common enemy (the Khartoum government), they were not united. Many southerners were well aware that the thinly populated expanse of southern Sudan lacked the physical or social infrastructure it would need to survive as an independent state. There was also a fear of possible domination by the numerically strong Dinka people, who formed the core of the SPLA. Accordingly, there were always southern leaders who were prepared to negotiate with representatives of the north or international mediators on the future form of the Sudanese state. The main issue was the relationship between religion and the state. To southerners it was essential that these be separated. According to the 1998 constitution, however, Sudan was a theocracy where God held supreme authority. The second crucial point was how much autonomy the south could be granted. These were exactly the same issues as half a century earlier, when the British had left Sudan. In 2003, it looked as though they might finally be resolved.

The situation in the rest of Africa was more uniform. The main exception was Southern Africa, where the impact of colonialism was deeper and slower to fade. The region's geographical position – halfway to the Indies and hence for centuries an ideal staging post for European vessels en route to Asia – had always had a major influence on South Africa in particular. European-style state structures were more strongly developed there than anywhere else on the continent. The transfer of power from the colonial state to the Africans took place later in South Africa than elsewhere (with the abolition of apartheid in 1994), and the aftereffects of this change were similarly delayed. The same was basically true of Zimbabwe and Namibia (see the previous section).

In Angola and Mozambique, both situated further up the coast, the independence struggle against Portugal had left deep scars. In both countries there were two competing armed groups which were unable to come to terms. The basic problem was the tradition of winner-takes-all ('all' meaning the state structures and the associated financial benefits). This encouraged the weaker party to keep on fighting. In Angola the result had been an endless civil war, which was impossible to resolve until rebel leader Jonas Savimbi was murdered in 2002. When peace was made in Mozambique soon after the Cold War ended, there was an attempt to resolve the tensions between the two camps by democratic means, but this was again thwarted by the winner-takes-all principle. The RENAMO movement, which at that stage represented a substantial part of the population, was not allocated a proportionate share of power. Although peace had officially been made, the situation in Mozambique was still extremely tense, with the chance of new outbreaks of violence. Angola and Mozambique remained divided, which was a threat to their unity as states.

This brings us to Central, East and West Africa. Of the states in these three regions, those in Central Africa are the weakest. There is, effectively, a political void in the heart of Africa, in Congo (Kinshasa). The repercussions this has had in the Great Lakes region and far beyond Central Africa are discussed in detail elsewhere in this book. Stability will not return to the region until Congo is revived as a state. The further development of Central

Africa and the surrounding countries will depend on this process, which in turn will depend on massive international support.

The problems in Congo have captured the world's attention because of that country's economic and strategic importance. However, the political situation in the countries to the north and northwest of Congo (known jointly in colonial times as French Equatorial Africa) is similar. In the Central African Republic, in particular, the state has been steadily disintegrating and has now practically ceased to exist. Nothing in the country works. A series of attempted coups were motivated by general disaffection, particularly among the military, some of whom had not been paid for two years. After the attempts in 1996 and 1997, in which hundreds were killed, the United Nations dispatched a peacekeeping force which was replaced by a special UN peacebuilding institute in 2000. However, there was not much the UN could do. Tension persisted between the various groups, especially between northerners and southerners. Nor could unpaid government employees and soldiers be expected to show much enthusiasm for their work. The Central African Republic was a seething cauldron in which everything that could go wrong did.

The situation on the other side of Congo, in East Africa, is substantially different. There are relatively strong states right on Congo's eastern border. Developments in Rwanda and Burundi are still dominated by fierce clashes between the two main population groups, the Hutu and the Tutsi. Uganda is calmer, but has its own civil war in the north. Thanks to a mixture of relatively good policies and good governance, the country is continuing to make progress. The rate of economic growth is five per cent a year, and poverty is on the retreat. The years of utter misery when Uganda was ruled by Idi Amin and Milton Obote are now fading memories under President Museveni. Yet Ugandan politics remains unpredictable. Political parties are still banned. There were presidential elections in 1996 and 2001, both won by Museveni. However, according to the constitution (which prescribes that a president may not stay in office for more than two terms), the Museveni era is due to end in 2006. This will be a critical juncture for Uganda, which has not had a peaceful change of government since it became independent.

Neighbouring Kenya finally made a fresh start with the 2002 election, which led to a change of power. Emilio Kibaki, the new president, launched reforms aimed at reducing poverty, unemployment, crime, corruption and mismanagement. Kenya's relatively strong civil society, which was instrumental in toppling the Moi regime, may also do a great deal to keep the current government on track. Even after decades of decline in all areas, Kenya is one of the few African countries likely to make progress in the near future. Though Kenyan society is extremely diverse, it has the potential for greater balance than most other countries on the continent.

Things were also going quite well in Tanzania. Admittedly, the ruling party lorded it over the divided opposition, but internally it had a culture of pluriformity. The presidency had already changed hands peacefully on two occasions, in 1985 and 1995. The expectation that this was the start of a lasting tradition brought political stability to the country. That had a positive impact on the economy, which grew faster than the population each year. Tanzania's main problem was the Zanzibar question – the relationship between the mainland and the island off the coast, which was very different. Members of Zanzibar's opposition, who had never accepted centralised Tanzanian rule, wanted to have the island's status within the union changed. The central government usually responded harshly, leading to clashes and human rights violations.

We will now cross the continent to look at our last region: West Africa. Poverty is more extreme here than in other regions; of the fifteen poorest countries in the world, no fewer than nine are in West Africa. The twenty or so countries in the region span the entire range of political development, from those that have been consistently stable (such as Senegal, and to a lesser extent Mali and Ghana) to those that have almost completely disintegrated under the impact of violence (especially Liberia and Sierra Leone). There are countries where governments change peacefully and more or less democratically (Senegal, Mali and Ghana once more) and ones whose rulers ruthlessly cling to dictatorial power (such as Togo and Guinea).

Yet West Africa appears to be in the grip of a steady, fairly general trend towards instability. Ethnic and religious tensions are on the rise, in small countries as well as in huge Nigeria. Here and there, unrest erupts into violence which can easily spill over into other parts of the region, starting with neighbouring countries. Refugees cross borders, as do rebel groups. The war in Liberia around the millennium spread to Sierra Leone, and later on Guinea, further to the north, also became involved. Traditionally stable Ivory Coast, to the east of Liberia, was not spared either. The country, which already had huge numbers of economic migrants from the Sahel within its borders, was flooded with refugees. In the 1990s the question of who was and was not an Ivorian became increasingly important, in daily life and in the political arena.

President Houphouët-Boigny, who had effectively ruled the country as an absolute monarch from independence until his death in 1993, was succeeded, in accordance with the constitution, by the speaker of the country's parliament, Henri Bédié. However, the incumbent prime minister, Alassane Ouattara, also laid claim to the post. After Bédié won the 1995 presidential election, the government adopted a new constitutional provision that residents whose parents were not both nationals of Ivory Coast could not run for president. The ruling elite claimed that Ouattara was a national of Burkina Faso. Tension over the nationality issue, together with financial mismanagement and corruption, posed an increasing threat to the country's stability. On Christmas Day 1999 the army staged a coup, the first in the nation's history. Bédié was deposed and General Robert Guéï assumed power. The transitional military regime promised to restore order and then hand over power to an elected civilian government once more. Another new constitution laid down even more stringent criteria for the presidency. In 2000 there were new presidential elections, in which only four selected candidates were allowed to take part. The turnout was extremely low. The proclaimed winner and new president of Ivory Coast was Laurent Gbagbo, who was entrusted with the task of restoring stability.

He did not succeed. In 2002 there was another coup attempt, which threw the whole country into turmoil. The territory of Ivory Coast was effectively divided into a northern part controlled by the Muslim 'New Forces', and a southern part controlled by the traditional Ivorian elite under President Gbagbo. The situation became even more complicated when armed groups of Liberians crossed the border into western Ivory Coast and new, brutal hostilities broke out.

France came to the rescue of its former colony. Its military stabilised the chaotic situation, and heavy pressure was brought to bear to find a political settlement. However, once an agreement had been reached none of the Ivorian parties to the conflict felt in was in their interest to implement it and restore national unity. The French were caught in the middle, able to prevent further bloodshed but not to hold the country together.

As for Liberia's role, commanders were said to have told their armed followers, 'Go and get your salaries across the border, in Ivory Coast.' This plan soon backfired, as the Liberians were pushed back into their own country by Ivorian groups. This increased the pressure on the Liberian government in Monrovia, which was already under attack by rebel groups. In mid-2003, the Liberian state collapsed once again. There was fighting all over the country and Monrovia, in particular, became a humanitarian nightmare.

The regional organisation ECOWAS – which over the years had built up quite some experience in conflict management – responded quickly. West African troops were again sent to Liberia to try to restore order. Again, Nigerian forces formed the core of the operation. Charles Taylor had no choice but to flee the country. He received political asylum in Nigeria. After several months the ECOWAS peacekeeping force was joined by the first UN troops, from countries around the world. It was hoped that the UN Mission in Liberia (UNMIL) would do the same job as UNAMSIL in neighbouring Sierra Leone; that is, give the country a future.

Developments in Ivory Coast and Liberia reveal several phenomena that are of broader significance to Africa as a whole. First of all, there is the fact that countries' domestic spheres are subject to increasing influence from neighbouring states. The surrounding region is of ever greater relevance to domestic politics. Interaction between African countries, which was minimal until the 1990s, is increasing, and this will have all kinds of consequences in the years to come. A second phenomenon is the remarkably rapid decline in stability. Better policies and better governance can improve the overall situation in a country fairly quickly, as Uganda under Museveni and Ghana under Rawlings have shown, but overall decline (for political, economic or other reasons) can set in even faster. Although there is a great deal of stability in Africa's patchwork of states, the states that make up that patchwork are individually fragile. Throughout Africa they face similar problems, which none of them can solve easily or quickly. Sometimes, things improve for a while only to deteriorate again. When development is as fragile as this, we cannot assume it will last. Recent developments have highlighted the variations on state development, but common underlying themes will determine the entire continent's future. For the time being, African countries will not move forward without disappointments.

International

uncertainty

How did the international community (more specifically, Western countries) react to the stalled process of state development in Africa and to cases of state disintegration in the early twenty-first century? To answer that question, we will first examine the new international phenomenon of Islamic terrorism and the fight against it. Its impact has been felt all over the world, including Africa.

On 11 September 2001, attacks by Middle Eastern terrorists brought death and destruction to New York and Washington. For the United States, it was a rude awakening from dreams of a new isolationism. The George W. Bush administration, which had been in power only a few months, found it could not ignore the world beyond the United States' borders. Without taking too much notice of other countries' opinions about how to take on the terrorist threat, Washington lashed out with the overwhelming might of its military. Regimes were ousted in Afghanistan and Iraq. The 'war on terrorism' became the first major chapter in the history of the twenty-first century.

How did all this affect Africa? The attacks of 11 September obviously raised the issue of whether African countries or individuals might be involved in terrorism. The African authorities were unanimous in condemning the attacks. President Abdoulaye Wade of Senegal called for an African pact against terrorism and his appeal was echoed by many African leaders. The attacks were even condemned by the government of Sudan, which Washington had suspected of villainy for years.

The official African response was thus positive, but the reaction from African Muslims was less unanimous. Emotions ran high in countries where there were large Islamic populations or tension between Muslims and Christians, above all in West Africa. Thousands died in confrontations between Muslims and Christians in Nigeria.

The attacks triggered off a debate about a possible connection between terrorism and poverty. Just as in the past there were those who suggested that outbreaks of fighting, intercontinental migration, environmental degradation and so forth were linked to poverty, some now attempted to link poverty and terrorism. This view simplistically divided the world into good and evil, with all the evil on one side under the heading of poverty and everything good on the other. One reason for making such a crude distinction was probably to give the rich an added incentive to eliminate poverty, lest they experience at first hand the adverse effects of poor people's misery. However, there was no substantive link between poverty and terrorism. Whatever the terrorists' problems were, lack of funds was certainly not one of them. Nor were there any known terrorist movements among Africa's poor.

Yet that was not the end of the matter – for there *was* a link between the operation of terrorist networks and certain types of country. In some failing states, terrorists had a free hand. Africa's most extreme example – Somalia, which had ceased to be a state – was probably the only 'country' in Africa that was used as a base by Al Qaeda fighters. It therefore seemed clear that there was a link between failed states and terrorism. Failed states not only harboured crime and instability within their borders but were also a threat to international security – a fact brought home to the world in no uncertain terms on 11 September 2001. Nearly every African country had features that made infiltration by terrorist networks relatively easy: a weak, ineffective state that in many cases did not even control the entire territory, porous frontiers, corruption (with ample opportunities for bribery and possibly even connivance by the authorities), the presence of religious fanatics and other malcontents, and international indifference. The attacks on the US were one more reason to stop ignoring problem states.

The George W. Bush administration, accordingly, turned its attention to Africa quite soon after the attacks. It realised that in recent years the US had become less and less aware of what was going on in Africa, including potentially threatening developments. American intelligence services started making up for lost time. In the meantime, continuing unrest in the Middle East was giving West Africa (Nigeria and the surrounding area) new importance as an oil supplier to the United States. Bush decided the time was ripe to make an appearance in Africa. In June 2003, he set out on almost the same tour of the continent that his predecessor Bill Clinton had taken in 1998, visiting South Africa, Botswana, Uganda, Nigeria and Senegal, in that order. (Unlike Clinton, he did not stop in Rwanda.) The entire visit took only a few days and produced little that was new. Ties with the large, strategically significant countries of South Africa and Nigeria were strengthened.

Entirely in the American tradition, efforts to improve standards of living in Africa were left largely to private organisations, rather than government. Still, the US did pledge additional aid for well-performing African countries and set aside fifteen billion dollars (to be paid out over a five-year period) for a new campaign against AIDS in Africa. Due to the ties between the Bush administration and the religious right, most of this aid was offered to African countries that took the ABC approach: first sexual *abstinence* before marriage (A), then *be faithful* (B) to your partner after marriage and if that isn't manageable, use *condoms* (C). This last element sparked off heated debate in the United States, because many politicians were opposed to recommending the use of condoms. They were joined by the Roman Catholic church, which announced with medieval zeal that condoms were not effective against AIDS, because the virus was too small and could slip through the rubber. In Africa and around the world, the quality of the measures against AIDS remained shockingly low. As a result, millions more died.

The United States had no new approach to failing and failed states, though these states had formed the main motive for its renewed interest in Africa because of their possible connection with terrorism. In 2003 the US refused to lead an international peace operation in Liberia, to the chagrin of the African countries that were sending troops there and the European countries with a military presence in the region (the UK and France were playing a central role in Sierra Leone and Ivory Coast respectively). Saddled with numerous military commitments around the world, Washington stuck to its policy of not sending ground troops to Africa. Without the military support of the world's only superpower, confronting Africa's major crises head-on became quite a complex proposition. Western countries trained and funded African countries and organisations so that they could take part in peace operations; the West African regional organisation ECOWAS was especially active in this area. In addition, Western powers sometimes sent troops of their own. The UN also played a prominent role in African peace missions.

These efforts were generally hampered by limited appreciation of the problems afflicting states in West and Central Africa (as well as Somalia). In areas where state structures were meagre or absent, the international community usually pinned its hopes for renewed stability and state development on forging agreements between local leaders through the right mix of pressure and support. However, these leaders could best be compared to warlords. Each one had his own band of young people, supplied with weapons and bereft of prospects. The leaders aimed chiefly to enrich themselves and to defend or expand their own authority. Their impoverished supporters had little on their minds but survival. Concepts such as the public interest played no role at all.

Most warlords were glad to take part in a peace process and a transitional government, as long as it gave them access to the public purse and international aid. But after the elections that every peace agreement called for, some leaders stayed in government and others had to go. Around the same time, the flow of international aid started to slow down. The losers of the elections would find themselves cut off from their sources of income and unable to appease their supporters. The obvious thing for them to do was to take up arms again. A state that has been destroyed can probably only be rebuilt with much deeper and longer-lasting commitment from the international community. Ordinary economic activity must be set in motion before elections are held, so that legitimate sources of income are available. In reality, international donors were not prepared to make this kind of commitment, though they had recently realised that they needed to be intensively involved in reconstruction for at least three to five years to set a country on the right track.

The international community was also uncertain how to approach African countries that were doing fairly well. The Millennium Development Goals supposedly made it clear where these countries should be headed (see chapter 9, pp. 285-286). There was also some theoretical consensus about how to help them along; donors had agreed to work within the general framework of the so-called Poverty Reduction Strategy Papers that each African country had drafted. However, there was pervasive doubt about whether the millennium goals were realistic for Africa. In practice, development assistance took almost every conceivable form.

One of donors' aims was to gradually improve Africans' access to rich-country markets. African production levels were sometimes responsive to these measures. The American trade initiative mentioned above boosted textile production in Africa, and when Europe became more open to African exporters, production of sugar increased. Even so, poor countries in other parts of the world often drew much greater benefit from new trade opportunities than the relatively uncompetitive African countries. This was especially true when it came to products with added value.

Direct aid to African countries, which had been provided in various forms since the 1960s, had achieved many small-scale successes. Its effect, however, was often quick to fade. Activities aimed at long-term improvement of the standard of living seemed prone to failure in the African environment, for numerous reasons discussed elsewhere in this book. The main hurdles included the policies and governance of African authorities, which were as poor as ever. Africa's state institutions worked badly, if at all. Moreover, there was little reason to expect that African leaders would do much to improve the lives of their people, since any significant reform would eat into their own status and income.

The fundamental obstacle posed by the elites became clearer and clearer as time went on. But what was a donor to do? Try to make African states work better? Or try to manoeuvre around the state entirely, in an attempt to tap into forces more favourable to development? The latter course might involve promoting local NGOs and creating new opportunities for the private sector in Africa. Some thought that civil society and business could counterbalance the power of the state, forcing it to do its job better and perhaps bringing greater balance to African societies.

This theory is intimately bound up with the role that the middle class had played in European state formation, and later in Asia. While European elites pursued their own narrow interests and the impoverished masses could not make themselves heard, it was the middle class that was able to represent the national or public interest, being made up of reasonably educated people who earned a living independently of the state. Taxes on their income funded state activities, and in exchange they demanded that the state perform its basic tasks adequately, because the continued prosperity of the middle class depended on public services: law enforcement, the protection of legal certainty, the provision of physical infrastructure, education, health care and so forth. In almost every part of the world that had achieved true development, the middle class and the state had spurred each other on to greater achievements.

This has not happened in Africa, because almost no countries have a powerful middle class. What are the chances that a 'civil society' promoted and funded by external forces could play such a role? The previous chapter (pp. 294-295) noted the contrast between African and Western civil-society organisations. There is an equally stark contrast between African civil society as a whole and the middle classes that played a role in the development of the wealthy Western countries. In the West, the middle class formed the foundation of the state by virtue of the taxes it paid, while Africa's civil-society organisations are not fundamental in any sense. And because these organisations often receive at least part of their income from non-African sources, their ties to their own states are fairly casual.

A final point: civil society is fragmented and, in Africa, often divided along ethnic or religious lines. African founders of civil-society organisations (and, after democratisation, new political parties) have tended to have other goals in mind than strengthening the fabric of their nation. They sometimes even pose an additional threat to stability, especially in states that have fallen into severe decline. In West Africa in particular, states may be endangered by the rise of Islam, including radical Islamism, along with fanatical Christian sects. If Africa's current state system continues to weaken, the dividing lines between Islam and Christianity may well determine where new national borders are drawn. Religious organisations in Africa are more likely to undermine than uphold existing states, especially if international tensions between radical Islam and the West continue to rise.

For all these reasons, it is probably wiser to look to the private sector as the basis of an African middle class. Substantial growth among businesses could allow people to escape patronage networks by providing an alternative source of income. Taxation of that income could also keep the state going. To protect the private sector and expand it where possible, businesses would then start demanding that the state provide public services for the benefit of society as a whole.

This rosy picture seems unlikely to become a reality any time soon. Apart from a few multinationals dealing in oil or other primary commodities, the international business community has kept its distance from Africa. It is difficult for African entrepreneurs to make much progress on their own, since they are caught between their family and friends on one side, clamouring for their share of any profits, and political and military leaders on the other, as eager as any mafioso to collect 'protection' money. Under such conditions, it would be difficult for anybody to build up an economically sound business of any real magnitude.

Still, Africa's civil-society organisations and businesses should not be entirely dismissed. Since the Cold War, African societies have been exceptionally dynamic, and many of the changes have been promising. Civil society has grown rapidly and the economic trend has improved, from decline in the 1970s and 1980s to stagnation since the 1990s. International support has stimulated both the economy and the expansion of civil society. It is too early to say whether this will lead to new social patterns and ultimately to better state performance. Nor is the verdict in on direct international support to African states, aimed at improving policies and governance. The global community can influence African societies by giving aid, but we cannot expect external forces to play a decisive role.

Since the continent's independence, the centre of gravity in Africa's patronage networks has gradually shifted from the international to the domestic sphere. If, as I suggested in the introduction, we should see Africa's elites as spiders in two webs, than it is the strength and the shape of their domestic webs that determine the fortunes of their states. Across Africa, those webs are extremely fragile and have been known to give way entirely. Relations with rich countries affect African states and their internal webs in both intended and unintended ways, for better and for worse. One unintended effect of international aid to states, for instance, is to stabilise patronage networks. We can see it in a positive or a negative light; it fends off total chaos, but perpetuates structures that hinder development. The power of good examples should be kept in mind, along with the more general need for African countries to exchange information and keep in close contact with representatives of the modern West. The effects of such activities vary from country to country and can probably never be fully enumerated, let alone measured. What is at stake is the drastic, qualitative transformation of African societies, in ways that encourage lasting increases in production and thereby set true development in motion.

CONCLUSIONS

The slow surge
of the past

In analysing events in Africa since the Cold War we have frequently

had to delve into the past – in some cases right back into the precolonial period. This historical approach to African problems is unusual. Yet there is a growing realisation that we
cannot fully comprehend contemporary African developments if we look no further than
the colonial era and the decades that have followed. In the twenty-first century, the period
of European colonialism in Africa is starting to recede from view. However important this
period may have been for Africa, it is more and more often recognised as just one episode
in a much longer history with persistent features and patterns. In order to understand
Africa's present-day situation, we must look not only at outside influences but also at long-
term, indigenous African elements.

This brings us close to what the French historian Fernand Braudel has called the *longue
durée* of history – the long, slow surge of the past, with events like ripples on the surface.[336]
The term is often understood to refer to socioeconomic structures, with political developments as the ripples. Indeed, this has been the approach taken in the few cases in which
Braudel's theories have been applied to African history. Bayart, Ellis and Hibou, for instance,
use a similar classification in their recent work. Abandoning the familiar division into 'precolonial', 'colonial' and 'postcolonial', they have adopted a classification mainly based on
economic criteria. They describe the period from after the depression of the 1930s to the
1970s, which was one of economic growth. This was followed by a period of economic
decline, which is still in progress.[337] This essentially logical basic system of classification
can be augmented by bringing in changes in political structures, so that we can better identify the underlying features of modern African history. This is where Africa's states come
in.

Africa's formal political structures have remained more or less intact since independence, but the way in which states function – or malfunction – has certainly changed. Since
independence, all African states have to a greater or lesser extent been gradually hollowed
out from within. These gradual political changes can also be seen as part of the *longue durée*
of African history. In this context, politics should not be seen as an isolated phenomenon,
but in relation to other domains, such as culture, the economy and social structures. The
erosion of African states since independence is mainly due to age-old African principles of
political culture, political economy and social relations. They date back to well before the
days of European colonialism in Africa, although they were sometimes profoundly influenced by it.

These age-old African features had a strong influence on the workings of the continent's states, in the sense that they made state institutions work differently – less effec-

tively by contemporary, non-African standards. I have referred to this interaction between the institutional legacy of the colonial period and its African environment as the Africanisation of the state.

The specific principles, or features, at work have been discussed at numerous points in this book. A first, crucial set of features could collectively be termed premodernism. These are the characteristics that prevent change, development or progress from taking place. Premodernism can be regarded as an interaction between politics, culture, economics and social relations, directed at maintaining the status quo. Although premodern systems involve a static perspective on the world and society, these systems can in many ways actually be quite dynamic – at least with respect to events, the ripples of history. Nevertheless, the end result for the population will never be substantially different; such societies continue to have low levels of both production and consumption.

In premodern systems, change was not valued, since economic growth was not an end in itself, as it is in modern societies. Instead, investment was seen in terms of redistributing existing resources. In practice, this often meant redistributing resources through the state, in the form of money, jobs or other favours. The emphasis was on consumption rather than production. There was no general awareness of a link between consumption and modern industrial production, which requires a certain work ethic, organisation and discipline. The African attitude towards modern consumption sometimes seemed more like that of the cargo cults of the Pacific Ocean, in which the acquisition of commodities was linked with religion and magic rather than production.

African entrepreneurs do not generally have a chance to build up a profitable, stable business. As soon as they make a profit, people close to them force them to share it. If the business and the entrepreneur's motivation survive this setback, powerful politicians show up to claim their cut. Any business with good prospects is absorbed, and eventually smothered, by political networks. Business decisions are made on a political rather than economic basis, keeping African economies uncompetitive. In the age of globalisation, this is a true disaster.

In the late twentieth century, as competition was becoming more and more important in other parts of the world, Africa's lingering preindustrial habits brought about relative decline. After 1970, Africa lagged further and further behind the rest of the world. This led to mounting instability in large parts of the continent around the millennium.

At the heart of Africa's societies we find a second important feature: the social structure known as patronage. Interpersonal relationships in Africa stress individuals rather than formal roles. Through their personal bonds, individuals form networks. At the cores of these networks are prominent persons ('patrons') surrounded by less prominent ones (their 'clients'). Patrons have social status and possess the power and resources to grant their clients favours, such as jobs. Links between patrons and clients are informal in nature, but because patrons nearly always make use of state power and government resources, their ties with clients often take on a formal character as well. Informal ties and networks are the reality behind otherwise meaningless official titles and hierarchies. Ties of dependence between patrons and clients create a social structure and afford the weakest in society some protection, but are also a source of corruption and an obstacle to democratisation. There are no general standards of conduct that apply to everyone. Furthermore, there are no mechanisms allowing clients to monitor their patrons' conduct. Patronage systems are therefore difficult to reconcile with the rule of law. They undermine the work of government and people's trust in the state.

There have been patron-client relationships in Africa since time immemorial. They were a natural response to the uncertainty and insecurity of premodern life. During the colonial period they grew stronger, because the colonial authorities usually dealt only with the patrons in local African structures. However, such patrons were sometimes hard to find, for there was a broad spectrum of political systems in precolonial Africa. These can roughly be divided into organised states (of varying size) and societies with no rigid formal structure. Where the colonial system of indirect rule could not immediately make use of the 'natural leader' of an existing African political structure, others grabbed their chance to become 'traditional chiefs' in the service of the colonial authorities.

Colonialism had various implications for patronage systems in Africa. First of all, they grew bigger. Initially, patronage was often limited to local networks within extended families, but in the colonial era these networks tended to expand, eventually reaching the distant capital of the colony. Besides expanding, the system grew stronger, thanks to the power of the colonial rulers. In colonial days, leaders (patrons) had derived their authority from being accepted by their subjects. There was an understanding, usually tacit, between patrons and clients. The situation resembled medieval European feudal systems, in which both lords and vassals knew where they stood. The balance of power was extremely unequal, but everyone depended on everyone else. A patron's authority, like a lord's, depended on his underlings' support, which was granted in return for protection and other favours. It was understandings such as these (whose terms varied from place to place) that kept many African political systems in equilibrium – an early version of what we would now call checks and balances.

This equilibrium was disrupted by colonialism. African leaders' power came to depend on agreements with the colonial rulers rather than with their subjects. If a local ruler's people revolted, the colonial authorities did what was necessary to keep him in power – provided, of course, that they wanted to continue making use of him. African rulers negotiated with the colonial authorities rather than with their own people. The indigenous African systems of checks and balances faded away. In much of Africa, colonialism destroyed local sociopolitical structures and made it even easier for African rulers to take an authoritarian attitude towards their subjects (which was already a tradition in many parts of the continent). In the preceding centuries, in most parts of the world rulers' power had gradually been reduced by the separation of powers and systems of checks and balances, but in Africa the trend was just the opposite.

As African rulers gained more control over their subjects, it reinforced a view of power that is now widespread in Africa, namely that power is all-pervasive. Postcolonial patron-client relationships may in some sense be governed by tacit understandings, but if so, then one of these understandings is that the patron can exercise power in whatever area he chooses (political, economic, social, etc.). There is no separation between the public and private spheres. Power is generally seen as sacred, even if the right to interpret the spiritual world is often reserved for individuals other than the ruler.

However, all this should be seen in perspective. Almost every type of political organisation could be found in Africa at one time. Moreover, the idea that power is all-pervasive is by no means solely African. The fact that it has become so dominant in postcolonial

Africa is not simply due to internal factors – colonialism is again very much to blame. In African eyes, the European colonial authorities had unlimited, all-pervading power. The first leaders of independent Africa inherited both traditions, African and colonial. In the years after independence the tendency for power to become concentrated, in combination with a social system based on patronage, caused African states to develop in their own unique way. Powerful networks of patron-client relationships sprang up, each with just one person at the apex. This pyramid structure cut across formal relationships between state institutions and obeyed a logic of its own. Informal networks spread throughout society.

It is tempting to add yet another feature to the list of constants in African history: the tenacity of subnational, 'ethnic' feelings, which have even grown stronger over time in some cases. These feelings undoubtedly have their origins in the precolonial period, but it is now also clear to what extent they were reinforced and frozen in place by the European colonial authorities.[338] In present-day Africa, ethnicity is still an important factor in the way states function. In itself, the existence of various levels of identity and loyalty (to one's country, province, town or village, neighbourhood and family) is a normal phenomenon found on all continents, but in some African countries ethnic affiliations are so strong that they undercut national identity. Yet the strength of ethnic ties seems to be not so much a part of Africanisation as one of its effects – one that has become more apparent as national structures have grown weaker.

The aforementioned features, to which still others might be added, continue to play an important part in the functioning of African societies.[339] They were not taken into account when more-or-less modern states were introduced, on a limited scale, in the colonial era. Structures were quite simply transplanted from the totally alien European context to the African one. When the Europeans left, these states had to fend for themselves in an African setting which had been disrupted by colonialism. The foreign body that was the European state was increasingly influenced by African ways of life. Although, with the exception of Somalia, none of these states actually ceased to exist, many came close. Especially after the end of the Cold War, as the influence of foreign powers waned, states became more 'Africanised', 'traditionalised' or 'premodernised'.

These terms – 'Africanisation', 'traditionalisation', and 'premodernisation' - should be used with the utmost caution, for what exactly do they mean? The features described above are far from uniquely African, for they can also be observed elsewhere in the world. Furthermore, they are not entirely due to indigenous African influences, but are also to some extent a colonial legacy. It was the colonial rulers who, when they left, handed over the reins of government to small, Westernised black national elites that were fairly isolated from their own African societies. In colonial states, just as in the states that replaced them, there had been no separation of powers. Power had been concentrated in the capital, and political and economic interests had been intertwined. These problems of the colonial state were exacerbated by the new African rulers.

Africa is so large and varied that not one of the features mentioned can fairly be said to be found in every African country or people. Moreover, the further we go back into the past, the harder it becomes to tell which features were most common.[340] Europeans have 'traditionally' been quick to call various African phenomena traditions. The British historian Eric Hobsbawm has even argued that in the initial period of European imperialism, from about 1870 to 1914, the Europeans 'invented' traditions for the indigenous peoples they governed.

Onto these conquered but unfamiliar societies the colonial rulers projected rigid characteristics which not only suited their ideological and administrative purposes but also acted as a psychological counterweight to far-reaching changes in European society that were creating a sense of loss and uprootedness.[341] While Hobsbawm's statement indicates the need for the utmost caution when identifying 'African traditions', it does not rule out the existence of African ways of life that truly do predate colonialism.

It is only logical that characteristic African notions of identity, loyalty, power, human relationships and society – notions that are probably centuries old – should continue to influence the states that the Europeans left behind. From this point of view, many current African developments make more sense. Presumably, the main significance of African independence was that it set off the Africanisation of politics. It was a turning point; from then on, the continent was headed in a new direction. The subsequent end of the Cold War served to bring the Africanisation process more clearly to the fore, but 1989 was not another turning point – Africa was still moving along the same path.

The position of African elites was the direct result of colonisation and, above all, decolonisation. The black national elites were given power over the new state structures. Apart from a Western education and links with the former colonial authorities, this was often the only thing they could rely on for survival. Nor did African countries have politically independent economic elites of the kind found in Western, Latin American and many Asian countries. Only a few, such as Ivory Coast, Kenya and Botswana, had middle classes with an economic base of their own. In most cases, the elites' only possession was the state, which they exploited for their own economic benefit. Potential political opponents likewise had no independent economic base. The only way they could afford a career in politics was to eat from the government trough. Thus the political economy of independent African states did not allow the emergence of a pluriform elite. The often inexperienced political parties were all assimilated into the ruling party, which ultimately coincided with the state and the economy.

These changes in the structure of African politics and society took place in almost every African country in the 1960s and 1970s. The rhetoric of socialism, anticolonialism and revolution, then a familiar part of international discourse, was often used to explain them, both by the Africans involved and by Western observers. However, this was a distortion of African reality, in which no such modern socioeconomic forces were at work. The roots of the process lay elsewhere – in Africa itself.

The features described above as being widespread in African societies were in keeping with the direction taken by African states under their new rulers. State institutions began to operate more in accordance with African society and culture, and African states became increasingly remote from the ideal of the modern Western state. By the turn of the century, this insidious process had more or less completely eroded state structures. Some countries – Somalia, Congo, Liberia and Sierra Leone – existed in little more than name. These were extreme but by no means exceptional cases; the disintegration of the state could be observed throughout Africa.

This erosion of the inherited 'modern' state followed a fairly consistent pattern, which after about twenty-five years culminated in general dysfunction, along with financial and moral bankruptcy. States that gained their independence around 1960 reached this low point in the 1980s, or in some cases around 1990. Countries that became independent later followed the same pattern, only with a time lag. The Portuguese colonies became independent in the mid-1970s, but as a result of the ferocious struggles for independence and the ensuing civil wars there was little of the states left. Far more significant was the delayed independence of Zimbabwe, Namibia and South Africa. The many Europeans who had settled in these countries made the situation there different from that in the rest of Africa. In these countries, colonialism can be said to have survived longer, in the form of apartheid. Only when apartheid was abolished and power was transferred to black governments could the state begin to be Africanised. In Zimbabwe this transition took place in 1980, so that the process reached its natural culmination in the opening years of the twenty-first century. This was reflected in President Mugabe's authoritarian style of leadership. Zimbabwe was followed ten to fifteen years later by Namibia and South Africa, where there is already considerable evidence of Africanisation.

From the 1980s onwards, there were national as well as international attempts to change the adverse situation that had been developing in African states since independence. The scale of these attempts grew ever greater in the 1990s. International donors focused on improving African policies and governance. They believed that African states had to put their financial houses in order, separate politics from the economy so that a private sector could emerge, introduce separation of powers as the basis for the rule of law, place checks on power through democratisation, fight corruption in order to make the state more efficient, and develop or strengthen state institutions. A large-scale operation began, with the aim of rebuilding Africa's states.

Why Africa failed

Attempts to restore African states to working order were largely the result of pressure from the international community, but were also backed by groups in the countries themselves. This shows just how interconnected African and international developments were, as we have seen throughout this book. However, if we look at the reasons for the lack of development in Africa since independence, it would be simplistic to conclude that internal and international factors were equally responsible. The general theories described in the introduction – modernisation theory and dependency theory – blamed the failure of African and other developing countries to develop (at least so far) on internal and external factors respectively. At the start of the twenty-first century we must conclude that, despite the lasting importance of the international environment, external factors cannot have been the overriding cause.

Dependency theory (including the latest version, antiglobalism) has proved untenable. Supposing for the sake of argument that international factors truly are chiefly an obstacle to development, many developing countries have still managed to overcome them. At no time in history were so many people on so many continents so well off as at the beginning of the third millennium AD. Prosperity came within reach of all parts of the world. Compare an arbitrarily selected pair of countries, one in Africa and one in Asia: Zambia and South Korea, for instance. When the Zambians became independent in 1964, they were on average twice as wealthy as the South Koreans. By the turn of the century, the South Koreans were, on average, a full twenty-seven times as rich as the Zambians.[342] Or take Kenya and Singapore, which thirty years ago were just about equally poor. Now Singaporeans earn an average of about 24,000 euros a year, while the average Kenyan earns about 340 euros a year, or one-seventieth of that amount.[343] If we take any comparable pair of countries, one African and one Asian, and look at what has happened to them over the past few decades, the difference is always stunning, and the Asian country always comes out on top. It would be absurd to attribute such huge differences to the international economic environment, which was essentially the same for all these countries.

It is often pointed out that, for political reasons, some Asian countries, especially South Korea and Taiwan, received much more aid than African countries. This is true to some extent, although African countries did not generally suffer from a lack of aid. The crucial factor, however, was what was done with the money, how profitably it was put to use. Here lay the great difference between Asia and Africa. Domestic circumstances in African countries were such that extra money would not have made any essential difference. A case in point is Nigeria, which for decades had several billion US dollars a year of 'extra' income from oil. The Nigerian elite became both extremely rich and extremely large by African standards. The result was a host of states within the Nigerian federation, each with a local elite and clientelist networks of its own, and internecine power struggles. This brought about chronic domestic instability, which led the army to stage repeated coups in an attempt to preserve national unity. The billions of extra dollars did nothing at all to raise ordinary people's living standards. When Nigeria became independent in 1960, about twenty-five per cent of the population was below the poverty line. By 2000 this figure had risen to around seventy per cent.

In an attempt to provide more palatable reasons for Africa's failure – factors that Africans 'could do nothing about' – people often mention the borders that were drawn rather arbitrarily by colonial rulers, sometimes while sitting in their capital cities in Europe. Naturally, a border that cut through an area inhabited by a particular group caused all kinds of problems for the people affected as well as for the authorities (even though the border was often very easy to cross). However, such problems cannot seriously be put forward as obstacles to statehood. Other parts of the world have shown that nationhood and development are perfectly possible even in geographical units whose borders are the result of historical contingency.[344]

Sometimes other geographical or environmental circumstances are cited, such as the fact that a country is landlocked or that it is not easy for people to live in a hot, humid climate. Yet numerous examples prove that this is of little relevance to a country's ability to modernise. If such theories were true, landlocked nations such as Switzerland and Austria or ones with extremely harsh climates, such as the Scandinavian countries, would be doomed to remain poor, whereas in fact they are the wealthiest countries in Europe.

The example of China shows to what extent domestic circumstances – especially the interaction between politics and culture – can determine a country's chances of modernisation. People in the West had long felt that the Chinese should be capable of becoming prosperous, given some of their more striking cultural characteristics such as industriousness, inquisitiveness, organisation, motivation and an emphasis on education. Chinese people living outside China showed the world what these virtues could achieve. In China itself, however, people could not take advantage of them, for the country's sociopolitical system was still premodern, still geared to maintaining the status quo.[345] This was true not only of the Empire but also of the Republic and the People's Republic, right through the twentieth century. It was only in the 1980s, when the state under Deng Xiaoping relaxed its grip on the economy and allowed free markets to develop, that the real Chinese revolution took place. These reforms fell on fertile soil, and since then China has changed dramatically. The country's socioeconomic development has produced not only victims, but also very many winners, and economic growth is now taking place at an astonishing rate. The idea that this might be due to the international economic environment or to China's geographical location or climate is baseless. The main contributing factors have been internal ones, both political and cultural.

So what can we conclude about Africa from this comparison with developments elsewhere? The continent has changed dramatically in all kinds of ways, but never truly modernised. Of course, this does not mean that Africa can never modernise – the potential to do so is probably universal – but internal factors have prevented this potential from being realised. The main reason for Africa's disappointing level of development is the Africanisation of colonial organisational structures. This insidious process, which was discussed in the previous section, took place almost everywhere in Africa and was largely unaffected by the international context.

The image of buildings from Africa's colonial days – mansions, office buildings, railway stations or hotels – that have succumbed to their surroundings is quite familiar, mainly from films and literature. Decades after the original owners abandoned it, the structure still stands, a mere skeleton, the wood stripped away, trees growing through the roof. Its physical remains are just a shell concealing a new function, one better suited to its tropical setting. Africa has taken possession of the alien intruder. Whole families live in what were once hotel rooms, clay huts have appeared on the balconies, the entryway has become a marketplace.

This process – call it 'Africanisation' – has affected more than just the material legacy of colonialism. The architecture of the state was also left in an African environment at the time of independence, and has undergone a similar process. The remains of colonial institutions – ministries, parliaments and courts – are still standing, but over the years they too have become mere shells, concealing an African reality that has taken possession of them and turned them to its own purposes. Outsiders dealing with African states would do well to remember: what you see is not what you get.

But even if the Africanisation of Africa's states is at the heart of the continent's development problems, might it not still be logical to blame the outside world – more specifically, Europe? After all, if European countries had not introduced colonial states to the continent in the first place, then no process of Africanisation could have taken place. However, the presence of modern, Western-type states is not in itself a development problem. Quite the contrary; results from other continents suggest that the presence of modern states with Western features is essential for development. Despite the unfortunate circumstances under which modern states were introduced in Africa, it was not those states but their African surroundings that caused problems for development.

In many parts of the world, the expansion of European power over the past several centuries, through colonialism or otherwise, set off local reactions that eventually promoted development. In Africa, however, it did not. For some reason, the continent was not receptive to it. That suggests Africa would also have been highly unlikely to have modernised on its own, without its involuntary exposure to European ways. It might have been a better place in many ways than it is now – more in balance, with greater self-esteem and dignity – but it would not be better off in a material sense. Colonialism left many scars in Africa, but it did not make the continent poorer. Instead, maybe it can be blamed for failing to put Africa on the road of material progress.

Plenty of change, but little progress

In order to understand recent African history we need to focus on internal factors. If we think of the new African elite as a spider in two webs, two networks (one internal, the other external), we must look more closely at how those elites interact with their internal networks. How do the new African elites run their countries?

With a few exceptions, African leaders have done poorly – not for themselves, but for their countries. Since this has been such a widespread phenomenon, there is no point in seeking explanations based on personal failings. The causes were systemic and lay in a combination of African sociocultural features and the historical background. A great deal has already been said in this book about sociocultural features. Domestic power, which is often seen as sacred and all-pervading, is based on extensive patronage networks. Rulers derive their support from 'clients', people who are tied to them by virtue of services rendered. This is also true of the security forces (the army and the police), whose members have personal ties with their leaders rather than formal, functional ones. The purpose of this system is to preserve the status quo, i.e. the authority of the leaders. These essentially premodern systems of political economy are thus geared to internal stability rather than development. In an age of globalisation, in which competition is increasingly important, they are causing Africa to lag further and further behind the rest of the world.

Africa's postcolonial leaders had no tradition or culture of leadership with its own sense of *noblesse oblige*, of rights and corresponding duties. They were not simply Africans, but also products of the recently departed colonial regime. These rulers, these new elites, did not see the state primarily as a means of developing their country but as a means of securing their own livelihoods. The democratic systems introduced by the colonial rulers at the last minute could not be maintained, since the opposition had no life of its own. Rulers had little difficulty in persuading members of the opposition to defect to the ruling party, where they could eat from the government trough. Only a few years after independence, Africa's originally pluriform political systems had become one-party systems. At the same time as the opposition was neutralised, the economy was incorporated into the state. So-called socialist systems of state enterprises, marketing boards and tariffs were sources of income for rulers and also provided the wherewithal for maintaining patronage networks.

This interaction between culture and history – which left African countries with a quite characteristic kind of political economy – produced the results described in previous chapters: abuse of power, corruption, a sprawling, expensive and inefficient bureaucracy, low competitiveness, an insubstantial private sector, poor economic performance, etc. As the state and the economy deteriorated, rulers' positions became less secure. African political life was full of risks. Leaders tried to stay in power until they died of natural causes. Their rivals tried to unseat them; if they succeeded, the ex-ruler often risked jail or execution.

Under such circumstances, long-term goals such as the development of the country were of minor importance. To African rulers, 'staying afloat was more important than going somewhere.'[346] Apart from decolonisation throughout the continent, African countries met none of the goals that they had set themselves on gaining independence. Economic development, social justice and autonomy/autarky failed to materialise.

Government activities that were designed to keep the ruler safe (the army, the police and the numerous security services) or to maintain a flow of income from abroad (contacts with the international community) were the ones that survived longest. In areas that were of little personal interest to the rulers (such as infrastructure, health care and education), states provided fewer and fewer services. The structural adjustment programmes imposed by the World Bank and the IMF only reinforced this trend. Governments created an investment climate that was unattractive to businesses, whether big or small, domestic or foreign. The governments of many countries harassed their citizens in all kinds of ways. All in all, it was no wonder that people showed little or no trust in government – instead, their attitude was one of distrust and fear. African states made no appreciable contribution to their people's welfare, instead preventing progress. In the course of the 1980s it became clear that the development of African states in the years since independence had been a failure. The impact of these failing states on the development of the continent was catastrophic.

Ultimately even the army and the police began to operate less effectively in many places. Throughout the continent, cities became more unsafe and crime rates rose, here and there to the point of actually threatening national stability. Ineffective states were sometimes unable to withstand pressure from rebel groups, especially in countries with a wealth of natural resources. In Liberia and Sierra Leone, regimes collapsed into violent anarchy. Disintegration of government institutions and social structures in general was the most extreme symptom of state failure. The 1990s saw sporadic outbreaks of civil war which proved difficult to halt or even contain. This partly reflected the new international environment since the end of the Cold War. African regimes could no longer rely on backing from major foreign powers, but were more and more often forced to fend for themselves and were less and less capable of doing so.

The striking trends of the 1990s included not only increasing violence within countries, but also the rise of what was considered classic warfare in the rest of the world – conflict between states. This had been unheard of in Africa for almost a century – throughout the colonial period and the first three decades of independence. The independent African states had largely abided by the principle of noninterference in each other's domestic spheres, as laid down by the Organisation of African Unity (the forerunner of the African Union). However, the collapse of the Eastern Bloc and the relative disengagement of the major Western powers from Africa gave African countries new scope to concern themselves with one another's affairs. Eritrea and Ethiopia actually went to war, and numerous Central African countries became embroiled in military conflict, usually allying themselves with rebel groups in other countries. Conversely, internal hostilities in African countries always proved to have an international component. Around the turn of the millennium, violent conflict in Africa had become a complex mixture of old and new features.

Yet not all of Africa displayed this tendency to lapse further and further into anarchy and violence. Across the continent – from Botswana to Tanzania to Senegal – there were states that remained fairly stable throughout the four decades following independence. In addition to years of decline they also experienced years of relative prosperity. There were also countries such as Uganda and Mozambique, which proved capable of impressive recoveries after years of chaos and warfare. Among the almost fifty African states there was considerable variety in quality of governance, stability and living standards.

Immediately after the Cold War, thanks to structural reforms, Africa's economies appeared to be heading in the right direction, with average growth rates of 5 to 6 per cent by the mid-1990s. Thereafter, however, growth slumped to an average of just 2.5 per cent and remained there into the twenty-first century. This was more or less on a par with population growth, so Africans were not really moving forward. Admittedly, some countries did quite a bit better, but they were counterbalanced by countries whose per capita income continued to shrink. In the age of globalisation, in which competition was increasingly important, Africa completely failed to become more competitive in relation to other continents. Except for oil, its share of the traditionally important commodities markets for raw materials fell. Nor was it able to capture substantial segments of new markets, at least not legitimate ones. Its share of the illicit drug trade did increase sharply.[347] The agricultural sector was not modernised, and there was no appreciable development in trades or industry.[348] The continent drew little private investment, and the flow of international aid decreased. While globalisation had a deep and rapid impact on the rest of the world, Africa failed to integrate into the global economy. Instead, it became even more marginal.

It is natural to view Africa's current situation from one of two seemingly contradictory perspectives. From the first point of view, the dominant theme is failure, with states and other organisations malfunctioning all over the continent. This image comes to the fore whenever Africa is compared with other continents, which have made impressive progress in the past few decades. Africa has not modernised, and is lagging further and further behind the rest of the world. However, if we abandon this comparative perspective, a different image emerges – that of a continent which is proceeding in its own, African way. States that seemed to be malfunctioning from one point of view (based on Western standards) suddenly appear to be functioning properly, in African terms.[349] From this perspective, Africa looks premodern, with no more than scattered links to the rest of the twenty-first century world. While the international setting has changed dramatically, Africa seems to have remained more or less the same.

This may be partly true, but by and large it overlooks the immense changes that have taken place there. In the second half of the twentieth century, the once empty continent – traditionally the domain of large herds of wild animals – was gradually populated by humanity. What had been tiny villages in 1900 often became cities with over a million people by 2000. In the twenty-first century, there were actually more Africans living in urban areas than in rural ones. What is more, they were young; more than half of them were under eighteen. In the cities, many young Africans came into contact with Western-style education or became acquainted with the outside world in other ways. Their respect for elders and for African traditions declined.[350] A gulf opened up between traditional African cultures and the world of young people longing to move forward. This caused intergenerational tension and many young people grew frustrated because modernisation was not taking place. Uprootedness and frustration formed an explosive mixture that led to chaos and misery through much of the continent. Mass migration, both internal and international, and above all the spreading AIDS epidemic disrupted African communities even further.

AIDS raged on uncontrolled. The message that had successfully reduced transmission of the disease in Western countries – prevention through safe sex – failed to hit home in Africa. There were various reasons for this, the main one probably being the strict African taboo on talking about sex. With a very few exceptions, African leaders failed to shoulder their responsibility for breaking this taboo. Some even sent the debate off in irrelevant directions, for example by questioning the cause of AIDS or overemphasising the importance of medicines, while the only thing that could really control the epidemic was prevention. The resulting confusion allowed AIDS to keep spreading swiftly, with disastrous consequences.

African states were incapable of tackling the continent's many problems effectively. The first to realise this were the international financial institutions, who discovered in the 1980s just how serious a financial mess the continent was in. A vast amount of money had been poured into Africa but had made no positive economic or social impact. On the contrary, conditions in Africa were deteriorating and its debts were increasing. There was clearly no point in continuing to support the bankrupt continent unless changes were made. In return for new loans, the World Bank and the IMF insisted that Africa must become more efficient. Just as elsewhere in the world, aid would have to yield returns. Ineffectual governments had to be thoroughly reformed, the private sector had to be promoted and measures were needed to encourage liberalisation and freer markets. The first results, however, were mostly disappointing. It became ever clearer that Africa's economic performance could not be seen in isolation from its domestic politics. In the absence of political change, economic reforms could not be carried through forcefully enough to have a substantial effect.

The breakthrough in the political sphere came at the end of the Cold War, when the worldwide wave of democratisation reached Africa. Encouraged by spectacular changes elsewhere, Africans took to the streets to call their leaders to account for the sorry state of their countries. Bowing to strong pressure, both domestic and international, numerous regimes agreed to liberalise their countries' political systems. One-party states were transformed into pluriform systems, and political parties and civil-society organisations sprang up like mushrooms. International donors also began to focus on using aid to improve the political situation in African countries. According to the development theory that prevailed after the Cold War, aid could only have a lasting impact in an environment of good governance and good policies. Where that was present, aid could be channelled through the government. Where it was not, donors were forced to limit themselves to small-scale activities in cooperation with civil society, in the hope that this would have some local impact. In places where the state had largely disintegrated, top priority was given to restoring state institutions.

In the mid-1990s, the combination of political change and gradually accelerating economic growth made Africa's future look a little brighter. South African leaders propagated the ideal of an African renaissance. Yet the mood soon darkened again, especially when extensive fighting broke out in Central Africa and the Horn. In many countries, moreover, the process of political and economic reform encountered major hurdles. It became clear that the road to better conditions in Africa would be a long and arduous one, assuming substantial improvement was even possible. Africa's position in the globalising world was marginal, and without further political and economic reform the continent would find it impossible to capture a larger share of the global economy. Young Africans were aware how hopeless the outlook was, and many attempted to migrate – the further from Africa the better. Others tried to build some kind of life for themselves, but hope often gave way to frustration. It was only a short step to violence and crime.

At the beginning of the twenty-first century, the idea of an African renaissance is a mirage to most Africans. Their daily lives are marked by poverty with little hope of change. They do not usually trust their leaders, let alone respect them. A sense of belonging, of community, is sought elsewhere – on a small scale among one's own 'ethnic' group, or on a larger scale as a member of one of the world religions. Islam, above all, is a magnet for malcontents. It is increasingly becoming a religion of protest against the West, the international system and modernisation, which many feel has brought Africa nothing but misery.

The postcolonial state: a comparison between continents

This book attempts to explain Africa's current problems by examining the interaction, in the years since independence, between the state structures left behind by the departing colonial rulers and certain central features of Africa's political, economic and social culture. Interaction between foreign and indigenous elements is not unique to Africa. The question then arises whether the Africanisation of the inherited colonial states is a concept whose relevance extends beyond Africa. What implications does Africa's experience have for other continents that have had to deal with European expansion? Obviously it is beyond the scope of this book to subject the whole world to thorough scrutiny. However, a brief glance at other continents may help make things clearer. The focus will be on the extent to which the European colonial powers introduced new state structures into their colonies, the 'cultural distance' between these structures and the local population and, where relevant, the role of the local elites that took charge of the newly independent states.

North America, Australia and northern Asia (Siberia) can be dealt with very briefly. There the indigenous population – native North Americans, Aborigines and the local Siberian population – were so thoroughly subjugated and massacred by the invading European colonisers that they were no longer able to influence the subsequent development of the state, which hence became totally European in form.

Latin America was conquered and colonised by the Spaniards and Portuguese in the sixteenth century, and the majority of the indigenous population fell prey to disease or warfare during this tragic period of European invasion. The survivors and their descendants were too few in number, and too powerless, to leave any mark on the development of the state. The cultural distance between indigenous Indian societies and the new states in Latin America may well have been as large as that between African societies and the colonial states in Africa, but the ratio of European settlers to local inhabitants was fundamentally different. All over Latin America, European colonists and their *mestizo* descendants were soon in the majority. In most of Africa, on the other hand, there was no appreciable settlement by Europeans, so that when the colonial powers officially departed, the original inhabitants 'had the place to themselves' once more and were able to exert considerable influence on the state structures that had been left behind. In the parts of Africa where

Europeans did settle on a fairly large scale (South Africa and Rhodesia/Zimbabwe), 'colonial influences' preserved state structures in their original form longer, delaying the Africanisation process by about twenty years in the case of Zimbabwe and thirty-five years in the case of South Africa.

Only in Latin American countries where the indigenous population formed a large proportion of the total, as in the Andes and Central America, did serious problems of state organisation arise, occasionally summoning the spectre of state failure. However, the state was never actually threatened or even challenged. In general, the makeup of the population in Latin America was such that the new state structures had little to fear from the indigenous inhabitants. Institutions could be set up without regard to local cultural or social conditions. Because the European invasion of the southern part of the western hemisphere took place so early (the first major phase of European colonisation there began right after the Middle Ages), the borders of the new states were largely determined by the physical and geographical features of the conquered regions. By 1600, less than a hundred years after the invasion began, the contours of the states that were to cast off Spanish rule two centuries later were already clearly visible in the patterns of habitation and political organisation of the conquered territories.[351] The history of these clearly demarcated states thus goes back some four centuries. The colonists and their descendants have remained in power the whole of that time. Border disputes and other local conflicts have sometimes led to fighting (between Ecuador and Peru, Peru and Chile, Chile and Argentina, Argentina and Paraguay and so on), but these hostilities have merely strengthened the states involved and contributed to their emergence as nations. At the turn of the millennium, in the age of globalisation, a number of these Latin American states began to forge serious cooperative bonds, one especially noteworthy example being Mercosur.

The picture in Asia was quite different and much more varied, even if we leave aside the parts that belonged to the former Soviet Union (Central Asia) and the Asian parts of the Middle East. The continent is so vast and has such a large population that it can hardly be treated as a single unit. However, one important characteristic of almost the entire continent is the decisive part played by indigenous cultures and state structures. These were so powerful that European colonialism was only able to gain more than a foothold in a very few places. Asian countries were certainly influenced by Western encroachment in all kinds of ways, but they did not allow Western state structures to be imposed on them. In essence, most of today's Asian countries were already in existence several centuries ago. European colonialism scarcely caused a break in Asian history. Only in a few parts of Asia, particularly in the Southeast Asian archipelago, were Western countries eventually (in the era of modern colonialism, around 1900) able to leave their mark on the development of the state. Malaysia and above all Indonesia are cases in point.

If we want to find a region of Asia where this book's thesis about Africa might also apply, Indonesia is perhaps the most likely candidate. The modern Indonesian state is a Dutch colonial invention.[352] When it became independent, the entire colony from Sabang in the west to Merauke in the east passed into the hands of a new, Dutch-educated elite. Most Europeans left. The political system underwent turbulent changes, and under President Suharto it reached a new equilibrium based on thoroughgoing centralisation and authoritarian rule. The functioning of the state was increasingly dictated by local cultural and social conditions.[353] Just as in Africa, economic decline brought the country's problems to the surface. However, Indonesia's decline in the closing years of the twentieth century was quite different from the erosion of state and administrative structures in Africa. Whereas Africa suffered from insidious, structural problems which got worse in the 1970s and 1980s, for Indonesia those same decades were a time of stability and economic growth. After that period of prosperity, a sudden recession came as a shock. There was a drastic change of policy, and what stability there had been was destroyed. Like other countries, Indonesia sought answers to the new challenges in economic reform, democratisation and decentralisation. Meanwhile its unity was threatened by violent domestic conflict and ethnicisation.

In the Middle East, some countries had historical origins of their own, whereas others were legacies of colonialism. However, this had little effect on their political structures. The model used in this book to describe Africa could in some respects equally well be applied to the countries of the Middle East, each with a national elite like a spider in two webs, one international and the other domestic. Yet one can immediately point to a number of major differences which greatly influenced the workings of the system; above all, the oil earnings of some Arab countries (and massive foreign aid to others), which meant that, unlike in poverty-stricken Africa, the ruling elites never really had to worry about money. However, the oil had to be sold to rich nations, so there were close ties between the Arab elites and the industrialised countries. The international web was so strong that Arab leaders scarcely had to concern themselves with their domestic webs.

As a result, the political systems in Arab countries were utterly dictatorial. The available money, of which there was no lack, was used by the elite for its own purposes, and the needs of ordinary people were ignored. Groups that attempted to voice their concerns were harshly suppressed, making it impossible for local forces to manifest themselves. For want of legal opportunities to express themselves politically, malcontents turned to religion. The government, naturally, could not do a great deal about that. Many people attempted to express their political and social dissatisfaction through Islam, which the secular states tried to suppress. With no prospects of material progress, large sections of the population felt desperate. They simply could not understand the position they were in. Why should they, the followers of the one true faith, have to live in such poverty while elsewhere in the world unbelievers could apparently afford whatever they wanted? Their anger and envy easily turned to aggression against their own rulers – stooges of the infidel Westerners – and against the West and modernity itself. Given a chance, they would replace the countries they had to live in with Islamic states in an instant, as Iranians did in 1979. Nowhere in the Middle East was there a gradual transformation of the state, as there was in Africa.

If we compare developments on other continents with those in Africa, we can draw the following conclusions. Postcolonial developments similar to those in Africa occurred in other former colonies only when there was something of a balance between the strength of colonialism and that of indigenous cultures. If colonialism was too strong or indigenous cultures too weak, local influence was extinguished altogether. In such cases, colonialism effectively became permanent. This was the situation in Latin America and to a much greater degree in North America, northern Asia and Australia, where the indigenous population was so thoroughly crushed that the situation was no longer even recognisable as a form of colonialism. In the Middle East, too, Arab elites could almost entirely ignore the local population thanks to their oil earnings and their ties with oil-buying countries. On the other hand, if colonialism was too weak or the indigenous societies too strong, as in much of Asia, colonialism had little impact on local structures. Of course, colonialism had a huge influence on Asia in many ways; it stimulated the modernisation of the continent. But it did little to disturb the continuity of most Asian states. Still, Asia was heterogeneous, and there were cases where indigenous resistance was weaker, as in Africa, enabling colonialism to leave its mark on the development of the state. The best example of this is the Southeast Asian archipelago. This shows that the thesis can have some relevance outside Africa.

An African renaissance?

Those with an interest in contemporary history are usually curious not only about what has happened, but also about where things will go from here. However, history is by no means the same thing as futurology. Sometimes, completely unpredictable events profoundly affect the forces that determine change. Moreover, what we might call structural changes – the slow surge of history – are, on closer inspection, not always so slow after all. One feature of the modernisation process in Europe since the Middle Ages has been that changes, including structural ones, have taken place in ever quicker succession. The global changes of the twentieth and twenty-first centuries have been especially rapid – faster than ever before.

We need only look at what happened in Africa in the course of the twentieth century. In 1900 the European colonial powers had only just become established there, and it looked as though they would remain in power for centuries. A new political structure was introduced – yet suddenly, long before the century was out, Africa became independent. For most of the rest of the century its countries were pawns in the Cold War. No-one reflecting on Africa's future in 1900 could possibly have foreseen all this. The speed of structural change will undoubtedly continue to increase in the twenty-first century. Today, when we speak of the challenges of the twenty-first century, we really mean the ones we are already facing. We have no idea what the rest of the century will bring.

We should therefore be cautious about making predictions. Still, we can say something about what the near future is likely to bring for Africa. This book has identified some dominant forces in the contemporary history of the continent, which will not suddenly disappear. They will continue to shape things to come, in combination with other forces as yet unknown.

Today's Africanised states, which we have come to think of as failing states, are unlike anything that previously existed on the continent. They are products of a unique historical process and are now functioning – or malfunctioning – under rapidly changing international and internal conditions. An example of an internal factor is the continent's rapidly growing population. In the days of precolonial African states, the continent was practically empty of people. Labour was therefore much more important to those states than land or other resources, which were relatively abundant. The situation has now changed drastically; the continent is starting to fill up with Africans. As a result, Africa's modern states no longer need to bind people to them; they have enough people already. Rather, it is land and other resources that are becoming scarce. This is a fundamental shift that cannot be reversed. If only for this reason, Africa's state structures will never again resemble those in the precolonial era. The same African forces may still be operating, but in an ever-changing setting. There can never be a return to the way things were.

So what will happen instead? Since the 1990s there have been efforts to help African states function better. As this book shows, there is a confrontation between the disintegration of states and attempts to build up state capacity. The outcome will have a decisive impact on the near future of the continent. What can we expect of efforts to restore and reconstruct African states? We must be realistic and accept that it will be difficult to achieve lasting results, since these changes, which have largely been forced on African leaders, are not falling on fertile sociocultural and historical soil. In China, simple changes of policy were sufficient to get modernisation going. In Africa, on the other hand, policy changes are necessary but by no means sufficient. Africa's social structures and cultures are particularly unyielding, with widely shared features that are outlined above: social systems geared to preserving the status quo, patron-client networks and a notion of power as all-pervasive. These features not only explain why the continent malfunctions, in that they form the main obstacle to development, but also explain how it functions, in that they describe how power operates in its societies. In the words of the Africanists Chabal and Daloz: Africa works.[354] If it is to improve its chances of developing, Africa will have to abandon many of its present features. The question is not even so much whether it is capable of changing – for societies and cultures always change – but rather how soon it will do so, what the direction of change will be and what force will drive the process.

Though we should be careful about making long-term predictions, improvement is certainly possible and indeed is already taking place. The last decade has seen an impressive degree of democratisation. This is also an instance of Africanisation of the state, only this time with the current of modernisation rather than against it. Originally, of course, democratisation was mainly a European phenomenon, but the democratisation of African states (based on Western models) can nevertheless be seen as Africanisation, since it gives Africans more influence over their own affairs. Not only has democratisation put the population in a closer and more effective relationship with the state, but it has also ensured that for the first time in the history of independent Africa the continent now has several former heads of state who have voluntarily relinquished power after losing elections and can still travel freely without fear of being imprisoned or murdered. A new, milder political culture is starting to emerge in Africa. As a result, rulers will feel less compelled to put their personal interests first (by embezzling state funds) and hence there will be less corruption. They will also focus more on long-term policies, such as freer markets, which often require sacrifices in the short term. More democracy, less corruption and better governance – there are those who believe that the positive impact of this dynamic is already visible.[355]

A second potentially important structural change has to do with the economy. Improved economic policies have halted the economic decline that Africa experienced in the 1970s and 1980s, replacing it with stagnation. In addition, a significant informal sector has emerged. The state and the economy are still quite intertangled and further liberalisation and privatisation are therefore necessary. The formal economy is in such a sorry state that people have no choice but to engage in economic activities of their own devising in order to make a living. This informal economy faces huge problems due to lack of organisation, training, credit and legal certainty, in combination with social pressure from family and friends. It therefore has difficulty moving beyond small-scale activities. However, its market forces and spirit of enterprise may lay the foundations for the dynamic, competitive private sector that African countries will ultimately need if they are ever to achieve economic power and prosperity. If vigorous centres of economic growth manage to develop in the informal economy, this will not only enable many people to escape from poverty but will also countervail the all-pervading power of politics and the state by allowing a middle class to emerge.

Nevertheless, the informal economy will not be able to develop fully without support from the state, which must provide the facilities and services on which a modern economy depends, such as law enforcement and infrastructure. The state and the economy must develop side by side and bolster rather than stifle one another. The informal economy must establish ties with the state that will gradually turn it into an 'ordinary', formal economy. This means that people who earn an income in the informal economy must ultimately pay taxes. Only then will the state regain the wherewithal to do such things as stimulate economic growth. This will also create the material ties between the state and its citizens on which any democratic system depends, for people who do not make a financial contribution to the state will never have a lasting say in how it is run. Africa's economic development cannot be seen in isolation from political, social and cultural change.

In this optimistic scenario, the African state might be ready for a development of the kind that Max Weber, the renowned (and still very relevant) late-nineteenth-century German sociologist, considered essential to modernisation. Africanised states, although they may have failed in performing the tasks of a modern state, have at least managed to bring the state and society together in a cultural sense. Weber said that, in order for a modern state to emerge, it must be emancipated from society. Instead of being tied to society in all kinds of obscure ways (as is now the case in Africa), it must stand above society as a visible institution and only be connected to it in clearly defined ways, for example by holding elections, collecting taxes and carrying out tasks that other organisations in society are not able or allowed to perform. Interaction between components of the state, and between the state and its citizens, should be purely functional and, in a sense, abstract. Such interaction should involve the performance of clearly defined tasks, the provision of services, and other transactions in which only objective factors (rather than personal ones) play a part. Africa's modernisation process will require the emergence of this kind of state.

It has been said that Africa's failure to modernise is largely due to the state's failure to become emancipated from society in the Weberian sense.[356] This raises the question of how this emancipation was supposed to come about, given that the state introduced by the colonial powers was so remote from society. If the state and society are not intertwined to start with, how can one be emancipated from the other? In fact, the Africanisation of the state since independence has brought the state and society closer together. It is only since about the end of the Cold War that African states have had the potential to try to stand above society in a healthy, functional manner – not as the 'foreign bodies' that colonial states used to be, but as truly African states. In some cases, of course, it is questionable whether there is enough of a state left to be emancipated in the first place. In any case, efforts to restore and build up well-run modern states must also be seen in this context of emancipation. The process can be encouraged and supported from outside, but will only succeed if the people of Africa are the driving force behind it. Democratisation and economic improvement are still the key.

What matters is what attitude Africa's people will take as they confront tomorrow's challenges. How will they cope with the intrinsic ambivalence of the modernisation process, of adopting and adapting some Western features while rejecting others? At the moment there is an ideological vacuum in Africa. African humanism, *négritude* and socialism merely evoke a sense of nostalgia for the good old days. Liberalism as an ideology is unlikely to win many converts in this part of the world. There is considerable frustration at the continent's failure to develop, and a tendency to blame this on external forces and systems which supposedly have the continent in a stranglehold. It is also all too easy to point the finger at Africa's history of slavery and colonialism. African leaders find it especially difficult to break free from these notions, because the supposed legacy of victimisation both has the potential to attract foreign aid and distracts from their own failures.

If the frustration and hopelessness of Africa's people mount, there is a danger that they will direct their energies even more destructively, into an ideology of protest that rejects modernisation altogether. Islam, which is spreading faster in Africa than anywhere else in the world, is a logical channel for feelings of discontent.[357] If the mood on the continent does indeed turn against the West and modernisation, then Africa's development, like that of the Middle East, may be set back decades. This could be counterbalanced by the ideology of the African renaissance, but it remains to be seen whether that movement will ultimately be strong enough.

Naturally, you would like to know what is going to happen to Africa in the coming decades. Will it develop along more or less Western lines after all, at least partly closing the gap that separates it from the rest of the world, or will its role grow ever smaller and the gap ever bigger? In that case, will Africa's entire state system collapse? Or might there be a two-tiered process of development, with 'islands' of relative modernity that can more or less keep up with the world economy, surrounded by large, backward areas that have missed the boat? Or is Africa simply too large and too fragmented for a single scenario, and will each region go its own way? I will venture a guess, but without attempting to look more than about twenty years ahead (up to around 2025), for we cannot even begin to imagine what will happen after that.

Despite the formidable cultural forces behind the erosion of Africa's postcolonial states, which have been discussed in such detail in this book, it is my prediction that Africa – with the probable exception of large parts of West and Central Africa – will not become any more unstable than it is at present. The independent states still have some power of their own. Since about 2000, international efforts have to some extent stabilised teetering state structures (in Sierra Leone and Liberia, for example), and this trend will continue. Violent conflict will remain, but that does not mean states will disappear.

Africans from all parts of society will obtain more of a say in running their countries. However, this will not have an immediate impact on their living standards, which will be much the same in 2025 as they are now. The number of poor people on the continent will greatly increase, not because Africans who are now better off will become poorer, but because the population will continue to grow rapidly. Opportunities for socioeconomic progress will remain extremely limited. At present there are no realistic answers to the huge challenges that Africa faces. The continent is still not at all competitive, and will attract little or no commercial investment from abroad. Investment on other continents may not always yield as much as investment in Africa, but will certainly be less risky. Africa will thus lag further and further behind the rest of the world.

Nor is there as yet any prospect of fighting the AIDS epidemic effectively. The disease will therefore continue to have a huge impact on society. The migration of large numbers of young men, especially from rural areas, will continue to have a disruptive effect. The continent will become increasingly urbanised. By the 2020s some of the world's biggest cities will be in Africa.

Turning back to the overall development of African countries, there will be some success stories in the years to come, but these successful countries will be at the risk of backsliding, for they will face essentially the same problems as other parts of Africa. Any progress they make will be fragile and uncertain. However, countries with reasonable governance that pursue satisfactory economic policies for more than ten years will have more lasting success, with potential for stable further development. Some of these countries will begin to emerge from 2010 onwards. Which ones they will be cannot be predicted at this stage. Their governments will display new, as yet unattested combinations of African and Western features. Just as there are now numerous modern Asian states which are partly Asian and partly Western in character (such as Japan, South Korea, Thailand, China, Malaysia and Singapore), there will be modern African states. Their effectiveness and stability will attract more and more foreign investment and trigger an upward spiral. These countries will act as models for their slower-moving neighbours and thereby make it possible for whole regions or even the entire continent to move forward. By then, however, we will have moved beyond our 2025 horizon.

All in all, the outlook for Africa is none too bright. There is no easy way out of the present situation, and few if any of the conditions for improvement are currently being met. What is more important, however, is that many Africans – including political leaders – are beginning to show the will to solve the huge problems Africa faces. And it is the strength of that will, more than anything else, that will determine whether or not there is an African renaissance.

Notes

1. UNDP, *Human Development Report 2003*, p. 5.
2. Note the low ranking of most African countries on the Human Development Index, which is compiled annually by UNDP.
3. Theroux, *Dark Star Safari*, p. 1.
4. Rostow also edited *The Economics of Take-off into Sustained Growth*. Other major works on modernisation are Apter, *The Politics of Modernisation*; Levy, *Modernisation and the Structure of Societies*; Black, *The Dynamics of Modernisation*; and Sinai, *In Search of the Modern World*. For a survey of modernisation theory, see Gendzier, *Managing Political Change*. Palmer and Colton, *A History of the Modern World* (many editions), is a general work of world history from the perspective of modernisation theory. Landes, *The Wealth and Poverty of Nations*, is similar but focuses on the discrepancy between wealth and poverty.
5. The leading representative of dependency theory was André Gunder Frank. His works include *Capitalism and Underdevelopment in Latin America* and *On Capitalist Underdevelopment*.
6. Bayart, *The State in Africa*; Chabal and Daloz, *Africa Works*.
7. Fatton, *Predatory Rule*; Bayart, Ellis and Hibou, *The Criminalisation of the State in Africa*.
8. For instance, Clapham, *Africa and the International System*.
9. World Bank, *The State in a Changing World*; World Bank, *Can Africa Claim the 21st Century?*
10. Rostow, *The Stages of Economic Growth*, p. 2.
11. Chapter 9, on poverty in Africa, discusses various definitions of the phenomenon.
12. Harrison and Huntington (eds), *Culture Matters*.
13. This is the definition given in Harrison and Huntington (eds), *Culture Matters* (p. xv).
14. This comes close to the influential, broad definition used by the anthropologist Clifford Geertz: culture as an entire way of life. Of course, countless other definitions can be found in scholarly writing. For a survey, see Breetvelt, *Dualisme en integratie* (*Dualism and Integration*).
15. Martin and O'Meara (eds), *Africa*, p. 78 (third edition).
16. Herbst, *Power and State Control in Africa*, p. 4.
17. Young, 'The colonial state and post-colonial crisis'.
18. Oliver and Fage, *A Short History of Africa*, pp. 191-199.
19. Smits, 'Financiële kenmerken van Afrikaanse staten' ('Financial characteristics of African states').
20. Goldsmith, 'Risk, rule and reason'.
21. Fatton, *Predatory Rule*.
22. Painter, *The Cold War*, is a useful survey of the Cold War period.
23. Clapham, *Africa and the International System*, p. 15; Jackson, *Quasi-States*.
24. Clapham, *Africa and the International System*, p. 20.
25. Marte, *Political Cycles in International Relations: Africa during the Cold War, 1945-1990*.
26. Wesseling, *Verdeel en heers* (*Divide and Rule*).
27. Chachage, *Environment, Aid and Politics in Zanzibar*, p. 71.

28. Dutch government memorandum, *Frankrijk en de Franse Communauté* (*France and the French Communauté*), taken from *Foccart parle. Entretiens avec Philippe Gaillard.* (*Foccart Speaks: Conversations with Philippe Gaillard*) Paris (Fayard / Jeune Afrique) 1995, p. 275.
29. Hancock, *The Sign and the Seal*.
30. Marte, *Political Cycles in International Relations: Africa during the Cold War, 1945-1990*.
31. For a comparative study of growth on various continents and in various periods, see Maddison, *The World Economy: A Millennial Perspective*.
32. Mamdani, *Citizen and Subject*.
33. Oliver and Fage, *A Short History of Africa*, p. 191.
34. World Bank, *World Development Report 1984*, table 4.
35. Regarding the relative importance of various economic sectors, see Bryceson and Howe, 'An agrarian continent in transition', and Bryceson and Jamal, *Farewell to Farms*.
36. Jackson and Rosberg, *Personal Rule in Black Africa*, p. 18.
37. Clapham, *Africa and the International System*, p. 165.
38. Figures are from various *World Development Reports* by the World Bank. They are not exact, but do give a reasonable indication of the size of the rapidly growing debt problem.
39. Callaghy, 'Africa and the world economy'.
40. UNCTAD, *Foreign Direct Investment in Africa*.
41. Clapham, *Africa and the International System*, p. 164.
42. Wickins, *An Economic History of Africa*, vol. 2.
43. Bryceson and Jamal, 'An agrarian continent in transition', p. 182.
44. Clapham, *Africa and the International System*, p. 171.
45. World Bank, *Adjustment in Africa*, p. 291.
46. *Landenreeks, Ivoorkust* (Ivory Coast), p. 40.
47. Azam, 'The uncertain distributional impact of structural adjustment in Sub-Saharan Africa', p. 111.
48. Husain, 'Structural adjustment and the long-term development of Sub-Saharan Africa', table on p. 162 (based on World Bank figures).
49. Adepoju (ed.), *The Impact of Structural Adjustment on the Population of Africa*.
50. World Bank, *World Development Report 1994*, table 1.
51. Wickins, *An Economic History of Africa*, vol. 1, pp. 241-2.
52. Rodrik, *Trade Policy and Economic Performance in Sub-Saharan Africa*, p. 6.
53. World Bank, *Africa's Growth Tragedy: A Retrospective 1960-89*.
54. Although in some respects the island state of Cape Verde (which is outside the scope of this book) was a few months earlier.
55. Decalo, 'Benin: First of New Democracies'.
56. Schumpeter, *Capitalism, Socialism, and Democracy*, ch. 21, p. 269 in the second edition (1947).
57. Dahl, *Polyarchy: Participation and Opposition*.
58. The overview provided in 1970 by Fortes and Evans-Pritchard in *African Political Systems* is still useful.
59. Well-documented examples of sacred power in Africa appear in Reefe, *The Rainbow and the Kings*, and De Heusch, *The Drunken King, or, The Origin of the State*.
60. On systems of checks and balances in West Africa, see Horton, 'Stateless societies in the history of West Africa'.
61. For a novelist's view of a precolonial society, see Achebe, *Things Fall Apart*.

62 Mamdani, *Citizen and Subject*.

63 Ake, *The Unique Case of African Democracy*, p. 239.

64 This categorisation comes from Bratton and Van de Walle, *Democratic Experiments in Africa*, p. 120.

65 Clark, *The National Conference as an Instrument of Democratization in Francophone Africa*.

66 The only possible exception is South Africa, where the Convention for a Democratic South Africa (CODESA) resembled a national conference. See Shubane, *South Africa: A New Government in the Making*.

67 Joseph, *Zambia: A Model for Democratic Change*.

68 Ethnicity is a loaded concept that is not easy to define in a generally acceptable and clear manner. In this context, it is sufficient to regard ethnicity as anything the authorities wish to describe as such (the top-down approach) or any such group to which a person believes or feels he belongs (the bottom-up approach).

69 Reyntjens, *Danse macabre*, pp. 12-13.

70 Reyntjens, *Danse macabre*, pp. 222-223; Longman, *Rwanda: Democratization and Disorder*, p. 287 et seq.

71 Reyntjens, *Danse macabre*, p. 262; Lemarchand, *Burundi: Ethnic Conflict and Genocide*.

72 Chabal and Daloz, *Africa Works*; Erdmann, *Neo-Patrimonial Rule*.

73 For a comparison of African 'feudalism' with, *inter alia*, medieval European feudalism, see Goody, *Technology, Tradition, and the State in Africa*, pp. 1-20.

74 Throup and Hornsby, *Multi-Party Politics in Kenya*.

75 Rueschemeyer, Stephens and Stephens, *Capitalist Development and Democracy*.

76 For an assessment of the intensity and scope of pluralism, see Bangura, *Democratization, Equity and Stability*.

77 Huntington, *The Third Wave*, pp. 315-316.

78 From a speech entitled 'Democracy and Social Justice', delivered in Seoul at a conference on democracy, free-market economics and development, 26-27 February 1999.

79 Mkandawire and Olukoshi (eds.), *Between Liberalisation and Oppression*.

80 Dutch Ministry of Foreign Affairs memorandum on conflict management (*Conflicthantering*), p. 13.

81 SPA status report on Eritrea, 14 May 1997, p. 3.

82 Lodge, 'South Africa: Democracy and development in a post-apartheid society'.

83 Diallo, *Mauritania. The Other Apartheid?*

84 Holm, 'Development, democracy and civil society in Botswana'; Hope, 'Development policy and economic performance in Botswana'.

85 Ottaway, 'Africa's "new leaders": African solution or African problem?', pp. 209-210.

86 Fatton, *Predatory Rule*.

87 Reno introduced the concept of the shadow state in *Corruption and State Politics in Sierra Leone*.

88 Young and Turner, *The Rise and Decline of the Zairean State*, p. 82.

89 In the words of Belgian journalist Colette Braeckman, quoted by Dutch journalist Dirk Vlasblom in the Dutch newspaper *NRC Handelsblad*, 17 October 1998, p. 35.

90 This was also the country's official name between 1964 and 1971.

91 As peculiar as, for example, 'Democratic People's Republic of Korea' (North Korea) and 'Great Socialist People's Libyan Arab Jamahiriya' (Libya).

92 See the list of Kabila's family members in positions of power in: International Crisis Group, *Scramble for the Congo: Anatomy of an Ugly war*, pp. 49-50.

93 International Crisis Group, *Scramble for the Congo: Anatomy of an Ugly War*, p. 47.

94 Dutch Ministry of Foreign Affairs memorandum on conflict management, p. 16.

95 Menkhaus, 'Somalia: political order in a stateless society', p. 220.

96 Edwards, *The Natural History of Revolution*; Briton, *The Anatomy of Revolution*; Davies, 'Towards a theory of revolution'; Wertheim, *De lange mars der emancipatie (The Long March of Emancipation)*, pp. 215-218.

97 Clapman, *Africa and the International System*, p. 70.

98 Bayart, Ellis and Hibou, *The Criminalisation of the State in Africa*.

99 Van Walraven, *The Pretence of Peace-keeping*.

100 For the classic description of the *poroh*, see: Dr Paul Julien, *Kampvuren langs de evenaar (Campfires along the Equator)*, pp. 107-127.

101 Ellis, *The Mask of Anarchy*.

102 Abdullah and Muana, *The Revolutionary United Front of Sierra Leone*, pp. 177-179.

103 'Small is nasty', in *Foreign Report*, 15 October 1998.

104 Dutch Ministry of Foreign Affairs, *Small Arms, Big Challenges*, memorandum, pp. 3-6.

105 Human Rights Watch, *Bulgaria: Money Talks – Arms Dealing with Human Rights Abusers*.

106 Bootsman, *De herkomst en financiering van wapens in het Grote Meren conflict (The Origins and Financing of Weapons in the Great Lakes Conflict)*.

107 Paul Collier, director of the Development Economics Research Group (DECRG) at the World Bank, has emphasised this issue; see the World Bank report *Economic Causes of Civil Conflict and their Implications for Policy*.

108 Kaplan, *The Coming Anarchy*.

109 Signer, 'Falen wordt je vergeven, succes niet' ('Failure can be forgiven, but not success'), in the Dutch newspaper *Trouw*, 30 November 2002; Polman, 'De vloek van het netwerk' ('The curse of the system'), in the Dutch newspaper *NRC Handelsblad*, 20 December 2002, p. 27.

110 Ellis, *The Mask of Anarchy* and 'Liberia's warlord insurgency'.

111 Van Walraven, *The Pretence of Peace-keeping*.

112 For a discussion of the various theories about the downing of the plane, see Prunier, *The Rwanda Crisis*, pp. 213-229. Much of the information in this section is taken from Prunier's book.

113 Prunier, *The Rwanda Crisis*, pp. 261-265.

114 For an eyewitness account of the corpses lying around for months, see Wagner, 'All the Bourgmestre's men: making sense of genocide in Rwanda', pp. 25-26.

115 Prunier, *The Rwanda Crisis*, p. 181.

116 Prunier, *The Rwanda Crisis*, p. 240.

117 Prunier, *The Rwanda Crisis*, pp. 168-169.

118 Percival and Homer-Dixon, *Environmental Scarcity and Violent Conflict: The Case of Rwanda*; Smith, 'Postcolonial genocide: scarcity, ethnicity, and mass death in Rwanda'.

119 Blok, 'Het narcisme van de kleine verschillen' ('The narcissism of minor differences').

120 See the detailed evaluation of the genocide, *The International Response to Conflict and Genocide: Lessons from the Rwanda Experience*.

121 For two completely different interpretations of Kabila's meteoric rise to power, see Vansina, 'The politics of history and the crisis in the Great Lakes', p. 38.

122 For a clear description and analysis of these events (in Dutch), see Vlasblom in the *NRC Handelsblad* newspaper, 17 October 1998 (p. 35), under the heading 'Verstrikt in de nieuwe tijd. Kabila en de geopolitieke kentering in Afrika' ('Caught in a new era: Kabila and Africa's geopolitical transformation').

123 In the words of Yerodia Aboulaye Ndombasi, who was later to be appointed minister of foreign affairs. The remark earned him an internationally circulated arrest warrant, issued in Belgium in 2000 following criminal charges filed by members of the Tutsi community in that country.

124 Based on the excellent report *Scramble for Congo* by the International Crisis Group.

125 With thanks to Jan Abbink, Ethiopia specialist at Leiden University's African Studies Centre.

126 Richard Pankhurst shows in *The Ethiopians* how nationalism (in the form of ethnic and tribal loyalties) has developed in Ethiopia, principally in terms of the relationship between Ethiopia and Eritrea.

127 For statistics on Sudanese refugees, see Van Baarsen, *The Netherlands and Sudan*, p. 30.

128 ICG, *Scramble for the Congo*, pp. 44-45.

129 For details of the size and strength of the various fighting forces in Congo, see ICG, *Scramble for the Congo*, p. 4.

130 UN, *Report of the Panel of Experts on the illegal exploitation of natural resources and other forms of wealth of the Democratic Republic of Congo*.

131 Bossema, 'Legers buurlanden plunderen Congo systematisch leeg' ('Armies from neighbouring countries systematically pillaging Congo').

132 ICG, *Scramble for the <$iCongo*, pp. 65-66.

133 ICG, *Scramble for the Congo*, p. 51.

134 ICG, *Scramble for the Congo*, pp. 60-63.

135 ICG, *Scramble for the Congo*, p. 65.

136 For information on individual countries and armed groups, see Bootsman, *De herkomst en financiering van wapens in het Grote Meren conflict* (*The Origins and Financing of Weapons in the Great Lakes Conflict*), pp. 11-21.

137 International Institute for Strategic Studies, *The Military Balance 1999-2000*; Bootsman, *De herkomst en financiering van wapens in het Grote Meren conflict* (*The Origins and Financing of Weapons in the Great Lakes Conflict*), pp. 22-27.

138 ICG, *Scramble for the Congo*, pp. 70-79.

139 Lindijer, 'De Afrikanisering van de hebzucht' ('The Africanisation of greed').

140 ICG, *Scramble for the Congo*, pp. 50-51.

141 Kane, *The Hour of Departure*, pp. 19-23.

142 This section draws heavily on a memorandum on refugees in Africa (*Vluchtelingen in Afrika*) largely drafted by the author and published by the Dutch Ministry of Foreign Affairs.

143 EMDAT database on disasters, CRED.

144 UNHCR, *Sexual Violence against Refugees: Guidelines on Prevention and Response*.

145 This was among the conclusions of the international evaluation report on the aid operation in Rwanda, *The International Response to Conflict and Genocide*. The report called on NGOs to establish a code of conduct, raise their own standards and exercise greater internal control.

146 Memorandum, Dutch Ministry of Foreign Affairs, *Humanitaire hulp tussen conflict en ontwikkeling* (*Humanitarian Aid between Conflict and Development*), pp. 45-53.

147 Memorandum, Dutch Ministry of Foreign Affairs, *Vluchtelingen in Afrika* (*Refugees in Africa*), pp. 84-85.

148 An outstanding analysis of the fundamental problems of conflict prevention is provided by Nathan, 'The four horsemen of the apocalypse: the structural cause of violence in Africa'.

149 Douma, Frerks and Van de Goor, *Major Findings of the Research Project 'Causes of Conflict in the Third World'. Executive Summary*.

150 For a list of possible measures to prevent, manage and resolve conflicts, see the Dutch Ministry of Foreign Affairs memorandum *Conflicthantering. Denken en handelen* (*Conflict Management: Thinking and Acting*).

151 UN, *Report of the Panel on United Nations Peace Operations*.

152 IMF, *World Economic Outlook 1999*, pp. 139 and 167.

153 Dutch Ministry of Foreign Affairs memorandum, *Effecten van economische globalisering* (*Effects of Economic Globalisation*), p. 3.

154 World Bank, *Can Africa Claim the 21st Century?*, p. 208.

155 ECOSOC, *Summary of the Economic and Social Situation in Africa*, 1999, p. 2.

156 World Bank, *Can Africa Claim the 21st Century?*, p. 208.

157 Rodrik, *Trade Policy and Economic Performance in Sub-Saharan Africa*, pp. 5-6.

158 IMF, *World Economic Outlook 1999*, p. 171.

159 IMF, *World Economic Outlook 1999*, p. 130.

160 Van der Heijden, *The Effectiveness of Economic Policy Reform, Foreign Aid and Debt Relief in Zambia*.

161 Bhinda et al., *Private Capital Flows to Africa: Perception and Reality*.

162 UNCTAD, *World Investment Reports*.

163 Bhinda et al., *Private Capital Flows to Africa: Perception and Reality*, pp. 25 and 29.

164 Bhinda et al., *Private Capital Flows to Africa: Perception and Reality*, pp. 29-33.

165 ECOSOC, *Summary of the Economic and Social Situation in Africa*, 2000, p. 2.

166 IMF, *World Economic Outlook 1999*, p. 139.

167 ECOSOC, *Summary of the Economic and Social Situation in Africa*, 1999, p. 3.

168 ECOSOC, *Summary of the Economic and Social Situation in Africa*, 1999, p. 3.

169 Signer, 'Falen wordt je vergeven, succes niet' ('Failure can be forgiven, but not success').

170 Signer, 'Falen wordt je vergeven, succes niet' ('Failure can be forgiven, but not success'); Polman, 'De vloek van het netwerk' ('The curse of the network').

171 In a speech at a meeting of the GCA in Dakar, October 1999.

172 Teunissen (ed.), *Regionalism and the Global Economy: the Case of Africa*, p. 35.

173 Whiteman, *Africa, the ACP and Europe.*

174 World Bank, *Can Africa Claim the 21st Century?*, p. 177, Box 6.2.

175 Robinson, *The Coherence of European Development Policies in Africa*, p. 27.

176 For a review of the loans, see Mistry, *Resolving Africa's Multilateral Debt Problem*, pp. 40-41.

177 IMF, *World Economic Outlook 1999*, p. 132.

178 IMF, *World Economic Outlook 1999*, p. 146.

179 World Bank, *Can Africa Claim the 21st Century?*, p. 154.

180 ECA, *Developing NICI Policies, Plans and Strategies*, pp. 4-6.

181 Okigbo, *Communication and Poverty: the Challenge of Social Change in Africa.*

182 ECA, *Developing NICI Policies, Plans and Strategies*, p. 5. According to the International Telecommunication Union (quoted in World Bank, *Can Africa Claim the 21st Century?*, p. 154), worldwide annual purchases of ICT goods and services around the turn of the century totalled five to six times Africa's total GNP.

183 World Bank, *Can Africa Claim the 21st Century?*, p. 155.

184 *Internet Development in Africa*, p. 5.

185 World Bank, *Can Africa Claim the 21st Century?*, p. 157.

186 RAWOO, *Local Perspectives on Globalization.*

187 Chabal and Daloz, *Africa Works*, pp. 63-76.

188 Comaroff and Comaroff (eds.), *Modernity and its Malcontents.*

189 Huntington, *The Clash of Civilizations and the Remaking of World Order.*

190 Davidson, *The Black Man's Burden.*

191 Of course, qualitative factors also played a role, in the form of collective ideas, memories, opinions and so on. These are discussed throughout the book.

192 Houweling, 'Demography, commodity chain position, state paralysis and structural reform in Sub-Saharan Africa', p. 26

193 Figures taken in part from McEvedy and Jones, *Atlas of World Population History.*

194 Adas, 'From avoidance to confrontation'. For a discussion of the relationship between Africa's low population density and the organisation of its states, see Stevensen, *Population and Political Systems in Tropical Africa* and Herbst, *Power and State Control in Africa.*

195 World Bank, *Can Africa Claim the 21st Century?*, table 1.2 on p. 16.

196 Houweling, 'Demography, commodity chain position, state paralysis and structural reform in Sub-Saharan Africa'.

197 A population pyramid is generally included at the end of each book in the *Landenreeks* (a series of country studies). The population pyramid for Kenya is on p. 58 of the appropriate volume.

198 *Mali (Landenreeks)*, p. 74.

199 *Senegal (Landenreeks)*, p. 31.

200 Data from the *Club du Sahel*, taken from a paper compiled for the Afri Cities 2000 conference in Windhoek, Namibia.

201 Clapham, *Africa and the International System*, p. 164.

202 The situation varied from country to country. In around half the countries, the projected urban growth rate for the 1990s was higher than it had been for the period between 1960 and 1990, but it was lower in the other half. For data on individual countries, see Rakodi (ed.), *The Urban Challenge*, pp. 68-69.

203 Potts, 'Shall we go home?'

204 Maps showing the natural environment in different parts of Africa can be found in Reader, *Africa: A Biography of the Continent.*

205 Television documentary, 'The elephants of Timbuktu' (National Geographic).

206 Hassing, 'Energie in Afrika' ('Energy in Africa').

207 Lensink, *Structural adjustment in Sub-Saharan Africa*, pp. 111-115.

208 Reed (ed.), *Structural Adjustment and the Environment.*

209 For example, around the turn of the century, the Netherlands spent 0.1 per cent of its GNP on environmental protection in developing countries.

210 Kaplan, 'The coming anarchy'.

211 UNDP, Human Development Report 1997 (N.B. the figures given are for 1994).

212 This quotation and other information in this paragraph are taken from the Dutch Ministry of Foreign Affairs memorandum *Vergrijzing en ontwikkeling (Greying and Development).*

213 Dutch Ministry of Foreign Affairs memorandum *Vergrijzing en ontwikkeling (Greying and Development)*, p. 21.

214 Van der Geest, 'Reciprociteit en zorg voor ouderen' ('Reciprocity and elder care').

215 More than five hundred such cases were recorded in Tanzania alone. Dutch Ministry of Foreign Affairs memorandum *Vergrijzing en ontwikkeling (Greying and Development)*, p. 23, based on data from Help-Age International.

216 World Bank, *Can Africa Claim the 21st Century?*, pp. 105-106 (figures taken from the UNESCO Yearbooks).

217 De Boeck, 'Lunda: een korte geschiedenis van oorlog, dollars en diamanten' ('Lunda: a short history of war, dollars and diamonds').

218 Van der Heide, 'Zuid-Afrika ziet nieuwkomers liever gaan' ('South Africa would prefer new arrivals to leave').

219 *Mali (Landenreeks)*, p. 45.

220 De Jong, 'De migratiecrisis' ('The migration crisis'), pp. 139-140.

221 For figures, see the Dutch Ministry of Foreign Affairs memorandum *Migratie en ontwikkeling (Migration and Development)*, p. 12.

222 World Bank, *Can Africa Claim the 21st Century?*, p. 109.

223 History of AIDS (internet).

224 World Bank, *Intensifying Action against HIV/AIDS in Africa*, frontispiece.

225 UNFPA, State of the World Population 1999.

226 UNAIDS 1999.

227 For the ten countries with the most AIDS orphans, see the table in *Internationale Samenwerking (International Cooperation)* 3, March 2000, p. 15.

228 World Bank, *Intensifying Action against HIV/AIDS in Africa.*

229 McEvedy and Jones, *Atlas of World Population History*, pp. 24-25.

230 UNAIDS 1999, pp. 14-15: fifty-five per cent of those infected with HIV are women.

231 Fredland, 'AIDS and development', p. 556.

232 UNFPA, State of the World Population 1999.

233 Caljé and Den Hollander, *De nieuwste geschiedenis* (*Contemporary History*), pp. 54-55; Kastelein, *Groei naar een industriële samenleving* (*The Growth of an Industrial Society*), pp. 69-87.

234 World Bank, *Can Africa Claim the 21st Century?*, table 1.2, with indicators showing evidence of a demographic shift, p. 16.

235 Landes, *The Wealth and Poverty of Nations*. If we examine the phenomenon more closely, there is of course plenty to say about it. See, for example, Iliffe, *The African Poor*, for a history of poverty in Africa.

236 Norberg, *Leve de globalisering* (*In Defence of Global Capitalism*).

237 According to Paul Collier, director of the Development Economics Research Group (DECRG) at the World Bank, as cited in *The Economist*, 13 May 2000.

238 Douma, Frerks and Van de Goor, *Major Findings of the Research Project 'Causes of Conflict in the Third World'.*

239 World Bank, *Voices of the Poor.*

240 World Bank, *Attacking Poverty.*

241 World Bank, *Attacking Poverty*, p. 23.

242 World Bank, *Attacking Poverty*, p. 4.

243 Dutch Ministry of Foreign Affairs memorandum, *Effecten van economische globalisering* (*Effects of Economic Globalisation*), p. 11.

244 World Bank, *Can Africa Claim the 21st Century?*, pp. 92-95.

245 World Bank, *Can Africa Claim the 21st Century?*, p. 94, box 3.2.

246 World Bank, *Can Africa Claim the 21st Century?*, p. 95, box 3.3.

247 World Bank, *Can Africa Claim the 21st Century?*, p. 113.

248 World Bank, *Can Africa Claim the 21st Century?*, p. 87.

249 World Bank, *Can Africa Claim the 21st Century?*, pp. 86-87.

250 Blackden and Bhanu, *Gender, Growth, and Poverty Reduction*, p. 25.

251 Blackden and Bhanu, *Gender, Growth, and Poverty Reduction*, p. 3; World Bank, *Can Africa Claim the 21st Century?*, p. 24.

252 Blackden and Bhanu, Gender, Growth, and Poverty Reduction, pp. 28-30.

253 World Bank, *Intensifying Action against HIV/AIDS in Africa.*

254 Blackden and Bhanu, *Gender, Growth, and Poverty Reduction*, pp. xviii, 92 and 107.

255 From the Annie Romein lecture given by development minister Eveline Herfkens on 8 March 2001 at Leiden University.

256 Bratton and Mattes, 'Africans' surprising universalism', p. 111.

257 Freedom House, Annual survey of freedom country scores, 1999.

258 A summary of the African human rights regime is provided in Ankumah, *The African Commission on Human and Peoples' Rights.*

259 Human Rights Watch, *Protectors or pretenders?*

260 Bratton and Mattes, 'Africans' surprising universalism', p. 111.

261 World Bank, *Global Development Finance 1999*, p. 101.

262 IMF, *World Economic Outlook 1999*, p. 200.

263 Mistry, *Resolving Africa's Multilateral Debt Problem*, p. 27.

264 Mistry, *Resolving Africa's Multilateral Debt Problem*, p. 21.

265 IMF, *World Economic Outlook 1999*, p. 204.

266 IMF, *World Economic Outlook 1999*, p. 199.

267 World Bank, *Global Development Finance 1999*, p. 76.

268 'The trouble with targets' in *The Economist*, 28 April 2001, pp. 35-36.

269 Dutch Ministry of Foreign Affairs memorandum, *Normverva(n)ging* (*Crowding out or pitching in. A new budgetary target for Dutch development cooperation*), R.J. van den Dool (ed.).

270 See the diagram in World Bank, *Can Africa Claim the 21st Century?*, p. 236.

271 For an overview for 1994, see the Dutch Ministry of Foreign Affairs memorandum *Afrika ten zuiden van de Sahara* (*Africa South of the Sahara: Regional policy Document*), appendix E, and *Geographical Distribution of Financial Flows 1994-1998*, OECD/DAC.

272 IMF, *World Economic Outlook 1999*, p. 132.

273 Lensink and White, *Aid Dependence.*

274 Mills, Greg, *Poverty to Prosperity*, p. 255.

275 According to Uganda's own National Household Survey. These findings were confirmed by the World Bank. See *Internationale Samenwerking*, vol. 1, no. 2, May 2001, p. 8.

276 World Bank, *Aid and Reform in Africa.*

277 Goldsmith, 'Foreign aid and statehood in Africa'.

278 World Bank, *Attacking Poverty*, p. 5.

279 UNDP, *Human Development Report 2001.*

280 Marres, 'Schaf ontwikkelingshulp af' ('Do away with development aid').

281 Goldsmith, 'Foreign aid and statehood in Africa'.

282 Hancock, *Lords of Poverty.*

283 Chabal and Daloz refer to this as 'the politics of the mirror' in *Africa Works*, pp. 117-118.

284 This section is largely based on a memorandum written by the author of this book for the Dutch Ministry of Foreign Affairs, *Tussen ownership en conditionaliteit in de ontwikkelingssamenwerking met Afrika* (*Between Ownership and Conditionality in Development Cooperation with Africa*).

285 World Bank, *Effective Implementation: Key to Development Impact*, better known as the Wapenhans report.

286 A well-known survey is the one carried out for the World Bank by Burnside and Dollar on the relationship between aid and economic growth. Their conclusion – which has not gone unchallenged – was that aid only leads to growth in a good policy environment. They argued that it would have no effect in an average policy environment, and that in a poor policy environment aid would in fact impair growth (*Aid, Policies and Growth*, 1997). A survey conducted in 2001 (*Aid and Reform in Africa*) yielded similar conclusions.

287 World Bank, *Adjustment in Africa*, cited in Collier, 'The failure of conditionality', p. 57.

288 Van de Walle and Johnston, *Improving Aid to Africa.*

289 Collier, 'The failure of conditionality'.

290 Asian countries reacted much more fiercely to these Western demands than those in Africa. The Malaysian prime minister Mahathir Mohamad, for example, accused the developed countries of trying to Westernise the world by setting conditions for trade and aid, a practice he described as a form of neocolonialism.

291 One of the many examples was the dispute between the IMF and the Ethiopian government in late 1997. Ethiopia asked for financial aid, but cited ownership as a reason not to comply with the condition that it should further liberalise its financial sector.

292 In 1997, for example, Eritrea appropriated cars intended for joint Eritrean-German projects and used them for other purposes, to the intense annoyance of the German donors.

293 The speaker of the Tanzanian parliament, in an interview with the author (1998).

294 World Bank, *Borrower Ownership of Adjustment Programs and the Political Economy of Reform*.

295 See the summary under the subheading 'Developing country responsibilities' in *Shaping the 21st Century*, pp. 14-15.

296 This theme is also discussed in detail in the policy document *Een wereld in geschil* (*A World in Dispute*) 1993, pp. 27-28, although it uses a slightly different wording: 'Tussen autonomie en aanpassing' ('Between autonomy and adjustment').

297 The World Bank's *World Development Report 1997* covers this in detail.

298 Hesseling and Kraemer, *Senegal/Gambia* (*Landenreeks*), p. 43.

299 Dutch Ministry of Foreign Affairs memorandum, *Afrika ten zuiden van de Sahara* (*Africa South of the Sahara*), p. 24.

300 In 2003, the Netherlands had diplomatic representations in Dakar, Bamako, Ouagadougou, Abidjan, Accra, Cotonou, Abuja, Lagos, Khartoum, Asmara, Addis Ababa, Kampala, Kigali, Nairobi, Kinshasa, Luanda, Dar es Salaam, Lusaka, Harare, Maputo, Windhoek, Pretoria and Cape Town.

301 Jan Pronk's policy is set out in the Dutch Ministry of Foreign Affairs policy documents *Een wereld van verschil* (*A World of Difference*) (1990) and *Een wereld in geschil* (*A World in Dispute*) (1993). The first of these documents was based on the Cold War context, while the second reflected post-Cold War developments.

302 Dutch government memorandum *Herijking van het buitenlands beleid* (*Foreign Policy Review*).

303 World Bank, *Assessing Aid*, also known as the Dollar report after its main author.

304 Dutch Ministry of Foreign Affairs policy memorandum, *De sectorale benadering* (*The Sector-Wide Approach*).

305 *SIPRI Yearbook 1999*, pp. 15-17.

306 Kaplan, *The Coming Anarchy*.

307 Anderson, *Imagined Communities*.

308 For details of how this happened in that classic nation-state, France, see Weber, *Peasants into Frenchmen*.

309 John Iliffe demonstrated this with reference to newly independent Tanganyika (later Tanzania) in Iliffe, *A Modern History of Tanganyika*, especially pp. 324-325.

310 See De Kadt's chapter of the advisory report by the Dutch Advisory Council on Government Policy entitled *Ontwikkelingsbeleid en goed bestuur* (*Development Policy and Good Governance*), pp. 255-257.

311 Gross, *The Civic and the Tribal State*, p. 106.

312 See for example Kaplan, *The Ends of the Earth*, pp. 86-87, for his experiences on the Togolese-Ghanaian border.

313 Bayart, Ellis and Hibou, *The Criminalisation of the State in Africa*, p. 29.

314 Bayart, Ellis and Hibou, *The Criminalisation of the State in Africa*, p. 15.

315 The World Bank played an important part in this. A milestone in the reassessment of the role of the state was the World Development Report 1997, entitled *The State in a Changing World*.

316 In the field of political economy this leads to Wagner's law, which states that, as the level of development rises, so does the state's share of the expanding gross national product.

317 For the role of the state in the modernisation of Asia, see the Dutch Ministry of Foreign Affairs memorandum *Het Aziatisch groeimodel* (*The Asian Growth Model*), especially p. 43.

318 The state was also necessary in order to compete internationally in the globalising world. See the Dutch Ministry of Foreign Affairs memorandum *Effecten van economische globalisering* (*Effects of Economic Globalisation*), p. 21.

319 Dutch Advisory Council on Government Policy, *Ontwikkelingsbeleid en goed bestuur* (*Development Policy and Good Governance*).

320 World Bank, *The State in a Changing World*, p. 29.

321 World Bank, *Voices of the Poor*; World Bank, *Can Africa Claim the 21st Century?*, p. 85.

322 In the Netherlands this led to a memorandum on economics and development entitled *Ondernemen tegen Armoede* (*In Business against Poverty*) (2000, with additions in 2002).

323 Thomas Isaac and Heller, 'The Campaign for Democratic Decentralisation in Kerala.'

324 Goldsmith, *Donors, Dictators and Democrats in Africa*, p. 419.

325 Villalón and Huxtable (eds.), *The African State at a Critical Juncture*.

326 Bratton and Mattes, 'Africans' surprising universalism'.

327 Bratton and Mattes, 'Africans' surprising universalism', p. 120.

328 Goldsmith, 'Risk, rule and reason: leadership in Africa'.

329 Goldsmith, 'Risk, rule and reason: leadership in Africa', p. 84.

330 Goldsmith, 'Donors, dictators and democrats in Africa', pp. 419-422.

331 Van Walraven, 'Of canvassing and carnival'.

332 Transparency International, *The Global Corruption Report 2001*, p. 88.

333 The first people to bring this to public notice in the Netherlands were probably the journalist Hans Moleman (in the daily newspaper *De Volkskrant*), with his article 'Ook het ANC kan een monster worden' ('Even the ANC could become a monster'), 30 August 2000, and politician Frits Bolkestein in 'Het stilzwijgen rond een gevallen held' ('The silence surrounding a fallen hero'), 4 September 2000.

334 Bayart, Ellis and Hibou, *The Criminalisation of the State in Africa*, pp. 49-68.

335 Moleman, 'Racisme is nog overal in Zuid-Afrika' ('Racism still rife in South Africa').

336 In fact, he identified three levels rather than just two. For more details, see Braudel, *The Mediterranean and the Mediterranean World in the Age of Philip II*.

337 This is briefly explained in Bayart, Ellis and Hibou, *The Criminalisation of the State in Africa*, p. xvii. Bayart's work, as well as that of Chabal and Daloz, has focused on long-term historical trends. Another relevant publication is Weiskel's analysis of Ivory Coast around the time of independence ('Independence and the *longue durée*').

338 Wright, 'What do you mean there were no tribes in Africa?'; Reader, *Africa: A Biography of the Continent*, pp. 615-616.

339 Some other authors have presented more elaborate lists of African traditions or characteristics that they believe still have a substantial impact on how African political systems and societies function. One interesting example is 'Does Africa need a Cultural Adjustment Programme?', by the Cameroonian author Daniel Etuonga-Manguelle.

340 For an attempt to reconstruct political traditions in one part of Africa (Western Equatorial Africa), see Jan Vansina, *Paths in the Rainforests*.

341 Hobsbawm and Ranger (eds.), *The Invention of Tradition*. Chapter 6, by Terence Ranger, specifically deals with the invention of traditions in Africa.

342 *The Economist*, 24 February 2001, p. 17.

343 From the Dutch daily newspaper *De Volkskrant*, 24 December 2002. Based on World Bank figures.

344 Take, for example, the absurd border between the Netherlands and Belgium, which cuts straight through Limburg, Brabant and Flanders.

345 Stover, *The Cultural Ecology of Chinese Civilization*.

346 Jackson and Rosberg, *Personal Rule in Black Africa*, p. 18 (also quoted in Clapham, *Africa and the International System*, p. 5).

347 Bayart, Ellis and Hibou, *The Criminalisation of the State in Africa*, pp. 3-4.

348 Modernisation of agriculture has always been necessary as a basis for industrialisation, in the West as well as Asia; see the Dutch Ministry of Foreign Affairs memorandum *Het Aziatische groeimodel* (*The Asian Growth Model*), pp. 4-5 and 14-15. However, Africa's agricultural sector was never modernised.

349 This is the essence of Chabal and Daloz, *Africa Works*.

350 See for example Ellis, *The Mask of Anarchy*.

351 Slicher van Bath, *Spaans Amerika omstreeks 1600* (*Spanish America around 1600*).

352 De Jong, *De waaier van het fortuin* (*The Fan of Fortune*).

353 Far from being called into question, colonial borders were actually the basis for political choices. Just as Eritrea was able to secede from Ethiopia, so Indonesia had to give up East Timor, which it had annexed in 1976.

354 Chabal and Daloz, *Africa Works*.

355 Goldsmith, 'Risk, rule and reason'.

356 Chabal and Daloz, *Africa Works*, pp. 131-137.

357 De Gier, 'Islam in de wereld' ('Islam in the world').

Bibliography

The list below includes all the publications cited in the notes, as well as a number of others that strongly influenced my thinking. The few works not written in Dutch or English were consulted in Dutch or English translation, as indicated. When English versions of works consulted in Dutch are known to exist, they are noted. Otherwise, an indicative translation of the Dutch title is given. All World Bank publications appear under 'World Bank', but many of them can also be found under the names of the individual authors.

The bibliography is divided into three sections:
• Books and articles
• Periodicals
• Memorandums from the Dutch Ministry of Foreign Affairs (including the development cooperation programme, DGIS) and other Dutch government bodies

Books and articles

Abbink, Jon, 'Breaking and making the state: the dynamics of ethnic democracy in Ethiopia'. In: *Journal of Contemporary African Studies* 13/1995/2. Pretoria (Africa Institute).

Abbink, Jon, 'Etniciteit en democratisering in Ethiopië' ('Ethnicity and democratisation in Ethiopia'). In: *Internationale Spectator* 49/1995/11, pp. 591-597. The Hague (Netherlands Institute of International Relations Clingendael).

Abdullah, Ibrahim and Patrick Muana, 'The Revolutionary United Front of Sierra Leone: a revolt of the Lumpenproletariat'. In: Christopher Clapham (ed.), *African Guerrillas*. Oxford (James Currey) 1998.

Acemoglu, Daron, Simon Johnson and James A. Robinson, 'The colonial origins of comparative development: an empirical investigation'. In: *The American Economic Review*, 91, no. 5, December 2001, pp. 1369-1400.

Achebe, Chinua, *Things Fall Apart*. London (William Heinemann) 1958. Later published in the Penguin Books series.

Adas, Michael, 'From avoidance to confrontation: peasant protest in pre-colonial and colonial South East Asia'. In: *Comparative Studies in Society and History*, 1981/23, pp. 217-247. Cambridge (Society for the CSSH).

Adejumobi, Said, 'Elections in Africa: a fading shadow of democracy?' In: *Africa Development* 23/1998/1, pp. 41-61. Dakar (CODESRIA).

Adelman, Howard and Astri Suhrke (eds.), *The Path of a Genocide: The Rwanda Crisis from Uganda to Zaire.* New Brunswick (Transaction Publishers) 1999.

Adepoju, Aderanti (ed.), *The Impact of Structural Adjustment on the Population of Africa: The Implications for Education, Health and Employment.* Portsmouth/London (Heinemann/James Currey) 1993. (UNFPA).

Advisory Council on Government Policy (WRR), *Ontwikkelingsbeleid en goed bestuur* (*Development Policy and Good Governance*). The Hague (SDU) 2001. (Report to the government, no. 58).

Advisory Council on International Affairs (AIV). *De worsteling van Afrika. Veiligheid, stabiliteit en ontwikkeling.* The Hague (AIV) 2001. (AIV advisory report,

no. 17). (Translated into English as: *Africa's Struggle: Security, Stability and Development*).

Aijmer, Goran, and Jon Abbink (eds.), *Meanings of Violence: A Cross-Cultural Perspective.* Oxford/New York (Berg) 2000.

Ajayi, J.F. Ade and Michael Crowder (eds.), *History of West Africa.* New York (Longman) 1972.

Ake, Claude, 'The unique case for African democracy'. In: *International Affairs* 69/1993/2, pp. 240-244. London (Royal Institute of International Affairs).

Ake, Claude, 'What is the problem of ethnicity in Africa?' In: *Transformation* 1993/22, pp. 1-14. Durban (University of Natal).

Ake, Claude, *Democracy and development in Africa.* Washington, D.C. (Brookings Institution) 1996.

Allen, Chris, 'Warfare, endemic violence and state collapse in Africa.' In: *Review of African Political Economy* 26, no. 81 (1999), pp. 367-384.

Anderson, Benedict, *Imagined Communities: Reflections on the Origin and Spread of nationalism.* London (Verso) 1983.

Anglin, Douglas G., 'International election monitoring: the African experience'. In: *African Affairs* 97/1998/389, pp. 471-495. London (Royal African Society).

Ankumah, Evelyn A., *The African Commission on Human and Peoples' Rights: Practice and Procedures.* The Hague etc. (Martinus Nijhoff Publishers) 1996. (Nijhoff Law Specials, 1996/16).

Appiah, Kwame, *In my father's house.* London (Methuen) 1992.

Apter, David E., *The Politics of Modernisation.* Chicago (Chicago University Press) 1965.

Ayoob, Mohammed, *The Third World Security Predicament: State Making, Regional Conflict, and the International System.* Boulder/London (Lynne Rienner) 1995.

Azam, Jean-Paul, 'The diversity of adjustment in agriculture'. In: Stephen Ellis (ed.), *Africa Now: People, Policies and Institutions.* The Hague (Ministry of Foreign Affairs) 1996.

Azam, Jean-Paul, 'The uncertain distributional impact of structural adjustment in Sub-Saharan Africa'. In: Rolph van der Hoeven and Fred van der Kraaij (eds.), *Structural Adjustment and Beyond in Sub-Saharan Africa: Research and Policy Issues.* The Hague (Ministry of Foreign Affairs) 1994, pp. 100-113.

Baarsen, M.V. van, *The Netherlands and Sudan: Dutch Policies and Interventions with respect to the Sudanese Civil War.* The Hague (Netherlands Institute of International Relations Clingendael) 2000. (Clingendael Conflict Policy Research Project).

Bailey, F.G., *Stratagems and Spoils: A Social Anthropology of Politics.* Toronto (Copp Clark) 1969.

Baker, Bruce, 'The class of 1990: how have the autocratic leaders of sub-Saharan Africa fared under democratisation?' In: *Third World Quarterly* 19/1998/1, pp. 115-127. London (Third World Quarterly).

Ball, Nicole, and Tammy Halevy, *Making Peace Work: The Role of the International Development Community.* Washington (ODC) 1996. (Overseas Development Council Policy Essay, no. 18).

Ball, Nicole, *Pressing for Peace. Can Aid Induce Reform?* Washington (ODC) 1992. (Overseas Development Council Policy Essay, no. 6).

Bangura, Yusuf, *Democratization, Equity and Stability: African Politics and Societies in the 1990s.* Geneva

(United Nations Research Institute for Social Development) 1998. (UNRISD Discussion Paper, 93).

Barkan, Joel D., and David F. Gordon, 'Democracy in Africa: no time to forsake it'. In: *Foreign Affairs* 77/1998/4, pp. 107-111. New York (Council on Foreign Relations).

Barnett, Tony, and Alan Whiteside, *AIDS in the Twenty-First Century: Disease and Globalization*. Houndmills etc. (Palgrave Macmillan) 2001.

Barro, Robert J., and Xavier Sala-i-Martin, *Economic growth*. Boston (McGraw-Hill) 1995; Cambridge and London (MIT Press) 1999.

Bayart, Jean-François (ed.), *La greffe de l'Etat. Les trajectoires du politique* (*The Transplantation of the State: The Trajectories of Politics*), vol. 2. Paris (Karthala) 1996.

Bayart, Jean-François, 'Civil society in Africa'. In: Patrick Chabal (ed.), *Political Domination in Africa*. Cambridge (Cambridge University Press) 1986, pp. 109-125.

Bayart, Jean-François, 'L'historicité de l'Etat importé' ('The history of the imported state'). In: Jean-François Bayart (ed.), *La greffe de l'Etat* (*The Transplantation of the State*). Paris (Karthala) 1996, pp. 11-39.

Bayart, Jean-François, *L'Etat en Afrique. La politique du ventre*. Paris (Librairie Arthème Fayard) 1989.

Bayart, Jean-François, Stephen Ellis and Béatrice Hibou, *The Criminalisation of the State in Africa*. Oxford (International African Institute) 1999.

Bayart, Jean-François, *The State in Africa: The Politics of the Belly*. London (Longman) 1993. (English translation of the original French edition: *L'État en Afrique. La politique du ventre*. 1989.)

Berman, Bruce J., 'Ethnicity, patronage and the African state: the politics of uncivil nationalism'. In: *African Affairs* 97/1998/388, pp. 305-341. London (Royal African Society).

Bevan, Phillipa, and Sandra Fullerton Joireman, 'The perils of measuring poverty: identifying the 'poor' in rural Ethiopia'. In: *Oxford Development Studies* 25/2000/3, pp. 315-337. Abingdon (Carfax).

Bhinda, Nils, et al., *Private Capital Flows to Africa: Perception and Reality*. The Hague (FONDAD) 1999

Black, Cyril E., *The Dynamics of Modernization*. New York (Harper and Row) 1966.

Blair, Harry, 'Civil society and building democracy: lessons from international donor experience'. In: Amanda Bernard et al. (eds.), *Civil Society and International Development*. Paris (OECD) 1998. (Development Centre Studies).

Blanton, Robert, T. David Mason and Brian Athow, 'Colonial Style and Post-Colonial Ethnic Conflict in Africa'. In: *Journal of Peace Research*, vol. 38, no.4, 2001, pp. 473-491.

Blok, Anton, 'Het narcisme van de kleine verschillen'. In: *Amsterdams sociologisch tijdschrift* 24/1997/2, pp. 150-187. Groningen (Wolters-Noordhoff). (English version: 'The narcissism of minor differences'. In: *European Journal of Social Theory* 1/1998/1, pp. 33-56).

Bobbitt, Philip, *The Shield of Achilles: War, Peace and the Course of History*. New York (Alfred Knopf) 2002; Penguin Books 2003.

Boeck, Filip de, 'Lunda. Een korte geschiedenis van oorlog, dollars en diamanten in de grensstreek tussen Angola en de Democratische Republiek Congo' ('Lunda: a short history of war, dollars and diamonds around the border of Angola and the Democratic Republic of Congo'). In: N. Telligen, *Africa-expert-*

bijeenkomst: Ghana, Mali, Mozambique, Sierra Leone, Congo, Rwanda (*Expert Meeting on Africa: Ghana, Mali, Mozambique, Sierra Leone, Congo and Rwanda*). Leiden (African Studies Centre and Dutch Ministry of Foreign Affairs, Sub-Saharan Africa Department (DAF)) 2000, pp. 83-88.

Bolkestein, F., 'Het stilzwijgen rond een gevallen held' ('The silence surrounding a fallen hero.'). In: *De Volkskrant*, 4 September 2000. Amsterdam (PCM).

Bootsman, A., *De herkomst en financiering van wapens in het Grote Meren conflict* (*The Origins and Financing of Weapons in the Great Lakes Conflict*). 2000 (thesis, unpublished).

Bosscher, Doeko, Hans Renner and Rob Wagenaar (eds.), *De wereld na 1945* (*The World since 1945*). Utrecht (Spectrum, Aula) 1996. (First edition: 1992).

Bossema, Wim, 'Legers buurlanden plunderen Congo systematisch leeg' ('Armies from neighbouring countries systematically pillaging Congo'), *De Volkskrant*, 26 April 2001. Amsterdam (PCM).

Bossema, Wim. *De trots van Afrika* (*The Pride of Africa*). Amsterdam (Meulenhoff) 1998.

Boutros-Ghali, Boutros, *An Agenda for Democratization*. New York (United Nations) 1996. (2nd edition).

Bratton, Michael 'Second elections in Africa'. In: *The Journal of Democracy* 9/1998/3, pp. 51-66. Baltimore (John Hopkins University Press).

Bratton, Michael, 'Beyond the state: civil society and associational life in Africa'. In: *World Politics* 41/1989/3, pp. 407-430. Lawrenceville (Princeton University Press).

Bratton, Michael, and Nicolas van de Walle, *Democratic Experiments in Africa: Regime Transitions in Comparative Perspective*. Cambridge (Cambridge University Press) 1997.

Bratton, Michael, and Robert Mattes, 'Africans' surprising universalism'. In: *The Journal of Democracy* 12/2001/1, pp. 107-121. Baltimore (John Hopkins University Press).

Braudel, Fernand, *La Méditerranée et le monde méditerranéen à l'époque de Philippe II*. Paris (Armand Colin) 1949. (3 vols). (Translated into English as: *The Mediterranean and the Mediterranean World in the Age of Philip II*). New York (Harper and Row) 1972.

Breetvelt, J.N., *Dualisme en integratie. Een studie van de factoren die een rol spelen bij het hervinden van identiteit bij opgeleide Afrikanen*. (*Duality and Integration: a Study of the Factors that Play a Role in the Rediscovery of Identity by Educated Africans*.) Kampen (J.H. Kok) 1989. Doctoral thesis.

Breytenbach, Willie, *Democratisation in Sub-Saharan Africa: Transitions, Elections and Prospects for Consolidation*. Pretoria (Africa Institute of South Africa) 1997. (2nd ed.).

Brinton, Crane, *The Anatomy of Revolution*. New York (Prentice Hall) 1952.

Bryceson, Deborah Fahy and Vali Jamal, *Farewell to Farms: De-agrarianisation and Employment in Africa*. Leiden (African Studies Centre) 1997.

Bryceson, Deborah Fahy, 'An agrarian continent in transition'. In: Stephen Ellis (ed.), *Africa Now: People, Policies and Institutions*. The Hague (Ministry of Foreign Affairs) 1996.

Bryceson, Deborah Fahy, and John Howe, 'An agrarian continent in transition'. In: Stephen Ellis, (ed.), *Africa Now. People, Policies, Institutions*. London (James Currey) 1996, pp. 175-197.

Buijtenhuijs, Robert, and Céline Thiriot, *Democratization in Sub-Saharan Africa 1992-1995: An Overview of the Literature*. Leiden (African Studies Centre) 1995.

Buijtenhuijs, Robert, and Elly Rijnierse, *Democratization in Sub-Saharan Africa 1989-1992: An Overview of the Literature*. Leiden (African Studies Centre) 1993.

Caljé, P.A.J. and J.C. den Hollander, De nieuwste geschiedenis (*Contemporary History*). Utrecht (Spectrum, Aula) 1996. (First ed.: 1990).

Callaghy, Thomas M., 'Africa and the world economy'. In: John W. Harbeson and Donald Rothchild (eds.), *Africa in World Politics*. Boulder (Westview Press) 1991.

Callaghy, Thomas M., 'Africa, back to the future?' In: *The Journal of Democracy* 5/1994/4, pp. 133-145. Baltimore (John Hopkins University Press).

Callaghy, Thomas M., and John Ravenhill, 'Vision, politics and structure: Afro-optimism, Afro-pessimism, or realism'. In: Thomas M. Callaghy and John Ravenhill (eds.), *Hemmed In: Responses to Africa's Economic Decline*. New York (Columbia University Press) 1993.

Cambell, Catherine, *Letting Them Die: Why HIV/AIDS Prevention Programmes Fail*. Oxford (James Currey) 2003.

Carothers, Thomas, 'The end of the transition paradigm'. In: *Journal of Democracy* 13 (January 2002), pp. 5-21.

Castells, Manuel, *The Information Age: Economy, Society and Culture*. Cambridge, Mass. (Blackwell) 1996-1998 (3 vols).

Causes of Conflict in West Africa: Synthesis Report. The Hague (Netherlands Institute of International Relations Clingendael) 1998.

Chabal, Patrick, 'A few considerations on democracy in Africa'. In: *International Affairs* 74/1998/2, pp. 289-303. London (Royal Institute of International Affairs).

Chabal, Patrick, and Jean-Pascal Daloz, *Africa Works: Disorder as a Political Instrument*. Oxford/Bloomington (James Currey/Indiana University Press) 1998. (African Issues Series).

Chabal, Patrick, *Power in Africa: An Essay in Political Interpretation*. London (Macmillan) 1992.

Chabal, Patrick. (ed.), *Political domination in Africa: Reflections on the Limits of Power*. Cambridge etc. (Cambridge University Press) 1986.

Chabal, Patrick, with David Birmingham, Joshua Forrest, Malyn Newitt, Gerhard Seibert, and Elisa Silva Andrade, *A History of Postcolonial Lusophone Africa*. Bloomington and Indianapolis (Indiana University Press) 2002.

Chachage, Chachage Seithy L., *Environment, Aid and Politics in Zanzibar*. Dar es Salaam (DUP) 1996.

Chole, Eshetu, and Jibrin Ibrahim (eds.), *Democratisation Processes in Africa: Problems and Prospects*. Dakar (CODESRIA) 1995. (CODESRIA Book Series).

Clapham, Cristopher, *Africa and the International System: The Politics of State Survival*. Cambridge (Cambridge University Press) 1996.

Clark, Gordon L., and Michael Dear, *State Apparatus: Structures and Language of legitimacy*. Boston (Allen & Unwin) 1984.

Clark, John F., 'The National Conference as an instrument of democratization in Francophone Africa'. In: *Journal of Third World Studies* 11/1994/1, pp. 304-335. Americus (Association of Third World Studies).

Clark, John F., and David E. Gardinier (eds.), *Political Reform in Francophone Africa*. Boulder (Westview Press) 1997.

Clough, Michael, *Free at Last? US Policy toward Africa and the End of the Cold War*. New York (Council on Foreign Relations) 1992.

Club du Sahel, *Africities 2000*. Paris, 2000.

Cockcroft, Laurence, *Africa's Way: A Journey from the Past*. London (Tauris) 1990.

Collier, David, and Steven Levitsky, *Democracy 'with Adjectives': Conceptual Innovation in Comparative Research*. 1996. (Unpublished paper, University of California, Berkeley, 8 April 1996).

Collier, Paul, and Jan Willem Gunning, 'Explaining African economic performance'. In: *Journal of Economic Literature*, 37/1999, pp. 64-111. Nashville (American Economic Association).

Collier, Paul, *The Political Economy of Ethnicity*. Oxford (Centre for the Study of African Economies) 1998. (Working paper series, 98/8).

Collier, Paul, and Anke Hoeffler, *Aid, Policy and Growth in Post-Conflict Societies*. World Bank Working Paper No. 2902. Washington, D.C. (World Bank) 2002.

Comaroff, Jean, and John L. Comaroff (eds.), *Modernity and its Malcontents*. Chicago (University of Chigago Press) 1993.

Conflicten in Afrika. Crisisanalyse en preventiemogelijkheden. Brussels (King Baudouin Foundation/Médecins sans Frontières) 1997. Report of the Commission on African Regions in Crisis. (English version: *Conflicts in Africa: Crisis Analysis and Options for Prevention*).

Crefeld, Martin van, *The Transformation of War*. New York (Free Press) 1991.

Crummey, Donald (ed.), *Banditry, Rebellion and Social Protest in Africa*. Portsmouth (Heinemann) 1986.

Dahl, Robert A., *On Democracy*. London/New Haven (Yale University Press) 1998.

Dahl, Robert A., *Polyarchy: Participation and Opposition*. New Haven (Yale University Press) 1971.

David, W. L., and P. A. David, 'Resolving the African development cathexia: empowerment of the people'. In: Feraidoon Shams (ed.), *State and Society in Africa: Perspectives on Continuity and Change*. Lanham etc. (University Press of America) 1995.

Davidson, Basil, *The Black Man's Burden: Africa and the Curse of the Nation-State*. New York (Times Books) 1992.

Davies, James C., 'Toward a theory of revolution'. In: *American Sociological Review* 27 (1962), pp. 5-19.

De Heusch, Luc, *The Drunken King, or, The Origin of the State*. Indiana (Bloomington) 1982. (Original French edition: *Le roi ivre ou l'origine de l'état*. Paris (Gallimar) 1972).

De Soto, Hernando, *The Mystery of Capital: Why Capitalism Triumphs in the West and Fails Everywhere Else*. London (Black Swan) 2001.

De Witte, Ludo, *De moord op Lumumba*. Louvain (Van Halewijck) 1999. (Translated into English as: *The Assassination of Lumumba*. New York (Verso) 2001).

Decalo, Samuel, 'Benin: first of new democracies'. In: John F. Clark and David E. Gardinier (eds.), *Political Reform in Francophone Africa*. Boulder (Westview Press) 1997, pp. 43-61.

Dedieu, Jean-Philippe, 'Les élites africaines, enjeu de la diplomatie scientificque des Etats-Unis' ('Africa's elites, the stakes of the United States' scientific diplomacy'). In: *Politique Etrangère*, 1 (2003), pp 119-131.

Dia, Mamadou, *Africa's Management in the 1990s and Beyond: Reconciling Indigenous and Transplanted Institutions*. Washington, D.C. (World Bank) 1996.

Diallo, Garba, *Mauritania: The Other Apartheid?* Uppsala (Nordic Africa Insititute) 1993.

Diamond, Larry, 'Is the Third Wave over?' In: *The Journal of Democracy* 7/1996/3, pp. 20-37. Baltimore (John Hopkins University Press).

Diamond, Larry, and Marc F. Plattner (eds.), *Economic Reform and Democracy*. Baltimore (Johns Hopkins University Press) 1995.

Diamond, Larry, *Developing Democracy: Toward Consolidation*. Baltimore (Johns Hopkins University Press) 1999.

Diamond, Larry, Juan J. Linz and Seymour Martin Lipset (eds.), *Democracy in Developing Countries*. Boulder (Lynne Rienner) 1988. (Vol. 2: *Africa*).

Dietz, Ton, and Dick Foeken, 'The Crumbling of the African State System' In: Gertjan Dijkink and Hans Knippenberg (eds.), *The Territorial Factor: Political Geography in a Globalising World*. Amsterdam (Vossiuspers UvA) 2001, pp. 177-200.

Dijkink, Gertjan, and Hans Knippenberg (eds.), *The Territorial Factor: Political Geography in a Globalising World*. Amsterdam (Vossiuspers UvA) 2001.

Dobkowski, Michael, and Isidor Wallimann (eds.), *The Coming Age of Scarcity*. Syracuse (Syracuse University Press) 1998.

Dool, R.J. van den (ed.), *Normverva(n)ging. Een bijdrage aan de discussie over de budgettaire norm voor internationale samenwerking*. The Hague (Ministry of Foreign Affairs) 1993. (Translated into English as: *Crowding out or pitching in: A new budgetary target for Dutch development cooperation*).

Douma, P.S., *The Origins of Contemporary Conflict: A Comparison of Violence in Three World Regions*. Clingendael Study 18. The Hague (Clingendael) 2003.

Douma, Pyt, and Klaas van Walraven, *Between Indifference and Naïveté: Dutch Policy Interventions in African Conflicts*. Conflict Policy Research Project. The Hague (Conflict Policy Research Project, Netherlands Institute of International Relations Clingendael) 2000.

Douma, Pyt, Georg Frerks and Luc van de Goor, *Major Findings of the Research Project 'Causes of Conflict in the Third World': Executive Summary*. The Hague (Netherlands Institute of International Relations Clingendael) 1999.

Douma, Pyt, *The Netherlands and Rwanda: A Case Study on Dutch Foreign Policy and Interventions in the Contemporary Conflict History of Rwanda*. The Hague (Conflict Policy Research Project, Netherlands Institute of International Relations Clingendael) 2000.

Drèze, Jean, and Amartya Sen, *Hunger and Public Action*. Oxford (Clarendon Press) 1989.

Easterly, William, *The Elusive Quest for Growth: Economists' Adventures and Misadventures in the Tropics*. Cambridge (MIT Press) 2001.

Economic Commission for Africa (ECA), *Developing National Information and Communications Infrastructure (NICI) Policies, Plans and Strategies*. Addis Ababa 2000.

Edgerton, Robert B., 'Traditional beliefs and practices – are some better than others?' In: Lawrence E. Harrison and Samuel P. Huntington (eds.), *Culture Matters: How Values Shape Human Progress*. New York (Basic Books) 2000, pp. 126-140.

Edwards, Lyford P., *The Natural History of Revolution*. Chicago and London (University of Chicago Press) 1927.

Ekeh, Peter, 'Colonialism and the two publics: a theoretical statement'. In: *Comparative Studies in Society and History* 17 (January 1975), pp. 91-112.

Ellis, Stephen (ed.), *Africa Now: People, Policies, Institutions*. London (James Currey) 1996. (Published in cooperation with the Netherlands Ministry of Foreign Affairs, DGIS).

Ellis, Stephen, 'Africa after the Cold War: new patterns of government and politics'. In: *Development and Change* 27/1996/1, pp. 1-28. London (Sage Publications).

Ellis, Stephen, 'Briefing: West Africa and its soil'. In: *African Affairs* 102 (2003), pp. 135-138.

Ellis, Stephen, 'Democracy and human rights in Africa'. In: *The Historical Dimension of Development, Change and Conflict in the South*. The Hague (Ministry of Foreign Affairs) 1994 (Poverty and Development Series, no. 9). An earlier version appeared under the title 'Democracy in Africa: achievements and prospects.' In: Douglas Rimmer (ed.), *Action in Africa: The Experience of People Actively Involved in Government, Business and Aid*. London/Portsmouth (Royal African Society/James Currey) 1993.

Ellis, Stephen, 'Liberia's warlord insurgency'. In: Christopher Clapham (ed.), *African Guerrillas*. Oxford (James Currey) 1998.

Ellis, Stephen, and Gerrie ter Haar, 'Religion and politics in Sub-Saharan Africa'. In: *Journal of Modern African Studies* 36/1998/2, pp. 175-201. Cambridge (Cambridge University Press).

Ellis, Stephen, *The Mask of Anarchy: Religious Aspects of an African Civil War and the Destruction of Liberia*. London (C. Hurst and Co. Ltd.) 1999.

EMDAT database on disasters, Brussels (Centre for research on the epidemiology of disasters (CRED), Université Catholique de Louvain).

Engelbert, Pierre, 'Pre-colonial institutions, post-colonial states, and economic development in Tropical Africa'. In: *Political Research Quarterly* 53 (March 2000), pp. 1-30.

Engelbert, Pierre, *State Legitimacy and Development in Africa*. Boulder (Lynne Rienner) 2000.

Engels, F., *The Origin of the Family, Private Property and the State*. Atlanta (Pathfinder Press) 1972. Original German title: *Der Ursprung der Familie, des Privateigentums und des Staats* (1884).

Erdmann, Gero, 'Neo-patrimonial rule: transition to democracy has not succeeded'. In: *Development and Cooperation*, 2002/1, pp. 8–11. Frankfurt (Deutsche Stiftung für internationale Entwicklung, DSE).

Etounga-Manguelle, Daniel, 'Does Africa need a Cultural Adjustment Program?'. In: Lawrence E. Harrison and Samuel P. Huntington (eds.), *Culture Matters: How Values Shape Human Progress*, pp. 65-77.

European Commission, *Democratisation, the Rule of Law, Respect for Human Rights, and Good Governance: The Challenges of the Partnership between the European Union and the ACP States*. Brussels (European Commission) 1998.

Evans, Peter B., Dietrich Rueschmayer and Theda Skocpol (eds.), *Bringing the State Back in*. Cambridge (Cambridge University Press) 1985.

Eyoh, Dickson L., 'African perspectives on democracy and the dilemmas of postcolonial intellectuals'. In: *Africa Today* 3-4/1998/45, pp. 281-306. Denver (Africa Today).

Eyoh, Dickson L., 'From economic crisis to political liberalization: pitfalls of the new political sociology for Africa'. In: *African Studies Review* 39/1996/3, pp. 43-80. Atlanta (African Studies Association).

Fatton, Robert, *Predatory Rule: State and Civil Society in Africa*. Boulder (Lynne Rienner) 1992.

Fieldhouse, David K., *Black Africa 1945-1980. Economic Decolonization and Arrested Development*. London (Allen and Unwin) 1986.

Fieldhouse, David K., *The Colonial Empires: A Comparative Survey from the 18th Century*. London (Weidenfeld and Nicolson) 1966: London (Macmillan) 1982, 2nd edition.

Fortes, Meyer, and E.E. Evans-Pritchard (eds.), *African Political Systems*. London etc. (Oxford University Press) 1970.

Franck, Thomas M., 'The emerging right to democratic governance'. In: *American Journal of International Law* 86/1992, pp. 46-91. Washington, D.C. (American Society of International Law).

Frank, Andre Gunder, *Capitalism and Underdevelopment in Latin America*. New York (Monthly Review Press) 1967.

Frank, Andre Gunder, *On Capitalist Underdevelopment*. Oxford (Oxford University Press) 1975.

Fredland, Richard A., 'AIDS and development: an inverse correlation?' In: *Journal of Modern African Studies*, 36/1998/4, pp. 547-568. Cambridge (Cambridge University Press).

Freedom House, Annual survey of freedom country scores, 1972-1973 to 1999-2000. New York (Freedom House) 2001.

Freund, B., *The Making of Contemporary Africa: The Development of African Society since 1800*. Basingstoke (Macmillan) 1998.

Frimpong-Ansah, John, *The Vampire State in Africa*. Trenton (Africa World Press) 1991.

Frobenius, Léo, *Histoire de la civilisation africaine* (*History of African Civilisation*). Paris (Gallimard) 1938.

Fukuyama, Francis, *Trust: The Social Virtues and the Creation of Prosperity*. New York etc. (Simon and Schuster) 1995.

Gambari, Ibrahim A., 'The role of foreign intervention in African reconstruction'. In: I. William Zartman (ed.), *Collapsed States: The Disintegration and Restoration of Legitimate Authority*. Boulder/London (Lynne Rienner) 1995.

Gates, Jr., Henry Louis, *Wonders of the African World*. New York (Knopf) 1999.

Geertz, Clifford, *The Interpretation of Cultures: Selected Essays*. New York (Basis Books) 1973.

Geest, Sjaak van der, 'Reciprociteit en zorg voor oud-eren. Een anthropologische vergelijking tussen Ghana en Nederland' ('Reciprocity and elder care: a comparative anthropological study of Ghana and the Netherlands'). In: *Tijdschrift voor Gerontologie en Geriatrie* 1998/29. Deventer (Van Loghum Slaterus).

Geest, Sjaak van der, 'Zorg om ouderen in Ghana' ('Elder care in Ghana'). In: N. Telligen, *Africa-expert-bijeenkomst: Ghana, Mali, Mozambique, Sierra Leone, Congo en Rwanda (Expert Meeting on Africa: Ghana, Mali, Mozambique, Sierra Leone, Congo and Rwanda)*. Leiden (African Studies Centre and Dutch Ministry of Foreign Affairs, Sub-Saharan Africa Department (DAF)) 2000, pp. 19-26.

Gendzier, Irene, *Managing Political Change: Social Scientists and the Third World*. Boulder (Westview Press) 1985.

Geschiere, Peter et al., De smalle marge van de onafhankelijkheid. Opstellen over Afrika (*The Narrow Margin of Independence: Essays on Africa*). Amsterdam (Bert Bakker) 1982. (Contact tijdsdocumenten).

Geschiere, Peter, *Village Communities and the State: Changing Relations among the Maka of South-Eastern Cameroon since the Colonial Conquest*. London, Boston and Melbourne (Paul Kegan) 1982.

Gier, J. de, 'Islam in de wereld' ('Islam in the world'). In: *Elsevier* 57/2001/40, pp. 50-51. Amsterdam (Bonaventura).

Gifford, Prosser (ed.), *The Christian Churches and the Democratization of Africa*. Leiden (Brill) 1995.

Gifford, Prosser, and William Roger Louis, *Decolonization and African Independence. The Transfers of Power, 1960-1980*. London/New Haven (Yale University Press) 1988.

Global Coalition for Africa, *Study on Transition to Democracy in Africa: Policy Issues and Implications*. Washington (GCA) 1996.

Global Coalition for Africa, *The Consolidation of Democracy*. Washington (GCA) 1997.

Global Coalition for Africa, *Urbanization in Sub-Saharan Africa: Policy Issues and Implications*. 2000. (GCA Document/PF/No.2/10/2000 for the Policy Forum in Abuja, Nigeria, 20-21 October 2000).

Goldsmith, Arthur A., 'Donors, dictators and democrats in Africa'. In: *Journal of Modern African Studies* 39/2001/3, pp. 411-436. Cambridge (Cambridge University Press).

Goldsmith, Arthur A., 'Foreign aid and statehood in Africa'. In: *Journal of Modern African Studies* 55/2001/1, pp. 123-148. Cambridge (World Peace Foundation).

Goldsmith, Arthur A., 'Risk, rule and reason: leadership in Africa'. Public Administration and Development 21/2001/2, pp. 77-87. New York (RIPA).

Goodwin-Gill, Guy S., *Codes of Conduct for Elections*. Geneva (Inter-Parliamentary Union) 1998.

Goodwin-Gill, Guy S., *Free and Fair Elections*. Geneva (Inter-Parliamentary Union) 1994.

Goody, Jack, *Technology, Tradition and the State in Africa*. Cambridge (Cambridge University Press) 1980.

Goody, Jack, *The East in the West*. Cambridge (Cambridge University Press) 1996.

Goor, Luc van de, Kumar Rupesinghe and Paul Sciarone (eds.), *Between Development and Destruction: An Enquiry into the Causes of Conflict in Post-Colonial States*. Houndmills etc. (Macmillan Press Ltd) 1996.

Gordon, A.A., and D.L. Gordon (eds.), *Understanding Contemporary Africa*. Boulder/London (Lynne Rienner) 1996. (2nd edition).

Gordon, David F., and Howard Wolpe, 'The other Africa: an end to Afro-pessimism'. In: *World Policy Journal* 15/1998/1, pp. 49-59. New York (World Policy Institute).

Gray, John, *False Dawn: The Delusions of Global Capitalism*. London (Granta Books) 1998.

Gross, Feliks, *The Civic and the Tribal State*. Westport/London (Greenwood Press) 1998.

Haggard, Stephen, Jean-Dominique Lafay and Christian Morrisson (eds.), *The Political Feasibility of Adjustment* in *Developing Countries*. Paris (OECD) 1995. (Development Centre Studies).

Hancock, Graham, *Lords of Poverty*. London (Mandarin) 1990.

Hancock, Graham, *The Sign and the Seal: A Quest for the Lost Ark of the Covenant*. London (Mandarin) 1992.

Harbeson, John W., and Donald Rothchild (eds.), *Africa in World Politics*. Boulder (Westview Press) 1991.

Harbeson, John W., et al. (eds.), *Civil Society and the State in Africa*. Boulder (Lynne Rienner) 1994.

Harrison, Lawrence E., and Samuel P. Huntington (eds.), *Culture Matters: How Values Shape Human Progress*. New York (Basic Books) 2000.

Hassing, Paul, 'Energie in Afrika' ('Energy in Africa'). In: *Energie- en Milieuspectrum* 10/1996, pp. 26-29. Utrecht/Sittard (Novem).

Haver Droeze, F., *Effecten van economische globalisering. Een terreinverkenning* (*Effects of Economic Globalisation: An Exploration*). Memorandum, Dutch Ministry of Foreign Affairs (SBO/PL) 1997.

Haynes, J., *Religion in Global politics*. London/New York (Longman) 1998.

Heide, L. van der, 'Zuid-Afrika ziet nieuwkomers liever gaan' ('South Africa would prefer new arrivals to leave'). In: *NRC Handelsblad*, 11 February 2000. Rotterdam (PCM).

Heijden, Hendrik van der, *The Effectiveness of Economic Policy Reform, Foreign Aid and Debt Relief in Zambia*. (ms., 2000).

HelpAge International, *Annual Review 1997/1998*.

Henley, David, 'Entrepreneurship, individualism and trust in Indonesia.' Unpublished paper for the Seminar on Indonesian Social History, Jakarta/Depok, 8-11 December 1997. Available at the KITLV (Royal Netherlands Institute of Southeast Asian and Caribbean Studies) library in Leiden, the Netherlands.

Herbst, Jeffrey, *States and Power in Africa: Comparative Lessons in Authority and Control*. Princeton, New Jersey (Princeton University Press) 2000.

Hertz, Noreena, *The Silent Takeover: Global Capitalism and the Death of Democracy*. New York (Free Press) 2001.

Hesseling, Gerti and Hens Kraemer, *Senegal/Gambia*. Amsterdam/The Hague (KIT Publishers, NOVIB, NCOS) 1996 (Landenreeks series).

Hobbes, Thomas, *Leviathan*, ed. by Michael Oakeshott, New York (Collier Books) 1962.

Hobsbawm, Eric, and Terence Ranger (eds.), *The Invention of Tradition*. Cambridge (Cambridge University Press) 1983.

Hodder-Williams, Richard, *An Introduction to the Politics of Tropical Africa*. London (George Allen & Unwin) 1984.

Hoeven, Rolph van der, and Fred van der Kraaij (eds.), *Structural Adjustment and Beyond in Sub-Saharan Africa: Research and Policy Issues*. The Hague (Ministry of Foreign Affairs) 1994.

Holm, John D., 'Development, democracy and civil society in Botswana'. In: Adrian Leftwich (ed.), *Democracy and Development: Theory and Practice*. Cambridge (Polity Press) 1996, pp. 97-113.

Homer-Dixon, Thomas F., *Environment, Scarcity, and Violence*. Princeton Press 1999.

Hope, Kempe Ronald, 'Development policy and economic performance in Botswana: lessons for the tran-

sition economies in Sub-Saharan Africa'. In: *Journal of International Development*, 10/1998/3, pp. 539-554.

Horton, Robin, 'Stateless societies in the history of West Africa'. In: J.F. Ade Ajayi and Michael Crowder (eds.), *History of West Africa*. New York (Longman) 1972.

Horton, Robin, *Patterns of Thought in Africa and the West: Essays in Magic, Religion and Science*. Cambridge (Cambridge University Press) 1997.

Hountondji, Paulin, *African Philosophy: Myth and Reality*. Bloomington (Indiana University Press) 1983.

Houweling, H., 'Demography, commodity chain position, state paralysis and structural reform in Sub-Saharan Africa'. Amsterdam (University of Amsterdam) 1999. (Paper for PSCW).

Howe, Stephen, *Afrocentrism: Mythical Pasts and Imagined Homes*. London/New York (Verso) 1998.

Human Rights Watch, 'Bulgaria: Money talks – arms dealing with human rights abusers', HRW World Report, vol. 11, no. 4, April 1999.

Human Rights Watch, *Arsenals on the Cheap: NATO Expansion and the Arms Cascade*. New York (Human Rights Watch) 1999. (HRW report).

Human Rights Watch, *Bulgaria: Money Talks – Arms Dealing with Human Rights Abusers*. New York (Human Rights Watch) 1999. (HRW report).

Human Rights Watch, *Protectors or Pretenders? Government Human Rights Commissions in Africa*. New York (Human Rights Watch) 2001. (HRW report).

Human, Piet, and André Zaaiman (eds.), *Managing towards Self-reliance: Effectiveness of Organisations in Africa*. Dakar (Gorée Institute) 1995.

Huntington, Samuel P., *Political Order in Changing Societies*. New Haven/London (Yale University Press) 1968.

Huntington, Samuel P., *The Clash of Civilizations and the Remaking of World Order*. New York (Simon and Schuster) 1996.

Huntington, Samuel P., *The Third Wave: Democratization in the Late 20th Century*. Norman/London (Oklahoma University Press) 1991.

Husain, Ishrat, 'Structural adjustment and the long-term development of Sub-Saharan Africa'. In: Rolph van der Hoeven and Fred van der Kraaij (eds.), *Structural Adjustment and Beyond in Sub-Saharan Africa: Research and Policy Issues*. The Hague (Ministry of Foreign Affairs) 1994, pp. 150-170.

Hyden, Goran, and Michael Bratton (eds.), *Governance and Politics in Africa*. Boulder (Lynne Rienner) 1992.

Hyden, Göran, *Beyond Ujamaa in Tanzania: Underdevelopment and an Uncaptured Peasantry*. London (Heinemann) 1980.

Hyslop, Jonathan (ed.), *African Democracy in the Era of Globalisation*. Johannesburg (Witwatersrand University Press) 1999.

Ihonvbere, Julius O., 'The state, human rights and democratization in Africa'. In: *Current World Leaders* 37/1994/4, pp. 59-80. Santa Barbara (International Academy).

Ihonvbere, Julius O., 'Where is the third wave? A critical evaluation of Africa's non-transition to democracy'. In: *Africa Today* 43/1996/4, pp. 343-368. Denver (University of Denver).

Iliffe, John, *A Modern History of Tanganyika*. Cambridge (Cambridge University Press), 1979.

Iliffe, John, *Africans: The History of a Continent*. Cambridge (Cambridge University Press) 1995.

Iliffe, John, *The African Poor: A History*. Cambridge (Cambridge University Press) 1987.

International Crisis Group, *Scramble for the Congo: Anatomy of an Ugly War*. Nairobi/Brussels (International Crisis Group) 2000. (ICG Africa Report, no. 26).

International Institute for Strategic Studies, *The Military Balance 1999-2000*. London (IISS) 2000.

Internet Development in Africa, University of Düsseldorf website, 2000.

Inter-Parliamentary Union, *Democracy: Its Principles and Achievement*. Geneva (Inter-Parliamentary Union) 1998. (Includes the Universal Declaration on Democracy).

'Is democracy possible in multiethnic states?' In: *INR Foreign Affairs Brief*. Washington, D.C. 1993. (Report from the US Department of State).

Italiaander, Rolf, De *nieuwe leiders van Afrika*. Utrecht (Bruna) 1962. (Original German edition: *Die neuen Männer Afrikas*. Düsseldorf (Econ Verlag/Dick Bruna) 1960). (Translated into English as: *The New Leaders of Africa*. Englewood Cliffs, NJ (Prentice Hall) 1961).

Jackson, Robert H., and Carl G. Rosberg, *Personal Rule in Black Africa: Prince, Autocrat, Prophet, Tyrant*. Berkeley (University of California Press) 1982.

Jackson, Robert H., *Quasi-States: Sovereignty, International Relations and the Third World*. Cambridge (Cambridge University Press) 1990.

Jackson, Robert, and Carl Rosberg, 'Why Africa's weak states persist: the empirical and juridical in statehood'. In: *World Politics*, 35, 1 (October 1982), pp. 1-24.

Jong, J.J.P. de, 'De migratiecrisis. Oorzaken, prognose en aanzet tot een beleidsdiscussie' ('The migration crisis: causes, a prognosis and an impetus for policy debate'). In: *Internationale Spectator* 55/2001/3, pp. 138-144.

Jong, J.J.P. de, *De waaier van het fortuin. Nederlanders in Azië en de Indonesische archipel 1595-1950 (The Fan of Fortune: The Dutch in Asia and the Indonesian Archipelago, 1595-1950)*. The Hague (SDU) 2000.

Joseph, Richard A. (red.), *State, Conflict, and Democracy in Africa*. Boulder (Lynne Rienner) 1999.

Joseph, Richard A., 'Zambia, a model for democratic change'. In: *Current History* 91/1992, pp. 199-201. Philadelphia (Current History).

Joseph, Richard, 'Africa: States in crisis'. In: *Journal of Democracy* 14, no. 3, July 2003, pp. 159-170.

Joseph, Richard, 'Nation-state trajectories in Africa'. In: *Georgetown Journal of International Affairs* 4 (Winter/Spring 2003), pp. 13-20.

Julien, Paul, Kampvuren langs de evenaar (*Campfires along the Equator*). Baarn (Mingus) 1993. (First edition: 1940).

Kabou, Axelle, *Et si l'Afrique refusait le développement?* (*And What If Africa Rejects Development?*) Paris (l'Harmattan) 1991.

Kadt, Emanuel de, *Back to Society and Culture: On Aid Donors' Overblown Concern with 'Governance' and Democratisation*. Utrecht (University of Utrecht) 1999.

Kane, Hal, *The Hour of Departure: Forces that Create Refugees and Migrants*. Washington, D.C. (Worldwatch Institute) 1995. (Worldwatch paper, no. 125).

Kane, Mohamadou, 'L'actualité de la littérature africaine d'expression française' ('Current developments in Francophone African literature'). In: *Réflexions sur la première décennie des indépendances en Afrique noire : Cahiers de présence africaine*, Special issue.

Kaplan, Robert D., 'The coming anarchy'. In: *The Atlantic Monthly* 273/1994/2, pp. 44-76. Boston (Atlantic Monthly Cy.).

Kaplan, Robert D., *The Coming Anarchy: Shattering the Dreams of the Post Cold War*. New York (Random House) 2000.

Kaplan, Robert D., *The Ends of the Earth: A Journey at the Dawn of the 21st Century*. New York (Random House) 1996.

Kapuscinksi, Ryszard, *The Emperor*. New York (Vintage Books) 1984.

Karl, Terry Lynn, *The Paradox of Plenty: Oil Booms and Petro-States*. Berkeley (UC Press) 1999.

Kastelein, T.J., *Groei naar een industriële samenleving. Inleiding tot 200 jaar sociale en economische geschiedenis* (*The Growth of an Industrial Society: An Introduction to Two Centuries of Social and Economic History*). Groningen (Wolters-Noordhoff) 1977.

Klein, Martin A., and G. Wesley Johnson (eds.), *Perspectives on the African Past*. Boston (Little, Brown and Co.) 1972.

Klein, Naomi, *No Logo: Taking Aim at the Brand Bullies*. New York (Picador) 2000.

Krasner, Stephen, 'Approaches to the state: alternative conceptions and historical dynamics'. In: *Comparative Politics* 16 (April 1984), pp. 223-46.

Kreijen, Gerard, *State failure, Sovereignty and Effectiveness*. PhD Leyden University 2004.

Kuitenbrouwer, Maarten, *De ontdekking van de Derde Wereld. Beeldvorming en beleid in Nederland 1950-1990* (*The Discovery of the Third World. The image and policy in the Netherlands 1950-1990*). The Hague (SDU) 1994.

Landes, David S., *The Wealth and Poverty of Nations: Why Some are So Rich and Some So Poor*. New York/London (W.W. Norton and Co.) 1998.

Lanschot, R. van, 'Het gaat Somalië zo slecht nog niet na het vertrek van de VN' ('Somalia not faring so badly after UN departure'). In: *NRC Handelsblad*, 10 April 1995. Rotterdam (PCM).

Lawrence, Robert Z., *Single World, Divided Nations?* Washington, D.C. and Paris (Brooking Institution/OECD Development Centre) 1996.

Leftwich, Adrian (ed.), *Democracy and Development: Theory and Practice*. Cambridge (Polity Press) 1996.

Lemarchand, René, *Burundi: Ethnic Conflict and Genocide*. Cambridge (Cambridge University Press) 1994. (Woodrow Wilson Center Series).

Lensink, Robert, and Howard White, *Aid Dependence: Issues and Indicators*. Expert Group on Development Issues. Stockholm 1999.

Lensink, Robert, *Structural Adjustment in Sub-Saharan Africa*. London/New York (Longman) 1996.

Levy, Marion, *Modernization and the Structure of Societies: A Setting for International Affairs*. Princeton (Princeton University Press) 1966.

Lijphart, Arend, *Democracies: Patterns of Majoritarian and Consensus Government in Twenty-One Countries*. New Haven (Yale University Press) 1984.

Lijphart, Arend, *Democracy in Plural Societies: A Comparative Exploration*. New Haven (Yale University Press) 1977.

Lindijer, K., 'De Afrikanisering van de hebzucht' ('The Africanisation of greed'). In: *NRC Handelsblad* 21-11-1998.

Lloyd, P.C., *The New Elites of Tropical Africa*. Oxford (Oxford University Press) 1966.

Lodge, Tom, 'South Africa: democracy and development in a post-apartheid society'. In: Adrian Leftwich (ed.), *Democracy and Development: Theory and Practice.* Cambridge (Polity Press) 1996, pp. 188-208.

Longman, Tom, 'Rwanda: democratization and disorder, political transformation and social deterioration'. In: John F. Clark and David E. Gardinier (eds.), *Political Reform in Francophone Africa.* Boulder (Westview Press) 1997, pp. 287-306.

Lynch, Katherine A., *Individuals, Families and Communities in Europe, 1200-1800: The Urban Foundations of Western Society.* Cambridge (Cambridge University Press) 2003.

Machiavelli, *Il principe.* 1532. Dutch edition: *De prins.* 1705. English title: *The Prince.*

Maddison, Angus, *Monitoring the World Economy 1820-1992.* Parijs (OECD) 1995.

Maddison, Angus, *The World Economy: A Millennial Perspective.* Paris (OECD, Development Centre Studies) 2001.

Makinda, Samuel M., 'Democracy and multi-party politics in Africa'. In: *Journal of Modern African Studies* 34/1996/4, pp. 555-573. Cambridge (Cambridge University Press).

Makumbe, John, 'Is there a civil society in Africa?' In: *International Affairs* 74/1998/2, pp. 305-317. London (Royal Institute of International Affairs).

Mamdani, Mahmood, *Citizen and Subject: Contemporary Africa and the Legacy of Late Colonialism.* Princeton (Fountain Publishers) 1995.

Mandel, Robert, *Armies without States: the Privatization of Security.* London (Lynne Rienner) 2002

Marres, Pieter, 'Schaf ontwikkelingshulp af' ('Do away with development aid'). In: *De Volkskrant*, 10 May 2001. Amsterdam (PCM).

Marte, Fred, *Political Cycles in International Relations: The Cold War and Africa, 1945-1990.* Amsterdam (VU University Press) 1994. (Doctoral thesis).

Martin, Phyllis, and Patrick O'Meara (eds.), *Africa.* Bloomington, Indianapolis (Indiana University Press) 1995 (third edition).

Maxwell, Gavin, *God Protect Me from My Friends.* London (Readers Union) 1957.

Mazrui, Ali A., *Cultural Forces in World Politics.* London (Currey) 1990.

Mbeki, Thabo, 'The African Renaissance, South Africa and the world'. 1998. (Address at the United Nations University, Tokyo, 9 April 1998).

Mbembe, Achille, *On the Postcolony.* Berkeley etc. (University of California Press) 2001.

McEvedy, Colin, and Richard Jones, *Atlas of World Population History.* Harmondsworth (Penguin Books) 1978.

McGowan, Patrick J., 'African military coups d'état, 1956-2001: Frequency, trends and distribution.' In: *Journal of Modern African Studies*, vol. 41, September 2003, pp. 339-370.

Médard, Jean-François (ed) *Etats d'Afrique noire : Formation, mécanismes et crise* (States of Black Africa: Formation, Mechanisms and Crisis). Paris (Karthala) 1991.

Médard, Jean-François, 'L'Etat néo-patrimonial en Afrique noire' ('The neopatrimonial state in Black Africa'). In: Jean-François Médard (ed.) *Etats d'Afrique noire : Formation, mécanismes et crise* (States of Black Africa: Formation, Mechanisms and Crisis). Paris (Karthala) 1991, pp. 323-353.

Mengisteab, Kidane, and Cyril Daddieh (eds.), *State Building and Democratization in Africa: Faith, Hope and Realities.* Westport, CT (Preager) 1999.

Menkhaus, Ken, 'Somalia: political order in a stateless society'. In: *Current History* 97/1998/619, pp. 220-224. Philadelphia (Current History).

Migdal, Joel S., *Strong Societies and Weak States: State-Society Relations and State Capabilities in the Third World.* Princeton, N.J. (Princeton University Press) 1988.

Mills, Greg, *Poverty to Prosperity: Globalisation, Good Governance and African Recovery.* Johannesburg (South African Institute of International Affairs) and Cape Town (Tafelberg Publishers) 2002.

Mistry, Percy S., *Resolving Africa's Multilateral Debt Problem: A Response to the IMF and the World Bank.* The Hague (FONDAD) 1996

Mkandawire, Thandika, and Adebayo O. Olukoshi (eds.), *Between Liberalisation and Oppression: The Politics of Structural Adjustment in Africa.* Dakar (CODESRIA) 1995. (CODESRIA Book Series).

Mohamoud, Abdullah Abdulkadir, *State Collapse and Post-Conflict Development in Africa: The Case of Somalia (1960-2001).* Amsterdam 2001. (Unpublished dissertation, University of Amsterdam 2001).

Molema, Hans 'Ook het ANC kan een monster worden' ('Even the ANC could become a monster'). In: *De Volkskrant,* 30 August 2000. Amsterdam (PCM).

Molema, Hans, 'Racisme is nog overal in Zuid-Afrika' ('Racism still rife in South Africa'). In: *De Volkskrant,* 31 August 2000. Amsterdam (PCM).

Mullins, A.F., Jr., *Born Arming: Development and Military Power in New States.* Stanford (Stanford University Press) 1987.

Mudimbe, V.Y., *The Invention of Africa.* Bloomington (Indiana University Press) 1988.

Musah, Abdel-Fatau, 'Privatization of security, arms proliferation and the process of state collapse in Africa'. In: *Development and Change* 33 (5) 2002, pp. 911-933.

Myrdal, Gunnar, *Asian Drama: An Inquiry into the Poverty of Nations.* New York (Pantheon) 1968. (3 vols.).

Nathan, Laurie, 'The four horsemen of the apocalypse: the structural cause of violence in Africa'. At http://ccrweb.ccr.uct.ac.za/two/10_2/p04_horsemen.html.

National Advisory Council for Development Cooperation (NAR), *Ontwikkelingssamenwerking tussen oorlog en vrede* (*Development Cooperation between War and Peace*). The Hague (NAR) 1996. (NAR advisory report, no. 111).

National Intelligence Council (NIC), *Global Trends 2015: A Dialogue about the Future with Nongovernment Experts.* Washington (NIC) 2000.

Norberg, *Leve de globalisering.* Antwerp and Amsterdam (Houtekriet) 2002. Original Swedish edition: *Till världskapitalismens försvar*, Stockholm (Timbro) 2001. British English edition: *In Defence of Global Capitalism.* Stockholm (Timbro) 2001.

Nwokedi, Emeka, *Politics of Democratization: Changing Authoritarian Regimes in Sub-Saharan Africa.* London/Hamburg (Lit Verlag) 1995.

Oakeshott, Michael, *Rationalism in Politics and Other Essays.* London (Methuen & Co.) 1962.

Obdeijn, Herman and Robert Ross, 'Afrika na 1945' ('Africa since 1945'). In: Doeko Bosscher, Hans Renner and Rob Wagenaar (eds.), *De wereld na 1945 (The*

World since 1945). Utrecht (Spectrum, Aula) 1996, pp. 425-448.

OECD/DAC, *Geographical Distribution of Financial Flows 1994-1998*. Paris (OECD) 1999.

OECD/DAC, *Shaping the 21st Century: The Contribution of Development Co-operation*. Paris (OECD) 1996.

Okigbo, Charles, *Communication and Poverty: The Challenge of Social Change in Africa*. Montreal 1999.

Oliver, Roland, and John D. Fage, *A Short History of Africa*. Harmondsworth (Penguin Books) 1995. (First edition: 1962).

Oliver, Roland, *The African Experience*. London (Weidenfeld and Nicolson) 1991.

Olsen, Gorm Rye, 'Europe and the promotion of democracy in post Cold War Africa: how serious is Europe and for what reason?' In: *African Affairs* 97/1998/388, pp. 343-367. London (Royal African Society).

Olson, Marcur, 'Dictatorship, democracy and development'. In: *American Political Science Review*, vol. 87, no. 3, September 1998, pp. 567-576.

Oomen, B., *Chiefs! Law, Power and Culture in Contemporary South Africa*. Amsterdam, doctoral thesis, 2002.

Osaghae, Eghosa E., *Crippled Giant: Nigeria since Independence*. London (Hurst and Company) 1998.

Ottaway, Marina (ed.), *Democracy in Africa: The Hard Road Ahead*. Boulder, CO (Lynne Rienner) 1997.

Ottaway, Marina, 'Africa's new leaders: African solution or African problem?' In: *Current history* 97/1998/619, pp. 209-213. Philadelphia (Current History).

Ottaway, Marina, 'Post-imperial Africa at war'. In: *Current History*, 98, no. 628 (May 1999), pp. 202-207.

Ottaway, Marina, *Africa's New Leaders: Democracy or State Reconstruction?* Washington DC (Carnegie Endowment for International Peace) 1999.

Otto, J.M., 'Ontwikkelingssamenwerking en goed bestuur' ('Development cooperation and good governance'). In: *Internationale Spectator* 51/1997/4, pp. 223-229. The Hague (Netherlands Institute of International Relations Clingendael).

Owusu, Maxwell, 'Democracy and Africa: a view from the village'. In: *Journal of Modern African Studies* 30/1992/3, pp. 377-397. Cambridge (Cambridge University Press).

Oyebade, Adebayo, and Abiodun Alao (eds.), *Africa after the Cold War: The Changing Perspectives on Security*. Trenton etc. (Africa World Press, Inc.) 1998.

Oyugi, Walter O. et al. (eds.), *Democratic Theory and Practice in Africa*. London (James Currey) 1988.

Painter, David S., *The Cold War: An International History*. London, New York (Routledge) 1999. (Making of the contemporary world series).

Palmer, R.R., and Joel Colton, *A History of the Modern World*. Boston (McGraw-Hill) 2001. (First edition: 1950).

Pankhurst, Richard, *The Ethiopians*. Oxford (Blackwell) 1998.

Pech, Khareen, 'Mobilisation of mercenaries'. In: *Jane's Intelligence Review*. 1 March 1997. Coulsdon (Jane's Information Group).

Percival, Valerie, and Thomas Homer-Dixon, *Environmental Scarcity and Violent Conflict: The Case of Rwanda*. Project on environment, population and security (EPS). 1995.

Polman, Linda, 'De vloek van het netwerk' ('The curse of the network'). In: *NRC Handelsblad* (Dutch daily newspaper), 20 December 2002, p. 27.

Potts, Deborah, 'Shall we go home? Increasing urban poverty in African cities and migration processes'. In: *The Geographical Journal*. 161/1995/3, pp. 245-264. London (Royal Geographical Society).

Prunier, Gérard, *The Rwanda Crisis: History of a Genocide*. London (Hurst and Co.) 1997.

Rake, Alan, *African Leaders: Guiding the New Millennium*. Lanham, Maryland, and London (Scarecrow Press) 2001.

Rakodi, Carole (ed.), *The Urban Challenge in Africa: Growth and Management of Its Large Cities*. Tokyo (UN University Press) 1997.

Ramondt, P., *De machtspolitieke betekenis van de netwerkmaatschappij* (*The Significance of the Network Society in terms of Power Politics*). Memorandum, Dutch Ministry of Foreign Affairs, 2000.

Ranger, Terence, 'The invention of tradition in colonial Africa'. In: Hobsbawm, Eric, and Terence Ranger (eds.), *The Invention of Tradition*. Cambridge (Cambridge University Press) 1983, pp. 211-262.

RAWOO, *Local Perspectives on Globalization*. Workshop report. Dar es Salaam, Tanzania, 10-11 September 1998.

Reader, John, *Africa: A Biography of the Continent*. London (Hamish Hamilton) 1997.

Reed, David (ed.), *Structural Adjustment and the Environment*. London (Earthscan Publications) 1992.

Reefe, Thomas Q., *The Rainbow and the Kings: A History of the Luba Empire to 1891*. Berkeley, Los Angeles, London (University of California Press) 1981.

Reno, William, *Corruption and State Politics in Sierra Leone*. Cambridge (Cambridge University Press) 1995. (African Studies Series, 83).

Reno, William, *Warlord Politics and African States*. Boulder (Lynne Rienner) 1998.

Reyntjens, Filip, *Danse macabre. Rwanda en Burundi, tussen haat en hoop* (*Danse Macabre: Rwanda and Burundi between Hate and Hope*). Antwerp (Icarus) 1996.

Richards, Paul, *Fighting for the Rain Forest: War, Youth and Resources in Sierra Leone*. Oxford (James Currey) 1996.

Rieff, David, 'In defense of Afro-pessimism'. In: *World Policy Journal*, 15/1998/99/4, pp. 10-22. New York (World Policy Institute).

Rimmer, Douglas (ed.), *Action in Africa: The Experience of People Actively Involved in Government, Business and Aid*. London/Portsmouth (Royal African Society/James Currey) 1993.

Robinson, Clive, 'The coherence of European development policies in Africa'. In: 'Europe and Africa: the search for a new partnership', *Development* 41/1998/4, pp. 27-33. Rome (Society for International Development).

Robinson, Pearl T., 'Democratization: understanding the relationship between regime change and the culture of politics'. In: *African Studies Review*, 37/1994/1, pp. 39-67. Atlanta (African Studies Association).

Rodney, Walter, *How Europe Underdeveloped Africa*. Londen (Bogle-L'Ouverture Publications) and Dar es Salaam (Tanzanian Publishing House) 1972.

Rodrik, Dani, *Trade Policy and Economic Performance in Sub-Saharan Africa*. Stockholm (Ministry of Foreign Affairs) 1998. (EGDI Studies in brief).

Ross, Alf, *Why Democracy?* Cambridge (Harvard University Press) 1952.

Ross, Robert, *A Concise History of South Africa*. Cambridge (Harvard University Press) 1999.

Rostow, Walt W. (ed.), *The Economics of Take-off into Sustained Growth*. London (Macmillan) 1963.

Rostow, Walt W., *The Stages of Economic Growth: A Non-Communist Manifesto*. Cambridge (Cambridge University Press) 1960.

Rouveroy van Nieuwaal, E. A. B. van, and D. I. Ray (eds.), 'The new relevance of traditional authorities to Africa's future'. In: *Journal of Legal Pluralism and Unofficial Law*, 1996/37-38. Littleton (Rothman). (special double issue).

Rozemond, Sam, *Privatisering van de veiligheid. Politieke aspecten (The Privatisation of Security: Political Aspects)*. The Hague (Netherlands Institute of International Relations Clingendael) 1998.

Rueschemeyer, Dietrich, Evelyne Huber Stephens and John D. Stephens, *Capitalist Development and Democracy*. Chicago (University of Chicago Press) 1992.

Rufin, Jean-Christophe, *L'empire et les nouveaux barbares (The Empire and the New Barbarians)*. Paris (Editions Jean-Claude Lattès) 1991.

Salih, M.A. Mohamed, and John Markakis (eds.), *Ethnicity and the State in Eastern Africa*. Uppsala (Nordiska Afrika Institutet) 1998.

Sandbrook, Richard, *The Politics of Africa's Economic Stagnation*. New York (Cambridge University Press) 1985.

Sandfort, Theo (ed.), *The Dutch Response to HIV: Pragmatism and Consensus*. London (UCL Press) 1998. (Social aspects of AIDS Series).

Sandifort, Mary-Ann, *De cholerafabriek (The Cholera Factory)*. Autobiographical account. Amsterdam (KIT Publishers) 2002.

Santiso, Carlos, *Strengthening Democracy and Good Governance*. Stockholm (IDEA) 1997. (IDEA discussion paper).

Saul, John S., 'For fear of being condemned as old fashioned: liberal democracy vs. popular democracy in Sub-Saharan Africa'. In: *Review of African Political Economy* 24/1997/73, pp. 339-353. Sheffield (ROAPE Publications).

Schaik, L. van, *Frankrijk en de Franse Communauté (France and the French* Communauté). 1997. Policy document, Dutch Ministry of Foreign Affairs, 1997.

Schilperoord, A., *Een inventarisatie van de inzet van niet-traditionele middelen van ontwikkelingshulp in conflictsituaties (An Inventory of Non-Traditional Means of Development Assistance used in Conflict Situations)*. 1997. Unpublished work placement report, 18 April 1997.

Schulpen, Lau (ed.), *Hulp in ontwikkeling. Bouwstenen voor de toekomst van internationale samenwerking (Aid in Development: Building Blocks for the Future of International Cooperation)*. Assen (Koninklijke Van Gorcum) 2001.

Schumpeter, Joseph A., *Capitalism, Socialism, and Democracy*. New York (Harper) 1976. (Second edition. First edition: 1947).

Schwab, Peter, *Africa: A Continent Self-Destructs*. New York (Palgrave) 2001.

Sen, Amartya, 'Democracy and social justice'. 1999. (Paper presented at the Seoul Conference on Democracy, Market Economy and Development, 26-27 February 1999).

Sen, Amartya, *Development as Freedom*. New York (Knopf) 1999.

Shin, Doh C., 'On the third wave of democratization: a synthesis and evaluation of recent theory and research'. In: *World Politics* 47/1994/1, pp. 135-170. Lawrenceville (Princeton University Press).

Shubane, Khehla, 'South Africa: a new government in the making?' In: *Current History* 91/1992, pp. 202-207. Philadelphia (Current History).

Siccama, J.G., *Conflicthantering. Denken en handelen (Conflict Management: Thinking and Acting)*. Memorandum, Dutch Ministry of Foreign Affairs, 1999.

Signer, David, 'Falen wordt je vergeven, succes niet' ('Failure can be forgiven, success cannot'). *Trouw*, 30 november 2002.

Sinai, I. Robert, *In search of the modern world*. New York (New American Library) 1967.

Skard, Torild, *Continent of Mothers, Continent of Hope: Understanding and Promoting Development in Africa Today*. London (Zed Books) 2003.

Slicher van Bath, Bernard H., *Spaans Amerika rond 1600 (Spanish America circa 1600)*. Utrecht/Antwerp (Aula) 1979.

'Small is nasty'. In: *Foreign Report*, 1998/2516. Coulsdon (Jane's Information Group).

Smith, David N., 'Postcolonial genocide: scarcity, ethnicity, and mass death in Rwanda'. In: Michael Dobkowski and Isidor Wallimann (eds.), *The Coming Age of Scarcity*. Syracuse (Syracuse University Press) 1998.

Smits, W., 'Financiële kenmerken van Afrikaanse staten' ('Financial characteristics of African states'). The Hague, unpublished paper in the collection of the Dutch Ministry of Foreign Affairs, 2001.

Snyder, Jack, *From Voting to Violence: Democratisation and Nationalist Conflict*. London (W.W. Norton and Co.) 2000.

Sogner, Sølvi (ed.), *Making Sense of Global History*. Oslo (Universitetsforlaget) 2001.

Sørensen, Georg, 'Conditionality, democracy and development'. In: Olav Stokke (ed.), *Aid and Political Conditionality*. London (Cass) 1995. (EADI Book Series, 16).

Sørensen, Georg, *Changes in Statehood: The Transformation of International Relations*. Houndmills etc. (Palgrave) 2001.

Sørensen, Georg, *Democracy, Dictatorship and Development: Economic Development in Selected Regimes in the Third World*. Houndmills etc. (Palgrave) 1991.

Spicer, Tim, OBE, *An Unorthodox Soldier: Peace and War and the Sandline Affair*. Edinburgh (Mainstream Publishing Company) 1999.

Spruyt, Hendrik, *The Sovereign State and its Competitors: An Analysis of Systems Change*. Princeton (Princeton University Press) 1996.

Steering Committee, Joint Evaluation of Emergency Assistance to Rwanda, *The International Response to Conflict and Genocide: Lessons from the Rwanda Experience*. (Synthesis report). Copenhagen 1996. (5 vols).

Stevenson, Robert F., *Population and Political Systems in Tropical Africa*. New York and London (Columbia University Press) 1968.

Stiglitz, Joseph E., *Globalization and its Discontents*. London etc. (Allen Lane) 2002.

Stiglitz, Jospeh E., 'Towards a new paradigm for development: strategies, policies and processes.' Ninth Raul Prebisch Lecture, delivered in Geneva (UNCTAD), 19 October 1998.

Stokke, Olav (ed.), *Aid and Political Conditionality*. London (Cass) 1995. (EADI Book Series, 16).

Stover, Leon E., Culturele ecologie van de Chinese beschaving. Utrecht (Spectrum) 1976. (Dutch translation of: *The Cultural Ecology of Chinese Civilization: Peasants and Elites in the Last of the Agrarian States.* New York (Pica Press) 1974).

Stuurman, Siep, *Kapitalisme en de burgerlijke staat. Een inleiding in de marxistische politieke theorie.* (*Capitalism and the Bourgeois State: An Introduction to Marxist Political Theory.*) Amsterdam (Socialistiese Uitgeverij) 1978.

Support by the United Nations System of Efforts of Governments to Promote and Consolidate New or Restored Democracies. New York (United Nations) 1995. (UN document A/51/761).

Tawney, R.H., *Religion and the Rise of Capitalism: A Historical Study.* Harmondsworth (Penguin) 1975.

Telligen, N. (ed.), *Africa-expertbijeenkomst: Ghana, Mali, Mozambique, Sierra Leone, Congo, Rwanda* (*Expert meeting on Africa: Ghana, Mali, Mozambique, Sierra Leone, Congo and Rwanda*). Leiden (African Studies Centre and Dutch Ministry of Foreign Affairs, Sub-Saharan Africa Department (DAF)) 2000

Terray, Emmanuel (ed.), *L'Etat contemporain en Afrique* (*The Contemporary State in Africa*). Paris (L'Harmattan) 1987.

Teunissen, Jan Joost (ed.), *Regionalism and the Global Economy: The Case of Africa.* The Hague (FONDAD) 1996.

The International Response to Conflict and Genocide: Lessons from the Rwanda Experience. Copenhagen (Synthesis report, Steering Committee, Joint Evaluation of Emergency Assistance to Rwanda) 1996. (5 vols).

Theroux, Paul, *Dark Star Safari: Overland from Cairo to Cape Town.* London etc. (Penguin) 2002.

Thomas Isaac, T.M., and Patrick Heller, 'The campaign for democratic decentralisation in Kerala: an assessment from the perspective of empowered participatory governance'. In: Archon Fung and Erik Olin Wright (eds.), *Deepening Democracy: Institutional Innovations in Empowered Participatory Governance.* New York (Verso Press). (to be published).

Throup, David, and Charles Hornsby, *Multi-Party Politics in Kenya.* Oxford (James Currey) 1999.

Tilly, Charles (ed.), *The Formation of National States in Western Europe.* Princeton (Princeton University Press) 1975.

Tilly, Charles, 'War making and state making as organized crime'. In: Peter B. Evans, Dietrich Rueschmayer and Theda Skocpol (eds.), *Bringing the State Back in.* Cambridge (Cambridge University Press) 1985.

Tilly, Charles, *Big Structures, Large Processes, Huge Comparisons.* New York (Russell Sage Foundation) 1984.

Tilly, Charles, *Coercion, Capital, and European States, AD 990-1992.* Cambridge (Blackwell) 1992.

Transparency International, *The Global Corruption Report 2001.*

UNAIDS, *AIDS Epidemic Update, November 2000.* Geneva (UNAIDS).

UNCTAD, *Capital Flows and Growth in Africa.* New York/Geneva (UNCTAD) 2000.

UNCTAD, *Foreign Direct Investment in Africa: Performance and Potential.* New York/ Geneva (UNCTAD) 1999.

UNHCR, *Sexual Violence against Refugees: Guidelines on Prevention and Response.* Geneva (UNCTAD) 1995.

UNHCR, *The State of the World's Refugees.* Geneva (UNHCR) 1995.

United Nations, *Preparing for Future Multilateral Trade Negotiations.* New York (United Nations) 1999.

United Nations, *Report of the Panel of Experts on the Illegal Exploitation of Natural Resources and other Forms of Wealth of the Democratic Republic of the Congo.* New York 2001.

United Nations, *Report of the Panel on United Nations Peace Operations.* New York 2000 (Also known as the Brahimi report).

United Nations, *Support by the United Nations System of Efforts of Governments to Promote and Consolidate New or Restored Democracies.* New York (United Nations) 1995. (document A/51/761).

Universal Declaration on Human Rights. New York (United Nations) 1948.

UNRISD, *States of Disarray: The Social Effects of Globalisation.* Geneva (UNRISD) 1995. (Report for the World Summit on Social Development).

Vansina, Jan, 'The politics of history and the crisis in the Great Lakes'. In: *Africa Today* 45/1998/1, pp. 37-44. Denver (GSIS).

Vansina, Jan, *Paths in the Rainforests: Toward a History of Political Tradition in Equatorial Africa.* Madison, Wisconsin (University of Wisconsin Press) 1990.

Verkiezingen en verkiezingswaarneming in Afrika (*Elections and election monitoring in Africa*). Leiden/The Hague (African Studies Centre and Dutch Ministry of Foreign Affairs) 1997. (Collection prepared for the joint study day of the African Studies Centre and the Ministry of Foreign Affairs, 18 February 1997).

Verkoren, O. and E.J.A. Harts-Broekhuis (eds.), *Tropisch Afrika* (*Tropical Africa*). Assen (Van Gorcum) 2000.

Villalón, Leonardo A., and Phillip A. Huxtable (eds.), *The African State at a Critical Juncture: Between Disintegration and Reconfiguration.* New York etc. (Lynne Rienner) 1998.

Viner, Jacob, *The Customs Union Issue.* New York (Carnegie Endowment for International Peace) 1950.

Vlasblom, D. and K. Lindijer, 'Verstrikt in de nieuwe tijd. Kabila en de geopolitieke kentering in Afrika' ('Entangled in the new era: Kabila and Africa's geopolitical transformation'). In: *NRC Handelsblad*, 17 October 1998. Rotterdam (PCM).

Waal, Alex de, 'Fucking soldiers'. In: *Index on Censorship.* vol. 31, no. 4 (2002), pp. 87-92.

Waal, Alex de, 'How will HIV/AIDS transform African governance?' In: *African Affairs*, vol. 102, no. 406 (Januari 2003), pp. 1-12.

Wagner, Michele D., 'All the Bourgmestre's men: making sense of genocide in Rwanda'. In: *Africa Today* 45/1998/1, pp. 25-36. Denver (GSIS).

Walle, Nicolas van de, *African Economics and the Politics of Permanent Crisis, 1979-1999.* Cambridge (Cambridge University Press) 2001.

Walle, Nicolas van de, and Timothy A. Johnston, *Improving Aid to Africa.* Overseas Development Council (ODC) Policy Essay no. 21. Washington, D.C. (ODC) 1996.

Walraven, Klaas van (ed.), *Early Warning and Conflict Prevention: Limitations and Possibilities.* The Hague (Kluwer Law International) 1998.

Walraven, Klaas van, 'Of canvassing and carnival: reflections on the political economy and culture of democratic politics in Africa'. (Paper presented at the annual meeting of the African Studies Association in Nashville, 18 November 2000).

Walraven, Klaas van, *Dreams of Power: The Role of the Organization of African Unity in the Politics of Africa, 1963-1993*. Aldershot (Ashgate) 1999. (African Studies Centre Research Series, 13/1999).

Walraven, Klaas van, *The Netherlands and Liberia: Dutch Policies and Interventions with respect to the Liberian Civil War*. The Hague (Netherlands Institute of International Relations Clingendael) 1999.

Walraven, Klaas van, *The Pretence of Peace-Keeping: ECOMOG, West Africa and Liberia (1990-1998)*. The Hague (Netherlands Institute of International Relations Clingendael) 1999.

Walraven, Klaas van, and Céline Thiriot, *Democratization in Sub-Saharan Africa: Transitions and Turning Points. An Overview of the Literature (1995-1996)*. African Studies Centre Research Report 65/2002. Leiden (ASC) 2002.

Walsh, Thomas G., and Frank Kaufmann (eds.), *Religion and Social Transformation in Southern Africa*. St. Paul, MI (Paragon House) 1999.

Warndorff, D., 'Waarom heb ik aids en mijn buurman niet?' ('Why do I have AIDS and not my neighbour?'), *Trouw*, 28-12-2002.

Weber, Eugen, *Peasants to Frenchmen: The Modernization of Rural France, 1870-1914*. Stanford (Stanford University Press) 1976.

Weber, Max, *Economy and Society: An Outline of Interpretive Sociology*. Berkeley (University of California Press) 1978. Original German edition: *Wirtschaft und Gesellschaft, Grundriss der Sozialökonomik, III. Abteilung*, 3 vols. 1922.

Weber, Max, *The Protestant Ethic and the Spirit of Capitalism*. New York (Sribner's Press) 1958. Original German edition: *Die protestantische Ethik und der 'Geist' des Kapitalismus*, 1905.

Weening, Heleen, *Conflictdynamiek in Liberia 1989-1998. Een analyse van de interventies van het Nederlandse ministerie van Buitenlandse Zaken (Conflict Dynamics in Liberia, 1989-1998: An Analysis of Interventions by the Dutch Ministry of Foreign Affairs)*. The Hague (unpublished student thesis) 1999.

Weiskel, Timothy C., 'Independence and the *longue durée*: the Ivory Coast 'miracle' reconsidered'. In: Gifford, Prosser, and William Roger Louis, *Decolonization and African Independence: The Transfers of Power, 1960-1980*. London/New Haven (Yale University Press) 1988, pp. 347-380.

Werbner, Richard, and Terence Ranger (eds.), *Postcolonial Identities in Africa*. London, New Jersey (Zen Books) 1996.

Wertheim, Wim F., *De lange mars der emancipatie (The Long March of Emancipation)*. Amsterdam (Kritiese Bibliotheek) 1977. Revised edition of *Evolutie en revolutie (Evolution and Revolution)*.

Wesseling, Henk L., *Verdeel en heers. De deling van Afrika, 1800-1914*. Amsterdam (Bert Bakker) 1991. (Translated into English as: *Divide and Rule: The Partition of Africa, 1880-1914*). Westport, CT and London (Praeger) 1996).

Wesseling, Henry L., *Europa's koloniale eeuw. De koloniale rijken in de negentiende eeuw, 1815-1919 (Europe's Colonial Century: The Wealthy Colonials in the Nineteenth Century, 1815-1919)*. Amsterdam (Bert Bakker) 2003.

Whiteman, Kaye, 'Africa, the ACP and Europe: the lessons of 25 years'. In: *Development Policy Review*, 1998/16, pp. 29-37. London (ODI).

Wickins, Peter Lionel, *An Economic History of Africa*. Cape Town (Oxford University Press) 1981-1986. (Vol. 1: *From the Earliest Times to Partition*, 1981. Vol. 2: *1880-1980*, 1986).

Wood, A. 'Could Africa be like America?' On www.worldbank.org (under 'ABCDE conference') 2002.

Wood, A., *North-South Trade, Employment and Inequality: Changing Fortunes in a Skill-Driven World*. Oxford (Clarendon Press) 1994.

World Bank, *A Continent in Transition: Sub-Saharan Africa in the Mid-1990s*. Washington, D. C. (World Bank) 1995.

World Bank, *Accelerated Development in Sub-Saharan Africa*. Washington, D.C. (World Bank) 1981. (Also known as the Berg report).

World Bank, *Adjustment in Africa: Lessons from Country Case Studies*. Washington, D.C. (World Bank) 1994.

World Bank, Africa region, *Intensifying Action against HIV/AIDS in Africa: Responding to a Development Crisis*. Washington, D.C. (World Bank) 2000.

World Bank, *Africa's Adjustment and Growth in the 1980s*. Washington, D.C. (World Bank) 1989.

World Bank, *Africa's Growth Tragedy: A Retrospective 1960-89*. Washington, D.C. (World Bank) 1995.

World Bank, *Attacking Poverty: World Development Report 2000/2001*. New York (Oxford University Press) 2001.

World Bank, *Can Africa Claim the 21st Century?* Washington, D.C. (World Bank) 2000.

World Bank, *Economic Causes of Civil Conflict and their Implications for Policy*. Washington, D.C. (World Bank) 2000

World Bank, *Globalisation, Growth and Poverty: Building an Inclusive World Economy*. Washington, D.C. (World Bank) 2002.

World Bank, *Governance and Development*. Washington, D.C. (World Bank) 1992.

World Bank, *Heavily Indebted Poor Countries (HIPC) Initiative: Status of Implementation*. Washington (World Bank) 2003.

World Bank, *Sub-Saharan Africa: From Crisis to Sustainable Growth*. Washington, D.C. (World Bank) 1989.

World Bank, *The State in a Changing World: World Development Report 1997*. New York (Oxford University Press) 1997.

World Bank, *Voices of the Poor*. New York (Oxford University Press) 2000. (Vol. 1: *Can Anyone Hear Us?* Vol. 2: *Crying Out for Change*. Vol. 3: *From Many Lands*).

World Bank, *World Development Reports*. New York (Oxford University Press). (Various years).

World Bank; C. Mark Blackden and Chitra Bhanu, *Gender, Growth and Poverty Reduction*. Special Program of Assistance for Africa, 1998 status report on poverty in sub-Saharan Africa. Washington, D.C. (World Bank) 1999. (World Bank Technical Paper, no. 428).

World Bank; Craig Burnside and David Dollar, *Aid, Policies, and Growth*. Washington, D.C. (World Bank) 1997.

World Bank; David Dollar et al., *Assessing Aid: What Works, What Doesn't, and Why*. New York (Oxford University Press) 1998.

World Bank; John Croome, *The Present Outlook for Trade Negotiations in the World Trade Organisation*. Washington, D.C. (World Bank) 1998. (Policy Research Working Paper, 1992).

World Bank; John H. Johnson and Sulaiman S. Wasty, *Borrower Ownership of Adjustment Programs and the Political Economy of Reform*. Washington, D.C. (World Bank) 1993. (World Bank Discussion Paper, 199).

World Bank; Mamadou Dia, *Africa's Management in the 1990s and Beyond: Reconciling Indigenous and Transplanted Institutions*. Washington, D.C. (World Bank) 1996.

World Bank; Shantayanan Devarajan et al. (eds.), *Aid and Reform in Africa: Lessons from Ten Case Studies*. Washington, D.C. (World Bank) 2001.

Wright, Donald R., '"What do you mean there were no tribes in Africa?": thoughts on boundaries – and related issues – in precolonial Africa'. In: *History in Africa* 26/1999, pp. 409-426. Atlanta (African Studies Association).

Wulf, Jurgen, 'Zambia under the IMF regime'. In: *African Affairs* 87/1988/349, pp. 579-594. London (Royal African Society).

Young, Crawford, 'The colonial state and post-colonial crisis'. In: Gifford, Prosser, and William Roger Louis, *Decolonization and African Independence: The Transfers of Power, 1960-1980*. London/New Haven (Yale University Press) 1988, pp. 1-32.

Young, Crawford, and Thomas Turner, *The Rise and Decline of the Zairean State*. Madison (University of Wisconsin Press) 1985.

Zakaria, Fareed, 'Democratic tyranny'. In: *Foreign Affairs* 76/1997/6, pp. 22-43. New York (Council on Foreign Relations).

Zartman, I. William (ed.), *Collapsed States: The Disintegration and Restoration of Legitimate Authority*. Boulder, London (Lynne Rienner) 1995.

Zoethout, Carla M. et al. (eds.), *Constitutionalism in Africa: A Quest for Autochthonous Principles*. Deventer (Gouda Quint) 1996. (SI-EUR series, no. 10).

Periodicals

Africa Confidential (Africa Confidential, London).

Africa South of the Sahara (Europa Publications).

African Development Reports (African Development Bank, Abidjan; 1989-2001).

African Development Reviews (published twice a year for the African Development Bank).

Amnesty International Yearbooks (Amnesty International).

Balance of Payments Statistics Yearbooks (IMF).

Country Profiles and Reports (Economist Intelligence Unit).

Country Reports (SPA).

Economic reports on Africa (ECA).

Global Development Finance (World Bank).

Human Development Reports (UNDP).

HRW World Reports (Human Rights Watch).

Landenreeks (KIT, NOVIB, 11.11.11).

Refugees at a glance (UNHCR).

SIPRI Yearbooks (SIRPI).

State of the world's refugees (UNHCR).

State of the world population (UNFPA).

Summaries of the economic and social situation in Africa (ECOSOC).

World Development Reports (World Bank).

World Economic Outlooks (IMF).

World Investment Reports (UNCTAD).

Memoranda from the Dutch Ministry of Foreign Affairs (including DGIS, the development cooperation programme) and other government bodies

Aan elkaar verplicht. Ontwikkelingssamenwerking op weg naar 2015. (Translated into English as: *Mutual Interests, Mutual Responsibilities: Development Cooperation en route to 2015*.).

Afrika notitie (*Memorandum on Africa*). 1999.

Afrika notitie. Sterke mensen, zwakke staten. (Translated into English as: *Memorandum on Africa: Strong People, Weak States*). 2003.

Afrika ten zuiden van de Sahara. Regiobeleidsdocument (*Africa South of the Sahara: Regional Policy Document*). 1998.

Het Aziatisch groeimodel (*The Asian Growth Model*). 1999. Policy Planning Unit, Secretary-General's Office (BSG/PL), J.J.P. de Jong.

Beleidsnotitie institutionele ontwikkeling (*Policy Document on Institutional Development*). 1999.

Bevordering van goed bestuur in het Nederlandse buitenlands beleid (*Promoting Good Governance in Dutch Foreign Policy*). 1999.

Conflicthantering. Denken en handelen (*Conflict Management: Thinking and Acting*). 1999. Policy Planning Unit, Secretary-General's Office (BSG/PL), J.G. Siccama.

Effecten van economische globalisering (*Effects of Economic Globalisation*). 1997. Policy Planning Unit, Secretary-General's Office (BSG/PL), F. Haver Droeze.

Frankrijk en de Franse Communauté (*France and the French Communauté*). 1997. Policy Planning Unit, Secretary-General's Office (BSG/PL), L. van Schaik.

De geschiedenis van vijftig jaar Nederlandse ontwikkelingssamenwerking, 1949-1999. 1999. (Translated into English as: *Fifty years of Dutch development cooperation*. 2000).

The Foreign Policy Review. 1995.

Hulp in uitvoering. Ontwikkelingssamenwerking en de herijking van het buitenlands beleid. 1995. (Translated into English as: *Aid in Progress: Development Cooperation and the Foreign Policy Review*).

Humanitaire hulp tussen conflict en ontwikkeling (*Humanitarian Aid between Conflict and Development*). 1993.

Internationale Samenwerking. Monthly magazine on development cooperation.

De machtspolitieke betekenis van de netwerk-maatschappij (*The Significance of the Network Society in terms of Power Politics*). 2000. Policy Planning Unit, Secretary-General's Office (BSG/PL), P. Ramondt.

Explanatory memorandum to the budget. Published annually.

Memorandum on Human Rights. 2001.

Migratie en ontwikkeling (*Migration and Development*). 1996.

Nederland en de Grote Merenregio (*The Netherlands and the Great Lakes Region*). 2001.

Normverva(n)ging. Een bijdrage aan de discussie over de budgettaire norm voor internationale samenwerking.

1993. R.J. van den Dool (ed.). (Translated into English as: *Crowding Out or Pitching In: A New Budgetary Target for Dutch Development Cooperation*).

Ondernemen tegen armoede. Notitie over economie en ontwikkeling. 2000 (supplemented in 2002). (Translated into English as: *In Business against Poverty: Memorandum on Economics and Development*).

Ontwikkelingen in Sub-Sahara Afrika. Marktpotentieel voor het Nederlandse bedrijfsleven (*Developments in Sub-Saharan Africa. Market Potential for the Dutch Business Sector*). 1999. Ministry of Economic Affairs.

De sectorale benadering (*The Sector-Wide Approach*). 2000. Sector-Wide Approach Support Group.

'Small arms, big challenges.' Pamphlet. 1999.

Tussen ownership en conditionaliteit in de ontwikkelings-samenwerking met Afrika. (*Between Ownership and Conditionality in Development Cooperation with Africa*). 2000. Policy Planning Unit, Secretary-General's Office (BSG/PL), Roel van der Veen.

Vergrijzing en ontwikkeling. Notitie over ouderen in ontwikkelingslanden. 1999. (In collaboration with the Ministry of Health, Welfare and Sport). (Translated into English as: *Greying and Development: Memorandum on Older People in Developing Countries*).

Vluchtelingen in Afrika (*Refugees in Africa*). 1996.

Een wereld in geschil. De grenzen van de ontwikkelingssamenwerking verkend (*A World in Dispute: Exploring the Boundaries of Development Cooperation*). 1993.

Een wereld van verschil. Nieuwe kaders voor ontwikkelingssamenwerking in de jaren negentig. 1990. (Translated into English as: *A World of Difference: New Frameworks for Development Cooperation in the 1990s*).

Abbreviations

ACP	African, Caribbean and Pacific (in connection with the Lomé Conventions and Cotonou Agreement)
AfDB	African Development Bank
AIDS	Autoimmune Deficiency Syndrome
ANC	African National Congress (South Africa)
ASC	African Studies Centre (Leiden)
ASEAN	Association of Southeast Asian Nations
AU	African Union (successor to the OAU)
CFA	*Communauté financière africaine* (African Financial Community)
CODESA	Convention for a Democratic South Africa
COMESA	Common Market for Eastern and Southern Africa
COSATU	Congress of South African Trade Unions
DAC	Development Assistance Committee (of the OECD)
DFI	Development Finance Institution
EAC	East African Community
ECA	Economic Commission for Africa
ECOMOG	ECOWAS Cease-Fire Monitoring Group
ECOWAS	Economic Community of West African States
EPLF	Eritrean People's Liberation Front
EPRDF	Ethiopian Peoples' Revolutionary Democratic Front
EU	European Union
FDI	Foreign Direct Investment
FONDAD	Forum on Debt and Development (The Hague)
FRELIMO	*Frente de Libertação de Mozambique* (Front for the Liberation of Mozambique)
GCA	Global Coalition for Africa
GDP	Gross Domestic Product
GEAR	Growth, Employment and Redistribution (South African policy)
GNP	Gross National Product
HIPC	Heavily Indebted Poor Countries
HIV	Human Immunodeficiency Virus
HRW	Human Rights Watch
ICG	International Crisis Group
ICT	information and communications technology
IDEA	International Institute for Democracy and Electoral Assistance (Stockholm)
IGAD	Intergovernmental Authority on Development (Horn of Africa)
IMF	International Monetary Fund (Washington)
KIT	*Koninklijk Instituut voor de Tropen* (Royal Tropical Institute; Amsterdam)
MAP	Millennium Action Plan (forerunner of NEPAD)
MINUCI	*Mission des Nations Unies en Côte d'Ivoire* (United Nations Mission in Côte d'Ivoire)

MLC	*Mouvement de libération du Congo*	
	(Movement for the Liberation of Congo)	
MONUC	*Mission des Nations Unies en République Démocratique de Congo*	
	(United Nations Mission in the Democratic Republic of Congo)	
MP	Member of Parliament	
MPLA	*Movimento Popular de Libertação de Angola*	
	(Popular Movement for the Liberation of Angola)	
MPR	*Mouvement populaire de la revolution*	
	(Popular Revolutionary Movement)	
NADAF	New Agenda for the Development of Africa in the 1990s (UN)	
NAFTA	North American Free Trade Agreement	
NAI	New African Initiative	
NAR	*Nationaal Adviesraad voor Ontwikkelingssamenwerking*	
	(National Advisory Council for Development Cooperation)	
NATO	North Atlantic Treaty Organisation (Brussels)	
NCOS	*Nationaal Centrum voor Ontwikkelingssamenwerking*	
	(National Centre for Development Cooperation)	
NEPAD	New Partnership for Africa's Development	
NGO	nongovernmental organisation	
NICI	National Information and Communications Infrastructure	
NIF	National Islamic Front (Sudan)	
NOVIB	*Nederlandse Organisatie voor Internationale Ontwikkelingssamenwerking*	
	(Netherlands Organisation for International Development Cooperation; Oxfam Netherlands)	
NPFL	National Patriotic Front of Liberia	
OAU	Organisation of African Unity (Addis Ababa)	
ODA	Official Development Assistance	
OECD	Organisation for Economic Cooperation and Development	
OPEC	Organisation of the Petroleum Exporting Countries	
PRSP	Poverty Reduction Strategy Paper	
QIP	Quick Impact Project	
RAWOO	*Raad van Advies voor het Wetenschappelijk Onderzoek in het kader van de Ontwikkelingssamenwerking*	
	(Netherlands Development Assistance Research Council)	
RCD	*Rassemblement congolais pour la démocratie*	
	(Congolese Rally for Democracy)	
RECAMP	*Renforcement des capacités africaines au maintien de la paix*	
	(Reinforcement of African Peacekeeping Capacities)	
RENAMO	*Resistência Nacional Moçambicana*	
	(Mozambican National Resistance)	
RPF	Rwandan Patriotic Front	
RUF	Revolutionary United Front (Sierra Leone)	
SADC	Southern African Development Community	
SADCC	Southern African Development Coordination Conference (SADC's forerunner)	

SPA	Special Program of Assistance for Low-Income and Distressed Countries in Africa (Washington)
SPLA	Sudan People's Liberation Army
SWAPO	South West African People's Organisation
TPLF	Tigray People's Liberation Front
UN	United Nations
UNAIDS	Joint United Nations Programme on HIV/AIDS
UNAMIR	United Nations Assistance Mission for Rwanda
UNAMSIL	United Nations Mission in Sierra Leone
UNAVEM	United Nations Angola Verification Mission
UNCTAD	United Nations Conference on Trade and Development
UNDP	United Nations Development Programme
UNESCO	United Nations Education, Scientific and Cultural Organisation
UNFPA	United Nations Population Fund
UNHCR	United Nations High Commissioner for Refugees
UNICEF	United Nations Children's Fund
UNITA	*União Nacional para a Independência Total de Angola* (National Union for the Total Independence of Angola)
UNMEE	United Nations Mission in Ethiopia and Eritrea
UNOMIL	United Nations Observer Mission in Liberia
UNOMOZ	United Nations Operation in Mozambique
UNOSOM	United Nations Operation in Somalia
UNRISD	United Nations Research Institute for Social Development
US	United States
USD	United States dollars
WHO	World Health Organisation
WTO	World Trade Organisation

Country index